T0319768

After the Breakup: Assessing the New Post-AT&T Divestiture Era

AFTER THE BREAKUP: ASSESSING THE NEW POST-AT&T DIVESTITURE ERA

Edited by BARRY G. COLE

COLUMBIA UNIVERSITY PRESS   NEW YORK

Columbia University Press
New York   Oxford
Copyright © 1991 Columbia University Press
All rights reserved

Library of Congress Cataloging-in-Publication Data

After the breakup : assessing the new post-AT&T divestiture era
edited by Barry G. Cole.
p.   cm.
Includes bibliographical references and index.
ISBN 978-0-231-07322-6
1. Telephone—United States.   2. Telecommunication policy—United States.
3. Competition—United States.
4. American Telephone and Telegraph Company.
I. Cole, B. G. (Barry G.)
HE8815.A34 1991   384'.06'573—dc20   90-40710
CIP

Casebound editions of Columbia University Press books are Smyth-sewn
and printed on permanent and durable acid-free paper

Printed in the United States of America

CONTENTS

PREFACE

On January 8, 1982, the AT&T divestiture consent decree was announced. A company with $150 billion in assets—more than General Motors, General Electric, U.S. Steel, Eastman Kodak, and Xerox combined—the country's second largest employer with over a million employees (bigger than the U.S. Army), and the nation's most widely held security with over three million shareholders, was to be broken up the first day of 1984. Peter Drucker predicted that, "few governmental actions since World War II will have such profound impact on American society, on American technology, and even on national security."[1] The *Economist* even suggested the divestiture "promises to affect, sooner rather than later, almost every household in the *world.*"[2] According to *Time* magazine, "the breakup has so many possible ramifications, few people even pretend to understand it thoroughly. . . . The only thing certain is uncertainty."[3] Many regulatory experts agreed. Edythe Miller, Chair of the Colorado Public Utility Commission and member of the National Association of Regulatory Commissioners' (NARUC) Committee on Communications, told the Congress "we seem to be embarking on a course with an unknown destination, uncertain as to exactly how we are going to get there."[4]

Predictions concerning the impacts of divestiture were often less than enthusiastic. Senate Communications Subcommittee Chairman Barry Goldwater characterized the AT&T breakup as "potentially the worst thing to happen to our national interest, particularly in the field of communications, that will ever or has ever happened."[5] Concerned that local phone rates might double in five years,[6] the House of Representatives by 1983 had introduced thirteen bills relating to universal telephone service.

What has been the actual impact of divestiture? AT&T claims it has been a great success. Current AT&T Chairman and CEO Robert Allen told the Federal Communications Bar Association in February 1989, "divestiture worked," and "myth-makers who predicted divestiture would produce doom instead of boom must have been disappointed when cadavers did not float to the surface." According to Allen, long-distance rates have dropped even 40 percent, local rates have not doubled, more households than ever are on the network, other long-distance and equipment companies now effectively compete with AT&T, and consumers have received more choices in products, more values, and lower prices.[7] In fact, suggests AT&T Vice Chairman Randall Tobias, "if you stand back and look at the total picture, you are hard pressed to find anybody hurt by divestiture." BellSouth's CEO John Clendenon agrees and argues that "all sinister things, like fears over finances going bad, have dropped by the wayside."[8]

Others, especially many outside the telecommunications industry, are more cautious in their evaluation of divestiture's impact to date. In reviewing divestiture's first five years, the *Philadelphia Inquirer*, January 1, 1989, concluded that, "given the disparate results of the breakup, all that can be said with certainty is that it changed everything that had to do with telecommunications." In a similar retrospective, the *Los Angeles Times* surmised "for consumers it's been a rough road. AT&T hasn't had an easy go of it either."[9] And in a *Washington Post* poll of over 1,000 respondents, taken in December 1988 to mark the fifth anniversary of the dismantling of AT&T, 39 percent still thought divestiture "a bad idea," while 30 percent had "no opinion." The *Post* suggested the "mixed feelings may partly stem from the fact that the impact has been unequally shared. . . . There have been 'winners and losers.' "[10]

Consistent with its mission, the Center for Telecommunications and Information Studies at Columbia University's Graduate School of Business initiated a major research project to help determine the existing state of knowledge about trends and developments since the AT&T divestiture in various essential elements in telecommunications. These were to include telephone network technology, pricing, service quality, efficiency and productivity, and household penetration levels, as well as innovation and new services, employment and wages, the degree of competition, and international trade in telecommunications. Concerning each of these subject areas, our intent was for research to form the basis of discussion—rather than simply opinion. In addition, an examination of post-divestiture regulatory and institutional change, albeit inevitably more analytical and less empirical, was deemed a necessary component. All costs relating to the project were to be met from the Center's general operating funds, which are received from widely diverse sources.

Having identified areas to be addressed, we were fortunate to enlist leading members of the research community who placed some "facts on the table" to promote an informed discussion. We then sought out distinguished individuals from government, industry, and academe to respond to the researchers' views of trends and developments since the AT&T divestiture. From the outset we determined that for this book the traditional approach of only publishing the principal research investigations, and utilizing respondents merely as a means of pretesting and fine-tuning the research, should be avoided. Instead, we would publish the reactions and reflections of all other participants, many of whom are outstanding researchers in their own right. This would not only take full advantage of their expertise, it would also provide the reader with a better understanding of whether a consensus exists as to what has happened subsequent to divestiture and where we may be headed.

The "chapter" format of research presenter, followed by reactions by three or four respondents is used throughout parts 2 through 4 of this volume. The sole exception is chapter 10 on Labor, Employment, and Wages, which has no respondents. The absence of discussants was the result of continuing labor negotiations in the telephone industry during 1989, and our desire to have Wallace Hendricks and Susan Sassalos delay completing their research for as long as possible to enable it to encompass 1989 settlements.

To open our volume, we envisioned a section on "Policymakers and Policy Initiatives." Our ideal wish list of contributors included the three major figures of the consent decree and the Modification of Final Judgement: William Baxter, Charles Brown, and Judge Harold Greene, as well as AT&T's long-time chief antagonist, MCI's William McGowan, current Federal Communications Commission Chairman, Alfred Sikes, and president of the National Association of Regulatory Utility Commissioners, Sharon Nelson. We were indeed fortunate to have all of them participate.

A conference component of the project was held on March 2–3, 1989 in Washington, D.C. Preliminary drafts of the research papers were presented, and respondents were able to express their initial reactions and suggestions for improvements. Sharon Nelson, Alfred Sikes, and William McGowan gave talks which formed the basis for their contributions. The conference featured an evening question-and-answer session in which the two principals of the divestiture agreement, William Baxter and Charles Brown, responded to a series of anticipated questions prepared and posed by Stanley Besen and Henry Geller, as well as to unpreviewed queries from the audience. Baxter and Brown later had the opportunity to review and fine-tune their responses to ensure they accurately portrayed their views and recollections.

Although Judge Harold Greene was unable to attend the March conference, he consented to join the project by answering a series of prepared questions. Originally, they were to be answered by Judge Greene in a face-to-face meeting with Besen, Geller, and me, but the additional responsibilities accruing to the Judge in connection with the "Iran-contra" trial of John Poindexter eventually made that impossible. However, Judge Greene generously used "a sudden burst of energy over [a] weekend" to draft written responses to our queries, and these too are included in chapter 1.

To promote a cross-referencing and interchange of ideas and information, throughout the project, all contributors were sent revised versions of the entire chapter in which he or she appears, prior to the manuscript being finalized. I also invited authors to request from the editor the text of any presentation in other chapters of the book which might be relevant to their own discussions.

It should be emphasized that the sixty-two contributors to this volume were invited to present their own research and analyses which may not necessarily represent that of their employers or respective organizations. A number of authors, particularly those in government, requested that a disclaimer be printed at the beginning of their particular presentations. To avoid unnecessary redundancy, a general disclaimer is hereby made for all contributors.

Undertaking a lengthy research project designed to produce a book can pose hazards. This is particularly true when the project entails (a) more than sixty geographically disbursed, extremely busy participants who are donating their expertise and energies on a spare time, pro bono basis, (b) a two-day, twenty-one hour conference in another city in which preliminary research findings are to be presented and discussed by these contributors, and (c) many thousands of pages of manuscript, graphs, and tables continuously being drafted and re-drafted and constantly being distributed around the nation to fellow authors on the same topic.

Fortunately, my task was made far easier than I had anticipated by many people who should be acknowledged. Foremost among this group are the sixty-one other contributors, who from the very beginning were enthusiastic about our goals and did their best to help us achieve them. They recognized the need to keep on schedule, and almost without exception met whatever deadlines I set, however unreasonable. They understood the inevitable restraints on total book and chapter length, and were willing to abide by whatever guidelines and final editing decisions I had to make. And they were receptive to my requests for updated statistics, and for further elaboration, and documentation.

Fellow principals and staff of the Center for Telecommunications and Information Studies also deserve both praise and thanks. Martin Elton, my partner in running the Center during Eli Noam's absence, aided in a number of ways to ensure the project received as much financial and staff support as possible, and cheerfully, often voluntarily, shifted priorities when necessary away from his own two-year research and book project on Integrated Broadband Networks which was nearing completion. Eli Noam, founding Director of the Center, who is on leave from Columbia University and is serving on the New York State Public Service Commission, helped conceptualize the project, delineate particular subject areas to be researched, and identify potential contributors. As usual, he made our initial brainstorming and planning sessions more stimulating and productive. Douglas Conn, Associate Director of the Center, displayed his knowledge of the field as a central participant in the formulation of the project and its execution. He was particularly helpful along with former Assistant Director Richard Kramer in organizing our two-day March 1989 Washington, D.C., conference. Rich and current Assistant Director Theresa Bolmarcich, handled their editorial stage office supervision with skill and humor.

The Center research staff for the book included at various times Mark Young, Michael McManus, Richard Nohe, Sherry Emery, Susan Miller, William Bodenlos, and Gianna Quach. In addition, Constantinos Stratos, Lynda Starr, and Warren Bareiss, who served as my graduate research assistants at the Annenberg School for Communication at the University of Pennsylvania during portions of 1988 and 1989, were most helpful in locating relevant research materials. Proofreading was ably done by Miguel Centeno, Miriamme Fields, Alan Goldman, Joanne Picciotto, Colette Pratt, Christine Robinson, and Judy Wong, and by my two favorite 1990 graduates, Tracy Cole and Kelly Cole.

Special thanks goes to Rhonda Harrison, who was able to decipher my handwriting and did yeoman service on the word processor during the final preparation of the manuscript, and to Helen Webbink, who deftly compiled a coherent and useful index to aid the reader.

Finally, my sincere gratitude to Everette Dennis, Executive Director of the Gannett Center for Media Studies at Columbia, and Gannett Associate Director John Pavlik for making equipment and expertise available, enabling us to prepare camera-ready charts and graphs at no cost. That expertise was supplied by Mark Thalheimer, Technology

Studies Coordinator, who treated the project as his own, and devoted many hours of his "free time," ultimately including a weekend, to enable us to meet our final publication deadline.

ENDNOTES

1. Peter F. Drucker, "Beyond the Bell Breakup," in *The Public Interest* (Fall 1984), no. 77.
2. "Stripping Ma Bell," *The Economist*, January 16, 1982.
3. "Click Ma Bell Is Ringing Off," *Time*, November 21, 1983.
4. 98th Cong., 1st sess., House of Representatives, Subcommittee on Telecommunications, Consumer Protection and Finance, "Hearings on the Prospects for Universal Telephone Service," Testimony of Edythe Miller, March 22, 1983, p. 153.
5. 98th Cong., 1st sess., House of Representatives, Committee on Energy and Commerce and U.S. Senate Committee on Commerce, Science and Transportation, "Joint Hearings on the Universal Service Protection Act of 1983 (S. 1660 and H.R. 3621)," July 28 and 19, 1983, p. 39.
6. AT&T prediction as cited in *US News*, January 25, 1982.
7. *Vital Speeches*, April 15, 1989.
8. *Fortune*, January 2, 1989.
9. Bruce Koppel, "Consumers Pay Toll for Bell Breakup," *Los Angeles Times*, January 1, 1989.
10. *Washington Post*, December 26, 1988 and *Washington Post Weekly*, January 9–15, 1989.

ABOUT THE CONTRIBUTORS

JOHN R. AKE is Assistant Vice President–Regulatory Support at Illinois Bell and is responsible for developing policy alternatives relating to pricing, costing, competitive strategies, and revenue requirements. He had previous telecommunications experience in the U.S. Air Force, in successive positions with Ohio Bell's network, information systems, and financial and regulatory departments, and with Ameritech Services. He currently serves on various United States Telephone Association Committees.

MICHAEL D. BAUDHUIN is Corporate Vice President–Communications Policies for American Telephone and Telegraph Company. Previously he was Vice President–Government Affairs for Bell Communications Research, Inc., representing the new Bell companies in legislative and regulatory matters during the 1982–1984 divestiture transition period. His recent papers delivered at academic and government related conferences have focused on privatization, deregulation and transnationalization of telecommunications, and the impact of the divestiture.

WILLIAM F. BAXTER is the William Benjamin and Luna M. Scott Professor of Law at the Stanford University Law School. He served as U.S. Assistant Attorney General, Antitrust Division from 1981 to 1983 and was a signatory to the 1982 consent decree which resulted in the breakup of the Bell System. He has published widely in the area of antitrust law, was a fellow at the Center for Advanced Study in the Behavioral Sciences (1972–1973), a visiting professor at Yale, and a member of the President's Task Force on Antitrust Policy (1969).

ALEXANDER BELINFANTE is an industry economist in the Industry Analysis Division of the FCC Common Carrier Bureau. He has taught economics and statistics at New York University, University of Wisconsin, Oshkosh, and the University of New Orleans and has written a number of papers analyzing telephone penetration. He is the editor of the quarterly "Monitoring Reports" of the FCC-State Joint Board (staff) and the author of the FCC's summaries of "Telephone Subscribership in the U.S.," which is published three times annually.

SANFORD V. BERG is Professor of Economics at the University of Florida, and the Executive Director of that university's Public Utility Research Center. He has published widely on business and economics topics, and is the co-author of a recent book on the regulation of natural monopolies. He has been a consultant on communications and environmental issues to various state and federal agencies, and his current research focuses on the impacts of technological change on regulation.

STANLEY M. BESEN is a Senior Economist at the Rand Corporation. He has taught at Columbia University, Rice University, and the University of California, Santa Barbara, and has served as co-editor of the *Rand Journal of Economics*, and co-director of the Network Inquiry Special Staff of the FCC (1978–1980). A former Brookings Economic Policy Fellow and Office of Telecommunications Policy Consultant (1972–1977), he has co-edited two books and authored numerous monographs and book chapters on telecommunications and media economics and regulation.

ROBERT T. BLAU is Director of Policy Analysis for BellSouth, where he is primarily responsible for identifying trends in regulation and evaluating their implications. He has held similar positions with Bell Communications Research, Inc., Communications Satellite Corporation, and Office of Plans and Policy and the Common Carrier Bureau of the FCC (1975–1979). His research and writings include topics relating to the analysis of public policy change and its relationship to growth in productivity.

WALTER G. BOLTER is the Director of the Bethesda Research Institute, Ltd. and Professor of Economics at Flagler College. He was formerly Chief Economist of the House of Representatives' Subcommittee on Telecommunications, Consumer Protection and Finance, and Chief of the Economics Division in the FCC Common Carrier Bureau. He has taught at the University of Maryland, George Washington University, and Georgia Tech, and has authored or co-authored four books and a number of articles and reports on economic and regulatory trends in telecommunications.

TIMOTHY J. BRENNAN is Associate Professor of Policy Sciences and Economics at the University of Maryland, Baltimore County. Prior to joining the faculty of George Washington University in 1986, he served eight years with the Antitrust Division of the U.S. Department of Justice, specializing in telecommunications, media, public utilities, and intellectual property. He has published widely on the AT&T divestiture, information services and price caps, and his current research interests include regulatory economics and the ethics and methods of policy analysis.

GERALD W. BROCK is an Adjunct Professor in the Telecommunications Program at George Washington University and a private consultant. He served as Chief of the FCC Common Carrier Bureau from 1987–1989, after holding several other senior FCC positions including Chief of the Bureau's Accounting and Audits Division. A former professor at the University of Arizona and former

Chairman of the Department of Economics at Bethel College, he has written an authoritative book on the telecommunications industry, and has authored a number of other publications in the fields of computer and communications.

CHARLES L. BROWN is a trustee of the Aspen Institute, Vice Chairman of the Board of Trustees of the Institute for Advanced Study at Princeton University, Chairman of the Colonial Williamsburg (Virginia) foundation, as well as a director of several major corporations. He was Chairman of the board and CEO of AT&T from February 1979 to August 1986, and led the company through the largest corporate reorganization in history. A Bell System employee since the age of eighteen, he also served as President of Illinois Bell and, later, as President of AT&T.

EDWARD F. BURKE is President of Canadian Connection, Ltd., an energy and telecommunications consulting firm, as well as Chairman of the Providence Rhode Island Water Supply Board. He was Chairman of the Rhode Island Public Utilities Commission from 1977 to 1988, and President of the National Association of Regulatory Utility Commissioners in 1981–1982. He served on the NARUC Committee on Communications and, as a member of several FCC Federal-State Joint Boards, was heavily involved in developing programs to increase telephone subscribership.

THOMAS E. BUZAS is Associate Professor of Marketing at Eastern Michigan University. He formerly taught marketing management, marketing research, and promotion management at the University of Florida, and has served as a consultant to the Florida Public Service Commission. He has published on applications of multivariate statistics in marketing and consumer responses to brands, and his current research interests include service quality issues, quantitative methods, decisionmaking and pricing.

RONALD G. CHOURA is Special Assistant to the Director of the Office of Planning, Policy, and Evaluation of the Michigan Public Service Commission, and the Michigan Project Director for the Governor's Telecommunications Task Force. He has been appointed to and has chaired the staffs of five FCC Federal State Joint Boards, and he continues to serve as Chairman of the Staff Subcommittee on Cost Allocations of the National Association for Regulatory Utility Commissioners. He has taught at Michigan State University and is a registered engineer.

THOMAS W. COHEN has been Senior Counsel of the U.S. Senate Committee on Commerce, Science, and Transportation since 1987, with particular interests in and responsibility for its Subcommittee on Communications. He served as Minority Counsel for the Committee between 1981 and 1987, and prior to joining the Senate staff, he was Assistant General Counsel for legislation in the FCC Common Carrier Bureau. He has also been a staff attorney and congressional lobbyist with Common Cause, and the Environmental Defense Fund.

BARRY G. COLE is Visiting Director of the Center for Telecommunications and Information Studies at the Columbia Business School, and Adjunct Professor at the Annenberg School of Communications at the University of Pennsylvania. He has served as founding Deputy Director of the Annenberg School Washington Program as well as a consultant to two FCC Chairmen (1970–1975), the U.S. House Subcommittee on Telecommunications, and the National Science Foundation. He has written extensively about communications policy and has been the co-recipient of two national book-of-the-year awards.

LAWRENCE P. COLE is the Manager of the Economics and Statistics Department of GTE Laboratories, Inc., with responsibilities for research in customer assessment methods and the emerging market structure in telecommunications. He has been Pricing Plans and Analysis Manager at GTE Telephone Operations, and a Statistical Staff Supervisor in Business Research at AT&T Long Lines. He is a member of the California Incremental Cost Task Force, and has published several papers on regulatory economics policy concerning costs and pricing.

A. GRAY COLLINS is Executive Vice President-External Affairs for Bell Atlantic, and directs its regulations, federal government, and industry relations activities. He was formerly the Vice President who headed the organization at AT&T and Bell Communications Research, Inc., responsible for developing and implementing the access charge plan, and determining rates necessary following the AT&T consent decree. As a current board member of the United States Telephone Association, he is involved in developing industry-wide positions on a variety of major policy issues.

MARK N. COOPER is Director of Research for the Consumer Federation of America, and focuses on economic analysis and survey research in the fields of energy, telecommunications, antitrust, and insurance. He also heads a private consulting firm, the Citizens Research, and has appeared as an expert witness before state and federal courts as well as a number of Public Utility Commissions. He has taught courses at Yale, the University of Maryland, and American University, and is the author of two books.

NINA CORNELL is currently a consultant based in Meetse, Wyoming, specializing in telecommunications and antitrust issues, particularly on the state level. She has been the Chief of the FCC Office of Plans and Policy (1978–1981), and has served on the staffs of both the Council of Economic Advisors and the Council of Wage and Price Stability in the Carter administration. She spent four years at the Brookings Institution, and has published widely and given expert testimony on telecommunications and regulatory economics.

ROBERT W. CRANDALL has been a Senior Fellow at the Brookings Institution since 1978, where he concentrates on the fields of industrial organization, antitrust policy and regulation. He has taught at the University of Maryland, George Washington University, MIT, and Northwestern University, and has served as Acting Director of the Council on Wage and Price Stability. He is the author of a lengthy list of books, papers, and articles dealing with economics and regulation of the telecommunications and the steel and automobile industries, and with environmental and health care policy.

ROWLAND L. CURRY is Director of Telephone Utility Analysis for the Public Utility Commission of Texas. He has extensive experience in the analysis of telephone service quality on both the state and federal levels, and is the longtime Chairman of the National Association of Regulatory Commissioners Staff Subcommittee on Telephone Service Quality. He also serves as a member of the NARUC Staff Subcommittee on Communications and on the staff of four FCC Federal State Joint Boards.

BRUCE L. EGAN is an independent industry consultant and an Affiliated Research Fellow at Columbia Business School's Center for Telecommunications and Information Studies. His primary research, consulting, and publishing areas are planning and policy analysis of emerging industry issues, including alternative forms of regulation, costing, pricing, and technology deployment strategies for digital communications networks. He was District Manager-Economic Analysis at Bell Communications Research Inc., and an economist at Southwestern Bell.

GERALD R. FAULHABER is Professor of Public Policy and Management at the Wharton School of the University of Pennsylvania and served as the first Director of Wharton's Fishman-Davidson Center for the Study of the Service Sector. He was formerly Director of Strategic Planning and Financial Management of AT&T, and has been AT&T's Director of Microeconomic Studies. His research and writing concern the microeconomic, management, and public policy aspects of service firms, and he has authored a well-known book on the background of the AT&T divestiture and the ferment in telecommunications policy.

SUSAN D. FENDELL, in her capacity as a staff attorney with the National Consumer Law Center, provides technical assistance and legal and economic analyses of utility matters to government agencies and nonprofit organizations. She previously worked with Legal Services of Upper East Tennessee and as an Assistant Attorney General with the Utilities Division of Massachusetts Department of Attorney General. She has authored utility reports concerning such matters as deregulation, telephone rate design issues, and cost allocation.

BAILEY M. GEESLIN is Vice President-Regulatory and Planning for New York Telephone. He previously served as Vice President-Marketing and Technology for the NYNEX Service Company, with responsibilities for developing new products and services and planning deployment of new technology for the NYNEX telephone companies. He is a former Dean of the Bell System Center for Technical Education, and has been an Assistant Vice President for New England Telephone, formulating regulatory and marketing strategies and directing rate case programs.

HENRY GELLER is a Markle Foundation Fellow and Director of Duke University's Washington Center for Public Policy Research. He served as the first Assistant Secretary for Communications and Information and Administrator of the National Telecommunications and Information Administration (1977–1981), as FCC General Counsel (1969–1970) and as Special Assistant to the FCC Chairman (1970–1973). He has published widely on telecommunications and media law and policy, and has assisted several foreign governments in their efforts to draft new communications laws.

JUDGE HAROLD H. GREENE was appointed to the U.S. District Court for the District of Columbia in 1978, after serving as Chief Judge of the Superior Court of D.C. (1974–1978) and Chief Judge of the D.C. Court of General Sessions (1966–1971). His Court retains jurisdiction for enforcing the 1982 Modified Final Judgement which resulted in and governs the AT&T divestiture. He has served in the Civil Rights Division of the U.S. Department of Justice, and is credited as the drafter of the 1964 Civil Rights Act and the 1965 Voting Rights Act.

BRUCE C. N. GREENWALD is a member of the Technical Staff at Bell Communications Research, Inc., and Visiting Professor at the Columbia University School of Business. He served in 1987–1988 as Staff Economist for the Presidential Task Force on Market Mechanisms (Brady Task Force), and has been a research economist for Bell Laboratories and Assistant Professor at the Harvard Business School. He has published several book chapters and many papers in the field of telecommunications, labor relations, and economic theory, and he has authored a book concerning the labor market.

ROBERT M. GRYB is President of the consulting firm, Customer Satisfaction Measurement. From 1966 to 1984 he was AT&T's Director of Business Research and Corporate Measurement, responsible for all service and product measurement in the Bell System, and was a member of the international committee which developed the ASCII code in the early 1960s. Beginning in 1949, he has also held various positions at New York Telephone, Bell Telephone Labs, and in 1960 he authored a seminal article on the capabilities of the telephone network for data transmission.

DALE N. HATFIELD is President of the consulting firm, Hatfield Associates, Inc., and Adjunct Professor at both the University of Colorado and the University of Denver. He has served as Deputy Assistant Secretary of Commerce for Communications and Information (1981–1982), Associate Administrator for Policy Analysis and Development at the National Telecommunications and Information Administration (1979–1981), and Chief of the FCC Office of Plans and Policy (1975–1977). He is the author of numerous papers and reports on trends in telecommunications technology.

WALLACE HENDRICKS is Professor of Economics and Labor and Industrial Relations at the University of Illinois at Urbana-Champaign. He has been a consultant for the U.S. Senate, the U.S. Department of Energy, the Illinois Commerce Committee, and the Illinois Department of Energy and Natural Resources. He has published broadly on collective bargaining and utility services, and is on the Board of Editors of *Review of Economics and Statistics, Advances in Labor and Industrial Relations,* and *Quarterly Review of Economics and Business.*

A. DANIEL KELLY is Director of Regulatory Policy of MCI Communications Corporation. He previously served as MCI's Director of Economic Analysis, on the trial staff of *U.S. v. AT&T* at the Antitrust Division of the U.S. Department of Justice, as Special Assistant to the Chairman of the FCC, and as a senior economist in the FCC Common Carrier Bureau and Office of Plans and Policy. His antitrust and telecommunications research has appeared in various academic and governmental publications, and he has provided expert testimony in federal and state proceedings.

GENE KIMMELMAN has been Legislative Director of the Consumer Federation of America, the nation's largest consumer advocacy organization, since 1984. At CFA, he heads a legislative and regulatory intervention program on a broad spectrum of consumer issues, and personally directs those aspects relating to telecommunications, product liability, and health care policy. A former staff attorney for Congress Watch, he is the author or co-author of numerous reports on telecommunications policy, and represents telephone users in ongoing proceedings concerning the aftermath of the AT&T divestiture.

JONATHAN M. KRAUSHAAR is a staff engineer in the Industry Analysis Division of the FCC Common Carrier Bureau. Since divestiture, he has been engaged in a variety of regulatory activities involving AT&T and the Bell Operating Companies, and has compiled FCC studies on fiber deployment activity, quality of service, and bypass. He has co-authored a number of other papers, including several on telephone traffic engineering, and holds three patents, two of which deal with telephone traffic measurement.

STANFORD L. LEVIN is Chairman and Professor of Economics at Southern Illinois University, Edwardsville. He served as a Commissioner on the Illinois Commerce Commission from 1984–1986, where he was heavily involved in telecommunications issues, and served as Chairman of the Commission's Telecommunications Policy Committee. He has served as a consultant to the Federal Trade Commission, has published widely in professional journals, has co-edited a book on antitrust, and has presented expert testimony on telecommunications before numerous regulatory agencies.

JOHN G. LYNCH, JR. is Associate Professor of Marketing at the University of Florida. He is a member of the Editorial Boards of the *Journal of Consumer Research* and the *Journal of Marketing Research,* and he has served as a consultant to the Florida Public Service Commission. His published research and research activities have centered on four general topics: the effects of memory and attention processes in consumer judgment and choice; context effects on decision making; validity issues in research methodology; and the measurement of values.

ELLIOT E. MAXWELL, as Assistant Vice President of Corporate Strategy for Pacific Telesis Group, heads a multi-disciplinary staff responsible for long range planning and the identification of critical policy issues. He previously served as Special Assistant to the Chairman of the FCC, as Deputy Chief of the FCC Office of Science and Technology, and as Senior Counsel to the U.S. Senate

Select Committee on Intelligence Activities. He has been a consultant to numerous organizations in the U.S. and Japan.

JAMES W. MCCONNAUGHEY is a Senior Economist in the Office of Policy Analysis and Development at the National Telecommunications and Information Administration. He held several similar positions in the FCC Common Carrier Bureau, and later was manager of the Research Studies Division at Bethesda Research Institute. He is the co-author of two books and various studies on telecommunications competition and deregulation in the U.S., and currently is examining U.S. competitiveness in global telecommunications markets.

WILLIAM P. MCGOWAN is a founder of MCI Communications Corporation and has been its Chairman since 1968, when MCI started in Washington, D.C. with only three employees. He is a member of the Board of Directors of Georgetown University, was named Telecommunications Executive of the Decade by the Communications Network organization, and received the Industry Achievement Award of the International Communications Association in 1986. Prior to founding MCI, he was a management and financial consultant, concentrating in high technology industries.

BRIDGER M. MITCHELL is a Senior Economist at the Rand Corporation where his research encompasses telecommunications, energy, econometrics, health insurance, and regulation policy. He has taught economics at Stanford University and UCLA, and he has been a Brookings Economics Policy Fellow at HEW. His books, articles, and monographs include major studies of local telephone demand and pricing, and methodologies for using incremental costs of local telephone service.

M. ISHAQ NADIRI is the Jay Gould Professor of Economics at New York University and a Research Associate at the National Bureau of Economic Research. His areas of specialization include the economics of technical change and productivity growth, investment theory and modeling, monetary economics, and quantitative analysis and applied econometrics. He has been a professor at Berkeley, Northwestern, the University of Chicago, and Columbia, and is the author of several books and a number of articles in academic journals.

SHARON L. NELSON, Chairman of the Washington Utilities and Transportation Commission since 1985, is the current President of the National Association of Regulatory Utility Commissioners. She served as Staff Counsel to the U.S. Senate Commerce Committee (1976–1978), and was legislative counsel to Consumers Union of the United States (1978–1981). She is the former Staff Coordinator for the Joint Select Committee on Telecommunications of the Washington State Legislature (1983–1985), past Chairman of NARUC's Committee on Communications (1987–1989), and has taught in secondary school.

ELI M. NOAM has been on leave from the Columbia University School of Business since 1987 and serves as a New York State Public Service Commissioner. The founding Director of Columbia's Center for Telecommunications and Information Studies, he has edited or co-edited a number of books, and is the author of the forthcoming two-volume *European Telecommunications and European Television*. He has published extensively in professional journals, has taught at the Columbia Law School and Princeton, and was an Advisory Board member for the federal government's FTS-2000 telephone network.

ROGER G. NOLL is Professor of Economics and Director of the Public Policy Program at Stanford University. He has served as a Senior Economist at the President's Council of Economic Advisors in the Johnson administration, a Senior Fellow at the Brookings Institution, and a Professor and Chairman of the Department of Economics at CalTech. Among his research activities is a lengthy list of books and articles on the economics of sports, the economics and politics of government R&D projects, and the economics and politics of regulation.

JERROLD OPPENHEIM is Assistant Attorney General in the Utilities Division of the Massachusetts Department of the Attorney General. He previously represented consumers as Director of Consumer Litigation for the Legal Assistance Foundation of Chicago, Director of Consumer Law for the legal services program in New York City, and Assistant Attorney General-In-Charge of Utilities for New York State. He has published widely in the field, and was Editor of the *Chicago Journalism Review* and *Evaluation Quarterly*.

LEWIS PERL is Senior Vice President of National Economic Research Associates and is responsible for studies relating to the economics of telecommunications, energy, and the environment. A former Assistant Professor at Cornell, his numerous papers, articles, and book chapters on telephone demand, costing and pricing, include the leading study on U.S. residential demand for telephone access, which has been used in many FCC and state regulatory proceedings. He consults for major telephone companies in the U.S. and abroad on the demand for and pricing of telephone services.

ALMARIN PHILLIPS is the John C. Hower Professor of Public Policy and Management at the Wharton School, and Professor of Law and Economics at the University of Pennsylvania. He is North American Editor of the *Journal of Industrial Economics* and has authored or edited seven books and an abundance of articles and comments dealing with industrial organization, regulation, and the economics of technological change. He has taught at Harvard, CalTech, McGill, and the London Graduate School of Business, and was a long time director of the National Bureau of Economic Research (1971–1983).

GLEN ROBINSON is the John C. Stennis Professor of Law and Goldsmith Research Professor of Law at the University of Virginia. He served as an FCC Commissioner from 1974–1976, and as U.S. Ambassador and head of the U.S. delegation to the World Administrative Radio Conference in 1979. He is co-editor of one of the standard texts on administrative law, and the author of numerous articles and book chapters on torts, administrative law and communications, the most recent of which concern the breakup of the Bell System, and the line item veto.

KENNETH G. ROBINSON, JR. is Senior Policy Advisor to the Chairman of the FCC. He previously served in similar positions over a ten-year period (1979–1989) with four U.S. Assistant Secretaries of Commerce for Communications and Information at the National Telecommunications and Information Administration. A former Justice Department Attorney, he is the author, co-author, or editor of many government reports and position papers relating to telecommunications, and he has written extensively on the AT&T divestiture in professional journals.

SUSAN C. SASSALOS is a doctoral student of business at the University of California at Berkeley. She is also a research intern at the Pacific Gas and Electric Company in San Francisco, where she is examining some of the consequences of deregulation. Her previous research has included analyses of executive compensation, the wage structure in the electronics industry and the effect of relative wages on attrition and productivity, and negotiations between unions and the labor relations departments of the telephone companies in 1983 and 1986.

LEE L. SELWYN is President of the consulting firm Economics and Technology Inc. and specializes in telecommunications pricing and regulatory policy. He has appeared as an expert witness in telecommunications regulatory proceedings in more than thirty states and at the FCC, and has served as a consultant for U.S. and foreign government agencies as well as for major corporate telecommunications users and user organizations. He has published widely on topics relating to telecommunications networks and services, market structures, and costing and pricing.

ALFRED C. SIKES has been Chairman of the FCC since August 1989. Prior to his FCC appointment, he served as Assistant Secretary of Commerce for Communications and Information and Administrator of the National Telecommunications and Information Administration from 1986–1989. An attorney and former owner of a broadcast management and consulting firm, he was an Assistant Attorney General to Missouri Attorney General John Danforth, and was a member of the Missouri Cabinet as Director of Consumer Affairs, Regulation and Licensing.

MARVIN A. SIRBU, JR. holds a joint appointment as an Associate Professor in Engineering and Public Policy, the Graduate School of Industrial Administration, and Electrical and Computer Engineering at Carnegie Mellon University. He previously taught at the Sloan School at MIT, where he directed its Research Program on Communications Policy. His recent publications have focused on the theory of compatibility standards for computers and communications, and how new communications technology impacts public regulation and corporate decision making.

SUSAN R. SMART will be Assistant Professor in the Department of Economics and Public Policy at the Indiana University School of Business beginning in Fall 1990. She is completing her Ph.D. dissertation at Stanford University on the political factors influencing decisions by state regulators concerning bypass of the public switch telephone network, and the impact of those decisions on local rates. She is also conducting research about the effects of water transport competition on the nineteenth century railroad cartels.

MARTIN G. TASCHDJIAN is Director of Strategic Marketing for US West. He previously has held positions at U.S. Sprint, in its strategic planning, regulatory affairs, and sales and marketing departments, at the National Telecommunications and Information Administration, and at Hatfield Associates, Inc. His recent research and publications focus on the interactions of technology change, competition, and public policy, and he has testified on those subjects in a number of state regulatory proceedings.

WILLIAM E. TAYLOR is Vice President of National Economics Research Associates, Inc., and directs its Cambridge office. At NERA, and previously at Bell Laboratories, and Bell Communications Research Inc., he has studied competition policies in telecommunications, economic issues concerning broadband network architectures, quantitative analysis of price cap and incentive regulation proposals, and antitrust problems in telecommunications markets. He has published widely in the field and has taught at Cornell University and MIT.

PHILIP L. VERVEER is a partner in the law firm of Willkie, Farr, & Gallagher, specializing in communications and antitrust law. He was the U.S. Department of Justice's first lead counsel in the investigation and prosecution of the AT&T 1974 antitrust case. Subsequently, he served with the Federal Trade Commission and then as Chief of the FCC Cable Television Bureau (1978–1979), its Broadcast Bureau (1979), and its Common Carrier Bureau (1979–1981), becoming the only person in the history of the agency to have held all three positions.

LEONARD WAVERMAN is Professor of Economics and Director of the Centre for International Studies at the University of Toronto. He is a member of the Ontario Telephone Service Commission, and has written extensively on the long-distance telecommunications market and efficiency aspects of regulation, as well as on industrial organization and antitrust. He is the Editor of *Energy Journal*, a former Editor of the *Canadian Journal of Economics*, and is currently working on a book (with Robert W. Crandall) on regulating telecommunications in a competitive environment.

DENNIS L. WEISMAN is Director of Strategic Marketing for Southwestern Bell Corporation, where he is responsible for telecommunications market demand studies. He has published widely in law and economic journals on the economics of regulated industries, with emphasis on telecommunications. He is a former District Manager-Demand Analysis for Southwestern Bell Telephone, where he testified in a number of regulatory proceedings on the issues of bypass, competition, and asymmetric regulation in the telecommunications industry.

RICHARD E. WILEY is a senior partner in the Washington, D.C. law firm of Wiley, Rein & Fielding. He has served as General Counsel (1970–1972), Commissioner (1972–1974), and Chairman (1974–1977) of the FCC, and in 1980 was head of the Reagan Administration's transition team for the Justice Department. He is a former member of the Council of the Administrative Conference of the U.S., former President of the Federal Communications Bar Association, and present Chairman of the FCC's Advisory Committee on Advanced Television Service.

JOHN R. WOODBURY is currently a Vice President of ICF Consulting Associates. He was formerly Associate Director for Special Projects in the Bureau of Economics of the Federal Trade Commission, Vice-President for Research and Policy Analysis at the National Cable Television Association, Chief of the FCC Common Carrier Bureau's Economics Division, and a Senior Economist with the FCC's Network Inquiry Special Staff. Among his publications are articles on the AT&T divestiture and a co-authored book on television regulation.

After the Breakup: Assessing the
New Post-AT&T Divestiture Era

Introduction

■

BARRY G. COLE

A number of books and scholarly articles have been written about the causes of and events surrounding the breakup of the Bell System.[1] This brief historical outline is intended to provide some background to promote a better understanding of various issues discussed in this volume, particularly those raised in chapter 1.

In September 1987, U.S. District Court Judge Greene, in reviewing the progress of the 1982 consent decree which broke up the Bell System in January 1984 stated:

> Although it may be difficult to recall this now, the fact is that for thirty years prior to 1984, the Congress, the courts, the Federal Communications Commission and state regulators wrestled with the problem of what to do about the Bell System monopoly, its arrogance in dealing with competitors and consumers, and its power to shut off competition. . . . In the meantime, competitors languished and the American ideal of free and fair competition remained absent from the telecommunications industry. When ultimately the decree . . . was negotiated between the parties [AT&T and the Justice Department],

and approved by the Court, it resolved the problem of claimed monopolistic conduct in telecommunications by going to its root.[2]

The root of the problem was the Bell System's "bottleneck" control over local telephone switches. In 1949, the Justice Department filed suit alleging that AT&T and its subsidiary Western Electric (Western) had conspired to monopolize the telephone equipment market, had excluded other manufacturers and sellers from that market, and had earned monopoly profits as a consequence.[3] The government sought the separation of Western Electric from the Bell System and a requirement that the Bell System buy its equipment by competitive bidding. Under circumstances later to be the subject of intense investigations by a House Subcommittee,[4] the Eisenhower administration terminated the suit in 1956 and entered a consent decree with AT&T[5] that Attorney General Herbert Brownell assumed would do AT&T "no real injury."[6]

The 1956 consent decree enabled AT&T to retain Western Electric, which even at the time of the 1984 divestiture was still manufacturing 80 percent of the telephone equipment supplied in the United States and most of AT&T's 827 million miles of copper wire. However, it did several other things which, although in 1956 seemed relatively insignificant, proved to be of increasing consequence to the Bell System. Henceforth Western Electric would be able to manufacture only equipment of the kind sold or leased for use within the Bell System. Moreover, AT&T and its Bell Labs subsidiary were required to grant to any applicant, including potential AT&T competitors, nonexclusive licenses (in return for reasonable royalties) to all of its existing and future patents, such as the transistor. In fact, a growing number of AT&T's emerging competitors were later able to take advantage of Bell Lab's new discoveries, while AT&T could not, because under the 1956 decree the Bell System was limited to furnishing common carrier communications service and facilities that were subject to public regulation. With the rapid convergence of communication and computer and data processing technology, AT&T's inability to engage in unregulated computer activities became increasingly significant, and the ability to draw the boundaries between permitted and forbidden activities by the regulated monopoly became more problematic.[7]

During the eighteen years following the 1956 consent decree, rapid technological change had reduced the minimum efficient scale upon which telecommunications activity could be undertaken, making competition possible in at least some market segments.[8] In addition, partly because of a belief by some key policymakers that AT&T's size made effective regulation impossible, public policy—particularly that formulated at the FCC—had been increasingly procompetitive. These factors had combined to result, sometimes inadvertently,[9] in the emergence of more fledgling competitors to the Bell System, in the equipment and long-distance markets, and more complaints concerning AT&T's resistance to their entry. In 1974, MCI filed its own private lawsuit seeking monetary damages for AT&T's alleged antitrust violations and history of discrimination.[10] Other similar suits followed.[11]

In November 1974, the Justice Department again sued AT&T for alleged violation of the antitrust laws. This time, the allegations of monopolization included the long-distance and customer premises equipment (CPE) markets, as well as the equipment markets addressed by the 1949 case.[12] The suit asked for major structural remedies, including the divesting of Western Electric originally requested by the Department in the 1949 suit, and the separation of AT&T Long Lines, the long-distance portion of the Bell System, from some or all of the local Bell Operating Companies (BOCs). The Justice Department's case had been prepared under the direction of Antitrust Division attorney Philip Verveer (a contributor to this volume) during the chaotic Watergate period, with its rapid turnover in the Attorney-General's office and a White House preoccupied with other matters. The suit was filed with the approval of Attorney General William Saxbe, but was never discussed at a Cabinet meeting, and President Ford did not remember having spoken about it with Saxbe.[13]

AT&T had taken an increasingly aggressive public stance against further inroads against its monopoly, particularly when John deButts became its Chairman in 1972. The following year, invoking the themes successfully used early in this century by AT&T's legendary Chairman Theodore Vail,[14] deButts told the National Association of Regulatory Utility Commissioners that AT&T had an obligation to oppose contrived competition and favor NARUC regulation. According to deButts, "given the nature of our industry, there is something right about monopoly, i.e., regulated monopoly." He told the state regulators "the time has come, for a moratorium on further experiments in economics —a moratorium sufficient to permit a systematic evaluation of the feasibility and desirability of competition in telecommunications."[15]

DeButts sought his "systematic evaluation" in the halls of Congress, through the introduction of H.R. 12323, the "Consumer Communications Reform Act of 1976" (CCRA), commonly called the "Bell bill." The bill sought to reaffirm the need for a unitary national telephone network to achieve universal telephone service; turn back the clock on equipment competition; make it more difficult for new competitors to enter the market; and make it easier for AT&T to set prices at levels comparable with those of the new entrants. In addition, the proposed law imposed clear limits on federal authority, thereby limiting the power of the FCC to move forward with some of its pro-competitive policies. DeButts told the Congress that in its centennial year, the Bell System was facing a degree of uncertainty concerning the future that matched the uncertainties that attended its birth. The FCC had usurped the role of Congress and had "redefined the aims of the country's telecommunications policy, changed its goals."[16]

The deButts strategy succeeded in making Congress more sensitive to the changing telecommunications landscape. The Bell bill was only the beginning of the legislation debate, with eleven major Congressional telecommunications bills introduced between 1976 and 1981. However, deButts' hope that Congress would reverse the direction of evolving policy was never realized. None of the bills were enacted into law, and in fact Congress was (and is still) unable to forge any consensus regarding telecommunications policy.

Meanwhile, the Justice Department's 1974 suit was not moving any faster than were telecommunications bills in Congress. The Department's complaint was assigned to Federal Judge Joseph Waddy. AT&T argued the U.S. District Court lacked jurisdiction because the relevant questions were already pending before the FCC. In November 1976, Judge Waddy ruled that his Court had jurisdiction, a ruling which was unsuccessfully appealed up to the Supreme Court.[17] In July 1978 Judge Waddy died of cancer, and the following month newly appointed U.S. District Court Judge Harold Greene inherited the AT&T case.

Judge Greene was thus the first of the three major principals of divestiture to assume his place on center stage. The drafter of the 1964 Civil Rights Act and the 1965 Voting Rights Act, and the person Attorney General Robert Kennedy called "the guy with the answers," Greene left his post as head of the Appeals and Research Section of the Justice Department's Civil Rights Division in 1967 to become Chief Judge of the District of Columbia Court of General Sessions. In 1978, when Judge John Sirica became Senior Judge, Harold Greene joined the U.S. District Court for the District of Columbia.

Judge Greene told both the government and AT&T that he was unwilling to postpone the litigation further because "the public has a right to have the important case started with dispatch." "There is just too much delay in complex antitrust litigation," continued Greene, and "I am unwilling to let this case fall into that pattern."[18] Greene made clear his desire to make the case a model of efficiency for the federal court system, which had been subjected to criticism aimed at both the

AT&T case and the government's 1969 antitrust suit filed against IBM, which was no closer to resolution. Greene made good his promise as he pushed forward through "many thousands" of documents, close to 350 witnesses and, over 24,000 pages of trial transcript.[19] To help speed up the process, the Judge forced the parties to stipulate the litigation issues.

The second principal to take center stage was Charles L. Brown, who succeeded deButts as AT&T Chairman and Chief Executive Officer in February 1979. Except for U.S. Navy service during World War II, Brown had been with AT&T all his working life, beginning at age eighteen with a summertime job digging ditches. Both his parents had also worked for the company. After a long steady climb up the lengthy Bell System ladder and service as president of Illinois Bell, Brown became President of AT&T in April 1977. It was clear to most observers that Brown and deButts were quite different personalities, and if and when Brown succeeded deButts as Chairman, AT&T's hard-line position, that competition is "contrived" and to be opposed, would soften.

Immediately upon taking office as AT&T's new head, Brown proclaimed "A New Realism." He told the National Telephone Cooperative Association, "Competition is here and it is growing. It's a fact of life in our business and has been for some time," and "AT&T is ready without preconceptions to explore alternative futures."[20] Brown desired a rapid resolution of AT&T's antitrust problems and wanted to move forward in the new competitive world. He soon was making conscientious attempts to work with the FCC, Congress and the Justice Department to undo some of the damage of the deButts' strategy.

The final principal to join Judge Greene and Charles Brown at center stage was William F. Baxter. A well-known law professor at Stanford University, Baxter was recognized as a believer in economic theory and the benefits of private enterprise, who opposed government meddling in the marketplace. His opposition to many antitrust cases was at times very outspoken. Yet, on the basis of those same economic theories, Baxter strongly believed the AT&T suit was valid and necessary, and should be vigorously prosecuted by the government.[21] He had thought and lectured about the case at Stanford, and had a definite conception of the desirable and appropriate resolution. When he came to Washington in 1981 to join the recently formed Reagan administration, Baxter had the chance to implement his ideas.

Officially, Baxter was "merely" the Assistant Attorney General of the Justice Department's Antitrust Division: he reported to Deputy Attorney General Edward Schmultz, and ultimately the Attorney General William French Smith. However, with respect to the AT&T case, both his superiors had recused themselves,[22] and thus for that particular litigation he was de facto Attorney General. Thus it was Baxter who, upon arriving in Washington, found himself the main object of attacks from those senior officials within the new Reagan administration who wanted the AT&T suit dropped. Leading that attack was Defense Secretary Casper Weinberger, who told a closed Senate hearing in March 1981 that because "the American Telephone and Telegraph network is the most important communications network we have to serve our strategic system in this country," it was "essential" it be kept together.[23] (A similar stance had been taken by the Eisenhower Defense Department to the 1949 Department of Justice AT&T antitrust suit, and was a factor in the decision by Attorney General Brownwell to enter into the 1956 consent decree without requiring any divestiture by AT&T.)

Commerce Secretary Malcolm Baldrige supported Weinberger in his attempts to have Baxter drop the suit. Baldrige feared divesting the operating companies and opening up the U.S. equipment market to foreign competitors would damage the American balance of trade position and would not help the development of U.S. industry. Baldrige believed Congress, not the courts, was the appropriate place to determine telecommunications policy and the need to restructure AT&T. He argued the dismissal of the Justice Department suit would help facilitate such legislative efforts.[24]

It did not take long for Baxter to make it clear he would resist attempts by Weinberger, Baldrige, and others to drop the AT&T case. The day after he received a letter from Deputy Secretary of Defense Frank Carlucci confirming "it is the position of the Department of Defense that the pending suit against American Telephone and Telegraph company be dismissed."[25] Baxter held his first press conference in which he vowed to "litigate [the case] to the eyeballs."[26]

Any inclination of the Reagan White House to order Baxter to change his mind and drop the case was tempered by memories of the disastrous results of Nixon White House attempts to interfere with the Justice Department's handling of the ITT case (the Dita Beard episode) and the Watergate investigation. The controversy which followed the dropping of the 1949 suit against Western Electric also suggested caution. James Baker, who was President Reagan's principal political adviser in 1981, told Secretary Baldrige and fellow Presidential Counselor Edwin Meese that dismissal of the case would have excessive negative political repercussions.[27]

Baxter believed that in order for genuine competition in telecommunications to exist, legislative or judicial action was needed to prohibit AT&T from using its "bottleneck" regulated local exchange monopolies, especially with respect to long-distance services, telecommunications equipment, and related information markets. In his view, since regulation limited AT&T's direct exercise of its market power in local exchange service, AT&T had the incentive (and ability) to discriminate against potential competitors in gaining access to the local telephone switches, by refusing, or at least delaying attachment, by giving inferior connections, and by overcharging those wishing to connect. Moreover, the Bell System had the ability to cross-subsidize AT&T's competitive services by shifting costs to its noncompetitive regulated local exchange monopolies, thereby enabling AT&T to drive efficient, low-cost competitors out of business.

Baxter's ideal solution was to separate—"quarantine"—the competitive and potentially competitive from the monopoly portion of AT&T, and then to require the divested local exchange companies to provide all long-distance carriers equal access and service to their bottleneck local facilities. To remove the danger of the divested local exchange companies repeating perceived past AT&T anticompetitive practices, Baxter wished to prohibit these regulated companies from engaging in the theoretically competitive long-distance, manufacturing and information services markets (prohibitions later to be called "line-of-business restrictions"). If these conditions were met, Baxter did not care whether the divested local exchange companies were all combined into a single company or into any other number.[28]

Baxter's desire to "litigate to the eyeballs" was tempered by his recognition that if the case continued and the inevitable appeals were filed, it would be at least four to six years before final disposition, and if the case were remanded for further proceedings at Judge Greene's level, it could take much longer.[29] Moreover, there was no certainty the Justice Department would win the case. Although willing, at least publicly, to accept legislation "containing appropriate competitive safeguards" as an acceptable alternative, it became clear that such legislation was having difficulty in Congress, and Judge Greene was not willing to grant a continuance of the case until Congressional differences could be resolved.[30] Finally, although Baxter had not been ordered to drop the case, opposition to its perpetuation from key members of the administration had not diminished. Therefore, Baxter saw an out-of-court settlement with AT&T that accomplished his major purposes as an increasingly attractive option.

At the same time, Charles Brown also had reason to be favorably inclined towards an out-of-court settlement based on Baxter's "clean but painful solution."[31] First, the litigation was costly, distracting, and, as Baxter had surmised, would probably take years to conclude. Second, the litigation outcome seemed less promising to AT&T when in September 1981 Judge Greene, after sixty-one days of the presentation of the government's case, denied AT&T's Motion to Dismiss and declared that "the testimony and documenting evidence introduced by the government demonstrates that the Bell System has violated antitrust laws in a number of ways over a lengthy period of time. The government has satisfied its burden, and the burden is now on the defendant to disprove what the government has done."[32] Third, two major efforts to reach an out-of-court settlement with the Department of Justice based on an injunctive rather than a divestiture approach (the "Quagmire I" and "Quagmire II" negotiations of November 1980–February 1981 and Fall 1981) had been both unsuccessful and frustrating. Fourth, although Brown could live with the "tough, doubly tough on the Bell system"[33] Telecommunications Competition and Deregulation Act of 1981 (S. 898), passed by the Senate by a vote of 90 to 4 in October 1981, he considered the companion bill introduced in December by House Communications Subcommittee Chairman Tim Wirth—"The Telecommunications Act of 1981" (H.R. 5158)—totally unacceptable. It was clear to Brown that inexorably "the Bell System was perceived in some quarters as too big, too powerful, too pervasive," and thus if Congress were able to agree upon relevant legislation, it would include elaborate injunctive decrees restricting AT&T's flexibility. And finally, the FCC's continuing procompetitive policies, coupled with restrictions on AT&T engaging in nonregulated, noncommunications activities posed by the 1956 consent decree, led Brown to conclude that "Time was not in the Bell System's favor" for, "soon the market opportunities created by our own technology might pass us by."[34]

The "quarantine theory" Baxter offered was an "immediate and comprehensive solution" which provided a means of diffusing the issue of AT&T's alleged size and operations, removed concerns regarding cross-subsidization, and eliminated long-distance competitors' complaints about equal access.[35] The Baxter solution would not only limit the level of uncertainty by ending a costly antitrust suit, it would avoid the danger of a negative judgment which could be used in dozens of private antitrust lawsuits which had already been brought by various parties against AT&T.[36] Most importantly, the Baxter resolution would lift the 1956 consent decree restrictions, while enabling AT&T to retain Bell Labs and Western Electric and to manage a nationwide network as a unified entity.

On January 8, 1982, almost a year after the AT&T trial had begun and just weeks before AT&T was scheduled to complete its defense presentation,[37] Baxter and Brown announced an agreement to settle the antitrust suit with the filing of a new consent decree which would supersede the one in force since 1956.[38] A plan of reorganization which would specify how AT&T would adhere to the new decree's objectives was required to be filed within six months of the Court's approval of the decree. Within eighteen months of the decree's acceptance by the Court, AT&T would have to complete its reorganization.[39] The date finally chosen for the reorganization to take effect was January 1, 1984.

The 1982 consent decree and plan of reorganization was based on the Baxter solution. AT&T would spin off its twenty-two wholly or majority owned Bell Operating Companies (BOCs), which would be regrouped within seven new distinct regional holding companies (RHCs).[40] This divestiture would eliminate AT&T's ability to disadvantage competitors in both the interexchange or the equipment markets. In the post-divestiture world, AT&T would be unable to subsidize its own interexchange service with revenues from monopoly local exchange service or obstruct competitors' access to the local exchange network. The BOCs would be restricted to providing only monopoly local exchange (intraLATA) services within approximately one hundred sixty-one local access and transport areas (LATAs).[41] Competitive interexchange service crossing LATA lines (interLATA service) would be provided by AT&T and competing interexchange (long-distance) carriers. Section II of the 1982 decree specifically ensured all interexchange carriers and information providers access "equal in type, quality and price to that provided to AT&T and its affiliates."

As for the equipment market, the AT&T divestiture of the BOCs meant that the incentive to exclude non-Western Electric equipment would be eliminated. In addition, the decree forbade the BOCs and their new parent RHCs from manufacturing equipment, thus removing any inducement to favor particular equipment manufacturers. To further help promote a competitive equipment marketplace, the decree included provisions to prohibit discrimination by the BOCs in equipment procurement.

When Baxter and Brown announced their divestiture settlement, many feared for the viability of the 22 divested BOCs. Numerous experts echoed the concern of Eric Schneidewind, Chairman of the Michigan Public Service Commission and member of the National Association of Regulatory Utility Commissioners' Communications Committee, that "the loss of telecommunications will make BOCs the railroads of the 1980s" which will retain "the least profitable, most capital intensive business (local residential service) while new technology and business opportunities will be lost to competitors."[42]

AT&T was widely perceived as retaining two-thirds of the revenue generating capability of the Bell System, with the ability henceforth to focus on the high-growth fields of telecommunications/computers, long-distance, and advanced equipment manufacturing. With over $35 billion in assets, the new AT&T was still twice the size of GTE, the most similar company, and it had retained Bell Labs and Western Electric.

On the other hand, the two-thirds of the assets of the old Bell System inherited by the newly divested BOCs were thought to consist largely of outdated equipment. Moreover, the BOCs were faced with escalating costs and the specter of going to the state Public Utility Commissions (PUCs) for local rate hikes, in part because of the loss of the parent company's support of local rates from long-distance revenues. In addition, concerns were raised that the impacts of technological change would extend to the local distribution plant, facilitating competitive alternatives to all BOC services and endangering the end of the traditional natural monopoly.

Such fears were expressed repeatedly in many of the numerous comments submitted to Judge Greene after he invoked the Tunney Act[43] to review the consent decree provisions. Before entering the decree, in his August 1982 *Modification of Final Judgement* (MFJ) opinion[44] the Judge revised and amended some of its provisions to help insure the future viability of the BOCs by (1) giving them control of the Yellow Pages and its more than $3 billion revenues a year, (2) allowing them to market (but still not manufacture) customer premises equipment, (3) giving them the Bell trademark, (4) prohibiting AT&T from using the Bell name or logo except in connection with Bell Labs, and (5) allowing the BOCs to seek permission, via a waiver, to enter nonregulated, competitive businesses. While Baxter believed "regulated utilities should not be fooling around in competitive markets,"[45] Judge Greene was reluctant to bar permanently a new Bell Operating Company (BOC) from nonregulated activities. Under Section VIII (C) of the MFJ, the BOCs would be allowed to file a "line of business" waiver request, which would be granted if Judge Greene found that "there is no substantial possibility that it could use its monopoly power to impede competition in the market it seeks to enter."[46]

Although Greene's modifications watered down Baxter's "quarantine" approach by blurring somewhat the lines between the new wholly competitive AT&T and the wholly regulated BOCs, and took some valuable assets from AT&T, the modifications were not contested by either Baxter or Brown. An appeal was filed and supported by a number of states which objected to aspects of the MFJ that affected state laws or regulations, but the appeal was denied by the Supreme Court.[47]

After the divestiture took effect on January 1, 1984, the BOCs and their new parents, the seven Regional Holding Companies (RHCs), took advantage of the opportunity to diversify into nonregulated activities, particularly publishing, consulting or financial services, software, and real estate. The RHCs also engaged in various foreign business ventures. According to Sam Ginn, President of Pacific Telesis, "operating companies felt their oats and thought that they could do almost anything. We could whip anybody in anything."[48] But consumers and state regulators worried that local toll telephone ratepayers would be cross-subsidizing such new ventures. And even if such a practice could be detected and prevented, diversification could still cost consumers if it caused Wall Street to view RHCs as risky ventures, thereby raising the cost of capital. This too would be, in effect, a cross-subsidy.[49] If the ventures failed, the basic phone network might also be at risk.

In his *Modification of Final Judgement* opinion, Judge Greene declared his jurisdiction would continue on indefinitely "for such orders or directions" as may be necessary for constructing, carrying out, modifying and enforcing the MFJ, and for punishing any decree violations. The judge also provided for a triennial reexamination of the line-of-business restrictions which prevent the BOCs from manufacturing telecommunications equipment, offering interexchange services, or providing information services.

Since 1984, the BOCs have attempted to have the line-of-business restrictions lifted, and by the time of the 1987 Triennial Review, the Department of Justice was headed by Edwin Meese, who as Presidential Counselor had joined Secretaries Weinberger and Baldrige in opposing Baxter's pursuit of the AT&T case. In a controversial reversal of its longstanding position, the Meese-led Department told Judge Greene that conditions had sufficiently changed to no longer make the prohibitions necessary.[50] But in his Triennial Review ruling Judge Greene determined the BOCs retained the monopoly over the local switches, the same "root" problem which had led to the antitrust violation of the Bell System and the ultimate AT&T divestiture. The Court said, "the actions of the BOCS still do not inspire confidence that, should the companies be permitted to enter [the lines of business] without limitation, they would treat competitors in an even-handed manner."[51] Judge Greene did allow the BOCs to offer "gateways" to information services which enable users to have convenient access to many information providers and to enable different services to have unified billing.[52] The following year he ruled BOCs may provide information transmission services, e.g., voice storage and retrieval services, which do not involve content generation or content manipulation.[53]

The BOCs appealed Judge Greene's 1987 Triennial Review ruling with partial success. In April 1990, a three-member panel of the U.S. Court of Appeals for the District of Columbia Circuit unanimously affirmed Greene's decision to retain the MFJ manufacturing and inter-exchange service line-of-business restrictions.[54] However, the appellate panel determined that because neither AT&T nor the Justice Department had opposed the lifting of some or all existing prohibitions on BOC information services, Judge Greene should have applied a "more flexible" public interest legal standard in deciding that uncontested issue. As a result, the District Court's information services ruling was reversed and remanded, and Judge Greene was instructed to undertake further proceedings to determine "whether the removal of the information services restrictions as applied to the generation of information would be anticompetitive under *present* market conditions" and would be "within the *reaches* of the public interest."[55]

In the meantime, as will be discussed in this volume, the BOCs continue to seek legislation to remove all MFJ line-of-business restrictions and to transfer to the FCC various powers of Judge Greene.[56]

This book opens with question and answer exchanges with the three divestiture principals, William Baxter, Charles Brown and Judge Harold Greene. Their thoughts and reflections were those of 1989, more then seven years after the 1982 consent decree, and more than five years after the actual AT&T divestiture.

ENDNOTES

1. See, for example: Steven Bradley and Jerry A. Hausman, eds., *Future Competition in Telecommunications* (Cambridge, Mass.: Harvard Business School Press, 1989); Timothy Brennan, "Why Regulated Firms Should Be Kept Out of Unregulated Markets: Understanding the Divestiture in *US v AT&T*" Antitrust Bulletin (Fall 1987), 32(3): 741–93; Gerald Brock, *The Telecommunications Industry: The Dynamics of Market Structure* (Cambridge, Mass.: Harvard University Press, 1981); Steven Coll, *The Deal of the Century: The Breakup of AT&T* (New York: Atheneum, 1986); David S. Evans, *Breaking Up Bell: Essays on Industrial Organizations and Regulation* (New York: North-Holland, 1983); Gerald R. Faulhaber, *Telecommunications in Turmoil: Technology and Public Policy* (Cambridge, Mass.: Ballinger, 1987).

And Fred Henck and Bernard Strassburg, *A Slippery Slope: The Long Road to the Breakup of AT&T* (Westport, Conn.: Greenwood Press, 1988); Robert Horowitz, *The Irony of Regulating Reform: The Deregulation of American Telecommunications* (New York: Oxford University Press, 1989); Roger G. Noll and

Bruce M. Owen, "The Anticompetitive Uses of Regulation: United States v. AT&T," in John E. Kwoka, Jr. and Lawrence J. White, eds., *The Antitrust Revolution* (Glenview, Ill.: Scott Foresman, 1989); Harry M. Shooshan III, *Disconnecting Bell: The Impact of the AT&T Divestiture* (New York: Pergamon Press, 1983); Christopher Sterling et al., eds., *Decision to Divest: Major Documents in United States v. AT&T 1974–1984* (Washington, D.C.: Communications Press, 1986); Alan Stone, *Wrong Number: The Breakup of AT&T* (New York: Basic Books, 1989); Peter Temin and Louis Galambos, *The Fall of the Bell System: A Study in Prices and Politics* (Cambridge: Cambridge University Press, 1987); W. Brooke Tunstall, *Disconnecting Parties: Managing the Bell System Breakup; An Inside View* (New York: McGraw Hill, 1985); Alvin Von Auw, *Heritage and Destiny: Reflections on the Bell System in Transition* (New York: Praeger, 1983).

2. *U.S. v. Western Electric Co.*, 673 F. Supp. 525 at 600 (1987).

3. *U.S. v. Western Electric Co.*, CA No. 17-49 U.S. Dist. Ct. Dist. of New Jersey, Complaint, January 14, 1949. Western Electric provided almost all of the Bell System's switching, transmission, and customer premises equipment. In 1949, with existing technology, these were the only areas in which competition was deemed viable. AT&T claimed the vertically integrated structure and exclusive buying arrangement with Western provided economics of scale, uniformity of voice signals and the ability to meet high engineering standards. See Richard H. K. Vietor, in Bradley and Hausman, *Future Competition*, pp. 46–48.

4. See generally 86th Cong., 1st sess., U.S. House of Representatives, Committee on the Judiciary, Antitrust Subcommittee, *Report of Antitrust Subcommittee on Consent Decree Program of the Department of Justice (Cellar Report)*, January 30, 1959. In 1958 (85th Cong., 2d sess.) the same subcommittee issued three volumes of hearings and documents relating to its investigation.

5. *U.S. v. Western Electric Co.*, CA No. 17-49, *Final Judgment*, 1956 Trade Cas. 68.246 (D.N.J. 1956).

6. U.S. House of Representatives. *Report of Antitrust Subcommittee on Consent Decree Program of the Department of Justice*, Memo of T. Brooke Price, AT&T Vice President and General Counsel.

7. This difficulty of defining boundaries led to the FCC's *Computer I, Computer II*, and *Computer III* inquiries. Regulatory and Policy Problems Presented by the Interdependence of Computer Communications Services and Faculties, 28 FCC 2d 267 (1971), *aff'd in part and rev'd in part sub. nom. GTE Serv. Corp. v. FCC* 474 F. 2d 724 (2d Cir. 1973). Amendment of Section 64.702 of the Commission's Rules and Regulations *(Second Computer Inquiry)*, 77 FCC 2d 384, *aff'd sub. nom. Computer & Communications Indus. Ass'n v. FCC*, 693 F. 2d 198 (D.C. Cir. 1982, *Cert denied*, 461 U.S. 938 (1983). Amendment of Section 64.702 of the Commission's Rules and Regulations *(Third Computer Inquiry)* 104 FCC 2d 958 (1986), *modified*, 2 FCC Rcd 3035 (1987), *further reconsid. denied*, 3 FCC Rcd 1135 (1988), *appeals pending sub nom. California v. FCC*, No 87-7230 (9th Cir.); *Illinois Bell Tel. Co. v. FCC*, No 88-1364 (D.C. Cir.) Also see Stone, pp. 202–16, 260–72.

8. Transmission end switching costs were declining through the use of

microwave, satellites, fiber optics, digital transmission, pocket switching and computer-based customer premises equipment. Ironically, Bell Labs was at the forefront of developments in transistors, microwave, and satellites which were central to the evolution of increased competition for AT&T.

9. For example, the emergence of MCI's Execunet Service. See Brock, *The Telecommunications Industry*, pp. 210–30, and *MCI Telecommunications Corp. v. FCC.* 561 F. 2d 365 (D.C. Cir., 1977).

10. MCI won the case, but its $1.8 billion trial verdict was later set aside by a federal appeals court, and a new trial for damages resulted in MCI receiving a much smaller amount. *MCI v. AT&T*, No 74 C 633 U.S. Dist. Ct., Northern District of Illinois, Eastern Division, June 13, 1980, Tr 11536-9 (Jury Decision). *MCI v. AT&T*, 708 F. 2d 1081 (7th Cir., 1983).

11. For example, in 1976 Litton Systems, Inc. filed a private law suit alleging AT&T had monopolized various markets for Private Branch Exchanges (PBXs) and other business terminal equipment. In June, 1981 Litton won a jury trial.

12. *U.S. v. AT&T*, Ca No. 74-1698 (D.D.C.) Complaint, November 20, 1974. The allegations of monopolistic abuses included refusals to deal with competitors, discriminatory practices, abuses of the regulatory process, and price setting designed to exclude competitors. See Noll and Owen, pp. 301–15.

13. Temin, p. 110. According to author Steven Coll, Saxbe admitted never having talked to President Ford about the filing. However, Saxbe claims he told Vice President Ford he thought the lawsuit was a good idea, and probably would file it if he were named Attorney General. Coll, p. 71.

14. Theodore N. Vail was President of AT&T from 1885 to 1887 and from 1907–1919. In his second administration Vail's successful strategy for building the natural monopoly of the Bell System was reflected in his statements in the 1910 AT&T Annual Report: "The telephone systems should be universal, interdependent and intercommunicating. . . . All this can be accomplished . . . under such control and regulation as will afford the public much better service at less cost than any competition or governmental-owned monopoly."

15. John D. deButts' speech to the National Association of Regulatory Commissioners, Seattle, Washington, September 20, 1973.

16. 94th Cong., 2d sess., U.S. House of Representatives. *Competition in the Telecommunications Industry.* Hearings of Subcommittee on Communications, "Hearings on Competition in the Telecommunications Industry," Testimony of John D. deButts, September 28, 1976, p. 19.

17. Judge Joseph C. Waddy, *Memorandum Opinion and Order on Jurisdictional Issues*, November 24, 1976, *U.S. v. AT&T*, CA No. 74-1698, 427 F. Supp. 57 (D.D.C., 1976); *AT&T v. U.S.*, AT&T, *Petition for Writ of Certiorari to the United States District Court for the District of Columbia*, January 6, 1977. Judge Waddy's opinion was appealed to the Court of Appeals and to the Supreme Court, but both Courts declined to hear the appeal.

18. Coll, pp. 130–31.

19. The Government presented close to one hundred witnesses to support its case. AT&T presented about three hundred fifty witnesses before the trail was terminated. *United States v. AT&T*, 522 F. Supp. 131 at 140.

20. Temin, p. 175.; Von Auw, p. 416.

21. William F. Baxter, "How Government Cases Get Selected—Comments From Academia," *American Bar Association Antitrust Law Journal* (Spring 1977), pp. 586–601.

22. Attorney General Smith had been a director of Pacific Telephone, and his Deputy Edward Schmultz decided a conflict-of-interest resulted from his law firm's activities concerning an AT&T pension matter.

23. 97th Cong., 1st sess., Senate, Committee on Armed Services, Hearings on S. 694, Testimony of Casper Weinberger, March 23, 1981. By June the new Reagan Defense Department had prepared a more detailed analysis of the potential impact of the Justice Department's divestiture approach. The analysis concluded that "the Department of Justice does not understand the industry it seeks to restructure" and divestiture "would have a serious short-term effect and a lethal long-term effect" upon the nation's ability to rely upon the nationwide telecommunications network.

24. 97th Cong., 1st sess., Senate, Committee on the Judiciary. "Hearing on DOJ Oversight: U.S. v. AT&T," Testimony of Malcolm Baldrige, August 6, 1981, pp. 4–13.

25. 97th Cong., 1st sess., House of Representatives. Subcommittee on Government Information and Individual Rights, "Hearings on Departments of Justice and Defense and Antitrust Litigation," Letter from Frank Carlucci to William F. Baxter (April 8, 1981), November 4, 1981, Appendix I.

26. DOJ Transcript of Press Conference of William F. Baxter, Assistant Attorney-General Antitrust Division, April 9, 1981, p. 29.

27. Bernard Wunder interview cited in Temin, p. 231.

28. 97th Cong., 1st sess. House of Representatives, Subcommittee on Government Information and Individual Rights, "Hearings on Departments of Justice and Defense and Antitrust Litigation," Testimony of William F. Baxter, November 4, 1981, p. 4.

29. Id., p. 23.

30. In August 1981, Baxter asked Judge Greene for an eleven-month continuance of the case to see whether appropriate legislation addressing the government's concerns could be passed. Greene's refusal to grant the continuance enabled Baxter to report to Cabinet members that he had tried to accede to their wishes for the Justice Department to go slow, but the matter was out of his hands.

31. Charles L. Brown, letter in *Telecommunications Policy*, June 1983.

32. Judge Greene, *Opinion*, September 11, 1981, p. 73, *US v. AT&T*, Ca No. 74.1698 (D.D.S.), 524 F. Supp. 1336 at 1381.

33. Brown quoted in "Matter of Telecommunications Legislation," *Bell Telephone Magazine*, Edition 4, 1981, p. 6.

34. "A Personal Introduction by Charles L. Brown" in Harry M. Shooshan III, *Disconnecting Bell: The Impact of the AT&T Divestiture* (Elmsford, N.Y.: Pergamon Press, 1984), pp. 4–5.

35. *Telecommunications Policy*, June 1983.

36. In 1979, a total of forty-nine private antitrust suits were pending against

AT&T. Brock, p. 295. As Gerald Faulhaber notes, the Justice Department suit was a catalyst for a number of these suits for "the combination of treble damages, the deep pockets of Bell, and free evidence from the Justice case was tempting to many firms." Faulhaber, p. 60. Moreover, AT&T had already lost the MCI and Litton Industries private suits. (See notes 12 and 13 above.)

37. The AT&T trial began on January 15, 1981, but then recessed. It resumed in earnest on March 4. AT&T began its defense on August 3, and was scheduled to complete its presentation of evidence on January 20, 1982. The litigation phase of the trial was slated to end three weeks later. *U.S. v. AT&T* 552 F. Supp. 131 at 140. If Judge Greene would have found AT&T guilty of violating the antitrust laws, a second or "relief" phase of the case presumably would have taken place to determine the proper remedy for such violations and appropriate means for preventing its recurrence.

38. The parties called their arguments a "Modification of the Final Judgement" and submitted it on January 8, 1982, to the District Court for the District of New Jersey which was overseeing the 1956 decree. On the same day they attempted to file with Judge Greene's Court a dismissal of the AT&T litigation. Judge Greene ordered the dismissal to be "lodged" and not "filed," thereby enabling him to review it before it took effect. Eventually, jurisdiction over all aspects of the case, including the lifting of the 1956 decree, was transferred to Judge Greene.

39. AT&T filed its Plan of Reorganization on December 16, 1982, just over four months after Judge Greene approved the decree (with amendments) on August 11.

40. In Appendix A of the consent decree, twenty-two of the twenty-four associated companies were identified as Bell Operating Companies. AT&T had less than 50 percent of the stock of the other two companies, Cincinnati Bell and Southern New England Bell.

41. The term local access and transport area (LATA) was created to avoid confusing the new post-divestiture exchange areas with those that existed prior to the Bell System breakup. In general, LATAs correspond to Standard Metropolitan Statistical Areas and are defined in Section IV of the decree as "areas serving common social, economic and other purposes, even when such configuration transcends municipal or other local governmental boundaries." Some geographically small states are single LATA states; Delaware has no separate LATA, but there are 11 LATAs within Illinois. No LATA could be drawn to cross state boundaries without the permission of the Court. Judge Greene allowed two "corridor" LATAs, one between New York City and northern New Jersey, and the second between Camden, New Jersey, and Philadelphia.

42. 98th Cong., 1st sess., House of Representatives. *The Prospect for Universal Telephone Service.* Hearings of Subcommittee on Telecommunications, Consumer Protection and Finance, "Hearings on the Prospect for Universal Telephone Service," Testimony of Eric Schneidewind, March 22, 1983, p. 15.

43. The *Antitrust Procedures and Penalties Act of 1974* (better known as the Tunney Act) was passed after the 1972 ITT Consent Decree and Dita Beard Scandal. It was designed to ensure antitrust settlements are in the public inter-

est and that steps leading to them are subject to public disclosure. Judge Greene's review of the decree submitted by the Justice Department and AT&T included the reading of written comments and reply comments and the holding of two days of hearings before his court.

44. *U.S. v. AT&T* 552 F. Supp. 131 (1982).

45. Coll p. 362.

46. Section VIII (C) of the MFJ, *U.S. v. AT&T* F. Supp 131 at 231 (1982).

47. *Id, affd. sub. mon. Maryland v. United States* 460 U.S. 1001 (1983).

48. *Washington Post,* December 28, 1988.

49. See Timothy J. Brennan, "Divestiture Policy Consideration in an Information Services World," *Telecommunications Policy,* September 1989, p. 245.

50. The department's conclusion was based, in part, on *The Geodesic Network,* an extensive commissioned study of the telecommunications industry undertaken by consultant Peter Huber and published by the Department in 1987.

51. *U.S. v. Western Electric Co.* 673 F. Supp. 525 at 551, (1987).

52. Id., pp. 591–92.

53. In his MFJ opinion Judge Greene modified the decree to prohibit AT&T from engaging in electronic publishing over its own transmission facilities for at least seven years. Electronic publishing was defined in Section VIII (D) of the MFJ as "the provision of any information which AT&T or its affiliates has, or has caused to be, originated, authored, compiled, collected, or edited, or in which it has a direct or indirect financial or proprietary interest, and which is disseminated to an unaffiliated person through some electronic means."

Judge Greene specified that upon request from AT&T the prohibition would be removed after seven years, unless the Court finds "competitive conditions clearly require its extension." Judge Greene supported the ban on the grounds that by using control of its interexchange network AT&T could discriminate against competing electronic publishers in various ways. The Court concluded the AT&T's "mere presence in the electronic publishing area was likely to deter other potential competitors from even entering the market." *U.S. v. AT&T* 552 F. Supp. 131 at 181–86. The ban was strongly urged by the American Newspaper Publishers Association (ANPA), who have long feared the potential inroads of a telephone company-based electronic yellow pages videotex type service on newspaper classified advertising revenues. The ANPA argued the need for diversity of information services and the danger of AT&T monopolization of the electronic publishing industry. The Justice Department maintained that the danger of AT&T monopoly portrayed by the ANPA had been eliminated in the consent decree's breaking up of AT&T's essential facilities bottleneck. However, Judge Greene's seven-year ban was well received in both Congress and the editorial pages of America's newspapers.

54. U.S. Court of Appeals for the District of Columbia Circuit. *United States of America v. Western Electric Company,* et al., 900 F. 2d 283 (1990).

55. In a footnote the appellate panel expressed its concern with "the practical difficulty of enforcing a merely *partial* repeal of information services ban" and "of determining whether the BOCs are using their rights to transmit the infor-

mation of others as a cover for generating their own." It thus ordered Judge Greene, in reconsidering the removal of the ban, to "consider whether the residual anticompetitive risks associated with lifting the restriction on generation of information are sufficiently great to outweigh the administrative burdens of the Court of policing, this limited prohibition." Idem., at note 29.

In May 1990 eight organizations, including MCI Communications Corp., the Independent Data Communications Manufacturers Association, and the Consumer Federation of America, announced their intention to appeal the reversal and remand of Judge Greene's information service ruling. The appeal would center on the "reformation of the decree's modification standard" and the billions of dollars that had already been made in the expectation that BOCs would not be permitted to engage in competitive markets dependent upon local access unless they could demonstrate their entry presented "no substantial possibility that they *could* impede competition." *Telecommunications Reports,* May 21, 1990, p. 1.

56. In May 1990, Senate Bill S. 1981, was approved by the Senate Commerce Committee. The bill would permit the RHCs/BOCs to conduct research and development, design and manufacture equipment now barred by the MFJ, and permit virtually any joint venture except with another RHC. Safeguards in the bill to preclude anticompetitive behavior include separate affiliate rules. However, the prospects of the legislation passing both Houses of Congress before the end of the Congressional sessions were considered remote. See, for example, *Communications Daily,* May 23, 1990, p. 1.

1
POLICYMAKERS AND POLICY INITIATIVES

1

Questions and Answers with the Three Major Figures of Divestiture

■

WILLIAM F. BAXTER

AND CHARLES L. BROWN

WITH STANLEY M. BESEN

AND HENRY GELLER

■

JUDGE HAROLD H. GREENE

Henry Geller: I pose my question to Charles Brown—although I would welcome Bill Baxter's answer. Looking back with hindsight, what factors that went into your decision to agree to divestiture do you regard as still very sound, and what turned out in your opinion not to be very useful?

Charles Brown: The factors that led me to make the decision centered around the very difficult situation AT&T was in at that time. What it amounted to was a series of alternatives; the divestiture was the least worst of them. As far as my expectations being realized, I think the relatively slow pace at which federal and state regulation is decreasing is a disappointment and a major factor in why the divestiture setup has not worked as well as it might.

Geller: Did you think it was inevitable, once the FCC authorized competition, that it was the proverbial slippery slope, with your competitors in toll successfully demonstrating your essential bottleneck? What would have happened, for example, if we had given you a Chinese menu and proposed that you divest three jewels only as benchmarks— one of them a jewel and two of them lesser companies—and cloned Western Electric?

Brown: Had we gone with some solution like that, I think probably either Bill Baxter, his successor, or Congress would be on our back for some other change a few years later. Although I might have been inclined to go along with such a thing in order to avoid complete disruption of the Bell System, I suspect it would not have lasted very long. There were other solutions, a number of which were acceptable to us. But each time we got into the Congressional mill, each solution got worse as Congress and its helpers operated on it. At the same time, Bill Baxter's people were constructing what we called Quagmires I and II, which were essentially injunctive relief: thou shall not do this, that, and the other, and thou shalt be separated one department from another, and the Bell Labs cannot talk to the Western Electric, and so on. As to that "solution," the longer it was worked on, the worse it got. So there were other answers, and had they stopped at an early enough stage, they might have been acceptable.

William Baxter: The slippery slope question intrigues me. I can imagine someone at AT&T deciding early on that there was a slippery policy slope out there, and that the way to head it off would be to afford manifestly equal interconnection to anybody who asked for it. If that had been done in some number of cases, and the practice had brought about a sufficient level of competition in the complementary activities, would pressure for divestiture have been fended off? It would have been an incredible feat of foresight to have done that, and to have run against what I believe are the inherent incentive structures that arise in a regulated industry where the industry is permitted to diversify across a regulatory boundary. Although it seems to me the slippery slope argument overstates inevitability as a theoretical matter, I do not think it overstates inevitability as a practical matter.

Brown: Just one point there. AT&T had been working on the interconnection matter long before the MFJ. This was not a simple piece of business. It took us some years to actually get the plan, the hardware and the software, and to put equal access into effect. We knew that this was necessary, and we were about doing it.

Stanley Besen: The theory of the case has been described as an "elegant" one in that it envisioned the separation of the naturally monopolistic from the potentially competitive part of the business. A related objective was to change and simplify the nature of the regulatory scheme. Yet, a rather substantial amount of regulation continues, and, in fact, in some people's views, regulation has actually increased. At the time of the negotiation leading to the MFJ, did you anticipate there would be a substantial increase in regulation, at least for a time? Alternatively, do you believe, despite the increase in regulation, there is less than there might have been had divestiture not occurred?

Baxter: Of course, the solution that might be called an "elegant" solution unfortunately was never tried. It was rejected by the Court right from the first with the political injunction against AT&T engaging in publishing, and there were some very ill-advised exceptions—the sale of customer premises equipment (CPE), and the disposition of the Yellow Pages. So what was tried was at best a rough approximation of the "elegant" solution, one that from the beginning had as one of its consequences much more extensive, continuing government involvement than might have been necessary if we had tried the "elegant" solution.

It was perfectly clear to me, for example, that you could not permit the companies to sell CPE without constant attention to a totally unprincipled line between manufacturing, research and development, design, and sales. That was an inevitable mess from day one.

Having said all those things though, I absolutely did not foresee, and would have been horrified had I been able to foresee, the extent to which regulation has continued. Certainly, I did not think it was going to go away tomorrow. But it definitely was my hope and expectation that once AT&T was severed from the local loops, it would expeditiously be deregulated and be regarded as being in the competitive sector. I still see no reason why that could not have happened, and I believe it should have happened.

Brown: I do not have anything to add to that. Both sides, of course, had the option to refuse these provisions inserted by Judge Greene. From AT&T's standpoint, by the time these exceptions surfaced, we were deep into reorganization turmoil, added to the turmoil of the three-ring circus which preceeded the MFJ decision. To visualize these decree changes, or points climbing up through the court ladder, while Bill McGowan [Chairman of MCI] and others were taking chunks of the market, was not a very savory prospect. I assume Bill Baxter had no taste for that either. We had traveled far enough, and these exceptions the Judge produced were not enough to force us through another long legal struggle.

Baxter: It is difficult to overstate the element of momentum that gets involved in a major litigation of this sort. Having aborted the litigation in January, and with the lawyers drifting to other matters, putting that litigation together again in August, eight months later, although not impossible, certainly was an unappealing proposition. I assume it would have been unappealing to AT&T as well.

Geller: Let me just follow up on one thing though. You said that the pure "elegant" theory got contaminated, but even without it, under the department's theory, you were still going to prescribe information services, manufacturing sale, and certainly manufacturing. AT&T said they were very motivated to have the decree because they were in the business of information movement and management. Did you not think the BOCs, the divested companies, would also want to be in the business of information management and information services, and that you were going to be immediately in a regulatory battle as they moved to try to do that over the years?

Baxter: It happened, yes indeed. It was no surprise to me that they wanted to be in those activities, although I was proposing a decree that said they could not be in those activities. And if that line had been drawn hard and sharp and with credibility from the outset, it seems to me the BOCs would have set about doing what would then have been the next best thing for them—really developing a kind of equal access that would promote development and investment in those information activities by an independent set of providers. But that line was never drawn with credibility, and the BOCs had every incentive, instead, to hang out as long as possible and see if they could not creep across that line. The situation created strong incentives not to bring equal interconnection into existence. And of course we are still waiting for Open Network Architecture (ONA).

Brown: AT&T has stood back from this one. It really did not make a critical difference to AT&T as long as the information barriers did not affect the core of the consent decree—the bans on manufacturing and long-distance. I do not think they do infringe on it in most cases.

I would like to point out something here. Some people have asked me what happened in these negotiations between Bill Baxter and myself. My answer has always been there were not any negotiations to speak of. There were these quagmires that were being constructed to come up with some sort of an injunctive consent decree, and there were a number of plans in Congress. We negotiated for many years on those. But the decree was what my lawyer called a two-pager. When the DOJ found out we might be willing to accept a decree which left the carrying out of the separation in the hands of AT&T, then it was a fairly clear track. It is very simple, short, and clear. So there was not much negotiation. We had a little fight about some things that I do not think Bill ever understood. But they were so peripheral and minor, compared to the things that really were the guts of the decree, that there were not many negotiations. Perhaps I have overstated that.

Baxter: No, I do not think you have. Once I studied the case, it seemed to me that we had a winning hand. Howard Treinens, AT&T's general counsel, came around in April 1981 and asked if there was a basis by which we might settle this. I said, "Yes, spin off all the local operating companies." And he kind of laughed and replied, "Well, I won't even talk to my management about that." And I said, "Fine." As the trial progressed, it seemed to me the heat got turned up and turned up. We were just about to go back to trial in January 1982, and my own guess was that the next session of litigation was going to be bad news for the company. When negotiations did not proceed as I wished with respect to the details Charlie mentioned, it seemed to me a good way of demonstrating that I was not under any time pressure was to take a vacation, which I did. And we finished up the decree by phone within the next three or four days. The remaining issues were not at all ones I regarded as details.

Besen: May I go back and see if I can understand the precise point you were making earlier when you talked about the revisions in the original decree as originally proposed? They obviously were not deal breakers; the deal went through. But I take it from your remarks here, they in fact caused some of the subsequent regulatory difficulties. Is that a fair statement?

Baxter: I think the most important thing about them was they indicated a state-of-mind on the part of the Judge that he was receptive to an endless succession of petitions—a kind of "Mother, may I?" game that was going to go on for a very long time. It was precisely the exhibition of that attitude on his part that sentenced us to having two regulators rather than one for a long period of time. Certainly, it was my notion that there would be a clean cut on the entry of the decree. The problem would be remanded to the FCC which had jurisdiction, and the Court would more or less step out of the picture. That is the way it should have worked, and I continue to be disappointed that it did not.

Geller: With the Triennial Review, at the end of that process, if there was a need for some revision, the matter would have gone over to the FCC and not remained with the Judge.

Baxter: Of course, the Triennial Review itself was a feature that was introduced at a much later period in time and fairly at the insistence of the Judge. No Triennial Review was needed with what Stan Besen referred to as the "elegant" solution.

Brown: To add to that, there seems to be continual confusion among industry watchers between regulation and the jurisdictional control of a consent decree.

Geller: Bill Baxter said he was sorry AT&T did not get the full deregulation the decree contemplated. And here we are, in 1989, with 43,000 route miles of fiber put in by MCI and US Sprint, and 80 percent cut over to equal access. Do you think that AT&T should have obtained more deregulatory benefits from divestiture than it has thus far?

Brown: I was not so naive as to think both the interstate and intrastate regulatory apparati would go away in a very short time. The elimination of the Civil Aeronautics Board example is a very rare one, and I certainly did not expect those particular organizations, federal and state, would go away. But I did think more deregulation would take place, that regulatory bodies would back off a lot faster than has actually occurred. Also, I have to clarify the idea that this was some sort of deal with the government by which we would give up the operating companies, and, as a reward or as a quid pro quo, get deregulated. One of the difficulties I faced was that we would not get a deal with anybody in the federal establishment except Bill Baxter. He was the only one who could sign an agreement and make it stick. So, the idea of having a "deal" with anybody else to do anything else was just not practical.

Geller: Congress would not come through?

Brown: That is another long story. They were not coming up with anything we felt we could live with and still do the job they and the people of the country expected us to do.

Geller: A follow-up for Bill: the Judge did put in a waiver, a specific waiver in Section VIII (C) of the MFJ which asks if the BOCs have a monopoly of bottleneck facilities such that they could substantially inhibit competition in the line of commerce? When he recently got to the issue of an infrastructure for videotex, he did not use VIII (C); he abandoned it and used the cost-benefit test—i.e. would the nation, competition, the consumer be better off? Back then, was consideration given to waivers being decided on a cost-benefit test rather than VIII (C) test? Was it flawed from the beginning?

Baxter: I do not think it was flawed by reason of VIII (C) as such. I do not see anything wrong with that. It was not a question of whether the BOCs continue to have a monopoly. Of course, they continued to have a monopoly, and they were going to continue to have a monopoly pending some enormous technological change that even now is not foreseeable. The real question was whether you were going to stick with the basic concept of the decree. Namely, you did not permit the BOCs, given their monopoly of great economic power, to integrate across the boundaries of that monopoly and into the provision of a wide range of complements. You confine the BOC as narrowly as possible to the very set of assets that gave rise to the scale economies, to the local loop with its joint product feature, that occasioned the problem in the first instance. So the problem, in my view, was not the monopoly test or cross-subsidization test so much as it was setting up a waiver procedure that destroyed credibility and created a bad state of mind on the part of everyone. We did not really mean to live by this flash-cut approach of the decree, and, of course, everyone would be around, hat in hand, with a series of waiver petitions.

Besen: I want to briefly return to the local rate question. I wonder if Charlie Brown is quite as sanguine about the impact of the decree on local rates as Bill Baxter apparently was.

Brown: Perhaps you will excuse me for my brashness in quoting Judge Bork here, but the Standard Oil breakup did not result in any reduction in the price of lamp oil. In other words, the Justice Department, due to its charter I presume, does not worry about things like that. They really weren't worried about local rates either. On the other hand, the principle of low local rates was what drove the Bell System for a hundred years. Having been concerned about that, we could see very clearly that the rates were going to have to go up under divestiture. I predicted eight to ten percent a year for four or five years, and that is just about what has happened. We also predicted, of course, that long-distance rates would come down sharply, which they have. But beyond that, the rate of change in how costs would be allocated and revenues divided was left in the hands of the regulators. More than five years later, we almost have the access charge matter straightened out. All during that five-year period there was a general concern about local prices going up. But, we could see it could be done without a rate shock, and it was.

Geller: In the MFJ, local access and transport areas (LATAs) were carved out—fairly large ones, and within them, they appear to be somewhat a barrier to competition. Just one example: the BOCs have a virtual monopoly on intraLATA toll, and just now that problem is coming to the fore in places like Iowa. At the time, did the Justice Department give consideration to the effect of the size of the LATA on competition within the LATA?

Baxter: Oh, most definitely. We worried about it a great deal. We worried about it, I suppose most explicitly, in conjunction with the several interstate LATAs we were persuaded we would have to create, and there was a trade-off there. I am not sure we cut it at exactly the right balancing point, but one had to define what was long-distance transportation in some way, and one had to also provide for points of presence. One important issue was at how many different points in the telephone network was an MCI or a US Sprint going to have to make a connection. Another way to put it, the question was, "How high up the switching hierarchy does the natural monopoly carry?" Manifestly, the local loops have monopoly characteristics, but as you proceed up the hierarchy, the amount of redundancy that has to be built into the more local trunks gives rise to a scale economy that derives from a law of large numbers. I did not want the other carriers to have to make interconnections in too many places and duplicate too much by way of local trunks. That was interrelated to the size-of-LATA question. I am not at all sure we got it right. Certainly we have thought about it and there was no question in our minds that, to the extent we gave the local operating company an enclave within the LATA, we were giving them a monopoly over whatever communication occurred within that geographic area.

Geller: Twenty-four percent of the toll revenues are intraLATA.

Baxter: I am not sure I knew that number, but certainly I was aware that a lot of communication existed there and we were committing it to the tender mercies of regulated monopoly. We had not succeeded in getting it across into what I was then visualizing as a more or less competitive sector, and that pained me.

Geller: To follow up on a previous question, we do have a waiver; we do have all kinds of regulations. Assistant Attorney General Rule said his staff is being used for regulatory purposes, and it is undermining other projects. The DOJ thought that matters such as information waivers ought to be turned over, for example, to the FCC. Since we have gone down that road, do you agree that, at this point, waiver requests ought to be shifted to the FCC?

Baxter: Well, I certainly do not want to take the position that the conclusion the department has reached in that regard is unreasonable or unjustified. Regardless of whether I would have made the decision exactly at that point in time, the argument is a perfectly plausible one. Humpty Dumpty will never be put back together again. The world is permanently changed. The Regional Bell Operating Companies (RBOCs) were at each other's throats before we finished working on the LATA problem. Representatives from the different BOCs came in to talk to us about LATAs, and they were competing, sometimes in rather unpleasant tones, before the decree was ever entered. So a kind of competition is out there in the world, a kind of yardstick possibility that will continue to operate as a check that did not exist before. For those reasons among others, it is not clear to me if it would be wrong to say, "Well, it did not come out exactly the way we expected. It has continued to be a regulatory morass, but at least give it back to the FCC. Let us get one of the regulators out of the picture." That does not seem to be an unreasonable conclusion at this point.

Besen: There have been a substantial number of recommendations by the DOJ and others for removal of some of the line-of-business restrictions. At the same time, a new regulatory scheme has been attempted that was not in place at the time of the negotiation of the MFJ, including the ONA and comparably efficient interconnection (CEI) provisions in the FCC's *Computer III* decision. I would like to hear both your views on the efficacy of this particular regulatory scheme and, in particular, how these views affect your retrospective vision of the decree you negotiated.

Brown: Do not ask me. As I should have said before, I have been retired for some two and a half years. I have not caught up with *Computer II* yet! I am not representing AT&T here and I just do not have any comment on that question.

Baxter: I think it is headed in very much the right direction. If the provision of these complementary activities is to occur in a competitive environment, then it has to occur in the hands of a plurality of companies. I do not want to talk about whether that means two or seven, but those competitors cannot face strongly divergent cost structures. I despise the term "level playing field," but I guess it is something like that. But a very interesting question arises. There is obviously some way, as a matter of electrical engineering, to provide equal interconnection to a set of competitors. The question is whether it is significantly more expensive, in real resource terms, than it would be for one company to provide the complement. That is really a question about the reality of asserted economies of scope on the part of the BOC. If it is really true that there are significant economies of scope there, then it follows, almost as a matter of definition, that you cannot have equal interconnection except at a cost significantly higher than the cost for a single company. That is pretty much a definition of the concept of economies of scope. We do not know that yet, and one of the really fascinating things will be to watch the FCC struggle with that problem, and perhaps eventually give us a very interesting answer to the question of how big were the economies of scope in the first instance.

Besen: That brings us back, of course, to the decree. Suppose the question were answered in the affirmative, so there were lots of scope economies.

Baxter: Then the decree looks less wise than it would in the contrary situation. The decree implicitly made a wager that the regulatory distortions of those portions of the economy, which could have been workably competitive, yielded social losses in excess of the magnitude of economies of scope that would be sacrificed by this approach. It was a wager, a guess. It would be absurd to pretend it was made on the basis of detailed econometric data. It was not; we did not have the data. Of course, all other courses from that point were also guesses. Clear proof was not about to become available any time soon. It was a judgment call, and I guess, in some senses, I do not yet know. Maybe we will never know whether it was right or wrong. Charlie?

Brown: A hell of a bet.

Geller: Divestiture opened our domestic market. It has been called "unilateral disarmament." In hindsight, suppose you knew there was going to be this foreign invasion with foreigners not reciprocating, was there some step, anything that could have been done to phase the invasion in, or was your concern exclusively antitrust? The antitrust train was leaving the station, and by God, that was it?

Baxter: Well, I would say neither of those things. I do not view trade deficits the way a lot of people do; I am reminded of a passage in Adam Smith's *Wealth of Nations* that starts off a chapter on international trade with a parable: your nation is greatly advantaged if you have large, deep, well-sheltered harbors. It goes on to say those harbors are worth a great deal less to you if no other country has decent harbors, because a great deal less shipping will occur. But nevertheless, he says, you can never advance yourself by dumping rocks in your own harbor. That seems to me to sum up the trade situation fairly well.

Geller: I am not uptight about trade deficits either, but the question I was raising was one of fair play in Olde England.

Baxter: The President has a 301 authority. And as I have tried to suggest, we are better off even if trade remains a one-way street than if it were a no-way street. I do not mean to say it might not make perfectly good policy sense for a President to cut off our own nose to spite our face in a way, and to halt that one-way trade as a device for attempting to open foreign markets. It is a costly device to use. One must keep in mind that one is losing while one is using that device. He is dumping rocks in his own harbor. It is a self-destructive kind of predatory behavior. But if it succeds in getting someone else's markets open, then it can make perfectly good sense. It certainly would not have influenced me in the negative to know I was going to increase international trade by taking the divestiture step.

Geller: It would appear Bill Baxter thinks, in the local exchange, we are dealing with the natural monopoly. But there is some indication that a number of people would like to take a crack at the local exchange and that monopoly. Charlie Brown, what do you think is the eventual outcome in this local competition? Is it just niche competition, or is it more? We have had *Computer I, II,* and *III.* Do we need "Divestiture II" to deal with unbundling access and the transport switch?

Brown: I really cannot predict. But it seems to me that the root of whether or not the operating companies are going to face competition lies in technology. And neither here today nor anywhere else have I been able to learn of any technology which would show a significant opportunity for an entrepreneur to compete successfully with a local operating company.

Geller: You do not think digital radio can do it starting ten years out, or digital cellular?

Brown: I do not see, in the next decade, any significant way of bypassing or competing successfully with the operating companies on any large scale, as long as they have a reasonable amount of flexibility to set prices which are related to costs.

Geller: Do you see them in any further problems that might lead to the unbundling or to even hardware unbundling of the local network?

Brown: I had not thought very much about that; it does seem a little bit farfetched to me unless they become hindered by political decisions which keep them from responding in a timely way.

Geller: And call location? Allowing New York Teleport to come directly in and where you separate the transport from the switch?

Brown: That is a version of bypassing [the main public switched network], and it does have some effect. But the effect is so minor on traffic flows and revenues that it is hardly a serious threat. Again, this assumes the BOCs are permitted to act and decide to do so.

Besen: At the end of the century looking back, what do each of you think will be the major benefits that have come from divestiture? What do you think will be the greatest drawbacks, and what do you think will be the balance sheet?

Brown: I would hope, as Bill and everyone else does, that in the post-divestiture world, we see the full benefits of competition and, so far as possible, get rid of the anchor—multiple anchors—of unnecessary regulation. That would do more than anything else to give us an improved balance sheet. I still hope and expect that will occur. As I said before, I think we have to stop confusing regulation with antitrust enforcement. But I believe that will come also, and I am optimistic about the future.

As far as the negatives are concerned, from what I hear listening to people where I used to work who know, the bulk of the residence and local small business customers have not seen net benefits from the upheaval. Their lot has been expense, confusion, and inconvenience in ordering service, getting repairs done, and generally dealing with the telephone system. This is what we expected and gave warning. However, it has been said you can even get used to hanging if you hang long enough, and so perhaps by the end of the century people will have learned to live with the current arrangements without making comparisons with the way things were.

I am perhaps old-fashioned in my belief that a telephone system designed and operated as a "system" has advantages over the results of when each of eight companies act out of self-interest. However, it certainly is the intention of the Regional Bell Companies and AT&T to make divestiture work. There is no incentive on the part of any of these companies, to have poor or more expensive telephone service. The urgency is all in the opposite direction. There will be a lot scrambling in between, but the incentives are there to make it function as well as it can for everyone.

Geller: What I would raise specifically is perhaps the benefits you get in toll might not be as strong as you think. You get a classic oligopoly, and you get sheltering under AT&T, and your Freddy Laker never really comes to the area. Looking back, the greatest benefit might be that you cloned AT&T seven times and got all the strategic planning, and it might be serendipitous. Would you have any comment on that, Bill?

Baxter: I understand the point, though I do not really agree with it. I think the bet has paid off; I think that AT&T's costs are down; I think what has happened to share prices in ensuing years is some evidence. Obviously, that is not a perfect test. I do not keep close track, but I would take a rough guess that if you take one share of AT&T stock and trace it through the split, the share price has gone up 500 percent since divestiture. Whatever it may be, it has risen a great deal more sharply than the market has over that period of time. I think the bet is paying off. I think we are getting the benefits of competition in the sense that AT&T is subject to less restrictive regulation—although still too much, as far as I am concerned. We have cloned AT&T, and we have seven other companies that can be used as standards of comparison with one another. I continue to think there is room for certain kinds of competition with the local loop. I think cellular has a very important future in that regard. Surely, it is one of the silliest things we ever did to limit local cellular to two licenses and give one of them to the wire line company. But in all those senses, I think we are moving in the right direction.

Brown: I think I would be remiss if I did not point out that the whole Bell System's performance, with respect to the mechanics of divestiture, deserves a tremendous amount of credit here. Only those of us on the inside understood the turmoil and the difficulty, both emotional and physical, in gettting that job done in two years. Bill also reminds me that very rarely are we given credit for taking care of the shareowner in this melee. There are lots of ways we could have divided up the company, but we did it in a way that spun off units in good financial shape and permitted them to do the job they had previously done, as well as get into new fields. I take no credit for what they have done, but I take credit for the fact that they have been spun off in condition to do it. The shareowner became a very important factor once AT&T decided to take this step because, as I kept on telling our people inside (ad nauseam I'm sure), "it's not our money." We were spinning off 75 percent of the shareholders' assets.

Baxter: I would certainly want to echo that. During that period of time, it was my clear impression that AT&T's management was very consciously devoted to the process of thinking through a sensible restructuring. Indeed, one of the great appeals to me of the decree approach was that I could let AT&T do the restructuring, subject to just a few constraints I had in mind. I was convinced the restructuring would be done a great deal better by AT&T management than it was likely to be done in the District Court, if it came down to that. The decree that had been worked on in the autumn and winter of 1980 seemed, to me, to have far less to recommend than the one with which we wound up.

Besen: We have reserved a block of time for questions from the audience.

Question: Almost from the time the consent agreement was signed, in fact, even a couple of weeks before signature, the regionals began pushing for the lifting of the MFJ restrictions on the lines of business. In the days and weeks that followed, some of them went into court and claimed because AT&T management was not negotiating for them, they should not have been bound by the agreement. What were your reactions to these actions by the different regionals? Had you expected something like that? Did it disappoint you?

Baxter: I guess it did surprise me. As a legal matter, I regarded their position as absolutely ludicrous, and I certainly did not expect it. I do not expect people to take such ludicrous legal positions, and I was surprised by it.

Brown: I was surprised also. It did seem like an extreme position.

Question: Mr. Baxter, you described the guesswork involved in determining what the marketplace looked like. Some observers claim either there were mistakes made, or the marketplace just changed in relation to the economies of scope. Can you give us a sense as to how you would evaluate that claim? What kind of benchmark judgment would you want to use, as a policymaker, to look back on the decree?

Baxter: It is very hard to determine. I would almost not know what to look at as a practical matter to assess the "lost" economies-of-scope side of the balance. I think it would be easier to get quantitative about the "saved" costs of mispricing complementary services. Certainly, one of the things that we have available to look at, and one that is very important, is the comparative price elasticities of local service as opposed to long-distance service. The sort of natural experiment we have conducted yields data that would tell us a lot about those elasticities. Residential service has certainly proven to be extremely inelastic, which I would have said was intuitively obvious in 1981. In economic efficiency terms, far more of the joint costs of the loop ought to have been put there in the first instance.

Question: My question relates to services that have not developed as well.

Baxter: Ah. Of course, those are pure losses. If one assumes they would have developed under some other circumstance, then the other circumstance, to that extent, is to be preferred. As I indicated a few minutes ago, I thought they would have occurred to a greater extent if we had not lost credibility about the flash cut.

Question: Has someone actually proposed that LATAs really are inappropriate and trample on intrastate jurisdiction, and thus they should be eliminated? Also, should we go back to intrastate regulation and interstate regulation, leaving interstate primarily to the MCIs and the AT&Ts? IntraLATA is now being opened up to competition and the local commissions have to deal with interLATA and intraLATA cases, and this seems to be a fairly heavy cost of regulation.

Baxter: I do not have any strong views on that one way or another. That is really a question of one's views of federalism, and I can see the argument for that position. I have never been a dyed-in-the-wool federalist myself. I understand, but I am not much persuaded by the argument that it should be okay if a state government wants to facilitate exploitation of its own population.

Question: Fourteen states are single LATA, and only thirty-six have multiple LATAs.

Baxter: I understand. It seems to me it is a perfectly plausible argument; I do not have any conviction one way or the other.

Geller: Gerry Faulhaber notes later in this volume [chapter 11] that AT&T developed a service-inward WATS that changed the entire scope of retail and other business in the United States. The BOCs—very strong companies, with considerable resources—are very good at developing new information services; these are not easy to do. People are losing considerable sums on many of them. The question is, are the MFJ restrictions precluding the development of some information service that might be akin to inward WATS?

Brown: I do not see how anyone could know. However, I am very skeptical of the notion that simply because the RBOCs cannot be manufacturers or sell long-distance service interLATA, talented people are therefore being prevented from innovating.

Question: Mr. Brown, to what extent did aspirations of getting into the computer business and related businesses affect the decision to accept this decree? And to what extent were you disappointed, during the first three years, after the decree went into effect—that is, before you retired—as to the progress in that area?

Brown: Of course, one of the pros with respect to accepting the theory was that it would be accompanied by relief from the 1956 restrictions. I have to tell you in that period of the late 70s to early 80s, the 1956 decree restrictions were giving us a very hard time. They were the cause of a good many strained solutions in the FCC, and they were giving us all sorts of costs and pain with respect to what the Bell Labs should develop and what it should not. Meanwhile, members of Congress were introducing all sorts of legislative ideas about Chinese walls between regulated and unregulated activities. So it was a mess and it was very essential to get rid of that if we really were to become competitive. I had no illusions about the difficulty of competing with IBM et al. That is a tough business with good companies which are well established. I was, and am, expecting continued movement of AT&T into a more successful position in the computer business. I have no doubt it will continue. I wished it had happened sooner. It has been an expensive process.

Baxter: I must also say getting rid of the 1956 decree provisions, which I also regarded as an abomination, was one of the attractive features of the 1982 agreement. I regarded it as something I had to give away, in the sense it was a bargaining chip on my side of the table rather than AT&T's. The truth was that I was as anxious, as was Charlie Brown, to get rid of the 1956 decree.

Question: Mr. Brown, as you were making your comments about local rates, it made me think of a boxer who has just gone through a fifteen-round bout. Under constant advisement from his trainer—you being his trainer—he wins in the fifteenth round on a technical knockout and comes back to the corner. The trainer, who is not sweating, has been watching the totally exhausted boxer and says, "I told you it was going to happen in the fifteenth round." I went back and looked at some of the press clippings of 1982–1984 and found your prediction.

You almost pinpointed local rate increases of precisely 8 to 10 percent a year; and no one else pinpointed increases as accurately. I am curious what your thoughts might be on predicting the next five years.

Brown: I had some background and knowledge on rate matters that other people did not have. You may recall that some people even had the gall to deny there was any toll to local subsidy. I also had the conviction it was within the regulators' control to ease off the subsidy in an orderly way, and that is what happened. As far the future goes, I am much more interested in my golf handicap, and probably could predict it better.

Question: Mr. Brown, you said there were some other outcomes that were acceptable, but other parties would have gotten involved and mucked them up. If I understood you correctly, those were not alternatives that Mr. Baxter was offering. He was offering Quagmire I and II as an alternative to this divestiture. Am I correct in saying the only place where the two sets came together was with this settlement?

Brown: Both the House or the Senate over a period of years were proposing certain things, some of which were mutually consistent. But then, as each body of Congress responded to stakeholders, the proposals began to diverge. This made the situation so bad, we could not really live with it. During this time, one solution, advocated by some people, was to have a consent decree short of divestiture. That is what the DOJ people were in the process of contructing in 1980–1981. They were trying to come up with something which would at least partially satisfy their desires and would also satisfy some the things which were being considered in the Congress and the FCC. I am sure Bill Baxter's heart was never in this. It was just a coincidence of things going on in parallel. When it became apparent that none of these solutions were going to work, we both stepped back to the simplicity of Bill's theory.

Question: But that presumes some of the things going on in the Congress had some chance of coming to fruition.

Brown: Yes. As you know, my predecessor started to bring the matter to the Congress on the basis that we were operating under an outdated 1934 Act and that Congress should have set the policy. Everybody had gotten involved, including the FCC, which was being overruled by the courts in critical ways. We were looking for some solution which would avoid the breaking up of the Bell System. *Some* of the things that were in *some* of the Congressional bills at *some* time were things we could live with, and those were the alternatives to which I referred. In any event, the process of trying to get acceptable legislation was exhausting and unproductive.

Besen: If AT&T had simply lost face and the litigation continued to run its course, what would the remedy have been at that point? What form would the whole thing have taken?

Baxter: I think it is very hard to tell. Certainly, I would have urged upon the Judge to decree precisely along the lines I urged on AT&T. But I think it is very unlikely that the Judge would have done that. I think the result would have been a sort of ceremonial fracturing of Western Electric and a few sacrificial operating companies here and there. In other words, something that looked much more like the decree I had seen in January 1981. But that is pure guess on my part. Who knows what the Judge would have been persuaded to do under those circumstances?

Brown: We were fairly convinced the Judge would operate on Western Electric. This is speculation also, but after reading and trying to analyze his moves and his questions, we expected that he would have forced the spin-off of Western Electric, perhaps in several pieces. As is obvious by our decision to enter into the consent decree, I did not want the largest company in the world to be reorganized by lawyers. The consent decree route let us reorganize it in a way we knew would work.

Question: This is addressed to both gentlemen. Do you have any advice for Congressional staff for drafting new legislation?

Brown: I believe it would be a real shame for Congress to jump into the middle of this complex matter and try to solve a problem that may not even exist. I do not speak for the current management of AT&T, but I expect they feel the same way. The thing ought to be given a chance to work rather than be interfered with by a piece of legislation full of compromises.

Baxter: Given the realities of the legislative process, I would be filled with despair at the prospect of new legislation. I think we were probably better off muddling through from where we are.

Question: I think it was widely believed Bell Laboratories was preeminent in the field of basic research. What was the thought process in terms of how to preserve that basic research capability, and how did that thought process enter into the eventual arrangement of the splitting of the Bell System?

Brown: The Bell Laboratories was split on essentially the same principles as the rest of the business. That is, those parts of the Labs dealing with local exchange matters were split off to what is now Bellcore, and those parts which were related to equipment manufacturing in the long-distance business were left with AT&T Bell Labs. Had we been forced to spin off Western Electric, I do not know how AT&T could have supported Bell Labs. It was certainly my contention—and has been that of my two successors—that the Bell Laboratories is a real asset to AT&T and to the country. My successors have continued to support the Labs. There is some discussion in this volume about the need to support research and development (R&D). AT&T was supporting the Bell Laboratories to the tune of about $2 billion at the time of divestiture. They are now supporting the Labs at a level of some $2.7 billion. The percentage of support related to the "R" part of R&D has remained about the same. In the order of 10 percent goes to Arno Penzias and his fundamental research people. So as long as AT&T has its health, I expect it will continue to support the Bell Laboratories and basic research.

Question: Just to follow up, it is conceivable that the amount of basic research has actually gone up.

Brown: It has. Just look at Bell Labs alone. Some of the RBOCs are doing basic research also.

Geller: I have one final question for Bill Baxter. As I recall, your deputy at Justice, Ron Carter, Chief Justice Rehnquist and others questioned the entire Tunney Act and MFJ process. They supported that you were really reviewing how the prosecutor handles his judgments on whether to prosecute or whether to settle, and that this was not a judicial function that could be given to an Article 3 court. Ron made a speech raising questions along these lines. What do you think of the Tunney Act process, and do you think it is something that is reviewable by the Supreme Court or a court of appeals?

Baxter: There are lots of things federal district judges do that are not very effectively reviewable by courts of appeals. I think Ron's point was flirtation with a separation-of-powers argument. I have been tempted by it again. It seems an arguable position, but was not one that seemed to me politically wise to push at that point.

Geller: Not then, but what about now?

Baxter: I do not have to write the brief now.

Questions Answered by Judge Greene

Question: Charles Brown has stated AT&T agreed to divestiture because the bargain struck by Theodore Vail no longer suited the different environment—that AT&T with its structure then was simply too big, and to move this huge monopoly into competitive endeavors such as those involving data processing (enhanced services) would mean continued harassment and claims of unfair competition. What would you characterize as the chief cause or causes of divestiture? In a nutshell, why did we break up AT&T?

Greene: I was, of course, not present during the discussions either within AT&T or between AT&T and the Justice Department, and I therefore do not know, of my own knowledge, what caused AT&T to agree to the divestiture. However, as best I can make out, there seem to have been at least three reasons for their decision. First, the company's management apparently realized it would be impossible in the 1980s for a giant corporation to maintain at the same time both a monopoly with secure profits and significant competitive enterprises, particularly those relating to computers and data processing in which AT&T was greatly interested. Second, and related to the first, was the apparent perception of Chairman Brown and other managers that the company would be unlikely to have a respite from attacks, no matter how the lawsuit was decided. The chances were the Bell System's competitors in long-distance and manufacturing, in particular, would continue and even step up their efforts in the courts, before the FCC, and in the Congress, and that this kind of defensive battle would never end. Third, AT&T management may have been convinced that the company would lose the government's antitrust suit, and they thought it best to settle before that happened.

Question: Some have described divestiture as an "experiment" or "gamble." Do you agree with that? With the theoretical argument and statistical data placed before the Court, as well as the record of AT&T's conduct, how much uncertainty and risk did you perceive when you approved the settlement of the case? To what extent was the decision based upon theoretical argument alone?

Greene: Let me answer this first of all by saying I did not regard divestiture as an experiment or a gamble. To the contrary, I was convinced then, and I remain convinced since, that the decree and the breakup was to be beneficial to the American public and the economy.
But even if I had not been so firmly convinced of that, it would have

been very difficult, as a matter of law, to reject the proposal submitted by the parties. The decree gave the government essentially all it had asked for when it filed the lawsuit. Given that circumstance, I would have been free under the law to reject the consent decree only if overriding and concrete reasons for such a rejection, plain for all to see, were present. The exact opposite was true. What flaws there were appeared to me to be relatively minor. Furthermore, of the 125 or so intervenors from all segments of American life—representatives of about half the states, most of AT&T's major competitors, all sorts of public interest and consumer groups—not one opposed the principles embodied in the decree.

Question: If AT&T had been found guilty at the conclusion of the trial, what remedies might have been available to you in fashioning relief? What factors would have weighed in the choice among them?

Greene: I cannot answer this question in the manner in which it is framed because I simply do not know whether ultimately I would have found for the government or, if I had, what the remedies would have been. There seems to be a general assumption I had decided to fight against AT&T because of the denial of the company's motions to dismiss and the explanations I gave at the time. The facts are much more straightforward and less Machiavellian than what has been credited to me.

The government, the plaintiff in the action, had made a prima facie case, and in the opinion I published at the time I recognized that fact. I then stated it was now the turn of the defendant, AT&T, to answer that case with its evidence, just as happens every day in hundreds of courtrooms. As for the explanation of my views, by way of an opinion, that was largely caused by AT&T itself. Before and at the time of filing its motion, AT&T's lawyers told me again and again that the company was entitled to know where it stood on each issue, so that it could concentrate its evidence on matters which were still being contested. After thinking about it, I came to the conclusion AT&T's counsel were right, and so I took the time and trouble to discuss all the proof that had been presented up to that time.

This effort was useful also in giving everyone, including the Court and the DOJ, a sort of road map of the status of the case. The department had been more or less improvising as it went along, and because of that, no one seemed to be entirely clear what was in the case and what was not. The opinion, incomplete as it was, served to present a picture of the entire case for the benefit of everyone.

Question: Are or should your actions be confined solely to antitrust considerations or can they appropriately take into account other factors? In particular, did concerns about the viability of the RBOCs and the effect of the decree on local ratepayers play an important role in your deliberations?

Greene: I have always placed antitrust considerations first and foremost in any decision regarding the antitrust decree. Clearly also, I did not want to take account of other policies that are in any way inconsistent with the antitrust laws, their objectives, or their purposes. But where other policies, particularly policies promulgated or endorsed by the Congress, such as universal telephone service, are complementary to or supportive of the decisions called for under antitrust principles, I saw no reason for not taking them into account. I might observe in passing that all the parties, including the Department of Justice and the Regional Companies, have strongly urged me from time to time to take such factors into account when this suited the particular purposes they were advocating at the time. At other times, of course, they object to such a course.

Question: Assistant Attorney General Baxter urged a strict quarantine approach for the divested Regional Companies—one that was modified in some significant respects by you after the Tunney Act process—e.g., sale of CPE, Yellow Pages. In his remarks in this volume, Baxter has argued that one important effect of those modifications was that they "sentenced us to having two regulators rather than one for a long period of time." Looking back, would you have any comment about your different tack?

Greene: Let me say first of all that I think very highly of Professor Baxter. Not only is he an outstanding lawyer and teacher and one of the nation's foremost antitrust experts, but it is also greatly to his credit that he was able courageously to face down the mighty Bell System at a time when he was only an Assistant Attorney General, and when most high officials in his own executive branch, including the heads of the Department of Commerce and Defense, were opposed to the lawsuit and to what he was about to do. Nevertheless, Professor Baxter is wrong in suggesting the continuing campaign of the Regional Companies to escape the line-of-business restrictions came about because the changes I required in the decree departed from the so-called quarantine theory. In my judgment, it is naive to think that the companies would not have made the same effort, just as vigorously and just as often, if what Professor Baxter calls a more "elegant" theory had been adopted. That that is so can easily be documented.

Professor Baxter himself has acknowledged he was surprised the companies immediately after divestiture began to push for lifting the restrictions on the basis of what he calls a "ludicrous" theory. Since that time, many requests have been submitted that had to be rejected because they were no better founded, either in theory or in fact. Even under the quarantine theory, the restrictions would not have been immutable, but would have been subject to motions, requests, demands for clarification, and the like.

The DOJ announced as early as 1982, when Professor Baxter was still Assistant Attorney General, that the line-of-business restrictions were to be removed once the rationale therefore became outdated. Can anyone seriously believe such a formulation, or any variation, would not have afforded the Regional Companies the same opportunity as now to file motion upon motion for removing or narrowing the restrictions, or that the exercise of the Court's duty to rule on such motions would not have given rise to the same charges of "regulation" that we hear today? I do not.

Question: Why did you insist on changes which departed from the theoretical underpinnings of the decree as it had been submitted?

Greene: I yield to no one in my search for elegance in expression, but as I was not operating in an academic setting, I also had to consider the practicalities of the situation, and I am not sorry I did. The marketing of customer premises equipment and the publication of the Yellow Pages which I authorized, but which the proponents of a more "elegant" solution deplore, gave the local companies little or no potential for anticompetitive behavior. That being so, why restrict them? Such restrictions would have been especially unfortunate because the companies were able in these fields to make significant contributions to competitive markets, particularly since without their participation, AT&T, then still with well over 90 percent of market share, would have been completely dominant. Furthermore, by permitting the local companies to enter these businesses, it was possible to achieve lower telephone rates for the average residential and business subscribers; for the earnings from these new enterprises could be used to subsidize these rates. I thought then and I still believe today that this was a useful contribution.

Question: Were you surprised by the quick separation in points of views by the RHC's from AT&T?

Greene: I can honestly say the quick separation in points of view between AT&T and the local companies was a great surprise to me. I assumed, along with everyone else, that the Bell company culture would prevail for a long time, even as to those who became managers of the local and regional telephone enterprises. During the trial, it was repeatedly emphasized that in this respect AT&T was like the Marine Corps: once a Bell employee, always a Bell employee. However, as it turned out, the Regional Company managers began almost from the first day—and in one instance even before the actual divestiture—to take aggressive action against their former parent. In a sense, this was troublesome because it created some uncertainty and obviously more litigation. Nevertheless, on balance, this was a wholesome development, and the Regional Companies deserve congratulations for deciding so swiftly and so decisively to stand on their own. In that respect, they performed valiantly and with foresight.

Question: There has been much water under the bridge since divestiture was first announced. In connection with waiver and equal access debates, you have given close scrutiny to various aspects of the operation of the telephone networks and to the markets they serve. The MFJ has consumed substantial amounts of your time and that of your staff. On reflection, do you believe that there have been problems in the administration of the decree? If you could do it again, would you have arranged anything differently to alleviate any problems of administration?

Greene: Of course, interpretation and enforcement of the decree have taken a great deal of my time, and I often wished it could be otherwise. But the decree, as submitted by the parties, provides explicitly that my Court shall have continuing jurisdiction for enabling any of the parties "to apply to this Court at any time" for orders or directions for construing, enforcing, or modifying the decree. When such applications are made, I could no more escape the obligation to entertain and decide them than I could escape the obligation to conduct criminal or civil trials, or to carry out any of the other duties imposed upon courts by the Constitution, statute, or other judgments and decrees.

It is difficult to visualize what arrangements could have been made for enforcement and interpretation other than action by the courts. Court decrees are enforced by courts, certainly not by the litigants themselves. To have transferred enforcement to the FCC—the only other conceivable entity on the horizon—would have been not only contrary to a hundred years of practice and precedent under the Sherman Act, but it would have been particularly inappropriate in this instance. It was the ineffectiveness of the FCC in coping with the problem of anticompetitive activity in the telecommunications industry that led to the antitrust suit and hence the decree in the first place.

Question: How did the concept of the Triennial Review come about? Would you have any comment or assessment of that process based on the actual experience?

Greene: The Triennial Review was strictly a Department of Justice idea, which I merely accepted. Professor Baxter's suggestion that the concept of such a review (1) was introduced at a much later time and (2) was introduced at the insistence of the Judge, is in error on both counts. The Triennial Review was proposed by his department when he was still there. The Review was intended to be a device for determining the status of the decree at a particular point in time, although it is not nearly as necessary now as it seemed when first proposed. The incessant stream of requests by the Regional Companies in effect compel an ongoing and continuing review.

Question: Were you surprised by the DOJ's reversal of policy in the Triennial Review? Would you have any comment on the effectiveness of the DOJ in implementing the MFJ?

Greene: Except for the quick independence of action displayed by the Regional Companies, my greatest surprise was the DOJ's reversal of policy. The department was the author and toughest protagonist of a wide-ranging and effective decree. In fact, the department initially objected when I suggested even relatively minor ameliorating changes. Insofar as the restrictions on the regional companies were concerned, the department wanted them as strict and as inflexible as possible.

In light of this background, it was quite shocking that the same department changed its entire attitude within a relatively short time, as new officials came in. Perhaps I should not have been so surprised because a similar flip-flop occurred in connection with the 1949 antitrust suit against the Bell System. That suit was ended by a consent decree at the behest of the then Attorney General several years later under circumstances that were investigated and severely criticized in Congress.

I might add that, although the present Department of Justice officials are taking an attitude totally at odds with that of their predecessors who wrote, sponsored, and explained the decree, in terms of the meaning of that document what is important, of course, is what its authors said at the time of its adoption, not what policies successor officials may advocate now.

As for the question of department effectiveness in implementing the decree, there is no evidence that the department has been guilty of bad faith. However, obviously any implementation and enforcement will suffer if they are undertaken by people who do not believe in the decree, and say so publicly at every opportunity.

Question: Even in the absence of trial evidence, you have made a strong distinction from the beginning with regard to content provision by telecommunications monopolies—the electronic publishing provision as to AT&T and the transmission-content delineation as to information services of the Regional Companies. Would you comment on this distinction and its importance?

Greene: The restriction on the provision of information services by the Regional Companies was not my idea; it was in the original decree submitted by the parties, although I did add a temporary prohibition on electronic publishing by AT&T. As the decree implicitly acknowledges, information services are as sensitive to discrimination and cross-subsidization as long-distance service and manufacturing. For that reason, the inclusion of the restriction on information services cannot be regarded as particularly controversial in terms of the decree as a whole. My Court authorized the removal of the restriction on the transmission of information services for very pragmatic reasons: as long as the Regional Companies are not involved with content, they have no incentive to discriminate with respect to transmission, and it may therefore be confidently predicted they will not do so.

On the broader question, it must be remembered that the First Amendment demands a diversity of sources of information for the American people. It is quite possible that the Regional Companies, with their bottomless pockets stemming from their ability to generate funds from captive ratepayers, and their monopolies on transmission, would be able to crowd out everyone else, to the detriment of a free press, if they were able to generate information content as well as to transmit it in competition with information generated by others. The purely economic consequences which would follow from a removal of the other restrictions would be augmented in the information field by adverse consequences of a quasi-constitutional nature if one group of companies were positioned to gain de facto control of news and information in the United States. This factor supports the antitrust rationale for the restriction on the generation of content-of-information services.

Question: The antitrust court, and particularly your extraordinary ability to handle this massive, complex case, were certainly needed to effect *structural* relief (divestiture of the bottleneck "tails"). Congress would not do it, and the FCC could not. But once that all-important task was accomplished, including supervising the cutover to equal access, a considerable part of what is now left has been termed by the DOJ as more akin to the regulatory process—such as the processing of requests for waiver of the line of business restrictions. Would you comment on whether such activities are more appropriate for the regulatory agency (FCC)?

Greene: It is quite true the DOJ and the Regional Companies have sought to affix the "regulation" label to the exercise of responsibilities by the court under the AT&T decree. But calling it regulation does not make it so. What the Court is doing is nothing more or less than the enforcement of the consent decree, essentially as the DOJ and AT&T wrote it. The "regulation" label, inaccurate as it is, fits in very neatly with the effort of some to transfer enforcement of the antitrust decree to the federal regulators in the hope this will result in its emasculation.

Question: If there were such a transfer, Congress could readily exercise its oversight of the activities of the regulatory agency. What would you say is the relationship between the antitrust court and the Congress? Would you have comment on the criticism voiced by some critics on the Hill that you are making policy properly reserved to the Congress?

Greene: What my Court is doing with regard to the decree is scrupulously in accord with the will of Congress as expressed in its legislation. The Court's role stems from the Sherman Act which explicitly authorized lawsuits against antitrust violators by the DOJ, among others. The Attorney General filed such a suit in my Court, and I entertained it, as I must under the statute. Eventually, the DOJ and the defendant settled that lawsuit on the basis of a consent decree, and I approved that decree as in the public interest, as I also had to do under another congressional mandate—the Tunney Act. As I stated earlier, the decree requires me to entertain applications from the parties for interpretation and enforcement, and I am doing that, too, as I must. It so happens that the decree was affirmed by the Supreme Court. Therefore, it stands out as a document explicitly sanctioned or approved at the highest levels of all three branches of government.

Some may now want a different policy. It is obvious it is Congress' prerogative to make or remake both antitrust and telecommunications law and policy as it sees fit. I do not have any doubt about that proposition; quite the contrary. In my view, as the elected representatives of the people, the national legislators are plainly entitled under our constitutional system to set broad policy on any subject under federal jurisdiction.

I do not agree, however, with the assertion the FCC is Congress' alter ego, and the Court should therefore turn the decree over to it. These claims are wrong as matter of law, since antitrust enforcement has never been delegated by the Congress to the FCC, and since the agency has no particular expertise in that area. The claim the FCC must be equated with the Congress is in error also as a matter of fact; the FCC has many times in recent years significantly deviated from the Congressional will.

Question: Both the antitrust court and the FCC necessarily act in the same areas at times. Would you comment on the relationship between the Court and the Commission? Has your view of the effectiveness of the FCC evolved over time, and if so, how?

Greene: As a consequence of the entry of the antitrust decree the Court necessarily affects telecommunications, and the FCC naturally is not happy, given the fact that points of friction have not been as severe as they could have been. I have bent over backward not to become involved in matters, such as rates, that were marginal to the decree but of real significance to the Commission. For example, early on I delayed again and again a deadline specified in the decree for the Regional Companies' provision of exchange access pursuant to tariffs approved by the FCC, because the Commission felt it needed more time. The only serious problem I can think of occurred when an FCC chairman made a public statement he was surprised by the "apparent acquiescence" of some of the Regional Companies in the ongoing administration of the decree, as if compliance of litigants with court orders were an occasion for regret. When this became a matter of public notoriety, the official stated all he had meant was that the Regional companies should file more briefs and pursue legislative remedies. That explanation may be taken with a grain of salt, as it would have been physically almost impossible for the Regional Companies to file more briefs than they were already filing. Their briefs, responses, oppositions, replies, supplemental memoranda, and attachments have consistently occupied more space in our courthouse than the filings of any other parties in any other litigation. And, of course, the Companies have not been shy about seeking legislation.

Question: What do you consider the greatest success of the MFJ? The greatest failure, if any?

Greene: The greatest successes of the decree seem to me to have been, first, the burst of innovation in telecommunications, which benefited both industry and the average consumer, and which far surpassed what the Bell monopoly had done in any comparable period; second, the appearance on the scene of a considerable number of vigorous, inventive, independent companies, particularly in manufacturing, but also in other telecommunications markets; third, the emergence of real competition in long-distance and the resulting substantial reductions in rates and the equally substantial increases in usage; and finally, the taking of the first steps toward the achievement of broad-based information services in this country. As for failure, I regard it as very unfortunate that the public has been inconvenienced with respect to installation, repair, the payment of bills, and the like, by the establishment of several telephone companies in place of the ubiquitous Bell System, and I wished it had been possible in advance to take steps to mitigate these problems. I also regard it as a failure the majority of the public has apparently not become convinced the emergence of competition is yielding benefits that outweigh that inconvenience, and a significant degree of public dissatisfaction therefore persists.

2

Policy Directions for the Future

■

WILLIAM G. MCGOWAN
ALFRED C. SIKES
SHARON L. NELSON

William G. McGowan

The three key figures in the settlement of the Government's 1974 case against AT&T have provided a fascinating insider's view of the deliberations that led to the breakup of the Bell System. The chapter 1 dialogue between William Baxter and Charles Brown, and the comments of Judge Greene are important reminders for today's policymakers of the forces that are shaping the structure of our industry. In a rapidly changing world, and even more rapidly changing industry, it is easy to lose sight of the lessons of the past.

It appears today many have forgotten the fundamental principle upon which divestiture is based: regulated bottleneck monopolies and competition do not mix. But before elaborating on that key principle, I want to highlight an important point touched upon by Baxter, Brown, and Judge Greene. When William Baxter's Antitrust Division and Charles Brown's AT&T asked Judge Greene to approve the consent decree, many viewed the action as a potential catastrophe. These critics failed to recognize the industry was already in a state of turmoil and divestiture was the only way out. Events since divestiture have shown the wisdom of the decision to divest.

Let's start with long-distance. My own company had been in business for roughly fifteen years prior to divestiture. During that time we had made important progress. We had secured some initial financing, and after lengthy delays we had approval from the FCC to construct a network. Later, we fought for—and received—permission from the D.C. Circuit Court of Appeals to compete in the switched services market. What we did not have was equal access or a nationwide network. As a result, our market share was minuscule—less than 5 percent—and we were the largest of AT&T's competitors!

The decision to break up the Bell System conveyed two extremely important benefits for competition. First, it mandated equal access. Years of proceedings and negotiations at the FCC had not achieved this result. Second, divestiture opened the door for major financing so we could build a nationwide network. MCI has spent over $5 billion on network construction and enhancement since divestiture, becoming national in scope in the process. I do not believe we would have been given this major commitment of funds so long as our major competitor in the retail long-distance market was also the major supplier of one of our essential ingredients—access to our customers. Moreover, at the time of divestiture, we were spending hundreds of millions of dollars to resell AT&T facilities needed in order to offer our customers ubiquitous terminations. Without external financing to build our own network, we would still be a captive customer of AT&T.

Since divestiture, impressive developments have occurred in the long-distance market. Prices have fallen dramatically and new services are being introduced almost daily. For the first time in the history of the industry, customers have a genuine choice. This is what competition is all about.

Instead of an overhead expense item, long-distance is now becoming a key productivity tool for management of firms of all sizes. Virtual private networks, broadcast FAX, and corporate data networks are changing the way business is done in both the manufacturing and service sectors. While some of these innovations may have come about without divestiture, I believe that the competition which divestiture has made possible continues to bring innovations to the market faster and at lower prices.

As an aside, it is worth mentioning that the FCC, which did so little to bring competition about before divestiture, has done very little to encourage it since. The FCC's original access charge decisions forced carriers to pay for equal access before they received it. As a result, many carriers were unable to obtain financing. For a full year after equal access conversions began, the FCC allowed hundreds of thousands of customers to be defaulted to AT&T. And in recent years, the FCC has allowed AT&T to ignore basic market rules—in effect deregulating AT&T without benefit of a public proceeding. At the same time, the FCC has refused to deal with important market structure issues that have not yet been resolved properly—equal 800 access, to cite just one example. Even if full competition had been theoretically possible without divestiture, FCC inaction or bungling likely would have killed it anyway.

Both Baxter and Brown lament the extent to which AT&T is still regulated. I have two reactions to that. First, AT&T has been substantially deregulated since divestiture. AT&T's tariff notice periods and cost support requirements are both substantially reduced compared to those in place at the time of divestiture. AT&T has made massive revisions to its rate structure and introduced literally dozens of new services and pricing plans. Most of these changes have been made without opposition from MCI. Second, markets become competitive overnight only in economics textbooks. A market position developed through a hundred years of monopoly abuse is difficult to attack— particularly when the most recent generation of regulators appeared to be rooting for the favored home team instead of the underdog.

Equipment competition has also blossomed since divestiture. Some competition had developed in terminal equipment even before the AT&T breakup. This initial competitive success was due to two factors. First, the interconnection problems involving terminal equipment were much simpler to resolve than those impacting long-distance. The FCC's equipment registration program succeeded in putting competitors on an even footing. Second, cross-subsidies by the Bell System were not an effective means of stemming terminal equipment competition because rivalry was based on features and functions. The competitors simply had better products to offer. Since divestiture, this competition has blossomed as more and more competitors have entered.

Baxter and Brown note that Judge Greene's decision to allow the RBOCs to market but not manufacture this equipment was in conflict with the theory of the divestiture. However, the Judge's action has apparently not had severe anticompetitive effects. The factors noted above likely provide the explanation—interconnection is not currently a problem and competition takes place over attributes other than price. This does not imply that problems will not develop in the future, particularly in the area of Centrex competition with private branch exchanges (PBXs), where cross-subsidy and interconnection problems are more likely to develop.

There was much less competition in the provision of network equipment prior to divestiture. The Bell System essentially foreclosed 80 percent of the market to competitors by handling that business to its own Western Electric. When MCI entered the long-distance market, we found virtually no sources of domestic supply for broad ranges of our needs. Now, only five years later, the situation is much improved. Digital Switch Corporation and Northern Telecom both manufacture large switches domestically. The area around Richardson, Texas, the location from which MCI directs the construction of its network, has become the Silicon Valley of telecommunications network equipment. Prior to divestiture, with large portions of the market foreclosed from competition by the vertically integrated Bell System, there was simply no market for these independent companies and the innovative diversity they bring to the market.

Electronic information services is another area in which competition has prospered since divestiture. This is a market that was in its infancy at the time of divestiture so it is difficult to say how it would have developed in a different context. Moreover, as Brown notes in his remarks, it is an area in which the Bell System was prevented from participating due to the 1956 consent decree, which settled an earlier government antitrust case. Nevertheless, it is an area which is progressing very rapidly—free from monopoly RBOC interference. As personal computers proliferate on workers' desks, at home, and in schools, large and small entrepreneurs are coming forward with myriad databases and interactive on-line services to meet the demand.

There are those who would have us adopt the French "Minitel" model for the deployment of information services in this country, but that would be a mistake. The French have given away terminals, at enormous cost, to 20 percent of the population. The wisdom of this decision is in doubt. Household usage for all but simple directory assistance declines after the novelty wears off. Business use of the Minitel system is strong, but in this country businesses already have access to all of the electronic information they want. In any event, recent decisions by Judge Greene allow the RBOCs to provide the same "gateway" functions performed by Minitel. The only element lacking in this country is the subsidization of simple terminals for households that do not have computers. The French experience suggests the benefit/cost ratio of this expensive activity is low. Even if it were high, cross-subsidization through the telephone company is simply not a good idea.

If performance has been disappointing in any area since divestiture, it is in the local exchange business. The RBOCs took advantage of the inevitable postdivestiture confusion to put through enormous local rate increases. At the interstate level they have consistently earned in excess of their already generous allowed rate of return. Their performance in the equal access implementation process was less than outstanding —prompting a Justice Department investigation at one point. Rather than do their best to encourage their customers to use their networks to the fullest, they have devoted valuable management time and untold dollars for efforts to escape from the provisions of the antitrust consent decree. And rather than find ways to become more efficient and cut costs, they are lobbying regulators to adopt incentive "regulation"—a code word for solidifying the enormous profits they now make.

The local exchange is one area where competition has not developed to any measurable degree. This is not surprising. The basis for the antitrust case and the divestiture that settled it was that the local exchange is a natural monopoly. Limited alternatives do exist for some of the functions performed by the local telephone companies. But the essence of the monopoly is its ubiquity—the ability to reach every customer in the local exchange area. The local loops and switches are the core of the monopoly and there is no technology in sight that will displace them. In the words of Charles Brown, "neither here today nor anywhere else have I been able to learn of any technology which would show a significant opportunity for an entrepreneur to compete successfully with a local operating company."

If there are any potential competitors for the local exchange, they are cellular radio and cable television. It is interesting that the RBOCs have spent so much money buying the non-wireline cellular franchises in each others' territories in a mutually beneficial effort to foreclose the possibility of cellular entry into the local exchange business. They are also busily lobbying Congress for the right to buy out, or drive out, their potential competitors in the cable industry.

This poor performance in the local exchange industry is not due to divestiture. Instead, the blame can be put at the doorstep of the regulators. Divestiture, by disentangling most competitive from monopoly lines of business in the Bell System, made effective regulation of the local exchange industry a serious possibility for the first time. Local exchange regulation is still a formidable job, but the payoffs for ratepayers from effective oversight of local telephone activities and control over their earnings would be enormous. That is why it is so sad that so many regulators are in favor of freeing the RBOCs from the competitive safeguards contained in the antitrust consent decree.

Allowing the RBOCs to integrate vertically again would lead to a reappearance of all the problems that plagued the industry prior to divestiture and would make effective control over monopoly earnings and anticompetitive behavior difficult or impossible. Holding out the possibility to the RBOCs of entry into the manufacturing, information services, and long-distance markets also distracts them from performing one of their most important duties—making the local exchange useful to their long-distance and information service customers.

In their chapter 1 comments, both Baxter and Brown recognize the problems with eliminating the so-called line-of-business restrictions. These necessary safeguards prevent the divested RBOCs from entering interLATA long-distance, manufacturing, or information services. It might be useful to speculate here on two alternatives for the future. One arises when the RBOC monopolies are contained and for the first time they actually take their monopoly utility responsibilities seriously. The second occurs if the RBOCs succeed, by virtue of their enormous economic and political power, in steamrolling Congress to lift the requirements of the decree.

The former alternative future is easy to speculate about. With the RBOCs doing their job to provide cheap and effective local and long-distance access service, all parts of the industry prosper and so do their customers. The progress that has been made since divestiture would continue and probably accelerate. If, on the other hand, the RBOCs are successful in their current drive to have the manufacturing and information services bans eliminated, the results are also predictable. (Even some of the RBOCs recognize that the long-distance safeguard cannot be removed.) All we have to do is review history. The history of the integrated Bell System is one of repeated episodes of government intervention designed to check monopoly abuses.

It all started in 1913 with the Kingsbury Commitment, in which the Bell System agreed to stop buying up all the independent telephone companies after complaints about AT&T's competitive tactics and interconnection practices. Then there was a lull in activity until the 1930s. Following the passage of the Communications Act, the newly created FCC began investigating certain monopoly abuses. A report was issued,[1] but with the distractions of World War II, nothing much came of it. Another lull followed until 1949, when the Justice Department filed an antitrust suit. This was settled in the 1956 consent decree, under which the Bell System agreed to limit itself to providing services only under tariff. Finally, the Justice Department filed its 1974 case culminating in the 1982 settlement.

This history suggests two things. First, it would violate the natural order of things to move so quickly to change the decree. The minimum period between major government actions appears to be at least fifteen years! For those who do not believe in exogenously imposed social cycles, the second point may be more persuasive: vertically integrated telephone companies simply do not know how to stay out of trouble. Perhaps this is why in their comments for this volume both Baxter and Brown express surprise at the attempts of the RBOCs to put Humpty Dumpty back together again so soon after the divestiture.

The RBOCs like to argue that change is warranted because things are different now. But the monopoly abuses of the old Bell System did not occur because the individuals involved were bad people. They occurred in large part because the monopoly structure of the industry was bad. The monopoly system allowed them to discriminate against competitors and to cross-subsidize any of their operations which faced competition.

There are those both in and out of government who argue that it will be different this time. They assert that either because of the new, more competitive industry structure, or because of innovations in regulation, RBOC abuses can be detected and controlled—or will not even be attempted. But I believe in the McGowan ironclad law of monopoly abuse, which goes something like this: unless prohibited, any monopoly will inexorably expand into closely related functions—which are often dependent on the monopoly for existence—using discrimination against competitors and cross-subsidization from its monopoly base to help it succeed in those new areas.

This behavior is a function of the American system, where corporate drives are basically the same as those of the people. We are taught to grow and expand our horizons. Corporations are inclined to grow and add new services. This is fine when a monopoly cannot be used unfairly to prevent others from bringing better and cheaper products to the market. But when there is a monopoly, this expansionism is exactly the sort of behavior the antitrust laws were designed to prevent.

As for regulatory innovation, we have two alleged candidates—accounting and ONA. New accounting tools are supposed to be able to police cross-subsidy even though regulators were unable to detect or prevent it in the pre-divestiture days. ONA is claimed to provide unbundled elemental access to basic switching and transmission functions within the monopoly network and thereby prevent discriminatory pricing or bundling.

ONA as an innovative procompetitive tool is easily dismissed by anyone familiar with the relevant proceedings at the FCC. The RBOCs are simply putting old wine in new bottles. They have done little to meet the demands of their customers and Baxter's skepticism over RBOC ONA efforts is well placed. Even if a new form of access were forthcoming, the RBOCs would still have control over both the nature and the timing of future changes to the network so important to the providers of electronic information services whom Open Network Architecture is supposed to protect.

As for accounting, the FCC "reforms" are a cruel joke. The FCC has fewer resources to deal with monopoly abuse now than it did at the time of divestiture. And even the best intentioned regulators cannot possibly prevent misallocations of common costs because the monopoly firms can make the fundamental decision to build "common" networks that benefit primarily their own competitive services.

Recognizing that they are playing from a very weak hand if the debate on where the public interest lies is limited to straight antitrust economic regulation principles, the RBOCs have attempted to divert the debate by talking about trade and competition. The old Bell monopolists used to justify anticompetitive behavior by claiming it somehow served the broader "public interest." Now the RBOCs are simply repeating the same old song-and-dance routine. To hear the RBOCs tell it, unless the line-of-business restrictions are lifted, American civilization as we now know it is in desperate peril. Here is a quote from one representative RBOC president: "the window of opportunity may pass, and so will the country's chance to regain economic preeminence. If that happens, the United States will be relegated permanently to the second rank of the world economy." This statement refers to the line-of-business restrictions on the RBOCs. In other words, because of the terms of the antitrust settlement, you can kiss America's economic future goodbye. That is simply self-serving RBOC hyperbole.

Our trade imbalance has been blamed on a number of things, from dumping and other unfair trade practices of other countries to our own fiscal mismanagement, the inflated value of the dollar for some years, our lack of international marketing expertise and even our own shortcomings in foreign language ability. But the emotional trade issue is being exploited by the RBOCs in a cynical and irresponsible effort to play on the justifiable concerns of the American people about the trade deficit. The trade issue is a straw man because RBOC entry into manufacturing and information services "content" would do little to redress the problem.

The main difficulty we face is not in services or in switches; it is in terminal equipment, which ran a deficit of around $2.7 billion in 1989.[2] But terminal equipment—telephones, cordless phones, facsimile equipment, answering machines, and the like—really is more in the nature of consumer electronics. And there is no reason to believe the RBOCs can compete in these product lines more effectively than other U.S. companies against overseas manufacturers, particularly our friends and trading partners in Asia.

The RBOCs have absolutely no experience in manufacturing—that went with AT&T at divestiture. To succeed in manufacturing, the RBOCs would have only two options: one is to cross-subsidize, and the other is to sell manufactured products to themselves at higher-than-market prices. Either way, American monopoly ratepayers would end up paying extra for the privilege of having the RBOCs in the manufacturing business.

This, of course, raises the specter of the same old monopoly abuses divestiture was supposed to cure. The RBOCs would be in the position to compete unfairly against other U.S. manufacturers, driving them out of business, stifling competition, and most likely making the trade problem worse, not better, by manufacturing offshore in joint ventures with foreign companies. In all three restricted lines of business, the RBOCs could play the dual role of bottleneck controller and competitor.

The RBOCs, of course, never tire of complaining about being unfairly boxed in, so to speak. They complain that their opponents simply do not want to compete. But since divestiture, Judge Greene has, in fact, relaxed the restrictions on the RBOCs. They can enter virtually any business they want. They are prohibited only from the three lines of business most readily susceptible to monopoly abuse—information services, telecommunications equipment manufacturing, and long-distance. And the RBOCs know full well that these restrictions would be dropped tomorrow if they divested themselves of their local telephone monopolies.

Unfortunately, the day of the monopoly is not over. In a modern reproductive miracle, involving a highly public—but hardly immaculate—conception, the monopoly gene has been passed along from Ma to Baby Bell. What will happen if the government ignores the lessons of the past and allows reintegration of monopoly local service with information services and equipment manufacturing? History gives us the answer.

Private antitrust cases were a large part of the pre-divestiture history of the Bell System. However, in their chapter 1 discussion of why AT&T agreed to divestiture, neither Baxter nor Brown mentions the pendency of private antitrust actions. I believe the private cases were a key factor in the decision to divest. Had AT&T been found guilty after a full trial—and both Brown and Baxter seem at least implicitly to agree that that was a likely outcome—under existing legal precedents

AT&T would have been faced with enormous liability for damages in the literally dozens of pending private antitrust cases. Not even AT&T's deep pockets could have protected shareholders against that outcome. The lesson here is simply that private antitrust played a powerful role in the breakup of the Bell System.

If the RBOCs are allowed to reintegrate, they will follow McGowan's ironclad law and abuse their monopolies. And with or without help from the government, the antitrust courts will be called into action once again. Everyone, except the lawyers and economists, will be better off if that does not happen.

Alfred C. Sikes

A number of things tend to make it hard for the government to operate as well as it should. First, everything takes a long time. The Justice Department's complaint challenging the vertically integrated structure of the old Bell System, for example, was filed in November 1974. The lawsuit survived through two judges, three national administrations, four Congresses, and five Attorneys General before it was finally settled in 1982. Here we are today, and many of the topics touched upon in this volume are basically the same old issues. We are now fifteen years down the road from the Justice Department's complaint, and much of the public policy agenda does not seem to have really changed.

A second problem with the way government works is that most of what government concentrates on is yesterday's or, at best, today's story—not what ought to be done in the future. There is limited vision, with all too many regulators and regulatees continuing to define their communications world in light of valid goals, but goals which have already been achieved—the attainment of universal voice telephone service, for example. Insufficient attention seems to be paid to expanding customer options and choices. Imagine how many tens of thousands of man-hours are expended daily chasing "fires" in what you could call "reactive government." Will Rogers said this was because most people have a hard time "getting their noses up more than about three inches from the moving highway." Having added word processors and FAX machines to the ubiquitous copiers, we all face the proverbial "paper blizzard." Sometimes I wonder whether we do not just have an "in-box government."

I do not mean to disparage the importance of handling people's day-to-day problems. Maintaining at least the perception—and preferably the reality—of responsiveness and fairness is critical to sustaining a political consensus.

We spend a great deal of time talking about marketplace solutions, but you cannot institutionalize competition by just talking about economic efficiency, productivity, innovation, and other abstract concepts. You have to make sure the people in the market believe the rules are generally fair, and that playing by the rules will ensure that you win or lose based on *your* own efforts. And so, the government has to contend with all the daily skirmishes and commercial firefights. That is just the way things are. By the same token, it is also important for the government—as well as the private sector—to do what is *hard:* namely, to try and anticipate both problems and opportunities.

One of the central issues—and one that is not being given sufficient attention, at least at the Federal Reserve level—is whether—and if so, how—we are going to amass the kind of communications assets this country will need to support the information economy. Decades ago, a consensus developed around the goal of assuring universal voice telephone service and the establishment of certain subsidies to achieve it. We decided to make sure everyone who wanted a telephone could get one. We decided to encourage that by underpricing residential service. And we decided to offset resulting revenue losses by overcharging business and long-distance callers.

Today, the FCC and the states in particular are tackling other issues. Much of the current debate surrounding "price caps," for example, addresses whether local phone companies may retain at least some of their gains attributable to new technology, greater operating efficiency, and innovation.

Both in the FCC's ONA proceeding, and in the ongoing debates about possible changes in the AT&T consent decree, the government is reviewing how phone companies will be able to expand their services, and under what set of competitive safeguards and ratepayer protections they can do so.

In *Telecom 2000,*[3] we talked mostly about the new communications and information technology. We talked about an "electronic neighborhood," in which people using the telephone with an information terminal could share information, concerns, and interests via an expansion of computer "bulletin board" systems that some people use today. We talked about a "video dial tone," which would open up new opportunities for valued program diversity, and maybe lead us to that elusive "video phone call." These new possibilities will not be inexpensive to achieve. Hundreds of billions of dollars in new investment will probably be needed over the next few years to extend the wonders of digital and opto-electronic communications nationwide, and to the residential telephone market.

A central question, when you consider such things as "video dial tone," is whether these services are going to appeal to enough people to result in a national consensus regarding an expanded definition of "universal service." I believe they are. Today, some new services are possible even though the basic transmission link to our nation's homes remains essentially the same as that twisted copper wire that Alexander Graham Bell used in his first test of the telephone in 1874.

The switches which guide and manage our communications are increasingly state-of-the-art computers, operated by very sophisticated software. And much of our long-distance traffic is being handled by the most modern fiber optics. Yet the pathway into most homes and businesses is not much different today than it was at the turn of the century —except, perhaps, that the wire used to be bare, and today it is vinyl-clad.

A logical question is "what are we missing?" The answer probably is "a great deal." The country has many impending electronic infrastructure needs—the need to provide American business and industry, for example, with the electronic tools—the "leverage technology"— needed to stay competitive in the world markets. There is the need to provide small business and residential customers with the communications links and services that they will demand in future years. Also, digital switches plus fiber optics could provide us full information video, plus high-speed data, as well as an ordinary phone. A patient could talk with his doctor while also transmitting his "vital signs." That is a good thing to have in a country with an aging population, health care costs that are running in the range of 10 percent of GNP and the priority need to restructure the system to address more long-term, chronic health care needs, and fewer acute service requirements.

A working mother, either at home or in an office, could both work and watch her child playing at home. That is a good thing to have when some three-quarters of women with school-age children also work outside the home. You want to ensure quality child care *and* make it possible for the country to benefit from the contribution of working women. The new technology could also enable a student to receive special tutoring help in the evening—at the same time that his or her father is using another terminal to pay the family's bills. That, too, is a good service to have when you look at today's—and especially tomorrow's—education requirements.

Some of these capabilities are now being used in highly controlled, experimental environments. But the "trick" here is getting them into everyday use more rapidly. And the "secret" to accomplishing that is either to subsidize them, or create the kind of marketplace environment in which economic incentives will drive their development, or both. If we, as a nation, want the telecommunications industry to make the kind of additional investments which we believe are needed, we must be prepared to permit investors to earn a fair—and competitive—return on their investment.

The government's risks and rewards assessments—and its resulting policies—have a major bearing on overall communications industry performance. Most agree, there is a pressing need to reassess much of that traditional balance. I understand the concerns regarding the potential for discriminatory access to essential communications facilities and the use of unfair, below-cost pricing. But the established telephone companies can bring a lot to our technologically dynamic communication marketplace. These firms constitute much of our telecommunications industry, and they have a history of accomplishment.

Some critics contend the established phone companies are simply not up to the challenge. They argue that even if the phone companies receive greater commercial discretion and more regulatory freedom, they nonetheless will not provide the kind of feature-rich and user-friendly communications networks which were described in the National Telecommunications and Information Administration's (NTIA's) *Telecom 2000* report.

Instead, those critics contend, the heavy hand of monopoly will simply extract additional profits, and not make the kind of future-oriented investments the country needs. These critics also suggest that the telephone company culture has been created by monopolized lines of commerce in a regulated environment. In short, they assert that the leadership of the local exchange carriers is incapable of open market behavior; incapable of marshalling resources in an economical and innovative manner.

In aggregate, GTE, the Bell companies, United, Contel, and the hundreds of other members of the United States Telephone Association represent more than 80 percent of the entire regulated U.S. communications universe. They represent not only enormous capital but very substantial human and technological resources as well. The established companies maintain extensive research and development operations. They have a long record of nearly unparalleled technological and commercial accomplishments.

So, if the established telephone industry cannot bring much to the competitive marketplace—as many of the more strident critics of regulatory and consent decree liberalization so often contend—our telecommunications prospects are not especially encouraging. I do not accept that all-too-commonplace contention. That, after all, was what many of the same critics said of AT&T, and yet that company has proved an increasingly formidable competitor, both at home and abroad.

If we expect telephone companies to improve their efficiency, to increase their productivity, then we need to provide incentives which reward those results.

If we want phone companies to be more innovative, we need to reexamine the traditional regulatory approach, which has often obliged firms to overprice innovative services and share any gains from successful services with ratepayers, while sometimes placing the costs of unsuccessful efforts on their shareholders. And, if we want to maintain the economic and technological integrity of the public switched telephone network, we need to allow phone companies the flexibility to adapt to changing market conditions and, where necessary, to compete fully with new entrants.

I do not think the "universal" infrastructure to support all future information services needs to be subsidized in most cases. At some point, hospitals, schools, and other public service institutions might subsidize them. But commercially viable services ought to be able to stimulate the necessary private investment, and carry most of the operating expenses. The public, and most of their elected representatives, know little of the choices and tradeoffs implicit in today's regulatory environment. They are only vaguely aware their local telephone service is relatively inexpensive compared, say, to cable TV, electricity, and other services. And, they are generally unaware of the services they might get from a different regulatory approach.

My colleagues on the Commission and I are committed to going forward with regulatory reform. There are problems created by outmoded regulatory laws—rules which are grounded on obsolete traditions which hold there will always be separate communications industries, each employing different and discrete electronic technologies. We are prepared to pursue regulatory changes which will afford established phone companies greater commercial and competitive discretion. We are also prepared to continue supporting appropriate changes in the AT&T consent decree, and we will be paying close attention to marketplace developments. But, let me add that those seeking regulatory reform must demonstrate the potential to actually fulfill the kind of promises outlined in *Telecom 2000*.

We will be interested in the extent to which established phone companies invest shareholder profits in new, possibly experimental, ventures. I appreciate the fact that there are limits on the kind of experiments that can be undertaken. I also understand the problems which arise when regulatory agencies, such as the FCC, do not act fast enough on proposals. For example, it should not have taken two and a half years to approve the GTE/Cerritos experiment. One of the priorities of the FCC will be to make certain that regulatory paralysis is not a problem.

At the same time, it is not clear to me that the established phone companies are taking complete advantage of the experimental and other commercial freedom they already have. More than a year ago, for instance, the AT&T consent decree court signalled its willingness to sanction Minitel-like offerings by the individual Bell companies. While most of the BOCs are experimenting with gateway services, we still await any such undertaking on a broad scale. Many of the "new" services that are just now being offered—call waiting, call-hold-on, and the like—are, in fact, not very different from those which the unified Bell System proposed in the late 1970s under the logo "Custom Calling II." The opportunities for providing significant new communications and information services are extraordinary. It is important that those opportunities not be available exclusively to those who use private networks.

In arguing for regulatory and consent decree reforms for many years, I have stressed the substantial opportunity costs which current restrictions impose. I have talked about telephone customers not receiving new service options, many of which are currently offered by phone companies abroad. But so long as the current debate focuses chiefly on hypothetical, not concrete and real new services, it will remain very difficult for us to succeed.

If regulatory reform is to succeed at a constructive pace, established companies and their management must be prepared to show all of us more of the fulfilled promises of communications and information technologies. I believe both the FCC and the state public utility commissions will respond better to concrete service proposals than to abstract advocacy.

Telecommunications organizations across the world—in France, Britain, West Germany, Canada, and Japan, for example—are clearly pursuing a 21st-century investment strategy. They are rapidly deploying the local fiber optic networks, advanced digital switching systems, and sophisticated information services that will be needed. In the United States, however, we do not always seem to be moving in this direction.

In Japan, NTT (Nippon, Telephone & Telegraph) is reportedly planning to deploy, by the 1990s, fiber optics directly to almost all the homes in Tokyo which have children. Incidentally, that choice of homes for both new and retrofit fiber installations is geared toward greater expected use of an NTT-developed, information services terminal—what they call the "family computer."

In France, France Telecom is continuing rapidly to expand its celebrated Minitel network, which reportedly reaches some 4.9 million subscribers. Moreover, France Telecom has little more freedom in its control of transmission content than the Bell companies are given under the AT&T consent decree. And, while the Bell companies are limited, most of the rest of the American telephone industry is not.

In Canada, Bell Canada has recently announced a major expansion in its long-run capital investment plans. The same is true in West Germany, where the Deutsche Bundespost—an entity that is about the same size as GTE—reportedly has integrated services digital network (ISDN) trials underway in seven West German cities. Yet in the United States, local telephone investment appears to be remarkably stable from year to year and, indeed, when inflation and higher labor costs are taken into account, may actually be slightly declining.

According to the most recent Commerce Department estimates, the established local and long-distance telephone companies—the regulated part of the overall industry—should account for some $159 billion in domestic service revenues in 1989, and they should generate at least $14 billion in profits.

For an industry with such very substantial revenues—and growing profits—the level and extent of innovation seems remarkably small. There are, of course, celebrated experiments such as the GTE/Cerritos project. Total outlays for that project reportedly are substantial but not a major financial undertaking for the company which currently ranks as America's largest public utility.

Many of the Bell companies in recent years have spent huge sums purchasing cellular mobile telephone properties, amounts that dwarf their expenditures on network innovations and experiments. And the track record for independent telephone companies—many of which have seen very substantial revenue and profit increases in recent years—is not markedly different.

Universal voice telephone service, at reasonable and affordable rates, has deservedly achieved almost constitutional status in our hierarchy of communications policy values. No regulator I know would countenance letting "bottleneck" monopolies use their facilities to hurt their new technology-driven competition. At the same time, it is important to keep the risk-reward dimension of the business squarely in mind, and to remember some of the most valued products we have today are the result of what initially were risky propositions. There are important reasons to let the phone companies remit the profits from their competitive services—what the Europeans call the "non-reserved" services—to their shareholders who bore the risk of the undertaking. And, there should not be rules against allowing phone company shareholders to capture some of the savings due to more efficient operations. Likewise, while phone companies should be required to allow others to access their customers through the network, those competitors should not be allowed to prevent the phone companies from offering new services which might require local network modernization.

The FCC is prepared, as part of our overall rate regulatory process, to give considerable weight to the need to accelerate the pace of local telephone exchange improvements and modernization. We place great store on the desirability of instituting the network and transmission changes today which will be needed to meet future demands.

Today's technologies can assure customers multiple service options—if all the suppliers have equal access into the home. We need to make the choice a concrete reality. If we just update our thinking, if we try to catch a new vision of what could be, then our laws and regulatory systems will soon catch up with that reality.

Making sure America continues to enjoy the communications services it wants and needs is, in the final analysis, up to the industry's leadership. It will be industry's vision of the rewards, along with sufficient courage to take appropriate risks, which will determine our future. The government, as I indicated, has to be prepared to do its part. It has to ensure the kind of policy environment conducive to new and beneficial investment. But the industry must be prepared to invest and invest more than ratepayer money.

I believe in the contributions which communications and information technologies can make to social and economic progress. I believe in the need to remain leaders in global telecommunications developments. And I believe I speak for my colleagues on the Commission when I say we will work hard at the FCC to create the kind of regulatory environment that makes those contributions possible.

Sharon L. Nelson

The future is much easier to create than it is to research, so I will begin by offering several predictions concerning the future of telecommunications. My first prediction is that advanced telecommunications will become increasingly important in rural life. The telephone will be used by farmers to gain prompt and accurate market information, to bring many "urban" conveniences to rural areas, and to provide important community services.

My second prediction is that advanced telecommunications will reduce hierarchy in organizations and greatly speed business transactions, particularly in financial markets—perhaps beyond our capacity to control. My third prediction involves the effect of advanced telecommunications upon important social issues. For example, the telephone may be seen as a channel for "safe sex"—an important issue to consider in the information services area. In addition, the telephone will become a window on the outside world for the elderly as they become less active.

My fourth prediction is that someone will soon figure out I am not really responsible for any of these first three predictions. I cribbed from an enlightening volume by the late Ithiel deSola Pool, entitled *Forecasting the Telephone: A Retrospective Technology Assessment of the Telephone.*[4] The book is a fascinating collection of predictions, that have been made over the years, on the effect of telecommunications on various elements of our social and political life.

The references to sex over the telephone date back to 1909. The predictions of the effect of telecommunications on organizations and finance date back to the 1910s, and the predictions on rural life also date back to the turn of the century. While many of the predictions have come true, I think it is also a lesson that we should be skeptical of utopian predictions about the immediate effects of technology on society. Things change, but the changes occur over time, as technology is assimilated into a rich culture. In our enthusiasm for the world of tomorrow, we need to remember it will be populated by the children of today. Their skills and their values will determine the extent to which the new technologies will be used, and the ends to which they will be applied. This suggests we might spend more time worrying about literacy and numeracy, and less time worrying about the relative market shares of competing corporate elephants.

Perhaps this focus is a product of my former life as a teacher. I want to focus on the three "R"s—only in this case my three "R"s for telecommunications represent three time periods—"reaction," the period following divestiture; "retrenchment," the period we now enjoy or endure; and "restructure," the period to come.

I characterize the period from divestiture up through roughly 1987 as the "reaction." First, the unthinkable was thought—the monolithic Bell System was dismembered. Confusion reigned as consumers dealt with the end of one-stop shopping. Getting a dial tone now required leasing or purchasing a phone, having a line hooked up by the local phone company, choosing a long-distance carrier (or having one chosen for you), and figuring out who would be responsible for repairs.

Following the announcement of the Bell breakup in 1982, many people thought the operating companies would not be financially viable. The RBOCs took advantage of that concern: From 1982 until two years after divestiture (1986), the RBOCs requested about $20 billion in new revenue from state regulators. State PUCs granted them rate increases equal to almost half that amount.[5]

These local rate increases tell only part of the revenue story, however. Despite concluding in early 1982 that divestiture should not affect local rates, the FCC by the end of that year introduced an access charge plan with the intent of shifting nearly $4 billion of non-traffic-sensitive (NTS) costs to local telephone users. The FCC said this action was necessary to avoid "bypass" and preserve the financial condition of local operating companies. According to the FCC's original plan, the charge for residential access would start at $2 a month in 1984, and would eventually rise to full cost of $8 a month by 1989.

Consumer groups attacked the plan as a massive transfer of wealth from residential consumers to large long-distance users and long-distance carriers. State commissions, acting through NARUC, challenged the plan in federal court. The House of Representatives easily passed the Dingell-Wirth Bill prohibiting access charges and requiring bypassers to make a contribution toward local loop costs.[6] The FCC responded to this pressure by scrapping its access charge plan a little over a month into the new post-divestiture environment. Companion legislation to the Dingell-Wirth Bill had significant support in the Senate *even after* the FCC dropped its plan. Access charges were delayed, although the concept of shifting the fixed costs of the local exchange plant to end users was not abandoned.

Almost before the ink had dried on the MFJ, local exchange companies began peddling state legislative proposals and referenda aimed at detariffing or deregulating services, or at reducing state regulators' authority to scrutinize affiliated interest transactions. Some of these efforts were successful. Illinois passed a law in 1985 allowing local telephone companies and interexchange carriers to self-certify services as competitive and to detariff them.[7] A number of states, including Iowa, Oregon, and Virginia, adopted laws essentially deregulating small telephone companies.[8] Local exchange companies succeeded in convincing the Nebraska legislature in 1986 to totally deregulate their services.[9] In 1987, Idaho and Vermont passed laws allowing their state regulators to establish local telephone rates under a "social contract."[10] Idaho Governor Andrus later vetoed that particular bill, but a variation on the theme has subsequently gone into effect. The Vermont Public Service Board, after extensive negotiations, finally approved a social contract rate regime with New England Telephone Company in December 1988. Several states adopted legislation organizing telecommunications services into various tiers, e.g., noncompetitive, emerging competitive, or deregulated services.

The Washington State Legislature in 1984 defeated a controversial proposal to detariff statutorily certain services and weaken our Commission's authority over affiliate transactions. After the defeat of that bill, we embarked on a cooperative, consensus-building effort to address the evolution of competitive market conditions in telecommunications through a bipartisan joint select committee of the state legislature. The legislation that resulted from these efforts was the Telecommunications Regulatory Flexibility Act of 1985 (or "Reg Flex" for short).[11] This law created a mechanism for reducing regulation of telecommunications where effective competition can be shown to exist, actually and factually. The act carefully balanced the needs of companies for pricing flexibility in competitive markets with the needs of ratepayers for protection from unrestrained monopoly pricing.

Since the act was passed, we have all but deregulated more than twenty long-distance companies, including AT&T. Pacific Northwest Bell (US West Communications) was granted permission to offer custom calling services under a banded tariff shortly after the law became effective. The Commission has detariffed a number of services provided by local exchange companies including Centrex, speed calling, billing and collection, and intercom services. Significantly, in 1989 we concluded an investigation of intraLATA markets. There we could not find effective competition. For example, US West's own evidence showed it retained a 99.3 percent market share in residential intraLATA toll. A companion to the "Reg Flex" Act deregulated cellular and shared tenant services, with a major exception if and when entities providing such services were to become monopolies.

A puzzling reaction to divestiture was some RBOCs' choice of elaborate corporate structures with many subsidiaries. This was surprising, in part, because AT&T and the BOCs had earlier resisted the FCC's efforts to force them to use separate subsidiaries to provide customer premises equipment and a variety of "enhanced" services that were competitive or potentially competitive. Within weeks of divestiture, the RBOCs were petitioning the court to allow them to engage in a wide range of activities, including data processing services, foreign trade, marketing unregulated communications equipment and services to government agencies, vehicle and fleet services, financial services, office equipment sales, procurement services, and real estate ventures. The RBOCs' new organizational structures created more complexity, more opportunities to shift costs, more ways to realize cross-subsidies, and a giant headache for state regulators.

The FCC's actions in this "reaction" period included Chairman Mark Fowler's "Back to the Future" speech.[12] Of course, the future that Mr. Fowler wanted to take us back to was a mythical one whose sole defining characteristic was a lack of regulation. Perhaps the future *is* as easy to regulate as it is to predict.

The public's reaction to the breakup was dissatisfaction and dismay. Early national surveys generally showed a substantial majority of Americans opposed the breakup. A more recent *Washington Post* survey showed critics of divestiture still maintain a plurality.[13] About 39 percent of those surveyed thought the AT&T breakup was a bad idea, while 31 percent believed it has produced positive results. (The other 30 percent did not express an opinion.)

The second period, beginning roughly in 1988, I call the "retrenchment." It represents a more focused policy debate on key issues facing us as we become an "information society."

The debate in this phase was inaugurated by the FCC's rulemaking on price caps. This rulemaking addressed the role of traditional rate-of-return regulation in the emerging telecommunications environment. The FCC argued, in its *Notice of Proposed Rulemaking*[14] (with the backing of NTIA and the regulated companies), that rate-of-return regulation is slow, deters innovation and promotes overinvestment. According to the FCC, price caps would encourage greater efficiency and innovation, reduce incentives to cross-subsidize, eliminate investment distortions, and be simple to administer.

In my opinion, which I have already shared with the House Telecommunications Subcommittee, the real objectives of price caps are twofold. First, they are intended to end the practice of pricing communications services on the basis of their cost at a time when industry costs are rapidly declining. Second, they are intended to shift the focus away from rising telephone company profit levels that will surely accrue under a declining cost scenario. At a conference sponsored by the University of Utah, an analyst with Morgan Stanley suggested that a coming wave of consolidation in the phone industry will reduce the number of phone firms (mostly independents) from 1,371 currently to about 150 by 1995, and in turn reduce operating overheads by 25 to 40 percent. One cannot be sanguine about predicting ratepayer benefits resulting from these increased operating efficiencies under a price cap regime.

Another development I view as positive is the new focus in many states on the quality and extent of the telecommunications infrastructure. The expanding role of information technologies and their application across all segments of economic activity has increasingly linked telecommunications with economic development. In 1988 and 1989, several states (including Washington) have undertaken projects that address perceived disadvantages in the availability, quality, and cost of rural services.

During this "retrenchment" period, we are now seeing a wave of rate reductions at the state level. According to FCC Summary Reports, state PUCs ordered rate reductions totalling $1.37 billion during 1988.[15] At the same time, however, the RBOCs began to renege on the compact established by the MFJ to use the substantial profits from Yellow Pages to support local service. The Colorado PUC's position was affirmed by its state Supreme Court.[16] Litigation is continuing in Washington.

Among other positive developments of this period, I count the RBOCs' rethinking of diversification. After some of them racked up big losses in their diversified enterprises, they began to refocus their attention on the businesses they know best. During the "reaction," the RBOCs' expansion strategy was indeed expansive. Now they seem to be responding to the *In Search of Excellence* notion of sticking to the knitting. US West has retreated from its effort to market equipment and services outside its fourteen-state region. Bell Atlantic has reduced investment in its chain of Compu-Shop computer stores and cut back holdings in its A-Beeper paging operation. Pacific Telesis has likewise begun to liquidate its Computer Store holdings and is backing away from its network management enterprise. Southwestern Bell has abandoned its Silver Pages venture and also pulled back from some of its directory efforts in East Coast markets.

The third phase, which I think we are now entering, I call the "restructure." In this period I see substantial changes in industry structure. In interLATA transmission, I expect to see further movement toward a stable oligopoly with the networks of the three major interexchange carriers overlaying smaller regional networks. In local service, I see the continuation of monopoly control of local access for the present, with perhaps some fringe competition from cellular in rural areas. "Mini-networks" based on various technologies will also continue to provide some competition for a portion of the usage of larger businesses in major cities but will still ultimately rely on the LECs' bottleneck. In equipment markets, it is reasonable to assume there will be continued robust competition and innovation.

Certainly one of the key issues in the restructure will be determining the appropriate market structure for and the role of regulation in fiber-based, broadband networks. The FCC tentatively concluded, in a *Further Notice of Proposed Rulemaking*,[17] that existing telco/cable cross-ownership restrictions are impeding innovative broadband services. The number of FCC Commissioners subscribing to these tentative conclusions steadily decreased. Although Commissioner Quello originally endorsed the agency's findings, he later tempered his position based first on his concern that lifting the ban might constrain free broadcasting in the U.S., and second, on several fundamental questions left unanswered in the *Further Notice:* how should cross-subsidization be prevented? Should the Congress, FCC, or states require structural separation of the telco's cable activities? Should the telcos be restricted to common carriage of video signals?

Commissioner Patricia Dennis also suggested that the tentative conclusions missed the mark, since they permitted telco entry into cable via the acquisition of existing systems, instead of limiting entry to the development of new systems. She also supported the concept of reciprocal entry by cable firms into the provision of two-way voice, data, and video services. There are also questions of significant regulatory jurisdiction to be resolved. The agency's tentative conclusions have been demonstrated to be hopelessly premature. Much further definition and study of these issues is obviously required.

Industries once entirely distinct from one another now appear to be on the verge of merging or colliding. The broadcast, publishing, and cable industries—traditionally viewed as affected with First Amendment values—are running smack dab into the traditional common carrier industry, viewed as affected with a public interest. Add to the brew concerns about American competitiveness in global (primarily equipment) markets and you have a major structural and regulatory dilemma.

Many public policymakers can be expected to participate in the structural issues debate. Given the clout of the present competing interests (and yet unborn ones), the outcome defies prediction. Congress is the only forum where these issues can be debated in a comprehensive way. Congress must not shy away from the task. My opinion is that regulation will accommodate and adapt to whatever is the emerging industry structure.

The FCC and state regulators can be expected to continue to simplify and streamline regulatory procedures and to use the efficiencies of competitive markets where possible. In pursuit of this, however, I hope we never fail to recognize that where monopoly persists, ratepayers *must* be protected by effective regulation. Monopoly ratepayers will continue to expect good service at *fair* rates. They should never be a source of free capital to finance speculative competitive ventures.

My final prediction is one of my own, which I offer hesitantly. The major communications issue of the future may have little to do with price caps, depreciation schedules, or lines-of-business restrictions. The preeminent issue for the future is privacy. If there ever was such a thing as an "unlisted" telephone number and address, it exists no longer. In the world of equal access and ONA, the telephone company no longer protects this information in any absolute sense. On the contrary, many companies are looking for innovative ways to exploit any information that comes into their possession. Whether regulators can offer any real protection to the public is debatable.

Privacy of unlisted numbers, caller ID, cellular communications, usage data, and the like are real issues. They are beginning to be addressed in state legislatures, and I think it is only a matter of time before they become a more central part of our national policy debate. Recent judicial nominees' video rental habits made good copy. Someday your pay-per-view or "976" habits may do the same.

Ironically, at the same time that the public may lose its expectation of privacy, regulated companies are increasing their expectation of privacy. The impact on public processes is severe. Published accounts of the Oliver North trial were disturbingly similar to the maneuvering that takes place in our hearing rooms every day. Like Judge Gessell, we state regulators struggle to balance the legitimate confidentiality concerns of one party against the due process rights of other parties, and the ultimate right of the people to be secure in the belief that government is there to serve the public. Can the people be confident when the public business is conducted behind locked doors? Can they accept as a matter of faith that justice is being done? As an attorney and public servant, I have my doubts. Where will this trend lead? I can only hope public servants will unite to resist efforts to "privatize" the public regulatory process.

To the extent that public processes may be inconsistent with competitive ventures, those ventures need to be isolated and insulated from unnecessary regulation and the public hearing process which is inherent to regulation. Amidst claims that structural separation of unregulated activities is inefficient, it may have been overlooked that without such separation, we are faced with a continuing need for similarly "inefficient" regulatory oversight. I hope those in a position to decide this issue will consider carefully the practical benefits to be derived from fully isolating the effectively competitive activities of regulated companies from their public service activities. If that isolation can be achieved at an acceptable cost, we may be able to return to a more open and rational administrative process in our regulation of the remaining monopoly activities.

I feel reasonably confident predicting that pressures on our traditional expectations of privacy will grow over the next five years or so. Prognostication beyond five years is always risky—all the more so in telecommunications, with constantly changing technologies—and is best left to the crystal ball gazers and science fiction writers. Recognizing this, my Commission recently invited a science fiction writer to share some insights—and predictions—with us at a roundtable on telecommunications policy.

Our science fiction writer, Rick Gauger from Bellingham, Washington, gave us some new vocabulary—phrases like "cyberpunk" and "recreational terrorism"—and a fairly unsettling vision of the future increasingly dependent on computers and telecommunications. Mr. Gauger's image of a telecommunications future is, as he put it, "Marshall McLuhan's global village—with teeth." In this future, you will be periodically awakened at odd hours of the night by random phone calls placed by computer hackers' telephone harassment programs—just for the fun of it. The thermostatic controls, lighting, and elevators in your "smart" building will be subject to similar random sabotage by computer-equipped malcontents with nothing better to do with their time. Your full-motion video phone answering machine or video messaging service will be constantly jammed by advertisements cleverly disguised as real messsages by marketers with access to a detailed database profile of your retail and personal habits. When the IRS electronically impounds your bank account because a festering computer virus erases the tax payment you keyed in months earlier, your bank will stop making the payments on your car—now due and payable daily. The bank will have no trouble repossessing your car, since your cellular phone conveniently keeps the cellular phone company's computer aware of the car's whereabouts at all times. Mr. Gauger's science fiction account is of the "Wired Nation" come to fruition and seriously over-ripened.

It would be comforting to sit back with a trusting smile and think, "We would never let it come to all that—we will legislate and regulate protections." Mr. Gauger anticipated that response, and pointed out that science fiction writers like Jules Verne wrote about air travel long before it became a reality. But even the science fiction writers failed to predict outcomes like international air piracy and the accidental shoot-downs of airliners by automated missiles.

At the beginning of my reflections I emphasized that technology evolves in the context of culture. The skills and values of today's children will help determine whether Mr. Gauger's chilling vision comes to pass.

We, as academic observers, policymakers, and regulators bear a heavy burden to consider the directions technology may take us, and to implement public policies that are likely to lead to a preferred, rather than a chaotic, future. To do this we must rationally and cooperatively assess future scenarios. And while regulatory bodies must continue to react to legitimate petitions by our regulated constituents for relief, it is time for us to take a proactive stance in formulating reasonable public policy goals and means to implement those ends. And finally, we must continue to stand for the consumer lest the consumer become the consumed.

ENDNOTES

1. Walker Report, FCC 1938; also FCC Final Report 1939.

2. Derived from data supplied by the Office of Telecommunications, International Trade Administration, U.S. Commerce Department.

3. National Telecommunications and Information Administration, U.S. Department of Commerce *Telecom 2000*, NTIA Special Report 88-21, Washington, D.C., October 1988.

4. Ithiel deSola Pool, *Forecasting The Telephone: A Retrospective Technology Assessment of the Telephone* (Norwood, N.J.: Ablex, 1983).

5. Gene Kimmelman and Mark Cooper, *Divestiture Plus Five: Residential Telephone Service Five Years After the Breakup of AT&T* (Consumer Federation of America, Washington, D.C., December 1988), pp. iii–iv.

6. HR 4102 "Universal Telephone Service Preservation Act of 1983" to amend the Communications Act of 1934 to assure universal telephone service within the United States and for other purposes, 98th Cong., 1st sess.

7. 1985 Illinois HB 1814 to add Article XIII and amend Sec. 4.3 of the "Regulatory Agency Sunset Act."

8. 1981 Iowa Acts Ch. 56 Sec. 4; 1987 Oregon HB 2660 added to ORS Ch. 757; 1986 Virginia HB 275 to amend Title 56 Ch. 19 Secs. 56.531–56.534, establishing the Small Investor-Owned Telephone Utility Act.

9. 1986 Nebraska LB 835 RRS 1943 (reissue 1987) Sec. 86.801–86.811.

10. 1988 Idaho HB 687 amending Title 62, Idaho Code, by the addition of a new Ch. 6, Title 62, Idaho Code (Telecommunications Act of 1988); amending Sec. 61.121; amending Ch. 6 Title 61 by addition of a new Sec. 61.622A; amending Ch. 6, Title 61 by the addition of 9 new Sec. 61.622B; also 1987 Vermont S114 30 V.S.A. to add Secs. 165, 220a, 220c, 220d, 227a and to amend Secs. 102, 203(S), 231.

11. Washington Laws 1985 Ch. 450 (Substitute SB 3305) amending various parts of RCW 80 and adding new sections to Ch. 80.36 RCW.

12. The contents of this speech were incorporated in Mark S. Fowler, Albert Halprin, James D. Schlichting, " 'Back to the Future': A Model for Telecommunications" 38 *Fed. Comm. L.J.* pp. 145-200.

13. "Remember Ma Bell?" *Washington Post National Weekly Edition*, January 9–15, 1989, pp. 6–8.

14. FCC Docket No. 87.313, In the Matter of Policy and Rules Concerning Rules for Dominant Carriers, Notice of Proposed Rulemaking, August 4, 1987.

15. Summary of Telephone Rate Cases, Industry Analysis Division, Common Carrier Bureau, FCC, April 24, 1990, table 3.

16. *Mountain States Telephone and Telegraph Co. v. The Public Utilities Commission of the State of Colorado*, 763 P 2d 1020 (Colo. 1988).

17. 3FCC Rcd 3195 (1988).

2
STRUCTURAL
ENVIRONMENT

3

Regulatory and Institutional Change

■

GLEN O. ROBINSON

■

PHILIP L. VERVEER

A. GRAY COLLINS

RICHARD E. WILEY

EDWARD F. BURKE

Glen O. Robinson

For all of its undoubted importance, the MFJ was not the beginning nor the whole of the transformation in telecommunications. Though the MFJ is currently at the center of controversy over regulatory policy, both it and the controversy now surrounding it are the products of changes in the economic, political, and legal environment of telecommunications that long antedated the breakup of the Bell System and are independent of it.[1]

I say "long antedated" with some hesitation. All things are relative, and relative to the magnitude of the transformation, the events took place in a rather short period of time. Virtually all of the important economic events occurred in less than a score years, and most of the major policy decisions within little more than a decade (roughly from the early 1970s to the early 1980s). Traditional accounts identify a series of major FCC decisions going back as far as *Hush-A-Phone*[2] in 1956, the *Above 890*[3] decision in 1959, *Carterfone*[4] in 1968, and continuing through the 1970s with such decisions as *Specialized Carriers*[5] in 1971, *Execunet*[6] in 1977, and culminating in *Computer II*[7] in 1980. I do not think any one of these decisions was a decisive influence in the evolution of telecommunications to its present state. However, if pressed to select one that could mark a critical turning in regulatory policy, I would choose the first *Execunet* case in 1977. It might not be the most important single decision in this period, but of all the decisions and events it more than any other signaled that the trend towards full competition would not be halted. Perhaps next in importance was *Computer II*, cutting loose the last vestige of terminal equipment regulation and creating the framework for competitive supply of services as well. After these two decisions were implemented, the antitrust case was almost anticlimactic.

The transformation of telecommunications policy has not been without its ironies. One is that the advent of competition has not diminished the importance or the magnitude of regulation, but merely altered its character. In fact, regulation has become far more active and energetic than anything seen in AT&T's salad days, when it was not only the center of attention, but virtually the only object of notice.

Prior to the 1970s, FCC regulation of interstate telecommunications consisted mostly of what it called "continuous surveillance."[8] This was a fairly laid-back form of regulation in which the Commission professed to regulate AT&T's interstate rates by taking credit for extracting voluntary rate reductions made possible by rapidly declining interstate service costs, which were in turn the product of technological improvements in long-distance transmission and switching capability. This regulatory policy changed somewhat in the mid-1960s, when the FCC embarked upon a formal investigation of AT&T's rate level and structure.[9] However, even the inauguration of formal rate proceeding, important as it was, did not alter the basic regulatory policy or the regulatory apparatus for implementing that policy. It was the introduction of competition that sparked the modern era of active FCC regulation.

Consider, as an illustration, the growth in the size of the FCC's Common Carrier Bureau. In fiscal 1970, a year that represents, if not the beginning of the modern era, at least the beginning of the beginning —the bureau's Washington staff numbered 131 persons out of a total Washington office complement of 1,098. Seven years later it grew to 244. That was not exceptional growth, perhaps, considering that the overall Washington staff grew to 1,596. Yet by fiscal 1989, when the overall Washington staff declined to 1,236, the Common Carrier Bureau continued to grow, to 297. The budget figures tell a roughly similar story. In 1970, Common Carrier activities accounted for roughly $2.6 million out of a total agency budget of $24.6 million; in 1977 the Common Carrier budget was $7.7 million out of a total of $56.9 million; in 1989 the Common Carrier budget rose to $21.3 million while the agency's budget was $99.6 million. Thus, as competition grew, the regulatory apparatus grew as well, growing even as a portion of the total: from around 10.5 percent in 1970 to about 21.4 percent in 1989.[10]

My brief career at the FCC, in precisely the middle of the 1970s, came at a particularly interesting time in the evolution from the old regime to the new. The earlier *Carterfone* and *Specialized Common Carrier* decisions had stirred enough political interest to prompt the occasional attention of Commissioners to the emerging issues of competitive policy in telecommunications. At the same time, the earlier initiation of formal rate proceedings drew some attention to traditional problems of monopoly regulation. As a result, issues that had once been virtually the exclusive preserve of the Common Carrier Bureau were starting to percolate up to the top levels of the agency. Nevertheless, despite this occasional notice of Common Carrier affairs, this period was still one where those affairs were subordinated to the concerns of mass communications; the most trivial controversy in broadcasting preempted all but the most important issues in telecommunications on the Commission's weekly agenda. Anyone interested in pursuing the emerging issues in telecommunications policy, whether they involved authorization of new competitive services or investigation of AT&T tariffs, had to resign to doing so in the company of a handful of staff specialists.

In part, the perverse ranking of priorities was a consequence of the sheer impenetrability of some of the issues then surfacing in telecommunications, as contrasted to the simplicity of broadcast regulation. Anyone could claim the requisite authority to make a judgment about, say, children's television. But trying to determine whether authorization of competition in private line services should include "FX" (foreign exchange) and "CCSA" (common control switching arrangement) services was a task far more perplexing. It was not, however, simply a matter of preferring to spend time on those matters you could understand instead of those you could not; it was also a matter of responding to what the political environment indicated was of primary concern. Professional bureaucrats are not politically accountable to the electorate; nor are political appointees, for that matter. But neither the bureaucrat nor the appointee are wholly insulated from or indifferent to popular sentiments. Agency officials may not closely follow the election returns but they do read newspapers, and like most ordinary people they are influenced by what they read about themselves; they like to be seen as doing things that others regard as important. It is no mystery then that, other things being equal, FCC Commissioners will tend to direct their attention to those things that have public salience. Herein lies much of the gravitational power of mass communications issues in the earlier era (and, to a still considerable extent, today). An FCC decision on broadcast network programming guaranteed newspaper notice and public attention. A decision on AT&T's rate structure might receive newspaper notice—in the back pages of the financial news— but little general public attention.

However, the pre-divestiture times were changing, without doubt. Competition brought new players into the inner circle of the regulatory community, and at the same time stimulated public interest in the community at large.[11] Stimulated by both communities, the FCC responded in the only way it knew how, with more activity of its own. Competition begat regulation, or at least more regulatory activity.

My discussion thus far has focused on the growth of *federal* regulation of telecommunications consequential to the evolution towards competition. I should comment upon *state* regulation where institutional change has been even more noteworthy. Unable to compile data comparable to the illustrative figures I cited for the FCC, I will do what most legal scholars do—tell a story.

Prior to my appointment to the FCC in 1974, my only firsthand experience with state telecommunications regulation was in Minnesota in the late 1960s where I first taught law. Minnesota was not then known to be in the forefront of activist regulatory states, but neither was it in the rear. In the field of telecommunications, Minnesota, traditionally a progressive state favoring the political transition of active economic regulation, was, if not dormant, at least very subdued. Having some interest in regulation at the time, I had occasion to inquire into the state's regulatory apparatus, circa 1969. I learned that Minnesota's Public Service Commission had a grand total of *three* persons assigned to the telephone-telegraph division responsible for regulating the local telephone company, Northwestern Bell. Of those three, one was a secretary, one an accountant, and the other a person of no particular calling who was assigned the task of reading Northwestern Bell's annual reports and other published matters. Minnesota was not in the vanguard, but some other states—Texas for instance—had no state regulation at all. Instead, the regulatory burden rested on the cities which were expected to exercise control through their franchising power, an aspect of their control over use of public streets.

The state regulatory presence became more noticeable in the 1970s, though I cannot honestly say I, as an FCC Commissioner, noticed it much. Perhaps it was my parochial attitude to think that all action—such as it was—took place at the federal level. It seemed to me, at the time, that the states' principal role was to quarrel with the FCC over how much local service should be cross-subsidized by rates on interstate service. Certainly that was the central agenda of NARUC, as was manifest from their utmost resistance to any FCC policy or decision that might adversely affect the subsidy.

It was, of course, such subsidy that made it possible for Minnesota to "regulate" Northwestern Bell with three staff members. The fact that intrastate service was heavily cross-subsidized by interstate service rates greatly reduced the need to maintain or increase intrastate rates, to the immense relief of local regulators who were neither well-disposed nor well-equipped to regulate. To be sure, some states like New York and California and a few others were reasonably active in their own right, independent of the FCC. Still, the structure of the industry made it unnecessary for them to bear the full burden of regulating local rates. With the entire system of local exchange and interstate service dominated by a single firm, it was relatively simple to shuffle the costs of the former to the latter, and with that shuffle to transfer the main burden of regulation on to the FCC. The mechanism of the subsidy was the separations and settlement arrangements which were deliberately manipulated to shift a disproportionate share of non-traffic-sensitive plant costs to interstate service. (The percentage of non-traffic-sensitive costs allocated to interstate service rose from 5 percent in 1952 to a high of 27 percent in 1982; the percentage of interstate use rose from about 3 to 7 percent in that period.)[12]

Of course, this cross-subsidization was premised on continuing AT&T's traditional monopoly. When the FCC began to authorize (limited) competition in interstate service markets, the subsidy was doomed. Amazingly, the subsidy continued to increase even as competition was being introduced. Between 1965 and 1975 the percent of non-traffic-sensitive costs (hence rate burden) which were shifted to interstate service had nearly tripled![13] Nevertheless, it was inevitable interstate competition would erode the basis on which the historic subsidy of local service rested by forcing interstate rates to be lowered towards cost of service. This put pressure on local rates, which in turn put pressure on local regulators.

As a supporter of the new competition, I was not then personally sympathetic to the states' concerns. Now that age has sweetened my disposition, it occurs to me that I might have been a little more understanding; I might have recalled my former home state of Minnesota and those three staff members of its State Public Service Commission who would be overwhelmed by the business of state regulatory responsibility in the new competitive era. It is small wonder the FCC's introduction of competition into interstate service and equipment markets in the 1970s was a traumatic event for state regulators.

Though competition inevitably would increase the states' regulatory activity, it seems remarkable that competition should also increase federal regulatory activity. The irony of this will not be lost on anyone who was educated to think of regulation and competition as substitutes, not complements, of each other. In the early years, the FCC viewed competition as an alternative to regulation. That is the way conventional economics sees it also. From that perspective, one would expect that as competition grew it would displace regulation. That is not quite what has happened, as I suggested earlier. As the role of competition in telecommunications has expanded, regulation has grown with it. In telecommunications, competition and regulation have turned out to be complementary goods, like bread and butter.

The character of regulation has changed, of course; the emphasis shifted from regulating AT&T's monopoly rates to regulating its competitive rates. Not "AT&T the Monopolist," but "AT&T the Competitor" became the focal point of regulatory concern. In a sense, the monopolist and the competitor were two sides of the same coin. The asumption was that AT&T's monopoly power in switched service markets gave it a competitive edge in specialized service and equipment markets. Be that as it may, the central point is that regulation shifted from its more or less static role of protecting *consumers*, to a much more dynamic role of protecting *competitors*. The fact the two roles were ultimately supposed to converge does not change the fact the character of the FCC's work changed dramatically. And as it changed, it also grew.

There has been deregulation. I do not mean to imply otherwise. Regulatory control over equipment supply has, for all practical purposes, disappeared. Interstate service regulation has diminished. *Computer II* and *Computer III*[14] later curtailed regulatory surveillance of competitive services. And the FCC's recent adoption of an incentive form of price regulation (price caps) for AT&T in lieu of traditional rate-of-return regulation promises a degree of deregulation for rates.[15] Yet, when the dust clears from these deregulatory activities, one must be struck by the fact that regulation seems to be a great deal more active and pervasive than in the monopoly era—*even at the federal level where competition is prevalent.*

I suppose, when one reflects upon it, that this is not really mysterious—ironic, but not inexplicable. Monitoring "AT&T the Monopolist" may have been a daunting challenge, but at least here the FCC could devote its total energies—such as they were—to the task. And the task was a well defined one. Protecting the consumer against monopoly overcharge or service inadequacies—the latter a rather minor problem—involves complexities that require intelligence, but not necessarily a lot of regulatory hands. Being able to concentrate on one entity does have its advantages. As Mark Twain once quipped, the admonition not to put all one's eggs in one basket is a fool's advice; it only scatters one's investments and one's attention. The wise man says—according to Twain—"put all your eggs in *one* basket—and *watch* that basket!" The FCC, however, chose to follow the wisdom of multi-basket diversification, hoping to spread the burden of regulation among multiple "market regulators" *cum* competitors. It soon learned the truth behind Twain's epigram. Increasing the number of players in the game only increased the number of players and plays to be watched, and to which it had to respond—or thought it had to respond. Hence we got more, if different, regulation along with more competition.

Witness the *Computer III* approach and the ONA rules, which are intended to promote the MFJ's provisions regarding equal access by all competitors to the network. ONA is designed to assure that all carriers have access to basic service elements (BSEs) on an unbundled basis, on essentially the same terms as enjoyed by BOCs themselves. The ONA rules provide a nonstructural alternative to the very costly structural requirements of *Computer II*. These new rules may be an improvement on the old. But they are not necessarily more deregulatory. Indeed, the implementation of ONA may well entail a degree of regulatory surveillance similar to that of the 1970s, before *Computer II*.[16]

So too with price caps. Though this scheme again seems to me superior to traditional rate of return regulation, it remains to be seen whether it will entail significantly less regulatory activity. Everything depends on how much continuing adjustment in the price cap the FCC finds is required by economic or political circumstances.[17] And we have reason to think from its report adopting the price cap scheme that the FCC intends to monitor the results of price cap regulation very closely. No doubt its assurances of "continuing surveillance"—to revive an old term—are a response to the considerable. political opposition to price cap regulation, but that simply underscores the point that political circumstances could undermine what otherwise seems to be a quite sensible measure of deregulation.

In theory, the antitrust suit should have relieved at least some of the awkwardness of this ironic situation, in which we had both the *Sturm* and *Drang* of competition and the depressing burden of regulation. Distrusting regulation in general (and the FCC in particular), the DOJ aimed at a "structural solution" that would permit competition to proceed without reliance on regulatory surveillance. A clean cut through this Gordian knot of intertwined competition and regulation required a breakup of AT&T in such a way as to separate the monopoly segments from the competitive segments, so the former could not disrupt the free play of competition. Once this was accomplished the regulatory task of the FCC would become marginal. State regulation of the local exchange monopoly would continue, but competition would supplant the need for regulation in all other markets, interstate and intrastate together.

Such was the theory. In practice it has not worked out quite so cleanly. States have taken on new regulatory responsibility,[18] and, as I have noted, there have been important curtailments in the FCC's regulatory surveillance. Yet there remains a significant amount of regulation precisely in the areas thought to be under competitive forces, and the aggregate level of regulation for the industry as a whole appears to have increased. Indeed, we now have a new regulator as a consequence of the antitrust suit, Judge Harold Greene. The irony marches on.

Of course, as indicated by his comments in the opening chapter of this volume, Judge Greene firmly believes the purpose of the MFJ was to make the industry safe *for* competition, not safe *from* regulation. There is something to be said for this view. Still, I rather doubt this was what the DOJ contemplated when it filed the case in 1974, or what it contemplated on the eve of the trial when the head of the antitrust division, William Baxter, promised to "litigate to the eyeballs" in order to get the relief requested.[19] As it happens, he got more than he wished and perhaps a bit more than was required. Certainly the *present* administration seems to think the relief obtained was more than required. The current Justice Department is one of the leading critics of Judge Greene's new regulatory machine.[20]

Proposals to divest Judge Greene of his authority over MFJ conditions are influenced not only by the questions of separation of powers and appropriate institutional responsibilities. In fact, the present controversy is generated less by Judge Greene's view of his role than by his substantive views on the basic policy questions—in particular his continued refusal to remove the general restrictions barring regional holding companies or their operating companies from equipment manufacturing, interexchange service, and information services. On the basic policy issue, I find it somewhat difficult to fault Judge Greene's judgment that these restrictions are entailed by the justification for the divestiture itself. If the Justice Department is correct in asserting that the restrictions are not necessary, it comes perilously close to saying that divestiture was an unnecessary exercise in the first place. If it is true that competition by the RHCs and BOCs is not a significant threat to competition, why was AT&T not allowed to continue to own and operate the BOCs?

This question is not answered simply by saying conditions were different in the early 1980s. Of course they were. But most of the changes that have occurred have not been the consequence of divestiture, but of an ongoing evolution towards competition that was set in motion by the FCC and by technological innovation wholly independent of and prior to the MFJ. The Justice Department's request for modifying terms of the MFJ that go to the very heart of its original case for divestiture is thus deeply ironic.

Irony aside, I have some doubt the affirmative case for permitting BOCs to enter these restricted fields is so compelling as to overwhelm the concerns that gave rise to the case.[21] However, my assignment here does not permit me to set sail on these troubled waters. I will limit myself to some abstract observations about antitrust and regulation and about institutional roles.

I expect the line-of-business restrictions will be phased out in time. The qualifier "in time" is, however, all important. To paraphrase Lord Keynes' celebrated quip: in time we are all dead. Experience with antitrust regulatory decrees in other cases is unfortunately not reassuring on this score. Consider as one illustration the consent decrees entered against eight major motion picture companies following *United States v. Paramount Pictures*,[22] a landmark in the film industry in much the way that the MFJ is in telecommunications. Following the Supreme Court's decision in 1948, ordering the separation of film production and distribution from theatrical exhibition, each of the Paramount defendants entered into consent decrees governing licensing practices, future acquisitions, and related matters. The individual decrees were entered between 1948 and 1952, but they, like the Supreme Court's earlier decision, rested on a complaint filed in 1938, based on practices as they existed in the 1930s.[23] More than fifty years after the complaint the decrees are still the subject of court actions to enforce or modify the original decrees.[24]

The problem of obsolescence is bad enough in a field like the motion picture industry; it is worse in a field like telecommunications where rapid technological change entails swift and important change in economic conditions, and they in turn demand responsive legal accommodations. To appreciate the problem here, one need only recall the 1956 *Western Electric* consent decree which forbade AT&T from competing in unregulated markets.[25] Whatever the merits of that restriction in 1956, the rapidly changing economic and technological conditions of the industry made it an anachronism by the 1970s, and threatened to retard the very competition it was intended to promote. The 1956 restrictions were, of course, eliminated as a condition of the 1982 decree. Whether they would have been eliminated otherwise is not clear. The FCC, recall, undertook to interpret the decree in its *Computer II* decision in a fashion that enabled AT&T to offer unregulated services and equipment; and the New Jersey District Court that had jurisdiction over the decree gave a similar interpretation. Still, it is not at all clear, that those interpretations would have prevailed over continued DOJ opposition.

The question of modification is confused by the uncertainty over burden of proof: what are the applicable standards for obtaining a modification? For contested modifications, the general standard, laid down by the Court in 1932 in *United States v. Swift*, is strict: "nothing less than a clear showing of grievous wrong evoked by new and unforeseen conditions should lead [a court] to change what was decreed. . . ."[26] It is debatable whether the *Swift* standard applies to the MFJ inasmuch as it contains a provision specifically addressing the criteria for modification which provisions arguably supplant the *Swift* standards. Also, one might argue that *Swift* was really intended to address only those cases where modification is opposed by the government. Here, of course, the government supports modification. However, all of this is probably moot. The MFJ itself provides that the restrictions will not be removed until there is no "substantial possibility" that a BOC could use its monopoly power to impede competition in the market it seeks to enter, and Judge Greene appears to be committed to an interpretation of this criterion that makes it roughly the same as the *Swift* standard.

Judge Greene may be reversed by a higher court, or by Congress. In 1986 the Court of Appeals for the District of Columbia affirmed his refusal then to make modifications.[27] However, more recently the Ninth Circuit remanded his Triennial Review Opinion's rejection of lessening MFJ restrictions on information services.[28] The outcome is uncertain, but my current expectation is that Judge Greene will adhere to his original opinion and will be affirmed. As to Congress, the most one could realistically expect is enactment of some version of current proposed legislation giving the FCC jurisdiction over the MFJ. This would be a dubious contribution unless Congress also gives some policy directions. Unfortunately, as we have learned from failed congressional initiatives in the 1970s (the famous "Bell bill" and the Van Deerlin "rewrite" of the entire Communications Act),[29] the odds of Congress taking meaningful action in this area are so small as to confound even Jimmy the Greek.[30]

Quite apart from the merits of the MFJ restrictions and the consequences of keeping them in place, one must be troubled that routine policy decisions are being made by a federal court judge. It is not that he is not knowledgeable in telecommunications policy. On the contrary, his opinions indicate he is uncommonly knowledgeable. And one could hardly say he lacks experience; I cannot think of any regulator in a position of comparable authority who has had a longer or more intense exposure to these particular issues. But this is not quite to the point of the question whether he should be engaged in this enterprise. Equally it is not to the point to ask whether the FCC and its state counterparts are preeminently expert or wise. For better or worse—and it is probably a bit of each—they are the ordained ministers of regulatory control.

To be sure, a court necessarily assumes some regulatory role as an incident of its adjudicatory powers—here, adjudication and enforcement of the antitrust laws. This is Judge Greene's defense of his present active role, as indicated in his remarks in chapter 1, and his defense is not without some merit. Given the complexity of the MFJ, it is not objectionable for the Court to retain jurisdiction to interpret and enforce the decree for a period of time sufficient to ensure that the mandate has been fully implemented. Yet, Judge Greene seems to have defined for himself a role beyond that of interpreter and enforcer of the MFJ—in itself a fairly capacious role—to that of policymaker, evaluating and acting on request for waivers of MFJ restrictions as deemed fit in the changing circumstances. Whatever the merits of the individual actions taken, Judge Greene's self-conscious effort to pronounce regulatory policy in this matter is troubling. Perhaps one should not place great weight on the manner of judicial expression, but it has not gone unnoticed by critical observers that Judge Greene's opinions on the MFJ restrictions have a style of reasoning hard to distinguish from that of the FCC, or any other agency engaged in the crafting of regulatory policy.

It may be the MFJ itself invites a kind of continuing judicial regulation with its Triennial Review program, but it surely does not demand it. On this score, the point-counterpoint between William Baxter and Judge Greene in this volume over where and when the idea for the Triennial Review program originated is largely irrelevant. Nor is it particularly relevant whether the Justice Department and AT&T *intended* active judicial oversight. An antitrust case that requires a whole new regulatory scheme as a means of enforcing the relief ordered is probably a case that should not have been brought in the first place. And if, after the fact, it turns out that the decree is becoming a basis for a new regulatory scheme, it should be abandoned.

Judge Greene is undoubtedly correct that with or without a formal review program a court must consider petitions for modification and change, which in turn requires periodic regulatory choices to be made. But as Baxter points out, Judge Greene seems to have created an environment that invites continued and detailed regulatory involvement given by the members of Judge Greene's rulings on the MFJ. Between July 1983 (when AT&T's reorganization plan was approved) and June 1990 (the latest reported decision as this is printed), there have been over forty separate opinions dealing with the interpretation, enforcement, or modification of the decree, over half of which resulted in some modification of the original terms of the MFJ.[31] Judge Greene's initial insistence on modifying the clean-cut terms of divestiture, and his subsequent willingness to entertain modifications on the basis of changing cost-benefit configurations, may or may not be sound as a matter of regulatory policy. But they seem out of character with the judicial role, and at least somewhat at odds with a central point of the case itself.

Whether or not Judge Greene remains an important player in the regulatory game in years to come, I would not look for the disappearance of regulation any time soon—not at the federal or the state level. I return to the ironic note sounded at the outset, that in this field competition and regulation seem to have become complementary not substitute goods. The present controversy over line-of-business restrictions on the RHCs and the BOCs may be special inasmuch as it involves an "outsider"—Judge Greene—in the regulatory game, but I doubt his leaving the game will terminate the play. For all the moves of the FCC away from traditional regulation, its regulatory energies seem to be as fully engaged as ever in monitoring the new competitive environment. And, of course, at the local level (intraLATA) most states have retained the traditional regulatory functions.

As usual in public affairs there is good news and bad news. The good news is that we have made exceptional progress in the past twenty years in telecommunications technology and services, and more is foreseeable. The bad news is that the future seems right now to be more in the hands of lawyers than in the hands of producers and consumers. To the ancient Chinese curse—"may you live in interesting times"—has been added a distinctively American twist—"and may your lawyers be fruitful and multiply."

Philip L. Verveer

As Glen Robinson has discussed, Judge Greene's District Court, the Antitrust Division of the Justice Department, the FCC, the state regulatory commissions, and the Congress all have contributed to the evolution of policy since the AT&T divestiture was announced in January 1982. The early days were marked by a good deal of institutional harmony, but the era of good feeling among governmental institutions with jurisdiction over telephony proved short-lived. From 1985 onward, there has been increasing conflict and uncertainty over respective roles, and more than a little misunderstanding, mistrust, and even meanspiritedness. The causes of the upset, I suggest, are, first, dramatically different views about the existence, extent, and social utility of scope economies in the offering of telephone service and the activities forbidden to the BOCs by the MFJ; and second, uncertainty—some genuine, some contrived for advocacy purposes—about the extent of the authority enjoyed by Judge Greene, the FCC, and the states. Some of these uncertainties and conflicts can be highlighted by briefly reviewing both Judge Greene's evolving role with the states, the DOJ, and the FCC, and the potential significance of the *Louisiana Public Service Commission*.[32]

During the initial Tunney Act review of the proposed consent decree, the FCC and several state regulatory commissions (as well as the FCC) argued that Judge Greene lacked the authority to enter the decree absent a finding by the regulators, in the exercise of their own jurisdiction, that the provisions of the proposed decree would serve the public interest. Relying principally on the supremacy clause, as well as Section 4 of the Sherman Act,[33] Judge Greene rejected these arguments[34] and concluded that "those provisions in the proposed decree which are necessary to vindicate the federal interest in the enforcement of the antitrust laws will be approved notwithstanding the fact that they may conflict with the state laws or interest."[35] However, in his opinion, Judge Greene indicated a willingness to accommodate state interests where possible, stating that "in its overall consideration of the public interest, the Court will also take into account that a particular provision may be merely peripheral to the federal interest but have a substantial adverse impact on state laws."[36] The District Court later cited the states' concerns in support of its decision allowing the divested BOCs to engage in the provision of printed Yellow Pages directories and the provision of CPE.[37] And subsequent to the MFJ, state regulators generally have been more sanguine about Judge Greene's continuing role than have decisionmakers at the FCC. The differing regulatory attitudes probably are due to differences in perceived jurisdictional overlaps. For many years, the FCC has claimed primacy over the states in substantive areas affected by the MFJ.

Relations between Judge Greene and both the DOJ and the FCC have been strained.[38] As Robinson suggests, continued presence of a powerful new player—viewed by some as an interloper—on the telecommunications federal regulatory scene made some tension between Judge Greene and other federal policymakers inevitable. But the continuing debate over Judge Greene's administration of the consent decree and the BOC line-of-business restrictions has been further fueled by a fundamental divergence of views with respect to the central tenets which underlie the decree—i.e., the notion that regulatory mechanisms are incapable of preventing anticompetitive behavior by the BOCs in adjacent competitive markets, and the related notion that the social costs of allowing BOC entry in such circumstances exceed whatever efficiencies may be associated with BOC integration into related markets.

The second Reagan administration's Justice Department, under Attorney General Edwin Meese, virtually abandoned the decree within three years of divestiture. While I will not attempt to set forth the evidence here, the rapid (in my view) and wholly unanticipated (to most observers) abandonment went beyond merely urging Judge Greene and the Congress to change the MFJ. It resulted in considerable laxity in the DOJ's administration of the decree from 1986 onward. As Charles Brown and William Baxter observe in chapter 1, this development was exceedingly unfortunate from the perspective of those who hoped the MFJ would quiet the competitive controversies which had wracked the telecommunications industry for decades. It created what economists sometimes call a "commitment issue," and predictably, the uncertainty has affected the conduct of the BOCs, their competitors, their suppliers, and their customers.

It seems clear, particularly in light of Mr. Baxter's and Judge Greene's comments in this volume, that the decree was entered on the basis of an informed judgment (or perhaps, as Mr. Baxter suggests, a calculated "wager") that, on balance, the procompetitive effects of the divestiture and the BOC line-of-business restrictions, as modified by the District

Court, would more than offset whatever efficiencies or other benefits might be lost by prohibiting BOC integration into related markets.[39]

Throughout the initial post-divestiture period, the Justice Department had rather aggressively maintained that position. But arguments advanced by the DOJ during the 1987 Triennial Review of the consent decree brought into full relief a complete metamorphosis in the department's view of the decree—of the efficacy of regulation, the wisdom of the decree's structural approach, and the appropriateness of the institutional arrangements for administrating the decree's provisions, in particular the BOC line-of-business restrictions. The department conceded that the BOCs retained monopoly control of the local telephone network within their respective regions,[40] and acknowledged "the BOCs' opportunities for discrimination and cross-subsidization still exist to varying degrees with respect to certain types of currently prohibited activities, especially activities within a BOC's region."[41] However, the department argued the level of risk to competition had been reduced as a result of "the divestiture and the independence of the BOCs from each other as well as from AT&T,"[42] developments that were, of course, part and parcel of the structural solution advanced by the department and embodied in the consent decree, *along with* the BOC line-of-business restrictions. In urging that the BOCs should be permitted to enter the immediately adjacent equipment manufacturing and information service markets, the department indicated a new-found faith in regulatory mechanisms, most of which predated the divestiture, together with certain new FCC programs which had yet to be fully developed or tested.[43]

As the DOJ began to abandon its support of the decree, the FCC simultaneously became more aggressive in urging that it, and not Judge Greene, should determine the extent to which the divested BOCs are permitted to enter adjacent competitive markets. In February 1986, Chairman Mark Fowler endorsed H.R. 3800, introduced by Representatives Swift and Tauke, providing for removal of the consent decree prohibitions on BOC entry into information services and equipment manufacturing upon a determination by the FCC, in consultation with the Secretary of Commerce and Attorney General, that such action would not harm competition or ratepayer interests.[44] Later in 1986, Chairman Fowler joined DOJ in supporting S.2565 (the Federal Telecommunications Policy Act of 1986) introduced by Senate Minority Leader Dole, to shift to the FCC the responsibilities of the Justice Department and the Court under the decree.[45] And upon the issuance of Judge Greene's 1987 Triennial Review decision, new FCC Chairman Dennis Patrick told the United States Telephone Association (USTA):

I am, quite frankly, surprised by the apparent acquiescence of some of the Bell Operating Companies in the ongoing administration of the MFJ. The Court has long since left the arena of antitrust law and assumed an ongoing regulatory role. Granting freedom here and denying it there, every day it seems the Court makes decisions that have critical impact upon the evolution of the network, and upon the public that network serves. These decisions are made without reference to the public interest standard and the specific statute the Congress enacted to direct federal communications policy, and without reference to other aspects of the industry that, along with MFJ related issues, provide an integrated picture that must, necessarily, be analyzed as an integrated whole.[46]

On the heels of Chairman Patrick's speech, the NTIA, under Al Sikes, filed a petition for declaratory ruling with the FCC, urging it to issue an order authorizing the BOCs to provide information services, and making an explicit finding that "the District Court's information services restriction represents a cumbersome, unnecessary layer of regulation in irreconcilable conflict with the requirements of the Communications Act."[47] On December 1, 1987, the FCC issued a public notice inviting public comment on the NTIA petition.[48] While certain of the BOCs continue to express support for NTIA's petition, a number of industry experts (including several BOCs) take the position that it is inadvisable and "counterproductive" for the FCC to precipitate a jurisdictional confrontation with the District Court. Despite the fact that Mr. Sikes is now the FCC Chairman, FCC action in response to the NTIA petition is not anticipated, and the BOCs have focused their efforts on getting Congressional action to remove MFJ restrictions.

The District Court was by no means mute in the face of such attacks. In an opinion issued in December 1987, Judge Greene noted (as he has in chapter 1 of this volume) that the consent decree "is one of the few judicial judgments to bear the stamp of authority of all three branches of government."[49] He added that he would "continue, as [he] has done in the past, to make every effort to avoid or minimize interference with FCC jurisdiction and operations where this can be done without jeopardizing the core provisions of the decree."[50]

The Court of Appeals has yet to shed further light on the jurisdictional relationship between the antitrust court and the FCC, in the context of the pending appeals of the District Court's Triennial Review decisions.[51] Barring an unlikely reversal by the Court of Appeals, it would appear the ball will remain with Judge Greene, unless and until Congress takes it away. For a variety of reasons, transfer of decree responsibilities to the FCC is likely to occur, if at all, at a measured pace. If the status quo continues, with Judge Greene retaining his current jurisdiction, the Bush Justice Department may be a "wild card" in the equation. Some movement back toward the pre-1985 DOJ support of various components of the MFJ is possible, although it is unlikely the DOJ will go back to its original aggressive defense of the MFJ restrictions.

Coincident with the MFJ's reconfiguration of the telecommunications industry, its major players, and the services those players were permitted to provide, the Supreme Court in 1986, in *Louisiana Public Service Commission*[52] overturned decades of jurisprudence and reconfigured the comparative authority of the FCC and state regulatory agencies. The timing could not have been worse. It came in a period of unprecedented technological change, telephone company diversification, and deregulation. The Court infused the dramatically altered regulatory terrain with an added degree of uncertainty. In fact, the direct public policy residue of the *Louisiana* decision is far more troubling and far more urgently in need of attention than anything which has fallen out of the MFJ.

The Communications Act does not provide clear definition of where federal authority over interstate communications ends and where state authority over intrastate communications begins.[53] Nevertheless, for decades the FCC had pushed out the limits of its authority. By the time the MFJ was approved and implemented, a fair statement of the prevailing jurisprudence was that federal authority must prevail over state authority if the economic efficiency of the telecommunications network is involved.[54] Individual state agencies and NARUC often appealed FCC preemptions, but almost always without success.

While its ultimate effect is still unknown, the *Louisiana* decision appeared to constitute a jarring adjustment in the distribution of federal and state regulatory authority. The Court determined that Congress granted the FCC a broad mandate to create a rapid and efficient telecommunications network, but not so broad as to prohibit any state action which frustrates the FCC's ability to create an efficient network. The Court found that Section 2(b) explicitly reserved broad authority to establish charges, including depreciation, to the states; the FCC could not preempt this authority by assuming it could take all necessary measures to further federal policy.[55]

In its Third Computer Inquiry, the FCC has attempted to preempt state regulation of enhanced services (an analogue to the MFJ's information services), state structural separation requirements for carriers providing basic and enhanced services, and state nonstructural safeguards inconsistent with federal policies.[56] With regard to the FCC's preemption of state regulation of enhanced services, the Commission has urged among other things that state regulation would jeopardize efficiency in enhanced service offerings. The agency claims the facilities used by carriers for basic and enhanced services are inseverable, and therefore cannot be subject to inconsistent regulation by separate authorities.

Overall, it is not excessive to fear the confusion and instability which has followed *Louisiana* has compromised some of the short-term promise of the divestiture, and of the widened authority to undertake gateway and related services bestowed on the BOCs by Judge Greene in his Triennial Review orders. Under most circumstances, one might expect the FCC or Congress to exert leadership in addressing a so obviously sub-optimal situation. It has not happened. Congress has shown no inclination to face the political hazards involved in reducing the authority of state commissions. The FCC, a good deal more insulated from politics, failed to react to *Louisiana* decisively because of conflicting doctrinal predilections. Throughout the Reagan administration, the FCC treated efficiency, defined in standard economic terms, as the summum bonum of common carrier policy. By the time of the *Louisiana* decision, it also had adopted the administration's federalist tendencies, notwithstanding the longstanding pattern of successful preemption of state regulation recited earlier. The Commission thus responded to *Louisiana*, not by defending its jurisdiction as aggressively as the decision would permit, or by appealing to the necessity for national rules to produce efficient outcomes, but by doing nothing.

In vacating and remanding *Computer III*, the Ninth Circuit did not do more than should have been expected of it to render Section 2(b) and the *Louisiana* decision suitable for the emerging milieu of nationally offered enhanced services. As a result, the Bush administration FCC will have to provide far stronger leadership on the issue than its predecessor. If it does not, the Supreme Court or Congress will have to revisit the preemption issue, and, during the interim, enhanced services will suffer for want of uniform national rules.[57]

Finally, a few comments are in order on Robinson's point that divestiture seems to have been accompanied by more rather than less regulation. Almost certainly in the last five years every state in this country has examined—many at a quite fundamental level—different ways to regulate or deregulate its telephone utilities. And, given the old Bell System's striking abilities in public advocacy and its nearly preternatural abilities at controlling, managing, and coordinating the public policy activities of its far flung operating companies, it is reasonable to believe we would be seeing much less diversity in terms of the state's approaches to regulation than we do today.

Robinson's point about the volume of regulatory activity is correct. We certainly seem to have more of it, but it is often less constraining. If one were to chart out carefully, at least at the federal level, the rate regulation of AT&T since 1984, I strongly suspect it would reveal activities less constraining than formal.[58]

On another level, the FCC has expended vast effort in trying to create accounting rules to allocate between regulated and nonregulated businesses the joint costs incurred by the local exchange companies subject to its jurisdiction.[59] But it is the consent decree itself which resulted in the increase of unregulated activities, which in turn led to the accounting rules. In fact, much of the additional regulatory activity since 1984 is a reaction to more activity by the local exchange telephone industry in the marketplace.

A. Gray Collins

As I think back on it now, divestiture was just one more episode in a continuing series of changes in the industry structure and the players of the telephone industry. I consider divestiture an event that merely sped up some things which were going to happen anyway.

A few days after divestiture was announced, the magnitude of the implementation problems began to become apparent. It only took a few hours for certain key leaders inside and outside the Bell System to recognize the seven regional companies and AT&T would become very competitive with each other. Almost immediately, questions were raised about the restrictions on the twenty-two operating telephone companies. The prevailing perception was they would not have the opportunity for growth and vitality that many felt were needed for a good business investment and a good place to work. Some concerns were expressed that the BOCs were being eliminated as the only effective competition for AT&T, and were being placed in a position where they would have to buy most of their equipment from AT&T, at least for the foreseeable future.

The task of divestiture was enormous. We had to divide up the physical plant, set up new corporations, assign people, issue stock; there was a multitude of this kind of activity. We had to implement access charges, and we had to bill those $20 billion of access charges using a new billing system that did not exist prior to divestiture. We also had to divide up Bell Labs and the AT&T headquarters. I want to focus on this partition of staff because in the institution that existed prior to divestiture, the BOC's were not stand-alone organizations.

In 1982, the newly created BOCs had no strategic or long-term planning capabilities. They were really the line-implementation organizations. The AT&T headquarters was the hub, the planner, the signal caller. We had to set up eight (AT&T and the seven regionals) separate corporations, and they had to stand alone and exist in the marketplace where there was increasing competition and uncertainty. And we knew the new corporations would end up competing with each other as they are today.

New organizations had to be put in place and policymaking and planning apparati established. Today, that might not appear to have been a major problem. But it must be remembered only the new Southwestern Bell and Pacific Telesis regions actually had organized central headquarters. What is currently the Bell Atlantic region was actually made up of seven jurisdictions and three formal telephone company organizations (four C&P companies, Bells of Pennsylvania and Diamond State, and New Jersey Bell). Among other things, we needed to install a management process, a marketing and product-line management process, a financial management process, a policymaking process, and a strategic planning process. I believe the tasks of implementing divestiture consumed the old Bell System for about two years. But we made it work.

Somehow, the nation had decided in the early 1980s, I believe by default, that competition in telecommunications and the information industry would be the national policy. Unfortunately, in my opinion, there was not, and still is not, a vision of what the policy should achieve. As a result, the industry structure continues to evolve in what I consider a most disadvantageous fashion. It evolved through a court process, based on antitrust law and without the vision of a fully competitive marketplace. As Glen Robinson points out, we have made great strides forward, but must we place the future of the nation's telecommunications infrastructure "in the hands of lawyers" instead of the producers and consumers?

Today, with divestiture, we have more major industry players in the game, and more regulation and more regulators. We have the FCC, DOJ, the Court, Congress, and the administration at the federal level, and the state PUCs and the state governments at the state level. All of these parties are involved in the regulatory process, and all of these parties have some oversight on our industry. Each of them has different perspectives and different interests, and rightly so, for they serve different primary constituencies.

In addition to more regulation and regulators, the relationships between these regulators, and the industry players have changed as well. Prior to divestiture, AT&T dealt with the FCC, Congress, the administration, and the Court. The BOCs handled the state relationships, including the PUCs, and state and local governments. At divestiture, we had to reorganize. The RBOCs had to create organizations to handle FCC/Federal Relations, while AT&T had to develop a state relations function.

At first, the newly established RBOCs attempted to use the Washington-bound Bellcore organization to focus their Washington activities. It did not work in those early days because seven Regional Companies were learning and struggling for identity. We would each go to see public policymakers and they would tell us that we did not have the same priorities, we did not have the same objectives, and we were divided. I would like to think we have learned our lesson. Today, the RBOCs are very close together on major issues, and we know it only serves our opponents when we are not unified. We are doing a better job of coming together. It might be time to try that coordinated Washington office idea again. I believe it would serve our interests.

The regulatory institutions have also changed their relationships to each other in the post-divestiture era. As I recall, conflict between the FCC and the state PUCs erupted a few weeks after divestiture. That process of conflict included subscriber line charges, separations, preemption by the FCC of deregulatory activities—particularly CPE, and the state regulators' involvement in preserving the Yellow Pages for the telephone companies. Conflict between Congress and the FCC intensified between 1986 and 1989. The FCC's decision to abandon the Fairness Doctrine in broadcasting, along with some FCC-Congressional personality conflicts, price caps, and subscriber line charges are all factors which have fueled the conflict.

The Washington art of "stakeholdering" through third parties has emerged and has been perfected since 1985. And as a result, the number of apparent players in the game and the number of points of view have multiplied. And as we all have found, each player has the opportunity to be disruptive because there are so many policymakers and policy forums.

We have two players who really were not very involved in policy matters before divestiture, Judge Greene and the DOJ. With their inclusion in the process comes confusion. The DOJ has said it was OK to do something, we did it, and the Court said we should not have done it. The whole policymaking process offers the opportunity for confusion, mischief, and delay. And frankly, I do not believe that to be in the best interest of the nation, the consumers, or the competing players.

It is my view, in spite of what some others in this volume may suggest, that markets and technologies *have* changed since 1982—or 1980 when we really got serious about studying antitrust and divestiture. Changes have occurred much faster than anyone could have possibly predicted six to eight years ago. The Information Age is upon us. It is already being implemented in other countries. And a local network is an efficient alternative for bringing the Information Age in the United States to the general public, and to business and government as well.

The RBOCs' competitors, acting as I would expect, are trying to delay and block the removal of the line-of-business restrictions on the RBOCs. They really do not want competition from RBOCs even with the appropriate safeguards. The result is that the nation's apparent policy of competitive structure is actually stalled, to the benefit of foreign providers and the detriment of consumers.

I believe the RBOC institutions have developed to the point where we now have a vision of what our business can be, and what we can offer in the way of products, services, and technologies in the future marketplace. I do not believe the institutions of the policymaker have developed as quickly and as completely as have the RBOCs. The competitive environment which we want to help create, and in which we wish to participate will be delayed until we get a better policymaking apparatus. That will probably happen when policy is made by persons more directly responsible to the public, as for example, Congress.

The RBOCs have developed their corporations while continuing to provide excellent service. It is already apparent that the RBOCs are preparing for a more competitive marketplace for communications services. We have the resources and the incentives to develop the communications infrastructure needed for the twenty-first century. The continuing restrictions first placed on us in 1982 are not in the national interest.

Richard E. Wiley

The most significant regulatory and institutional change since divestiture, in my judgment, is the presence (some might be tempted to say "omnipresence") on the telecommunications and information scene of

Judge Harold Greene. Since 1984, like it or not—and there are many takers on both options—the Judge has been the single most important individual and authority in the field.

The "easy" reaction to this circumstance is that Judge Greene is a self-appointed and self-important judicial and regulatory czar, who has arrogated to himself all the policymaking power possible while, concomitantly, removing it from the rightful holders of authority, Congress and the FCC. Given the centrality and significance of the Judge's role, and all the public attention that has surrounded his activity, it is not surprising that such an opinion is held by many people—and not just by those who want so much to see the AT&T consent decree, the object of Judge Greene's constant attention, go away.

However, it seems to me there are a number of "hard" responses to this view of the Judge and his continuing activity relative to the decree. These responses, reflecting perhaps certain institutional failings or miscalculations on the part of other entities, may be both distasteful and disputatious. Nevertheless, they must be confronted.

The first and most obvious point to be considered is that the Judge was not the author of the MFJ. Instead, he merely approved and entered the decree which, in large measure, was the product of the litigating parties, AT&T and the Department of Justice. It also was a document agreed to, however reluctantly perhaps, by the heads of all the RHCs. For what it may be worth, I personally have always had some misgivings concerning the wisdom of the divestiture, and I obviously am far from alone in this viewpoint. But the fact is that both AT&T and the Justice Department desired an end to the government's prolonged antitrust action against the company, and believed the MFJ represented an appropriate resolution.

Given all that was involved in the litigation and the settlement, is it reasonable to expect that it all would end so soon? The 1956 AT&T consent decree endured for over twenty-five years (indeed, it was terminated only with the entry of the MFJ). As Glen Robinson points out, if Justice is now correct in asserting that the line-of-business restrictions on the RBOCs are no longer necessary, the department comes very close to saying that the divestiture of AT&T was really not necessary in the first place.

Rightly or wrongly, AT&T was broken up for the sake of intercity competition. And the DOJ's demand for drastic structural relief reflected its fundamental distrust of the efficacy of both federal and state regulation of the huge carrier. The result of this distrust was to thrust on Judge Greene the responsibility to enforce the structural solution crafted by the department and the company.

One must now ask what has changed since 1984 that might justify a termination of the decree. Is it technology, marketplace conditions, regulatory developments, or, in reality, is it simply the attitude of the DOJ and other federal governmental bodies toward the basic concepts which underlie the consent decree? In my judgment, the latter is clearly the case.

The second "hard" fact that must be faced is that, over the last two decades, there has been a general absence of Congressional leadership in the development of overall telecommunications policy. While Congress in the 1980s has passed modern deregulatory legislation for such industries as banking, airlines, railroads, and motor carriers, it utterly failed to do the same in the communications field. The creaky old Communications Act of 1934—enacted prior to the advent of television, computers, satellites, and all the other technological marvels of the last half century—is still the governing statutory regimen. Accordingly, in the absence of comprehensive Congressional direction, the FCC crafted its procompetitive and deregulatory course, and the AT&T consent decree was entered—together, they represent the primary communications policy determinants over the last twenty years. But, given the reality of legislative inaction, it seems to me unfair and unrealistic to blame Judge Greene (or, indeed, the Commission) for an alleged "power grab." Nature, after all, does abhor a vacuum.

Third, it must be recognized the FCC and the RBOCs themselves may hold some of the important keys to bringing the MFJ and the line-of-business restrictions to an end. In particular, if ever effectuated, the nonstructural safeguards contained in the Commission's *Computer III* effort, and especially the ONA concept, ultimately could convince Judge Greene that at least the information services restriction is no longer necessary.

However, these competitive protections must be "real." In this regard, I would agree that ONA—given the limited time that the RBOCs were accorded to develop it—should be viewed as very much an evolutionary concept. The FCC, state regulatory agencies, and the regional companies all must cooperate in making such an evolution efficacious if they are to gain the confidence of the Court and various industry participants. Should Congress prematurely remove Judge Greene's authority over the consent decree, it could be argued that the incentive on the part of the RBOCs to mature the ONA concept, and to effect a truly competitive enhanced service marketplace might be somewhat lacking.

The fourth "hard" fact is that the Court's oversight of the consent decree has not been a static one. While the pace of change understandably may not have satisfied the RBOC community, Judge Greene's waiver grants and decisions, like his "Gateways" order, exemplify a continuing willingness to modify the decree (either on the merits or in the face of political pressure, depending on your perspective). I would expect additional changes or clarifications ahead.

In the final analysis, I anticipate that the MFJ and Judge Greene's involvement in it are both of finite duration—sometime during the decade of the 1990s, the end may come. As always in the telecommunications field, technology holds the greatest promise for bringing such a development to fruition. Hopefully, further technological advancements will continue to mandate a competitive industry which, in turn, will allow government (at all levels and in all branches) gradually to withdraw its regulatory hand. Incidentally, how soon this might be true with respect to the MFJ's long-distance prohibition, likely to be the last restriction to go, remains a question mark, given the uncertainty of competition's future at the local level.

One final comment: while life has occasionally cast me on the other side of regulatory and policy issues from the regional carrier family, I must pay some well-justified tribute to what these companies have accomplished since 1984. Predicted by many at the time of the divestiture to be "tomorrow's railroads," the RBOCs have made the whole concept of the consent decree work better than anyone might have expected. More or less from scratch, the carriers have developed their fledgling corporate enterprises into some of the largest and most dynamic companies in America. The fact that many significant federal government officials today are calling for an end to the MFJ restrictions also demonstrates conclusively that they have learned quickly and effectively to play the so-called Washington "lobbying game."

Thus, the future would seem to be with the RBOCs—a future, as indicated, that someday may be MFJ-free. In the meantime, however, the presence and impact of Judge Greene continues.

Edward F. Burke

I was intrigued by Glen Robinson's account of the Minnesota Commission and its three so-called telecommunications specialists in the mid-1960s. I would have been happy to have such an enormous staff to help me. During my tenure as Chairman of the Rhode Island Public Utilities Commission from 1977 to 1988, I had on my staff only one telecommunications specialist. Fortunately, I also had two top-notch CPAs on my staff, who eventually became very knowledgeable in the intricate field of telecommunications revenue allocation and related matters. Unfortunately, for many years no other New England Public Utility Commission employed any CPAs. This became a matter of growing importance in the post-divestiture era with the increasing need for careful scrutiny of cost allocations between the regulated and nonregulated sectors of NYNEX, to prevent cross-subsidies flowing from monopoly activities to nonregulated ventures.

It was a simpler age in 1977 when I joined the Rhode Island Commission, seven years before divestiture, but the seeds of competition had been sown, and litigation and FCC inquiries were already the harbinger of major changes in the structure of the telecommunications industry. It was clear to me, as I grappled with my first telephone rate case, that rapid technological advances were about to transform the industry radically, and a new Information Age was emerging.

I and many of my colleagues felt grossly ill-prepared to meet the challenges with which we were confronted, in regulating telecommunications, in dealing with the significant difficulties being faced by the nuclear power and natural gas supplies, and in ruling on requests for skyrocketing utility rate increases at a time of high inflation and serious unemployment. Small wonder resignations under fire and decisions by governors not to reappoint commissioners were commonplace. Calls for regulatory change and reform filled the halls of state legislatures. How we commissioners were to cope with this crisis of confidence, and how we were to master our multiple and burgeoning responsibilities became our top priority.

We in Rhode Island had one advantage over some of our colleagues in other states. As the smallest state, we had long since learned that we could not or should not try to go it alone. In fact, our legislature provided a special fund of $20,000 per year to be used at the discretion of the PUC Chairman to foster regional cooperation in regulatory matters. Clearly, I felt this was of paramount importance in relation to telephone issues. Since New England Telephone (NET) was operating in five New England states, and making rate filings for new equipment which were substantially similar in each, it made sense to consolidate hearings to pool the several states' limited resources, and to look at the big picture of NET and beyond that, to its parent AT&T. I considered the piecemeal state-by-state approach to be parochial, ineffective, and unsuited to modern times.

As early as 1977, we in Rhode Island asked NET to outline long-range company plans and to compare the modernity of plant in Rhode Island to that in other NET states. We worked to develop cooperative analysis of regional and national telecommunications among the New England states through our regional New England Conference of Public Utilities Commissioners. We worked closely with our Attorneys General; we finally convened in 1979 several regional hearings relative to the attachment of non-Bell equipment to the telephone system and the level of credits to be applied for using non-Bell telephones in ratepayer residences. Needless to say, this effort was met at first with resistance by NET.

We also became increasingly aware that such issues as modernization of plant, the treatment of new services, rural telephone pricing and quality of service, and the onset of and necessary transition to competition, were issues of national as well as regional concern. Through the many forums and publications of NARUC and especially through its Committee on Commumications, we shared our experiences and concerns and groped for common solutions.

The late 1970s and early 1980s saw increased staffing support for the NARUC Communications Committee. Extensive study sessions were devoted to the issues I have mentioned, as well as to the role of modern communications systems in economic development. Consumer groups pressed us with concerns about the possible demise of universal service due to burgeoning rates, and the need for lifeline or special economy service.

In 1981, one major event helped to galvanize state regulators and forced us to utilize, collectively, the skills and networking mechanisms which we had been developing. I refer to the concerted effort of AT&T's large telephone companies to divert Yellow Pages' revenues from state regulatory control. The lobbying effort on behalf of this legislation which nearly passed was enormous. Lobbyists in Washington imported local telephone officials by the carload.

It took a major effort by state regulators, working at first individually and then collectively, to defeat this incredibly bad piece of legislation. To be sure, we had allies among the consumer groups and within Congress, but it was the last ditch "do or die" outcry from state commissioners and certain governors, mayors, and local legislators, whom state regulators recruited to the effort, which in the end averted disaster. We learned from this adventure that state regulators could unite and, when they did, they could have an impact.

All this was a forerunner to the dramatic events which took place early in 1982, when the proposed consent decree between AT&T and the Justice Department was announced. I had just assumed the presidency of NARUC, and I am proud of the part we played. We did not wait for events to transpire. We felt it vital to reassess and restructure the role of the state regulator in order to meet the challenges of divestiture, competition, and advancing technology.

To that end, I called a meeting of state regulators in Washington within three weeks of the January 8, 1982 announcement. Over one hundred commissioners and staff responded. We analyzed issues and developed an overall strategy. I must stress that the process included countless hours of efforts by regulators operating in a manner of cooperation and coordination which, in retrospect, seemed impossible to obtain. It required dialogue with AT&T, the Justice Department, Judge Greene, members of Congress, the public, and the media.

NARUC recognized it would be impossible to prevent divestiture, and perhaps imprudent to try. However, it was essential to ensure that the local operating companies—the BOCs—be assured appropriate staff, sufficient initial cash flow, and necessary freedom of action to enable them to remain economically viable and to function effectively in the post-divestiture period.

To that end, we were in the forefront of the successful effort to modify the consent decree to leave Yellow Pages' revenues to the BOCs and to allow them the privilege of selling, if not manufacturing, terminal equipment. We felt these measures were essential because of the continuing central role of the BOCs in the American telephone network. Some of us would have preferred to further "unshackle" the BOCs, and this remains a continuing item of discussion and debate on the NARUC agenda.

We also availed ourselves the opportunity to comment on the plans of reorganization which AT&T submitted to the Justice Department and, ultimately, to the Court. I believe we helped AT&T to make uncertain modifications in the plan of reorganization in the public interest. We especially appreciated that Charles Brown of AT&T interrupted a trip to a college reunion to speak at our February 1982 NARUC meeting in Washington. It was a beneficial visit. He convinced us of his desire to be evenhanded in the division of materials and personnel between post-divestiture AT&T and the new RHCs and their BOCs.

Finally, we worked closely with AT&T, the independent telephone companies, the Justice Department, and the FCC to attempt to smooth the path toward divestiture. I think these efforts were somewhat successful. We all remember the initial concerns after the announcement of the consent decree relative to possible deterioration of service quality. A number of problems did develop, especially in relation to installation and servicing of large terminal equipment systems by AT&T. There was also some confusion as to responsibility and accountability for terminal equipment and wiring. But I think it is fair to say such problems have been significantly less than anticipated. As discussed elsewhere in this volume, quality of service across the United States seems to this point at least to have remained essentially high.

Of course, the spirit of cooperation between federal, state, and industrial policymakers in smoothing the path to transition was greatly influenced by the firm guidance of Judge Harold Greene. I believe he performed many affirmative acts in his oversight position. While I greatly admire the Judge, it seems to me an unhealthy situation for any individual, no matter how talented or dedicated, to have such a central role relative to the telecommunications industry.

NARUC also made its voice heard in the halls of Congress. We thought there was a need for comprehensive communications legislation if universal service at affordable prices was to be maintained. To that end, we worked closely with Senator Packwood and members of his committee and Congressmen Dingell and Wirth and some of their colleagues, in the development of legislation to deal with problems related to bypass and to the special concerns of smaller, high-cost factor telephone companies. We were guided by a prevailing view that the FCC's plans for end-user access charges (later renamed subscriber line charges), if fully implemented, would have an unnecessarily severe impact on residential customers and could eventually make telephone service unaffordable for millions of Americans.

While these efforts did not succeed, the overwhelming passage by the House of the Universal Telephone Preservation Act bill (H.R. 4102) in November of 1983,[60] and the potential passage of a NARUC-supported Packwood bill in the Senate in early 1984, had a salutary effect. It led to a discussion between FCC Chairman Mark Fowler and Senator Dole and Senate leaders, who were anxious to head off Congressional action at the onset of divestiture. The result was the famous "go-slow" letter to the FCC which requested no flat-rate end-user charges on residential and single line business phones in 1984, a four-dollar cap on such charges until at least 1990, and a reduction in proposed interconnection charges. The letter also noted with approval, the actions which the FCC had taken in recognizing "certain low-income telephone customers who make few interstate calls might be unable to afford any flat monthly charge." Also noted were Commission efforts to explore "lifeline" service alternatives, and the planned monitoring of possible threats to "continued universal availability of affordably priced telephone service."[61]

The letter was issued just in the nick of time. The Packwood bill lost by a mere two votes. Chairman Fowler and his fellow Commissioners acceded in essence to the major requests of the Dole letter signatories and most importantly, deferred imposing flat-rate end-user charges on residential and single-line business customers until at least 1984.

In short, some members of Congress and Chairman Fowler bought time. Perhaps it was important to buy that time. We in NARUC adjusted immediately to this turn of events, and we four Commissioners representing the states on the Federal State Joint Board on Separations, lobbied to have our jurisdiction enlarged to encompass the access charge docket as well. This effort, which was supported by the NARUC Executive Committee and included extensive discussion with Chairman Fowler and his staff, resulted in substantial success. On April 2, 1984, the FCC announced:

> The Commission, while reaffirming its basic access charge principles, has asked for additional public comments and Joint Board recommendations on certain aspects of the following: the plan for implementing end user charges for residential and single-line business subscribers; the framework for a lifeline exemption or other assistance for low income subscribers; additional assistance for small telephone companies.

The FCC also asked the Joint Board to undertake a comprehensive review of the existing separations procedures for all central office equipment (COE) and recommend changes in these rules. Issues involving the allocation of interexchange plant costs were also referred to the Joint Board. Later, other more specialized Joint Boards were established.

The discussions among state regulators and then between their representatives and Chairman Fowler and his colleagues, were, I think, historic. We in NARUC were determined to continue our efforts to challenge federal preemption issues in the courts and our later success in the *Louisiana Public Service Commission* case. The case was good for state regulator morale, and we also sought comprehensive telephone legislation. However, we resolved to make divestiture work, and attempted to work cooperatively with the FCC on issues which could not wait for legislative or judicial determination.

It was not easy. Some of my state colleagues preferred rhetoric, fruitless legislative initiatives, and litigation to compromise and consensus, but most of us pressed on. A personal rapport which gradually evolved between the three Fowler-led FCC commissioners and their four state counterparts and their staffs on the Joint Boards, was most important. So too was the bipartisan composition of the Joint Boards. For example, when conservative Republican Mark Fowler and solid Democrat Edward Burke and our colleagues reached consensus on key issues, it helped to convince other parties in Congress and in the states that our recommendations had merit.

I think our Joint Board access charge decisions helped to alleviate concerns relative to bypass. We heeded the requests of the industry concerning the immediate dangers of depooling and deaveraging by incorporating in our orders many of their internally agreed-upon suggestions. I am especially proud of the success of the federal lifeline programs, which were truly federal-state products. These helped to preserve and extend universal service and, by 1990, are being used by more than 3 million subscribers.[62]

That, I submit must be the goal of the process. It is not easy for state regulators to downplay local interests and vote in the national interest. However, I think that is what we attempted to do. We were not always successful, but I believe that our sincerity and our dedication to developing nationally acceptable policies were perceived by most of the interested players, and helped to create a climate of reasonableness.

Looking back over the post-divestiture period, I have one major regret. It seemed to me in the period after the announcement of the approval of the MFJ in August 1982, that state regulatory processes needed to be modified to relate to the holding company structure under which the local BOCs were to function after January 1, 1984. In 1983, Rhode Island Governor J. Joseph Garrahy wrote his fellow governors in the states in which NYNEX affiliates were to operate:

> I suggest that the time has come to address common concerns relative to a regional company on a regional basis. It would appear that the rate of return to which New England Telephone is entitled ought to be uniform throughout the five state region. Certainly common costs throughout the five state region ought to be apportioned fairly amongst the states.

He went on to propose that rate filings in the five states be synchronized as to time, in order to allow coordinated review and pooling of technical resources by Attorneys General and other public interest advocates. I hoped there would be regional hearings.

Despite very strong editorial support in a number of newspapers and from segments of the regulatory community, we never achieved our goal. That goal would have made sense not only for the NYNEX situation, but also in the other RHC areas. At least I can say that there has been some state-to-state cost allocation analysis cooperation with regard to the Regional Holding Companies and their local telco affiliates, and NARUC continues to advocate close regional cooperation on cost allocation, competitive service, and diversification-related issues.

By and large, I remain an optimist. I agree with Robinson that, although state regulation has and will continue to change in form and focus, it still will remain important and significant to the stability of the industry for years to come. My successors in state regulation will continue to be hard pressed by their multiple responsibilities. There will be no miracle answers, but I know they will preserve and contribute significantly to major telecommunications policy decisions. They are, for example, hard at work analyzing the many issues surrounding ONA. I hope those of us who preceded them in the 1980s will have made their task easier.

ENDNOTES

1. I have reviewed some of the major events and decisions in Robinson, "The Titanic Remembered: AT&T and the Changing Worlds of Communications," *Yale Journal on Regulation* (1980), 5:517.

2. *Hush-A-Phone Corp. v. FCC*, 238 F.2d 266, 269 (D.C. Cir. 1956) (AT&T tariff prohibiting attachment of passive device to telephone handset as unreasonable restriction on customer phone use).

3. Allocation of Frequencies in the Bands Above 890 Msc., 27 FCC 359 (1959), modified, 29 FCC 825 (1960).

4. Use of the Carterfone Device in Message Toll Tel. Serv., 13 FCC 2d 420 (1968).

5. Specialized Common Carrier Servs., 29 FCC 2d 870, 31 1106 (1971), *aff'd, Washington Util. & Transp. Comm'n v. FCC*, 513 F.2d 1142 (9th Cir.), *cert. denied*, 423 U.S. 836 (1975).

6. *MCI Telecommunications Corp. v. FCC*, 561 F. 2d 365 (D.C. Cir. 1977) *(Execunet I)*; see also *MCI Telecommunications Corp. v. FCC*, 580 F. 2d 590 (D.C. Cir.) *(Execunet II), cert. denied*, 439 U.S. 980 (1978).

7. See Amendment of Sec. 64.702 of the Commission's Rules & Regulations (Second Computer Inquiry), 77 FCC 2d 384 (1980), *aff'd sub. nom. Computer & Communications Indus. Ass'n v. FCC*, 693 F.2d 198 (D.C. Cir. 1982), *cert. denied*, 461 U.S. 938 (1983).

8. For a brief discussion see Policy and Rules Concerning Rates for Dominant Carriers, 4 FCC Rcd 2873, 2884-86 (1989); G. Brock, *The Telecommunications Industry* (Cambridge, Mass.: Harvard University Press, 1981), pp. 179–80.

9. See AT&T, 2 FCC 2d 173 (1965) (initiating investigation into interstate rate return); AT&T, 9 FCC 2d 30 (1969) (decision in initial phase 1-A of investigation).

10. Figures are from the official budgets and FCC annual reports for the years in question. The fiscal 1989 total budget figure of $99.6 million excludes a special $1.2 million indefinite appropriation to relocate an FCC monitoring facility from Ft. Lauderdale to Vero Beach, Florida.

11. An indication of just how much changed in public attitude from the 1970s to the 1980s is given by the public reaction to the FCC's 1983 residential telephone access charge decision. When the FCC announced its decision there was a public demonstration in front of the FCC's building. By contrast when,

nearly a decade earlier, the FCC allowed AT&T to raise its rates, the only person outside the industry to notice was Ralph Nader.

12. See Crandall, "The Role for U.S. Local Operating Companies," in R. Crandall and K. Flamm, eds., *Changing the Rules: Technological Change, International Competition and Regulation in Communications* (Washington D.C.: Brookings Institution, 1989), pp. 114, 123. I interpret this continued transfer of cost/rate burden as simply due to the continued increase in productivity of interstate service relative to local exchange service. The transfer was at war with the emerging policy of promoting competition which had to undermine the rents from interstate markets that were used to support local service.

13. See Crandall, supra.

14. Amendment of Sec. 64.702 of the Commission's Rules and Regulations (Third Computer Inquiry) 104 FCC 2d 958 (1986), *modified*, 2 FCC Rcd 3035 (1987), *further reconsid. denied*, 3 FCC Rad 1135 *vacated and remanded, California v. FCC*, 905 F.2d 1217 (9th Cir. 1990).

15. Policy and Rules Concerning Rates for Dominant Carriers, 4 FCC Rad 2873, 3379 (1989). Essentially price cap regulation sets average rates for defined groups ("baskets") of services according to a retail price index minus a "productivity" factor of 3 percent. The basic idea is to create an incentive for the regulated firm to invest in efficient methods and technologies by allowing the firm to retain part of the cost savings realized by its efficiencies. This overcomes the opposite bias in rate of return regulation. In a sense, price cap regulation returns the FCC to its old "continuing surveillance" form of rate regulation. For a good short description of the price cap concept of rate regulation see Noll, "Telecommunications Regulation in the 1990s," in P. Newberg, ed., *New Directions in Telecommunications Regulation* (Durham, N.C.: Duke University Press, 1989), 1:36–42. The future success of the Commission's ONA initiatives was put into question by the Court of Appeals holding (supra note 14) that the *Computer III* decision to permit the BOCs to integrate their regulated and unregulated activities were unlawfully arbitrary and capricious, and that FCC's preemption of state regulation of enhanced services exceeded its jurisdiction under the Communications Act.

16. The ONA and the regulatory surveillance problems are briefly discussed in Noll, supra at 43–46. See also the summary of Gerald Brock, Chief of the FCC's Common Carrier Bureau, in Hearing on Modified Final Judgment Before the Subcomm. on Communications of the Senate Comm. on Commerce, Service and Technology, 100th Cong., 2d sess., pp. 159–63 (1988).

17. See Noll, supra at 42.

18. The Supreme Court's surprising (and in my view incorrect) refusal to allow the FCC to preempt state regulation of carrier depreciation of telephone equipment, see *Louisiana Public Service Commission v. FCC*, 476 U.S. 355 (1986), suggests that states may play an even larger role than had been contemplated by the FCC. That suggestion was reinforced by the Ninth Circuit's 1990 ruling on *Computer III* (supra note 14).

19. For the Antitrust Division's theory and strategy under Baxter's leadership, see P. Temin, *The Fall of the Bell System: A Study in Prices and Politics*

(New York: Cambridge University Press, 1987), pp. 217–49. (Baxter's famous threat to litigate to the eyeballs is quoted on p. 225.)

20. See, e.g., "Ringing the Bells," *National Journal*, February 4, 1989, pp. 272–77. The Justice Department has joined with the regional RHCs in seeking to overturn Judge Greene's refusal to modify the MFJ, both in court and in Congress. See Hearings on S.H. 52565 Before the Senate Comm. on Commerce, Science, and Transportation, 99th Cong., 2d sess. (1986); *United States v. Western Electric Co.*, No 83–5388 (D.C. Cir.).

21. See Robinson, supra note 1 at 536–40. Whether to relax or eliminate the line-of-business restrictions is a matter of evaluating the benefits of more competition in the restricted fields against the risk that BOC entry would distort competition because of their control of the local exchange network. The latter question is critically dependent on the effectiveness of the FCC's ONA scheme, about which we know nothing yet. The former question must be broken down according to the different lines of business. Probably the strongest case for BOC entry is in the field of information services where there is a significant possibility that the BOCs could spur what seems to be an underdeveloped market. At the same time one should recognize that information services can be and are provided by independent suppliers; if the market is underdeveloped, it may be simply that consumer demand does not match technological potential. It is not obvious how the BOCs could rectify this "problem"—if it is a problem.

22. 334 U.S. 131 (1948).

23. For a short description of the *Paramount* litigation and subsequent consent decrees see *United States v. Loew's Inc.*, 1988–2 Trade Cases ¶68,360.

24. It is reported that Judge Palmieri, who until his death in 1989 was responsible for administering the decrees (as he had been since the early years of their history) ruled on as many as seventy-four petitions by *Paramount* defendants in a single year! See Hammond and Melamed, *Antitrust in the Entertainment Industry*, Gannett Center Journal, pp. 138, 156 (*The Image Factory*, Gannett Center for Media Studies).

25. *United States v. Western Electric Co.*, 1956 Trade Cases ¶68,246 (D.N.J. 1956). The 1956 decree, the outcome of an antitrust action initiated in 1949, forbade AT&T from offering non-communications services or products except as an incidental aspect of a tariffed (regulated) communications venue.

26. 286 U.S. 106, 119 (1929).

27. See *United States v. Western Electric Co.*, 797 F.2d 1082 (D.C. Cir. 1986).

28. See *United States v. Western Electric Company*, et al., 900 F.2d 283 (1990).

29. Officially styled the "Consumer Communications Reform Act of 1976," the "Bell bill" was drafted and promoted by AT&T. The initiative was correctly seen to be a ratification of AT&T's traditional views on the glory of monopoly and the unworkability of competition, and as such was doomed almost from the outset. The Van Deerlin rewrite effort, a broadly pro-competitive measure, supplanted the Bell bill on the legislative agenda. But it proved too ambitious. For a history of both efforts see Temin, supra at 113–31.

30. This negative prediction is perhaps overstated. I would not look for any Congressional *policy* guidance, but, short of such policy guidance, Congress might take "meaningful" action by transferring jurisdiction over the MFJ from Judge Greene to the FCC, as has been proposed. Nevertheless, even that limited action seems unlikely at the present time.

31. This number is based on a Westlaw search for reported decisions, adjusted to exclude opinions dealing with purely procedural matters having no substantive implications.

32. An extended version of my discussion is contained in a Columbia University Center for Telecommunications and Information Studies' Working Paper.

33. 15 U.S.C. § 4.

34. Arguments advanced by the states were based upon the 10th Amendment, Sec. 2(b) of the Communications Act, and the state action exemption from the antitrust laws initially articulated in *Parker v. Brown*, 317 U.S. 341 (1943).

35. *United States v. AT&T*, 552 F. Supp. 131, 153–60 (1982) *aff'd sub nom.*, *Maryland v. United States*, 460 U.S. 1001 (1983).

36. Id. at 160.

37. Id. at 192, n. 250. In their submissions to the Court several states maintained the proposed decree's prohibition of such activities would undermine the financial viability of the BOCs or produce substantial increases in local telephone rates. I tend to disagree with William Baxter's suggestion in chapter 1 that allowing the BOCs into CPE and Yellow Pages, and departing from "the quarantine theory" caused the institutional frictions we have witnessed since divestiture. The Court's action may have served to accelerate the process, but I agree with Judge Greene that the BOCs would still have pressed to escape the line-of-business restrictions.

38. In approving the MFJ, the Court noted the FCC's preliminary conclusion, in its amicus curiae brief, that "the basic settlement appears to be fair and reasonable" and accordingly concluded that "the court need not and will not decide specific questions of possible conflict at this time." 552 F. Supp. at 211, citing brief of FCC as amicus curiae at 9. However, Judge Greene's Court made it clear that while there is no reason to anticipate a conflict between the decree and federal regulation, if such a conflict were to arise, "in view of the Commission's limited authority in regard to the structural matters in the telecommunications industry, the judgement of an antitrust court would prevail." Id. at 212.

39. Indeed, in 1982, the Department was (perhaps rightly) convinced the "wager" embodied in the consent decree was sufficiently well-calculated that it should be applied across the board (i.e., to prohibit any and all BOC diversification into competitive markets).

40. The Justice Department's consultant, Dr. Peter Huber, found that "only one-tenth of one percent of intraLATA traffic volume, generated by one customer out of one million, is carried through non-regional company facilities. . . . " 673 F. Supp at 540 (citing Huber Report at 3.9, table IX.5.).

41. Report and Recommendations of the United States Concerning the Line

of Business Restrictions Imposed on the BOCs by the MFJ, February 2, 1987, p. 5.

42. Id. at 4. That seven independent companies emerged from the divestiture was a function of a choice made by AT&T. The consent decree would have permitted AT&T to spin off its local exchange assets in a single company had it chosen to do so. Thus, the Department's heavy reliance on yardstick or benchmark competition in the Triennial Review filing represented a new appreciation for its value.

43. In 1982, the Justice Department stated that its alternative settlement proposal—the so-called "regulatory alternative"—"did not approach even remotely the effectiveness of the proposed modification in achieving conditions that would assure full competition in the telecommunications industry." DOJ Competitive Impact Statement, 47 Fed. Reg. at 7170, 7181 (1982). During the ensuing Tunney Act proceedings, the Department was even more explicit on this point, stating that, "Indeed, the very basis for divestiture is that the competitive problems inherent in the joint provision of regulated monopoly and competitive services are otherwise insoluble." Response of the United States to Public Comments on Proposed Modification of Final Judgement, 47 Fed. Reg. at 23336 (1982).

In rejecting the arguments advanced by the Justice Department and the BOCs, Judge Greene said the regulatory safeguards and FCC proposals upon which Justice's revised position relied "are entirely inadequate: they either predate the decree and were found at the trial to be ineffective; they are not sufficiently comprehensive; they contain large loopholes; or they are a long way from being promulgated, let alone being implemented." *United States v. Western Electric Co.*, 673 F. Supp. 525, 579 (D.D.C. 1987). The Court also expressed considerable dismay at the Justice Department's abandonment of the line-of-business restrictions. Id. at 536, n.40.

44. A similar bill, H.R. 3687, introduced by Rep. Wyden, would have removed the consent decree restrictions, to the extent permitted by state regulators in each jurisdiction in which the BOCs operated, subject to regulations designed to prevent cross-subsidization of the BOCs unregulated services.

45. In support of the proposed legislation, Assistant Attorney General Douglas Ginsburg urged that "the present dual regulatory system be restored to a unitary system based on the expert agency—the Commission—that can best assure that the regulatory regimes embodied in the [D]ecrees are implemented in a manner consistent with other telecommunications-related regulations." Testimony of Douglas H. Ginsburg, Assistant Attorney General, Antitrust Division, Concerning S. 2565, the Federal Telecommunications Policy Act of 1986 before the Committee on Commerce, Science and Transportation, United States Senate (September 10, 1986), p. 6. Mr. Ginsburg further argued that permitting the FCC to administer the decrees would allow "important factors to be taken into account in carrying out the [D]ecree's regulatory schemes that cannot now be addressed by the [D]ecree court, such as the national security interest, the interests of local telephone users, and the significant role of telecommunications and international trade." Id. pp. 7–8.

46. *The American Spirit in Telecommunications*, address by Dennis R. Patrick, Chairman, Federal Communications Commission, Before the United States Telephone Association 90th Annual Convention (October 13, 1987), p. 6.

47. Petition for Declaratory Ruling of the National Telecommunications and Information Administration (November 24, 1987) at 28.

48. FCC Public Notice, Mimeo. No. 768 (December 1, 1987).

49. *United States v. Western Electric Co.*, 675 F. Supp. 655, 661 (1987).

50. Id.

51. *United States v. Western Electric Company et al*, No. 87–5388 et al. (D.C. Cir.) April 3, 1990 (slip opinion).

52. *Louisiana Public Service Commission v. FCC*, 476 U.S. 355.

53. In Secs. 1 and 2(a) of the Communications Act of 1934 [47 U.S.C. SS151, 152(a)], Congress vested exclusive authority to regulate interstate telecommunications in the FCC, but Sec. 2(b) [47 U.S.C. S 152(b)] of the Act reserved to the states' jurisdiction over "charges, classifications, practices, services, facilities, or regulations for or in connection with intrastate communication by wire or radio of any carrier." This dual regulatory scheme has proved enigmatic because interstate and intrastate communications are not readily distinguishable; in fact, both types of communications utilize the same facilities.

54. See *North Carolina Utilities Commission v. FCC*, 537 F. 2d 787 (4th Cir.), *cert denied*, 429 U.S. 1027 (1976) ("NCUC I") and *North Carolina Utilities Commission v. FCC*, 552 F. 2d 1036 (4th Cir. 1976), *cert denied*, 434 U.S. 874 (1977) ("NCUC II") for important examples of the expanse of federal authority.

55. 476 U.S. at 374.

56. Third Computer Inquiry, Order on Reconsideration, 2 FCC Rcd. 3035 (1987). In June 1990, *Computer III* was overturned by the Ninth Circuit *California v. FCC*, 905 F.2d 1217, partly on the grounds that the FCC had overstepped its jurisdiction over intrastate services.

57. This is not to say that the FCC's regulation of the juncture of basic and enhanced services (ONA and comparably efficient interconnection in the current *Computer III* context) invariably has been better than the state equivalents. In some instances, in my view, the state agencies have proposed major improvements. See, e.g., Florida Public Service Commission Order No. 21815 in Docket No. 880423-TP, September 20, 1989 (Information Services).

58. See, e.g., AT&T Communications Tariff 12, 4 FCC Rcd. 4932 (1989).

59. Joint Cost Order, 2 FCC Rcd. 129B, recon. 2FCC Rcd. 6283 (1987), *further recon.* 3 FCC Rcd. 6701 (1988). Appeal is pending in the D.C. Circuit as *Southwestern Bell Corp. v. FCC*, Nos. 87–1764 and 89–1020.

60. U.S. Congress, House, Committee on Energy and Commerce Report No. 98–479, "Universal Telephone Preservation Act of 1983" (98th Cong., 1st Sess.), November 3, 1983.

61. The letter, urging reconsideration and delay until after the 1984 elections, was drafted by Senator Dole and signed by thirty fellow senators.

62. We had our perilous moments. I was prepared to dissent from the major Joint Board decision of March 1987, which increased the subscriber line charge

to residential subscribers to an ultimate level of $3.50 per month. I left the room and walked off to write my dissent when it appeared that I was the lone holdout for reducing the top level below $3.80. Mark Fowler followed me. After some tough talk he agreed to lower the cap to $3.50. I faced my moment of truth. There had been substantial concessions made to my views relative to "Link-Up America" provisions, and the extent of the monitoring process relative to the effectiveness of our orders. I decided that consensus remained important, so I agreed to concur with my colleagues in voting a $3.50 maximum.

4

The State of Competition
in Telecommunications

■

BRUCE L. EGAN

AND LEONARD WAVERMAN

■

STANFORD L. LEVIN

■

LEE L. SELWYN

NINA CORNELL

MARTIN G. TASCHDJIAN

JOHN R. WOODBURY

Bruce L. Egan and Leonard Waverman

Not surprisingly, there are many opinions regarding the state of competition in telecommunications. There are many submarkets to consider, each with a very different potential for the manifestation of competition as commonly defined in economics. Competition, of course, is a matter of degree, and there is a great deal of confusion regarding the criteria to determine the level of competition in any given market at any given time. For this reason we focus on empirical observations using the available data to evaluate competition since divestiture.

One of our main purposes is to make the same data available to others for their own interpretation. Space constraints preclude attempts to examine causality in any detailed fashion. This is appropriate considering the limitations of reported data and the short history since the AT&T divestiture. Moreover, economic causality is difficult to evaluate, and the divestiture itself is just one major event among a host of other exogenous and entirely random factors, such as tax reform, low inflation, high growth, technical change, and numerous judicial and regulatory decisions which are in large part responsible for what we observe.

Of critical importance to most economists in evaluating competition are the actual and potential number of market suppliers and buyers, and the ease with which suppliers may enter the market. There are many possible measurements, including the counting of suppliers, and evaluating entry barriers and the ready capacity of alternative suppliers. A traditional structural approach looks at market share at a point in time and over time to evaluate competition. Strict market share calculations are not good indicators of the state of competition in any market. Price movements are also important indicators of competitive conditions, and financial performance and profitability are also relevant.

Beyond the usual indicators, other behavioral considerations include the presence or absence of joint ventures and other partnerships among firms or groups of firms, productivity, product/service introduction and innovation, and progress in technology adoption. Even were data available on all such factors, an analysis of competition is complicated by transition dynamics and institutional, regulatory, and other exogenous factors for which there are often no data at all.

The post-divestiture marketplace features a wide range of submarkets, only some of which are closely related. Various categories of telecom products and services can be substitutes or complements, depending on income levels or other characteristics of users. Various network services are often used in combination by certain residence and business customers, while many others consider them as substitutes and choose one or another. For example, some businesses use switched and dedicated lines in relatively fixed proportions, while others view them as close substitutes based on price. We proceed to look at data on each category separately, recognizing that only net effects are revealed among a host of complex cross-elastic relationships. The market categories examined are: toll network services, including switched and nonswitched network services; local network services, including access lines and usage; access services for toll calling; customer premises equipment; network switching and transmission equipment; cellular mobile telecommunications; public or pay telephone equipment and services including alternative operator services; and information services.

Since divestiture, the telecommunications industry has become one of the fastest growing markets in the economy. However, there are large differences in the growth rates of different submarkets. There also appears to be a strong correlation between growth rates and competitive conditions (i.e., the highest rates of growth appear in sectors with the most competition).[1] This correlation exists for several reasons. First, the pressures for entry usually occur in market segments with high growth prospects. Second, competition drives down price and this increases demand. Third, it is easier to support new entrants in very high growth industries. Correlation, however, is not causation; thus it is necessary to consider whether entry constitutes a perhaps short-lived competitive fringe, or genuine long-run price/quality rivalry. Industry "shakeouts" typically follow boom periods, and such situations should be monitored closely.

The top portion of table 4.1 presents data on growth rates in local, toll, and access volumes for the 1984–1988 five-year period. These growth rates are significantly affected by federal and state rate changes mandating local price increases and toll and access service price decreases. The history of these price changes is given in table 4.2. The increase in the price of local and the fall in the price of interstate toll and access reflect the rebalancing of rates that has taken place. Obviously, the aggregate demand response to such large rate and rate-structure changes represents a significant part of observed growth in toll and access service since 1984, and not just inherent structural differences in long-run growth rates. Within the overall industry, growth in local telephone service since divestiture, especially for voice lines and usage, is quite sluggish, with the growth in voice toll and access services being two to four times greater. Such slow growth in the presence of unprecedented postwar economic expansion could indicate local service is a very mature and largely saturated market, whose future is likely to be most closely related to population growth. The same is true of voice toll and access services, but large rate reductions make them appear very high-growth markets. Data services, on the other hand, even local service, show very high growth rates (see figure 4.1). This is not due to divestiture or changes in regulation, but simply reflects shifting demand.

The bottom half of table 4.1 provides information on the levels of "industry" revenues (some 90 to 95 percent of the market, see table

TABLE 4.1

Industry Data

Network Market Segment Growth (%)
(year over year)

	1984	1985	1986	1987	1988
Access lines[a]	—	2.6	2.6	3.4	3.2
Local usage[b]	—	2.1	0.5	0.8	0.5
Toll usage[c]	—	8.0	6.3	8.3	9.4
Access usage[d]	—	10.5	8.3	15.2	13.0

Note: Comparisons of switched toll and access are difficult to make partly due to differences in measurement and reporitng and bypass.

[a] RBOCs plus the 18 largest independents (Source: Annual Reports/FCC Statistics).

[b] Subscriber line usage data (Source: FCC Tier 1 companies, Joint Board Monitoring Report, CC. Docket No. 80-286, p.198, 12/88).

[c] Based on AT&T data, for switched service only. Non-reporting carriers are usually higher growth and private and bypass usage is excluded, causing the estimates shown to be lower than actual.

[d] Interstate (Source: FCC report on Interstate Switched Market, March, 1989).

Industry Revenues ($B)

	1984	1985	1986	1987	1988
Total[e]	113.7	124.6	131.2	134.2	142.0
Local[f]	75.3	82.6	87.7	91.5	96.7
Toll[g]	38.4	42.0	43.5	42.7	45.3
Access[h]	25	27	23	22	25.2

[e] Based on data for approximately 90% of the market (Source: Annual Reports/FCC).

[f] RBOCs plus the 18 largest independent companies, includes local service, intraLATA toll, access (Source: Annual Reports/FCC).

[g] Includes top 5 carriers or about 95% of market (AT&T, MCI, US Sprint, NTN, Allnet).

[h] Author's estimate.

notes). Total revenues, so measured, rose by 24 percent in 1984–1988, with local exchange carrier (LEC) revenues increasing 28 percent, and toll revenues (interLATA) increasing 18 percent. Significant repricing must be taken into account when evaluating these data. The overall financial health of the industry during the five-year period is indicated in tables 4.3–4.5. Table 4.3 shows the market/book values of the pub-

TABLE 4.2
Telephone Prices
(annual rate of change)

	Local	*Intrastate* *Toll*	*Interstate* *Toll*	*Access*[a]
1984	+17.2	+3.6	−4.3	—
1985	+8.9	+0.6	−3.7	−8.1
1986	+7.1	+0.3	−9.5	−14.3
1987	+3.3	−3.0	−12.4	−21.7
1988	+4.5	−4.2	−4.2	−8.5
Total	+41.0	−2.7	−34.1	−52.6

Source: FCC price index study 1989.
[a]Interstate only.

licly traded shares of major firms for 1984–1988, as well as for the S&P 400; table 4.4 provides key financial data for the total industry, and for the LECs and interexchange segments. Table 4.5 (p. 127) shows the industry growth in telecom plant in service and also provides data on capital turnover rates. Several important observations may be made from these data. The first is that operating cash flow and net income

TABLE 4.3
Market/Book Ratios for Telephone Company Equities

	Market/Book Value				
	AT&T	*GTE*	*United*	*S&P 400*	*RBOC's*
1984	1.43	.96	1.17	1.51	.94
1985	1.78	1.24	1.32	1.86	1.16
1986	1.98	1.47	1.45	2.16	1.41
1987	2.00	1.28	1.61	2.13	1.46
1988	2.69	1.55	2.53	N/A	1.50

Source: All data from Annual Reports (except S&P 400).

Note: Market/Book = $\dfrac{\text{(stock price) x (shares outstanding)}}{\text{shareholder's equity}}$

TABLE 4.4
Telco Financial Data ($M)

Industry Total

	Annual Revenues	Operating Cash Flow	Net Income	Deprec. Expense	Dividends	Capital Expends.	Debt Ratio (%)	Rate of Return (%)
1984	113711.0	25781.3	9869.5	13427.3	10349.5	21843.3	35.5	7.49
1985	123584.6	29342.3	10219.8	15766.8	8744.7	24217.7	35.1	6.77
1986	130828.9	30754.7	10203.3	17969.4	9905.5	26287.9	33.8	7.81
1987	134187.4	30130.8	10516.3	20630.6	10291.3	24899.1	34.2	7.70
1988	141472.0	31637.5	11906.6	21593.7	12110.6	25272.0	34.0	8.22

LEC Subtotal

	Annual Revenues	Operating Cash Flow	Net Income	Deprec. Expense	Dividends	Capital Expends.	Debt Ratio (%)	Rate of Return (%)
1984	75303.0	23207.4	8587.6	11927.2	7910.5	18224.6	43.18	7.40
1985	82432.3	25938.2	9645.3	13647.6	5953.6	20401.2	42.19	6.80
1986	87578.0	27289.4	10104.8	15418.8	6320.7	21047.9	41.43	8.03
1987	91382.6	27301.3	10113.0	17804.0	6797.6	20325.7	41.73	7.79
1988	96128.5	28176.8	10368.6	18652.3	8582.4	20740.4	41.00	8.00

Interexchange Subtotal

	Annual Revenues	Operating Cash Flow	Net Income	Deprec. Expense	Dividends	Capital Expends.	Debt Ratio[a] (%)	Rate of Return (%)
1984	38408.2	2573.8	1281.9	1500.2	2439.0	3618.8	39.0	8.36
1985	41152.2	3404.1	574.5	2119.2	2791.1	3816.5	35.1	6.52
1986	43250.9	3465.4	98.5	2550.6	3584.8	5239.9	38.8	6.05
1987	42804.8	2829.6	403.3	2826.6	3493.8	4573.4	38.4	6.96
1988	45343.5	3460.7	1538.0	2941.4	3528.2	4531.6	38.4	9.83

Source: Company reports for five largest IXCs, twenty-five largest LECs (about 95% of market).

Key: Debt Ratio = Long-term debt/invested capital.
     Rate of Return = Net income/invested capital.

[a] AT&T and MCI.

(total industry) expanded significantly between 1984 and 1988 (22 and 21 percent, respectively). Operating cash flow grew for both LECs and interexchange carriers (IXCs). Net income was significantly down for IXCs in 1985, 1986, and 1987, reflecting problems for MCI and particularly for US Sprint, but recovered nicely in 1988 and 1989 (not shown). In fact US Sprint turned its first profit in 1989. Capital expenditures have risen appreciably since pre-divestiture. Much of the capital spending in earlier years (1984–1986) was to pay for equal access required by the MFJ and remains high due to aggressive network modernization programs. Table 4.5 shows gross investment for the industry rose steadily between 1984 and 1988, increasing 28 percent overall, and net investment increased about 15 percent. The steady increase in telephone plant has occurred for local and toll carriers.

Note that the ratio of long-term debt to invested capital has decreased, and that depreciation has increased 50 percent. These facts, combined with relatively low inflation and taxes, have allowed the industry to rapidly replace and modernize their plant without sacrificing profits or dividends. Dividends fell somewhat for LECs in 1985 but otherwise have grown steadily for both LECs and IXCs.

Currently, almost two-thirds of industry cash flow is from depreciation. The very important financial effect of recent increases in allowed depreciation rates is a result of both divestiture and competition. It is difficult to imagine that such rapid increases in depreciation would have been allowed by regulators if AT&T still owned the majority of local distribution and manufacturing facilities as a vertically integrated entity.[2] Of course, the simultaneous effects of positive exogenous economic factors which reduced pressure on regulated rate levels certainly is also responsible for the favorable financial picture.

Most financial information concerning the various subcomponents of the "industry" and broad aggregates such as LECs is from public accounting data and may not provide a particularly accurate economic evaluation. However, the data is presumed reasonably consistent across firms, allowing for comparison of nominal financial results. As long as such comparisons are made among firms within a given narrow industry segment, the actual economic conditions underlying the data are likely to be similar for all of them. Of course, the institutional environment may favor certain firms over others, and the most obvious cases will be mentioned. The data presented for each industry segment to yield insights into indicators of competitive activity include market structure, growth, capacity, prices, new products and services, productivity, and technology adoption.

Table 4.6 (pp. 128–29) shows the key financial results for the three major interexchange carriers for the period 1984–1988. On average, total toll revenues have grown by about 4 percent per year, even with the substantial price reductions that were detailed in table 4.2. Cash flow, net income, capital turnover, and capacity additions have all risen rapidly since divestiture, but are beginning to slow down. Construction spending has peaked and is on the decline as significant capacity expansion, particularly in fiber optics plant, has occurred.[3] Depending on one's definition of usable toll capacity in place, by 1989 intercity capacity was two to five times that at divestiture, but this is the result of competitive entry, not the divestiture itself.

Figure 4.1 shows the growth in various toll market segments since divestiture—in residence, business, 800 Service, international, and data—and indicates the strong relative growth of business toll services, especially 800 Service and data. Again, remember how prices have fallen. Table 4.7 (pp. 130–31) gives estimates of fiber optic installations in the toll market since divestiture for major IXCs. Fiber-miles in service

FIGURE 4.1

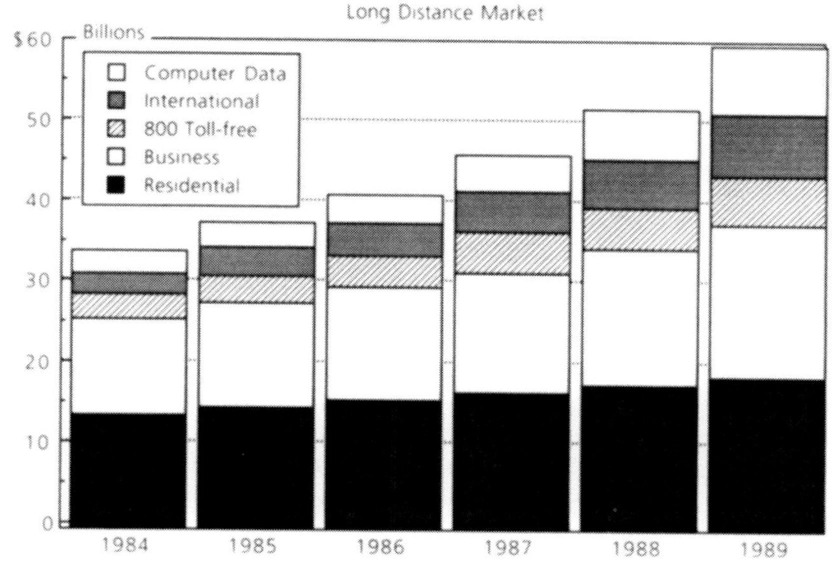

Long Distance Market

Source: *New York Times* May 22, 1989 Paine Weber.

increased from 456,000 in 1985 to 1.89 million in 1988. In 1989 the figure reached 2.18 million. Advances in electronics will lead to even greater capacity without new lines. This growth is remarkable.[4]

Table 4.8 estimates the market share for interexchange carrier (state and interstate toll) revenues since divestiture and shows a steady decline in AT&T's share of the interstate market from 91 percent in 1984 to 78 percent in 1988. The interstate market remains even more competitive (deregulated) relative to intrastate markets, as is reflected in AT&T's lower market share of interstate switched access minutes of 67 percent in 1988 as compared to 80 percent in 1984. This has no doubt been partly a result of progress in conversion of the public network to equal access. The effects of equal access are indicated in table 4.9. Note that by the end of 1988, AT&T's share of premium and all minutes of interstate toll use were nearly identical.

Since divestiture, the number of IXCs has expanded rapidly from 123 in 1984 to 577 by the end of 1989.[5] Even though most are resellers, there has been a large number of facilities-based entrants. Along with new firms came a proliferation of new toll service offerings, including many from AT&T as a competitive response.

Data on market shares or investment do not capture the full flavor of the degree of competition (or lack of it) in any market. Market share is but one descriptive statistic of the nature of competition. One cannot be unimpressed, however, by the sharp fall in AT&T's share of the interexchange market (table 4.9), by the competitive service offerings in terms of quality (fiber optics), and the range of services and price (although here AT&T is greatly constrained). The obvious response is to say that the market is competitive. Yet the "market" is an aggregate and the toll market is geographically specific. Some observers conclude, and we agree, that AT&T's market domination is confined to lower profit markets (i.e., rural, low-volume, and short-haul private line long-distance services), where competition is not vigorous. But in those markets where AT&T is dominant, its domination encompasses both residential and business customers.[6]

Few markets—and certainly not those with sunk investments such as in fiber optics—can be "perfectly" competitive. The case is not whether the interexchange market fits some textbook version of competition but whether it fits into those sectors we deem competitive enough for ex post evaluations of firm strategies, or into the ex ante regulatory box we view as irredeemably not competitive. We believe the interexchange market is generally in the ex post category—i.e., competitive enough that with few rules (far fewer than in the FCC's 1989 price caps order, which is really closer to rate-of-return regulation

TABLE 4.5
Telco Investment ($M)

Industry Total

	GPIS	NPIS	DR(%)	DE(%)	RETS	ADDS
1984	207953.9	159686.7	23.21	6.46	7818.7	21843.3
1985	225377.8	168715.8	25.14	7.00	8278.5	24217.7
1986	243168.0	175685.1	27.75	7.39	8977.4	26287.9
1987	253494.0	180041.1	28.98	8.14	10299.8	24899.1
1988	267264.7	181855.7	31.96	8.22	9963.8	25272.0

LEC Subtotal

	GPIS	NPIS	DR(%)	DE(%)	RETS	ADDS
1984	186043.0	143591.9	22.82	6.41	7223.4	18224.6
1985	200845.1	151195.7	24.72	6.80	7632.7	20401.2
1986	213927.0	156194.1	26.99	7.21	8015.5	21047.9
1987	222395.5	159855.0	28.12	8.01	9003.8	20325.7
1988	231177.3	160233.0	30.69	8.07	8810.8	20740.4

RBOC Subtotal

	GPIS	NPIS	DR(%)	DE(%)	RETS	ADDS
1984	145481.8	113560.3	21.94	6.05	5216.8	13872.7
1985	156243.6	118589.0	24.10	6.54	5328.1	15458.8
1986	166862.0	122378.2	26.66	6.92	5614.1	15750.7
1987	172877.4	124468.5	28.00	7.88	6114.0	14735.0
1988	180900.8	126095.4	30.30	7.96	6003.7	15315.7

Interexchange Subtotal

	GPIS	NPIS	DR(%)	DE(%)	RETS	ADDS
1984	21910.9	16094.7	26.54	6.85	595.2	3618.75
1985	24532.7	17520.1	28.58	8.64	645.8	3816.54
1986	29241.0	19490.9	33.34	8.72	961.9	5239.94
1987	31098.5	20186.1	35.09	9.09	1296.0	4573.39
1988	34087.4	21622.7	36.57	8.84	1153.0	4531.60

Source: Company reports.

Key: GPIS = Gross plant in service. DE = Depreciation expense/GPIS.
NPIS = Net plant in service. RETS = Plant retirements.
DR = Depreciation reserve/GPIS. ADDS = Plant additions.

TABLE 4.6
IXC Financial Data ($M)

AT&T

	Annual Revenues	Operating Cash Flow	Net Income	Deprec. Expense	Dividends	Capital Expends.	Debt Ratio (%)	Rate of Return (%)
1984	34935.00	2255.50	1107.06	1148.44	1222.00	1514.00	36.36	9.2
1985	36770.00	3025.61	974.09	1661.10	1273.00	1791.08	32.36	7.7
1986	36514.00	3476.80	1307.30	1790.04	1245.00	2483.83	33.57	9.9
1987	35219.00	3163.60	1472.80	2028.57	1287.00	2497.76	33.25	10.9
1988	35407.00	2662.00	1689.00	2029.00	1290.00	2800.00	31.38	11.8

MCI

	Annual Revenues	Operating Cash Flow	Net Income	Deprec. Expense	Dividends	Capital Expends.	Debt Ratio (%)	Rate of Return (%)
1984	1959.29	377.84	59.20	264.57	0.00	1157.12	60.30	1.90
1985	2542.27	643.00	113.30	347.15	0.00	1000.10	56.27	3.76
1986	3592.00	398.00	−448.00	451.00	0.00	1074.00	67.95	−11.38
1987	3939.00	523.00	88.00	471.00	0.00	619.00	66.31	2.19
1988	5137.00	929.00	346.00	549.00	0.00	896.00	66.33	7.93

US Sprint [a]

	Annual Revenues	Operating Cash Flow	Net Income	Deprec. Expense	Dividends	Capital Expends.	Debt Ratio (%)	Rate of Return (%)
1984	1245.00	−68.00	114.60	80.00	NA	925.00	NA	14.32
1985	1345.00	−253.00	−490.00	99.00	NA	1000.00	NA	−4.10
1986	2345.20	−418.20	−700.00	281.80	NA	1101.00	NA	−3.20
1987	2672.20	−846.50	−1154.90	308.40	NA	996.00	NA	−41.80
1988	3405.40	−122.50	−467.10	344.60	NA	728.20	NA	−15.90

Source: Company reports.

Key: Debt Ratio = long term debt/invested capital.
Rate of Return = net Income/invested capital.

[a] Data for 1984–1986 represents predecessor companies.

TABLE 4.7
IXC Fiber Optic Deployment

	Approx. Current Invest. ($M)	Route-Miles				Fiber-Miles			
	1985	1985	1986	1987	1988	1985	1986	1987	1988
NTN Partners:									
Consolidated Network	310		292	352	352	3504	3504	3864	3864
Litel	881		950	1210	1210	13730	17274	22280	22280
Microtel	800		950	967	1127	8000	9500	9670	17158
SouthernNet	188		895	895	—	1880	8950	8950	—
Southland Fibernet	277		277	277	—	2770	2770	2770	—

Southern & Southland

LDX Net	—	670	1379	1172	1172	1080	33096	11720	11720
WilTel	—	214	2899	—	—	2140	58077	—	—
LDX & Wiltel	—	—	—	—	—	—	—	—	—
NTN Subtotal:	—	—	—	4244	5177	—	—	104923	131865
AT&T	584	3340	7642	7945	9038	48094	133171	152457	186887
MCI	1758	5677	10893	18000	23324	136248	261432	432000	704731
GTE Sprint	823	2560	5580	8775	10975	79200	167400	245700	264680
US Telecom	—	1200	—	—	—	24000	—	—	—
US Sprint	1670	4100	10000	18195	22090	98400	190000	497224	575562
Electra	50	493	493	493	493	10194	10194	10194	10194
Lightnet	280	2200	5000	5300	5300	52800	120000	127200	127200
Mutual Signal Corp.	32	0	0	420	420	0	0	4200	4200
Norlight	50	0	0	670	670	0	0	8040	8040
RCI	7	580	580	796	413	6960	6960	7202	2618
Teleconnect	30	0	0	320	400	0	0	1920	2400
Totals	5285	20150	40183	70031	73123	455896	889157	1497857	1886512

Source: FCC Fiber Report, February 17, 1989.

TABLE 4.8
Interexchange Carriers Market Shares
(% Revenue)

	1984	1985	1986	1987	1988
AT&T	90.96	89.35	84.42	82.28	78.09
MCI	5.10	6.18	8.31	9.20	11.33
US Sprint	3.24	3.27	5.42	6.24	7.51
NTN	0.00	0.36	0.81	1.35	2.21
Allnet	0.70	0.84	1.04	0.92	0.87

Source: Annual reports, company data.

Note: Top five firms estimated to be 95% of total interexchange market revenues.

than price caps), one can allow real competition.[7] The lack of competition in some interexchange markets does require some oversight, but we are convinced that a judicious price cap regulatory approach can protect captive customers, encourage competition, and still not unduly hamper the actions of AT&T.

There are about 1,370 local telephone companies, of which BOCs

TABLE 4.9
AT&T Share of
the Interstate Market (%)
(end of year)

	Premium Minutes	All Minutes
1984	94	80
1985	88	77
1986	79	73
1987	74	70
1988	69	67

Source: FCC report on Interstate Switched Access, March 1989.

and GTE represent about 85 percent of the total market. Table 4.10 gives key financial data on the seven RBOCs and eighteen of the major independent companies which collectively serve about 90 percent of the total number of local service subscribers in the U.S. The RBOCs have increased cash flow by 23 percent from 1984 to 1988 and have maintained dividends near 1984 levels. If 1984, the year of financial transition, is excluded, dividends have increased steadily since 1985. Net income has risen 30 percent (1988 over 1984) and depreciation expense increased over 60 percent (again 1988 and 1984 comparisons). Data for the eighteen independent LECs aggregated on the bottom portion of table 4.10 show steady cash flow, declining net income, and steadily increasing dividends.

Examination of revenue shares of the top twenty-five LECs since divestiture[8] reveals no indication of serious competition among LECs for the basic local service market, and little for intraLATA toll and other local services. This implies stable market shares of incumbent firms, which thus far only seem sensitive to exogenous regional growth differences. Furthermore, as noted, the RBOCs' and many LECs' market value, net income, cash flow, and profits have increased since 1984 and remain high, all in the face of relatively low growth in the quantity of services sold. The data indicate that no major new local service companies have entered the market, at least not sufficiently to lower any major LEC's market share substantially. This is despite the fact there is no MFJ prohibition against IXCs or other LECs from providing local service in competition with the incumbent dominant LEC. Further evidence of LEC market power is the continued growth of market penetration in spite of a more than 40 percent rise in rates for basic local service since divestiture.

The lack of competition at the state and local level is due to many factors, primarily regulatory policies which do not encourage entry. The incumbent LEC enjoys the relative comfort of rate-base regulation. While most states do not grant exclusive certificates of necessity and convenience to the incumbent LEC, regulatory barriers exacerbate entry barriers of up-front sunk costs with assets fixed and immobile, and very high business risk for new entrants with no rate base, customer base, or cash flow. It is not clear if local competition would flourish in the absence of regulation, but we would certainly expect to see more entry if regulatory protection were removed. The only true test, of course, is to see what would happen without regulation. Where niche local exchange competition has emerged, a host of regulatory, legal, and technical roadblocks continue to face the new entrant.

TABLE 4.10

LEC Financial Data ($M)

RBOCs

	Annual Revenues	Operating Cash Flow	Net Income	Deprec. Expense	Dividends	Capital Expends.	Debt Ratio (%)	Rate of Return (%)
1984	57829.1	17982.9	6805.9	8783.8	5484.1	13872.7	41.2	7.6
1985	63365.5	20148.9	7534.0	10212.2	4556.6	15458.8	39.8	8.1
1986	67390.1	21233.4	8135.9	11531.0	4914.0	15750.7	38.3	8.5
1987	70187.3	21166.2	8372.4	13627.6	5272.4	14735.0	39.3	8.5
1988	74197.4	22235.7	8914.5	14397.6	5392.4	15315.7	40.0	8.5

Independent LECs

	Annual Revenues	Operating Cash Flow	Net Income	Deprec. Expense	Dividends	Capital Expends.	Debt Ratio (%)	Rate of Return (%)
1984	17494.9	5102.6	1744.9	3122.7	1207.1	4333.9	46.4	6.4
1985	19259.2	5640.4	2071.4	3460.4	1427.7	4927.3	47.7	6.5
1986	20329.2	5747.4	1935.7	3865.0	1570.0	5284.4	47.6	6.6
1987	21344.9	5753.8	1713.1	4178.7	1685.8	5576.7	47.9	5.7
1988	22471.0	5803.6	1535.1	4369.8	1760.7	5490.6	48.0	6.2

Source: Annual reports/company reports for RBOCs and 18 largest independents (about 90% of market).

Note: Some data represent non-telco operations due to consolidated reproting (non-telco activities estimated in 1988 to be no more than 10% of revenues). Data for GTE and United is net of Sprint and US Telecom, respectively.

Key: Operating cash flow = net income + depreciation + deferred tax + other.
Debt ratio = long-term debt/invested capital.
Rate of return = net income/invested capital.

Arguably there are some large new niche competitors in the business local service market. Two of the most prominent are Metropolitan Fiber Systems, Inc., and Communications Teleport. The track record of such firms is still in the start-up phase, however, and thus far they are primarily bypass suppliers. In 1989, these two suppliers announced plans to expand to a number of cities, including New York, Chicago, San Francisco, Los Angeles, Boston, and Houston.[9] These two firms plan to compete against each other, as well as against the LECs.

Another interesting case of potentially important post-divestiture competition were the so-called Shared Tenant Service (STS) providers. These were firms that chose natural aggregates of local subscribers in large buildings or campus complexes, and basically resold LEC service, usually through the use of private remote switching or multiplexing equipment. Accurate data on such private arrangements are not generally available. Such activity grew rapidly in 1984 through about 1986, but recently thereafter it fell off and even declined to the point where it now receives little attention even in the trade press. The likely explanation is that while this new market was initially perceived as substantial, as often is the case with new and untested markets, there was little true potential, given the environment. It proved to be difficult for a STS provider, even in partnership with a building owner or contractor, to contract for a break-even penetration rate among tenants. Furthermore, in some states, litigation brought by LECs and regulators or other groups against the STS industry resulted in delays and even some orders to terminate operations, for fear of cream-skimming the LECs.[10]

Overall we believe the local service market is still a monopoly, though there are some pockets of competition for business customers. We emphasize the true nature of feasible competition will only be known when local service and access are correctly priced in relation to cost, and regulatory barriers are removed.

Access services represent a huge market, strictly a product of regulatory decisions of the early 1980s. Before divestiture, access charges were an implicit part of retail toll prices, except in the case of a few fledgling toll carriers. After divestiture, AT&T and other IXCs had to pay large per-minute fees to LECs whenever a toll call was placed using LEC local connections. Table 4.1 (p. 120) provides data on LEC access revenues since divestiture. Mandated access tariff rate levels have gone from 17.3 cents per minute of toll use in 1984 to 9.8 cents by 1989.[11] The decrease is primarily due to concomitant increases in local Subscriber Line Charges. The many different rate levels for intrastate access are similar to interstate rates, both in level and structure. Access charges represent almost a third of LEC revenues and almost half of AT&T's annual operating expenses. Average switched toll rates nationwide are about thirty cents per minute.

The main reason for analyzing "access" separate from other LEC markets is that it is uniquely competitive for large users, and many bypass substitutes exist and their numbers are growing rapidly. As is the case with toll service, smaller users in many geographic markets still have no ready alternative to LEC switched access services. In recognition of potential bypass competition, the FCC has significantly reduced interstate access charges on originating switched toll traffic. Some evidence of relative price elasticity in LEC access services is the fact that access service revenues remain steady despite large annual rate declines.

Due to significant early measurement problems and rate reductions since 1984, it is difficult to evaluate real growth rates for LEC access services. Before divestiture, as noted, LEC access charges were part of retail toll prices, which made it more difficult, even for large users, to avoid paying them for switched services. The post-divestiture environment provides large customers with a number of alternatives for obtaining cheaper access services, including WATS, 800 Service, private bypass, and interconnect services. As new IXC toll service options grow, even moderate and small customers will begin to have alternatives to full-priced LEC switched access service. AT&T's new small-customer 800 Readyline Service is an early example.

No solid data source on private bypass of LEC switched access charges exists, and thus it is difficult to estimate market share declines, especially in the face of fairly rapid overall toll service growth partially caused by dramatic rate declines. One method for estimating LEC bypass is available from the FCC Bypass Monitoring Reports in CC Docket 87–339. The 1988 year-end report puts bypass at $3.7 billion annually for the RBOCs and GTE. An NTIA report[12] estimates compound annual growth rates for bypass networks at 20 percent for the period 1985–1990. Table 4.11 provides some data on the growth of microwave radio and satellite systems. In 1989, about 16,000 domestic common carrier point-to-point microwave systems are in operation, licensed to almost 1,325 carriers, and the annual growth in facilities is substantial. Private (non-common-carrier) systems have also proliferated. As of July 1989, there were about 18,000 domestic satellite earth stations authorized by the FCC, and since 1984 over 12,000 applications for new earth stations had been filed, and about 1,500 for modification of existing stations. The U.S. Department of Commerce forecast sales for satellite ground stations to reach $900 million by 1991, includ-

TABLE 4.11
FCC Microwave Facilities Applications

1986	1987	1988	1989	1990
8,593	7,928	6,400	7,000[a]	13,000[a]

Source: FCC Radio Facilities Division (Common carrier point-to-point service.)
[a] Estimates.

Very Small Aperture Terminal Market ($M)

1984	1985	1986	1987	1988
59.7	73.5	62.6	92	151.4

Source: Dataquest.

ing very small aperture terminals (VSAT), direct broadcast satellites (DBS), and television receive only (TVRO) markets, but other private satellite, radio, copper, and fiber telecom systems vendors have also grown rapidly, well into double-digit growth since divestiture. This growth has, by definition, reduced LEC market share, at least for high volume customers.

Recent FCC pricing rules have allowed LECs to rapidly lower originating access rates to try to stem the competitive tide, but high rates obviously persist at about ten cents per minute. This trend will continue and thus LEC access services, at least for interstate service—which is 75 percent of the market—is effectively competitive, and we recommend deregulation of these markets. In some specific markets (e.g., small and rural customers), access services, like toll service, may still be dominated by one supplier. In state jurisdictions where the market structure for toll and access more closely resembles the monopoly model, we believe a more gradual transition to deregulation is appropriate.

The CPE market was already quite competitive by 1984 due to some important regulatory decisions, especially *Carterfone* (1968) and *Computer Inquiry II*, which detariffed CPE and forced structural separation of AT&T from its CPE division, known at the time as American Bell. Today, there are numerous buyers and sellers, none of which currently exercises market power. Even the industry giant AT&T is only an average supplier, as evidenced by the number of competitive-bid contracts it wins. Foreign imports of CPE dominate the market, and foreign production capacity is so large as to prevent the U.S. from ever again dominating the market to the extent of forcing higher market prices. Table 4.12 shows factory shipments of broad categories of CPE since 1984.

We cannot estimate market share by supplier for "POTS" telephones because there are simply too many of them. That market is competitive. Table 4.13 provides some market share data for all telecommunications equipment, including the equipment used by telcos. The data do not pertain only to the CPE market, but they do show low concentration on a world or U.S. basis. Of greater relevance to our analysis of competition in the CPE market are the data in table 4.13 showing market shares in the PBX market. PBXs are much more sophisticated than "POTS" telephones, and as such, less vendors will exist. Even though market shares of the top four PBX vendors exhibited stability over the 1984 to 1987 period, industry experts recognize the ferocious competition that has existed in this market even with its high start-up costs and exit barriers (the software for an unsuccessful PBX has zero salvage value). If PBXs are a competitive market (and they are), other CPE equipment is clearly a competitive market now.

Two issues remain. First, the BOCs are not allowed to manufacture equipment. Second, ISDN and other developments require more sophisticated CPE. We would be inclined to allow RBOCs to manufacture; given intense competition already, they can only add to it. However, some narrow regulatory rules may be acceptable to prevent favoritism of one's own manufacturing division.[13] As CPE becomes more sophisticated, entry costs rise. Yet, the market is huge and the number of potential producers is large and we see no serious problems for competition.

The present Congressional hearings into broad safeguards, such as cost allocation rules or separate subsidiaries for BOC permission to manufacture equipment, really ignore the enormous competition in CPE, and the inability of any vendor to predate against other suppliers so as to wield long-run market power. Submissions to the House Committee argue the BOCs could subsidize the R&D and software costs for new equipment and thus dominate the equipment market. There is little ground to believe that "deep pockets," wherever financed, will ensure success in the CPE market. Whatever the failures of domestic regulatory policy in fostering competition in other areas, in the case of CPE they have been a very significant stimulus. To some, deregulation of CPE, coupled with BOC line-of-business restrictions, have gone too far and leave the U.S. in a poor competitive position in the interna-

TABLE 4.12
U.S. Factory Shipments of Telephone and Telegraph Equipment ($M)

	1984	1985	1986	1987	1988
Private branch exchange equipment	1,603.7	1,720.8	855.9	1,222.0	1,300.0
Other switching and switchboard equipment	1,410.6	1,660.7	1,851.9	1,816.1	1,850.0
Carrier line equipment	1,917.3	2,329.5	2,833.0	2,737.0	2,745.0
Telephone sets	846.7	1,218.6	783.7	875	NA
Teleprinters	294.1	270.8	361.2	NA	NA
Modems	848.3	829.5	1,228.2	1,078.1	1,155.0
Voice frequency equipment	301.7	328.3	243.0	196.2	175.0
Other telephone and telegraph equipment	4,161.4	3,371.5	2,857.5	3,027.8	3,000.0

Source: U.S. Department of Commerce.

tional arena. The U.S. share of the current world CPE market is only about 20 to 25 percent. Most of the rest is from the Far East, and prices have plummeted as a result. Residence customer CPE comes almost entirely from overseas manufacturing facilities, and even for large scale business systems domestic production is estimated to be less than 25 percent of the U.S. market.

For a long time before divestiture, LECs depended on Centrex, a central-office-based business system, to compete with on-premises PBX systems. The displacement of LEC Centrex by competitive PBX sys-

TABLE 4.13
CPE Market Share Data

*World's Market Top Ten Telecommunications
Equipment Manufacturers*

Rank	Company	Headquarters	1986 Sales ($B)
1	AT&T Technologies	USA	10.20
2	Alcatel NC	Belgium	8.00
3	Siemens	W. Germany	5.40
4	NEC	Japan	4.50
5	Northern Telecom	Canada	4.40
6	IBM	USA	3.30
7	Motorola	USA	3.10
8	Ericsson	Sweden	3.10
9	Fujitsu	Japan	2.10
10	Philips	Netherlands	2.00

*Full Product Line Equipment Manufacturers
(1987 US Market = $103B)*

AT&T	12.0%
Alcatel	10.0
Siemens	8.0
Northern Tel.	6.0
Ericsson	5.0
NEC	3.0
Philips	—
Fujitsu	—
Italtel	—
Other	55.0

TABLE 4.13 (continued)

PBX Market Shares

	1984	1985	1986	1987	E1992
AT&T	19.00%	26.00%	22.00%	21.00%	22.00%
Northern Telecom	21.00	22.00	21.00	20.00	20.00
IBM	18.00	15.00	18.00	17.00	20.00
Mitel	9.00	8.00	9.00	10.00	9.00
NEC	7.00	7.00	8.00	9.00	9.00
GEC/Fujitsu	NA	NA	NA	8.00	7.00
Other	26.00	22.00	22.00	15.00	13.00
Total Revenues ($B)	3.5	3.67	3.42	3.39	NA

Source: NTIA Telecom 2000, Gartner Group Reports.

tems since divestiture has been substantial, indicating that even when the LEC enjoys a significant physical advantage of being the sole supplier of Centrex (they own all the central office switching machines), there are ready market substitutes. Recently however, Centrex is making a comeback as a way for business customers to obtain digital service and ISDN, and this could develop into a market advantage for LECs. Nonetheless, recent ONA regulations, which promise to unbundle LEC interconnection arrangements, will likely allow for a competitive alternative.

It is hard to envision a freely operating CPE market returning to a monopolistic structure, and therefore we believe any residual regulation is probably unnecessary.

The embedded base in large-scale network switching and transmission systems represents a huge investment of over $230 billion, and includes some 22,400 network switch locations and several billion circuit miles of transmission capacity. Estimates of sales and shipments (1984–1988) for network equipment are given in table 4.14. Currently in the U.S., shipments are about $15 billion, of which about a third is switching equipment, and the rest is electronic devices and components (about $2 billion) and transmission systems.

The data in table 4.15 show that the U.S. market for switching and fiber optics is highly concentrated, featuring two major suppliers in each segment. It is difficult to measure the impacts of divestiture on sales and purchases of network equipment. However, sales of Northern Telecom switching equipment increased sharply after 1983. And, in-

TABLE 4.14
U.S. Shipments of Network Communications Equipment ($M)

	1984	1985	1986	1987	1988
Telephone switching and switchboard equip.[a]	5,871.2	7,7714.3	7,180.0	7,480.5	
Carrier line equip. and modems[b]	8,369.5	8,348.1	4,062.2	3,815.1	
Other telephone and telegraph equip.[c]			3,891.1	4,227.2	
Comm. systems and equip. (excl. broadcast)[d]	9,258.5	10,708.0	11,216.5	11,363.2	
Central office equipment[e]	2,856.9	4,332.8	4,525.0	4,442.5	4,500

Source: U.S. Dept. of Commerce, Bureau of Census.

[a] SIC Code 36611.   [c] SIC Code 36614.   [e] Estimate.
[b] SIC Code 36613.   [d] SIC Code 36631.

roads have been made in the device and components sector, as well as in microwave and satellite technology, since there are many suppliers and some significant new firms.

The nature of production in the market for large-scale switching and transmission systems features very high start-up costs and substantial scale requirements, both static and dynamic.[14] Competition is still evident, however, even with only two major firms since the products of each remain very close substitutes. Moreover, the "competitive fringe" includes a substantial number of large foreign firms licensed to serve the U.S. market. As a result of technical progress and competition, unit prices for transmission and switching capacity are falling, and market power, if it exists, is not evident from current behavior and performance of major firms. What is more, we expect the dominant firms' share of the domestic switching and transmission equipment market to begin to fall as foreign competitors continue to enter and as technology evolves. Competition is really at a global level and on a world basis, four-firm concentration ratios (albeit not measured for the markets in which they can today sell) are lower. We therefore feel the market for central office (CO) switching equipment appears very competitive. Barring future trade barriers or collusion in LEC procurement practices, this market should continue to feature competitive characteristics.

The growth rate in cellular communications services is the highest

TABLE 4.15
Market Share Data
Network Equipment

U.S. Switch Market (1989)

AT&T	53.00%
Northern Telecom	40.00
GPT-Stromberg	3.00
Siemens	2.00
Ericsson	1.00
NEC	0.50
Fujitsu	—

Source: *Business Week*, May 2, 1989.

U.S. Fiber Optics Cable Market Share

1985		*1988*	
AT&T	37%	AT&T	52%
Siecor	32	Siecor	30
ITT	13	Alcatel	8
Ericcsson	9	Pirelli	4
Northern Telecom	4	Northern Telecom	2
Others	5	Others	4

Source: ElectroniCast Corporation.

of any major new telecommunications market since 1984, but this is not a result of divestiture. In 1984, there were only 50,000 cellular subscribers, and by 1989 there were about 3,500,000. Table 4.16 and figure 4.2 provide data on market share since 1984 for both cellular service and equipment.[15] Price competition for cellular customer equipment is fierce by any measure, and today's average unit price is a small fraction of what it was in 1984. Prices for service have fallen too, but not substantially. Some have argued that those service price declines are insufficient. One possible reason for less competition on the service side is that only two competitors were designated by the FCC to operate in any given locale. Another problem is that cellular is provided over scarce radio spectrum and traditional ownership or control over spectrum use bestows certain market power advantages. Like other

TABLE 4.16
US Cellular Switching Systems Market
(% share of system contracts)

	1985[a]	1986[a]	1987[a]	1988[b]	1989[b]
Motorola	50.0%	40.1%	36.9%	33.1%	31.1%
AT&T	33.0	32.4	32.8	26.2	25.6
NTI/GE	8.4	12.7	12.3	12.0	15.6
Ericsson	2.8	9.5	9.7	10.5	14.4
Harris	2.8	—	—	—	—
NEC	2.8	2.5	3.0	2.8	2.3
Astronet	—	1.9	4.1	8.8	5.6
CTI/EF Johnson	—	.6	0.05	—	—
NovAtel	—	—	0.05	5.1	4.6
Plexsys	—	—	—	1.1	0.5

Source: *Cellular Business* Magazine.
[a]Based on top 90 markets.
[b]Based on top 306 markets.

markets using scarce radio spectrum, some sort of regulation is necessary, since auction markets are not used and early mistakes were made in the process of regulating this new market.

Service price competition is possible with two suppliers. We see it in the provision of central office equipment, where many real and potential market entrants exist. The same is not true for cellular service. Service prices vary widely city-by-city. Presumably the cost structures are similar (at least for cities of similar size); therefore the ability to regionally segment this market will allow for the potential of monopoly abuse, and it is imperative the two major service suppliers in a given area not be able to coordinate pricing policy.[16] U.S. market share data on cellular service is not particularly meaningful for two reasons —it is a young market in transition, and entry is restricted. There has also been a trend of holding companies buying up cellular franchises, and the high prices paid are indicative of current and future monopoly rents which accrue to the owner of the cellular licenses. Some believe this could result in coordination of pricing and innovation, and perhaps fewer service options. But it has not seemed to affect dramatically the radio paging business or cable TV, both of which also have similar local monopoly possibilities. In the case of cable TV, however, the local area franchise does bestow market power and may be more valuable than

FIGURE 4.2

U.S. Cellular Market

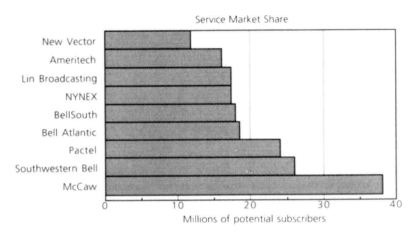

Source: *Business Week* September 21, 1987.

Equipment Market Share

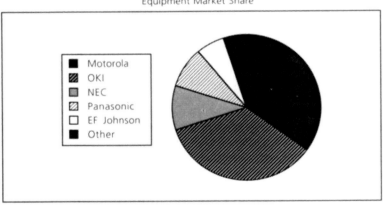

Source: *Cellular Business Magazine.*

the license for local radio spectrum use for paging and cellular service.

The cellular market at retail service and equipment level is competitive, and cellular telephone prices continue to plummet. The wholesale market, however, is not competitive due to local duopolies in spectrum. This probably explains why retail service prices have not fallen significantly. Until this duopoly situation is changed, regulation is necessary.

Public telephone service has also been a very high-growth market since divestiture, with some locales experiencing stiff competition in public telephone sets and services. But information on prices and service is confusing or nonexistent, and although such problems will likely be alleviated eventually, for now, reduced regulation and lack of good consumer information has in fact often resulted in *higher* market prices. However, this does not necessarily mean monopoly profits, as cost structures are not known and the present market may reflect the fact that old prices were set too low. On the other hand, it could be an indication that deregulation has allowed premises owners to garner local monopoly rents where demand is very price inelastic.

Table 4.17 provides estimates of sales and market share data for customer owned coin operated telephones (COCOTs) and public telephone services. This COCOT part of the market is very competitive since the only real monopoly power lies with the owners of the locations the COCOT vendor desires to use. Of course, there is no data on these local monopoly rents, and in the absence of good regulatory solutions, recent calls for broad reregulation should be viewed with caution. The FCC has proposed requiring COCOT vendors to inform customers of rates and charges for COCOT services, and such minor regulations may be appropriate.

A very important market segment is Alternative Operator Services (AOS), which for the first time competes with telco operators. By 1989,

TABLE 4.17
Public Pay Phone Vendors Market Data (1988)

Pay Phone Vendors	Market Share Estimates (units)
Segments	Approx. % Share (units)
BOCS	80%
Independent Telcos	10
Private	9
	(range is 5 to 15%, depending on region)
AT&T	1
Total number of units: approx. 2 million	

Source: Telecom Services, Inc.

AOS sales were $800 million, or almost 9 percent of the total market for operator services.[17] This also appears to be a very competitive influence and as it develops will provide a ready alternative and some discipline to the AT&T and LEC operator services markets.

The partially deregulated COCOT and AOS markets, while competitive in many aspects, will not be able to be completely deregulated for reasons of emergency service and potential for local monopoly abuse. However, we know of no existing proposals for reregulation that are worth implementing, and prefer the current approach of minimum residual regulation.

The market for information services broadly defined includes such services as facsimile, E-mail, paging, audiotext, videotext, computing, electronic publishing, database, transaction services, and the like.[18] By all accounts, information services' growth potential is enormous and regulatory initiatives such as ONA and the recent MFJ court ruling allowing BOCs to provide gateways for other vendors will significantly stimulate demand. The "market" and its subcomponents is quite competitive, usually featuring many suppliers and price competition. What remains limited is ubiquitous distribution networks and this is where the LECs can help. For now, BOCs are not allowed directly to provide information services as they enjoy a competitive advantage owing to their ubiquitous distribution network. This restriction should eventually be lifted when alternative distribution networks develop and LEC interconnection becomes easy and open under the new ONA guidelines.

Until the Nirvana of competition arrives, there are certain principles for "good" residual regulation, including nondiscriminatory access, unbundling of services and nondiscriminatory pricing rules. Wherever noncompetitive elements remain in telecom markets, they are either because of bottleneck facilities or because of regulation. Those competitors who lease facilities from the bottleneck providers (be these thin interexchange markets or thick local markets) require nondiscriminatory unbundling to effectuate competition. Of course nondiscrimination and interconnection is ultimately a two-way street. As competition increases to the point where alternatives for LEC facilities become available, market forces should increasingly be relied on, and asymmetric rules favoring new competitors should be relaxed.

Stanford L. Levin

Perfect competition exists primarily in textbooks and perhaps a few isolated markets. Economists have long sought to define "workable" or "effective" competition to describe markets which are generally competitive but which do not meet the strict definition of perfect competition. While these terms now often have unfavorable connotations, and have been used and abused in reference to telecommunications regulation, the necessity for such a definition remains.

A definition of effective competition must focus on competitive behavior; if the structural conditions for perfect competition were met, there would not be a problem. Thus, the distinction between competitive behavior and competitive structure is particularly relevant for telecommunications.

This is not to say that structural characteristics such as the number of sellers, the degree of product differentiation and market growth have no place in such a definition. However, other characteristics, including the independence of the sellers, responses to competitive actions, the lack of collusion, and the presence of systematic predatory pricing are, in practice, more likely to be the determinants. "The basic characteristic of effective competition is that no one seller (or group of sellers) has the power to choose its level of profits by giving less and charging more. In workable competition, this power is kept in check by rival sellers offering or threatening to offer effective inducements."[19]

It is also important to consider the extent of competitive supply for a particular service. For example, if competitors could absorb much or all of the market demand, it is much less likely that any firm would have a significant ability to increase price, even if market share and other variables might suggest otherwise.

This type of behavioral approach has two major advantages. First, it uses broadly based determinants of competition. It is not necessary to rely solely on one or two measures, such as market share or concentration. The competitive evaluation is based on a wide range of indicators, including structural measures, but also incorporates entry, other firms providing competitive goods or services, and observed behavior.

Second, this analytical approach eliminates the need to draw definite industry boundaries, something that takes up much energy and is often not truly resolved in most antitrust analysis. This behavioral approach focuses on competitive conditions for a particular good or service. It directly and indirectly incorporates all other products or services which may be in competition and considers how firms interact with each other while focusing on the ultimate behavior of the firms. Such an approach makes the analysis both simpler and more complete, considering what is directly at issue: whether a particular product or service is sold under effectively competitive conditions. A market definition, in the antitrust sense, is therefore not required, and the term "market," used here for convenience, does not have the antitrust meaning.

In addition, this approach also permits the behavior of markets which are not regulated to be included in the evaluation. For example, cellular service in some jurisdictions is deregulated, while it is subject to full regulation in others. If the markets where cellular service is deregulated exhibit competitive behavior, this must be of major importance in the evaluation. Based on structural or even other behavioral criteria, a preliminary evaluation that the cellular market is not effectively competitive would have to be reassessed if the market is, in fact, exhibiting competitive behavior when it is not regulated.

Evaluating competition means, in part, evaluating pricing in various telecommunications markets. If markets are effectively competitive, pricing should be similar to pricing in comparable competitive markets. For telecommunications, this requires an understanding of pricing by firms producing multiple products and incurring joint and common costs. Among the many intraLATA telecommunications services, certain ones are relatively important or sufficiently different to warrant some brief analysis. The issue is to see if these services are provided under conditions of effective competition, and if not, why not.

The lack of useful data for this analysis is striking, although upon further reflection it is not surprising. For those services that have become significantly more competitive since divestiture, six years is just long enough to begin to generate sufficient time series or cross-section data to permit analysis of post-divestiture changes. In addition, the data available, including those presented by Egan and Waverman, are often not particularly useful in assessing effective competition. For example, minutes of use data may be available to allow the calculation of "market shares" for message toll service (MTS). MTS, however, is not a good product market, as there are many other close substitutes, especially for large users. In addition, minutes of use figures, even if they pertained to an economic market, are of only limited usefulness in assessing effective competition and a much broader array of indicators should be used.

Customer premises equipment, including both telephone instruments and PBXs, was becoming increasingly competitive before divestiture; divestiture simply accelerated the trend. The market looks competitive structurally, with many sellers and frequent entry and exit, as well as behaviorally, with strong price competition and falling prices over time. Customers are offered a wider range of choice and more sophisticated products at lower prices than before divestiture. Given the international nature of much of the CPE market, suppliers can easily shift capacity and products to the U.S., greatly limiting the ability of any one firm to affect price. The provision of CPE also illustrates very clearly the importance of the customer being able to change equipment at relatively low cost, with almost universal compatibility.

After some initial concern caused by customer confusion and equipment problems, the CPE market has more or less vanished from public concern. There is little interest in generating data, and customers simply take the market, with its wide array of products, for granted. There is no evidence that customers view this market any differently than any other nontelecommunications market with a substantial degree of competition. The CPE market appears to be effectively competitive with the predicted consequences.

The situation for private networks is similar to that for CPE. There are many potential providers of these networks, including many of the major telecommunications companies. Because of the private nature of the market, little in the way of data is available. At the same time, customers are free to choose between regulated services and their own networks. Customers approach private networks much as they do any other service purchased in a competitive market, and, as for CPE, the lack of concern suggests that this market is working just as an effectively competitive market should.

Cellular telecommunications is provided by not more than two companies in each major metropolitan area. It is an example, however, of how resale, plus what appears to be fairly elastic demand for a service with many broad alternatives, is delivering effective competition through competitive behavior. There were some start-up service quality problems, which sometimes linger, but this is not surprising for a rapidly growing business based on new technology. More importantly, these service quality problems are not the result of an indifferent monopoly provider, and all providers are sensitive to complaints and appear to be working hard to improve quality.

Cellular providers seem to compete aggressively on price to build customer bases. Not only have equipment prices declined substantially in the past five years, but usage prices are stable or declining. Profits are not yet widespread, in spite of large investments. All of this suggests an aggressively competitive market.[20]

In some markets cellular service is regulated and in others it is not.

While data have not yet been generated to compare these two types of markets, one future research project will no doubt examine whether continued regulation has improved or hindered behavior and performance in the cellular market.

The philosophy behind pay telephone competition is that it should provide for more phones, sometimes in areas not served by a monopoly provider, while competition might result in lower prices (depending on whether the pay phone services benefit from a subsidy under regulation). Customer-owned coin or pay telephones are subject to different regulation in different jurisdictions, ranging from being banned de facto in some states, to being unregulated in others. In evaluating competition, the first issue is whether these phones are allowed, and the second issue is whether the market is effectively competitive.

Even states that do not ban private pay phones create vastly different competitive conditions. For example, pay telephone service provided by Southwestern Bell in Missouri is over twice as expensive as private pay telephone service provided by Southwestern Bell in Texas. It is not surprising, therefore, that by 1989, private companies had only 200 phones in Missouri compared to 33,000 for Southwestern Bell. In contrast, Illinois' liberal approach resulted in 10,000 out of a total 77,000 pay phones in the Chicago area being privately owned.[21]

Whether private pay phone competition is sufficient to restrict price is a complex issue. Some states regulate the price that private pay phone operators may charge, usually limiting the price to that of the regulated local exchange company. Other states, such as Illinois, do not regulate the price but rely on competition. One result of this latter policy is that pay phones are available in locations that could not support them previously, but sometimes at prices that are higher than the regulated company's price.

The competitive issue is not the number of pay phone providers, since they seem to appear when regulators remove entry barriers. Rather, the problem is that many pay phone locations serve customers with relatively inelastic demand, thus conferring to the owner of the pay phone or to the owner of the location some ability to increase prices in these locations. This is generally accomplished by raising prices and paying larger commissions to the location owner. While some providers charge lower prices, the problem is with those who charge higher prices. To some extent, this problem may be transitory, as customers begin to understand the situation and avoid higher-priced private pay phones. At the same time, the location owners may find that the extra revenues are more than offset by poor customer relations. If location issues can be dealt with satisfactorily, and regulatory restriction and pricing basis in the form of local exchange carriers are eliminated, there can probably be effective competition in pay telephone.

Centrex is an example of a service subject to strong competition from PBXs primarily, as well as other standard business access offerings. Once declared dead, Centrex has found new life, usually with reduced prices and less regulation. The market shows all the signs of effective competition, and as with cellular service, a good research project would be a comparison of Centrex services in states with more and with less regulation.

Other central office based services with good substitutes, such as speed dialing and voice messaging, look like Centrex. Still others, such as call waiting, appear to have poorer substitutes for most non-business customers. Regulators, however, have used such services in many cases to exact substantial subsidies to support local service. While the market for these services may not be effectively competitive, customers would probably not fare worse than they do under regulation.

The enhanced services market is too small and too regulated to allow any clear competitive evaluation at this time. While there seems to be little inherent impediment to an effectively competitive market, demand for these services is still low in most areas. It does not seem to be easy to enter, however, although the lack of competition due to low demand makes it difficult to draw conclusions on pricing.

One major difficulty for enhanced service providers is that they are dealing, usually under regulated tariffs, with local exchange telephone companies who may, in some cases, also be competitors. On the other hand, MFJ restrictions may prevent local exchange companies from entering some segments of this market. Intuitively, this market should be effectively competitive as it matures. This will require working out, perhaps through Open Network Architecture, some method of allowing competition and service provision between local exchange companies and enhanced service providers. At the same time, the market will need to grow to provide a true test of effective competition.

It is helpful in analyzing the interexchange market to revert to the pre-divestiture perspective of long distance. While divestiture has created artificial LATA boundaries and has perpetuated equally artificial state boundaries, the regulatory treatment in these various jurisdictions has been different, allowing some useful conclusions about competitive behavior. In one of the few empirical studies to quantify the results of pricing flexibility, Mathios and Rogers found that flexible state regulation resulted in lower intrastate interLATA toll rates than rate-base regulation.[22] These states have experienced entry by a variety of companies, and the Mathios and Rogers study confirms the appropriateness of considering competitive behavior rather than structure, as AT&T often still retains a significant market share of some (perhaps economically meaningless) markets.

In those states which do not provide pricing flexibility, the markets are not effectively competitive. Indeed, even in those states with pricing flexibility, there may still be regulatory restrictions on entry, reporting requirements, or pricing bands which inhibit competition. The evidence to date, both from the Mathios and Rogers study and from more anecdotal sources, suggests that in the absence of regulatory and MFJ restrictions, the interLATA intrastate toll market would be effectively competitive.

In an update of their study, Mathios and Rogers extend their analysis to the intraLATA toll market.[23] They find that in states allowing toll competition, including competition from resellers, rates are 7 to 10 percent lower than in the more restrictive states. Once again, this study, along with other anecdotal evidence, confirms the intraLATA market may be effectively competitive. In states where it is not, regulatory barriers may be the reason. The elasticity of supply is important here, as it is with interLATA toll. Competitors have the capacity to handle a large portion of the toll business, severely restricting any one firm's ability to increase price. This is particularly true for large customers, where any "one-plus" advantages are less important.

The interLATA interstate market is controlled by the FCC's policy of dominant firm regulation, where entry is relatively free and prices for all but AT&T are not regulated. AT&T's prices, however, have been subject to traditional rate of return regulation, with a recent partial switch to price cap regulation. This regulatory interference prevents any judgment on effective competition from directly observing the interstate market. However, since competition seems to be working in markets which are smaller and perhaps inherently less competitive than the interstate market, including competition based to a great extent on resale in the intraLATA market, a reasonable tentative conclusion from state experience is that the interstate market would be effectively competitive in the absence of regulation. Certainly, the limited useful data available do not support claims of natural monopoly in toll. In any case, the natural monopoly hypothesis can only be confirmed by allowing competition to function unhindered by regulation.

There is little competition for local exchange services. This may be for two reasons. First, some local exchange services, particularly residential access, have been priced significantly below most measures of cost in most jurisdictions. Unless prospective costs for new entrants are sufficiently below historical costs, entry will be unlikely, even if it were allowed. Second, it is possible that some aspects of the local exchange exhibit the cost characteristics of a natural monopoly, although this is difficult to confirm without a market test. In addition, most regulatory jurisdictions provide regulatory barriers to competition, creating or enhancing the bottleneck control of the local exchange carrier.

There are, however, several states that allow some types of local exchange competition. Few are as open as Illinois, but New York, Washington, D.C., and other cities as well as Chicago, do have some local exchange competition. This tends to focus on large customers in areas where regulated tariffs are probably not significantly below cost. What is surprising is not the dearth of local exchange competition but that there is any at all, given the typical regulatory hurdles. While there are not any effectively competitive local exchange services today, there could be some in the future if regulatory restrictions are relaxed.

Some of the customer disappointment about post-divestiture telecommunications may be a result of continued regulation and court restrictions and not a result of a failure of competition to deliver what it promised. Indeed, in the toll market, for example, competition, when allowed, does seem to fulfill its promise. In a related effect, continued regulatory and court oversight seems to siphon competitive energies into regulatory and legal battles. Competitors often suggest, directly or indirectly, that if they do not get all of the business, or that if the local exchange carrier or AT&T gets any business, somehow the market is not competitive. Removing regulation when appropriate will channel energies into a more productive competitive arena, benefiting consumers by helping to achieve an effectively competitive market.

In many markets, the single biggest impediment to effective competition may be regulation, and in some of those markets there is already evidence to suggest a move to reduce or eliminate regulation would carry little risk. Appropriate policy, however, would not deregulate until other constraints are substantially eliminated. Other services, including local exchange access, for example, are not at this time effectively competitive. In these markets appropriate policy might include alternative forms of regulation but probably not deregulation.

Lee L. Selwyn

Divestiture is unquestionably the seminal telecommunications *policy* event in our generation, but divestiture did not create, nor is it now creating, a "competitive" market except in limited industry segments. Like the sorcerer's apprentice who chopped the enchanted broomstick into many pieces only to discover that each was possessed with all of the power of the single prototype, the breakup of the Bell System into seven regional offspring served only to create seven monopolies where there had been but one. Moreover, while there has been much attention on the seminal *policy* event, the seminal *technological* events—the development of ultra high capacity fiber optic transmission systems, digital switching, and common network control systems—so increase the economic scale of local exchange carrier network architecture that over time industry concentration cannot help but increase.

It is in this context that efforts to "prove" the presence of "effective competition" must be evaluated. To their credit, Egan and Waverman do not themselves advance a definition of "competition markets," but nevertheless either assert its existence based upon their interpretations of broad trends or, worse, seek to explain its failure to develop in certain market segments on the basis of regulatory intransigence. Sandford Levin speaks of "workable" or "effective" competition as describing "markets which are generally competitive but which do not meet the strict definition of perfect competition." One cannot help but agree that it would be overreaching to require the "perfect competition" academic market model be shown to exist before deregulation could be considered. But the fact that there is no formal academic model to describe the economic structure of the telecommunications network services marketplace cannot justify the adoption of vague notions of "generally competitive" in formulating tests of market condition. Levin seems to settle on a traditional antitrust definition of "effective competition"—"the ability of a firm to increase prices." By examining price movements over the post-divestiture years, Levin argues, it should be possible to see whether or not "effective competition" has actually become a reality.

Of course, even assuming one had *good* data upon which to apply Levin's "pricing behavior" standard, the test would be valid *if and only if* all of the *apparent* pricing changes could be attributed to the development and presence of "effective competition" as opposed to some other explanatory factor(s). Yet while Levin discusses pricing behavior and other conditions extant in a number of industry segments, he fails entirely to establish a nexus between perceived pricing behavior of individual suppliers and the actual competitive condition of the marketplace. Egan and Waverman fall into this same trap as well.

Efforts to assess the degree of effective competition in the inter- and intraLATA long-distance markets on the basis of pricing behavior require a more extensive examination of price changes than is implicit in Levin's discussion. And Egan and Waverman, for their part, seem to ignore price changes altogether in drawing conclusions from the data they have assembled.[24] For one, the level of dominant carrier rates is far more heavily influenced by regulatory action than by any competitive pressures. The 40 percent-plus reductions in interstate MTS rates cited in both the Levin and Egan and Waverman papers *is not attributable either to the divestiture or to the entry of "competition" per se;* it is instead the direct result of shifting to Subscriber Line Charges and of the Commission's requirement that the dominant interexchange carrier—AT&T—pass through all reductions in carrier access charges to end users of its toll services.[25]

Differences in intrastate toll rate levels are far more attributable to state access charge and overall rate design policy than to the presence (or lack thereof) of competition. California and New York each have little or no intraLATA toll competition, even though rates in the two jurisdictions are at virtually opposite ends of the spectrum: California has high intraLATA toll rates but prohibits intraLATA competition, while New York, in which LATA competition has been allowed for many years, has some of the lowest intraLATA usage charges in the country pursuant to a Public Service Commission policy initiative that began as far back as the mid-1970s.[26]

While it may generally be correct that MTS rates are lower in states which allow toll competition, it is probably incorrect to attribute that pricing condition to the presence of competition itself. States which have examined intraLATA competition policies have recognized that competitive entry requires a realignment of toll and access charges, so as to eliminate the uneconomic pricing practice of loading non-traffic-sensitive cost recovery and other unrelated cost burdens onto toll usage charges. Toll rates are indeed lower in states that allow toll competition, not because of the presence of competition per se, but because the regulatory agencies in those jurisdictions have affirmatively realigned dominant carrier rate levels precisely to achieve this result.

Both Egan and Waverman and Levin correctly observe there is little competition in the provision of basic local exchange network access. Levin seeks to explain this condition not in terms of the pervasive scale and scope economies which exist—and which are increasing in magnitude—in the local network infrastructure, but by the suggestion that competition has failed to develop because local exchange services have traditionally been underpriced. Egan and Waverman similarly dismiss the possibility of fundamental economic and technological impediments to competition at the local exchange level, instead holding regulators responsible for this condition: "The lack of competition at the state and local level is due to many factors, the primary one being regulatory policies which do not encourage entry." But in the same paragraph Egan and Waverman seem to change their position completely: "While most states do not grant exclusive certificates of necessity and convenience [sic] to the incumbent LEC, entry barriers in terms of up-front sunk costs with assets fixed and immobile, and very high business risk for new entrants with no large customer base or cash flow."

Surely Egan and Waverman are not "blaming" regulators for high up-front sunk costs of immobile assets or for the fact that start-up firms (by definition) do not have a customer base? It is, of course, these very natural monopoly conditions—the enormous investment in the basic LEC infrastructure, immobile assets, high entry barriers, the captive LEC customer base—that accounts for the lack of effective competition in the local exchange. And these conditions are all *permanent* fixtures that will not erode with time. Indeed, as the scale of modern digital and fiber optic technology grows, the likelihood of effective entry by a start-up competitor becomes even more illusory.

Even in those jurisdictions in which entry into the market for local exchange services has been permitted—e.g., New York, Chicago—actual penetration is minimal, and has had little, if any, perceptible financial impact upon the dominant local exchange monopoly. The lack of growth in LEC revenues since 1984 cited by Egan and Waverman is not the result of "competition" eroding their markets, but is instead a compelling demonstration of the effectiveness of rate-of-return regulation in reflecting the increasing asset productivity on the part of the LECs in prices for LEC monopoly services. While geographically specialized metropolitan fiber optic networks, such as New York Teleport, and other *niche market* providers may continue to expand, the LECs have already demonstrated sufficient softness in the pricing of their own high-capacity digital services that the financial attractiveness of the fringe competitors' services, vis-a-vis those offered by the LECs, can only fade.

Egan and Waverman contend the market for business access services is competitive. They suggest large users have the ability to obtain access services from sources other than the LECs. The inability of Egan and Waverman to obtain any solid data source on private bypass is not, as they seem to believe, the result of an unorganized marketplace. It is instead directly attributable to the fact the type of "bypass" they believe to be so rampant is, in reality, virtually nonexistent. The reason, of course, is that the capital investment and recurring operating costs associated with a dedicated, customer-provided access arrangement are no match for the substantially lower costs of providing equivalent capacity on a common carrier network. This is especially true when modern fiber optic transmission technology, with its high fixed costs and almost insignificant variable costs, is involved.

Both Egan and Waverman and Levin are clearly correct in stating the CPE segment of the telecommunications marketplace has become competitive. But in reaching that generally undisputed conclusion, they ignore what is perhaps the key element in achieving effective competition in this industry segment—the unbundling of CPE from the monopoly local network access "bottleneck." That unbundling, of course, had nothing in particular to do with divestiture; the FCC had started down this policy path more than a decade earlier. If we want to achieve increased competition in other market segments—e.g., enhanced services and long-distance—we should not forget what the CPE experience has taught.

Interestingly, despite the dramatic drop in AT&T/BOC market shares from their near-100 percent level at the beginning of this decade, the CPE market has been through its "shake out" and appears to have come to rest at a fairly concentrated state. Gone are the "mom and pop" "interconnect" vendors or small, specialized PBX and key system manufacturers; return the BOCs and AT&T. Another factor in the future CPE marketplace is the reemergence of Centrex as an economically viable alternative to customer premises systems. Loaded with advanced digital switching features coupled with the advantages of flexibility, turnkey operation, and often highly aggressive pricing, Centrex and Centrex-like services could become a formidable competitor to future CPE sales. Moreover, BOC reentry into the Centrex market may provide further incentives to exert market power over "bottleneck" services required for CPE alternatives, services such as PBX trunks and direct inward dialing.

Levin asserts: "The situation for private networks is similar to that for customer premise [sic] equipment." This claim is not supported by any empirical evidence, and in point of fact is patently false. Even at the interLATA level, which is arguably the most competitive of the network services markets, AT&T retains an overwhelming market share. Because it maintains twice as many analog and three times as many digital points of presence as MCI, its nearest competitor, AT&T is uniquely able to offer private network customers ubiquitous coverage on a far more efficient basis than any of its rivals. At the intraLATA level, most so-called "private networks" are actually constructed out of private line and special access services or leased fiber optic facilities furnished *by the very LECs with whose services Levin believes these networks compete!* Moreover, having posited a "pricing behavior" test, Levin ignores the pervasive strategic pricing and market management practices of the LECs with respect to "private network" services; if the private network marketplace were "similar to that for CPE," competition would force the *price* relationships between analog and digital services, and between single voice channel and high capacity services to cost. The LECs' ability to keep the apparent break-even point well above the *technological* relationship belies Levin's overly simplistic "explanation" of the condition of this market segment.

In discussing the state of competition in cellular, Levin concludes that the presence of two cellular carriers plus resellers in each market, together with a relatively elastic demand, "is delivering effective competition through competitive behavior." He observes (without actually citing any data), "Cellular providers seem to compete aggressively on price to build customer bases. Not only have equipment prices declined substantially in the past five years, but usage prices are stable or declining." In point of fact, there have been *hardly any* price reductions or price competition for cellular *service;* the price decreases that have occurred have come exclusively in *cellular telephones.* Indeed, under Levin's behavioral approach to assessing the degree of competition in a market, one would be forced to conclude there is virtually no effective competition in the provision of cellular service, as evidenced by the enormous difference in price movements between the undeniably competitive cellular telephone equipment market and the profit-maximizing duopoly structure that was created by the FCC. What has occurred in the five years since divestiture has been an unprecedented run-up in the market value of cellular *franchises.*

The decision to open private pay phones and operator services to competitive entry can only be described as "a solution in search of a problem." The fundamental monopoly character of these services is not altered by multiple supplier entry, because, as Levin correctly notes, the public utility monopoly is simply replaced by local monopolies under the control of the owner of the property (such as a hotel or airport terminal) on which the pay phone or access to the operator service is provided. Prices to consumers have not fallen; they have increased. And the availability to consumers of information as to the prices and options offered by pay phone and AOS suppliers—clearly an essential attribute of a competitive marketplace—is minimal to nonexistent. The jury is clearly still out on this experiment with "competition," but one may easily conclude, on the basis of actual pricing behavior, that nothing remotely close to "effective competition" has emerged as of this point in time.

Nina Cornell

The discussions of Bruce Egan and Leonard Waverman and of Stanford Levin attempt to utilize standard economic principles to consider the state of competition in a number of telecommunications services. Both examinations, however, suffer from the failure to analyze the effect on competition of that which is unique to competition or potential competition in telecommunications—the bottleneck monopoly enjoyed by the local exchange companies. This omission is somewhat surprising in a volume about divestiture, for it was the bottleneck monopoly over the local exchange that resulted in such a drastic remedy as divestiture to solve the antitrust problems. As both presentations comment in places about whether the restrictions that accompanied divestiture are still warranted, the omission of any analysis of this issue is even more startling.

Egan and Waverman do list some steps needed to try to ensure that local exchange companies do not use their bottleneck monopoly to erect barriers to entry. But nowhere do they show why these steps are needed. Because Egan and Waverman present a large amount of data, most of my comments will focus on them. The conclusions about how to analyze competitiveness in these markets and the necessary regulatory changes needed, however, apply equally to Levin.

The local exchange companies have been and remain the only source of switched interconnection with end users of telecommunications services. Although some large users may route certain services, at least in part, past the local exchange carrier by using a bulk connection between two points, no customer can avoid the local exchange carrier when local switching is required. Moreover, even this ability of a small number of customers (although potentially a large share of total traffic) to sidestep the local exchange carrier is limited in a number of ways. First, no customer has yet been able to avoid the local exchange carrier completely, but can only move some of its telecommunications usage to a bulk facility. Second, even for bulk facilities, not all locations can be served by any carrier but the local exchange carrier, because of very high costs of obtaining the necessary rights of way. This is especially a problem in some cities, where the majority of large users are found.

Finally, in a number of those locations where alternative providers could offer the end user substitute bulk facilities, the alternative provider often must use the conduits or other right-of-way structures of the local exchange carrier. This opens the important and largely unaddressed issue of the local exchange carrier's price for use of its right of way, relative to the price for use of its bulk facilities.

The question of pricing by the local exchange companies for use of their bottleneck monopoly facilities is not limited to the pricing of the use of their right-of-way structures relative to the pricing of their own bulk facilities. In fact, today, most local exchange companies are not required to use nondiscriminatory pricing for virtually any of their offerings to potential competitors relative to their own "competing" services. Not only are they not required to do so, but on those occasions when I have been able to examine a local exchange company's cost data, I have found that local exchange companies rarely pay the same amount as their potential competitors for the bottleneck elements.[27] Most often, the local exchange company implicitly pays itself less for these elements, at least for the services offered to customers who might be the most likely first target for potential competitors.

The existence of the local exchange companies' bottleneck monopoly and the absence, at least so far, of serious regulatory constraints on discriminatory and unduly bundled pricing raise very strong issues of barriers to entry and exit. Unfortunately, Levin essentially ignores these issues entirely. Egan and Waverman do touch upon the bottleneck question, and they call for nondiscriminatory access, unbundling, and nondiscriminatory pricing of access. All of these are essential and are needed now, regardless of later deregulation, if telecommunications markets are to achieve their potential in terms of technological development and expanded services. But Egan and Waverman do not appear to have a genuine appreciation of the extent to which the local exchange carriers are failing to follow these principles, or how large the task will be to change that outcome. As a result, Egan and Waverman's conclusions about the competition facing specific services are almost always wrong, and their suggestions for regulatory treatment for those services would likely lead to substantial abuse of monopoly power. This can be best illustrated by looking at some of the analyses they provide of particular service offerings.

In reference to STS, Egan and Waverman conclude those who initially entered this market failed to judge correctly the potential for profitable operation given the "environment." The implication is that the major cause of the failure of this industry segment was lack of tenant interest. In fact, it was the local exchange company regulatory litigation which changed almost completely the potential of the STS market. The original premise of STS was that the tenants of a building would share a PBX or similar device, and as a result would economize on the number of lines needed to the central office; calls between and among tenants would be switched at the shared PBX. But this plan was allowed in only a very few places, and local exchange companies won regulatory rules permitting them to force possible major inefficiencies into the intended offerings. They were able to achieve such victories in essence because of their control over the bottleneck monopoly of the local exchange. In the process, nondiscrimination lost. It is hard to understand why a corporation is allowed to "share" a PBX among its employees, but separate tenants within a building, who collectively have the same amount of traffic as that corporation, are not.

Egan and Waverman are perhaps the most flawed in their discussion of access. They reach the surprising conclusion that the access market is effectively competitive—indeed, according to them, "uniquely competitive for large users." They base their claim of competitiveness on two factors: the trend in access revenues, relative to the trend in other revenues of the local exchange carriers; and the growth in so-called "bypass."[28]

The trend in access revenues in Egan and Waverman's table 4.1 does indeed show that access revenues rose in 1985, fell sharply in 1986, fell slightly more in 1987, then rose in 1988 to slightly above 1984 levels. However, to conclude that the trend must be due to competition ignores the data shown in table 4.1 on growth in access usage, and further evidence of the precipitous decline in access charges. Using their data on the revenues and price movements in access confirms their data on the growth in minutes of use of access shown in table 4.1: it has been one of the fastest growing services of the local exchange companies. The decline in the price of access, however, has been even more rapid. Moreover, access growth has been greater than toll growth. If the revenue trends were due to a large increase in access substitutes, it should be reflected by growth in toll volumes exceeding the volume of access usage. That the numbers show the opposite demonstrates the *lack* of competition in access.

The other pillar of support for their conclusion is growth in "bypass." "Bypass" only becomes significant if it is interpreted to include several lines provided by the local exchange carriers themselves, namely local exchange private lines, special access facilities (the tariff term for local exchange company-provided bulk facilities that do not use the local exchange switch), and cellular radio usage. But to include such services as part of "bypass" renders the terms meaningless from a policy perspective for two reasons. First, some of the use of these services is not a substitute for use of switched network. Private line and special access facilities are sometimes used as a substitute for switched services, but they are also often used to carry types of traffic that cannot pass over the switched network. Cellular radio usage is only occasionally a substitute for use of the regular wireline telephone system, because much more often, cellular traffic would not exist if the cellular telephone network had not been developed.

Second, the overwhelming share of "bypass" that comes from the offerings of local exchange carriers only means that each local exchange carrier faces significant competition from itself, unless there recently has been a very sudden increase in the use of facilities not provided by the local exchange carriers to carry traffic, that could just as easily— but at a higher price to the user—have gone over the local exchange carriers' access facilities. This is far from the normal definition of competition.

In fact, access is not a service subject to competition. The authors note, "access charges represent . . . almost half of AT&T's annual operating expenses." They also imply rates are far above cost at about ten cents per minute. It is hard to believe that AT&T Communications, a large and sophisticated company, would not have moved massively away from local exchange company-provided access if competitive substitutes at lower prices were available for such a large element of its costs! Clearly, the evidence in the marketplace itself speaks eloquently to the absence of effective substitutes for access, particularly switched access. Without effective substitutes, there is no effective competition. Unlike some of the other services discussed, moreover, there is not a set of regulations which, if imposed on the local exchange company, would significantly change this conclusion, at least not in the near or middle term. Requiring nondiscriminatory pricing of the use of local exchange companies' right-of-way structures could increase actual competition for bulk transport facilities. Switched access services, however, are squarely part of the heart of the bottleneck monopolies of the local exchange companies.

Finally, although Egan and Waverman talk only about access as it relates to the interLATA market, access is also used by toll carriers in the intraLATA market. In the intraLATA arena, not only is access part of the bottleneck monopoly, but the local exchange carriers discriminate against their potential toll competitors both in terms of price and quality. Local exchange carriers have almost universally retained a monopoly on the ability to offer most customers "1 + dialing."

Egan and Waverman conclude that all forms of customer premises equipment are sold in very competitive markets, and, to quote them, "it is hard to envision a freely operating CPE market returning to a monopolistic structure, and therefore we believe any residual regulation is probably unnecessary." It is accurate that among the manufacturers of customer premises equipment, competition is vigorous. This is not the end of the story, however. In their discussion of customer premise equipment, particularly their discussion of Centrex-type services,[29] the authors ignore the fact the local exchange companies not only *do* have the ability to predate against other suppliers, but are actually doing so now with regulatory blessing. They do so by charging very different rates for the bottleneck monopoly local exchange wires that physically link customers with the central office. A customer who subscribes to a Centrex-type service pays far less for each wire than does a customer who uses a PBX.

Rates for PBX trunks in some jurisdictions can be as much as twenty times or more the rate per wire charged for "intercommunications lines," one of the tariff terms for at least some of the wires used by Centrex-type services. The result of this price discrimination has been the comeback for these services, as Egan and Waverman note.

The price discrimination that has permitted the rejuvenation of these services in the market is even more chilling in light of what the authors note is the possibility that Centrex-type services may be "a way for business customers to obtain digital service and ISDN, and this could develop into a market advantage for LECs." The current ONA regulations have not eliminated tariff restrictions that limit the availability of certain tariffs to certain kinds of users. As long as the local exchange carriers are allowed to decide which users get favorably low and which get unfavorably high rates for identical functions, they have a very powerful ability to predate, contrary to Egan and Waverman's claims. Such price discrimination is a barrier to effective competition.

Even more ominous would be the entry into manufacturing by the RHCs under the present circumstances. Clearly, for these markets to support competition as vigorous as it might be, the present pattern of differing prices for lines depending upon the type of terminal equipment or depending upon which vendors' intercommunications service is used must end. Such a change, however, will not come easily. The present pattern of discriminatory local exchange rates, particularly business local exchange rates, has been sanctioned for years, and regulators do not see the full importance of change.[30]

Egan and Waverman do not give a consistent analysis of the competitiveness of public telephone service. At one point in their discussion, they claim it is basically a competitive service subject to reduced regulation, and at another point a service subject to reregulation.

As the authors note, entry by private pay telephone service providers has been somewhat of a mixed blessing for consumers to date, and in a number of cases, the rates charged by the private payphone operators are higher than those of the local exchange companies. The authors seem to believe the cause for this may be monopoly power by premise owners.

Although premise owners may have significant market power, there is another reason for the higher prices by private payphone operators: price squeezes they are under from the local exchange company. In those states where I have been able to examine relevant data, local exchange companies charge private pay phone providers more for the lines to, and for minutes of use of the local exchange network, than they charge users of their own pay phones. Perhaps the most blatant example is in Massachusetts, where NET has been constrained for years to charge ten cents per local call over its payphones, while it charges private payphone vendors eleven cents per "message"—and many local calls consist of more than one "message." If a price squeeze as obvious as that in Massachusetts is hard to eliminate, it does not bode well for the attainment of nondiscriminatory access and pricing alluded to by Egan and Waverman.

Egan and Waverman apparently define "Nirvana" as competition everywhere, and perhaps the adoption by regulators of their suggestions for individual markets. Contrary to their belief, however, the requirements of nondiscriminatory access, unbundling of services, and nondiscriminatory pricing rules are not just needed "until the Nirvana of competition arrives," but in order to establish the conditions for competition to be given a fair market test. The implication of their argument is that adoption of these nondiscriminatory and unbundling rules will be sufficient to abolish the bottleneck monopolies of the local exchange companies. I believe closer examination of the reasons for the bottlenecks would suggest otherwise. The proposed rules are necessary to see where competitive activity could bring benefits to the public, but will not be sufficient to permit total deregulation in the foreseeable future.

Martin G. Taschdjian

The issue of the state of competition in the telecommunications industry is of more than passing academic interest. Billions of dollars rest on the outcome of public policy decisions on this subject.

Egan and Waverman have made a sterling attempt to marshal data to determine competitiveness of the various standard "markets" in telecommunications. (I continue to gag on the notion of "submarkets.") But they, like Stanford Levin, present a problematic definition of relevant markets. In both cases, the menu of products, services, technologies, and jurisdictions which they examined for competitiveness, are not markets in any sense of the word. Instead, both discussions have accepted the traditional industry definitions of markets with little or no recognition of their artificiality. Professional economists in particular should be more careful about their usage.

Egan and Waverman also confuse the markets with the players in the markets. For example, the treatment by public policymakers of interstate toll as a market separate from intrastate toll has led to much mischief. Another example is the tendency to identify the IXC "market" with AT&T. This confusion leads Egan and Waverman into logical difficulties. They conclude that the IXC market is sufficiently competitive so that the FCC price cap order is too restrictive a regulatory regime.

The implication is that the FCC is overregulating a workably competitive market. But in fact, AT&T is the only IXC subject to the price cap order. No other IXC is regulated by the FCC in any meaningful sense. So either AT&T *is* the IXC industry and is dominant, which the authors argue is not the case, or the industry is largely unregulated already. But they imply that this is not the case. Below, I propose a means of assessing the issue of level of competition more objectively.

Turning to the local exchange carrier "market," Egan and Waverman touch on the interesting phenomenon of slow growth in local service. Their conclusion about local usage per access line is corroborated in table 4.18 and raises an important point. Where has the local usage gone since divestiture?

I do not believe that growth has simply stopped. One possible answer is that before equal access, feature Group A access was counted as local usage. Alternatively, it seems the growth in local usage is being captured by entities other than the local exchange carriers.

Some candidates: (1) the dramatic penetration of PBX and key systems, documented by Egan and Waverman, has drained traffic which once used the public switched network and made it essentially internal, private traffic; (2) traffic is being captured by radio-based systems such as cellular and SMR (Specialized Mobile Radio), which offer alternatives to the local exchange; (3) some of this traffic undoubtedly is going to private systems, or to shared tenant services, LANs (local area network) and WANs (wide area network).

TABLE 4.18
Percent Change in Local Call Volume
per Access Line

	1980–1984	1984–1986
Ameritech	8.2%	0%
Bell Atlantic	3.4	0
BellSouth	2.4	2.5
NYNEX	13.3	1.1
Pacific	16.2	0
Southwest Bell	7.8	−1.1
US West	5.5	0.3
Cincinnati Bell	3.7	0.5
SNET	7.3	4.5

Source: Sonneville Associates, *Macro Analysis of Telco Enterprises,*
1988, p. 56.

Turning to Sanford Levin's paper, I find his reliance on the notion of "workable competition" flawed because it is not defined operationally. The traditional definition he adopts—a situation of rivalry or potential rivalry among suppliers—boils down to a tautology. I would offer instead a practitioner's definition which distinguishes between short-run and long-run workable competition. In the short run, a market is workably competitive when each of the vendors, faced with the marginal customer, has a roughly *equal opportunity to fail* to make the sale. Markets that seem to pass this test are CPE and private networks.[31]

In addition, there are important aspects of competition which divestiture was intended to foster that are not addressed either by Levin or Egan and Waverman. *AT&T vs IBM:* there is strong competition in the standards arena, but little in the area of goods and services. *AT&T vs LECs:* competition is a battle for customer control and who will be the "dumb pipe."

Finally, there is the serious underlying policy issue which is addressed only tangentially. "When is it appropriate to deregulate a dominant firm?" This long-run issue has not arisen in previous waves of deregulation of airlines, trucking firms, or banks, because those industries were (arguably) structurally competitive.

Current efforts at deregulation are targeted at industries which until recently had been deemed natural monopolies. The telephone industry, CATV, and electricity are examples. Under this kind of industry structure, deregulation follows a pattern of: entry permission; "greenhousing" of competition (continued regulation of the former monopolist with little or no regulation of the fringe entrants); and finally, relaxation of regulation of the (formerly) dominant firm.

It is the transition from the greenhouse stage to the deregulation stage that requires standards for decisions. The (de)regulator faces the possibility of error from two sources—what statisticians might call Type I error and Type II error.

Type I error results from regulating as a monopolist a firm which is in fact competitive. The costs associated with such error include the direct and indirect costs of regulation, as well as the foregone benefits of competition on resource allocation, innovation, etc. Type II error results from deregulating a firm which is in fact noncompetitive. The costs here are from two sources: first, the welfare losses resulting from any predation by the dominant firm as it seeks to drive out competitors; second, welfare losses due to monopoly pricing by a now-unregulated monopolist.

In general, the costs of Type I error are likely to be less than the costs of Type II error because of differences in reversibility conditions. It is probably easier to deregulate a firm that is competitive than to re-regulate once deregulation has been accomplished. The type of cost/benefit analysis needed parallels that of building a dam in a scenic area. One can build the dam later, but once built, the area can never be recovered and the costs of tearing down the dam are high.

It is important therefore that the decision to deregulate a dominant firm be done only after careful analysis, not willy-nilly or on the basis of uninformed "theology." There are two questions which a regulator pondering a deregulation of a dominant firm must answer: if I deregulate, will the firm raise its prices to the monopoly level? If I deregulate, will the firm use its market power in less competitive segments of the marketplace to cross-subsidize and exclude competitors in other segments?

In a 1981 article, Landes and Posner derive a formula which can be extended to answer the first question.[32] The Landes and Posner formula cannot directly answer the second question. But if the answer to either question is yes, deregulation would be undesirable. Therefore, passing the Landes and Posner test is a necessary but not sufficient condition for deregulation.

The Landes and Posner formula is:

$$L = \frac{MS_D}{e_{(D/M)} + (1 - MS_D)e_{(S/F)}}$$

where:

$$L = \frac{price - marginal\ cost}{price}$$

MS_D = Market share of the dominant firm.
$e_{(D/M)}$ = Market elasticity of demand.
$e_{(S/F)}$ = Supply elasticity of the competitive fringe.

This formula relates the Lerner index of monopoly power to market share, but has as a critical argument the elasticity of supply of the competitive fringe. The variables in the Landes and Posner formula fall into three classes:

A) Technical/policy: The left-hand variable L represents the Lerner index, which is a measure of the ability (or need) to set price above marginal cost. Traditionally, prices above marginal cost reflect market power. However, in the presence of economies of scale, some deviation of price from marginal cost is needed to satisfy the firm's break-even constraint. The extent of the needed deviation is a combination of technical and policy analysis.

On a per unit basis, to satisfy the break-even constraint, prices should exceed marginal cost by the ratio that average costs bear to marginal costs. (It is also possible to incorporate Ramsey pricing into this framework.) This can be shown to equal:

$$\frac{Average\ cost}{Marginal\ cost} = 1 + \frac{Fixed\ cost}{Variable\ cost}$$

These kinds of calculations are readily knowable.

B) Market data: In this category is the measurement of the market share of the dominant firm. While there can be great variations in this measure, there are usually "zones of reasonableness."

C) Parameters: There are two parameters in the Landes and Posner formula; the market elasticity of demand, and the supply elasticity of the competitive fringe. For a regulated dominant firm, the market elasticity is usually known, at least within some range. This is a result of regulation. When a regulated monopolist seeks to change rates, it usually must estimate the revenue effects of the rate change, and this requires a knowledge of the market demand elasticity.

More problematic is the elasticity of supply of the competitive fringe. Fringe firms tend to be very diverse in geography, accounting procedures, technology, and extent of diversification. Moreover, they usually view the type of data needed to estimate a fringe supply function as proprietary.

Nevertheless, this is a crucial parameter. A dominant firm seeking deregulation will argue that the fringe supply elasticity approaches infinity—i.e. that the market is perfectly contestable. As a consequence, deregulation can safely occur (under the standards of the question above) at a high market share.[33] Opponents of early deregulation on the other hand, will argue that the fringe elasticity approaches zero.

The extent to which market forces constrain price increases by the dominant firm is crucially dependent, therefore, on the value of the fringe supply elasticity. There are two ways of dealing with this problem.

One way is simply to try values for the fringe supply elasticity for some acceptable value of L and see whether the value that would allow deregulation at the current market share is believable. An alternative is to derive elasticity of supply under the assumptions that the competitive fringe firms are price takers and profit maximizers, and that the market clears.

The amount supplied the fringe is the difference between total market demand and the demand satisfied by the dominant firm. At the limit price (Pl), the competitive fringe sells nothing, but as the dominant firm sets a price above the limit price, the quantity supplied by the competitive fringe is represented by the difference between the market demand curve and the demand curve facing the dominant firm. We can therefore trace out a fringe supply curve which is related to the difference in the elasticity of demand of the market and the elasticity of demand of the dominant firm. Knowing the demand and supply elasticities, plus a value for L, it is possible to solve for the market share that the dominant firm should have before it could be deregulated without fear that prices would be increased.

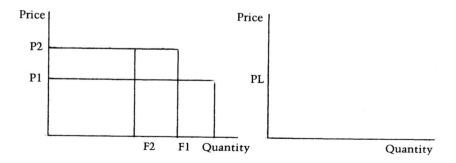

Putting this all together, the Landes-Posner formula can be written as:

$$L = \frac{MS_D}{2e_{(D,M)} - (MS_D)e_{(D,D)}}$$

Note that when a firm is a monopolist, $MS_D = 1$ and $e_{(D,M)} = e_{(D,D)}$, so the equation reduces to:

$$L = \frac{1}{e_{(D,M)}}$$

Let us develop an example of how the formula might be applied. Suppose we have a hypothetical dominant firm and market with the following price elasticities of demand:

Service	Firm Elasticity	Market Elasticity
A	−0.66	−0.2
B	−0.46	−0.2
C	−0.18	−0.1

The next piece of information needed to apply the formula is a value for the Lerner index. Estimates of this ratio of fixed costs to variable costs depend on the time horizon and the interpretation of accounting data. For illustrative purposes, if the ratio of fixed to variable costs is 0.32, the market share that warrants deregulation is as follows:

Service	L	Threshold Share	Market Elasticity	Firm Elasticity
A	.32	16%	−0.2	−.66
B	.32	15%	−0.2	−.46
C	.32	6.8%	−0.1	−.18

Given these threshold market shares, the original form of the Landes and Posner model can be used to calculate the supply elasticities of the comparative fringe firms, these are shown below:

Service	Threshold Share	Fringe Supply Elasticity
A	16%	1.39
B	15%	1.09
C	6.8%	0.42

It is clear that the fringe supply elasticity is not so high that it can act as an effective constraint on the ability of a dominant firm (defined as a firm with market share above 70 percent, according to some) to increase its prices. Moreover, these are not unreasonable numbers for an industry with high costs of entry.

This methodology can help the regulator seeking tools to assess deregulation. We leave it to public policy practitioners to apply the model and draw conclusions about (1) whether any given firm is ripe for deregulation, or (2) the form such deregulation may take.

John R. Woodbury

At the outset, one might reasonably ask why policymakers should care about the state of telecom competition. One answer might bear relation to the First Amendment: a more competitive telecommunications marketplace is likely to foster First Amendment values in the provision of information services. I think it is fair to assert that there is an apparent general belief that competition is a necessary condition for such a goal.[34] Further, there is a corresponding belief among many that competition is not sufficient, that something more is required—although that "something more" is never made clear. Nonetheless, if the market is more competitive, I presume First Amendment experts would agree the policy role for government is less intrusive than would otherwise be the case.

A second answer to the question posed is that the degree of competition tells us something about the need for various kinds of regulations. In this regard, I would amplify on a point made in passing by Egan and Waverman. In assessing how well telecommunications markets have performed since both divestiture and deregulation, a finding that some telecommunications markets are still characterized by market power does not necessarily herald the failure of deregulation. Nor does it necessarily signal the need for continued regulation. Many real-world firms likely possess some degree of market power, and an absence-of-market-power criterion would lead one to recommend the regulation of price and entry in so many more markets, that even the most ardent regulator might feel uncomfortable.

I raise this issue because I detect a sense among some authors of this volume that deregulation is only appropriate when an industry is fully competitive.[35] Among others, I detect a sense that deregulation is appropriate only if the market would be declared obviously competitive under the Justice Department's merger guidelines. But from an economic standpoint, deregulation is appropriate if consumers would be better off—or at least no worse off—than under the existing or alternative regulatory regimes. And if regulation is sufficiently costly to consumers, even the exercise of substantial market power in a deregulated environment might be a better alternative for consumers.

Equally important, regulation is not an all-or-nothing proposition, as has become particularly apparent in telecommunications; regulatory intervention can extend from less intrusive (and presumably less costly) forms such as antitrust and price caps to the more intrusive and costly rate-of-return regulation and line-of-business restrictions. The task of determining which regulatory form is appropriate requires an assessment of the costs and the benefits of each. More to the point, assessing the degree of competition in telecommunications markets can provide some information about the extent of any benefits from restraining the prevailing degree of market power. Given the costs of regulation, the more competitive the market and the better the market performs, the less likely it is that more intrusive regulation is the policy solution that best serves consumers.[36]

For markets in which product or process innovation is relatively unimportant, idealized competition is the inability of any single firm or group of firms to raise the market price above marginal costs. Because the ideal may be attainable only at great costs, the appropriate question to ask of telecommunications markets may not be how they differ from ideal competition but rather how they differ from monopoly. By contrast, in markets in which innovation is important, the industry organization that best promotes the interests of consumers may be one characterized by substantial power over price by a single firm or group of firms.[37]

Rendering even the more straightforward judgments about power over price is fraught with pitfalls on the kind of data that can be used as evidence. Unfortunately, neither the Egan and Waverman study nor the Levin analysis fares well in characterizing the empirical indices of competitive behavior. Levin devotes more space to the topic than Egan and Waverman, but in the end he leaves the reader empty-handed.[38] Advising that their purpose is to provide enough data to permit the reader to make a judgment regarding the state of competition, Egan and Waverman offer only a brief but incomplete catalog of empirical factors to consider. As a result, the probability of making a judgment error is quite high. A few examples may help to illustrate my concerns.

Levin and Egan and Waverman suggest that an industry in which prices are falling is one that is performing well, but neither ever tells us what permits that inference. Falling prices may be a consequence of process innovations that lower the costs of producing a service. As a result of the innovations, the industry can produce more of the service at a lower price. Thus, if falling prices are the result of process innovations, one might conclude that the industry in the innovation dimension was performing well (although one might reasonably ask against what benchmark one can judge that performance).

But consumer demand might be such that the primary effect of the same innovation is the release of resources to other sectors, with little change in output and price of the service in question. In that case, we presumably would not conclude industry performance was deficient even though it would fail the falling price test of Egan and Waverman and Levin. Worse yet, if the industry is characterized by service innovations, which provide consumers with better services at a higher price, the falling price test would lead one to conclude incorrectly that the industry is performing poorly. In addition, falling prices may have nothing to do with innovation, but may instead simply reflect declines in the cost of some of the inputs used to produce the service.[39]

If Levin and Egan and Waverman propose the falling price test on the assumption that beneficial deregulation should reduce prices, then the test is still flawed. What if, prior to implementing deregulation, we could have correctly predicted, for example, that CPE would be offered in a competitive market, but nonetheless that prices would rise instead of fall? Would maintenance of regulation be appropriate economic policy? If the price rise were due to artificially low prices mandated by regulation and not market power, then an increase in price would benefit consumers (although the political salability of deregulation may be reduced). If prices rise because input costs increase, we would surely not conclude that the market is performing poorly. If the postderegulation increase in price were due to market power that had been restrained by regulation, maintaining regulation may still not be the consumer welfare maximizing policy (because of the costs of regulation).[40]

Egan and Waverman also suggest that the financial performance of market participants is a useful gauge of market performance, and expend a considerable amount of space describing that performance. Yet, they fail to tell us why what is good for MCI is good for the country. In fact, good financial performance is not necessarily indicative of a well-functioning market. In unregulated markets characterized by monopoly, excess profits, which could be characterized as good financial performance, are symptomatic of that market power. In well-functioning competitive markets, financial performance depends upon the ability of the firms to satisfy consumer demands. Those firms that tend to serve those demands better do relatively better financially. In such markets, the existence of firms that are performing poorly or failing financially in and of itself has no significance for consumer welfare.[41]

Neither Egan and Waverman nor Levin provide any discussion of market definition, in either its product or geographic dimensions. Levin apparently concludes that the need for that exercise is obsolete, since one can measure directly whether firms are behaving competitively. However, he offers the reader no measurement metric, presumably because none is readily available. Egan and Waverman offer no market definition discussion, presumably because their stated purpose is to present the data so that individual readers may render their own conclusions. But they offer the reader no data upon which market judgments might be made.

For example, consider the discussion of cellular phone services. Egan and Waverman and Levin both treat cellular phone service as a separate product market, without offering the reader any reason why this might be the case. In particular, it would not be separate if a small increase in the price of the service (as opposed to the equipment) led to substantial declines in use. For example, local exchange service might be a good substitute for cellular service. Given the FCC spectrum limitation on entry, cellular providers may be mere "fringe" competitors of local exchange services. In that case, the price for cellular services would largely be dictated by the price of local exchange service and the cellular specific costs: cellular providers—even if they merged—would remain price takers rather than price makers. No price or even antitrust regulation of cellular would be required, except perhaps to prevent the local exchange from acquiring any of the cellular licenses. The acquisition of cellular licenses by local telcos is something the FCC in its wisdom not only permitted, but encouraged as a matter of policy.

It may well be that cellular services are in a distinct product market: a small increase in the price of cellular service may not result in a substantial decline in the use of cellular. But one reason for the existence of a distinct cellular market may be regulation induced. By limiting the amount of spectrum available to cellular, the FCC guaranteed that cellular service would be artificially scarce relative to its demand. Given that scarcity and at the consequently high regulation-induced price of cellular service, few consumers view cellular as a substitute for local exchange. If the FCC instead had allocated significantly more spectrum for cellular, or better yet, had permitted entrepreneurs to purchase adjacent spectrum for cellular service, the price for cellular might have been far more competitive with local exchange service.[42] If so, cellular might have broken the local exchange monopoly, thereby permitting us to more easily do away with the MFJ.[43]

Interestingly, each study reaches different conclusions regarding the state of cellular competition, differences that highlight the significance of market definition in market power analysis. Levin asserts almost tautologically that the market is competitive because the two cellular providers "compete" with the local exchange. Egan and Waverman express concern over the fact that there are only two cellular providers per area, a concern that makes policy sense only if cellular is in a distinct market. They do stop short of recommending conventional rate-of-return regulation, but puzzle about how to make the two providers compete. If cellular providers are earning apparent excess profits, either because of market power, spectrum limitation on cellular services, or some combination of the two, the FCC could always amend the licenses of those using other nearby spectrum to permit those licenses to offer cellular. Price or other behavioral regulations are not the only possible responses to the perceived "problem."

Not surprisingly, Levin argues that the interstate long-distance services are effectively competitive, but offers little in the way of corroborating evidence. Egan and Waverman are clearly impressed with the dramatic fall in AT&T's market share since divestiture,[44] but not sufficiently impressed to recommend complete deregulation. They cite one study which concludes that in many "low-profit" markets, AT&T continues to have a market share of customers in excess of 75 percent.

First, it seems that Egan and Waverman may have fallen into the trap of concluding that deregulation is only appropriate when the market is competitive. Second, if these high share markets are indeed "low-profit" markets, the scope for the exercise of market power might be quite limited.

Third, Egan and Waverman have committed the analytical sin of inferring market power from a high share of sales or customers alone. In particular, it may well be that an unregulated AT&T would be unable to raise price for any sustained period in these "problem" markets. Other competitors might have sufficient capacity to quickly expand the amount of toll service they provide into those markets. The FCC's John Haring and Kathy Levitz have observed that AT&T has only a 40 percent share of all long-distance assets, while MCI has 29 percent; US Sprint, 18 percent; and other providers, 13 percent.[45] Indeed, one current financial concern is the growing excess capacity in the long-distance business.

When gauged by capacity, then, the share of AT&T suggests that in most markets, an unregulated AT&T may not possess excessive market power.[46] And AT&T's share seems comparable to that of other large firms—such as General Motors, IBM and Xerox—regulated only by the antitrust laws. One can only hope the twisted 1989 version of price caps foisted on the FCC and AT&T by Congressional critics will be a very temporary phenomenon.

At the dawn of airline deregulation, many economists—including myself—regarded the airline industry (and the trucking industry) as close to a real world analog of contestability as we were likely to see. As a result, anticompetitive problems were expected to be exceedingly rare. There quickly developed among policymakers, particularly at the Department of Transportation (DOT), which until 1989 had the power to disapprove airline mergers, a "don't worry, be happy" antitrust approach to the airline industry. Even as evidence began to accumulate that structure still seemed to matter for airline industry performance, a DOT official described the industry as one in which the possession of market power was technically impossible.

As a result of the "don't worry, be happy" policy, DOT approved a raft of mergers—some of which were opposed by the Department of Justice, and which likely resulted in higher fares and fewer choices for some consumers. Because of DOT's knee-jerk reliance on contestability, even in the face of contrary evidence, praise for airline deregulation has given way to clarion calls for reregulation.

Levin clearly falls into the "don't worry, be happy" mold. Although Egan and Waverman are far more substantive and cautious, they nonetheless carry a risk of avoidable policy error as a result of their failure to specify carefully their analytical optic, their inclusion of some largely irrelevant criteria in their competition assessment, and their exclusion of some relevant criteria.

I am concerned that obviously mistaken analyses will lead to consumer harm. The Levin approach would likely take us down the path followed by DOT, adopting a hands-off policy which is sure to have the effect of permitting the development of market power. As with the airline industry, deregulation will wrongly be blamed for the ills of the telecommunications industry brought on by the failure of antitrust.

If Egan and Waverman's analytic prescriptions are followed, there is no doubt some antitrust and deregulation mistakes will be made, although it is difficult to predict how serious they will be. If the mistakes are serious enough, the damage could be almost as great as that from following the Levin prescription. I would simply hope our policeymakers engage in a more careful competitive analysis of telecommunications markets before deciding whether to act, and what action to take.

ENDNOTES

1. This is not true for cellular radio as discussed later, where demand growth is exceptional but only two basic service providers exist in any regional market.

2. For a detailed account of the recent telco investment activity and the role of depreciation, see Bruce L. Egan and Lester D. Taylor, "Capital Budgeting and Technology Adoption in Telecommunications; The Case of Fiber," Center for

Telecommunications and Information Studies, Working Paper #349, Columbia University, September 1989.

3. For more detailed data on investment for individual firms since 1984, see table 2.1 in Bruce L. Egan and Leonard Waverman, "The State of Competition in U.S. Telecommunications," Center for Telecommunications and Information Studies, Working Paper #350, Columbia University, September 1989.

4. According to FCC estimates, if state-of-the-art electronic and photonic devices were used on the 1988 installed base of fiber, the network capacity would be ten times that of AT&T's pre-divestiture network. With current devices and components for transmission systems and the amount of "lit" (active) fiber transmission lines, capacity is at least doubled.

5. The FCC recently released market-share and other key statistics in the new 1989 Statistics of Communications Common Carriers, Industry Analysis Division, May 1990. At the end of 1989, AT&T's reported market share was at 64 percent for interstate switched minutes. Furthermore, AT&T's toll traffic has grown at an average annual rate of about one-third that of all other carriers combined. See FCC Report, *Long Distance Market Shares*, March 20, 1990.

6. Multinational Business Systems, November 1987, pp. 6 and 15.

7. See L. Waverman, "U.S. Interchange Competition," in Robert Crandall and Kenneth Flamm, eds., *Changing the Rules: Technological Change, International Competition and Regulations in Communication* (Washington, D.C.: Brookings Institution, 1989).

8. For more detailed data for major LECs and IXC firms, see Egan and Waverman, table 3.8, supra at note 3.

9. See *Communications Week*, June 26, 1989, p. 15.

10. Much of the early market for STS providers was the significant profit opportunity from reselling access to long-distance service, and with the substantial toll and access charge price cuts their margins were squeezed. Many states since 1986 have chosen to regulate or prohibit STS operations, and the FCC has declined to preempt such regulation.

11. For details of the exact price changes for access services see table 4.0, supra at note 3.

12. NTIA report, *Telecom 2000*, 1988, p. 343.

13. A safeguard against subsidies might be not to allow RBOCs to sell equipment to themselves, which may already apply in today's situation where they have an equipment sales division selling to the telephone company for internal use, and this cost enters the rate base.

14. For any telco, once it has selected one or two vendors for certain kinds of equipment—e.g., central office switches—costs of conversion to other vendors may make it unlikely new suppliers will win contracts.

15. For more detailed data information see supra at note 3.

16. See Proceeding 1.88-11-040 before the California PUC on the state of competition in cellular.

17. See table 8.1 in Egan and Waverman, supra at note 3.

18. For data on local networks and information services growth since 1984, see tables 9.0, 9.1, 10.0 in Egan and Waverman, supra at note 3.

19. Les Seplaki, *Antitrust and the Economics of the Market* (New York: Harcourt, Brace, Jovanovich, 1982), p. 36.

20. See, for example, "Cellular Telephone Business Is Full of Hang-ups," *St. Louis Post-Dispatch*, February 19, 1989.

21. "Private Companies Stymied," *St. Louis Post-Dispatch*, February 19, 1989.

22. Alan Mathios and Robert P. Rogers, "The Impact of Alternative Forms of State Regulation of AT&T on Direct Dial Long Distance Telephone Rates," Bureau of Economics, Federal Trade Commission, Working Paper Series No. 159, December 1987.

23. Alan Mathios and Robert P. Rogers, "The Impact of State Price and Entry Regulation on Intrastate Long Distance Telephone Rates," Bureau of Economics, Federal Trade Commission, November 1988.

24. Egan and Waverman note that AT&T's toll revenues have increased some 2 percent over the 1984–1988 period, and compare this small revenue growth to enormously higher growth rates for MCI and US Sprint. One cannot help but be impressed, however, with the fact that, *even in the face of a 40 percent price decrease,* AT&T was still able to maintain steady revenues; indeed, when the significantly lower access charges are factored into the calculation, AT&T's *net revenues,* like its overall level of usage, experienced considerable expansion. As for MCI and US Sprint, it is certainly easy to ascribe high growth *percentages* to start-up firms with minimal base period demand. According to data cited by Egan and Waverman, AT&T interstate minutes of use increased by some 36 percent over the 1984–1988 period, from 73 billion to over 99 billion.

25. The majority of the increase in the price of basic residential service that Egan and Waverman cite in their table 4.2 can be attributed to the interstate Subscriber Line Charge (SLC), which had nothing specifically to do with the divestiture itself. Offsetting these increases are significant *reductions* in toll charges that are also incurred by residential customers. It is a distortion of the facts to limit a comparison of pre- and post-divestiture residential telephone bills to local services only; had Egan and Waverman included an amount for toll usage *that reflected the significant rate decreases that took place over the same period of time,* their results would have looked considerably different.

26. See, e.g., New York Public Service Commission Cases 26426, 27089, 27100, 28425, 28710, 28961, 28978.

27. One of the somewhat puzzling facts about regulation of local exchange companies is that, despite the fact that they have a monopoly over most of their service offerings, all cost data is confidential. Access to such data is very limited, and outsiders who do gain access are not allowed to use it for any purpose other than a particular regulatory or judicial proceeding.

28. "Bypass" is actually just a pejorative name for competition.

29. I use the term "Centrex-type services" to refer to all services offered by local exchange companies that offer intercommunications services through the central office switch. Within the various BOCs, these services go by such names as ESSX, Centron, and the like. In most jurisdictions, Centrex is the name given

to a tariffed offering that is now grandfathered: no new customers may sign up for it. Despite differences in name, however, all Centrex-type services share the characteristic with Centrex that the user most often has a separate wire to the central office for each telephone number that is a part of the system.

30. Egan and Waverman, in their discussion of local exchange competition, repeat the dubious assertions of the local exchange companies that local rates are subsidized. This claim has been used as part of the reason to erect the complicated pattern of differing local exchange rates for different "classes" of business customers. To date, such claims of subsidy have been supported by relying on very questionable allocations of costs to local exchange, including the argument that the local loop is "caused" by local exchange usage. The local loop is a cost that is incremental to almost all the *collection* of services offered by the local exchange company, not to just one of them. To quote Dennis Weisman, "how many sins of man have been committed under the term 'cost based pricing.' . . . For the economist that term means something very specific; all the other [measurements] are simply meaningless manipulations of data designed to some predetermined outcome. You can call them costs, [although] it really doesn't mean anything in the economic efficiency sense of the term."

31. Although it appears that many arguably competitive industries price far above marginal costs—see Robert E. Hall, "The Relationship between Price and Marginal Cost in U.S. Industry," *Journal of Political Economy* (1988), 96:921–47.

32. William M. Landes and Richard A. Posner, "Market Power in Antitrust Cases" *Harvard Law Review* (March 5, 1981), 94:937–96.

33. Carl Shapiro and Robert Willig, "InterLATA Capacity Growth and Market Competition." Paper presented at the 13th Telecommunications Policy Research Conference, Airlie House, Va., 1985.

34. I am ignoring the possibility that in some cases (e.g., natural monopoly) the market structure that best promotes First Amendment goals is far from obvious.

35. Perhaps this view has its origins in airline deregulation for which the industry to be deregulated displayed every sign of being highly competitive.

36. This kind of cost-benefit analysis suggests that retaining or imposing rate-of-return regulation simply because an industry failed an anti-trust "test" for permitting a merger is a flawed policy because it ignores the rising costs associated with more intrusive regulation. As a result of these rising costs, the optimal form of regulation may well result in the possession of some market power by the regulated entity. Put differently, the costs of eliminating *all* market power may be far greater than the benefits. We may want to challenge "significant" mergers in such an industry, but that is a far less costly policy than rate-of-return regulation.

37. For example, it seems on the one hand that the debate regarding the deregulation of interLATA interexchange service is largely one about the pricing power of AT&T. On the other hand, the controversy regarding the wisdom of the line-of-business restrictions is argued (at least by the RBOCs) in the arena of innovation. Antitrust economists seem much more comfortable about ren-

dering judgments about the degree of pricing power than about the market structure that best promotes innovation, probably because we know so little about innovation processes.

38. For example, Levin asserts that the contestability theory has greatly reduced the antitrust significance of market structure and has emphasized instead the degree of "competitive behavior" which is characterized by "independence of sellers, responses to competitive actions, [and] lack of collusion" among other measures. Levin also contends that the antitrust definition of competition should focus more on the ability of the firm to raise price rather than structural conditions. Nowhere does he tell the reader, for example, how we should go about measuring the degree of collusion, of seller independence, or of power over price.

39. Presumably, Levin and Egan and Waverman do not mean to suggest that an industry with falling prices is more likely to be competitive than monopolistic. Competition and monopoly models typically lead to predictions about price levels, not about price trends.

40. In a curious twist, Egan and Waverman maintain one indicator of the market power of the local exchange companies (LECs) is the 40 percent increase in basic local service rates since divestiture, rates that presumably were approved by the local regulators.

41. Perhaps the focus on financial performance is a residue of rate-of-return regulation which could result in an allowed return being less than the competitive return. Monitoring the financial performance of the regulated firms could assist the regulators in determining whether the allowed return was too low (or too high).

42. Surprisingly, Egan and Waverman assert erroneously that ownership of a scarce resource like spectrum automatically confers market power. I am certain that any major market radio station owner would vigorously contest that view.

43. In this regard, it will be interesting to observe the outcome of the New Zealand experiment, which anticipates relying on cellular service as a constraint on the market power of the wireline local exchange.

44. It is not clear that AT&T's market share contains any useful information regarding its likely behavior in the deregulation era. Unlike its competitors, AT&T's price changes have until recently required prior FCC approval.

45. John Haring and Kathy Levitz, "What Makes the Dominant Firm Dominant?" OPP Working Paper Series, Federal Communications Commission, April 1989.

46. However, if one did regard toll service as being highly differentiated by carrier, the sales or customer market shares would carry greater weight. But the analysis still would not end with the share distribution.

3
SERVICE ISSUES

5

Pricing of Telephone Services

■

ROGER G. NOLL

AND SUSAN R. SMART

■

ALMARIN PHILLIPS

RONALD G. CHOURA

DENNIS L. WEISMAN

SUSAN D. FENDELL

Roger G. Noll and Susan R. Smart

The decade of the 1980s provides an excellent opportunity for studying the political forces that shape the development of economic regulatory policies. The changes in federal telecommunications policy during this period, especially the most financially significant divestiture ever accomplished under the antitrust statutes, amount to nothing short of a cataclysmic change in the underlying philosophy of government involvement in the industry. Moreover, as the FCC has moved towards deregulating interstate telecommunications services, the largely cooperative federal-state relationshp in telecommunications regulation has all but dissolved, while the relative influence of state regulation has increased. As a result, for the first time since state regulation was adopted more than a half-century ago, state regulators have had to develop comprehensive policies about pricing and competition. These developments provide something of a natural experiment for testing hypotheses about the political and economic forces that shape state regulatory policies.

Until late 1981, while the FCC was clearly moving to increase the role of competition in the industry, the eventual result of procompetitive policies—the vertical separation of the local telephone companies from AT&T—was regarded as a long shot. Indeed, during both the late Carter and early Reagan years, the Antitrust Division of the DOJ was under considerable pressure from other influential members of their administrations to abandon the quest for wholesale divestiture. Both the FCC and the NTIA, while believing AT&T had violated the antitrust laws, did not support the scope of divestiture favored by the DOJ, and the DOJ opposed total divestiture. Instead, it favored a minor divestiture, such as spinning off one large operating company, combined with injunctive relief and more stringent regulatory rules to protect against anti-competitive actions by AT&T in the future. This position had considerable support in Congress and among state regulators.

As the Reagan administration took the reigns of power, pundits first believed the case would be settled with a whimper, much as the Eisenhower administration quickly settled the Western Electric case when it took office. When Assistant Attorney General for Antitrust William Baxter promised to "litigate to the eyeballs," it was widely expected that other members of the Reagan administration, working with Congress, would undermine the pending case by enacting legislation which would force the case to be dropped. This almost occurred in the summer of 1981, when Baxter was forced to put the case on temporary hold as Congress came within a whisker of passing legislation.[1]

The importance of these developments is that when divestiture was announced in the settlement agreement of January 1982, it was a largely unanticipated event that was forced upon the states. At the end of 1981, the FCC's procompetitive policies had not yet had much of an effect on local telephone service and other activities in the domain of state regulators. Moreover, state and federal regulators had managed to retain a largely cooperative relationship in defining the boundaries of state and federal authority, including the allocation of the industry's revenue requirements between them.[2] In large measure this was because a vertically and horizontally integrated AT&T managed to work out many of the inherent conflicts between federal and state officials. With AT&T Long Lines and the BOCs advocating essentially identical policies, compromise and coordination among regulators were more easily accomplished.

In hindsight, the seeds of disruption in federal-state regulatory relationships were sowed long before divestiture, and state regulators ought to have been aware of them before December 1981. Perhaps most regulators even recognized that the world had been permanently and dramatically altered a decade earlier when the FCC began to allow competition in long-distance, domestic satellites, and customer equipment. But in 1981, whatever the deeply held views of state regulators, state regulatory policy remained essentially unchanged. Yet these policies could not remain unchanged in the 1980s, for procompetitive policies were becoming financially significant to the local telephone companies, and through divestiture, the policy integrating power of a vertically integrated AT&T quickly disappeared.

The primary effect of divestiture and federal deregulation was reduced prices for customer equipment and for services that were becoming competitive.[3] In order to maintain the financial health of local telephone companies, other prices had to be increased to offset the revenue loss from competitive products. The policy question facing state regulators in the 1980s was how to apportion the inevitable rate increases. The twin issues to be decided were the pattern of price increases, and decisions about whether to disallow or disadvantage competition where possible for the purpose of sustaining supercompetitive prices in these services, so that prices elsewhere could be held down.

The telecommunications sector has persistently experienced declining real prices for as long as detailed price data have been collected. Table 5.1 shows the average annual rate of change in several price indexes for the half-century before competition and divestiture, and the first few years thereafter. Throughout the entire period, telecommunications prices rose substantially less rapidly than all consumer prices, and less than prices for the other major utility services, gas, and electricity. During the late 1970s and early 1980s, all prices increased more rapidly than they had in the previous three decades; however, the relative price of telecommunications services continued to decline at approximately the same rate it had before. Meanwhile, the relative price performance of the other utilities deteriorated in comparison to telecommunications.

A focal point of the policy debate regarding telecommunications pricing has been the rate charged to residences for basic monthly service. Table 5.2 shows the average monthly residential rate for unlimited service from a sample of cities for the period 1940–1988. From

TABLE 5.1
Annual Rates of Change for Various Price Indexes

	1935 to 1988	1978 to 1988
CPI all goods and services	4.2%	6.1%
CPI all services	4.6	7.5
CPI telephone services	2.2	4.3
CPI piped gas	3.8	7.1
CPI electricity	2.4	6.2

Source: Industry Analysis Division, Common Carrier Bureau, "Trends in Telephone Service," Federal Communications Commission, February 15, 1989, p.4.

1940 to 1970, local residential rates increased very slowly, averaging approximately the same annual rate of increase as is reported for all telephone services in table 5.1. During this thirty-year period, the basic rate increased by only 70 percent (a little less than 20 percent per decade, taking into account compounding). Since 1970, the rate of increase has been much more rapid. The basic monthly rate increased fifty percent during the 1970s, and then doubled in the 1980s.

The period since 1970 corresponds to the new era of competition in telecommunications; however, the differences in price trends reflect more than this. Competition was not plausibly a major factor affecting most telecommunications services until the late 1970s. Until the *Execunet* decision in 1978, AT&T's competitors were too small and too limited in the services they offered to have much of an effect. Competition in customer equipment was permitted shortly after long-distance competition, and it also became important only in the late 1970s.

During the 1970s the Ozark Plan governing separations was in place. This plan established a new formula for taxing long-distance services to help pay for the costs of the local exchange. Between the late 1960s and 1984, the fraction of non-traffic-sensitive local exchange costs paid from long-distance revenues increased from 10 to 26 percent, at which time the FCC froze the federal share at 25 percent. Had Ozark not been in place, by the early 1980s nearly another dollar per month of local exchange costs would have been collected somewhere else in the price structure, and most probably in large measure from the basic monthly rate. One implication of these data is that local exchange costs rose substantially more rapidly in the 1970s than the rate of increase in local service rates.

TABLE 5.2
Charge for Unlimited Local Service

January		January		January		October	
1940	$3.44	1955	$5.29	1970	$5.87	1983	$11.58
1941	3.63	1956	5.34	1971	6.16	1984	13.35
1942	3.70	1957	5.37	1972	6.51	1985	14.54
1943	3.83	1958	5.44	1973	6.79	1986	16.13
1944	3.84	1959	5.60	1974	7.14	1987	16.66
1945	3.84	1960	5.64	1975	7.31	1988	16.59
1946	3.84	1961	5.70	1976	7.77		
1947	3.87	1962	5.71	1977	7.98		
1948	4.09	1963	5.75	1978	8.16		
1949	4.20	1964	5.76	1979	8.19		
1950	4.47	1965	5.78	1980	8.32		
1951	4.69	1966	5.77	1981	8.82		
1952	4.83	1967	5.71	1982	9.73		
1953	5.18	1968	5.72	1983	11.14		
1954	5.18	1969	5.79				

Source: James L. Lande, "Telephone Rates Update," Industry Analysis Division, Common Carrier Bureau, Federal Communications Commission, February 3, 1989, p. 16. Monthly rate increased 50 percent during the 1970s, and then doubled in the 1980s.

Note: Data excludes equipment rental, but includes estimates of state and local taxes. Data for 1983–1988 do not include maintenance of inside wiring. Data for 1940–1983 (January) from AT&T; remaining data from FCC survey of 95 cities.

Table 5.3 provides additional detail on the trends in the different types of telephone services during the period of competition and divestiture. As is apparent in the table, basic residential service experienced two major rate shocks during this decade. The first, from 1980 until 1982, probably had very little to do with federal policy changes. The period 1978–1981 witnessed unusually high inflation in the United States; moreover, interest rates reached all-time peaks. The effect on telecommunications prices was delayed by regulatory lag. In the early 1980s, however, all categories of service show a rate catch-up to accommodate inflation. The second rate shock occurred in 1984–1986, and probably was a direct consequence of divestiture, competition, and accommodating FCC policies. Unlike previous periods of large increases in local service prices, the mid-1980s saw dramatic reductions in prices for interstate services, with the drop in real prices averaging about 10 percent per year.

TABLE 5.3

Changes in Telephone Price Indexes, 1978–1988

Year	CPI	All Telephone Services	All Local Charges	Monthly Residential Service	Interstate Toll	Interstate Toll
1978	9.0%	0.9%	1.4%	3.1%	−0.8%	1.3%
1979	13.3	0.7	1.7	1.6	−0.7	0.1
1980	12.5	4.6	7.0	7.1	3.4	−0.6
1981	8.9	11.7	12.6	15.6	14.6	6.2
1982	3.8	7.2	10.8	9.0	2.6	4.2
1983	3.8	3.6	3.1	0.2	1.5	7.4
1984	3.9	9.2	17.2	10.4	−4.3	3.6
1985	3.8	4.7	8.9	12.4	−3.7	0.6
1986	1.1	2.7	7.1	8.9	−9.5	0.3
1987	4.4	−1.3	3.3	2.6	−12.4	−3.0
1988	4.4	1.3	4.5	4.5	−4.2	−4.2

Source: Industry Analysis Division, Common Carrier Bureau, "Trends in Telephone Service," Federal Communications Commission, February 15, 1989, p. 5–7.

The state regulation component of the local service rate shock appears to have been over by the end of 1986. Table 5.4 shows some further details of how states altered basic access rates during the divestiture period. Since 1986, the basic state rate has actually declined; however, it has been more than offset by small increases in the Subscriber Line Charge (SLC), which is administered by the FCC, and by state and local taxes. Precisely the same pattern is seen for monthly business rates, for installation charges, and for so-called "lifeline" rates. For pay telephones, all of the rate shock apparently took place in 1984, the year of the divestiture, when prices rose by about one-third.

A common belief at the time of divestiture was that the BOCs were the major losers. In the MFJ, this belief was manifested when Judge Harold Greene, responding to requests from state regulators, gave the local companies Yellow Pages, cellular telephones, and the right to retail customer equipment. Apparently the same concern caused state regulators to give an initial rate relief to the BOCs that quickly proved to be excessive. Table 5.5 shows the amount of rate increases given to BOCs in each year since divestiture. After receiving revenue increases of $5 billion in 1984–1985, the BOCs were then required to give back nearly $2 billion in 1987–1988.

TABLE 5.4
Local Rate Levels for October of Years Shown

	1983	1984	1985	1986	1987	1988
Residential rates.[a]						
Unlimited service	$10.50	$12.10	$12.17	$12.58	$12.44	$12.33
SLCs		0.00	1.01	2.04	2.66	2.67
Taxes	1.08	1.25	1.36	1.51	1.56	1.59
Total	11.58	13.35	14.54	16.13	16.66	16.59
Lowest generally available rate	5.37	5.62	5.75	5.96	5.81	5.62
SLCs		0.00	1.01	2.04	2.66	2.67
Taxes	0.56	.58	0.70	0.84	0.94	0.91
Total	5.93	6.20	7.46	8.84	9.41	9.20
Connection[b]	35.01	43.71	44.32	45.63	44.04	42.98
Taxes	1.75	2.19	2.22	2.28	2.20	2.11
Total	36.76	45.90	46.54	47.91	46.24	45.09
Business Rates[c]						
Representative rate	29.15	32.73	33.40	34.25	33.65	33.42
SLCs		0.00	1.01	2.04	2.68	2.69
Taxes	3.35	3.76	3.96	4.17	4.18	3.95
Total	33.50	36.49	38.37	40.46	40.51	40.06
Average charge for 5-minute same zone daytime business call	.085	.090	.090	.092	.092	.091
Connection[c]	56.04	68.91	70.90	73.01	72.23	72.30
Taxes	3.08	3.79	3.90	4.02	3.97	3.89
Total	59.12	72.70	74.80	77.03	76.23	76.19
5-minute pay phone call	.168	.212	.222	.225	.228	.230

Source: Lande, table 2, p. 15.

[a] The residential rates shown in this table do not include touch tone services.

[b] The business rates include touch tone service. The "representative" rate is the single line rate for unlimited service where offered, and the measured service rate with 200 messages in other cities.

[c] Connection charges do not include drop line and block charges.

The preceding descriptive material provides the background for our investigation of state pricing decisions after divestiture. Obviously, the real action in post-divestiture price changes occurred in the period 1984–1986. It is during this period that we ought to be able to detect

TABLE 5.5

Bell Operating Company Rate Requests and Outcomes

Year	Rate Increases Requested ($M)	Rate Increases Granted ($M)	Rate Requests Pending ($M)
1984	4,023.7	3,875.5	3,672.3
1985	1,627.2	1,154.9	1,437.3
1986	643.7	290.0	322.6
1987	146.3	−519.0	124.7
1988	378.9	−1,366.4	219.5

Source: Industry Analysis Division, Common Carrier Bureau, "Trends in Telephone Service," Federal Communications Commission, February 15, 1989, p. 11.

how the economic and political circumstances of the states affected their adjustment in pricing policy to accommodate the new realities.

By the time divestiture was implemented in 1984, the challenge facing state regulators contained the following elements. First, the divestiture agreement prohibited the BOCs from participating in a wide variety of competitive markets, thereby reducing the effective power of state regulators in regulating these markets even in cases where they retained some authority.[4] Second, in implementing divestiture, the FCC renounced the policy of burdening services in the federal jurisdiction with an ever-growing subsidy of services in the jurisdiction of the states. Third, divestiture imposed the "equal access" requirement on local telephone companies, with the effect of requiring them to undertake massive investment plans. Together these new federal policies undermined the historical pricing policies of the states. The first requirement reduced the current and prospective profits of local telephone companies from services that were becoming competitive. The second requirement reduced subsidy flows from federal to state services. The third requirement imposed new costs because it forced premature retirement of switches that could not cheaply be converted to equal access. Thus, prices for monopoly services regulated by the states had to be increased—and relatively quickly—or local telephone companies would be forced to experience significant reductions in profits.[5]

The economic theory of politics, particularly the "new institutionalism" in economic models of policy formulation,[6] provides two insights that are particularly useful to understanding how regulatory policy adjusts to major changes in a regulated industry. One is that, because majority-rule decisionmaking is inherently unstable, democratic political processes are designed to make policy change slow and difficult. The second is that, because in large democracies a single voter is essentially powerless, policy decisions tend to accord greater weight to the preferences of organized groups, which can coordinate their political actions. These two insights suggest several hypotheses about the response of state regulated prices to divestiture and deregulation. First, local telephone companies ought to have fared relatively well. Politically astute state regulators should be more responsive to regulated firms located in the state than to either unorganized customers or national telecommunications firms with principal places of business elsewhere. Second, because ex ante prices reflect the historical political forces in a state, state regulators can be expected to minimize the extent to which changes in federal policy force changes in the structure of state-regulated prices. This implies that the states would strive to maintain the status quo with respect to cross-subsidies. The means for retaining the status quo are to erect barriers to competitive services in the state jurisdiction, and to use carrier access charges for long-distance and other services within the states as a means to generate revenues to offset some local service costs. Third, to the extent that price increases for basic access services were necessary, the pattern should be a "spread-the-pain" policy across customer classes, in an effort to keep price increases below the threshold for motivating political response.[7] Fourth, reflecting the more ambivalent views of business towards regulated price increases,[8] changes in prices for business services would be expected to be larger than changes in residential prices. Fifth, reflecting the change in political representation that has occurred since the pre-divestiture price structure was adopted,[9] prices should be expected to increase more rapidly in rural areas than in large cities. Sixth, any connection between these changes in prices and the service-specific costs of local telephone companies would be coincidental, and driven by the new constraints facing state regulators owing to such factors as federal procompetitive policies and the competitive opportunities created by new technology.[10]

Superficially, the first hypothesis is supported by the initial round of state rate hearings after the announcement of divestiture and several facilitating policy changes by the FCC. Local telephone companies responded by proposing massive rate increases for basic local service, most of which were granted by state regulators (table 5.5). The subsequent profit performance of the divested BOCs was sufficiently strong that, two years later, large rate reductions were ordered, and the BOCs all but stopped asking for further price increases.

The second hypothesis is confirmed by the initial reactions of most states to the attempt to introduce competition against local telephone companies. Peter Huber's report to the DOJ documents the tendency of most states to prevent competition in intraLATA long-distance and in many competitive forms of network access.[11] The exceptions seem to be related to the creation of relatively narrow competitive niches to serve intensive business users of telecommunications services, such as the metropolitan area fiber optic networks in New York City. Again, this is consistent with the interest-group model of regulatory processes, whereby well-organized groups with intense interests in regulatory policy are provided for. But for most customers, competitive alternatives for local services are generally not permitted, or are not feasible given the nature of regulatory restrictions. Examples are the absence of equal access requirements for facilitating intraLATA long-distance competition, the presence of "block or pay" rules or similar provisions to prevent intraLATA long-distance competition, and restrictions or prohibitions on shared tenant service, whereby groups of residences or small businesses could form a cooperative local system for purchasing access and other services from either local telephone companies or their competitors.

The third, fourth, and fifth hypotheses pertain to the pattern of price changes during the 1980s. To examine whether the patterns and trends in rates conform to these expectations, we have collected single-line service rates for business and residential customers for all BOCs. Single-line business service reveals the price structure for small businesses that generally will not want, or have the opportunity to acquire competitive services. The data were taken from the 1980s series of *Exchange Service Telephone Rates*, an annual compilation of telephone prices assembled by NARUC. Data were collected for all BOCs for the years 1980 through 1988, except for 1984 when the NARUC compendium was not published. From 1980 through 1983, the NARUC data report rates as of June 30 of the year in question; since then, the rates are those that apply as of December 31 of that year. Data were obtained on all states except Alaska and Hawaii, plus the District of Columbia, and on fifty-four separate companies.

Each operating company has separate rates for each type of service and for each of several size categories of local service areas. However, the size categories differ from company to company. To facilitate comparisons among states, rates were collected from each company according to a predetermined set of hypothetical sizes of local service areas.

Ten sizes were used, beginning with the smallest reported area and the rate for an area with one thousand customer terminals, and ending with a locality of one million terminals. The bottom three size categories represent small towns and rural areas.

Many states have no large cities or, if they do, do not offer flat-rate basic service in large metropolitan areas. These states do not quote rates for large local service areas. Hence, sample sizes are larger for rates in small areas than in large ones. In addition, some states report rates for sizes of local areas that do not correspond to any actual communities served by a company within its jurisdiction. These rates were included in the sample only for exchange sizes that are smaller than the largest exchange. The rationale for this decision is that regulators are less likely to have thought through pricing policies for an exchange size that has never existed in the state, but will have given thought to an exchange size that some community has passed through and others may soon enter.

In a few states, the NARUC data pertain to more than one local operating company. Each company within a state is reported as a separate observation, so that more companies are included in the sample than there are states. All of the local companies in the sample are part of the Bell System because, since 1985, only BOCs are included in the NARUC survey.

Table 5.6 reports the average rates for a single-line residential and business service in each year for the ten size categories of local service areas. These averages are unweighted by the number of customers or communities of each size category in each state, and so do not represent the average prices actually paid by customers nationwide. Instead, the table shows the trends in state decisions about price structure. The last three columns show the change in rates between 1980 and 1986, between 1983 and 1986, and between 1986 and 1988 for each size of locality. The last row shows the difference in price in each year between the smallest and largest communities.

The patterns are consistent with the expectations described above concerning the political forces for rate reform. As the decade begins, both business and residential rates are higher in large areas, even though large areas have lower costs of service.[12] This is especially true for business service, for which rates were about twice as high in large localities as in small ones for the entire period before divestiture (through 1983). In all categories of service prices rose dramatically from 1980 to 1986, a trend that was detectable before divestiture was announced. Given the lags in regulatory processes, the 1982 and 1983 data probably do not reflect any effects of *U.S. v. AT&T*; the settlement was an-

TABLE 5.6
Rates for Single-Line Service: Averages for All Companies

Business

Size of Locality (No. of Terminals)	Pre-Divestiture		Divestiture Plans		Post-Divestiture Plans				Change 1980–86	Change 1983–86	Change 1986–88
	1980	1981	1982	1983	1985	1986	1987	1988			
Smallest	$14.33	$15.23	$17.04	$19.98	$25.18	$26.04	$25.83	$25.63	$11.71	$6.06	$-0.41
1,000	14.71	15.62	17.44	20.31	25.45	26.29	26.08	25.87	11.58	5.98	-0.42
5,000	16.33	17.26	19.02	21.80	26.68	27.41	27.19	26.99	11.08	5.61	-0.42
25,000	19.23	20.23	22.08	25.33	29.69	30.34	30.00	29.77	11.11	5.01	-0.57
50,000	20.97	22.14	24.39	27.54	32.32	32.78	31.99	31.74	11.81	5.24	-1.04
100,000	22.93	24.11	26.27	29.64	34.47	34.72	34.22	34.04	11.79	5.08	-0.68
250,000	25.29	26.96	29.25	32.52	37.66	38.05	37.55	37.27	12.76	5.53	-0.78
500,000	27.82	29.54	30.78	34.43	39.08	38.86	38.74	38.33	11.04	4.43	-0.53
750,000	27.91	29.20	33.43	35.23	38.61	37.69	37.49	36.95	9.78	2.46	-0.74
1,000,000	31.55	34.21	34.06	37.56	38.40	37.34	37.22	36.33	5.79	-0.22	-1.01
Difference	17.22	18.98	17.02	17.58	13.22	11.30	11.39	10.70	-5.92	-6.28	-0.60
No. of Companies	50	50	51	50	48	48	48	48			

Residential

Size of Locality (No. of Terminals)	Pre-Divestiture		Divestiture Plans		Post-Divestiture				Change 1980–86	Change 1983–86	Change 1986–88
	1980	1981	1982	1983	1985	1986	1987	1988			
Smallest	$6.49	$6.69	$7.42	$8.64	$10.68	$10.92	$10.78	$10.67	$4.43	$2.28	−0.25
1,000	6.60	6.82	7.54	8.76	10.78	11.01	10.86	10.76	4.41	2.25	−0.25
5,000	7.05	7.25	7.97	9.20	11.15	11.36	11.21	11.11	4.31	2.16	−0.25
25,000	7.84	8.05	8.82	10.11	11.95	12.13	11.96	11.85	4.29	2.02	−0.28
50,000	8.26	8.54	9.43	10.73	12.60	12.71	12.52	12.40	4.45	1.98	−0.31
100,000	8.70	9.02	9.92	11.21	12.94	13.07	12.86	12.78	4.37	1.86	−0.29
250,000	9.38	9.72	10.56	11.76	13.64	13.76	13.54	13.44	4.38	2.00	−0.32
500,000	9.87	10.31	10.97	12.27	13.99	13.95	13.68	13.56	4.08	1.68	−0.39
750,000	9.74	10.02	11.33	11.95	13.12	13.11	12.94	12.76	3.37	1.16	−0.35
1,000,000	9.56	9.94	10.37	11.41	13.08	13.28	13.27	12.98	3.72	1.87	−0.30
Difference	3.07	3.25	2.95	2.77	2.40	2.36	2.49	2.31	−0.71	−0.41	−0.05
No. of Companies	52	53	54	54	51	51	51	51			

Source: National Association of Regulatory Utility Commissioners, *Exchange Service Telephone Rates*, 1980 through 1983, and *Bell Operating Companies Exchange Service Telephone Rates*, 1985 through 1988.

nounced in January 1982, but the details were not completed for almost another year. Yet prices increased substantially during the early 1980s, reflecting primarily the effects of inflation and high interest rates, rather than the effects of divestiture and the procompetitive policies at the FCC.

For both business and residential service, the magnitudes of price increases were approximately the same for all sizes of localities during the early 1980s; however, after 1983, business prices in the smaller areas experienced larger increases, both absolutely and percentage-wise, than they did in the larger areas. The effect was to reduce sharply the disparity in prices between small and large communities. For business customers, the difference in prices between the largest and smallest communities fell by about one-third between 1983 and 1986. For residential customers, this reduction was about one-fourth and spread more evenly over the decade. Then in 1987 and 1988, small price reductions were spread more or less equally among all communities, thereby preserving the changes that had just taken place in relative rates. Thus, on a nationwide basis, the trend since 1983 was to reduce the extent to which small towns and rural areas are differentially advantaged in the price structure. This pattern is consistent with the expectation that redistricting can be expected to have reduced the relative influence of rural areas. Nevertheless, the price increases in the early 1980s exhibit no such tendency. Moreover, even by 1988, substantial benefits to smaller communities remained. Prices are still lowest in areas with the highest costs. In fact, the narrowing of price differences by the size of the local area is probably rather small compared to the magnitude of the subsidy to small communities.

Finally, price increases have been substantially larger for business customers than for residential service. (The price cuts in 1987 and 1988 were a little larger for business customers, but not as a fraction of the 1986 prices.) The most interesting aspect of this comparison is that in all but the smallest communities, business rates are now above all extant estimates of the average cost of service. These data confirm the hypothesis that, as a political matter, price increases for small business are more palatable than increases in residential prices.

One difficulty in interpreting table 5.6 is that relatively few states have localities with as many as one million terminals; hence, the averages for small communities are not strictly comparable to the entries for large communities. Tables 5.7, 5.8, and 5.9 report the same data as in table 5.6, but for three categories of states, according to the size of the largest local service area. The results are quite different when the states are so categorized.

Table 5.7 shows prices for states with no large exchanges. (A local exchange of 100,000 terminals corresponds to a population of about 200,000.) Here rates in all size categories have generally risen more rapidly than the national average; however, the pattern of increases has not produced as much of a narrowing of the price differentials between communities of different sizes. This is consistent with table 5.6, which shows that most of the narrowing in rate differentials is accounted for by smaller price increases in the largest communities, none of which is located in the states summarized in table 5.7.

Table 5.8 shows the same data for states in which the largest local service area contains either 250,000 or 500,000 terminals. For the 1980–1986 period, rate increases were greatest for the small exchanges and smallest for the largest exchanges. Most of the reduction shown in the "Difference" row is accounted for by smaller price increases in the largest exchange (500,000 terminals). But the pattern of increases during 1983–1986 was much different than it was during 1980–1983. In the earlier period, the change in prices was approximately equal in all communities; however, in the later period the magnitude of price increases was larger in the smaller localities, especially for business services. Finally, the 1987–1988 rate reductions were essentially equal for all exchanges, except the largest exchange category. The effect was to take back about one-fourth of the reduction in the gap in business prices between large and small exchanges that had opened in the 1983–1986 period. Three-fourths of the reduction in the gap for residential services was taken back. This is not consistent with the hypothesis of declining rural influence; however, the largest price cuts did go to communities in the mid-range of exchange sizes, which correspond to smaller standard metropolitan statistical areas. These results are consistent with the hypothesis.

Table 5.9, showing the states with the largest local service areas, exhibits a small change in the spread in rates between the smallest and largest communities. During 1980–1986, price increases tended to be greater for larger communities, except for relatively small increases for businesses in the very largest areas. Moreover, virtually all of the reduction in the differences in business rates between small and large communities took place before 1983, and it was confined solely to exchanges with one million terminals. The gap between small exchanges and other larger exchanges increased during the 1980s. Finally, the 1987–1988 price reductions were smaller in these states.

Comparison of all the tables reveals that price increases are generally lower in the states with large communities. Indeed, rates in small communities were *lower* in the states with no large cities in 1980–

TABLE 5.7
Rates for Single-Line Service: States With No Large Cities

Business

Size of Locality (No. of Terminals)	Pre-Divestiture		Divestiture Plans		Post-Divestiture				Change 1980–86	Change 1983–86	Change 1986–88
	1980	1981	1982	1983	1985	1986	1987	1988			
Smallest	$13.04	$13.77	$15.44	$18.56	$25.55	$26.42	$26.22	$26.35	$13.38	$7.86	$−0.07
1,000	13.94	16.64	16.14	19.28	25.99	26.87	26.66	26.80	12.92	7.59	−0.07
5,000	16.66	17.24	18.66	21.25	27.73	28.18	27.95	28.10	11.52	6.93	−0.08
25,000	19.70	20.57	22.36	25.29	32.32	32.64	32.03	32.05	12.94	7.35	−0.59
50,000	22.14	23.33	25.90	28.26	36.72	36.85	36.20	36.24	14.71	8.59	−0.61
100,000	23.14	24.15	26.10	28.80	35.56	36.05	35.70	35.71	12.91	7.25	−0.34
Difference	10.10	10.38	10.66	10.24	10.01	9.63	9.48	9.36	−0.47	−0.61	−0.27
No. of Companies	12	13	13	14	12	12	12	12			

Residential

Size of Locality (No. of Terminals)	Pre-Divestiture		Divestiture Plans		Post-Divestiture				Change 1980–86	Change 1983–86	Change 1986–88
	1980	1981	1982	1983	1985	1986	1987	1988			
Smallest	$5.99	$6.05	$6.78	$7.87	$10.40	$10.76	$10.69	$10.75	$4.77	$2.89	$−0.01
1,000	6.23	6.31	6.96	8.13	10.54	10.90	10.84	10.89	4.67	2.77	−0.01
5,000	7.02	7.05	7.68	8.87	11.30	11.57	11.49	11.55	4.55	2.70	−0.02
25,000	7.96	8.08	8.83	10.07	12.53	12.80	12.72	12.78	4.84	2.73	−0.02
50,000	8.56	8.89	9.85	10.98	13.90	14.13	14.05	14.12	5.57	3.15	−0.01
100,000	8.78	9.42	10.20	11.38	13.60	13.95	13.80	13.80	5.17	2.57	−0.15
Difference	2.79	3.37	3.42	3.51	3.20	3.19	3.11	3.05	0.40	−0.32	−0.14
No. of Companies	12	13	13	14	12	12	12	12			

Source: National Association of Regulatory Utility Commissioners, *Exchange Service Telephone Rates*, 1980 through 1983, and *Bell Operating Companies Exchange Service Telephone Rates*, 1985 through 1988.

TABLE 5.8
Rates for Single-Line Service: States With Mid-Size Cities

Business

Size of Locality (No. of Terminals)	Pre-Divestiture		Divestiture Plans			Post-Divestiture			Change	Change	Change
	1980	1981	1982	1983	1985	1986	1987	1988	1980–86	1983–86	1986–88
Smallest	$16.48	$17.61	$19.54	$23.68	$29.50	$31.78	$31.01	$29.71	$15.30	$8.10	$–2.07
1,000	16.82	17.97	20.07	23.94	29.76	31.96	31.18	29.87	15.14	8.04	–2.09
5,000	18.17	19.41	21.45	25.12	30.70	32.95	32.15	31.24	14.78	7.83	–1.71
25,000	21.42	22.82	24.78	28.61	33.68	35.77	34.96	34.34	14.35	7.16	–1.43
50,000	23.14	24.59	26.81	30.82	34.82	36.43	35.56	34.65	13.29	5.61	–1.78
100,000	25.41	26.97	29.38	33.28	37.70	39.22	38.27	37.42	13.81	5.94	–1.80
250,000	26.98	28.79	31.16	35.01	39.55	41.21	40.37	39.47	14.23	6.20	–1.74
500,000	31.12	33.42	33.81	38.47	41.09	41.96	42.39	40.94	10.84	3.49	–1.02
Difference	14.64	15.81	14.27	14.79	11.59	10.18	11.38	11.23	–4.46	–4.61	1.05
No. of Companies	19	18	18	17	17	16	16	18			

Residential

Size of Locality (No. of Terminals)	Pre-Divestiture		Divestiture Plans		Post-Divestiture				Change 1980–86	Change 1983–86	Change 1986–88
	1980	1981	1982	1983	1985	1986	1987	1988			
Smallest	$7.26	$7.50	$8.01	$9.77	$11.99	$12.69	$12.31	$11.85	$5.43	$2.92	$-0.84
1,000	7.38	7.62	8.18	9.86	12.08	12.74	12.37	11.90	5.36	2.88	-0.84
5,000	7.76	8.01	8.58	10.19	12.30	12.98	12.60	12.18	5.22	2.79	-0.80
25,000	8.52	8.79	9.37	11.01	13.10	13.68	13.28	12.90	5.16	2.67	-0.78
50,000	8.96	9.24	9.96	11.63	13.40	13.82	13.41	13.06	4.86	2.19	-0.76
100,000	9.57	9.83	10.62	12.24	14.06	14.52	14.10	13.86	4.95	2.28	-0.66
250,000	10.09	10.42	11.09	12.64	14.76	15.25	14.85	14.66	5.16	2.61	-0.59
500,000	11.00	11.54	11.56	13.41	15.55	15.39	15.22	15.27	4.39	1.98	-0.12
Difference	3.74	4.04	3.55	3.64	3.56	2.70	2.91	3.42	-1.04	-0.94	0.72
No. of Companies	19	19	19	18	18	17	17	19			

Source: National Association of Regulatory Utility Commissioners, *Exchange Service Telephone Rates*, 1980 through 1983, and *Bell Operating Companies Exchange Service Telephone Rates*, 1985 through 1988.

TABLE 5.9

Rates for Single-Line Service: States With Largest Cities

Business

Size of Locality (No. of Terminals)	Pre-Divestiture		Divestiture Plans		Post-Divestiture				Change 1980–86	Change 1983–86	Change 1986–88
	1980	1981	1982	1983	1985	1986	1987	1988			
Smallest	$12.98	$13.96	$15.82	$17.71	$21.07	$21.22	$21.46	$21.06	$8.24	$3.51	$-0.16
1,000	13.08	14.06	15.92	17.81	21.26	21.40	21.64	21.26	8.32	3.59	-0.14
5,000	14.29	15.23	17.20	19.20	22.47	22.56	22.80	22.07	8.27	3.36	-0.49
25,000	16.78	17.58	19.61	22.41	24.61	24.73	24.91	23.81	7.95	2.32	-0.92
50,000	18.26	19.19	21.62	24.36	28.14	28.20	27.18	26.90	9.94	3.84	-1.30
100,000	20.04	21.06	23.42	26.38	30.60	30.28	30.14	30.03	10.24	3.90	-0.25
250,000	22.81	24.43	27.10	29.67	35.64	34.72	34.72	34.75	12.08	5.22	-0.14
500,000	24.79	25.97	28.61	31.32	37.57	36.71	36.50	36.36	11.92	5.39	-0.35
750,000	27.79	28.11	31.99	33.86	38.61	37.69	37.49	36.95	10.49	3.83	-0.74
1,000,000	30.18	32.07	30.33	34.88	38.40	37.34	37.22	36.33	7.16	2.46	-1.01
Difference	17.20	18.11	14.51	17.17	17.33	16.12	15.76	15.27	-1.08	-1.05	-0.85
No. of Companies	19	19	20	19	19	20	20	18			

Residential

Size of Locality (No. of Terminals)	Pre-Divestiture 1980	1981	Divestiture Plans 1982	1983	1985	Post-Divestiture 1986	1987	1988	Change 1980–86	Change 1983–86	Change 1986–88
Smallest	$6.07	$6.36	$7.29	$8.22	$9.72	$9.65	$9.65	$9.51	$3.58	$1.43	$−0.14
1,000	6.11	6.41	7.34	8.27	9.80	9.73	9.72	9.59	3.62	1.46	−0.14
5,000	6.41	6.68	7.65	8.59	10.09	10.01	10.00	9.84	3.60	1.42	−0.17
25,000	7.15	7.37	8.36	9.39	10.67	10.59	10.56	10.34	3.44	1.20	−0.25
50,000	7.49	7.75	8.82	9.92	11.40	11.31	11.26	11.04	3.82	1.39	−0.27
100,000	7.88	8.13	9.26	10.33	11.80	11.71	11.64	11.44	3.83	1.38	−0.27
250,000	8.64	8.98	10.07	10.96	12.57	12.48	12.41	12.16	3.84	1.52	−0.32
500,000	9.12	9.49	10.65	11.64	13.17	13.19	12.99	12.52	4.07	1.55	−0.67
750,000	9.61	9.80	11.00	11.65	13.12	13.11	12.94	12.76	3.50	1.46	−0.35
1,000,000	9.33	9.60	9.80	10.93	13.08	13.28	13.27	12.98	3.95	2.35	−0.30
Difference	3.26	3.24	2.51	2.71	3.36	3.63	3.62	3.47	0.37	0.92	−0.16
No. of Companies	21	21	22	22	21	22	22	20			

Source: National Association of Regulatory Utility Commissioners, *Exchange Service Telephone Rates*, 1980 through 1983, and *Bell Operating Companies Exchange Service Telephone Rates*, 1985 through 1988.

1981, but were *higher* by 1985–1988. As a result, most of the narrowing of the price differential between large and small communities is due to the fact that rates have increased more rapidly in states with no large local service areas. To the extent that federal policy is the force behind the trends in prices, it is causing the differential to narrow primarily by pushing up prices more rapidly in states that do not have large cities. Only in the middle category of states has there been a substantial narrowing of price differentials between small and large communities since divestiture.

The pattern of price changes after divestiture is consistent with the third and fourth hypotheses. For each customer class (residence and small business), most states have more or less increased prices across the board, as predicted by the "spread-the-pain" view. And increases have consistently been greater for businesses than for residential customers. In small and medium-sized states, prices have increased a little less in communities with 100,000 terminals or more, as is consistent with the hypothesis concerning the relative decline of the political importance of rural constituencies; however, as of 1988, this effect was still relatively small.

Finally, in the most populous states, relative rates in small and large communities have not changed very much, and price increases have been lower than in other states. Apparently regulators in these states are under less pressure to raise rates generally, and have had the greatest success in preserving the old pattern of cross-subsidies within the rate structure. The somewhat surprising result is that rural customers now pay lower prices in the most urbanized states, where their political influence is presumably not as great.

The last bit of data regarding post-divestiture price decisions by the states is the pattern of carrier access charges for interLATA toll within the states, as shown in table 5.10. These are the prices charged by local telephone companies for connecting customers to their long-distance telephone company for intrastate long-distance calls between LATAs. As shown in the table, these charges are substantially lower in the largest states, but the meaning of these data is difficult to ascertain. Generally speaking, interLATA carriers have interconnection interfaces with local exchange carriers only in larger cities. Hence, the shorter mileage distances typically connect customers in larger cities to their long-distance carrier, whereas the longer distances are for connections to smaller cities or rural areas. In general, the price structure is consistent with the view that smaller states faced a greater rate shock from divestiture and deregulation, and so imposed a bigger surcharge

TABLE 5.10
Carrier Charges for Premium Switched Access for Intrastate
InterLATA Toll, 1987

Local Transport Distance in Miles	AVERAGE TOTAL COST OF SWITCHED ACCESS PER MINUTE OF USE BY SIZE OF LARGEST METROPOLITAN AREA			
	Small	Medium	Large	Average
under 1	$.065	$.062	$.051	$.059
2	.072	.063	.054	.062
6	.072	.066	.054	.062
11	.076	.067	.057	.065
16	.082	.070	.059	.069
21	.082	.070	.059	.069
31	.091	.079	.068	.078
51	.101	.089	.076	.087
101	.111	.096	.081	.094
Total Number of States[a]	7	15	20	42

Source: MCI Communications, Inc.

[a] Eight states and the District of Columbia have a single LATA and, hence, no established carrier access charges for intrastate interLATA toll.

on long-distance interconnection as part of a general "share-the-pain" strategy.

The data also are consistent with a tendency for less populous states to impose a greater price increase for longer distance (and, on average, more rural) service. This reflects a constraint imposed by federal policy, which permits long-distance carriers to provide bypass lines to their customers. This option is economically far more attractive when the customer is a relatively short distance from the carrier's point of presence in the LATA. Unfortunately, the data provide only weak evidence for these hypotheses, for the observed price differences might reflect only differences in costs. Larger states presumably have larger traffic volumes for interLATA calls, regardless of the length of local transport, and so may achieve greater economies of scale. Because pertinent cost information is virtually nonexistent, the conclusions drawn from these prices must be regarded as speculative.

The last hypothesis concerning prices is that only through inadvertence will they reflect costs of service, other than through the requirement that total revenues equal total costs. As with transport costs for carrier access, the actual costs of local service are a matter of considerable uncertainty and controversy. An assessment of this debate is beyond the scope of our discussion. Suffice it to note that the range of estimates is very large. For our purposes, we can simply use estimates of the average cost of local service provided by local exchange carriers (LECs) in various rate hearings during the mid-1980s. Average costs can be compared with prices to determine whether a class of customers is, on balance, subsidized. The estimated average monthly cost from LECs is in the range of $25 to $30 for most states, with lower estimates of under $20 for companies primarily serving only large cities, and high estimates of over $40 from the least densely populated states. These data indicate that in larger urban centers, BOC data would show average costs in the neighborhood of $20. Cost estimates from LECs tend to be at the high end of the range of estimates, so that they can be used as a conservative baseline for identifying customer classes that pay more than average cost for access service.

The comparison between these estimates and the price data in tables 5.6 through 5.9 is interesting, because it indicates for one class of customers—small businesses in areas serving more than 40,000 terminals—divestiture and deregulation may have driven prices away from costs. In these areas, business customers were paying more or less the cost of serving them in the early 1980s (with prices perhaps above average cost in the largest cities); however, by 1985, business customers in all but the smallest areas were paying prices substantially above any estimate of their average costs. Indeed, in localities with more than 250,000 terminals, the price of small business service is between $10 and $20 a month more than estimates average cost.

Much less can be said about residential service prices. The data in tables 5.6 through 5.9 exclude the FCC's customer access charges. If these are added to the prices in the table, residential prices in communities with over 100,000 terminals fall into the range of controversy concerning average costs; however, there is no controversy that for the smallest localities prices were substantially below costs in 1986, yet they were reduced in 1987 and 1988. Thus, divestiture can be said initially to have driven residential prices toward costs, but the effect was small compared to the tendency for small-business prices to be pushed above average costs, and proved to be transitory.

Of course, none of these trends has had much of an effect on the efficiency of the market for access to the telecommunications network. Both residential and small-business demand for service is highly insensitive to price. By contrast, carrier access charges for long-distance companies, to the extent that they exceed the traffic-sensitive costs of access, do create inefficiencies. Thus, the primary import of the pattern of single-line price differences and their relationship to costs is what they reveal about the politics of allocating cost responsibilities among classes of customers. It is unambiguously clear from these data that business customers in all but the smallest communities are paying more than the average cost of service, and that residential and business customers in small exchanges continue to receive a very large subsidy.

In summary, the first responses of state regulators to the new policy environment created by divestiture and federal deregulation reveal the complexity of the politics of regulatory policy. The price increases and the protections against competition which states have given to local exchange carriers provide support for the traditional "capture" theory of regulation. But it is apparent that state regulation of telephones does more than help out regulated firms.

The special provisions for large users in larger states provide support for the influence of organized buyer interests in shaping regulatory policy. The data on single-line pricing also reveal a pattern of pricing that is responsive to another form of political influence—the possibility that the price performance of a regulated industry could be used by a political entrepreneur as a symbol of the overall policy preferences and performance in office of an incumbent politician. The "share-the-pain" pattern of price increases, and the differential increases between residential and business users, are consistent with the response-threshold characterization of the susceptibility of regulatory policy issues to becoming politically salient.

Finally, the somewhat larger price increases for rural customers provide only weak confirmation of the view that declining representation of rural interests should cause the structure of prices to shift against them. However, this effect is quantitatively very small. Most likely this reflects the fact that the impact of federal policy changes on state regulation has thus far been too mild to force serious reevaluation of the overall pricing policies practiced by the states, or that regulatory officials still adhere to the long-standing policy of using telephone prices to redistribute income to rural communities.

State regulation does not show much of a tendency to move prices toward costs of service, or toward other forms of more efficient prices such as Ramsey pricing. This conclusion is tentative, of course, because so little is known about costs. Trends in the rate structure suggest a movement of rural and residential prices toward costs. But urban business prices are moving away from average costs, and rural prices are not moving much closer to urban prices despite higher costs in rural areas. The difference in business rates across cities is especially strong evidence against the proposition that pricing efficiency is a major force in state regulatory policy.

The prospects are very good for further exploitation by researchers of state decisions about telephone regulation after divestiture to develop a richer model of the politics of regulation. By collecting more data about pricing, policy institutions, and the economic structure of states, a more sophisticated test of political theories of regulation is clearly feasible. It is apparent that the changes in federal policy of the 1980s provide a rich natural experiment for improving our knowledge of the dynamics of regulation by the states.

Almarin Phillips

Roger Noll and Susan Smart provide a study containing interesting and incontrovertible facts about post-divestiture trends in the prices of telecommunications services. They then explain these facts in terms of several hypotheses suggested by the "economic theory of politics." While I have no objection to explorations of this kind, I find it easy to restrain my enthusiasm for the outcome.

The main problem is that the hypotheses put forth by Noll and Smart are not really operational; it is easy to conduct tests that would either confirm or refute them. This difficulty is compounded because, as I show below, the pricing events described in their study can be as well explained by old-fashioned, elementary microeconomics as by the proffered "economic theory of politics."

Before addressing the explanatory value of Noll and Smart's hypotheses, I want to note two more homely hypotheses about the American political behavior. The first is that it is risky in the American political system "to get too big for your britches." This applies to firms and to politicians alike. It is an element in the American scene that AT&T seems not to have learned, despite a prolonged sequence of events that attested to this very fact. AT&T had ample evidence of the mounting pressures for change—*Above 890*, the response to *Telpak*, *Carterfone, MCI*, and *Specialized Common Carriers* to name a few— but it did little to alter its conduct. Then it found to its dismay in late 1981 that the handwriting was on the wall. We ended up with a remedy that might well have been avoided if the company had been more introspective about its place in society and, on its own initiative, instituted more modest reforms.

The second hypothesis concerns what I will call the "kick them while they're down (or going down)" syndrome. This behavior appears in the political and regulatory responses to the cataclysmic downfall of a powerful player. Many of Charles Brown's remarks in chapter 1 suggest that AT&T was late discovering this type of behavior, too. Attainment of the goals AT&T sought through divestiture has surely been far more difficult than had been anticipated when the terms of the settlement were arranged in January 1982.

Let me turn now to Noll and Smart's analysis. Noll and Smart's fourth, fifth, and sixth hypotheses are the easiest to criticize. Instead of saying in the fourth that businesses have experienced larger rate increases than residential subscribers because of "the more ambivalent views of business towards regulated price increases," one could more simply attribute the phenomena to the fact that the demands of businesses are generally less price elastic than are those of residential users. And why ought this be true? Not ambivalence at all, I think, but rather because of familiar aspects of the derived demands for inputs that Alfred Marshall clarified about a century ago. If this were not enough, one could add the supplementary note that businesses, to a degree, can internalize the network externality of their having a telephone through the prices charged for goods and services.

Noll and Smart argue that the larger relative price increases in rural areas are attributable to "the change in political representation . . . since the pre-divestiture price structure was adopted." Well, maybe, but there are other equally inviting explanations. It was in the rural areas that the costs of service were (and are) the highest. The cross-payments from the pre-divestiture intrastate-interstate separations process and from intrastate toll pooling arrangements were essential to offset those high costs. The events of the late 1970s—*Execunet II* and the deregulation of CPE, for example—and then divestiture made it clear that this type of revenue sharing would end. The inevitable move of rates towards costs obviously meant that rates would go up most where the ratio of price-to-cost was the lowest (and vice versa).

The sixth hypothesis is either poorly stated or faulty. It is indeed true that "new constraints facing state regulators" have "driven" some of the rate changes for specific services. Overall, however, Noll and Smart show what they claim cannot be shown. Their data and other information indicate that rate changes can be explained by the magnitude of the differences between revenues from specific services and perceived (but inaccurately measured) service specific costs and/or to differences in demand elasticities. This is true of the general rebalancing between toll and local services and the rate of restructuring within local services. Operator assisted services, maintenance, and installation charges have gone up to reflect costs; rural rates have gone up more to reflect relatively higher costs; business rates—especially small businesses with no bypass alternatives—have gone up more than residential rates because of elasticity consideration. Moreover, with "competitive" interexchange service, AT&T is no longer in the position of being able to internalize the gains in toll traffic that may flow from low access (local) rates. Hence, its incentives for supporting high cost local service to foster interexchange service have been weakened.

I do not question the accuracy but do question the relevance of the first hypothesis, that "politically astute state regulators should be more responsive to regulated firms located in the state. . . ." The problem is that the state regulators lost the battle against rate rebalancing even as AT&T lost its battles. For the most part, NARUC and AT&T fought as one and lost as one. And the second hypothesis, that "states . . . would strive to maintain the status quo with respect to cross-subsidies," if it is different from the first, tells the same story.

The third hypothesis is that a " 'spread-the-pain' policy across customer classes" would prevail "to the extent price increases for basic access services were necessary." Given that Noll and Smart go to some length to explain divergences in price increase across customer classes, one must wonder what this means. If they mean that the rates for all basic local services went up due to general prices, with some going up more than others, they are, of course, correct. But then "spread-the-pain" does not mean anything beyond there having been a general component to the cost increases that affected all basic services. And that, too, is correct even if somewhat ambiguous.

I also have some reservations about interpreting the price trends and political factors noted by Noll and Smart as forecasts of things to continue into the future. Although the facts to date do seem clear, I question whether the regulatory framework and industry structure that gave rise to these so-called trends are themselves sustainable. Is what Noll and Smart show us anything like an equilibrium in either the economic or the political sense? I suspect it is not.

Congruent with the "kick them while they're down" syndrome, the deregulation that AT&T anticipated at the time of the MFJ has not materialized. While price cap regulation now seems assured, AT&T will still be subject to far more rate regulation than are its rivals. Similarly, and also contrary to what had been anticipated, the deregulation of AT&T with respect to enhanced service offerings has not yet materialized, whatever one thinks of *Computer Inquiries II* and *III*. Less noted, but perhaps of no less consequence, AT&T may be bearing a disproportionate part of the cost of service to low-traffic density areas, and to low-volume subscribers. This results from AT&T's carrier-of-last-resort responsibilities and the continuation of rate averaging for ordinary MTS.

I am certain the costs of serving high-density routes and, in fact, the costs of serving large volume customers generally are well below the prevailing rates. This relationship between rates and costs is creating continuing pressure for selective rate reductions, with competitive emphasis on the areas and the customers where large volumes of traffic and significant contributions to profits may be gained. As this continues, we will see greater rate disparities among visible customer groups, with a small number of subscribers receiving high rates (for low call volumes). The availability and the prices for enhanced services will be similarly distributed, with obvious failures to achieve near-universality. Moreover, with the continued handicapping of "dominant firms" —AT&T and the BOCs—I doubt that the structural outcome will reflect comparative efficiencies. More importantly, I also consider it unlikely that the continuation of these trends will reflect the character of regulation, as the structure of the industry will continue to change, partly as a consequence of the rate changes now being observed. Unfortunately, while I make this general prediction with some confidence, I have no idea of the nature of the changes that will occur.

This leads to an additional criticism of Noll and Smart's political analysis. Their "economic theory of politics" is invoked post hoc to explain the past. So far as I can see, it is very limited in its application as a predictive device to forecast the coalitions, the organizations and the political and regulatory pressures that will develop in days to come. It does not tell us in advance which groups will be effective in creating a "saleable political commodity," or help to predict what is likely to happen to the regulatory structure.

Finally, Noll and Smart see divestiture and recent FCC policies as moves "towards deregulating interstate telecommunications services" and as "procompetitive policies." I believe this is an inaccurate representation of the changes that have occurred. All one needs to do is spend an hour or so studying FCC decisions under the rules of *Computer Inquiries II* and *III*, or its handling of pricing issues in AT&T's Tariff 15 to know that we are a long way from deregulation and open competition. The handling of the FTS 2000 matter is another case in point.

Overall, I end up with the feeling that political theories may be useful in explaining the attacks on AT&T in the 1960s and 1970s, but that these theories add little to the explanation of what has happened in telecommunications market places since then.

Ronald G. Choura

Noll and Smart address an important issue today in telecommunications. However, I find myself in disagreement with a substantial portion of their conclusions. Like many authors who review the regulatory process, Noll and Smart only look at a portion of the facts and base conclusions on desired results, instead of looking at the same facts the regulators used to make their decisions. My perspective is that of a state or federal staff regulator.

There is no question state and federal regulators, prior to the early 1970s, coexisted with little conflict. AT&T and the BOCs were able to work out many of the problems associated with the two regulatory jurisdictions. Compromises between the interexchange and exchange carriers helped significantly in maintaining harmony between state commissions and the FCC. If obtaining these compromises is considered "running the process," then AT&T did just that prior to 1980. However, AT&T was losing some of its control by the late 1970s.

AT&T's loss of control over state and federal regulators began with the concern that costs were being allocated unfairly with respect to both the intrastate jurisdiction and between services. On the state side, this concern was first evidenced in the early 1970s, with the issues of license contracts between AT&T and the BOCs, the integration of Alaska and Hawaii rates to those of the mainland states, and allocation of central office circuits plus cable and wire facilities between the state and interstate jurisdiction. As early as 1973, state regulators were asking the FCC to set up a Joint Board, as provided for in paragraph 410(c) of the Communications Act of 1934, to review many of these cost-allocation issues. The FCC did set up a Joint Board for the Alaska and Hawaii issues in the 1970s, and later again in the mid-1980s (in Docket 83-1376). And after significant pressure, the FCC finally set up a Joint Board to look at all the cost-allocation issues in June 1980 (in Docket 80-286). Most of these events occurred prior to the announcement of the divestiture settlement.

The states were very vocal about the settlement agreement AT&T worked out with the Justice Department. In fact, state regulators did not like many of the original decree conditions, such as the LATA boundaries, allocation of Yellow Pages and assets to be transferred to AT&T. If it were not for the Justice Department and Judge Greene deciding in favor of the states position, AT&T would have done things differently. Reflecting this division of opinion, the discussions and negotiations between the regulators and AT&T were very much less than friendly during the 1982–1989 period.

As for the allocation of costs between the federal and state jurisdiction, the only real issues raised during divestiture were the cost of divestiture and the cost of implementing MFJ-mandated equal access service. Again, the final outcome differed significantly from what AT&T had advocated. Federal and state regulators were philosophically light years apart on the proper long-distance cost allocation procedures, and only the intervention of Congress led to an eventual compromise settlement.

Noll and Smart indicate that states faced significant rate increases at the time of divestiture. In fact, rate increase requests began in the early 1970s, at a time when the country was suffering from an economic recession and telephone companies were facing cutbacks in employees and expense spending. Most telcos were earning below authorized rates of return and were going to file rate increases whether divestiture occurred or not. Pre-divestiture rate increases were the result of a number of factors, such as rural upgrade programs for multi-party to one-party; upgrades from electromechanical to electronic equipment; the need to expand equipment to meet the increasing demand for telecommunications in the economic development of the country; the introduction of competition in selected services markets which forced rate restructuring; and the consumer demand for a higher quality of telephone service in all areas, not just urban. These factors and others contributed to significant differences of opinion between state and federal regulators, which are not explored by Noll and Smart.

Noll and Smart discuss how the regulation of telecommunications is a political process and mention various factors driving that process. I agree strongly that telecommunications regulation is a political process, but it is not limited to the factors addressed by Noll and Smart. There are many other important externalities that also drive the process. One consideration not mentioned is coverage by the local media. Is telecommunications being covered, or are other concerns such as nuclear abandonment, water problems, sewer problems, or electrical energy problems attracting more attention? An absence of telecommunications coverage by the media usually enables the industry to control the process more.

Yes, economics also drives the process. The "bottom line" is among the most important, if not the number one factor. If rates are increasing for any user group, that group usually gets concerned. And the greater the financial importance of telecommunications to the user, the more vociferous the user will be in trying to reduce or eliminate the proposed rate increase. If rates are going down, users and consumers generally do not get as aroused.

Noll and Smart cite divestiture and federal deregulatory policies as the primary catalysts for change. There is no question these have been extremely significant influencing factors. However, other factors may have been equally important. We are facing an information explosion, and the telecommunications industry is an integral part of information delivery. Increasingly, people need and demand telecommunications in order to conduct daily business. The more users depend upon telecommunications service and notice the effects of service changes, the more they will learn how the telecommunications policy process works and how to manipulate it in order to achieve their own goals. For example, the new enhanced service providers (ESPs) want to find a way to access the telecommunications network more cheaply. Most of them are large corporations with lobbyists and people who are well-educated in the regulatory and governmental arena, and they have learned the policy process very well. They were thus able to avoid paying access charges paid by the majority of carriers or competitors to AT&T.

Noll and Smart state that business rates are rising. Although rates are going up for some business customers, the real question is "which business rates?" Are these higher rates paid by small businesses who have not figured out how to manipulate the policy process to their advantage? What about the rates for the big businesses? General Motors and IBM have not experienced rate increases. Those contract rates, such as Tariff 15 mentioned by Almarin Phillips, have decreased to levels significantly below average cost. It is the large companies who benefit the most from the federal subscriber line charge implementation on the local residential and small business customer—who now pays billions of dollars once paid by big business. These large companies can negotiate special contracts for telecommunications service and get basic Centrex service at per-line cost below those paid by residential and small business customers. None of these costs are considered by Noll and Smart.

Noll and Smart conclude that service costs have little or no role in state regulation. That is not true for those states in which state commissions require cost filing. For years, Michigan, like many other states, has required cost study support to be provided for new service offerings as well as for backup to major rate restructurings. State commissions also have developed intrastate cost allocation procedures for intercompany settlements, even separating out individual service cost. In Michigan, we are making the process open to public review by setting specific open proceedings to review the cost allocations.

Issues of cost and cost allocation are becoming increasingly important and will merit even more attention as the political process becomes less opaque. Once the customer and businesses learn how cost allocations work, understand all those little acronyms the telephone people use, and know how to play the game with the state regulators, their interest in costs will become even greater. This will be especially true if competition continues to exist in only a portion of the telecommunications service market. In this environment, customers as well as the competitors will be concerned about cross-subsidization.

The real issues seem to be whether the prices businesses and residential customers pay for telecommunications services have been increasing or decreasing, and the overall economic effect of the current trend of deregulation on the telecommunications infrastructure in this country. The readers of this volume should be able to make their own judgments based on the services they buy and use. What is your opinion? On a per person basis for the access to telecommunications services, do you think it is cheaper to live in New York City or in Lansing, Michigan? The question becomes very simple. Is telecommunications easier and cheaper to provide in the big urban areas or in the small rural communities? There are a wide variety of cost studies generating numerous different figures. It is necessary to ask if the people who develop the figures develop them correctly and depict the true picture, rather than producing and manipulating them for self-serving ends.

We regulators see all kinds of cost studies. For example, four or five years ago, when there was no competition in pay phones, telephone companies went before every state commission and claimed a rate increase to twenty-five cents per call was absolutely necessary, to avoid continuing to lose money on every call from public telephones. Now telcos are saying public pay telephones make money, and providers can afford to pay substantial commissions to keep the telephones in business owners' locations. When COCOTs threatened their markets, the telephone, companies submitted cost studies with only two or three line items. Whereas, they had included everything except the kitchen sink only five years before. What happened to all those other line items? This illustrates why cost studies will become an important part of the policy process in the future.

The primary issue here is very clear; as competition is introduced in the big markets, there is an incentive for telecommunications providers to cross-subsidize the competitive service offerings with service revenues from the less competitive markets. That is the essence of the Noll and Smart discussion. The telephone companies and regulators feel they have to cross-subsidize somewhere, and thus the question becomes how far and how fast they can do it and still survive politically. Basically, competition drives prices either to cost or to anticompetitive pricing—which one of them I am not certain.

State regulators are left with two options to avoid anticompetitive pricing: either initiate cost studies and address the problem to make sure it does not happen, or get out of the business of regulation and leave the customers to fend for themselves. Both courses of action are being pursued on the state level. The last few years have seen half of the regulators getting out of the business of regulation, and the other half conducting extensive cost studies to try to prevent the anticompetitive and captive customer abuse activities.

Unquestionably, small business and residential customers are going to get hit hard because they have not yet learned how to lobby effectively for their concerns. Big businesses in the competitive areas will fare well because they have the resources and technical expertise to get what they need, such as special contract deals for Centrex and Tariff 15s.

Noll and Smart assume state regulators are not concerned about costs. I disagree. The number of resolutions NARUC passed in 1988 and 1989 with regard to costs demonstrates that regulators do care. They will continue to do so as they get better information and as cross-subsidization becomes more prevalent with the introduction of more competition in selected markets of the existing dominant carriers.

Dennis L. Weisman

Noll and Smart's analysis is both insightful and thought-provoking, and is one with which I find myself in substantial agreement. If one writer were to suggest a "shadow title" for their discussion, it might be something like "Neither Political Rents Nor Monopoly Rents Are Parted With Easily." This seems to represent the central theme. My comments will, of necessity, cover some aspects of regulation and competition in order to do the pricing issue justice.

In the beginning of their study, Noll and Smart make the salient point that, until the FCC embarked on procompetitive policies and certainly prior to divestiture itself, the policies governing intrastate and interstate telecommunications were closely aligned. However, if once upon a time the FCC and the state public service commissions were marching to the same drummer, they certainly are not today. This raises the question of whether the regulatory structure currently in place is actually sustainable.

I contend that technology and competitive entry in telecommunications markets are rapidly blurring any meaningful distinction between interstate and intrastate telecommunications. Arguably, the only entities that possess LATA maps today are the regulators and the declining portion of the industry they regulate. The history of telecommunications regulation over the last two decades is fraught with examples, from *Above 890* through *Carterfone* to *Execunet*, of technology pushing competition further and faster than the regulatory and judicial decisions initially envisioned.

A recurring theme, and one that figures prominently in the comments of William Baxter and Charles Brown in this volume, is that there are "too many regulators" in telecommunications today. While the inference has been that Judge Greene—the "third and uninvited" regulator—should perhaps step out of the picture because he is upsetting the balance of power, it is entirely possible that two regulators are, in fact, one too many. If one looks carefully at the current structure of telecommunication regulation, it seems peculiar that there is a separation of powers between control over market entry and control over ratemaking. This is by no means a new phenomenon, but it is perhaps more critical today than it was in the past. For example, the effect of the FCC's *Above 890* decision in 1959 was to sanction competition in both interstate and intrastate telecommunications markets. And yet, the ratemaking powers for intrastate telecommunications were reserved for the state Public Service Commissions, who were not necessarily as enamored with the benefits of competition as was the FCC.

The dichotomous regulatory structure is not unlike a tandem bicycle, with the rider in front and the rider in back pedaling in different directions. Each rider may have a perfectly good reason for pedaling in the direction he has chosen, but the end result is still the same—pedaling in place with little progress over the desired route. Whatever this regulatory structure yields, and regardless of the good intentions of those who believe "their policies are serving the public interest," it is less than clear the collective social good is being served by this morass of regulatory authority.

Coalitions of individual users are building their own private networks and thereby bypassing not only the common carriers, but the regulatory process as well. The effect of this proliferation of private networks is a degree of fragmentation of our telecommunications infrastructure far beyond that which we would expect with economically efficient rates structures in place, and with a consensus on the direction of telecommunications policy. Increasingly, users cite "regulatory uncertainty" as one of their primary reasons for bypassing.

Telecommunications, quite unlike other regulated industries, such as natural gas and electric power, is a service jointly consumed in a spatially diverse manner. In this respect, telecommunications is probably more like air travel than it is like electric power or natural gas and we can conceive of the telecommunications network as the "skies" through which messages travel. Suppose commercial air travel were regulated in the same way as telecommunications—i.e. on a jurisdictionally specific basis. The FAA directs all eastbound commercial aircraft to fly at odd altitudes (e.g., 33,000 or 35,000 feet) and all westbound aircraft to fly at even altitudes in order to diminish the likelihood of midair collisions. Safety is the principal motivation for regulating air travel in this manner and there is some obvious logic in this type of regulation. But suppose a (hypothetical) state aviation administration (SAA) summarily decides to reserve the authority to regulate intrastate air travel. In doing so, the SAA decides the public interest is best served if eastbound commercial aircraft fly at even altitudes, and westbound aircraft fly at odd altitudes. I think it is clear there is a very high social cost indeed when interstate and intrastate regulation are out of sync with one another in this fashion.

The dichotomous regulation of state and interstate telecommunications presents a similar problem. This is why the insight of Noll and Smart regarding consistency between state and federal regulatory policies is so critically important. As long as the two sets of regulators were in policy harmony with one another, it was as if we had only one set of regulators and the structure was sustainable. Although many observers would look at the state of telecommunications regulation today and say that the dichotomy serves as checks and balances, separation of powers or "little laboratories"—I do not believe it is really any of these. It is a gridlock that will be broken in a most inefficient manner due to the distorted economic incentives being propagated through this multi-tier regulation.

I will move on from the benchmark of regulation today to the trends in local service rates, for which Noll and Smart provide some interesting data. Although state regulators appear to set prices according to some Ramsey pricing rule, unfortunately, the elasticities they use are not price elasticities, but political fallout elasticities. The Ramsey pricing rule states that, should departures from marginal costs be necessary in order to sustain a firm subject to a specified profit constraint, welfare losses are minimized when the departures from marginal costs are set in inverse proportion to the absolute values of the price elasticities of demand. In other words, departures from marginal cost are greatest in the least elastic markets, and least in the most elastic markets. This so-called Ramsey-Optimal rule is not generally practiced in the telecommunications industry today; if it were, toll and switched access prices would be set at much lower levels and basic local service rates set at much higher ones. In fact, quite the opposite is true, and this has resulted in welfare losses estimated at about $10 billion annually in telecommunications markets.[13] Another interpretation is that it costs society about $10 billion annually because telecommunications prices are set in accordance with a Ramsey-Political as opposed to a Ramsey-Optimal pricing rule.

The central theme of Noll and Smart suggests, instead of following a Ramsey-Optimal rule for setting telecommunications prices, regulators "appear" to be setting prices in a manner that minimizes "political fallout." We could define a political fallout elasticity as the ratio of the percentage change in votes (or electoral support) to the percentage change in the price of particular telecommunications services. Prices set in a manner to minimize political fallout—or equivalently in inverse proportion to the absolute value of the political fallout measures —are therefore set according to a Ramsey-Optimal pricing rule.

From the Noll-Smart analysis, it appears that price elasticities of demand for specific telecommunications markets run exactly opposite to the political fallout elasticities. It is important to inquire why this occurs. Local rates for telephone service have always been a politically charged issue. When the performance of regulatory commissioners in protecting the "public interest" is held up to public scrutiny, their stance on local rate increases almost always receives the most attention. Although we may want to say "no, it really does not work that way," the data is, at the very least, seemingly consistent with the Ramsey-Political rule. We may not be able to accept the hypothesis, but we certainly must fail to reject it.

One very interesting dimension of the Noll-Smart analysis is the hypothesis that state regulators do not rely upon costs of service to any great (or perhaps discernible) extent in setting rates. Ronald Choura vigorously challenges this hypothesis, and emphasizes that the Michigan Commission requires Michigan Bell to file very extensive cost studies. There are, of course, literally an infinite number of different cost study methodologies, including studies of fully distributed, incremental or embedded costs. Rates based on any one of these cost studies could legitimately be referred to as "cost-based," but this is quite misleading. It can be truly said some of the greatest sins of man have been committed under the guise of "cost-based pricing."

For the economist, the term cost-based pricing means something very specific—prices that are based on some measure of marginal or incremental cost. The key attribute, of course, is that the relevant measure of costs is grounded in the principle of causality. All of these other measures of cost—based on some fully distributed cost methodology—are little more than meaningless manipulations of data (or revenue requirements) designed to rationalize some predetermined outcome. One can call them costs, it really does not matter what one calls them, but they are meaningless, or worse, from the perspective of economic efficiency.

Choura goes on to castigate Michigan Bell for filing cost studies for coin phones that showed dramatic differences before and after competition entered the market. I do not know the details of the example in question, but he raises an issue that should be addressed. I submit that his complaint is simply a manifestation of cost studies that are not grounded in sound economic principles. Arbitrary cost methodologies can be used to justify virtually any rate structure. The inference, of course, is that the cost study was conducted in such a way as to advantage Michigan Bell vis à vis its competitors in the coin-phone market. Assuming the cost study were able to be altered in this manner (in fact Michigan Bell did so), and given that the Commission has authority both to require and review specific cost studies (as it most surely does), then Choura has only succeeded in attesting to the Commission staff's inability to properly monitor the output of an arbitrary costing methodology.

Another area for discussion is the prospect for change in state regulation and how this will drive change in the pricing of telecommunications services. Competition will be the major factor influencing changes in pricing at the state level, and we are already starting to see signs of the dam breaking. Peter Huber's report, which examined the nature of competition in the telecommunications industry, concluded that the telecommunications marketplace is poised for significant, profound and surely irrevocable changes.[14]

As for the equity/efficiency aspects of telecommunications pricing, I believe that once competition is allowed in a market, there ceases to be any meaningful equity/efficiency pricing tradeoff. This does not imply that some form of subsidy is not warranted, but such measures should be targeted to economically disadvantaged households, as needed, rather than to the service class as a whole (i.e., one party flat-rate residence service). Competitors frequently argue that incumbent firms should be required to set prices with a view toward equity considerations as defined in the regulated monopoly era. These statements, however, are frequently little more than thinly veiled attempts to promote their own interests by enjoining the regulated carriers to inefficient prices that in turn favor their own services. Since competition is most intense precisely for those customer classes supporting the majority of the cross-subsidies, any attempt to maintain this level of subsidy in competitive markets will only result in the burden of the revenue requirement falling disproportionately on those customers for whom regulators hold the most steadfast equity interest—small business and residence rate-payers.

What about the prospects for convergence between Ramsey-Political and Ramsey-Optimal pricing? There are two primary forces that will serve to cause price elasticities and political fallout elasticities to converge. First, state legislatures are increasingly interested in attracting new businesses to their states in order to promote economic development. To the extent that economically efficient pricing is a key factor in the location decisions of businesses, regulators could be expected to look upon such a rate structure more favorably. Second, competition will ultimately cause the political interests of the regulator to be more closely aligned with the economic efficiency interests of the economist. In other words, what the regulator views as equitable pricing under competition will increasingly begin to look like economically efficient pricing.

Some rather significant changes in the structure of telecommunications pricing will occur over the next five years. The vast majority of costs are caused not in providing actual use over the network but in providing the option of use. When costs are incurred in providing the option of use, while services are being sold primarily on the basis of actual use, "transactions asymmetry" exists. This is a source of financial risk for firms in competitive or transitionally competitive markets, such as telecommunications, because capital is being deployed with the expectation that demand will materialize to recover investment. The more competitive the market, the greater the financial risk for any individual firm. We should therefore expect firms subject to increased risk to alter the structure of their sales transactions in a manner that brings about a greater degree of "transactions symmetry," which in turn will reduce their overall level of market risk.

The implications of this "transactions symmetry" hypothesis for the future of telecommunications pricing are two-fold. First, an increased emphasis will be placed on the use of two-part and multi-part tariffs, where the first part of the tariff is a buy-in or option fee, and the second part is usage charge that varies inversely with the price of the option. Second, there will be an increased use of explicit contracts between carriers and customers. In large measure, these explicit contracts serve the role that the "regulatory contract" served prior to competition (i.e., to restrict competition and thereby reduce market risk). Undoubtedly these transactions changes will occur first in the high risk or competitive segments.

Optional calling plans are probably just the beginning of this phenomenon. These plans incorporate buy-ins or option fees for the purchase of blocks of calling time, or simply offer discounts off the standard usage price. Extended area service and expanded local calling scopes, wherein intraLATA toll is shading into local service, are further examples of this trend.

Finally, as Almarin Phillips suggests, the carrier of last resort issue will figure prominently in the evolving telecommunications marketplace. We are not that far away from the time when carriers will charge their customers for the option of standing by as carriers of last resort. This is a prime example of a situation in which regulators will be forced into efficient pricing in order to preclude inequity for residential and small business customers. This is because failure to charge for carrier of last resort services in a competitive marketplace will actually result in a flow of subsidies from residual customers to bypassers. Under strict usage sensitive pricing, those customers partaking of bypass and private networks—predominantly large and medium business —will receive a de facto "free insurance" policy for stand-by service, paid for by small business and residence customers who do not have such an array of options. While regulators will probably view this as inequitable, it is also economically inefficient. Customers using competitive alternatives should pay directly for stand-by options that insure service provisioning, but impose substantial costs on the carriers.

Susan D. Fendell

Roger Noll and Susan Smart postulate that recent rate increases are essentially due to various political and economic forces. To the extent that the RHCs have significant influence over regulators and those who appoint them, Noll and Smart are correct.

The RHCs are enormous corporations, each with approximately a billion dollars in revenue each year. In contrast, residential consumers are less organized and have fewer resources than large businesses, be they large business customers or the BOCs. Indeed, the resources, both political and economic, of the RHCs and AT&T should never be underestimated. Compared to consumer groups, their funding is limitless.[15] Compared to legislators and regulators, the RHCs and other companies' longevity is eternal. Even with respect to the courts, the telephone industry is overpowering in money, lawyers, technical expertise, and to a certain extent, persistence.

Furthermore, these corporations employ brilliant tacticians. For example, telephone companies sponsor legislation permitting, though not requiring, the regulating agency to deregulate telecommunications services or companies. This variety of legislation is difficult to lobby against because it does not require deregulation, but merely allows the agency with the most familiarity with the subject to consider deregulation as an "alternative." This type of legislation also curries favor with regulators, who, of course, have no doubt as to their ability to be just, reasonable, and wise in their determination when to deregulate.

The telephone companies are also masters of public and press relations. They have access to widely viewed advertising, not only in the form of telephone bill inserts, but also (more importantly perhaps) on television and radio. Local newspapers are hungry for pre-written editorials, and most reporters (on small and large papers alike) are woefully ignorant of the telephone issues currently being debated, except for the little information gleaned from company spokespeople and press releases.

Additionally, charitable donations provide telephone companies an inexpensive means of garnering community support. The telephone companies also improve their relations with their communities by establishing consumer councils composed of community leaders, who usually have little or no expertise in telecommunications. The overt purpose of these councils is to provide the companies with community feedback on their services. However, these councils also conveniently provide the companies with an allegedly neutral forum in which to feed community leaders a steady stream of pro-company information, usually about the wonders of new services.

The motives of companies for establishing links with consumer groups should not be misinterpreted. A 1988 AT&T document on the management of consumer affairs spells out the company's motives and tactics:

> The advisory committee (on consumer affairs) began its work by focusing its mission and clarifying its objectives. The committee

agreed that it should only address organized consumer movements, not consumers as end users. Further, it was agreed that the overriding goal of consumer affairs should be to help AT&T achieve its business objectives. . . . Mitigating the negative influence of national consumer organizations on AT&T's business objectives should be the number one priority for consumer affairs.

The document goes on to say that liaison work with national consumer organizations (specifically naming the American Association of Retired Persons (AARP) and United States Public Interest Research Group (US PIRG), among others) is "imperative" and "will produce less opposition from these organizations and their leaders."[16]

Perhaps the telephone industry's public relations coup is the shaping of the language used to discuss its essentially self-interested deregulation initiatives. While the term "deregulation" may conjure up images of corporations attempting to avoid societal oversight in order to reap higher profits, the terms the industry uses to describe its deregulation initiatives invoke images of the public good. The terms by which various forms of deregulation are known include: social contract, incentive ratemaking, price caps, alternative regulation, and streamlined regulation. Social contracts might be more accurately referred to as "retention of excess earnings plans."

Together, deregulation and the rate increases granted to the local BOCs in the years proximate to divestiture have combined to raise local rates and raise the overall bill of residential customers. In August 1989, the FCC reported the average telephone ratepayer was paying 52 percent more for flat-rate local telephone service than just prior to divestiture.[17]

The BOCs, which offer a combination of competitive and monopoly services, naturally seek to lower the prices of their more competitive services and make up the difference by raising the prices of monopoly services. According to the Federal-State Joint Board, local service charges (including subscriber line charges) increased at an annual rate of 1.9 percent for the first ten months of 1988, while the price of interstate toll calls fell at an annual rate of 1.5 percent, and the price of state toll calls fell at an annual rate of 4.8 percent.[18]

The BOCs and others claim that sufficient competition exists to alleviate the need for regulation to control prices. Advocates for residential customers disagree on the following premises. First, effective competition does not exist for most telecommunications services. Most persons agree that basic local exchange service is not competitive. Second, more than the presence of competition is necessary to justify the abandonment of regulation of what has become a basic necessity.

Telephone companies are not seriously competing for the residence market. The rate changes since divestiture confirm this. They also confirm that residential customers lack political and economic power comparable to the BOCs and big business customers. For example, business customers use long-distance services more than residential customers. Charges for local exchange service account for less than half of the average monthly bill of small businesses.[19] Since divestiture, long-distance phone rates dropped 33 percent, while local rates increased in an average of 47 percent.[20] According to a study performed for the Small Business Administration, those interstate and intrastate toll reductions that have occurred tended to favor business customers[21]

Telephone companies are competing for big business customers who use high-tech services. Digital switches are not being deployed by the BOCs just to provide equal access, but to provide end-to-end digital connectivity to allow for error-free data communications. With business usage and revenues—both local and long-distance—growing faster than residential usage,[22] the BOCs are merely responding in a rational manner to current market conditions.

The legitimate fear that monopoly services will cross-subsidize the more competitive service offerings is another reason why consumer advocates oppose deregulation. Many consumer advocates believe basic local service has been subsidizing long-distance and enhanced services. For years, residential rates were set on a residual basis. Thus, basic local exchange service was, and is, often unjustly saddled with common and joint costs not directly attributable to any particular service.[23]

Cross-subsidization also occurs due to the manner in which rates of return are set. The level of the rate of return reflects the risk of investment. Services that are competitive are more risky than services which are not, yet the same rate of return is incorporated in the rates of all services. This unfairly burdens basic local exchange ratepayers—the BOCs' monopoly customers—with the risk associated with competitive services.

In addition, residential ratepayers subsidize business services when the investment costs incurred to provide data and enhanced services for business are allocated to basic local exchange service. Digital switches and fiber optics just are not necessary to provide plain old telephone service (POTS); therefore, the costs associated with switch replacements and other "modernization" should not be allocated to those services. Similarly, if depreciation rates are accelerated to account for the rapid replacement of plant and equipment to meet competition or the needs of high-tech business customers, the customers of noncompetitive, basic services should not bear the higher expenses associated with that acceleration.

Many telephone company advocates, including Dennis Weisman, suggest that rates for competitive services must be set at marginal cost to optimize social welfare. However, cross-subsidies cannot be determined or prevented in the telecommunications industry if the rates for competitive or enhanced services are based on marginal costs. This is because whenever a large amount of undepreciated jointly-used equipment exists, the marginal cost of a service will always be less than its stand-alone and fully embedded costs.

Weisman also advocates Ramsey pricing. Ramsey pricing allocates overhead costs to those least able to avoid such costs. The proponents of marginal cost-based pricing and Ramsey pricing ignore the fact the adoption of such pricing schemes by commissions represents a severe distortion of their traditional regulatory role, which is to protect monopoly customers from exploitation.

A preferable means to set prices and to control cross-subsidization is for regulators to determine the stand-alone cost of providing each of a utility's services, and then determine the savings achieved by jointly offering the services. Those savings should then be allocated to the services based on the stand-alone costs of each.[24]

Ronald Choura notes that the Michigan Commission requires its utilities to submit detailed cost studies. However, the mere presence of cost studies does not uncover and prevent cross-subsidization. As Weisman states, "some of the greatest sins of man have been committed under the guise of 'cost-based pricing.'" Nonetheless, such studies should not be abandoned altogether or limited to incremental costs. Carefully structured, and with all assumptions exposed, stand-alone cost studies provide useful benchmarks for setting rates.

Unfortunately, most state utility commissions and the FCC permit cross-subsidization either through reliance on residual pricing or the allocation to basic local exchange service of costs associated with competitive business and enhanced services. This means that, if rates are frozen or prices capped at their current levels, rates for basic local exchange service will remain unfairly high.

Advocates for residential customers also oppose price caps and similar approaches to deregulation on the grounds that they do not recognize that telecommunications is experiencing declining costs. For example, the cost of fiber optic cable, which the companies are installing in lieu of or in addition to copper cable, has fallen dramatically. Moreover, the companies claim new technology reduces the cost of maintenance and the building space required to house switches.[25] Walter Bolter and James McConnaughey in this volume describe additional cost reductions the telecommunications industry is experiencing.

Because the telephone industry is a declining cost industry,[26] the BOCs and other telecommunications companies prefer to avoid regulation that examines their profits. At the same time, consumers have an interest in maintaining routine regulatory review of utility profits and expenses to ensure that rates are no higher than the minimum necessary to meet constitutional requirements.

Provisions that tie rate increases to the CPI or similar indexes are particularly unjust.[27] There is simply no evidence that the CPI or any other such cost index is related to the cost of providing telephone service.[28] For the first ten months of 1988, the overall annualized CPI rose by 5.0 percent. During the same period, the CPI for telephone services increased at an annual rate of 0.1 percent.[29] A study by the New York State Public Service Commission staff indicated that if a price cap model allowing for such an indexing were in effect from 1978 to mid-year 1987, the rates for AT&T would have exceeded actual rates by approximately 150 percent. Even with a productivity adjustment of 3 percent per year, price cap rates would have exceeded actual rates under cost-of-service regulation by 70 percent.[30]

Consumer advocates have additional concerns with the trend toward deregulation. Universal service is yet to be achieved,[31] and the FCC's Lifeline and Link-Up programs are of questionable efficacy in attaining that national goal.[32]

Those of us who question the benefits of deregulation and point to the dangers of cross-subsidies will have a difficult time proving such cross-subsidies flourish where deregulation is permitted. Because the BOCs control—either directly or indirectly—information critical to such analyses, regulators must establish information-keeping guidelines for the companies that will allow the impact of deregulation to be monitored. The utilities must be required to keep adequate records of the expenses, investment, revenues, and network usage associated with both deregulated and regulated services. If the utilities fail to maintain such data, they will be able to evade review.[33]

One other issue in telephone pricing is local measured service (LMS). Suffice it to say many persons believe LMS raises the cost of providing local service and is particularly detrimental to low-income customers who rely on fixed monthly incomes. Telephone companies prefer mandatory LMS for a variety of reasons, particularly its revenue-enhancing abilities. But LMS has gotten a bad name and has even been outlawed in some states, so the companies have taken a different tack to achieve the same ends. They do this by proposing rate plans that so limit the primary calling area (that area which can be called without unit or toll charges under flat-rate service) as to effectively implement measured service. Again, the companies are master linguists, cloaking their rate design strategy in terms of offering more options, while in reality laying the groundwork for charging higher prices for basic flat-rate telephone service that encompasses the customer's community of interest.[34]

The success of the BOCs and other telecommunications companies in pressing their ratemaking agendas to augment profitability is due, not to the inherent "rightness" of their positions, but to their economic and political power. Large business users are able to obtain their goals of lower rates for essentially the same reasons: they are economically and politically powerful and their agendas coincide with those of others in the same position. Residential customers, on the other hand, are powerful in neither sense: as monopoly customers, they lack the power of the pocketbook; as diverse, unorganized individuals they lack political clout.[35] At most, residential customers may be represented in rate cases by an underfunded, understaffed state agency.

Because the resources of consumer advocates are infinitesimal compared to the RHCs, only a strong, organized consumer movement can halt the trend of lower rates for big business at the expense of higher rates for residential customers.

ENDNOTES

1. For an account of the near termination of the case in late 1980 and early 1981, see Peter Temin, with Louis Galambos, *The Fall of the Bell System* (New York: Cambridge University Press, 1987).

2. For more details about how divestiture disrupted the relationship between federal and state regulators, see Roger G. Noll, "State Regulatory Responses to Competition and Divestiture in the Telecommunications Industry," in Ronald E. Grieson, ed., *Antitrust and Regulation* (Lexington, Mass.: Lexington Books, 1986).

3. For details about the effects of divestiture on prices, production costs, and market shares for competitive products and services, see Roger G. Noll and Bruce M. Owen, "*U.S. v. AT&T:* An Interim Assessment," in Stephen P. Bradley and Jerry A. Hausman, eds., *Future Competition in Telecommunications* (Boston: Harvard Business School Press, 1988).

4. For details on how and why the DOJ insisted on placing numerous constraints on the BOCs, see Roger G. Noll and Bruce M. Owen, "The Anticompetitive Uses of Regulation: *U.S. v. AT&T,*" in John E. Kwoka, Jr., and Lawrence J. White, eds., *The Antitrust Revolution* (New York: Scott, Foresman, 1989).

5. An interesting issue is whether AT&T and the BOCs ought to have absorbed some of the revenue losses imposed by divestiture. After all, the pre-

divestiture AT&T was responsible for installing switches that were not capable of providing equal access without expending funds to alter or replace them. And, as post-divestiture pricing developments indicate, the vertically integrated AT&T had changed its local operating companies' supercompetitive prices for equipment (see Noll and Owen [1989b]). By allowing BOCs to continue to recover the costs of providing equal access, regulators were essentially rewarding pre-divestiture AT&T stockholders for the company's antitrust violations. Nevertheless, state regulators may not have been able to force the BOCs to absorb these costs. The reason is that *U.S. v. AT&T* was settled, rather than litigated to conclusion. Hence, AT&T and its operating companies were not actually convicted of violating the law, and the settlement agreement contained no requirement that the company ought to be punished. Thus, state regulators would have faced at least a long legal struggle and possibly ultimate defeat in court had they tried to prevent the full recovery of these costs. In any event, for whatever reasons, no state elected to fight this battle.

6. For more complete developments of this approach to the study of regulation, see Roger G. Noll, "Economic Perspectives on the Politics of Regulation," in Richard Schmalensee and Robert Willig, eds., *Handbook of Industrial Organization*, vol. 2 (New York: North-Holland, 1989); and Wesley A. Magat, Alan J. Krupnick, and William Harrington, *Rules in the Making*, (Washington: Resources for the Future, 1986), ch. 3. In his discussion for our analysis, Almarin Phillips suggests two additional hypotheses: "do not get too big for your britches" and "kick them while they are down." While we admire Phillips' imaginative turn of a phrase, we had difficulty following the proofs of his theorems.

7. For further analysis of why regulators especially seek to avoid visible price increases, see Paul L. Joskow, "Inflation and Environmental Concern: Structural Change in the Process of Public Utility Price Regulation," *Journal of Law and Economics* (October 1974), 17:291–327.

8. Like consumers, most businesses do not regard telephone prices as an important element of overall business costs. In industries in which telecommunications services are used intensively, interest-group arguments pertain: they will seek special price breaks for themselves, not overall reductions in prices for everyone. For other businesses, the signalling aspect of telephone prices is not as straightforward as it is for consumers. Higher telephone prices can be interpreted as signalling a generally favorable stance towards business. Hence, business may interpret a price hike for them (and the debate about it in a campaign) as indicating that the incumbent is inclined to work for their interests on matters of greater importance to them than monthly telephone rates. As long as the price increases for business customers are not substantially out of line with rate changes for residential customers, business users, then, might be expected to accept them.

9. In the 1960s, the Supreme Court issued a series of decisions regarding the constitutional requirements for legislative representation. In both the U.S. House of Representatives and state legislatures, legislative districts differed considerably in population, and in general the effect was to overrepresent rural constituencies compared to urban areas. The impact of the Court's decisions was that

by the early 1970s, House districts within a state and in both chambers of a state legislature had to be virtually identical in population. Only the U.S. Senate, by virtue of its definition in the Constitution, was exempted from this requirement. The result was a substantial shift in the political influence of rural constituencies, and more so in urbanized states than in the federal government.

10. The beneficiaries of regulation would prefer efficient pricing, all else equal, because efficiency maximizes the net economic welfare created by the industry and hence the wealth that the beneficiaries might be able to receive from regulation. Unfortunately, not all else is equal; the normal circumstances is that rules which maximize the welfare of the beneficiaries of regulation inevitably create inefficiency, so that efficiencies become at best of secondary interest to regulators. See Noll, supra at note 6.

11. For details about the anticompetitive actions of the states after divestiture, see especially Appendix B of Peter Huber, *The Goeodesic Network* (Washington, D.C.: U.S. Department of Justice, 1986).

12. The most recent study estimates that the annualized average incremental capital cost for local access and usage was $90 to $103 in communities with 10,000 lines ("small urban"), but only $54 to $78 in communities with 40,000 liens. See Bridger M. Mitchell, *Incremental Capital Costs of Telephone Access and Local Use* (Santa Monica, Calif.: Rand Corporation, 1989), p. 41. This translates to a monthly difference of about $3.

13. John Wenders and Bruce Egan, "Implications of Economic Efficiency for US Telecommunications Policy," *Telecommunications Policy* (March 1986), 10:33–40.

14. One of the more dramatic findings of this report is that the amount of private capacity in telecommunications today now exceeds that available from common carriers. This is a very significant finding, and is supported by some insightful research by Peter Grandstaff and John Watters at Southwestern Bell.

15. For example, Legal Service programs, which are dedicated to providing legal representation to poor people across the country on all civil matters (not just utility issues) have a total funding of only $305 million per year. The smallest of the seven Baby Bells, with assets of over $20 billion, earns profits of about $1 billion a year.

16. October 31, 1988 draft of *A Final Report: The Management of Consumer Affairs at AT&T*, AT&T Advisory Committee on Consumer Affairs.

17. Industry Analysis Division, Common Carrier Bureau, FCC, "Trends in Telephone Service," August 16, 1989, p. 9.

18. Staff of Federal-State Joint Board, "Sixth Monitoring Report," in CC Docket 80-286, reported in *National Association of Regulatory Utility Commissioners Bulletin*, January 30, 1989, p. 21.

19. *Telecommunications Reports*, September 12, 1988, p. 8.

20. "FCC Date Shows Taxes, SLCs Make Up 30 Percent of the Local Phone Bill," *State Telephone Regulation Report*, September 7, 1989, p. 9.

21. *Telecommunications Reports*, September 12, 1988, p. 4. See also *Wall Street Journal*, July 6, 1989, p. 64.

22. In 1986, business revenues grew 8 percent in the long-distance market,

but residential only grew 5 percent. *Business Week*, February 16, 1987, p. 28.

23. Long before divestiture, administrative proceedings discussed the costs incurred to accommodate toll calling. For example, a local call could be made just by dialing three or four digits. Toll calling required investment in new equipment that could switch the additional digits necessary to make toll calls. In addition, single wire iron conductors had to be replaced with paired copper conductors so that speech could be clearly heard over long distances. Thus, there is debate as to whether long-distance has been subsidizing local service or whether it is actually the other way around.

24. Other economists recognize that alternative means must be found to correct the current inequitable allocation of costs associated with enhanced services. See Nancy J. Wheatly, Dr. Lee Selwyn, and Patricia D. Kratvin, *Telecommunications Modernization: Who Pays?*, The National Regulatory Research Institute, September 1988.

25. See New England Telephone and Telegraph Co., D.P.U. 86-33, Phase II, Testimony of John A. Foresto, Exh. NET 98 at 16 and Transcript 48, p. 54.

26. The cost of providing telecommunications service has been falling by about 2 to 5 percent annually. *Telecommunications Reports*, August 15, 1988, p. 7. See also *Financial World*, April 18, 1989, p. 33.

27. Just as outrageous are social contracts that "freeze" local rates but permit adjustments in rates due to changes in taxes, separations, and labor contracts. The cost of each of these items is unlikely to decrease in the foreseeable future. Under these social contracts, local ratepayers lose the primary benefit of social contracts: protection against future rate increases.

28. The Consumer Federation of America (CFA) reported that the telephone industry historically earned a return over two points less than the Standard & Poor 400. CFA estimated that a straight CPI price cap would result in rates 20 percent higher over five years, and about 50 percent higher over ten years than traditional regulation.

29. The CPI for the local service component of telephone services, including subscriber line charges, increased at an annual rate of 1.9 percent, while the CPI for interstate toll calls fell by 1.5 percent and state toll calls by 4.8 percent. *National Association of Regulatory Utility Commissioners Bulletin*, January 30, 1989, p. 21. The increase of 1.9 percent in the CPI for local service is still far below the increase in the overall CPI of 5.0 percent.

30. *Comments of the State of New York Department of Public Service*, Policy and Rules Concerning Rates for Dominant Carriers, CC Docket No. 87-313, pp. 16-17. AT&T prepared its own study comparing price caps and cost-of-service regulation, which indicated that consumers would realize lower rates under price caps. However, as the Consumer Federation of America points out, AT&T's study makes certain untenable assumptions, including a continuous decline in the evening and weekend discount under regulation.

31. The penetration rate for poor minority households ranges from 57.1 percent to 82.2 percent. United States Department of Commerce, Bureau of the Census, *Current Population Survey*, November 1983 to March 1989.

32. Problems with the programs include overly restrictive eligibility require-

ments and other factors that have led to limited low-income participation. See Staff of the Federal-State Joint Board, "September 1988 Monitoring Report," in Docket No. 87-339.

33. As Nina Cornell indicates in the previous chapter, companies will attempt to inhibit the preparation of intervenors' cases by designation of documents as "proprietary" or "competitively sensitive." Regulators should establish a standard for designating materials as "secret." The standard should be strict and the burden of showing a compelling need to maintain secrecy should be placed on the utility attempting to keep the information confidential. Furthermore, the regulatory agency should not limit public access to materials any more than is absolutely necessary under the circumstances.

34. The contraction of primary calling areas is not cost-justified according to BOC testimony. US West witnesses testified that it costs no more to place a call going ninety miles than one going less than a mile if both calls are interoffice calls. This testimony seems to assume either that the costs being referred to are marginal costs or that the network is fully depreciated.

35. Small business users have had uneven success. They benefit to the extent that their interests coincide with large business users, e.g., lower long-distance rates. Small business customers also benefit to the extent that rate classes are not categorized by amount of use, but type of use, e.g., residential versus business.

6

Service Quality

■

ROWLAND L. CURRY

■

JONATHAN M. KRAUSHAAR

ROBERT M. GRYB

JOHN R. AKE

THOMAS E. BUZAS,

STANFORD V. BERG,

AND JOHN G. LYNCH, JR.

LAWRENCE P. COLE

Rowland L. Curry

The divestiture of the telephone operating companies from the AT&T system had the potential to disrupt voice and data communications throughout the nation and significantly affect service quality. The industry began the implementation of equal access for all interexchange carriers in accordance with the Court's orders. Moreover, at the same time, the telephone companies were having to adapt to changes in equipment operations caused by the 1983 deregulation of CPE. The transition produced customer confusion and limited discontinuities in the operations of the system, but the network remained intact. In many instances, AT&T and the BOCs had to sort out deeply entangled facilities; the companies even used tape on switching office floors to designate ownership and operating responsibility. It is a significant tribute to American planning and technology that the divestiture was accomplished with as few snags as actually occurred.

A characteristic of telephone service quality analysis is that success is measured in terms of the lack of attention paid to the quality of the service offered. There are exceptions, for example, when a customer notices the clarity of a transcontinental circuit or an exceptionally efficient installation. However, in today's technological society, we have grown to expect good performance, and poor performance has become the memorable exception. A "regulatory" perspective sometimes fails to give credit where it is due; the telephone companies in the United States created a reliable and advanced technical communications system through a century of hard work and dedication to the provision of good service.

An effective service quality evaluation process must consist of standards, measurement, and analysis. A standard can be defined as something established by authority as a rule for the measure of quantity, weight, extent, value, or quality. Standards set the criteria for judgment; measurement produces the data; and analysis uses these data to provide a judgment on whether the criteria were met. These three sequential elements must exist in a tight correspondence, and must be used in carefully controlled and monitored applications. Loose or weakly specified standards cannot produce reliable performance judgments, no matter how good the data and analysis. Without standards, the evaluator has no benchmarks or criteria with which to compare actual results. Accurate and consistent measurement is essential to ascertain the current status of any activity. And, to evaluate a program effectively, the evaluator must conduct feedback analysis of the measurement compared to the standard, in order to determine whether change should take place.

Regulators attempting to evaluate the quality of telephone service following the divestiture appear to be faced with a shortage of uniform nationwide standards, inconsistent measurements, and very little analysis. The fact is, however, there has been continual and extensive evaluation by utility analysts at the micro level, consisting of the level of engineering, installation, and maintenance of switches and facilities. Evaluation at the micro level has assured continuation of acceptable service quality despite a general lack of analysis at the macro level, the overall level of network performance.

It is important to recognize this micro/macro evaluation distinction when comparing the nature and operational level of service evaluation among services, providers, and regulators. Significant differences can be seen in the evaluation perspectives of: (a) regulators and utilities, (b) federal and state regulators, and (c) local and interexchange services. Regulatory analysts, by necessity, cannot become steeped in the detailed analysis performed by the utilities. At the same time, regulatory analysis is often more objective than that done by the utilities. The same comparison of perspective can be found between state and federal regulatory agencies; the states often analyze issues in greater depth than the FCC, but in many instances, the FCC has a more "forest view" perspective.

For a variety of reasons, most regulatory analysis of telephone service quality has been oriented toward LECs, with very little service quality evaluation of interexchange carriers. State regulatory agencies have adopted service standards over the past fifty years or more, but only a few specifically applied to long-distance service. Most rules have been oriented toward customer connection with the local exchange. This is partly because it has only been since the emergence of interexchange competition and the divestiture that there has been the potential for separate standards for interexchange carriers. Further, most of the interexchange carriers are either nonregulated or are operating in a more competitive environment, and regulators have shown little interest in pursuing added standards for them. Finally, some state regulators who have attempted to measure service performance of interexchange carriers have encountered difficulty in determining the source of specific inadequacies. In order to maintain a comprehensive mechanism for the evaluation of telephone service quality, all three components of evaluation need to exist for all comparative segments—utility and regulatory, local and interexchange, and federal and state. The following sections will discuss the three components of evaluation—standards, measurement, and analysis—and their application to the question of divestiture's effect on service quality.

Utility regulatory agencies function as administrative law bodies which are given certain powers by constitutional or legislative mandate. In discussing standards, it may be helpful to examine the relationship among the levels of authority under which the rules are established: i.e., whose rules are they? Telephone service quality standards can be grouped into the following five categories for the purpose of this discussion:

Legislative   A specific standard is mandated by law.

Administrative There is no specific legal requirement, but the appropriate regulatory agency adopts formal rules or orders which establish standards governing the provision of service for all utilities.

Tariff   There is no specific legal standard or formal administrative agency rule, but each individual utility's tariff contains criteria that control the provision of service in a contractual sense.

Industry Standard   None of the above authorities have approved standards, but a utility has its own internal or industry-accepted standards which control the provision of service.

Nonexistent   Folklore prevails; no legislative or regulatory agency standards exist, and the utility has no written documentation on standards for the service.

Standards may be established at any one of these levels of authority. In practice, all five of these categories exist for various services and regulatory agencies. Generally, the "higher" levels of authority set standards establishing broad requirements, while technical details are found in utility procedural documents.

State regulatory agencies are generally given authority by their respective state legislative bodies to assure that regulated carriers provide an adequate level of service. Currently, thirty-one state regulatory agencies have adopted formal telephone service quality standards which are applied to local exchange carriers. A smaller number of regulatory commissions have approved standards that apply to interexchange carriers. Performance standards in the state range from brief to voluminous. Typically, the formal state standards fall into two general categories; customer service and technical standards.

Performance standards related to customer service vary greatly from state to state, but usually include one or more of the following: location, retention of records, filing of periodic reports, tariff regulations, customer information, billing procedures, handling of complaints, disconnection practices, customer deposits, directory requirements, pay telephone provision. Technical network standards exist in many states, and may include the following: engineering and construction standards; party line provisioning; emergency operation (batteries, generators); maintenance requirements, reports; testing methods, test lines; service order completions, commitments; trouble reports (volume of reports, commitments for repair, clearing time); operator answer time;

dial tone speed; call completions (or blockages and failures); and transmission and noise quality.

Because state regulatory agencies function in an oversight capacity, the standards established by those agencies are generally less stringent than those set by the utilities themselves for a particular item of evaluation. As an example, telephone utilities might adopt a 98 percent standard for their own individual business offices in order to ensure compliance with the state PUC standard of a lesser 95 percent. Conversely, a state PUC might establish a lesser standard for a particular performance item knowing there is significant variation in the capabilities of the many LECs under its jurisdiction.

The NARUC has adopted Model Telecommunications Service Rules that contain suggested guidelines for both customer service and technical service quality standards. The model rules are basically patterned after existing rules in place in various states, and are offered as a guide for other states that desire to adopt standards. The NARUC model rules are modified as necessary to track industry issues and technology. Changes are developed by NARUC staff subcommittees, and must formally be adopted by the Committee on Communications and the Executive Committee of NARUC.

The FCC has not adopted any specific standards for service quality performance of telephone utilities. In order to assure adequate performance, the federal agency depends on the existence of state service standards, on utility industry standards, and on requirements contained in the approved tariffs of the utilities. The FCC has used various monitoring plans during past years to analyze the level of interstate service quality offered by local exchange and interexchange carriers.

As a result of the proposal to utilize price caps as an alternative form of regulation for telecommunications carriers, parties have recommended that the Commission adopt minimum service quality standards, and the FCC staff has begun analysis of that recommendation. NARUC and consumer advocacy groups have argued the FCC plan to replace rate-of-return regulation with a price cap plan will encourage reductions in network investment and maintenance expenses, thus degrading the level of service quality. The utilities have argued they must maintain high levels of service quality to be successful, and service quality is unlikely to decline as a result of the price cap approach. As of this writing, the FCC has expressed its intent to refrain from establishing standards for service quality, and instead to require periodic monitoring reports from the utilities.

Measurement, as used in this discussion, involves the use of various instruments (e.g., test equipment or auditing techniques) to produce data that reveal the nature and level of service quality. Three groups generally "perform" measurements of telephone utility service quality; customers, regulators, and the utility itself.

Historically, surveys of the perception of service quality by utility customers were considered as a useful, but rather subjective and nontechnical measurement. In addition, few customers had the expertise to perform measurements using sophisticated test equipment. However, as interexchange carriers and complex premises equipment vendors have begun serving major customers, technical gauges from the "customer" group have gained credibility. Large customers often have staff with technical skills to perform reliable tests and measurements on the facilities connecting the customer to the utility.

Nontechnical customer opinion surveys have become an increasingly accepted form of measurement for service quality. Typically, a utility will engage a consulting firm to poll customers who have had a recent transaction (installation, repair, etc.) with the utility. That survey will show the customer's perception of service, and may be used to evaluate diverse practices ranging from operator staffing to worker neatness. While state regulatory agencies recognize the value in such polling, it is generally viewed as being too subjective to be used as a tool for regulatory analysis.

Understandably, the vast majority of performance measurements are conducted by the utilities themselves. With approximately 1,370 local exchange telephone companies operating in the United States, the amount of continual testing necessary to keep the network functioning properly is staggering. Telephone companies of all sizes must perform periodic measurement and analysis on network facilities. Tests range from individual component specifications to overall network performance testing. With newer analog and digital electronic technology, much of the testing is done at a centralized location, and repair forces are dispatched as needed. Some computerized systems are able to dial repeatedly into test terminations to determine the percentage of call completions, and others are able to test subscriber lines during off-peak periods at night. Such systems are not limited to the larger BOCs, but also are used by smaller telephone companies with modern systems. Some of the performance measurement data collected by the utilities are provided to regulatory agencies to assess service quality, either on a routine reporting basis or by special request. The data are generally limited to a small number of broad performance categories the agency believes best reflects the overall condition of the utility's service.

Service performance measurement for regulatory purposes must be consistent, not only within one utility's operation but, ideally, across the operations of all utilities within the regulatory agency's jurisdiction. Measurement of performance must be oriented toward the ultimate analysis of the data and the standards to be applied. If various telecommunications utilities use similar but different methods of measurement for a particular performance category, analysis and comparison of the results with a published standard are difficult. As an example, one utility may report on service orders worked within five days, and another may use the measure of three days.

In addition to the difficulties caused by inconsistent measurements, regulatory analysts face a dilemma in determining the authenticity of utility data. Many performance measurements are based on large numbers of events (e.g., service orders, trouble tickets, or completed calls), to which only the utility itself has access. Such measurements cannot be duplicated by the regulatory agency; therefore, some level of assurance is required for the regulator to accept the data. In order to address this concern, evaluators occasionally conduct desk or field audits of the performance data provided by the utility, and data filings may be required to be accompanied by sworn statements of authenticity by utility representatives. In addition, there is an increased use of management audits of utilities for regulatory purposes, within which the data collection procedures are generally addressed.

Tests and measurements may be performed by the regulatory agencies themselves. State regulatory agencies which have reported having field testing programs in place are: Alabama, Arkansas, Florida, Georgia, Illinois, Indiana, Missouri, Nebraska, New York, North Carolina, Ohio, Oklahoma, Oregon, South Carolina, Tennessee, Texas, Virginia, West Virginia, and Wyoming. Those programs may include call completion, operator answer time, and facility testing elements. In addition, almost all regulatory agencies track the number of customer complaints received against telephone utilities. Those complaints are often categorized by issue, resulting in patterns of complaints such as noisy lines or calling failures. Patterns detected through customer contacts can lead to additional measurements and investigations by the utility or regulatory staff.

The third element of evaluation—analysis—refers to the comparison of measurements with approved standards. Without analysis, the establishment of standards and the compilation of measurement data are meaningless. To an engineer, this element represents the feedback of a measurement of the output of a device in order to establish control on the input.

In order to support a reasonable conclusion, an analyst must be assured that the measurement data are consistent. Data gathered under inconsistent assumptions reduce the probability of an accurate conclusion. Inconsistent measurements pervade telephone service quality data collected by the various telephone utilities and reported to state and federal regulators. Within a given jurisdiction, a regulatory agency may adopt sufficiently detailed instructions to ensure that the utilities provide consistent measurements in a particular category. Among different jurisdictions, however, inconsistencies cause great problems for analysis.

As an example, one of the most useful measures in service analysis is the "Trouble Reports per One Hundred Lines" category. In-depth analysis of this index has shown that various utilities exclude certain types of reported calls from this measurement. Many of the exclusions are reasonable, such as a customer contact which is not truly a trouble report. However, some utilities have been found to exclude over twenty varieties of calls, while others exclude only a few. This difference in procedures has resulted in significant differences in results.

Inconsistencies in measurement are clearly found in other areas such as service order provisioning, where some utilities collect data based on the percentage of orders filled within three days, and others record the percentage of orders filled within five days. In most cases, the measurements can be translated to a common denominator if an approved standard is present.

Another difficulty for the utility analyst is the "masking" which occurs when data are aggregated into a statewide, companywide, or nationwide result. Individual companies, states, or exchanges can be experiencing significant service problems, yet aggregated measurements show no adverse indications. One operator service location in a large state may be experiencing substandard performance during particular periods of the month or year. However, after combining that operating unit with others in the state, and averaging the performance for all the days of the reporting period, the substandard performance will not be seen.

One solution for the masking problem is the technique of reviewing the percentage of entities meeting a particular standard. While this requires "an index of an index," it can improve the performance analysis caused by large data aggregation. As an example of this technique, assume that an approved standard requires the utility's switching offices to provide a dial tone within three seconds 95 percent of the time during busy hours. It is more meaningful for an analyst to know that only 80 percent of the offices met the standard, than it is to know that the dial tone speed percentage aggregated for all offices was 94.5 percent.

Telephone utilities often aggregate many individual performance measurements into a single composite index for comparison purposes. The composite figures invariably contain assumptions and weightings which may be disputed. For instance, one utility combines its "trouble report" index with its "service order installation" index and other performance data to produce an "exchange maintenance index." That index appears to be helpful to the utility in comparing exchanges or operating districts. However, it is not particularly helpful to a regulatory analyst who must compare the performance of that utility with regulatory performance standards.

Unfortunately, regulatory analysts of telephone service quality are cursed with a void of knowledge when evaluating the impact of divestiture. In order to evaluate the effects of an event, it is critical to know what was happening before and what was happening after the event took place. Individual states possess performance data for their respective BOCs, and there are some studies which show bits and pieces of the pre-divestiture and post-divestiture service quality picture; however, there are very little meaningful measurement data that track clearly across the divestiture divide.

In 1976, the FCC Common Carrier Bureau's Special Studies Branch released its Quality of Telephone Service Survey, a study of nationwide telephone service quality offered by the Bell System. That special report included ten basic measurements that reflected significant indices of service quality. The study report compared the performance of each geographic operating area with benchmarks based on industry objectives in seven of the ten categories to determine areas of weakness, and a "weakspot" analysis was compiled. The 1976 study was updated on a semiannual basis until it was discontinued in 1981.

Figures 6.1a–6.1d contain summary graphs of nationwide data provided in the FCC Quality of Telephone Service Survey in overlapping periods from January 1974 to December 1980. Spanning the entire Bell System, these graphs show performance in ten categories: unfilled orders—main total; unfilled orders—main over thirty days old; unfilled regrades—over thirty days old; percent toll and assistance answers over ten seconds; percent DDD incoming trunk—equipment blockages and failures; percent dial tone over three seconds during busy hours; percent regular installations not completed within five days; percent regular installation appointments not met (for company reasons); customer trouble reports per one hundred stations; and percent repeated repair reports.

The FCC publication of these performance measurements was accompanied by a "weakspot" analysis, in which the performance in

FIGURE 6.1a

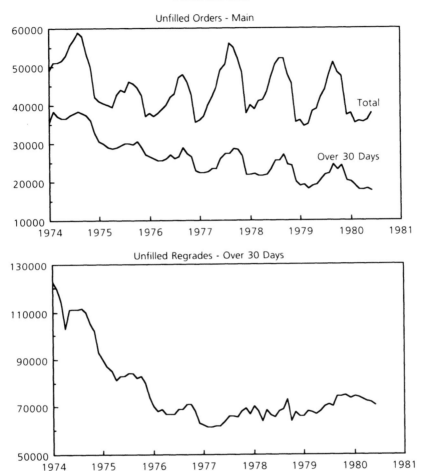

Source: Bell System.

seven of the categories was compared to FCC "benchmarks." These benchmarks were not formally adopted FCC standards. The failure to achieve the benchmark level in a category resulted in a "weakspot" in the affected area for that time period.

FIGURE 6.1b

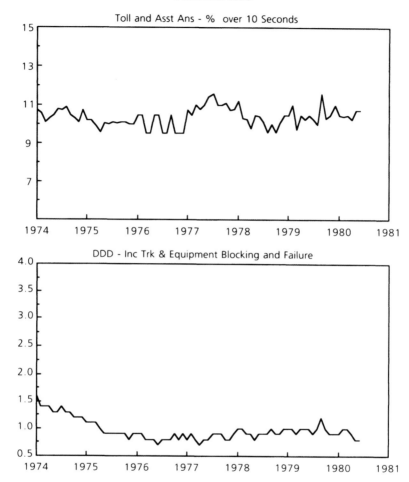

Source: Bell System.

Table 6.1 contains a sample of the Summary of Total Weakspots for the entire Bell System for the period from January through June, 1978. Each Bell System operating area was evaluated separately. For that period, there were a total of nineteen weakspots, four of which were

FIGURE 6.1c

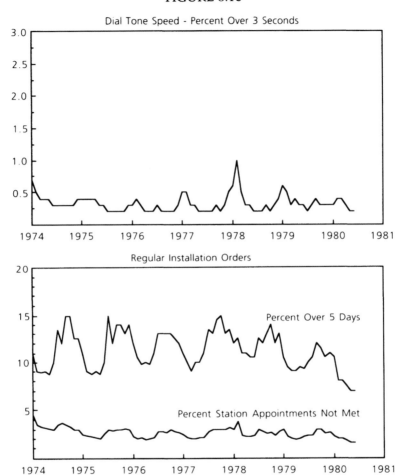

Source: Bell System.

shown for South Central Bell in Kentucky, and three each in New England Telephone (Rhode Island) and Pacific Bell (Los Angeles). The strength of the FCC's pre-divestiture report was not in its aggregated, nationwide data, but in the specific analysis of weaknesses in regions of the country.

FIGURE 6.1d

Source: Bell System.

The FCC's Memorandum Opinion and Order, released on December 23, 1983, approving the transfer of facilities associated with the divestiture, required the divested BOCs to provide service quality data on a semiannual basis. A 1989 FCC paper by Jonathan Kraushaar, entitled "Report on the Quality of Service for the Bell Operating Companies"

TABLE 6.1
Total Weakspots Quality of Service Area Report

New England		Illinois	
Maine	0	Chicago	0
New Hampshire	0	Suburban	0
Rhode Island	3	State	0
Vermont	0	Northwestern	
Massachusetts	0	Iowa	0
New York		Minnesota	0
New York City East	0	Nebraska	0
New York City West	0	North Dakota	0
Suburban	1	South Dakota	0
Upstate	0	Southwestern	
New Jersey	0	Arkansas	0
Pennsylvania		Kansas	0
Philadelphia	0	Missouri	0
Eastern	0	St. Louis	1
Central	0	Oklahoma	0
Western	0	N.E. Texas (inc. Dallas)	0
Chesapeake and Potomac		S.E. Texas (inc. Houston)	2
Washington, D.C.	0	W. Cent. Texas (inc. San Antonio)	0
Maryland	0	Mountain	
Virginia	0	Arizona	0
West Virginia	0	Colorado	0
Southern		Idaho	0
North Florida	0	Montana	0
South Florida	0	New Mexico	0
Southeast Florida	0	El Paso (Texas)	0
Atlanta	0	Utah	0
Georgia (excl. Atlanta)	2	Wyoming	1
North Carolina	0	Pacific Northwest	
South Carolina	0	Washington–Idaho	0
South Central		Oregon	0
Alabama	0	Pacific	
Kentucky	4	Bay	0
Louisiana	1	Northern	0
Mississippi	0	Los Angeles	3
Tennessee	0	Southern counties	0
Ohio	0	Nevada	0
Michigan		Southern New England	0
Outside	0	Cincinnati	0
Detroit	0		
Indiana	1	Total	19
Wisconsin	0		

FIGURE 6.2

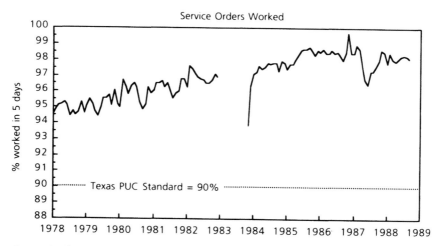

Service Orders Worked

Source: Southwestern Bell.

has been released by the Common Carrier Bureau's Industry Analysis Division. Later in this chapter, Kraushaar provides a summary and analysis of that study.

Many state regulatory agencies have collected service quality data that reflect various performance indices related to the Bell operating divisions prior to 1984, and continuing through 1988. For example, performance results in four key categories for Southwestern Bell's Texas operations are shown in figures 6.2 through 6.5.

Most of the performance measures show general improvements over time. Southwestern Bell has generally met most of the Texas PUC service quality standards during the past ten years. The analysis of Southwestern Bell's Texas performance data shows several trends and events of interest as described in the following paragraphs. However, no significant impact of divestiture is evidenced.

Figure 6.2 tracks Southwestern Bell's provisioning of customer service orders, with the index showing the percentage of "regular" service orders filled within five days. The only remarkable trend of these data during the past ten years is the general, gradual improvement in the percentage of service orders completed within the specified period. No negative trends were visible about the time of divestiture.

Figure 6.3 shows the trend of operator answer time, measured as the percentage of instances over ten seconds. The Texas PUC standard for

FIGURE 6.3

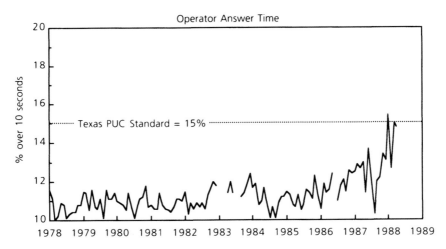

Source: Southwestern Bell.

this service measure is 15 percent, and until 1988, Southwestern Bell operated well within this objective. There is no noticeable trend in the 1983–1985 time period, across divestiture.

Figure 6.4 shows Southwestern Bell's Texas performance in the category of Trouble Reports per one hundred Stations/Lines. Prior to the deregulation of customer premises equipment, the performance measure "Trouble Reports per 100 Mainstations" was one of the most often used indices. The deregulation of CPE resulted in the elimination of many of the trouble reports for the regulated utility. This reduced the number of trouble reports per line. At about the same time, however, the base or denominator of the measure was drastically reduced through the change to "Trouble Reports per 100 Access Lines." The end result of the combined changes was that the BOC's performance index improved significantly in that area during 1984. This change was not due to an improvement in service, but rather a change in reporting methods, and was not directly related to divestiture.

Figure 6.5 illustrates the utility's performance in the category of "Out-of-Service Troubles Cleared Within Eight Working Hours." In 1979, the utility was having a difficult time with this measure, due in large part to the existence of buried air-core plastic cable throughout the state. The utility embarked on an aggressive plant replacement program, and there has been a gradual improvement in the category

FIGURE 6.4

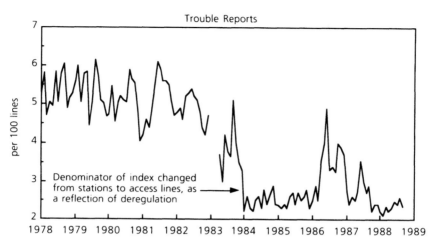

Source: Southwestern Bell.

FIGURE 6.5

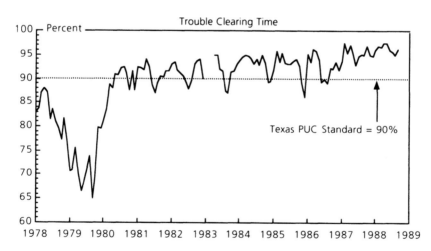

Source: Southwestern Bell.

since that time. No significant variation was seen as a result of divestiture.

The most significant impact of the divestiture on service quality would be expected in the interLATA toll network. After all, little was changed in the realm of local exchange operations. The most abrupt change took place in the splitting of the toll network into inter and intraLATA. Prior to divestiture, the LATA concept did not exist; there is no pre-divestiture interLATA network performance for comparison. In addition, many of the pre-divestiture service standards applied to the overall telephone system are meaningless when used to evaluate AT&T or any other interexchange carrier. Traditional standards related to service orders and trouble reports per one hundred lines have no relevance in evaluating the divested AT&T.

AT&T has placed added emphasis on network quality, and the company is moving toward digitalization of the network, with features such as Dynamic Non-Hierarchical Routing (DNHR) and Common Channel Signaling (CCS) as major improvements. AT&T continues to employ an aggressive service monitoring program, which consists of automatic measurements and customer surveys.

The competitive nature of the interexchange marketplace has certainly provided incentives for the continuation of satisfactory, if not improving service quality. Competitors such as US Sprint have based massive customer marketing campaigns on the technical excellence of their network, and that has clearly made an impression on AT&T.

Very little data is available from AT&T regarding service quality, and it does not report semiannual information to the FCC in the same manner as the BOCs. AT&T does report some measurements to state regulatory agencies. However, it has not provided data that would track meaningful measures across the threshold of divestiture.

It is clear that the divestiture of the BOCs from AT&T has had no catastrophic effect on nationwide service quality. However, lack of consistent data from the pre-divestiture era to the post-divestiture era makes it difficult, if not impossible, to quantify precisely the effects on a nationwide basis. And much more data are available to analyze the BOCs than AT&T. It is important to also recognize the forces of CPE deregulation during the same time period further complicate any analysis.

Critics argue that the AT&T divestiture should never have taken place, that the result of the consent decree was to dismantle the most reliable telephone system in the world. It is a tribute to the technical planning and talent of the telecommunications industry that the massive task was accomplished with no apparent long-term setbacks in service quality or network performance.

The preservation of adequate national telephone service quality depends on the ability and willingness of federal and state regulatory agencies, the courts, and the Congress to work in harmony to establish policies which encourage telephone utilities to continue improvements in their operations. In an era of increasing regulatory flexibility, regulators must maintain service evaluation standards, measurement, and analysis to ensure the public interest is protected.

Jonathan M. Kraushaar

Rowland Curry aptly points out some of the problems in collecting quality of service data, focusing in particular on the problem of specifying uniform standards. The present FCC quality of service monitoring program was established to respond to the general concern about service quality following divestiture, and relies on a technique for analysis which was designed to address precisely the problem of dealing with data in which the imposition of detailed uniform standards was not feasible. It illustrates the obvious limitations and constraints in rapidly setting up a monitoring program after divestiture.

In the December 1983 authorization for transfer of ownership associated with divestiture, conditions were specified that the Commission would collect quality of service data, among other things, to determine divestiture's impact. The 1983 order gave the Common Carrier Bureau the opportunity to work with the companies to determine what data would be filed.

There were, of course, a number of constraints on requiring service quality data collection. These included the deregulatory environment, and the fact the companies were undergoing a tremendous amount of upheaval just to get their operations in order. Moreover, many of the state PUCs already monitored quality of service. Because it was infeasible to ask for new data not already being prepared, the companies were asked to provide information on the general categories of data they collected for internal use and for the state commissions. Material to be used in the monitoring program was limited to those data categories which were provided by all the Bell companies.

Despite the uniformity in data categories, it was recognized that there were various differences among the companies in how data was prepared and assembled. Imposition of detailed standards at all levels would have prevented the timely availability of baseline data. As a result, efforts focused on new ways to evaluate the existing data in a meaningful manner. It is hoped the analysis technique I will describe will be helpful to others in examining data from different companies, with possible variations in measurement standards.

The FCC monitoring program focused on local operating company data in particular for two reasons. First, all interexchange service is limited by access into the local networks. Second, the greatest concerns voiced at the time of divestiture were about how the local carriers were going to perform.

The quality of service items currently being monitored are broadly organized into five main categories: (1) customer satisfaction levels; (2) percent of switching machines performing at or above dial tone speed objectives; (3) percent of offices meeting all transmission objectives; (4) percent of calls encountering equipment failure or blocking; and (5) percent of on-time service orders.

Customer satisfaction levels are determined by company surveys, which are an outgrowth of pre-divestiture methods developed by Bell Laboratories. Percent satisfaction levels for residence, and small and large business subcategories are requested. Some companies also provide data for a medium business subcategory. Data has been summarized in two FCC reports in March 1989 and June 1990. Several minor changes were made to data presented in the June 1990 report. For example, Pacific Bell's general business subcategory was classified in the March 1989 report as medium business and reclassified in the June 1990 report as small business.

Due to their subjective nature, these surveys generally are not expected to provide conclusive results when changes in the quality of service are slight or gradual. Nonetheless, the companies place a high reliance on these surveys. In accordance with the Commission's general policy not to place new burdens on the carriers, and to use existing measures whenever possible, the survey results have been incorporated into the monitoring requirements along with the following other more objective gauges.

The length of time it takes for a customer to obtain dial tone, sometimes referred to as dial tone delay, is historically one of the most obvious and immediate causes for customer dissatisfaction. All companies monitor it with fairly consistent objective standards. Severe dial tone delay in a number of central offices during the late 1960s was one of the factors leading the Commission's Docket 19129 investigation of AT&T. Eventually a pre-divestiture general standard of a three-second dial tone delay became well established, and the companies now provide the FCC with data on the percentages of central offices failing to meet it.

The primary variation noted among companies relates to the way they measure and calculate standard compliance. Although such variations may be expected between companies, each company is required to document any changes in its standards when it files any new data. Dial tone delay is becoming less significant in an environment of electronic switching machines, in which the failure mode may be loss of an entire office, rather than increased dial tone delay. Nonetheless, it continues to provide historical perspective and illustrates the impact of new technology and investment on service quality.

The four major components of transmission quality are noise, balance, loss, and distortion. Perceptible noise or inadequate signal amplitude are obviously objectionable. Balance and distortion measurements are also needed, although problems in these areas may be harder for customers to identify. Information on the percentage of offices meeting all company established transmission level standards associated with these four criteria, as well as the standards themselves, have been requested by the FCC.

Although the measured transmission characteristics and the techniques for collecting and processing the data are similar for all reporting companies, it is not clear that all companies are basing their transmission quality measurements provided to the Commission on all four components. Some companies may be reporting the percentage of measured central offices that meet only one or two of the key criteria. In addition, Pacific Bell did not provide transmission quality data for a number of reporting periods I will be reviewing. Furthermore, there is some concern about subtle problems relating to other companies' understanding of the requirements for this category of data. And finally, there may be variation in the objective criteria which companies use to determine whether an entity is categorized as passing or failing transmission tests.

The FCC also monitors the percentage of on-time service orders. This measurement reflects the date promised to the customer, and is not a uniform standard time interval for all companies. As with many of the other data elements, the underlying reports from the BOCs do not always use the same formats, definitions, and reporting categories. For the purpose of summarizing the data, however, the reported results for on-time service orders will be shown in three overall categories: residence, access, and a "catch-all" labeled "Special/Business."

The final category of service quality being reported to the FCC is the percentage of calls which cannot be completed due to equipment problems or lack of adequate facilities. Historically, the toll network has been designed so that typically less than one percent of all calls encounter such problems. For local networks this percentage may be slightly higher, but should not exceed 5 percent. End-to-end blocking is difficult to evaluate since more than one trunk connected in tandem may be used in completing calls. A relatively new system called Service Evaluation System II (SES II) is used by some of the operating companies. This system monitors a sampling of calls traversing the network and evaluates the status of each call just prior to completion. Since not all companies use this system, it is not possible to assure complete consistency for this data category in the FCC's monitoring program.

Companies not using SES II employ another equipment-based measurement parameter, which indicates the percentage of offices not meeting company-established performance levels. Although these data also deal with calls not finding their way through the network, they have a different meaning than the SES II results, are numerically somewhat higher, and are not provided separately for interLATA and intraLATA calls. They are included in place of the SES II results for interLATA calls. The data in this category are based on a sampling process that may differ from company to company, but which the FCC has not evaluated. Despite the above imperfections, data for this category may provide a broad indication of trends in call completion rates.

All RBOCs have provided data to the Commission, although a number of companies do not provide certain data subcategories. The data first were compiled in 1985, and continue to be submitted to the FCC semiannually. Although the quality of existing service measurements are too aggregated to pinpoint localized problems, one would expect significant service quality problems to be more global in scope and to probably occur over an extended time period. Rather than evaluating absolute levels for the five measurements, adverse changes can be detected by examining changes in each of the data.

In addition to simple data trending, a technique of indexing has been used by the Commission to help standardize results and determine the presence of general trends in company results. The approach is based on the premise that the magnitude of a change in service quality from one reporting period to the next, which may be influenced by many extraneous factors (including subjective perceptions) is less significant than what kind of a change occurred. This technique should help to deal with variations in individual company procedures in preparing the data submitted. The validity of results only depends on individual company consistency in its own procedures.

The indexed results reflect changes from 1985 baseline data. Each subcategory is assigned a "+1" if the current data element reflects improved performance relative to the corresponding item in the baseline period. Similarly, if the current data reflects poorer performance, the index is assigned a "−1." If there is no change, the respective index is assigned a zero. Data elements not provided by the carriers in the FCC's March 1989 report discussed here, but which were provided previously, automatically result in a "−1" index. A second result not penalizing the carriers for missing data was also calculated. Data not provided in 1985, but provided subsequently, results in a zero in the baseline index. This reduces the maximum attainable score and should encourage all required data to be filed.

All the subcategories under each main category are then averaged. A "+1" is assigned to the main category if the subcategory average is greater than zero, and a "−1" is assigned if the average is less than zero. A zero results if the subcategory average equals zero. The results of the process, assuming no penalty for missing data, is shown in table 6.2. All resulting main category indices could be added to provide a single overall index.

The quality of service data presented is intended to be viewed in the context of the Commission's original concerns about broad future service deterioration trends associated with the divestiture. The individual reports provided by the companies tend to make interpretation of short-term variation difficult, since the indices almost always register over 90 percent. Nonetheless, a key concern of the commission is to compare current and baseline results and to identify any adverse long-term trends.

In table(s) 6.2 (and 6.3), the individual quality of service indicators are grouped into five summary indices for all companies up to and including the reporting period, January–June 1988. (Table 6.3 includes a penalty for missing data.) In order to better evaluate the data provided to date, the data for each of the individual measured items associated with the seven regional holding companies were averaged. These results, based on revisions in the source data, have been trended and are displayed in figures 6.6 to 6.9.

These aggregated data show improvements in the areas of customer perception, transmission quality, dial tone speed, and blocking since the data were first collected in 1985. In the area of on-time service performance, there is a noticeable, although small, decline in the on-time service provisionary category for residential customers. Customer perception results appear somewhat less variable than when they were first provided: however, business perceptions appear to have improved

TABLE 6.2
Quality of Service Data Analysis

Trends Composite Index[a]
First Half 1988 Data – End of Year 1985 Data

	Customers Satisfied	Dial Tone Speed Objective	Trans- mission Quality	On Time Service Orders	Call Com- pletion
US West					
Northwestern Bell	0	1	−1	0	0
Pacific NW Bell	1	1	1	−1	1
Mountain Bell	1	1	−1	1	0
SW Bell	−1	1	1	1	−1
Bell South					
Southern Bell	1	1	−1	−1	1
South Central Bell	1	−1	1	1	1
NYNEX					
New York Telephone	1	1	1	1	1
New England Telephone	1	1	1	1	1
Pacific Telesis					
Pacific Bell	1	0	0	−1	0
Bell of Nevada	1	−1	1	−1	0
Bell Atlantic					
C & P Cos.	1	1	1	1	1
Bell of Pennsylvania	1	1	−1	1	1
New Jersey Bell	1	1	1	1	1
Ameritech					
Illinois Bell	1	−1	−1	0	0
Indiana Bell	1	1	1	1	0
Michigan Bell	1	1	1	1	0
Ohio Bell	1	1	1	1	0
Wisconsin Bell	1	−1	0	1	0

Note: +1 indicates index has improved.
−1 indicates index has deteriorated.
0 indicates no change from baseline or data missing.
[a] No penalty for missing data.

more than residential perceptions. A noticeable decline in data for the second half of 1989 is apparent in a number of categories. This may be attributable to the telephone strike in late 1989; however, more subsequent data would be needed to confirm this fact.

TABLE 6.3
Quality of Service Data Analysis

Trends Composite Index[a]
First Half 1988 Data – End of Year 1985 Data

	Customers Satisfied	Dial Tone Speed Objective	Trans- mission Quality	On Time Service Orders	Call Com- pletion
US West					
Northwestern Bell	−1	1	−1	0	0
Pacific NW Bell	0	1	1	−1	1
Mountain Bell	1	1	−1	1	0
SW Bell	−1	1	1	1	−1
Bell South					
Southern Bell	1	1	−1	−1	1
South Central Bell	1	−1	1	1	1
NYNEX					
New York Telephone	1	1	1	1	1
New England Telephone	1	1	1	1	1
Pacific Telesis					
Pacific Bell	1	0	0	−1	0
Bell of Nevada	1	−1	1	−1	−1
Bell Atlantic					
C & P Cos.	1	1	1	1	1
Bell of Pennsylvania	1	1	−1	1	1
New Jersey Bell	1	1	1	1	1
Ameritech					
Illinois Bell	1	−1	−1	0	−1
Indiana Bell	1	1	1	1	−1
Michigan Bell	1	1	1	1	−1
Ohio Bell	1	1	1	1	−1
Wisconsin Bell	1	−1	0	1	−1

Note: +1 indicates index has improved.
−1 indicates index has deteriorated.
0 indicates no change from baseline or data missing.
[a] Includes a penalty for missing data.

These observations may suggest a greater general responsiveness to business customer problems, but may also reveal a greater sensitivity by business customers to service quality levels. While perception surveys are an important part of company quality monitoring programs,

FIGURE 6.6

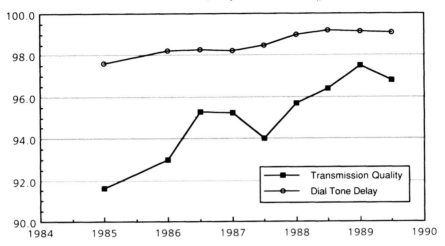

Transmission Quality & Dial Tone Delay

Source: FCC "Update on Quality of Service for the Bell Operating Companies"
Common Carrier Bureau, June 1990.

FIGURE 6.7

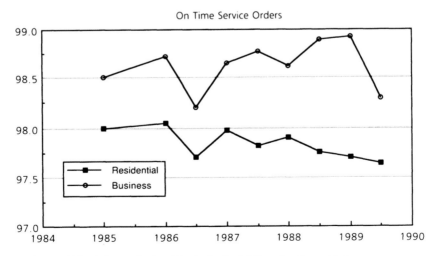

On Time Service Orders

Source: FCC "Update on Quality of Service for the Bell Operating Companies"
Common Carrier Bureau, June 1990.

FIGURE 6.8

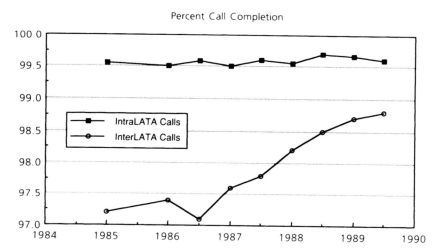

Percent Call Completion

Source: FCC "Update on Quality of Service for the Bell Operating Companies"
Common Carrier Bureau, June 1990.

FIGURE 6.9

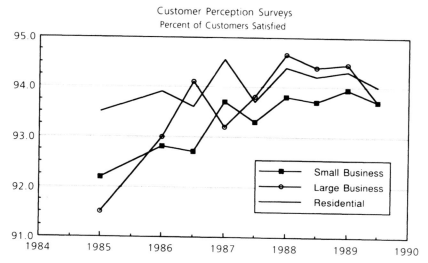

Customer Perception Surveys
Percent of Customers Satisfied

Source: FCC "Update on Quality of Service for the Bell Operating Companies"
Common Carrier Bureau, June 1990

the significance of these measures when taken alone should be viewed carefully, since they tend to be less objective and may be influenced by many extraneous factors, such as a customer's past experiences with service and his general expectations. In addition, customers may not be able to identify problems and service perceptions of local carriers separately from problems and perceptions of interexchange carriers.

Another concern relates to the robustness of the data and significance of small changes in the results. It appears that the companies are currently operating in a range of performance well above that which would elicit a significant amount of customer complaint. Therefore, small fluctuations in this range may not have any clear significance, but continuing small declines could serve as an alert to adverse trends. In addition, individual adverse elements may easily be masked. The results from, and responsiveness in, restoring service in the case of a natural disaster or fire is generally not reflected in this kind of data. Finally, the extent of any trend may be more difficult to assess than the presence of a trend.

Although a technique has been presented to deal with the problem of variations in standards alluded to by Curry, and objective standards of each company are supposed to remain fixed, it is possible they may change. The companies reporting data have generally indicated that their procedures and standards for preparation of the quality of service have not changed; however, in some cases the character of the underlying data appears to suggest otherwise. Because the indexing process for each company relates to performance in a limited number of distinct categories relative to 1985 baseline results, comparison between companies should be made with caution.

It is true that the present monitoring system contains some reporting inconsistencies, and is subject to both limitations in our state of knowledge and practical limitations in observing large complex real world systems. However, the observed trends in service quality appear to be supported by the companies' significant investment in fiber facilities and the significant amount of new switching equipment deployment associated with equal access requirements following divestiture. Also evident in the data are differences in trends for large business and residential customers. It is interesting to note, for example, there is a slight decline in the on-time service order category for residence subscribers. To the extent that Curry's observation of lengthening operator service response time, and the slightly poorer response to residential customer service orders mentioned above involves a greater reliance on people resources, this may also reflect changes in the way people and capital resources are being managed. Of course, further study would be required to confirm this possibility.

Given the limited data series and the level of aggregation, it is difficult to predict to what degree and how quickly the data now being collected will respond to changes in future quality of service. The FCC data presented here and any results derived therefrom, should thus be used with caution and should not be a substitute for more detailed data that may be collected elsewhere (e.g., by the state PUCs). It should also be clearly understood the data being received are not appropriate to address the existence of localized problems. And while it is not the intent of the data collection to compare the performance of individual companies, analysis suggests there are differences in performance patterns of the companies since the measurement process was begun.

Robert M. Gryb

From its very inception, the telephone industry has been undoubtedly the most measured business in the world. From the earliest days of Theodore Vail, telephone company employees were held accountable for the quality of service rendered to their customers.

In the Bell System, prior to divestiture, every district manager in every telephone company in the system received (on a monthly basis) reports on the level of customer satisfaction in his district for the various services for which he was responsible. This included satisfaction with installation, repairs, operator services, directory services, local calls, toll switch calls, and many other important types of service. Prior to divestiture, six million customer interviews were done per year to provide input to those managers to help them better manage their business and serve the customer.

The spirit of competitiveness between districts, divisions, regions, and companies in the telephone business in achieving the highest possible levels of service, while simultaneously achieving high scores on productivity measurements, was an incredible driving force. Accomplishing the "balanced job" was no myth—it was the most prevalent basis for employee merit ratings, and the most important motivator for operations managers throughout the telephone industry.

Over the years, the number and types of service measurements grew with the complexity of the business. Most were born from necessity—to balance loads, allocate resources, engineer additions, or train or assign personnel, for example. The goals and objectives of what might be called "standards" came about by two self-propelling forces. First, customers' levels of expectations kept changing, based on their past experiences. If customers became used to experiencing every call going through in ten seconds, they expected it, and became annoyed if it took longer. Couple this with the fact every good manager was staking his or her career and salary on getting better results than their peers, and you have the reason why telephone service in the United States has been the best in the world.

Without in any way denigrating the importance of the regulatory process, there is no question in my mind that when it comes to levels of service, the forces I described are 99 percent of the reason for the excellent levels of telephone service that still exist. Rowland Curry has said, "We have grown to expect good performance, and poor performance has become the memorable exception."

There were periods of time, especially the late 1960s, when growth in some major cities so far exceeded the planners' expectations that service took a turn downward, rather than its usual continuing upward trend. This triggered the FCC's twenty-city report on ten service indicators with "weakspot" levels. These levels were the equivalent of a ninety index, which fell far below the ninety-six level that was needed to meet the internal objectives of the Bell System. As the service in these cities improved, the report grew to cover seventy-five areas, rather than just twenty cities, but most of the twenty cities were included in the areas. Finally, weakspot failures became so rare that the seventy-five-area report was dropped in favor of exception reporting, if and when necessary.

What has divestiture really changed? It has not changed the concepts of ever-improving service, because of the continued existence of two factors mentioned earlier. First, higher levels of expectation due to new technologies such as faster electronic switching, better transmission on fiber optics, and more customized features, to name just a few. And, second, the persistent attitude on the part of the telephone companies that achieving higher levels of service is still the paramount motivator. However, the kinds of customers and their needs and expectations keep changing and getting more complex. Now the question is, "Who determines what are the right levels of service?" Curry asks, "What is good?" When a benchmark for a service measurement is set, it is always based on what is achievable, as shown by the distribution of a great many management units. It is essentially what customers have grown to expect.

Measurements are very, very expensive. Just think about the process.

If you measure (1) every time a phone goes off hook and a dial tone is given, (2) every time a trunk is seized and terminating lines get rings, (3) every time repeat attempts are made, (4) every time a call is made to repair and why, (5) every time a call is made to a business office and why, it is not difficult to imagine the costs involved in such a measurement process. Prior to divestiture, AT&T and the BOCs collected 130 service measurements every month. Some were simple, such as dial tone speed which was done by machine. Others involved human service observing of operators, business offices, repair bureaus, and even switched calls during set-up time. The costs for doing this were difficult to identify, because the measurement process was so woven into the operations comprising the business. However, we believed it could have been as high as several hundred million dollars per year. Even if it was half that amount, it was still an enormous expense.

There was (and is) much to be said for reducing these costs by eliminating expensive processes such as human service observing, and focusing on those factors which are really the most important—to manage the business efficiently, and to provide service which meets customers' expectations. Great strides have been made, and I am sure great savings have been achieved, by reducing the number of measurements and the manner of collecting data. Instead of deciding or telling customers what they should want or what is "good" for them, the telephone industry has moved toward the process of asking the customers, "How did we do?" and if it was not good enough, "Why?" and "What could we have done better?" Load balancing and speed of connection measurements may still be needed for efficient design and administration, but when it comes to judging quality of service and making sure in every location customers get service the way they want it, why not let the customer be the judge?

The kind of service measurements included in the FCC and NARUC service standards of the past in no way touch upon the real concerns of customers today. Problems of getting service installed and repaired, public phones, billing procedures, all have changed. If customers do not have the option to switch to another supplier, then they should have a voice in what they expect, and how well they are being served. Experience has shown this can be done accurately, and in a manner the customers appreciate. Of course, if they do have options, then the regulatory need for such data is moot, although well managed businesses will still need and use the data effectively.

I believe that monitoring service quality means gaining an understanding of the customer's point of view, and recognizing the fact that each customer, whether a residence, a small business with some data and FAX, or a large corporation with a vast network, should have the ability to express how well his expectations are being met. If federal and state regulatory agencies still feel a need for a service monitoring process, they should be wary of the costs as well as the frailties of some of the historic internal methods. It would seriously be better to consider a new way of keeping pace with changing customer expectations and what is really happening to them.

AT&T's divestiture of the BOCs was achieved remarkably smoothly, and I think service quality measurements played an important part in achieving the changes gracefully (i.e., with relatively few problems in the day-to-day operations of the business). There are few, if any, businesses in the world which have better measurements of the service they provide than has the telecommunications industry.

John R. Ake

Rowland Curry's treatment of the service quality issue framed the problem as a transaction between two groups—the regulator and the regulated. Of course, that reflects a monopoly perception of the telecommunications business. Today, and not necessarily as a result of divestiture, one of the most significant changes that telephone companies face is the growing power of the customers, who now have the opportunity to "vote with their feet." There are several examples, such as the Hinsdale, Illinois disaster, where telephone companies have permanently lost business as a result of temporary service disruption. A new term has been floating around: "vendor diversity." In plain English, it means, "don't put all your eggs in one basket." That is a major problem if you are an exchange carrier in a region where there are growing numbers of alternative local service arrangements.

At Illinois Bell, the two largest customers by an order of magnitude are MCI and AT&T. This is significant when you consider that the Ameritech region includes the likes of General Motors and Ford. The MCI and AT&T accounts dwarf the automobile accounts by many multiples. These accounts are so important that we hold regular meetings with Joe Reed of AT&T and Ron Spears of MCI, and when they call we pay attention. In fact, Ron has his own index which he uses to remind us of how we are doing, and I will assure you the "Spears" index is more important than any number of individual measurements.

The telecommunications industry has become very internally focused, often overlooking lessons we can learn from trends in other industries. For example, one of our other neighbors and customers in Illinois is McDonalds, the hamburger people. They devised a system called QSC that made them unique in the fast food business. "Quality, Service, and Cleanliness" became the corporate credo which Mc-Donalds drove back into the supplier chains—into the beef business, the potato business, and the dairy business. This seemingly simple phrase produced tremendous changes in quality levels and in the way those businesses developed and delivered their products. Similar changes are occurring today in the telecommunications business as a result of pressure from companies such as AT&T, MCI, and GM. These customers can and do impact our perception of our service, and the quality level we provide.

I have no empirical evidence for residence and small business customers, but I can relate the trends I sense in the industry. At the time immediately after divestiture, these smaller customers were concerned because they had to make decisions about issues they could previously ignore. Some people do not like to make decisions; some just do not like change. I believe, however, that we have weathered that storm, and the service quality delivered by local exchange carriers is as good or better than it was prior to divestiture.

Where does all this lead us? Away, I believe, from the need for service quality levels and toward a growing faith that the competitive nature of our markets will successfully motivate market participants to provide what customers demand.

There has been a great deal of recent discussion, within and about the local exchange carrier industry, as to the industry's motivations under various alternative forms of regulation. Specifically, the fear arises that increased earnings flexibility will encourage carriers to deliberately degrade service quality and thereby convert expense dollars, otherwise destined for network maintenance, into net income. The argument goes further to conclude that the monopoly environment makes the carriers immune from customer reaction.

If you think about it, this concern is illogical in today's increasingly competitive environment. First, customers do have choices, and the number of those options is increasing constantly. Second, carriers, of whatever type, are, for the most part, switching over to a "pay for what you use" pricing format. Under such arrangements, the call has to be completed quickly and with no "quality" problems in order for the serving carrier to, first, get paid for the service and, second, not experience inordinate "reorder" levels which serve only to drive up cost of operation. The structure does not really exist, on a widespread basis anymore, under which a carrier can sit back and collect revenues, indifferent to the network quality provided.

Thomas E. Buzas, Sanford V. Berg, and John G. Lynch, Jr.

Our fellow contributors to this chapter thus far have made a number of important points about the quality of local telephone service. Six can be summarized as follows:

1. Companies and regulators take numerous technical measures related to service quality (Rowland Curry, Jonathan Kraushaar, Robert Gryb).

2. Measures are taken with respect to at least three classes of customers: residential, small business, and large business (Kraushaar).

3. There are, however, problems with a lack of consistency in the measures of service quality across regulatory body, company, and time (Curry, Kraushaar).

4. Companies also use consumer inputs, such as surveys, which regulators find too subjective for purposes of regulation (Curry, Kraushaar, John Ake).

5. Analysts need to be concerned about whether the standards are defined appropriately and whether the right things are being measured (Curry, Gryb).

6. Researchers and regulators must pay close attention to how the measures being taken should be combined into an overall index of quality (Curry, Kraushaar).

We shall discuss points 6, 2, and 4. In the present context, the question is whether service quality has improved or deteriorated since divestiture. In the broader context, we are interested in customer and regulator evaluation of company performance.

The answer to the post-divestiture service quality question would be clear if all indicators were improving over time for all classes of customers. Unfortunately, they are not. Curry plots Southwestern Bell's performance in several dimensions of service quality. Post-divestiture performance appears superior on several criteria, but performance seems to deteriorate for operator answer time. According to Kraushaar, customer perceptions, dial tone performance, transmission quality, and on-time service orders for business customers either improved or remained the same following divestiture, but on-time service orders for residential customers decreased.

Since the indicators are mixed, we need some method of combining performance on the separate dimensions into a summary index. We agree with Curry that the process for determining appropriate weights for the different criteria is difficult and subjective. These difficulties have driven regulators to seek simple solutions that finesse complex measurement issues. An illustration is the index used by Kraushaar to ascertain whether quality declined or increased following the AT&T breakup. He rewards a company with a plus if performance has improved in comparison with the previous period, and penalizes with a minus if performance has declined. He then averages the pluses and minuses. The beauty of this approach is that it gets around the problem of different methods used by the various companies in preparing the data submitted. However, this approach has two important drawbacks.

First, Kraushaar's method treats all dimensions as equally important, in that the same "+1" and "−1" scores are used for changes on all five dimensions. Conceivably, these five dimensions *are* all equally important in the eyes of regulators. It is likely, however, that they are not.

Second, Kraushaar's procedure treats the magnitude of any change from the previous period as irrelevant—all that matters is whether the change reflects an increase or a decrease. For the sake of argument though, consider Kraushaar's table 6.2, where call completions dropped for Southwestern Bell, while dial tone delay, transmission quality and on-time service orders improved. Arguably, a large drop in call completions might outweigh small increases in the others. The plus/minus procedure would not reflect this information.

The question then is how to develop a rule for integrating different levels of performance on several criteria. One approach is to avoid the assignment of an explicit formula. That is, leave evaluation to the best judgment of regulators. In this case, the weights will be implicit, yet just as subjective as any explicit weights might be. Moreover, a wealth of behavioral research shows decisionmakers are inconsistent in the application of their own implicit weights.[1] Inconsistent evaluations will send confusing signals to companies. In particular, effort may be spent improving performance in the wrong areas for which rewards may not materialize. In addition, undeserving companies may be rewarded and others unfairly penalized for changes in performance indicators.

Thus we agree with Curry that the determination of the weights for different criteria is a crucial issue. There are, basically, three approaches to determining the weights. First, in a competitive market, one could directly relate performance on the different criteria to marketplace choice in the form of a revealed preference analysis or by hedonic pricing analysis.[2] But with regulated monopolies like local telephone service, residential customers have no option to patronize alternative vendors, so this form of analysis is unavailable for this class of customers. To the extent commercial customers have telecommunications options and exercise these options, this form of modeling is available.

Second, one could ask customers about their preferences. It seems beneficial to ask some large commercial customers about their evaluations. As Ake suggests, they likely have investigated the possibility of telecommunications alternatives, and are quite knowledgeable about the importance they attach to different criteria. On the other hand, we are less sanguine about the value of asking residential customers about their preferences regarding the various dimensions of telephone service quality. First of all, they have no incentive to think about these matters, since they do not have the option of choosing different local telecommunications suppliers, nor can they realistically contemplate doing without service altogether. Thus it is unlikely that they have given much thought to the relative importance of the different dimensions of telephone service quality. Even if they had, consumers are ill-equipped to relate performance levels to end benefits. Of course, if we ask consumers to make tradeoffs they will. But, research on behavioral decision theory over the past decade has shown that when prior opinions about the tradeoffs do not exist, the revealed weights are highly unstable and susceptible to minor changes in the elicitation procedures, including question, wording, order, format, and context.[3] In contrast, recent research has shown that respondents who have high levels of expertise or prior knowledge in the value domain being measured are *not* susceptible to these same distorting effects of momentary salience, question wording, format, etc.[4]

Thus, for residential customers, the third available alternative to determine weights, modeling telecommunication experts' views of consumers' tradeoffs among different levels of performance on various technical demensions of quality seems the best (albeit not perfect) approach.[5] There are several ways to do this.[6] Modeling can use methods of conjoint analysis, information integration theory, and policy capturing. We have used one variant, hierarchical conjoint analysis,[7] to model the preferences of thirty-nine employees at six organizations: the Florida Public Service Commission (FPSC) and five local telephone companies operating in the state of Florida.[8] The thirty-eight rules covered in the study are listed in exhibit 6.1. In brief, we found: (1) a linear function provided a good fit, within the ranges of performance considered, to the experts' tradeoffs; (2) the thirty-eight criteria differed in importance with a one-percentage point improvement for the most important dimension receiving a weight 130 times greater than the least important (table 6.4); and (3) there were no significant differences among the weights based on employer.

Although the incremental weights are subjective, there was substantial agreement about them among experts at the FPSC and at the five telcos, so it appears to be a subjectivity we can tolerate. Partly based on our results, the New York and Florida PSCs are examining the possibility of including our model as part of the normal regulatory process.

If comparable weights were available to Curry and Kraushaar, it might be possible to say whether overall quality has improved or declined. At present, the most that can be said is that performance goes up on some and down on others, but probably has not deteriorated since divestiture.

Let us now turn to consumer surveys about service quality. From the standpoint of behavioral theory, the fact that residential customers have no occasion to make choices among competing local telephone companies renders residential ratings of quality and satisfaction far less meaningful than similar measures in competitive markets. Residential evaluations might be relevant in areas that involve individual, highly salient events for which responsibility can be unambiguously attributed to the regulated company. For example, consumer evaluations of installation and repair services and of operator assistance may be very useful. However, there is no competition among local telephone companies and thus the basis for comparison is unclear. Would consumers rate the telephone company relative to its past performance, as Gryb believes, or to the electric company or even to Sears?

Kraushaar and Gryb have noted that differences between companies or change over time may reflect shifts in perspective, such as changes in expectations, rather than differences in quality. Note that, depending upon one's purpose, one might *want* consumers to rate, for example, telephone installation relative to electricity installation or to appliance installation. Furthermore, the perspective appropriate to regulators may not be the perspective managers find most useful. The point is not that

---

EXHIBIT 6.1
38 FPSC Rules with Published Standards of Performance

Rule Cluster 1: Dial Tone Delay

1. Dial Tone Delay: 95% of all calls shall receive a dial tone within 3 seconds.

Rule Cluster 2: Call Completions

2. Intraoffice: 95% of all calls to numbers with the same first 3 digits as your own shall be completed.
3. Interoffice: 95% of all calls to numbers with different 3-digit codes but within your home exchange shall be completed.
4. EAS: 95% of all calls to different home exchanges must be completed.
5. Intracompany DDD: 95% of all toll calls within your local company's service area shall be completed.

Rule Cluster 3: Answer Time

6. Operator Answer Time: 90% of all toll calls to a toll office shall be answered within 10 seconds after the start of an audible ring.
7. Directory Assistance: 90% of all calls to Directory Assistance shall be answered within 20 seconds after the start of an audible ring.
8. Repair Service: 90% of all calls to Repair Service shall be answered within 20 seconds after the start of an audible ring.
9. Business Office: 80% of all calls to Business Offices shall be answered within 20 seconds after the start of an audible ring.

Rule Cluster 4: Adequacy of Directory and Directory Assistance

10. Directory Service: A directory conforming to FPSC rule 25–4.040 shall be published within 12–15 months since the last published directory.
11. New Numbers: 100% of all new or changed listings shall be provided to directory assistance operators within 48 hours after connection of service, excluding Saturdays, Sundays, and holidays.

Rule Cluster 5: Adequacy of Intercept Services

12. Changed Numbers: 90% of all calls to numbers that have been changed shall be answered automatically within 20 seconds.
13. Disconnected Service: 100% of all calls to numbers to disconnected numbers shall be answered within 20 seconds by a recording informing the caller that the number reached is not in service.
14. Vacation Disconnects: 80% of all calls to numbers temporarily disconnected at the customer's request shall be answered within 20 seconds.
15. Vacant Numbers: 100% of all calls to vacant numbers shall be answered

EXHIBIT 6.1
(continued)

within 20 seconds by a recording informing the caller that the number reached is not in service.

16. Disconnects Non-Pay: 100% of all calls to numbers disconnected due to nonpayment shall be answered within 20 seconds by a recording informing the caller that the number is not in service.

Rule Cluster 6: Installation Service

17. 3-Day Primary Service: 90% of requests for Primary Service in any Calendar month shall normally be satisfied within an interval of 3 working days after the receipt of application.
18. Appointments: 95% of appointments kept that are set within time frames of 7–12 A.M., 12–5 P.M., or 5–9 P.M., or for a specific hour of the day.

Rule Cluster 7: 911 Service

19. 911 Service: 95% of all calls to 911 Service answered within 10 seconds.

Rule Cluster 8: Repair Service

20. 24-Hours Restoral: 95% of all customers shall have service restored within 24 hours of reporting trouble.
21. Appointments: 95% of Repair Service appointments kept that are set within time frames of 7–12 A.M., 12–5 P.M., or 5–9 P.M., or for a specific hour of the day.
22. Rebates—Over 24 Hours: 100% of customers whose service is interrupted for more than 24 hours shall be given prorated rebates.

Rule Cluster 9: Public Telephone Service

Sub-Cluster 9a: Functioning of Public Telephones

23. Serviceability: 100% of public telephones must meet all service standards applicable to service to other customers.
24. Telephone Numbers: 100% of all public coin phones must have identified station telephone numbers.
25. Receive Calls: 100% of all pay phones—except in prisons, schools, and hospitals—must be able to receive incoming calls.
26. Dial Instructions: 100% of all public telephone stations should have legible and clear dialing instructions, including notice of the lack of availability of local or toll service.

Sub-Cluster 9b: Enclosure of Public Telephones

EXHIBIT 6.1
(continued)

---

27. Accessibility to Handicapped: 100% of all stations installed since January 1, 1987, must be accessible to the handicapped.
28. Cleanliness: Normal maintenance shall include inspection and reasonable effort shall be taken to insure cleanliness and freedom from obstructions of 95% of all coin stations.
29. Lights: 100% of all public telephones must be lighted during hours of darkness when light from other sources is inadequate to read instructions and to use the instrument.

Sub-Cluster 9c: Coin Operations of Public Telephones

30. Pre-Pay: 100% of all coin-operated public telephones allow Pre-Pay. They provide a dial tone, require coin deposit prior to dialing (except for calls to operator or 911 as discussed in 32 and 33 below), and automatically return any deposited amount for calls not completed.
31. Coin Return: 100% of all coin stations shall return any deposited amount if a call is not completed, except messages to a Feature Group A access number.
32. Coin Free Access-Operator: 100% of all public telephones shall have coin free access to the Operator.
33. Coin Free Access-911: 100% of all public telephones shall have coin free access to 911 Service.
34. Coin Free Access-Directory Assistance: 100% of all coin stations shall allow coin free access or coin return access to Local Directory Assistance.
35. Coin Free Access-Repair Service: 100% of all coin stations shall allow coin free access or coin return access to Repair Service.
36. Coin Free Access-Business Office: 100% of all coin stations shall allow coin free access or coin return access to the Business Office.

Sub-Cluster 9d: Directory Security of Public Telephones

37. Directory Security: 100% of all coin stations have directories available. When there are three or more coin stations in one area, there must be a directory for the local calling area for every two stations. Otherwise, there must be a directory for every station.

Sub-Cluster 9e: Address/Location of Public Telephones

38. Address/Location: 100% of all public telephones have their locations posted, and the identifications of locations coordinated with the appropriate 911 or emergency center.

TABLE 6.4
1985—Generic

Cluster	Rule	Results	Difference	Weight	Score
1. Dial tone delay	95%	99.8	4.8	.1172	.56256
2. Call completion					
Interoffice	95%	100.0	5.0	.0786	.393
Intraoffice	95%	99.5	4.5	.0813	.36585
EAS	95%	99.5	4.5	.0600	.27
DDD-company	92%	98.8	6.8	.0372	.25296
3. Answer time					
Operator	90%	98.0	8.0	.0114	.112
Directory assistance	90%	96.2	6.2	.0078	.04836
Repair service	90%	97.8	7.8	.0082	.06396
Business office	80%	98.8	18.8	.0070	.1316
4. Directory					
Directory service	100%	100.0		.0298	
New numbers	100%	100.0		.0105	
5. Intercept services					
Changed numbers	90%	100.0	10.0	.0114	.144
Disconnected	100%	100.0		.0188	
Vacation	80%	80.0		.0037	
Vacant	100%	100.0		.0186	
Non-pay	100%	97.4	−2.6	.0304	−.07904
6. Availability of service					
3–day primary	90%	97.1	7.1	.0342	.24282
Appointments	90%	95.7	5.7	.0470	.2679
7. 911 Service	95%	95.0		.0885	
8. Repair service					
24–hour restoral	95%	96.9	1.9	.0170	.0323
Appointments	95%	96.9	1.9	.0213	.04047
Rebates	100%	100.0		.0024	
9A. Functioning of public telephones					
Serviceability	100%	97.3	−2.7	.0234	−.06318
Telephone numbers	100%	98.2	−1.8	.0163	−.02934
Receives calls	100%	100.0		.0092	
Dial instructions	100%	100.0		.0241	

TABLE 6.4 (continued)
1985—Generic

Cluster	Rule	Results	Difference	Weight	Score
9B. Enclosure					
Handicapped	100%	100.0		.0057	
Cleanliness	95%	100.0	5.0	.0037	.0185
Lights	100%	100.0		.0050	
9C. Coin operations					
Pre-pay	100%	100.0		.0114	
Coin return	100%	98.2	−1.8	.0063	−.01134
Operator	100%	100.0		.0021	
Directory assistance	100%	100.0		.0046	
911 Service	100%	100.0		.0015	
Repair service	100%	100.0		.0011	
Business office	100%	100.0		.0013	
9D. Directory	100%	94.4	−5.6	.0009	−.00504
9E. Address/location	100%	99.4	−.6	.0198	−.01188
Total weighted score:					2.71646
Rating (wt. score + 5.9244)					8.64086

consumer input is meaningless, but that asking the questions in a manner that is meaningful to regulators is not an easy task.

Earlier comments in this chapter represent an important attempt to examine the impact of divestiture on local telephone service quality. Although the bottom line is somewhat mixed, service quality has probably not deteriorated since divestiture. But the comments also underscore the importance of developing better indicators of industry performance. We have described one such effort where the weights for one-percentage point improvements were derived from telecommunications experts. We look forward to seeing future analyses of the value of service quality. Of course, the costs of achieving different levels of performance must be factored into the analysis as well.

Lawrence P. Cole

Rowland Curry has presented figure 6.2., "Service Orders Worked," which indicates that on the eve of divestiture the bottom fell out of a series reported by Southwestern Bell to the Texas PUC, but it later recovered and resumed its pre-divestiture trend. This, of course, is an example of the type of evidence used to determine whether divestiture affected any aspect of service quality. An economist or statistician will examine a data series more extensively where something appears to happen coincident with the event of interest, in order to determine what actually happened. When Curry did that, he satisfied himself that whatever happened with respect to telecommunications service quality was not related to divestiture.

Figure 6.3, entitled "Operator Answer Time," also depicts an index Southwestern Bell reports to the Texas Commission. Again, Curry finds nothing that needs investigation. I look at that series and see a slope coefficient that is horizontal from 1978 until mid-1984, and then I see what may be a sharp upturn in that slope. Although there may not be enough information here yet, there are techniques for testing whether the slope coefficient has, in fact, changed. Then it is a question of whether the trend is attributable to divestiture, or one of the other events, noted by various authors in this volume, that occurred in this period, including CPE deregulation and equal access activity.

Trends in customer satisfaction measures, such as those we at GTE found starting to show up in the monthly surveys we take throughout our serving territories, can be at least partially attributed to divestiture. We ask a variety of questions on these surveys: some are about very specific aspects of services, and some address an overall quality rating. Those numbers, cited in the press and elsewhere, show about 85 or 90 percent of the customers giving the telcos a "good" or "excellent" rating on a subjective scale of "excellent," "good," "fair," "poor," and "bad."

As indicated in figure 6.10, these studies began to show a decline in customer satisfaction with their bills during mid-1985 to mid-1986 for four GTE telcos; but this growing dissatisfaction was purely an issue of confusion. Divestiture meant the local exchange carrier portion of the bill had to become distinct from the interexchange carrier portion, even if the customer did not change long-distance companies. Certainly, other events contributed to confusion on the bills: CPE and inside wire deregulation, the imposition of customer access line charges, and equal access balloting, with the whole timetable of the latter having been tailored to the divestiture. So it would be very difficult to disentangle the effects due to divestiture per se. In any case, we did a great deal of focus-group type research to find out what would help customers better understand their bills. When the findings were implemented, the problem disappeared.

FIGURE 6.10

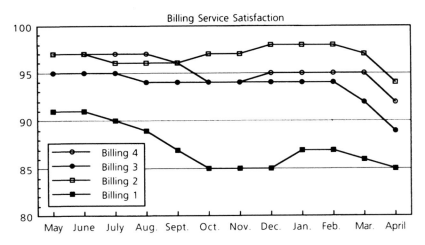

Source: GTE.

We carry on extensive customer perception measurement. Figure 6.11 shows the overall quality ratings for nine GTE companies on a scale of one to five for a typical month. Suppose these were available for the RBOCs over the whole post-divestiture period, so that one could do some analysis of them (figure 6.12). One interesting undertaking would be to examine of the relationship, if any, between the behavior of the RBOCs' quality ratings over the five-year period, and their earnings performance as reported in the national business press (figure 6.13).

There are some obvious hypotheses to test in this area. Quite apart from any possible functional relationships between earnings and quality, there is also a question of how the RBOCs' quality ratings relative to one another have varied over time. Presumably a pre-divestiture view would have found them to be fairly tightly bunched due to the central administration of the Bell System. Would we now expect to find more dispersion between the highest ranked and the lowest ranked RBOC? And would that be a direct consequence of divestiture?

Also as a result of divestiture, long-distance customers may deal with as many as three carriers in order to complete a single call. In that connection, I call your attention to a series of articles in the *IEEE Communications Magazine* for October 1988, an issue entirely devoted to quality and other aspects of standards and measurement of service quality in a very informative way. In one of those articles, "National

FIGURE 6.11

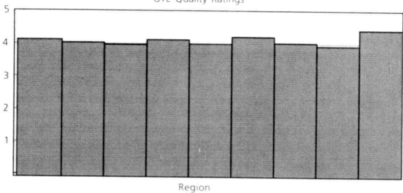

GTE Quality Ratings

GTE Quality Ratings

Region

Source: GTE.

FIGURE 6.12

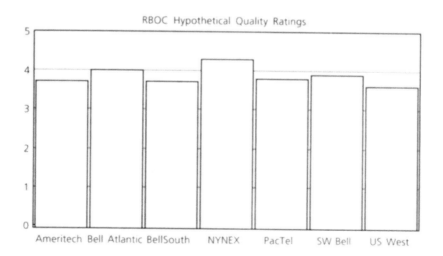

RBOC Hypothetical Quality Ratings

FIGURE 6.13

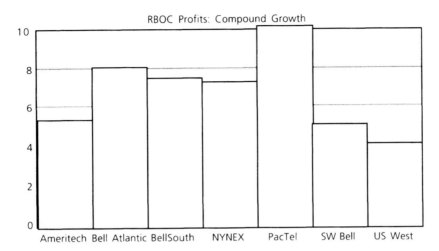

Source: *Fortune*, January 2, 1989.

Performance Standards for Telecommunications Services," Melvin N. Woinsky states:

> The multicarrier, multivendor structure for providing telecommunications services clearly calls for national standards to support compatibility and interoperability. The pieces must 'plug together' in order for service to be provided. A need for performance standards, however, is not as evident. Long-distance end-to-end services are competitive and it can be argued that the performance level is a characteristic of the service to be determined by customer needs and willingness to pay in a free market environment. Standards should not impede competition based on service performance level nor unnecessarily restrict the price/quality options available to customers, nor should standards impede the introduction of beneficial new technology.

I think this view echoes Robert Gryb's remarks about the customer perception measures being more important than some of the traditional quality measures. And it is the customer's determination of quality that ought to count. There may be needs for various standards for technical reasons, but those standards should not limit the range of quality options that can be offered.

From the point of view of those who work in the area of the statistical validation of the service quality measures, the questions that naturally arise are, "Why this particular set? Why four versus five measures? What is the research basis for these particular items? Also, what is the connection between these measures and what truly concerns customers?"

We have studied some aspects of what constitutes a quality contact between a customer and a customer service order center (CSOC). Some PUCs have standards that require 80 percent of the calls coming into a CSOC to be answered in 20 seconds. This may be a perfectly valid standard, but how important is it to customers? No one wants to be put on hold for a long period of time, either to get a sales pitch or to have music played at him, but it is clear that other things may be more important to customers than the specified twenty seconds. Thus, if, as suggested, increased FCC service quality monitoring is one of the results of price caps, there should be a discussion devoted to which measures are used, how many, and why.

Thomas Buzas, Sanford Berg, and John Lynch usefully remind us of the fact that service quality is multidimensional. They then assert, "Since the indicators are mixed, we need some method of combining performance on the separate dimensions into a summary index." This is not at all obvious. Why do we need an index? And, if we do need something that somehow incorporates the many dimensions of quality, why should it be anything other than the overall quality rating perceived by customers, as measured as best we can with state-of-the-art survey methods?

Consider the thirty-eight dimensions of service quality used in the Florida study reported by Buzas, Berg, and Lynch. How would the threatened "possibility of including our model as part of the normal regulatory process" work in Florida? If quality falls below the standard set by the PUC along one or more of those dimensions, must those dimensions be directly and individually addressed by the company, or must the index be improved? Suppose the index fell, but no standard was violated, except maybe a standard for the index value itself. Could the company then get the index back up to snuff without improving service quality along the dimensions whose decline led to the fall of the index in the first place? Could it raise quality along dimensions that were relatively easy and inexpensive to improve, or could it shore things up along those dimensions it knew mattered most to its customers? (These two sets are not necessarily mutually exclusive.)

Note these questions are analogous to the many questions asked about the proposed use of price indices in implementing price cap regulation plans. That suggests the imposition of the Buzas, Berg, and Lynch quality monitoring scheme could be accompanied by upper and lower bands on service quality changes and baskets of quality dimensions.

Implicit in the last question above is the presumption, among others, that some of the items in the Florida list do not matter much to customers. In general, our research indicates that customers do not give half a hoot, much less two, for some of the commonly imposed regulatory standards of service quality. Now, maybe the Florida list is based on careful study of what Florida residence and business customers really care about, and those thirty-eight items are all significant. But one gets the impression from the analysis that the list consists of items that the regulators think consumers should regard as important, and furthermore, that consumers are not even considered competent to determine their relative importance.

I have a difficulty understanding why asking residential customers about their preferences regarding the various dimensions of telephone service quality is not the best of the three alternatives offered by Buzas, Berg, and Lynch. Note that I refer to *preferences*, not *judgments* about technical matters. It seems to me to be definitional in a market economy, especially in market segments where customers have no choice of service providers, that it is totally inappropriate to ask anybody else. Whose interest is regulation supposed to be protecting where competition is lacking? And since when have customers been required to have any particular competence in order to have a preference? (Many of us who do not know much about art, know what we like when we see it.)

In fact many customers have dealt with other providers in other locations where they have resided, or they may work in areas served by a different company than the one that serves their residence. They also may have dealt with more than one interexchange provider. Furthermore, doing business with a phone company is not unlike doing business with several other service industries. Therefore, I think customers have an adequate experiential basis for evaluating service quality. As for consumers being ill-equipped to relate performance levels to end benefits, they are not alone. Nor will they be, until studies establish relationships between objective performance levels based on measures that engineers and regulators are fond of and customer ratings of service quality. Presumably the latter are the end benefits that count: customer satisfaction with what they get, relative to what they pay.

ENDNOTES

1. For example, see C. Camerer, "General Conditions for the Success of Bootstrapping Models," *Organizational Behavior and Human Performance* (1981), 27:411–22.

2. Sherwin Rosen, "Hedonic Prices and Implicit Market Product Differentiation in Pure Competition," *Journal of Political Economy* (1974), 82:34–55.

3. Logically equivalent ways of asking about preferences yield different preference orderings, and dimensions that are made momentarily salient or that can be easily articulated receive disproportionate weight. James R., Mita, and Sujan Bettman, "Effects of Framing on Evaluation of Comparable and Noncomparable Alternatives by Expert and Novice Consumers," *Journal of Consumer Research* (1987), p. 14. Baruch Fischhoff, Paul Slovic, and Sarah Lichtenstein, "Knowing What You Want: Measuring Labile Values," in T. Wallsten, ed., *Cognitive Processes in Choice and Decision Behavior* (Hillsdale, N.J.: Erlbaum, 1980), pp. 117–42. Timothy D. Wilson, Dana Dunn, Dolores Kraft, and Douglas J. Lisle, "Introspection, Attitude Change, and Attitude-Behavior Consistency: The Disruptive Effects of Explaining Why We Feel the Way We Do," in L. Berkowitz, ed., *Advances in Experimental Social Psychology* (Orlando, Fla.: Academic Press, 1989), 22:287–343.

4. James R., Mita, and Sujan Bettman, "Effects of Framing on Evaluation of Comparable and Noncomparable Alternatives by Expert and Novice Consumers," (1987), p. 14. Feldman and Lynch, 1988. J. Wesley Hutchinson, "On the Locus of Range Effects in Judgment and Choice," in R. Bagozzi and A. Tybout, eds., *Advances in Consumer Research* (Ann Arbor, Mich.: Association for Consumer Research, 1983), vol. 10. John G. Lynch, Jr., Dipankar Chakravarti, and Anusree Mitra, "Distinguishing Contrast Effects Caused by Changes in Mental Representation from Those Caused by Changes in Response Language," Working Paper, University of Florida, 1989. Timothy D. Wilson, Dolores Kraft, and Dana Dunn, "The Disruptive Effects of Explaining Attitudes: The Moderating Effect of Knowledge about the Attitude Object," *Journal of Experimental Social Psychology* (1989), p. 25. These distorting effects all operate in the process of constructing tradeoffs at the time of measurement, but those with high levels of expertise need only retrieve tradeoffs that existed prior to measurement and that are accessible in memory.

5. Ideally, these experts' judgments would be informed by various measures of customer satisfaction with service, but would not treat these measures as defining quality. Technical knowledge allows such experts: (1) to have some understanding of how levels on measured technical dimensions relate to end benefits; (2) to factor in externalities, as for example, when certain customer groups would not choose to pay for certain dimensions of quality, and this decision affects others who call them (Eli Noam, "Questions by Commissioner Noam Concerning the Establishment of Economic Incentives to Quality Performance by New York Telephone as Part of the General Treatment of its Rates," NYPSC Report to Hon. J. Michael Harrison, Administrative Law Judge, 1989); (3) to respond to questions about tradeoffs without undue distortions due to normatively irrelevant details of the questioning procedure.

6. For a well-written nontechnical explanation of the basic approach, see Paul Green and Yoram Wind, "New Way to Measure Consumers' Judgments," *Harvard Business Review* (July–August 1975), 53:108.

7. Jordan Louviere, "Hierarchical Information Integration: A New Method

for the Design and the Analysis of Complex Multiattribute Judgment Problems," in Thomas Kinnear, ed., *Advances in Consumer Research* (Provo, Utah: Association for Consumer Research, 1984), 11:148–55.

8. Thomas E. Buzas and John G. Lynch, "A Formula for the Comprehensive Evaluation of Local Telephone Companies: Report to the Florida Public Service Commission," University of Florida, Public Utilities Research Center, Working Paper, 1989. Thomas E. Buzas, John G. Lynch, and Sanford V. Berg, "Regulatory Measurement and Evaluation of Telephone Service Quality," University of Florida, Public Utilities Research Center, Working Paper, 1989.

7

Innovation and New Services

■

WALTER G. BOLTER
AND JAMES W. MCCONNAUGHEY

■

ELLIOT E. MAXWELL
JERROLD OPPENHEIM
BAILEY M. GEESLIN
THOMAS W. COHEN

Walter G. Bolter and James W. McConnaughey

Prior to divestiture, under the AT&T monopoly regime, users came to expect "one-stop shopping" and "end-to-end service." In this environment, new network offerings were introduced on a highly restrained basis. These were also largely predictable, and terms and conditions of supply were often *not* reflective of technical limitations. Service innovation was not a carrier priority, but, instead, was a by-product or incidental result of supply-driven technical innovation or a response to limited competition. For instance, the operational improvement aspects of touch-tone were its prime motivation, not the new service possibilities that this new form of dialing facilitated. In short, customer demand assumed a relatively minor role in service development or introduction.

As the local provider for more than 80 percent of the nation's telephone subscribers and over 95 percent of long-distance customers, the Bell System wielded considerable influence in determining the direction and rate of change of innovation pre-divestiture. Bell Laboratories received enormous payments for conduct of basic research and systems engineering from all the BOCs and AT&T's Long Lines Division. In 1982 alone, the BOCs' "license contract" expenditures totaled $464.5 million for fundamental research and systems engineering (R&SE).[1] Historically, substantial "specific design and development" (SD&D) payments were also made to Bell Labs by Bell's manufacturing arm, Western Electric. For example, in 1979 SD&D accounted for 60 percent of the Labs' research budget, while the remaining 40 percent represented R&SE disbursements.[2]

In general, the perceived need for network improvements, rather than a recognition of customer demand, appeared to drive innovation in the telecommunications industry for at least two-thirds of this century. Where competition did exist, technical and service imperatives were often redirected. And, even when an effort to be innovative in a services sense occurred, the design often appeared to be left to engineers rather than marketers, sometimes with disastrous results.

Most industry observers agree the current rate of innovation in telecommunications is exceedingly brisk. For example, NTIA finds in its 1988 landmark assessment of the industry that "[e]xponential technological and commercial growth today characterizes telecommunications."[3] Similarly, MCI's industry pioneer Willam McGowan observes there has been an "explosion in services," citing, inter alia, his company's increase in core offerings from five to sixty since divestiture.[4]

Major users and the RBOCs also have characterized the rate of innovations as rapid. Indeed, in contrast to historical constraints on their options, International Communications Association members acknowledge the existence of a much wider choice of attractive communications equipment and services today.[5] Finally, Judge Harold Greene concludes, "as predicted by classic antitrust doctrine, innovation has flowered during the post-divestiture period."[6]

Despite this apparent widespread consensus, careful analysis of the events of the post-divestiture period may suffer from imprecise use of concepts and terminology. Service innovations present very considerable obstacles to recognition and precise measurement. A glance at table 7.1, "Telecommunications Mileposts," underscores some of the complexities that may be encountered. For example, the appearance of (OUT)WATS, which was introduced in 1961, and (IN)WATS, which was inaugurated four years later, clearly gave rise to a number of effi-

Table 7.1
U.S. Telecommunications Mileposts: Service and Equipment

Year	Event	Year	Event
1844	First commercial telegraph system (Washington, D.C.↔Baltimore)	1948	First microwave radio relay system cutover (N.Y.↔Boston)
1876	A.G. Bell awarded telephone patent	1951	Beginning of direct long-distance customer dialing
1879	First telephone switchboard (New Haven, Conn.)	1955	Colored phones offered (Bell System)
1882	First underground cable laid	1956	First transAtlantic telephone cable
1889	First public pay phone installed	1958	Hi-Speed Data Phone service inaugurated (1200 bps)
1892	First automatic switchboard (LaPorte, Ind.)	1960	Electronic switching systems developed
1896	First telephone dial (Milwaukee, Wis.)	1961	WATS, Telpak introduced
1905	First unattended central office	1963	Touch-Tone (push button phone) service begun
1915	First transcontinental call (N.Y.C. to S.F.)	1964	Facsimile machines in infancy
1918	First carrier (transmission) system	1965	First commercial international telephone service by satellite ("Early Bird"); AT&T 800 Service initiated
1920	First automatic toll board		
1926	Nonblack telephones offered (Independents)	1966	Data transmitted 4800 bps
1927	First international telephone call (N.Y. to London)	1970	Picturephone service offered
1930	Data transmitted 600 bits per second via telephone	1972	First commercial analog electronic switching system
1940	Coaxial cable introduced		
1947	Transistor unveiled by Bell Labs		

Table 7.1 (continued)

Year	Event
1974	First private line digital communications service (data transmitted 56 Kbps)
1976	First commercial digital electronic switching system
1977	First full-service lightwave communications system (Chicago)
1978	CCIS, digital PBX introduced; mobile cellular phone service started in Chicago
1979	Local area networks (LANs) inaugurated
1980	Launching of Ku-band geosynchronous satellites made customer premises applications (e.g., VSATs) feasible
1981	Shared tenant services (STS) introduced
1982	Electronic mail service introduced
1983	Single mode fiber optics developed for use in local loop beginning in 1984; tariffed T-1 links provided by AT&T
1984	Interstate access charge services offered; phased interexchange equal access initiated as part of MFJ decree; air-to-ground communication system granted experimental license
1985	First central office local area network (CO-LAN) offered (by Bell of Pennsylvania)
1986	First "external" ISDN trial (Illinois Bell and McDonald's Corp. in Oakbrook, Illinois)
1987	Electronic Data Interchange (EDI) unveiled (computer transmission of business documents); digital Centrex launched; low cost "FAX" and PC FAX boards emerging
1988	AT&T Open Network Architecture plan approved by FCC; RBOC ONA plans approved in part; numerous Comparably Efficient Interconnection (CEI) plans approved for former Bell System members relating to information gateway services
1989	Interactive 900 Services offered (e.g., polling)

cient new applications of telecommunications. But were these "special purpose" or discount services fully innovations *before* their special uses developed?

Similar problems of timing apply to the introduction of touch-tone dialing. Touch-tone dialing was technically possible in 1963, with the introduction of the push button telephone. But during the 1980s the age of digital switching and information services began to dawn and the capabilities of this equipment expanded many fold. Notably, "high speed" data phone service made its debut in 1958 with a 1200 bits per second capability. In contrast, DS-3 dedicated data services today feature speeds of 45 megabits per second. Did innovation, as it related to the touch-tone feature, appear twice, or, should the term apply only to the use of a new option?

Table 7.1 illustrates the slow pace of service introduction and marketing in the demand area, when compared to the industry's emphasis on technology or supply parameters. This applies for even the most simple or trivial changes. For instance, it took approximately fifty years after the initial commercialization of telephony for the first nonblack telephones to be offered (i.e., by the Independents in 1926). Even with this "innovation" in evidence, another thirty years passed before the Bell System provided colored telephones in 1955. But nearly twenty-five *more* years were required for "Mickey Mouse" to make his appearance in the industry (i.e., as an innocuous plastic case for the basic telephone in the mid-1970s). At that point, Mickey was already in his fifties.

A corresponding history applies in the case of many services. As table 7.1 shows, the appearance of data transmission at 600 bps over telephone lines occurred in 1930, about fifty years after the introduction of commercial voice service, but another forty years went by before a visual offering was instituted (picturephone). Now it appears that about twenty-five more years will have to pass before all three services will be available concurrently over the public switched network, i.e, with the full application of the ISDN. Finally, note that the new service frontier of transcontinental service (New York to San Francisco) was breached in 1915 or about 40 years after birth of the Bell System, but Bell required another 40 years before making dependable, reasonably priced transoceanic service available over cable. Yet, innovative ("transindustry") electronic mail only made its appearance about twenty-five years later in the early 1980s, or at about the time that the Bell System was breaking up.

As shown by the difference between the "transmission capability" supply line of figure 7.1 and the accompanying plot of "service de-

FIGURE 7.1

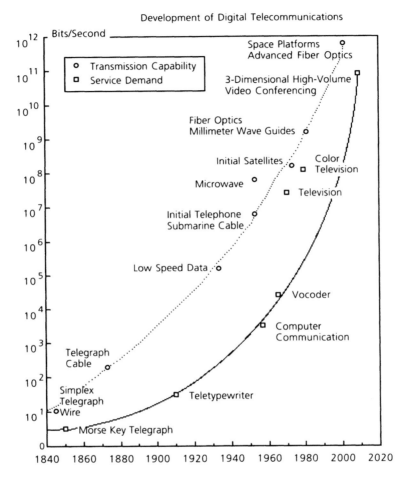

Development of Digital Telecommunications

mand," a lag in facility applications for the telecommunications indus-try has at some points exceeded a decade. Recently, the gap between the incidence of technical possibility and the practical application of industry capabilities has lessened. This has reflected the increased pres-ence of competitive pressures and heightened industry awareness of the need for greater responsiveness to users' requirements. For instance, widespread utilization of facsimile technology, which first appeared in the 1960s, has required "just" two decades. Moreover, commercial exploitation of cellular radio has taken only slightly more than a decade, after cellular's technical feasibility was established in the late 1960s. Cellular implementation has been directly impacted by the FCC's determination that competitive provision, albeit only two providers, would be an appropriate means of fostering widespread deployment of this technology. Finally, in several instances, custom calling and CLASS services have been tariffed in less than ten years after their initial development. In this instance, competitive pressures, from terminal equipment and enhanced service suppliers, were an important impetus toward more rapid deployment.

Of course, the process of translating the capabilities of the network after divestiture into a service-related form generally seems to be improving when compared to historical norms. This also applies to current attempts to define service building blocks or BSEs in the context of the FCC's plans for ONA. Indeed, this effort may be completed in the space of only a few years. But, even here, accolades for the industry's supply enthusiasts may not be in order. Notably, the technological or facility-focused breakup of the Bell System took place without *any* prior attention or even mention of the ONA applications or customer oriented process.

The pre-divestiture period of high engineering or technological innovation and low service application had an impact that was economywide because of its effects on dependent or served industries. Utilization of computer technology languished for well over a decade before high-speed data links became available. Similarly, in the 1960s and 1970s, firms in banking, manufacturing, and other areas found it necessary to develop private networks specially suited to their service needs because of slow industry application of available technology.

While the steady stream of technological advances during the predivestiture period were impressive, these developments pale in comparison to telecommunications' post-divestiture facility revitalization, both in terms of the pace and scope of change. Plant replacement has been implemented at a brisk pace ever since the industry realized that the new environment would be characterized by multiple supply. Indeed, in the case of the Bell companies, conditions of competitive supply are a *prerequisite* for their participation in toll and other markets. Thus, digital technology is currently supplanting most analog installations in the toll and local networks. This is remarkable when one considers that the network was basically engineered for analog transmission from its inception.

Facility changeover is having fundamental effects on industry switching, transmission, and terminal equipment capabilities. Currently local telephone companies, led by the BOCs, are actively evolving their public switched plant toward the ISDN. Taken as a whole, ISDN implementation represents technological innovation pushed forward on a massive scale. In the near term, ISDN will offer integrated standard voice, medium-speed data, facsimile, and telemetry services. In later stages, it will be able to accommodate highly desirable broadband applications, such as video and high-speed data.

Clearly, the proportion of switching systems already digital has risen dramatically from the level existing at divestiture. According to the USTA, in 1985, 4,251 of the 20,093 Central Office Switches in service in the U.S. were digital. By 1987, digital switches were 7,381 of the 19,712 Central Offices.[7] Optical fiber transmission facilities have shown rapid expansion as well as shown by table 7.2, which indicates, during the post-divestiture period 1985–1987, that interexchange fiber miles increased fourfold. During the same interval, the number of fiber miles installed by the BOCs more than tripled. In fact, as recently as 1982, there was virtually no fiber in service.

A report for NASA prepared by IGI Consulting, Inc., predicts cable costs will go as low as $0.12 per meter by 1995 (figure 7.2) while NET expects fiber prices in 1994 to be only half as high as they were in 1986.[8] Southwestern Bell is forecasting annual price reductions of 10 to 15 percent for fiber cable by 1993, as well as annual reductions of 10 to 15 percent in prices of digital loop carrier systems, 15 to 20 percent in optical device prices, and 37 percent in laser prices.[9]

A decline in prices has also been experienced by terminal equipment for fiber systems. This is due in part to the fact that manufacturers' input prices have been rapidly declining. For instance, high-quality

TABLE 7.2

Estimated Fiber Optic Miles Deployed by Major Service Providers, 1985–1988

| | Fiber-Miles (000s) | | | |
	1985	1986	1987	1988
Major Interexchange Carriers	455.9	889.2	1,486.1	1,886.5
Seven regional Bell operating companies	497.1	880.7	1,192.0	1,548.5
Metropolitan fiber systems	NA	NA	NA	12.2
Total	953.0	1,769.9	2,678.1	3,447.2

Source: Jonathan M. Kraushaar (FCC), *Fiber Deployment Update, End of Year 1988*, February 17, 1989.

FIGURE 7.2

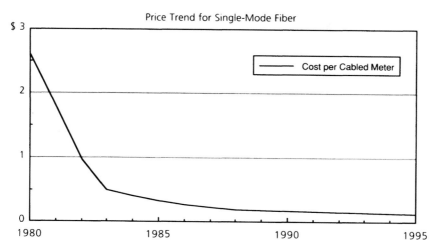

Price Trend for Single-Mode Fiber

Source: Bethesda Research Institute.

light emitting diodes (LEDs) have dropped in price from $200 to $10 in recent years. Digital switching costs are also declining. For example, these systems fell 17 percent between 1986 and 1989. While this is not as impressive as the savings experienced in fiber costs, the outlook for switching equipment economies is also quite positive.

Not unexpectedly, carriers' *operating* costs are likewise experiencing a downward trend. This directly reflects installation of the newer technologies, especially the lower provisioning and maintenance costs associated with fiber optics. But the ongoing evolution to a digital network will imply *both* a reduction in current costs and an increase in capacity. In turn, these will lead to realization of recurring future economic benefits, as providers experience increased revenues and lower costs for expansion and rearranging their networks.[10]

The declining cost of fiber optic cable is not the only aspect of the new technologies from which carriers are deriving a cost advantage. In fact, the savings these firms are experiencing from technical improvements are even more impressive than the reductions in manufacturers' equipment prices. These technical improvements have generally enhanced the performance and capacity, and lowered the cost of lightwave transmission systems since divestiture.[11]

For instance, the recent trend of bit rates times repeater spacing, as that measure of operating capacity applies to systems in commercial

FIGURE 7.3

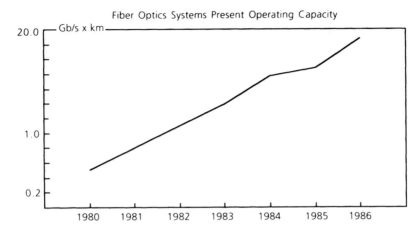

Source: Bethesda Research Institute.

use, is shown by figure 7.3. Notably, the vertical scale for the figure is exponential, reflecting the fact the improvements have been exponential, and it is simply impractical to capture these on a linear measure. Overall, this parameter has actually improved by a factor of ten approximately every three years, while the cost of optical fiber capacity has been decreasing at a similar rate. The resultant unit cost reductions are illustrated by the same chart.

Switching capacity has also been increasing, albeit not as rapidly as that for transmission. For instance, Patrick White of Bell Communications reports "the 1ESS switch, first introduced in the mid-1960s, could process 115,000 calls per hour, while its successor, 1AESS handles 240,000 calls per hour. Current generation digital switches, such as the DMS 100, can process 330,000 calls per hour."[12] Taken together with developments in transmission, switching feature progress and capacity increments leave open the possibility for a tremendous influx in new services development.

Another potential gauge for gleaning how quickly technical progress is taking place is labor productivity. For example, as shown by table 7.3, employment in the Bell companies by the end of 1988 had declined 14.8 percent from its 1983 level. On the other hand, customers served, as measured by the number of access lines, had risen 14.7 percent, leading to an overall labor productivity gain of more than 30 percent. Overall, this gain was registered in the first year, but between

TABLE 7.3
Labor Productivity Gains for Bell Companies Lines Per Employee

Number of Access Lines
(thousands)

	1983	1984	1985	1986	1987	1988
Ameritech	14,114	14,337	14,555	14,755	15,094	15,469
Bell Atlantic	14,358	14,677	15,090	15,509	16,056	16,541
Bell South	13,612	14,000	14,500	15,000	15,700	16,400
NYNEX	12,829	13,226	13,623	13,962	14,415	14,851
Pacific Telesis	10,930	11,307	11,630	12,063	12,525	13,090
Southwestern Bell	10,329	10,650	10,898	11,083	11,105	11,340
US West	10,610	10,871	11,167	11,332	11,613	11,878
Bell Totals	86,782	89,068	91,463	93,704	96,508	99,569

Number of Employees

	1983	1984	1985	1986	1987	1988
Ameritech	95,238	77,514	74,883	77,538	78,510	77,334
Bell Atlantic	80,600	77,788	73,036	77,358	80,950	81,000
Bell South	120,174	96,000	92,300	96,900	98,700	110,280
NYNEX	117,042	94,900	89,600	90,200	95,300	97,400
Pacific Telesis	97,647	76,881	71,488	74,937	71,877	69,502
Southwestern Bell	74,000	71,900	71,400	67,500	67,100	69,900
US West	73,000	70,765	70,202	69,375	68,523	69,765
Bell Totals	657,701	565,748	542,909	549,808	560,960	560,181

Lines per Employee

	1983	1984	1985	1986	1987	1988
Ameritech	148	185	194	190	192	200
Bell Atlantic	178	189	207	211	198	204
Bell South	113	146	157	155	159	163
NYNEX	110	139	152	155	151	152
Pacific Telesis	112	147	163	161	174	188
Southwestern Bell	140	148	153	164	165	175
US West	145	154	159	163	169	170
Bell Totals	132	157	168	170	172	178
Cumulative Gain		18.9%	27.2%	28.8%	30.3%	34.9%

Sources: Company annual reports and forms 10K.

1984 and 1988 average Bell productivity in this area still improved by 16 percent.

The post-divestiture experience shows the telephone network to be already feature rich and to possess diverse capabilities. The technologies already in place have capacity to serve far in excess of historical demand growth or the rate of service introduction by industry providers. And, as shown by figure 7.4 (for fiber optics), the unit economies being generated consistently take hold at fairly low traffic levels. These effects are likely to be accentuated as network revitalization proceeds to completion in the early 1990s. Moreover, as gleaned from figure 7.5, the transfusion of new equipment will have been largely financed *before* its full benefits are realized, since amounts are being reserved currently at accelerating rates to pay for these installations.

In general, the industry seems to be witnessing a speedup of technical innovation and supply improvements from a traditional span of decades to just a few years. Thus, the need to stimulate applications or demand is likewise accentuated. The magnitude of GNP that was lost prior to divestiture due to lagging application over a period of perhaps twenty-five to fifty years, could not be potentially at stake before we reach the next century, or possibly even before 1995. This points to the critical need to develop policies which ensure that service innovation also greatly exceeds pre-divestiture levels.

FIGURE 7.4

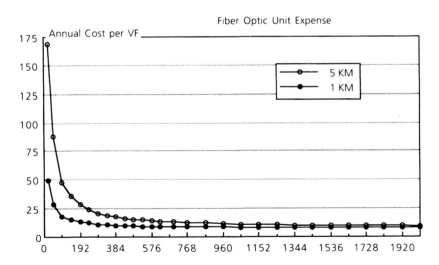

Source: Bethesda Research Institute.

FIGURE 7.5

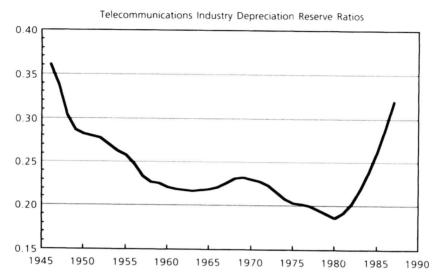

Telecommunications Industry Depreciation Reserve Ratios

Source: Bethesda Research Institute.

Since divestiture, business users have benefited from a proliferation of choice and opportunity offered by more efficient, productive suppliers, but there has been turmoil in the new operating environment and the difficult loss of "one-stop shopping." Fortunately, in the post-divestiture era, customer demand has assumed a more important role in determining the direction of service and product development. By definition, multiple entry into a given market presents users with more choice and therefore more leverage in their dealings with suppliers. Indeed, most established carriers today publicly stress their commitment to their customers, citing, inter alia, their "market driven" strategies,[13] "rededication to customer service,"[14] "responsive[ness] to customer needs,"[15] "commitment to service,"[16] and "customer satisfaction."[17]

Yet, despite the rhetoric, many within the industry still exhibit supply-driven tendencies to an important degree. For example, on the eve of divestiture, ISDN was referred to as a "grand design for tomorrow's telephones," and it was observed that:

The big push for the digital network has come from the telephone companies in developed nations, which look to it as a new source of revenue at a time when much of the growth in communications is going to new specialized carriers.[18]

AT&T was identified as the "driving force behind ISDN," and a French electronics firm remarked that "there will be no turning back."[19]

ISDN in its incipient stage would seem to be appropriately classified as "technically feasible but no demand." Although not as blatant in its disregard for customer input as picturephone, this network concept nonetheless is clearly an example of a "technology push" innovation. Dubbed the "great economic hope of most telephone companies" by a British Telecom marketing director, ISDN has been very slow to win approval of users, despite an increasingly rampant industry push toward its application.

Indeed, a spring 1988 survey of large nonresidential users found there had been no significant movement among corporate network planners in either adding or expecting to add ISDN capability through the end of 1989.[20] Often bewildered or skeptical users have adopted their own interpretations of the ISDN acronym, ranging from "I Still Don't (K)Now" to "Innovations Subscribers Don't Need" to "It's So Damn Near." More recently, a few large customers (e.g., McDonald's Corporation and American Express) have pioneered the use of ISDN capability.

The outcome of ISDN implementation is yet unknown. Recent interest by some users may qualify the concept as bona fide serendipity, but at this point the outcome is still unclear. In fact, three basic ISDN scenarios appear plausible, underscoring the pivotal importance of public policy guidance in this area. One scenario is characterized by "market failure," whereby the lack of a quick consensus on standards would retard development of a public ISDN, resulting in disparate, incompatible private enhanced networks. A second scenario has a public ISDN emerging on a "piecemeal" basis, targeting large cities and featuring a shared facilities architecture rather than complete integration of voice, data, facsimile, and other services. Finally, the third scenario envisions full conversion to broadband ISDN as the technological "dream" is brought to fruition, namely, full deployment and integration based on universally accepted ISDN standards. These standards would support open entry, a myriad of wideband video and high-speed data offerings, integrated packet and circuit switching, and value-based (rather than cost-based) pricing.

Failure to develop an appropriate public policy infrastructure for the new Information Age or utilize the competitive catalyst could result in parallel development of all three scenarios, at an enormous waste of R&D funds, public monies, manufacturing resources, and public network operating systems. The possibility exists that full conversion might *never* be achieved without the necessary public guidance.

The demand for services provided via ISDN is a key element to the success of the concept. The cost to end users may not be the determining factor since the price of a service is not always the criterion used to select among alternative service offerings. Service quality and reliability are often more important than cost considerations. Technical criteria, such as the capability to interface different technologies and terminal types among users, are critical factors in other situations. And, if diverse routing is required by users, alternate suppliers can be used to provide such a feature.

Beyond ISDN, high rates of change have occurred in recent years in the U.S. telecommunications sector, and even greater rates are expected from now until the year 2000.[21] Both domestic and international telecommunications markets are growing substantially. A number of specific markets have enjoyed particularly robust growth. As shown by table 7.4, electronic information industry revenues, particularly computerized databases, have increased significantly since the pre-divestiture era. The U.S. business information services sector is projected to reach $15 billion by 1992.[22]

Several other markets have been gaining in popularity. Facsimile machines' plummeting pricing (some quality units now cost under $2,000) have fueled that brisk market. Although sales of personal computers, facsimile hardware, and software products only totaled $13 million in 1987, the figure may reach one-quarter *billion* by 1991. The number of VSATs grew by over 50 percent from 1987 to 1989 as a spate of customers have become convinced of the medium's cost effectiveness and reliability. Similar to FAX, T-1 has existed for a quarter of a century, but has only caught on since divestiture as companies set up high-quality, cost-effective private networks to replace the Bell System's end-to-end offerings.

Two markets may prove to be the most impressive in terms of growth. With respect to electronic mail, the number of in-house electronic messaging subscribers totaled 5.6 million in 1987, an increase of approximately 40 percent from the previous year. The number of messages in 1987 averaged 62.9 million per month, with 67 percent accounted for by private mail boxes. Compared to long-distance telephone calls and mail, fast-growing electronic mailbox usage currently comprises less than one percent of total U.S. message volume as this country enters the Information Age.

Another emerging service is electronic data interchange (EDI). EDI is the computer-to-computer transmission of business documents, such

TABLE 7.4
Electronic Information Industry Revenues

*Computerized Databases
(1982 and 1987)*

	1982 ($M)	% of Total	1987 ($M)	% of Total	Growth Rate (%)
Financial	304.5	29.1	835.2	28.6	22.4
Economics and econometrics	90.7	8.6	198.1	6.8	16.9
Industry-specific	28.2	2.7	73.4	2.5	21.1
Credit	290.0	27.7	513.9	17.6	12.1
Audience measurement	16.4	1.6	35.9	1.2	17.0
Product movement	20.1	1.9	76.9	2.6	30.8
Demographics	6.5	0.6	22.8	0.8	28.5
General business and industry	10.0	0.9	30.5	1.0	25.0
Industrial directories and catalogs	1.8	0.2	8.4	0.3	36.1
News	35.3	3.4	267.2	9.1	49.9
Scientific and technical	68.0	6.5	162.0	5.5	19.0
Library support	17.6	1.7	34.9	1.2	14.7
Legal	94.0	9.0	266.8	9.1	23.2
Government	9.0	0.8	22.4	0.8	20.0
Real estate	28.0	2.7	40.8	1.4	7.8
New professional services (medical, pharmacists, etc.)	11.3	1.1	146.5	5.0	66.9
Consumer	10.5	1.0	178.5	6.1	76.2
Other	5.0	0.5	10.1	0.4	15.1
Total	1,046.9	100.0	2,924.3	100.0	22.8

Source: *Huber Report,* Section 7.1.

as purchase orders, invoices, and advance shipping notices, in standard formats. Potential benefits include shorter procurement intervals for manufacturing materials, lower purchasing costs, and increased buyer productivity. Pacific Bell, Southern Bell, and South Central Bell are attempting to use EDI to provide enhanced billing services to customers, such as presenting monthly inventories of all BOC-provided services and equipment.

ONA is a form of equal access for enhanced service providers instituted by the FCC in response to a burgeoning market. Highly acclaimed as a concept, ONA as developed by the FCC has been criticized for its lack of specificity and for its slow development. Some claim that the RBOCs, subject to MFJ restraints, have eschewed rapid implementation of ONA in favor of CEI plans designed to help themselves, and *not* their competitors.[23]

The pivotal importance of ONA is widely recognized by the telecommunications industry. The Regional Companies see a significant market opportunity in successful implementation of the process. For example, an executive at Southwestern Bell observed:

> Increasing the use of the network—even by just one percent—promises far more revenue potential than anything we could gain by providing enhanced services ourselves. . . . ONA can aid economic development by creating a telecommunications market rich in Information Age services. New businesses or existing businesses considering relocation will look at whether an area offers a progressive environment that promotes the advantages of the Information Age.[24]

Enhanced service providers are also cognizant of this potentially lucrative market. Potential users regard the process as a means to have their information service needs better met. Public policymakers at the FCC envision ONA as an "equal access" approach to promoting competition, and assuring a more rapid and efficient delivery of Information Age services to the public.

The concept is a key element in the FCC's *Computer III* program of relaxed regulation, which was vacated and remanded by the Court of Appeals in June 1990. Notably, without its successful implementation, separate subsidiary requirements will be retained for enhanced service provision by Bell companies. This network architecture and its interim counterpart, CEI, represent essential elements of the much touted broadband ISDN network of the 1990s and beyond.

Local telephone companies have not passively accepted entry into their traditionally secure markets, and have turned to network developments in the attempt to meet the challenge. Centrex was initially offered by the local exchange carriers in the early 1960s as an alternative to PBXs, that is, switching equipment located on a customer's premises. In the 1970s, PBX began its resurgence as microprocessor technology advanced and the FCC's procompetitive policies gathered momentum. The FCC's decisions in the areas of equipment registration, rate unbundling, and cost-based pricing fostered considerable competitive entry. As a result, by the 1980s, there was much greater emphasis on meeting customer needs and growth in the PBX sector, particularly respecting equipment offered by competitors of the Bell System.

Apparently, in an attempt to meet changed marketplace conditions and combat incursion of new competitors, the Bell System launched a marketing program in the late 1970s that has been termed a "migration strategy." Under this new strategy, Centrex was deemphasized as an offering. Instead, marketing focus and development of new features were shifted to Bell's recently upgraded CPE project line (e.g., Dimension PBX). Within a few years, Centrex systems' growth and customer acceptance suffered through increasing replacement by Bell's electronic PBXs.

The divestiture altered these conditions and incentives dramatically. These new regional companies and their BOCs inaugurated an energetic program to innovate, i.e., to remarket and upgrade their Centrex services. Resurgence of Centrex growth is expected to continue as a result of this sales push, corollary actions (e.g., a lowering of the minimum 100-line requirement formerly imposed on Centrex users), and technological enhancements in the late 1980s. In addition, central office local area networks (CO-LANs) have been developed to enhance existing Centrex lines to allow the BOCs to provide an alternative offering to LANs obtained from independent suppliers.

The structure of the U.S. telecommunications sector today is the product of major technological forces, increased competitive entry, and a myriad of facilitating public policies instituted by federal and state agencies, the courts, and the U.S. Congress. The relatively simple era of few choices, fewer suppliers, rental phones, electromechanical networks, and extensive regulation has been superseded by a competitively inspired greater diversity of offerings, multiple sources of supply, sophisticated CPE for sale to users, digital electronic networks, and relaxed regulation.

As we have indicated, during the early post-divestiture era, options have widened significantly for users, and customers have strengthened their role in impacting the rate and direction of innovation; clearly demand has become more important in shaping technological advance in the industry. However, the supply factor and strategic view of the impact that competition may have remains the pivotal consideration in new service and product development in the telecommunications sector. Established carriers have effected a dramatic upgrading and rapid expansion of facilities in vigorously responding to competitive pressures in the 1980s. As a result, the industry is currently faced with excess network capacity and unexploited capabilities. These facilities are likely to be utilized efficiently only if "outside applications" (e.g., by new entrants) supplement those contemplated by traditional suppliers.

Consolidation is a structural fact in key markets, whether by merger, acquisition, joint venture, or withdrawal. For example, in interexchange markets, a second tier of companies has formed new corporate combinations reminiscent of the bolstering of MCI and US Sprint in the early eighties. Never crowded, the ranks of large switching equipment manufacturers were thinned by ITT's abandonment of the market. PBX, key system, and modem vendors have all been beset by market "shakeouts."

Over an extended horizon, there is evidence that conditions of (incipient) economies of scale and scope may arise in the industry, especially after telecommunications traverses the first decade after divestiture. Unexpectedly, this situation is a direct result of new competition and the accommodating Bell System divestiture, which have been the catalysts for existing carriers to overexpand and sharply upgrade the scale of their plant. These programs, when complete, will position traditional suppliers to meet competitive threats and forestall further entry. In addition, these firms believe their upgraded capabilities are justified because they can be employed in meeting new customer requirements. Yet, in many instances, these perceived needs can only be characterized as being a remote likelihood or distant fruition. Thus, they will apparently not be the bases for fully loading in a timely manner the facilities that are coming on line.

Given these network conditions, there is a need to direct public policy toward encouraging the near-term utilization of huge network and other resources which would otherwise be left idle. Importantly, from society's viewpoint, the benefits of such exploitation are essentially "free." However, without intervention, this plant is likely to be left underutilized over the next several years. If this is the case, the increased industry and national economic growth, service options and operational economies, and other benefits that could have been derived from our paid-for and greatly enhanced communications network will simply be lost forever.

At the same time, vertical integration has become fashionable again as service providers seek to recapture the "one-stop shopping" capability of the pre-divestiture period and preempt their competitors. The RBOCs, AT&T, and many independent telephone companies have indicated their belief in this corporate goal.[25] For example, BellSouth and Ameritech telephone companies have combined their service and CPE operations pursuant to *Computer III.*

Despite the much publicized specter of bypass, the nation's local exchanges apparently remain securely in the grasp of the BOCs and the Independents in their respective operating territories. This has slowed the pace of innovation significantly. There are no compelling signs that exchange carriers will lose their grip on local markets. Entry, whether real or imagined, has clearly helped to spur the BOCs and other LECs to modernize their networks, and to become leaders in implementing many of the so-called bypass technologies such as fiber optics, digital switching, cellular radio, and short-haul microwave.

The road to ISDN and UIS-type[26] comprehensive solutions, once navigated, should reaffirm the public switched network as the undisputed backbone of this nation's telecommunications capabilities. High supplier concentration will likely remain or even heighten in interexchange services, large switching equipment, and many CPE markets. A brisk rate of innovation should be evident in these markets, born of the reactions of financially and otherwise solid oligopolists to the clashes of less stable, but more adventuresome legions of competitors characteristic of the early and mid-1980s. Market instability should lessen, but so will "derring do" as "me too" pricing and other forms of mutual interdependence may evolve.

Thus, a key to maintaining a lively pace of new service and product development will center on the nature and extent of the access afforded competitors to the "network of the future" and the role of competition itself. The ability of alternative facilities providers to enter without restriction, and public policymakers to encourage competition in the enhanced information services resale market, will determine whether the network's capacity and capabilities are utilized on a timely basis. In turn, these should, in large measure, determine whether the Information Age is properly fueled for the journey ahead.

Elliot E. Maxwell

Walter Bolter and James McConnaughey argue that competition spurs innovation—few people would disagree. Unfortunately Bolter and McConnaughey present little empirical evidence on the central question of how innovation has been affected by the MFJ and related regulation.

If one measure of innovation is the bringing of new services to market, there are several ways one could demonstrate the delays introduced into the process by the MFJ and regulatory requirements. One simple method would be to measure the intervals between the filing of proposed MFJ service waivers with the DOJ, and a favorable decision by Judge Greene. That delay would be a direct consequence of the MFJ. A preliminary review of the twenty waivers filed by Pacific Telesis Group and approved by the District Court between 1984 and 1987 shows a total delay of 4,131 days. For those who wish to offer services in increasingly competitive markets, these numbers provide little comfort. Similarly, in the federal or state regulatory arena, one could calculate the time it takes a service proposal to move through the regulatory system by examining when CEI or ONA plans are filed, and when they are authorized.

My thesis is this: the MFJ, FCC, and public utility regulations, established to govern the activities of the BOCs, have discouraged these companies from offering new products or services, or engaging in development activities that typically lead to new products and services. The practical effect has been to exclude the local exchange companies from competing in a number of markets to which they would bring considerable skills and resources, and to reduce competition and innovation by these large, technologically competent and well-capitalized firms. Although it may be argued that this reduction in competition has led to increased innovation by other firms, one should hesitate to restrict *actual* entry, and therefore competition, on the *theoretical* basis that the restriction will promote competition.

The negative effects of regulation are illustrated in many cases. Among the most glaring was the long delay in the FCC authorizing cellular radio service. Yet, there are other illustrations of the impact of regulation on innovation. One area of particular interest, given the convergence of telecommunications and computing, is the regulation of enhanced services.

In 1980, the FCC noted the need to examine issues surrounding protocol conversion subsequent to issuing its *Computer II* rules. However, the first protocol processing waiver, one providing little freedom for the BOCs to meet market needs, was not granted to a BOC by the FCC until 1984. Other data-oriented services, the so-called "Custom Calling II" features, had been proposed by AT&T in the late 1970s and early 1980s. The AT&T proposals involved offering the services on an integrated basis, rather than through separate subsidiaries, and were rejected by the FCC as being inconsistent with the emerging *Computer II* ruling. Potential competitors told the FCC that they would be dissuaded from entering the marketplace if AT&T were allowed to compete on an integrated basis—i.e., in the same way others would provide such a service—and the FCC accepted this line of reasoning. Following divestiture, the FCC's prohibition on integrated provisioning of these services was applied to the BOCs, just as it had been earlier imposed on AT&T.

The results of this FCC experiment in promoting competition were not encouraging. Several years passed and the services in question still were not generally available. The Commission eventually concluded its strategy of excluding the BOCs had been unsuccessful, and it adopted *Computer III* rules, eliminating the separate subsidiary requirement and allowing the BOCs to provide the services on an integrated basis.

However, *Computer III* created newer complications. Under the *Computer III* rules, the BOCs had to file interim plans for these services, and indicate how they would provide competitors with CEI to underlying BOC facilities. This resulted in further delays. In addition, competitors sought to delay integrated provision of services by advocating an FCC ban on BOC information service provisioning until ONA was implemented. And most recently, the Ninth Circuit vacated and remanded the *Computer III* decision and we are, at least temporarily, back to *Computer II* and separate subsidiaries.

MFJ proceedings also contributed to delay. Even though the FCC had found BOC provisioning of these data services to be in the public interest, Judge Greene was unconvinced. The MFJ still barred the BOCs from providing information services. Not until March 1988 did the District Court allow the BOCs to make a general offering of information transmission, storage, and retrieval services. Judge Greene based his decision on the grounds that BOC participation was the only way the new services would be made available to the mass market—a rationale strikingly similar to that invoked by the FCC in adopting *Computer III* several years earlier. If Judge Greene and the FCC were correct, the years of delay had deprived the public of useful new services to which the BOCs brought unique strengths.

This example provides only an anecdotal measure of the impact of the MFJ and regulation on innovation. But it understates the problem. The uncertainty about the effect of regulation and judicial intervention on these data services continues. The D.C. Circuit's remand of Judge Greene's Triennial discussion on information services may lead to significant changes in the MFJ ban, but that may not be known for some time. Even after FCC and MFJ approval, there are nagging questions about how to offer such services economically. For example, some aspects of these services raise possible interLATA questions. The District Court has held that the MFJ requires a BOC to place a gateway processor in every LATA to avoid any interLATA carriage, regardless of whether that is the most economically efficient way to provide the service. No similar configuration requirement exists for any non-BOC competitor. What is the social impact of this requirement? Does it mean the service will be priced too high for the casual user? Will the interLATA prohibition have the effect of preventing these services from being offered successfully to the mass market? The delay and uncertainty surrounding such questions, faced only by the BOCs, are terrible impediments in the planning and offering of innovative products and services. When proposed new service offerings must compete for resources within a BOC, the prospect of regulatory delay or legal disapproval associated with the offering is often enough to remove the proposed new services from the BOC's list of top priorities.

I have focused on the MFJ's prohibitions on information services because of the great potential the RHCs possess to provide mass market telecommunications services. Former Assistant Attorney General William Baxter obviously thinks the RHCs should not be in information services, so the problems I raise are irrelevant to him. According to Baxter's comments in this volume, it would have been better had Judge Greene continued to "just say no" to any BOC role in the information services area.

Yet during the first Triennial Review of the MFJ, the two parties to the decree, the DOJ and AT&T, agreed that flatly prohibiting a BOC role in information services was inappropriate. The DOJ took the position that the information service ban should not have been written. AT&T said that the ban was imposed due to a mistaken analogy with the problems in the long-distance market that had triggered divestiture.

The information services prohibition was premised on fear that BOC participation might result in anticompetitive behavior in the information services market. The BOCs had the "incentive and ability" to discriminate against their competitors, and regulatory solutions to the "incentive and ability" issues were impossible. This thesis may be "elegant," in Baxter's words, but it is wrong. It is belied by the results of the RHCs' involvement in CPE distribution, where the same "incentive and abilities" could be said to exist.

Although the initial settlement agreement between AT&T and the DOJ proposed to exclude the RHCs from distributing CPE, the District Court rejected the prohibition thesis and allowed RHC distribution. Critics claimed that the BOCs would misuse their freedom, for example, by providing more favorable connections to RHC-provided PBXs than to PBXs offered by competitors. But this has not happened. Similarly, in theory, GTE has the same incentives and even a greater ability to act anticompetitively than the BOC. GTE participates directly in the local exchange market, the information services market (Telenet), the intraLATA market (US Sprint), and in the manufacturing of telecommunications equipment. But here too, the real world and actual behavior of GTE has provided little empirical support for the prohibition thesis. It is also worth noting the nation's expert agency in telecommunications, the FCC, has not adopted a strategy of prohibition in the case of information services. Rather, it is defining a regulatory response via "comparably efficient interconnection" requirements and ONA plans.

The very processes for change in both the MFJ Court and at the regulatory commissions also impede innovation. When one of the seven RHCs obtains a waiver from the MFJ Court or an approval from the FCC, the other six can and often do follow with exactly the same proposals. This "me too" mentality is the cheapest and fastest way to obtain permission to enter a particular market. What has been created is a government stamp of approval on one particular procedure and course of action. There is a great regulatory cost in seeking approval for an alternative way of providing the service, even if that alternative approach is more effective in the long run.

The MFJ also affects innovation due to its definition of manufacturing. The MFJ has always prohibited the RHCs from engaging in the manufacturing of telecommunications equipment. The District Court has now interpreted the definition of that "prohibition" to include barring the RHCs from the "design and development" of such equipment, although they are permitted to engage in "research."

Most authorities believe there is an important connection between levels of R&D, productivity, and innovation. Michael Noll of the University of Southern California has published a series of papers on AT&T and BOC spending on R&D.[27] He observed that the BOCs were now spending about 1.4 percent of their revenues on research, much less than AT&T's expenditures both before and after divestiture, and much lower than other firms. (For example, Hewlett Packard spends 10.5 percent of sales on R&D.)[28] Other studies have shown that the BOCs' expenditures on R&D per employee are relatively small compared to industry averages.

Why are the BOCs not spending more? As a March 1989 NTIA report noted, "The AT&T consent decree's manufacturing restriction, particularly as it is currently construed, is creating uncertainties which appear to deter research and development on the part of the Bell companies."[29] It is not surprising that expenditures are not growing when the activities to be funded may carry with them potential criminal liability.

BOC innovation has also been negatively affected by challenges to the ability of BOCs to obtain economic returns from innovation in the telecommunications equipment arena. If the BOCs were to be prohibited from retaining economic rights to their discoveries due to a broad interpretation of the definition of "manufacturing," they clearly have less incentive to invent. If they were to encourage activity in a prohibited area, they would face punishment by the Court. It is a striking irony that the RHCs may be forced to warn their employees against wasting time on innovation.

The present legal construction of the manufacturing prohibition presents yet another challenge to the RBOCs' ability to innovate. The definition of "manufacturing" is based on a simple linear view of telecommunications equipment manufacturing: research, design, development, then fabrication, with the RHCs allowed to perform research and to issue generic specifications. Many suppliers see the development process as requiring substantial interaction between purchasers and suppliers. Yet the RHCs are prohibited from engaging with suppliers in any design activities that concern the implementation of generic specifications.

As NTIA noted, the uncertainties about the distinction between permissible and impermissible research and design activities "appear to be adversely affecting the ability of Bell company suppliers to interact with them efficiently. Both the pace at which innovations are being brought to market, and the overall cost of that process, appear to have been adversely affected."[30] In this regard, the BOCs differ from other telecommunications service suppliers around the world who "can and do work actively and affirmatively with their suppliers in ways that would almost certainly be ruled illegal under prevailing interpretations of the AT&T consent decree."[31]

Brief mention should also be made of the negative effects of a particular type of regulation on innovation. Under rate-of-return regulation, incentives to develop and deploy new services are dampened. Profits are limited to a set return on assets, and the deployment of profitable new services does not increase profits unless they also increase the asset base. Thus, there are limited incentives to deploy new services or make a non-capital-intensive investment to bring new services to market.

Rate-of-return regulation also arguably creates incentives for firms to shift costs from competitive markets to monopoly markets, therefore subsidizing competitive profits at the expense of monopoly ratepayers. A switch to incentive-based regulation such as price caps would be desirable, in order to eliminate any incentive to shift costs (which could not be recouped from monopoly ratepayers) and to encourage service deployment by allowing the firm to profit from the fruits of its own creativity.

Any discussion of telecommunications innovation today must examine carefully the impact of the MFJ and regulation. Regulation of essential monopoly services continues to be necessary, and certain safeguards may be required to prevent anticompetitive behavior by a dominant supplier. But no matter how well-intentioned, regulation should not be immunized from critical review. If telecommunications is to be part of the engine for societal progress, and if innovation is to be the fuel for the engine, we cannot allow unnecessary or counterproductive governmental policy to be the sand in the gas tank.

Jerrold Oppenheim

It is easy to assume innovation is an unmitigated blessing. The telephone itself was a spectacular innovation, and it is difficult to imagine what American life would be like today without such innovations as the transistor, the assembly line, and the personal computer. But innovation has its drawbacks. After all, one consequence of the transistor is "boom boxes" in city streets; the assembly line brought a new form of boredom to the workplace; and computers made possible error on a scale never before imagined.

The first response raises caveats about two aspects of technological development in telecommunications. First, to the extent that faster innovation is a product of competition, there are negative economic consequences that may outweigh the benefits achieved. (This conclusion is underscored when social disadvantages of innovation, such as threats to privacy, are considered.) Second, the history of telecommunications innovation teaches that those who benefit from innovation are often the last to pay for it.

The policy conclusion I draw is that regulation of telecommunication remains essential to (1) protect the public from deleterious consequences of innovation and competition, and (2) apportion fairly the costs of innovation to those who benefit from it. The relatively free forces of the marketplace cannot be relied upon to perform these functions.

The proliferation of novelty phones—shaped as dogs, cars, even a red high-heeled shoe—illustrates the point that some innovations may be worth more than others. The innovations of digital switching and touch-tone signalling make possible such useful services as credit card shopping at home, bill paying and banking at home, appliance control by telephone (so you can turn on your home air conditioner as you leave the office), a display of the phone number of the person calling, and even games at a distance. A glass fiber cable can already carry 100–

250 times as much as a copper cable; telephone engineers predict this will rise to 1,300 times copper's capacity. The fiber cable innovation may bring us switched video services in the next decade and ultimately full-motion broadcast-quality TV, dial-from-anywhere security cameras to watch for fire and burglary or to check up on the teen-age party upstairs, dial-from-home videocassette libraries that save trips to the video store. The telephone companies' fiber optic entry into the cable television business is also on the agenda.[32]

As Bolter and McConnaughey document, some telecommunications innovations have already arrived more broadly for consumers. These include facsimile transmission, computer-based services such as banking by teller machines and shopping by modem, audio services such as tax information lines and recorded "Yellow Pages" information.

However, there is a darker side to innovation. For example, the increased regulatory emphasis on competition made it possible for AOS to enter the marketplace on a broad scale as resellers of long-distance service. Their "added value" is little more than a surcharge on captive customers. Resulting proceeds are then shared with such customer captors as hospitals, hotels, and private pay phone operators. Thus, a hospital signs up with an AOS, then reaps new revenues as the AOS charges higher rates than the hospital did before for the same service and pays the hospital a commission based on the higher rate. It is difficult to recognize what additional level of service to consumers the innovation of increased charges purchases. In Massachusetts, consumers have complained about paying seventy-five cents via an AOS for pay phone calls that ordinarily cost twenty-five cents, and about being charged $3.45 for a call that without an AOS would have cost $1.00.[33]

As Sharon Nelson discusses earlier in this volume, another serious drawback to telecommunications innovation is its potential to erode privacy and First Amendment freedoms. Tomorrow's telephone system, with digital switches and fiber optic cable to nearly every home, could become a super cable television system, doing everything cable TV does now and more. It is also not unreasonable to project it will remain a natural monopoly—there will only be one telephone cable system entering each home—and the BOCs will attempt to free themselves of almost all common carriage obligations[34] as cable operators have successfully done.[35] This could mean that local monopolies would have unfettered control over what a subscriber could receive from a community's only carrier of television, only source of movies (movie theaters having been displaced by videocassettes), only carrier of news (newspapers by then having been converted to teletext, a transition that has been predicted since 1971),[36] only carrier of Congressional sessions, town meeting debates, and classified ads—and perhaps the only carrier of pictures from inside your home to the local police (watching for burglars, of course). Not only could local monopolies thus control access to information, they could maintain records of information and entertainment habits of its customers. Indeed, they would arguably need it for billing purposes.[37]

Thus, even before we reach economic issues, we see that telecommunications innovation requires management on behalf of the public to prevent antisocial results. Much telecommunications innovation, for better and for worse, is at least partly due to competition—including competition spawned by divestiture. But perhaps we assume too easily that competition leads to greater innovation. As Bolter and McConnaughey suggest, for example, divestiture may not have significantly changed the innovation structure in the telecommunications industry. On the other hand, the lack of change may merely reflect the failure of divestiture to stimulate much competition. AT&T, after all, continues to dominate the long-distance (toll) market, controlling 70 to 80 percent of it.

There is an alternative explanation, however, to any failure of divestiture to stimulate innovation: competition may retard innovation. As J.A. Schumpeter has said, "The introduction of new methods of production and new commodities is hardly conceivable with perfect—and perfectly prompt—competition from the start. . . . As a matter of fact, perfect competition is and has always been temporarily suspended whenever anything new is being introduced. . . ."[38] By requiring short-term perspectives and by failing to reward innovations that are easily duplicated, "competitive markets may hinder efficiency in production by stifling technological advances."[39] The great success of Bell Labs during AT&T's monopoly days may provide evidence for this point.[40] So deregulating telecommunications carriers to stimulate innovation may have the opposite result. On the other hand, the bureaucracy usually spawned by monopoly and oligopoly is not famous for its tolerance of new ways of doing things.[41]

Be this as it may, the competition that may spawn innovation requires examination. Not only is the innovation itself a mixed blessing, but innovation-spawning competition is also far from an unmitigated blessing on consumers.

I do not mean to imply there are no consumer benefits from competition. The outcome of the deregulation of telephone set sales (which predates diverstiture) is a vivid illustration of the potential power of competition. At the same time telephone set technology was developing and marketers were providing a bewildering new variety of choices, prices dropped like a spent rocket. It is hard to recall that, as late as 1980, the rental payments to New York Telephone over the fifteen year life of a telephone set would total $212.40[42] although sets could then be purchased for $25. Today low-quality sets can be purchased for less than the 1980 New York one-year rental cost of $14.16.

However, competition has consequences in addition to dropping some prices. Ordinary competitive markets do not guarantee to meet all demand, nor do they assure just, reasonable or stable prices—indeed, volatile prices and shortages are part of the normal competitive cycle. In contrast, the goals of regulation include justice, stability, guaranteed service, and universal service. Competition may produce many important benefits in certain contexts, as, for example, diversity and efficiency, but these regulatory goals are not among them.[43]

This is not to say that regulation, at least as developed to date, is without blemishes. As Roger Noll suggests in this volume, it is, in fact, as messy, slow and as often controversial as any political process. However, as Winston Churchill concluded in describing democracy to the House of Commons in 1947, the alternative is worse.

Even if we determine that, for the general society, competition-induced innovation is generally worth the price, the first specific sector of society to benefit from a telecommunications innovation is often the last to pay for it. A telecommunications utility has the incentive to lower prices to customers with high elasticities of demand (especially in its competitive markets), and recover the resulting lost income by raising prices to customers with low elasticities of demand in monopoly markets. In this way, captive monopoly residential consumers can be required to pay costs of innovations enjoyed only by customers in other, more competitive (or simply more price elastic) sectors.

Such cross-subsidy in the telephone business is a very old problem. It seems as though each technological advance was paid for in large measure by those who did not need to use it. Two historical examples make the point. AT&T began improvements to telephone plant very early in order to improve long-distance service. Indeed, the purpose of the complete integration of local and long-distance calling into one network in the 1890s was to expand the long-distance business, although the costs for the resulting upgrading of the local network were largely assigned to the local business.[44] Similarly, the national conversion to seven-digit dialing and 1+ long-distance dialing did away with the ease of three, four and five-digit dialing in many localities, in order to make direct dialing of long-distance calls possible everywhere. Direct dialing also required additional investment in the local portion of the network for equipment to recognize, route, and bill for the additional digits. Additional costs are and will continue to be imposed as the area code numbering system is changed to defer exhaustion of local office numbering codes. Indeed the entire fixed plant is very different than it would be if it had been constructed only for local calling.[45]

There is nothing inherently wrong with these innovations. They only become problems with respect to pricing. The question of which service—local or long-distance—should pay what portion of the fixed plant costs is almost impossible to answer without controversy when the services share the plant in unquantifiable proportions. This battle has been fought for at least eight decades.[46]

New digital services offer another current example of the difficulties created by the potential for cross-subsidy among services rendered by joint and common plant. High-speed data services and new custom calling services such as call identification and call tracing were made possible by the introduction in 1981 of digital switching machines, essentially the computerization of central office switches (this advance also made touch-tone service much more economical to provide on a marginal cost basis). Thus, the new switches provide ordinary local and long-distance service and also make possible new digital services.[47]

According to one telephone company study of this new switching technology (figure 7.6),[48] this advance increased the company's current incremental investment per line by $52. Thus, assuming that the older analog machines continued to render acceptable basic local and long-distance voice service, the incremental investment cost per line of digital service is $52. (There are also some offsetting savings in circuit equipment used to translate digital signals to analog or back, but these are not germane to basic voice service.) However, digital services are optional services for which the customers have relatively high elasticities of demand. Therefore a utility offering both optional, high elasticity digital and essential, low elasticity local monopoly service has an incentive to cross-subsidize digital services with local service revenues.[49]

Telephone companies will often contend that, on the basis of economies achieved by the new technologies alone, their investment in digital switching is justified on behalf of local and toll services. However, these economies are often created by such means as artificially raising the depreciation expense ascribed to it. Indeed, increased depreciation rates are ascribed to innovation but largely collected from users who do not use or need the innovations. The industry's depreciation reserve ratio, for example, increased by 56 percent from 1980 to 1986 (from 18.6 percent to 29.0 percent), due to telephone companies' need to replace equipment more frequently to keep up with technological

FIGURE 7.6

Investment Allocated to POTS

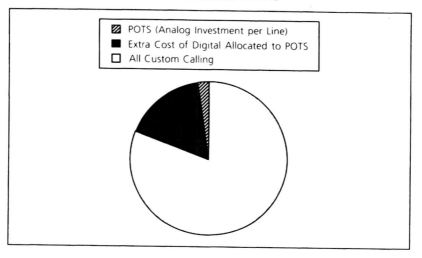

Sources: Mass. D.P.U. 86–33, Ex. NET-120 (Incremental Cost Study)—Book 1, Tab C2, p. 3, @ 3CCS, (April 1986); Book 3, Tab 22, p. 196; Book 3, Tab 10, p. 136.

innovation. However, the bulk of this expense is allocated in rates to basic local subscribers via assignment to local switching machines, although the local machines thus depreciated more quickly are rendering perfectly adequate basic grade service.[50] Even so, telephone company data show the digital machines are not economical for voice service alone (figure 7.7).[51] At least one Bell company spokesman, in response to this presentation, acknowledges that new technology has higher unit costs.[52] He argues that the extra costs are justified by the value of the new functions performed by the innovative technology.[53]

To the extent that new functions are thus the justification for the new technology, the incremental costs of the new technology should not be recovered from ratepayers other than those who benefit from the new functions. Although the digital machines are, by one accounting, somewhat less expensive to maintain, this is more than offset by their much greater capital cost. Furthermore, counting recurring software costs ("right to use" or "RTU" fees) as additional maintenance erases the digital machines' maintenance advantage as well (figure 7.7). Nevertheless telephone companies have installed digital machines in place of analog machines. Such innovation may be as much a product

FIGURE 7.7

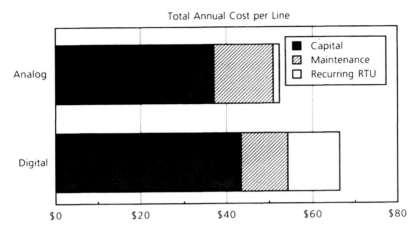

Total Annual Cost per Line

Sources: Mass. D.P.U. 86-33, Ex. NET-120 (Incremental Cost Study)—Book 1, Tab C2, pp. 3,4,6, @ 3CCS, (April 1986); DR ATTCOM-35.

of telephone companies' ability to find a monopoly customer base to finance it as of any other factor. The immediate beneficiaries of telecommunications innovation are thus often the last to pay for it.

My comments should not be interpreted as arguing against innovation, competition or divestiture. Rather I have argued for the maintenance of vigilant regulation alongside innovation, competition, and divestiture. All of this should be guided in accordance with consensual social values such as economic equity, privacy, adequate supplies of essential services, and prices for essential services that are just, reasonable, stable, and least-costly.

Bailey M. Geeslin

The dawning of the Information Age is presenting new opportunities and creating new challenges for the industry as well as its customers. I will offer an insider's perspective on a few of those opportunities and challenges which will affect the rate of deployment of innovative new services.

Consider the following fundamental change in network usage, the staple of the public networks supplied by the telephone companies: the growth potential of network usage is limited and it is obvious that "voice grade usage" is a mature business, continuing to grow, but within predictable growth limits. Many telecom managers agree that from a financial and economic perspective future viable business growth in the transport of information will be represented by the phenomenon of Information Age "applications"—the use and packaging of telecommunications network functionalities by enhanced service providers into retail end-user services.

However, the characteristics of Information Age applications versus voice grade transmission are startling and have a profound effect on the management of the business as well as regulation. Take, for example, the effects on marketing. With the voice grade network, the product of transmission of information on the supplier's side is the same as the product of a telephone call from the consumer's side. That is, the network companies are retail businesses dealing directly with consumers. The product as seen by both parties is identical: the transmission of voice information.

The Information Age is changing that fundamental product perception. In the Information Age, applications of telecommunications services go well beyond voice grade transmission. The transport of voice information—indeed the transport of information—ceases to be the product that is bought by the telecommunications services customer. Two examples will help crystalize this concept.

A very simple example is accessing a database, which is done frequently at work as well as at home. The product being bought here is definitely not the transmission of information. The product being bought is a screen of information, either on a monitor or through a printer. A more complex example is sophisticated health monitoring services such as those contracted for by a county health department. The customer using this Information Age application may not even be the one who is paying the bill, and again, the transport of information is no longer a retail product.

This change in telecommunications products from retail to wholesale affects both the people who deal with the industry and the industry which deals with the people wanting to use its services. Both have a lot to learn about marketing Information Age applications.

First, consider the effect of wholesaling on a telecommunications business which thinks of itself as a retail business. With the redefinition of the transport product by the Information Age application, the retailing telephone company often looks upon people who want to use its services as intruders and rejects them, sometimes rather rudely. The history of the old Bell System has proved this to be true in the past, and that tendency still exists with some of its current successors.

The problem with this less than amicable relationship is not one-sided. Sometimes the people knocking on the door, wanting to use the network, do not try to gain entry very politely. Users of network services in applications in which transmission is apparently not the primary product very often say that they have problems doing business with the telephone companies. The users feel that one of the problems which leads to resentment is that they must go to the Bell people and convince them to provide services, even when the use of the service by the users may be a good deal for Bell. But is anything wrong here? Bell companies do that with vendors all the time. Building sound business relationships is part of management's job.

Sound industry/network user relationships do not end with understanding customer focus, and shifting retail/wholesale markets. The telecommunications industry must feel comfortable that there are a number of reputable retailers in business using their services. In addition, retailers must feel comfortable that they are getting a fair deal from the wholesalers; they must like and use the industry's services and see terms as reasonable. The onus is also on the company to modernize the network so that the "wholesale" machine is producing what users are seeking. This leads to another misperception.

There is a tendency today to define the capacity of the network in terms of voice grade telephone calls. This tendency leads to a belief that the capacity of the network is well beyond that which will ever be used. However, the use of network capacity of bandwidth for services other than voice telecommunications will not leave an excess inventory of capacity. On the contrary, the capacity problem being faced right now is not one of excess, but rather a lack of bandwidth beyond 2.4 kilobits on an end-to-end basis through the switched network. Aside from the 56-kilobit services used primarily with personal computers, there is very little end-to-end capacity to provide Information Age services such as point-to-point full-motion video. This requirement to invest in increased end-to-end capacity leads to a final phenomenon. That is, the telecommunications networks in the United States have the characteristics of infrastructure. Infrastructure traditionally provides capabilities prior to identifiable assessable applications for its use.

That causes great difficulty in convincing upper management to invest in new network capabilities. With the prevailing short-term business orientation in this country (as well as the regulatory restrictions of rate-of-return or profit regulation), very often senior management wants names, addresses, social security numbers, and checking account numbers of the customers who are going to pay for this investment. This concern on the part of management is only justified to the extent that regulation will not allow returns to the company's shareholders which are commensurate with the risk incurred (incentive regulation in the form of price regulation would reduce the risk concerns of management). This is certainly true when you examine the major trends toward services with increasing bandwidth and the growth of data usage in this country. Regulatory risk aside, the investments in the infrastructure which are required to satisfy wholesale markets are in my opinion risky, but worth making. These capacity and usage trends are a good barometer of what will be a healthy and vibrant partnership between the telecommunications industry and enhanced service providers, if both the industry and the users "step up" to meeting the challenges which will accompany the opportunities.

As we move into the Information Age, there are many opportunities for both the industry and the users of network services. However, both the industry and the users of the industry's services must work at developing business relationships. The industry must strive to understand and service our wholesale markets and to modernize the network, within regulatory constraints. Retailers have to develop a reputation as good business partners and providers of services which will benefit the community. Together, the industry and the users of telecom services can make the Information Age a reality.

Thomas W. Cohen

It is clear that one of the chief reasons for ending AT&T's monopoly in the equipment and long-distance markets was to foster greater innovation. Moreover, the increased innovations presumably would more closely match the needs and demands of users, and would come on the market more rapidly. There was a strong belief that while "mother" was useful for a network to develop, once that network had developed, the customer, not "mother," knew what was best.

Prior to divestiture, AT&T controlled the pace of technological development and innovation. Virtually every product in the telephone network was developed and made by Western Electric. Those few products which came from the outside were either of little consequence or had to pass AT&T's extremely rigorous—some say, unreasonable—standards. As Walter Bolter and James McConnaughey indicate, Ma Bell decided when a new feature would be offered and who could use it. In other words, the American consumer had no choice. He had to wait for something other than a black telephone, yet was brought the Picturephone without wanting it.

The downfall of the old system did not come from some government policymakers adding up the number of innovations in the telephone network, and deciding that something should be done. Rather, it came about in a typically American fashion. Other firms saw the profits that could be made, and recognized that the technology was available to offer competing products. Much of this technology, somewhat ironically, came from AT&T's Bell Labs. When these new firms came to the government seeking permission to offer various new goods and services, it was many years before the government let them in. It was many more years before they were able to compete on an even footing. In fact, it was not until divestiture that outside providers had a fair opportunity to sell to the telephone company, or interconnect to provide service.

If one were to test whether the old AT&T was, in fact, providing state-of-the-art products and services, one might look at what happened just after divestiture was announced. In the switch market, for example, Northern Telecom quickly shot ahead of Western Electric in selling to the local telephone companies. A major cause was that the AT&T switch was not the most innovative. It took AT&T several years to update its product and regain the lead in switch sales to the local telephone companies. It appears that greater competition has its rewards.

The U.S. telecommunications market is far different today than it was even a decade ago. There are well over one thousand more services, and the consumer (which in certain instances may be the local telephone company) is largely king, getting almost all he wants. However, policy concerns and debates remain.

Elliot Maxwell in this chapter forcefully argues that the manufacturing restrictions of the MFJ may limit certain efficiencies that come from integrating the research, development, manufacturing, and marketing operations. The model used in the MFJ, however, has precedent in the telephone operations in other countries, such as Germany and France. Moreover, the MFJ restriction seeks to strike a balance between the evils that arose from vertical integration in the old Bell System, and any advantages that might come from such integration. While we may be missing some economies, there is little doubt that we are avoiding the costs the old structure imposed. We still lack the necessary and sufficient remedies to deal with the incentives and abilities of the telephone monopolist to self-deal or cross-subsidize. At the same time, there is good reason to continue to refine the MFJ to try to reduce uncertainty and help speed the introduction of new products and services.

I have heard no one cogently argue that the U.S. telephone network has fallen behind that of the rest of the world, or that it is in danger of doing so. But consider the following: total amounts spent on R&D have risen, construction budgets also are increasing, and new services and products are constantly coming onto the market. Just look at the size of any of the trade shows, and the frequency of product announcements. There are now over fifty companies and firms around the U.S. testing ISDN services and products.

The twin policies of competition and divestiture have thus become largely successful. That does not mean that continued vigilance is unnecessary. For example, with the old AT&T, the standards process required little coordination. Today, with the great number of providers, significant coordination in the setting of standards is essential. There is also the need for the government to ensure that trade laws are effectively administered and enforced.

The U.S. telephone network is fundamental to our nation's industrial future. The telephone industry is to be congratulated for ensuring this network remains the finest in the world. There is every reason to believe that the industry will continue to innovate, and bring users the products and services to guarantee the network remains state-of-the-art.

ENDNOTES

1. See Walter G. Bolter, Jerry B. Duvall, Fred J. Kelsey, and James W. Mc-Connaughey, *Telecommunications Policy for the 1980s: The Transition to Competition* (Englewood Cliffs, N.J.: Prentice-Hall, 1984), p. 176. This book was sponsored by the Washington Program of the Annenberg Schools of Communications.

2. Notice of Inquiry, In the Matter of License Contract Agreements and Other Intrasystem Arrangements of the Major Telephone Systems, CC Docket 80-742, FCC 80-700, released February 6, 1981, at 30.

3. National Telecommunications and Information Administration (NTIA) *Telecom 2000: Charting The Course For A New Century*, Special Publication 88-21, October 1988, p. 4.

4. See "McGowan knocks FCC's 'piecemeal deregulation,' " *Network World*, February 6, 1989, p. 48.

5. See, e.g., "ICA urges caution in deregulatory efforts," *Network World*, January 30, 1989, pp. 1 and 37.

6. Address, Communications Week Symposium, December 8, 1988, pp. 3–8.

7. *Telephone Statistics 1988* (Washington, D.C.: United States Telephone Association, 1988), 1:21.

8. New England Telephone and Telegraph Company, Depreciation Rate Study (1987), Intro., p. 12, filed with the Massachusetts D.P.U. in Case No. 86-33.

9. Myron Keller, area manager for loop technical planning, Southwestern Bell, at the Fifth Annual Bypass Conference sponsored by Phillips Publishing, Inc., April 4, 1988.

10. The important savings in current costs manifest themselves in virtually every area of operation. For example, power costs are reduced due to the low energy consumption of fiber systems. Installation costs also fall because of the lower number of repeater sites, and because cables are small and lightweight, require less security protection, and can be converted from one type of use to another merely by changing electronics. In addition, the lower number of repeater sites leads to savings in maintenance costs, which are even further reduced because optical cables are less susceptible than other technologies, such as microwave, to corrosion and electrical or radio interference. Moreover, the greater processing power of the digital switches used with optical cables offers opportunities for automatic remote diagnostics, as well as automatic record keeping and traffic tracking, all of which contribute to maintenance savings. Notably, New England Telephone, which has extensively studied the relative cost savings, reports that "fiber system maintenance costs were approximately one-fifth of those of copper cable facilities." See James McDade, response to data request No. BTUG 5-77 for New England Telephone, MA D.P.U. Case No. 86-33.

11. R. W. Dixon and N. K. Dutta, "Lightwave Device Technology," *AT&T Technical Journal* (January/February 1987), p. 80.

12. Patrick White, Testimony for New England Telephone and Telegraph Company, Massachusetts D.P.U. Case No. 86-33, January, 1987, pp. 20–21.

13. "Annual Forecast," *Telephony*, January 16, 1984, p. 58 (quote attributed to GTE chairman and CEO).

14. Id., January 14, 1985, p. 61 (executive vice president, Central Telephone System).

15. Id., January 13, 1986, p. 42 (chairman, Bell Atlantic Enterprises).

16. Id., January 12, 1987, p. 54 (chairman and CEO, BellSouth).

17. Id., January 18, 1988 (executive vice president, Contel).

18. "A Global Data System is Seen as Telephones Use More Digital Gear," *Wall Street Journal*, December 23, 1985, p. 1.

19. Id.

20. "Users Aren't Getting The ISDN Message, Study Reveals," *Communications Week*, May 30, 1988, p. 22 (Coopers & Lybrand survey of one hundred users at the annual International Communications Association (ICA) conference in Anaheim, California.)

21. NTIA, *Telecom 2000*, p. 4.

22. Link Resources, July 1988 estimates.

23. See, e.g., "The RBHCs should be urged to get on with it," *Network World*, February 6, 1989, p. 46.

24. Remarks given by Richard J. Vehige, Southwestern Bell Assistant Vice President, before the Columbia University Center for Telecommunications and Information Studies Seminar, June 29, 1987, p. 2.

25. See, e.g., "The CPE Marketplace Is a Dog-Eat-Dog World," *Telephony*, May 11, 1987, pp. 30–54.

26. UIS, or Universal Information Services, is AT&T's goal of providing modern, sophisticated services on an "equal access" basis for its customers.

27. Michael Noll, "Bell Systems R&D Activities," *Telecommunications Policy* (June 1987) and "The Effects of Divestiture on Telecommunications Research," *Journal of Communications* (Winter 1987).

28. Noll, "Bell Systems R&D Activities," pp. 161–68.

29. NTIA, The Bell Company Manufacturing Restrictions and the Provision of Information Services, U.S. Department of Commerce, March 1989, p. 4.

30. Id.

31. Id. While some foreign PTTs, as Tom Cohen will point out, do not fabricate equipment, there is no PTT that is prohibited from engaging in developmental activities with its potential suppliers as are the BOCs.

32. New England Telephone Co. (NET), *1987 Depreciation Study*, Ex NET-93 in Mass. D.P.U. 86-33, 159, 171, 337, 466–67.

33. *International Telecharge*, D.P.V. 87-72, slip op. at 3-5, 8-9 (Mass., October 11, 1988); Comments of the Attorney General in D.P.V. 88-45 at 20 (Mass., April 20, 1987).

34. See generally, *Applicability of the Common Carrier Concept*, Order Institution Proceeding (New York Public Service Commission Case 89-C-099, May 24, 1989).

35. See *Century Communications Corp v. FCC*, 835 F. 2d 292 (D.C. Cir. 1987), *cert. den sub nom. Office of Communication of United Church of Christ v. FCC*, 1085. Ct. 2014, 100 L. Ed. 2d 602 (1988) (rules requiring carriage of certain stations invalid under First Ammendment).

36. Chicago Tribune Educational Services Dept. *Big City Newspaper* (1971).

37. See generally re cable tv privacy concerns, J. Oppenheim, "The Coaxial Wiretap? Privacy and the Cable," *Yale Journal of Law and Social Action* (1972), 2:282.

38. J. A. Schumpeter, *Capitalism, Socialism, and Democracy*, 3d ed. (New York: Harper, 1950), p. 105.

39. B. L. Copeland, Jr. and A. Severn, "Price Theory and Telecommunications Regulation: A Dissenting View," *Yale Journal on Regulation* (1985), 3:53, 82.

40. See, generally, L. S. Reich, *The Making of American Industrial Research* (New York: Cambridge University Press, 1985).

41. See H. H. Gerth and C. W. Mills, *From Max Weber: Essays in Sociology* (New York: Oxford University Press, 1946), pp. 52–54, 196.

42. Witness J. Hopley at Tab B in N.Y.P.S.C. Case 27710 (1980). Mr. Hopley argues that New York Telephone's sale price would have been $33 if maintenance, depreciation, and an alleged subsidy to local service were deducted {Innovation session tr. at 10.} (He might have also included the company's

insurance, income taxes, and cost of money). Assuming so *arguendo*—and there is some validity to the claim about maintenance—the facts remain that (1) under the anti-competitive regulatory structure consumers paid $212 rather than $33 and (2) New York Telephone's $33 price would still have been 32 percent above the market price of $25.

43. For example, a Southwestern Bell executive argues that there should be no mandatory carrier of last resort obligation in competitive markets. D. L. Weisman, "Competitive Markets and Carriers of Last Resort," *Public Utilities Fortnightly*, July 6, 1989.

44. N. H. Wasserman, *From Innovation to Innovation* (Baltimore: Johns Hopkins University Press, 1985), p. 39 and n. 33; M. D. Fagan, ed., *A History of Engineering and Science in the Bell System/The Early Years* (Bell Telephone Labs, 1975), pp. 198–99, 202–04. The added cost for local service due to the new two-wire system was about 35 percent. D. Gabel, "Technological Change, Contracting and the First Divestiture of AT&T," Columbia Center for Telecommunications and Information Studies (February 1989), p. 7.

45. R. Gabel, "Allocation of Telephone Exchange Plant Investment," in *Adjusting to Regulatory, Pricing, and Marketing Realities* (East Lansing, Mich.: 1983), p. 468 (Ex. AG-35 in Mass. DPU 86-33); M. D. Fagan, ed., *A History of Engineering and Science in the Bell System/The Early Years* (Bell Telephone Labs, 1975), pp. 1007–08.

46. New York Telephone Co., 2 PSC (2d Dist.) 710 (1910). In the latest phase of the battle, average local flat rate bills jumped 47 percent since divestiture while interstate long-distance rates dropped 30 percent. *State Telephone Regulation Report* 9, September 7, 1989. See FCC CC Dockets 78-72, 80-286.

47. New England Telephone Co. (NET), *1987 Depreciation Study* (Ex-NET-93 in Mass. D.P.V. 86-33) 154–55, 157, 159, 181–82, 359; NET, *Incremental Cost Study* (Ex. NET-120 in Mass D.P.V. 86-33), Book 3, Tab 11, pp. 138–39.

48. New England Telephone Co., *Incremental Cost Study* (Ex. NET-120 in Mass. D.P.U. 86-33), Book 1, Tab C2, p. 3 and Book 3, pp. 136, 196 (April 1986). Total investments required per line are $271 per line (digital) v. $219 (analog growth), making assumptions in favor of the economics of digital machines.

49. In this instance, a utility makes a $52 incremental investment that is not essential to basic local or long distance voice service. Then the telephone company asserts that no incremental investment in switching is needed for digital data services and that only $6.18 (12 percent of the incremental investment) is due to Custom Calling, services that it could not physically provide without the $52 incremental investment in new technology. In so claiming, it lays the foundation for a relatively low "cost-based" price for digital services, raising prices of other services to cover the investment costs that might fairly have been allocated to digital services instead.

50. R. Gabel, "Who Pays the Freight? The Development and Allocation of Telephone Depreciation Expense," in D. W. Wirick, ed., *Proceedings of the 6th NARUC Biennial Regulatory Information Conference* (National Regulatory Research Institute, 1988), 3:563, 569, 575.

51. New England Telephone Co. (NET), *Incremental Cost Study* (Ex. NET-

120 in Mass. D.P.V. 86-33), Book 1, Tab C2, pp. 3, 4, 6 at 3 CCS; DR ATTCOM-35 in Mass. D.P.V. 86-33.

52. New York Telephone manager John Hopley {Innovation Session tr. at 10-11f}. Accord, pre-filed Fifth Stage Testimony of New York Telephone Co. Vice President Bailey Gesslin in N.Y.P.S.C. Case 28961 at 18 (1989).

53. Geeslin testimony supra note 22, at 18, 20-22. Geeslin also argues that the business risk of presenting new services should be shifted from the company to the ratepayers (at 16-20, 26, 27), but this begs the question of which ratepayers (if any) should bear the additional costs in rates.

8

Advances in Network Technology

■

MARVIN A. SIRBU, JR.

■

BRUCE C. N. GREENWALD

DALE N. HATFIELD

A. DANIEL KELLEY

Marvin A. Sirbu, Jr.

A vast army of researchers in dozens of companies continues steadily to advance the state of the art in telecommunications across a broad front. Thus, it would be presumptuous to attempt to review all of the developments in telecommunications technology that have occurred since divestiture. My objective is something at once more narrow, and more speculative. I will consider the question of how the evolution of technology since 1984 would have differed had there not been a divestiture.

I formulate the question in this way for several reasons. First, it would be misleading to attribute the new technologies which have appeared since 1984 to divestiture. This is the post hoc ergo propter hoc fallacy. In evaluating the breakup of AT&T it is important that we not attribute too much to it. Virtually all of the technologies implemented since 1984 were being actively pursued in industry research laboratories prior to divestiture. Thus, divestiture has primarily affected the rate at which existing technologies have been deployed, and to a much lesser extent it has created incentives for the development of new or different technologies. Of course, we know from the theory of the learning curve that changes in volume lead to numerous incremental, but cumulatively important, changes in technology; in this sense, faster deployment has led to technological change as well. Similarly, major new research stimulated by and undertaken since divestiture takes more than these last six years to be deployed.

Moreover, divestiture is only one of many changes in public policy over the last decade; certain decisions by the FCC, such as *Computer III*,[1] have had as much or more impact on technology than the MFJ.[2] Furthermore, I would argue that *Computer III* was not just itself a response to the MFJ; it would have been needed in light of the inherent weaknesses in *Computer II*,[3] with or without divestiture.

Finally, by formulating the question in this way, I hope to reduce the problem to manageable proportions by focusing on how the technologies deployed since divestiture are different than what might have been had there not been an MFJ. However, while narrowing the scope, this device also makes our task somewhat more speculative, for I now have a counterfactual: how do I know what would have happened even without divestiture?

The antitrust complaint against AT&T charged the company not only with monopolizing the interexchange market, but also with impeding competition in the supply of network equipment. Several of the most significant impacts of the MFJ follow from the separation of Western Electric, AT&T's manufacturing arm, from the RBOCs, and the consequent change in incentives for both AT&T and the operating companies.

The market for customer premises equipment in the United States was fully competitive prior to the consent decree as a result of the *Carterfone* decision of 1968[4] and the registration decision of 1976.[5] In this environment, competitors attacked AT&T's market for PBXs and the central-office-based, functionally equivalent Centrex service. As noted by Walter Bolter and James McConnaughey in the previous chapter of this volume, for a variety of reasons AT&T adopted the strategy of trying to migrate users from Centrex to PBXs. Beginning in the late 1970s, it stopped enhancing the functionality of Centrex, and through various pricing policies encouraged Centrex users to buy a PBX. By 1984, the market for Centrex stood at 8.3 million lines, while the installed base of PBXs totaled 21 million stations.[6]

After the announcement of the consent decree, the incentives of the

RBOCs and AT&T were no longer the same. While the RBOCs could sell and service CPE, they were prohibited from engaging in manufacturing; AT&T retained all manufacturing operations. As a consequence, many of the RBOCs concluded that they had more to gain from selling and servicing Centrex than from selling PBXs. For some, such as Bell Atlantic, defending Centrex was critical: more than 52 percent of the business lines in Washington, D.C. were Centrex lines; the loss of this business to PBXs would strand millions of dollars of undepreciated investments.

At the time divestiture was announced in 1982, PBXs had the advantage over Centrex in four major areas: call signaling features, management features, networking capabilities, and data. In each of these areas, as a result of pressures put on them by the RBOCs, the switch manufacturers have upgraded their products in order to make them more competitive. Let us look at each area in turn.

The introduction of stored program control switches—such as the Rolm CBX or the #1ESS central office switch—means that it is possible to introduce many new features for the convenience of users just by altering the software. Services such as call forwarding and speed dialing were the first. By the early 1980s, however, the number of such features that might be ordered with a PBX had reached into the hundreds: "camp-on-busy," variable and fixed call forwarding, remote call pickup, and many more. Centrex lagged far behind in the number of such features typically available. Much of this gap has been made up in the years since divestiture.

In the management area, PBXs were providing reams of detail on telephone usage—station message detail recording (SMDR)—to aid in accounting and system management, while Centrex continued until after divestiture to provide only toll records, and often not in easily manipulable form. In 1982, reassigning a telephone number to a new room for a Centrex user might have required a written purchase order to the telco, two weeks, and a service charge of up to $100. By contrast, most PBXs provided the corporate telecommunication manager with a terminal from which he could reassign numbers instantly with a few keystrokes. Beginning in 1985, the RBOCs began offering customer controlled reconfiguration (CCR) capabilities which offered similar control.

Elsewhere in this volume is mentioned the history of the "subsidy" which flowed for many years from long-distance service to the BOCs. Prior to divestiture, a large user could escape this tax on switched toll services (MTS) by configuring a network of leased lines between company locations, and routing intracompany traffic on its "private network." The federal government, with its FTS (Federal Telecommunications System) network was and continues to be the largest operator of such a private network, and has saved billions of dollars in the process. For obvious reasons, the BOCs were slow to equip Centrex to manage such networks, thereby providing further incentive to users to switch to PBXs. The repricing of switched long-distance since divestiture has reduced somewhat the advantages of leased-line networks, diminishing this motivation for switching. But more importantly, in response to customer demand, the RBOCs have required from the switch vendors improvements in the capabilities of Centrex in this area. Thus, we have seen a wide range of feature enhancements to Centrex, which I believe can be directly traced to the new incentives created by divestiture. The result has been a compound growth rate for Centrex of 6.8 percent from 1984–1989, while the installed base of PBX lines peaked at 2.6 million in 1988 and is projected to decline 4 percent by 1990.[7]

We turn next to the area of data capabilities. Rolm was the first, in 1976, to introduce a PBX that used digital rather than analog techniques to switch calls. Rolm touted its product as eventually making it easier to use the PBX for switching data as well as voice within the firm. AT&T had delayed developing central offices based on digital switching, correctly arguing that they would be uneconomic compared to dedicated data switching systems such as port switches or local area networks. Unfortunately, in a classic example of selling the sizzle not the steak, Rolm and other PBX vendors successfully sold hundreds of digital PBXs because of their data potential, which was seldom utilized in practice.

For the BOCs, the only solution was to convert as rapidly as possible to digital central office switches that could offer comparable capabilities. The rapidity of conversion to digital central office switches by the RBOCs is, I believe, another major consequence of divestiture. It is a result of the confluence of several forces originating with divestiture, not merely the need for a digital Centrex capable of competing with digital PBXs. As a result of the MFJ, the RBOCs were faced with massive capital investments to meet the access requirements. In many cases, they concluded that it would be cheaper to simply accelerate the replacement of outdated step-by-step and crossbar central offices with new digital switches, rather than invest in costly adjuncts or access tandems. Moreover, as noted in more detail below, the rapid increase in the use of digital fiber optic transmission capability, itself a result of divestiture, also made digital switching more attractive. Terminating a digital transmission link on an analog switch requires costly channel banks, whereas with a digital switch less expensive digital interfaces are required.

Of course, digital switching would have been phased in even without divestiture. By 1983, Western Electric had already spent more than one billion dollars developing the #5ESS digital central office switch. The continuing decline in digital logic costs, which has produced dramatic improvements in price versus performance in the computer industry, has similarly affected telecommunications switching. However, the RBOCs went from a negligible fraction of their lines terminating on digital switches on January 1, 1984[8] to more than 36 percent by 1989. This rapid rate must be attributed in part to divestiture.[9]

At the same time, the RBOCs' switch market has shifted from a virtual monopoly with AT&T, to a duopoly, with Northern Telecom and AT&T splitting over 90 percent of the sales. Half a dozen U.S. and foreign firms split the remainder, with no vendor yet showing clear signs of emerging as the RBOCs' third major supplier. The competition for these digital switch sales has been extremely intense, with switch prices dropping from $400–500 per line to $100–200 per line. In part, this represents a "give away the razor, sell the blades" strategy; the initial capital cost of a switch is only a small fraction of what a vendor expects to receive eventually from the BOC. Additional line cards, new software releases, maintenance contracts, and other continuing revenue sources provide the bulk of the profits. Once a totally new switch is put in place, it generally stays in place for twenty to forty years while virtually all of its components are swapped for newer printed circuit boards, thus ensuring that the initial sale locks in a substantial future revenue stream. It is unlikely Northern Telecom would have succeeded in wresting half of the market away for Western Electric had divestiture come seven or eight years later, when most of the digital switch commitments would have already been made.

While the move from monopoly to duopoly has surely driven down switch costs, it has raised new issues of compatibility and standardization. For example, the manner in which Northern Telecom switches were designed, to provide 56 kbps. service, was different from the method chosen by AT&T.[10] Multiple switch designs result in increased training and adaptation costs. As a result, if one looks closely at the composition of switch sales among the seven Regionals, one generally finds each region aligning with one manufacturer. Thus, the great bulk of NYNEX's digital switch purchases have been from Northern Telecom, while Bell Atlantic seems to prefer AT&T.[11]

With the introduction of stored program control switching in the

1960s, the telephone industry began a gradual shift from services implemented in hardware—e.g. electromechanical relays—to services implemented in software. As suggested by the discussion of Centrex above, there are hundreds of new features and services which customers are demanding from their telecommunications system that software can readily provide. With the current generation of technology, the BOCs are dependent upon the central office switch manufacturers for the implementation of new software-based services. Thus, in order to offer a service like "camp-on-busy" the carrier must request that the switch vendor provide a new software release for the central office incorporating such a service. As the basis for competition in telecommunications became increasingly dependent on the rapid implementation of software-based services, the BOCs found themselves intolerably dependent upon the responsiveness of the switch manufacturers. Moreover, the MFJ prohibited the normal business response of integrating backwards into switch manufacture. As an alternative, the BOCs began work in 1985 on a new model for how switching and software-based services ought to be provided in the network of the future, which has been called the "Intelligent Network."

In today's network, virtually all the software, which determines the services offered by the network, runs in the central office switches. Because the switches must respond in real time to hundreds of thousands of requests for service per hour, switching system software is incredibly complex, expensive, and almost completely controlled by switch vendors. In the Intelligent Network model, the switch is seen as a highly intelligent server, responding to instructions from an attached processor. The distinction is much like that governing the separation of window managers from application programs in the computer world: machine vendors are responsible for providing an operating system that provides simple command primitives for controlling the computer display; the application programmer then calls on these window management primitives—e.g., open a window, draw a line, shade a polygon, etc.—to produce complex pictures through repeated use of these primitive operations. Indeed, in modern distributed computer systems, the application program might run on a completely different machine than the window manager. By separating the display functions into client and server layers, applications can be quickly developed by third parties without having to make changes in the complex, hardware-specific server software.

In much the same manner, in the Intelligent Network model, the vendor's switch would be capable of executing numerous primitive operations—collect the number dialed, complete a circuit between two

FIGURE 8.1

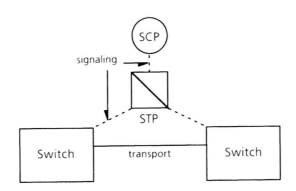

Intelligent Network

numbers, etc. The application programs that link together these primitives to provide sophisticated services would reside on separate machines, programmed by the BOCs themselves and communicating with the switch via digital communications protocols such as Signaling System Seven (SS7).[12]

A block diagram of such a system is shown in figure 8.1. The Service Control Point (SCP) represents the attached processor. Given the dialed digits collected by the switch, the SCP could then decide, based on the called and calling number, the time of day, or any other criteria which had been programmed, exactly how to route the call. AT&T is already using a very similar model for providing advanced 800 Services and Software Defined Network.

The Intelligent Network concept is an inevitable response to the demand for more rapid introduction of new and customized call handling services. It is an extension to telecommunications of the same model of layering of software functionality that we are seeing in the corporate world, with back-end databases responding to standardized queries from numerous different applications generated by MIS (Management Information Systems) departments and end users.[13]

Moreover, with the Intelligent Network model, the carrier is no longer totally dependent upon the switch supplier for providing new services because the SCP is under the carrier's control. The local exchange carrier can introduce new services more quickly and make them available throughout its network without reprogramming every central office. As the set of primitives provided by the switch vendors becomes more standardized, problems of coordinating new offerings across heterogeneous switches are reduced. Indeed, even if there had not been a divestiture, we would likely have seen some evolution to redistribute functionality between switches and SCPs. The same reasons of flexibility led AT&T to introduce the first systems of this type in 1979, and caused MCI and Sprint to follow suit in 1988.[14]

Ameritech first initiated the Intelligent Network concept, post-divestiture, in 1985, under the title: "Feature Node/Service Interface." In addition to facilitating service creation by the operating companies, the Intelligent Network, with attached processes able to control switches remotely, is potentially the basis for a true ONA.

The Intelligent Network represents a profound change in the architecture of the network and will not be implemented quickly. Unlike MCI and US Sprint, which are also moving their networks in this direction, many of the BOCs' switches are still electromechanical[15] and cannot be reprogrammed to support the new architecture.[16] Older SPC switches will need substantial increases in processing power, along the lines of Northern Telecom's SuperNode processing upgrade.[17] A complete transition to the Intelligent Network, like the shift from analog to digital, will take decades. In addition to the resistance of switch vendors, which can be expected as this strategy threatens their role, there are substantial technical barriers to overcome, such as ensuring that removing call processing logic to a remote processor does not introduce unacceptable call processing delays.[18] Bellcore has announced a phased schedule, with the first IN components to be specified and agreed to by 1990 and available by 1993, with other components to be defined by 1992 and available by 1995.[19] The challenge for the carriers is to find a reasonable compromise between a desire to "have it all" and the need to set targets which are realizable in a timely fashion.[20]

While some such services can be provided to the largest users by customer premises equipment (e.g., PBXs), smaller users and smaller branches of large firms typically do not have the traffic volume to justify the fixed capital expense, or the expense of providing twenty-four-hour a day maintenance at far flung locations. The shift to an Intelligent Network software architecture is an inevitable response to the growing demand from customers for more rapid introduction of new network services. That response has been accelerated, however, by the change in the relationship between local exchange carriers and switch vendors caused by the MFJ.

Integrated Services Digital Network, or ISDN, is an umbrella term that describes the long-term trend to convert the world's telecommunication networks from analog to digital. The International Consultative Committee for Telegraph and Telephone (CCITT), the world body that coordinates telecommunications standards development, first began working on ISDN in 1976. The first drafts of ISDN were completed in 1984. Thus, the move towards ISDN considerably predates divestiture. The three key elements of ISDN are: communications channels that are digital end-to-end; a signalling channel associated with each access line, which can be used both for signalling to the network and for end-to-end signalling between customer terminals; and the interleaving of bit streams through a standard interface for user access, in order to accommodate a broad scope of services.

Divestiture has both positively and negatively affected the rate of implementation of ISDN technology. The technology encompassed by ISDN is exactly what the carriers need to provide a digital Centrex service that can compete with digital PBXs. Following divestiture, the BOCs had to rely on independent manufacturers to supply both the central office switch and handsets and terminals needed to provide digital Centrex. The BOCs need the impetus provided by a worldwide standard to persuade both switch vendors and terminal manufacturers to produce the necessary equipment. The BOCs have thus been ardent supporters of both the ISDN concept and ISDN standardization. Unfortunately, without the power of an integrated AT&T to set standards, divestiture can probably be blamed for a two-year delay in the development of standards for the ISDN CPE interface with the network.[21]

At divestiture, AT&T Communications was granted the existing CCS network. The BOCs had to start from scratch to develop their own CCS systems, which has also served to delay the introduction of ISDN services. On the other hand, the BOCs have had strong incentives besides ISDN for proceeding with CCS deployment, such as the lucrative 800-number services market. The greater the success of the competitive carriers as a result of divestiture, the greater the value of a BOC CCS-based capability for providing 800-number service.

One consequence of the divestiture was to create seven RHCs for the BOCs where before there had been one. This regionalization has affected technology development in several ways, and may have even more profound effects in the future.

The differences in the territories served by the RHCs have led to differential emphasis on technologies. Where in the past AT&T may have forced all of the BOCs to adopt a common approach, divestiture has made divergence easier. We have already addressed regional divergence in the selection of switch supplier. The average number of lines per switch in the predominantly rural US West region is half the number in the more urbanized Ameritech region.[22] This leads to a difference in the distribution of switch technology and the preferred suppliers.

The regions are also competing head-to-head in cellular mobile telephone service; many of the "non-wire" licenses have been bought by out-of-region RBOCs. If one examines the new R&D laboratories set up outside the framework of the commonly-owned Bellcore, one finds, at NYNEX for example, a significant effort in cellular telephony research.

In April 1989, Pacific Telesis became the first BOC to acquire a cable television operation outside its franchise area.[23] To date, cable television operators have generally shied away from implementing the technologies that would allow them to compete head-to-head with the telephone companies in the provision of voice and data services. As telephone companies acquire cable systems, perhaps this will change. Under the current FCC Cable/Telco cross-ownership rules (which are themselves up for discussion), a local exchange carrier cannot own a cable television operator within its service area. When AT&T was integrated, this rule eliminated 80 percent of the country, and most major markets. With regionalization as a result of divestiture, the situation has changed dramatically.

Divestiture has clearly stimulated competition in the interexchange market. AT&T's share of interstate switched traffic, in minutes, went from 80.0 percent at the end of 1984 to 71.2 percent by the third quarter of 1987 and 66.8 percent in the first quarter of 1989.[24] Much of the improvement in market share came about as a result of the implementation of equal access and the associated balloting process.[25]

In order to service the growth in traffic expected as a result of equal access, the competitive carriers such as MCI and US Sprint were obliged to make massive investments to increase capacity in their networks; and the technology of choice as clearly optical fiber. In the period 1985–1989, US Sprint installed 24,000 route miles of fiber, MCI 18,000 miles, and AT&T 17,500 with typically 10-32 fibers per route mile, or more than 1.5 million miles of fiber (figure 8.2).[26] Operating at data rates as high as 1.7 Gbps., a single pair of optical fibers can carry more than 25,000 voice conversations simultaneously! If each of the fibers were equipped with the electronics to run at these rates—which they are not—it would amount to more than a factor of three increase in interstate network capacity since divestiture.

There have been substantial improvements in the technology of optical fiber systems a result of the massive investment in fiber. The price of optical fiber has dropped dramatically, to as low as twenty cents per meter.[27] Electro-optic components, such as lasers and detectors have been dropping in price at rates greater than 30 percent per year. The tremendous improvement in price performance has greatly

FIGURE 8.2

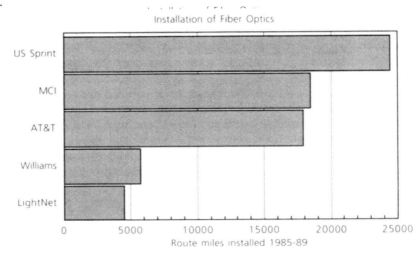

Installation of Fiber Optics

Route miles installed 1985-89

Source: Kessler Marketing Intelligence.

accelerated interest in fiber all the way to the home on the part of the local exchange carriers.[28] All of this is clearly a result of divestiture's impact on interexchange competition.

Along with equal access came equal access charges and a reduction in the price difference between AT&T and its competitors. Competition for large customers has shifted from price to service with both AT&T and its competitors introducing customized offerings for large businesses and various forms of virtual private networks. The growth in these software-based services is another consequence of heightened interexchange competition.

The 1980s have also witnessed a dramatic growth in private networks: leased lines tied together by customer-owned tandem switches and PBXs. The growth of private networks has several causes, not all of them related to divestiture. The policy of taxing switched toll service usage to pay for non-traffic-sensitive local plant provided a large financial incentive to escape the tax through the use of leased lines for over fifty years. Had subscriber line access charges been phased in more rapidly—a decision in the hands of the FCC and Congress, not Judge Greene—the growth of private line networks would likely have been significantly less. Competition in CPE led to the availability of end-user equipment capable of switching and managing large private networks, thus facilitating their growth. To some extent, the confusion created by divestiture led many companies to think about creating their own private networks as a way to reduce their dependence on the suddenly fragmented carrier industry.

To discourage investments in local bypass transmission technologies by their customers, virtually all of the BOCs greatly accelerated their investments in local interoffice and feeder fiber capacity. They also hoped to preclude a wave of intraLATA competitors who were freed to enter the marketplace by the more relaxed entry policies adopted by some states following divestiture.

The proliferation and variety of CPE, ranging from residential handsets and telephone answering machines to corporate PBXs and voice mail systems, is often attributed to divestiture. Such a view is not supported by the facts. *Carterfone* preceded the MFJ by fourteen years. As a result of the registration decision and *Computer Inquiry II*, the marketplace for CPE had become fully competitive before divestiture. By 1985, AT&T's share of the PBX market had dropped to 25 percent. If divestiture impacted the technology of CPE, it was to require PBX manufacturers to incorporate much more sophisticated call routing capabilities in order to deal with multiple carriers and bypass.

Finally, we should consider what impact the MFJ's ban on BOC and AT&T involvement in information services has had on technology development. The BOCs have not hesitated to call attention to widespread use of videotex services in France and bemoan the restrictions on their participation embodied in the MFJ. Here it is worth returning to our counterfactual: what would have been the situation in the absence of divestiture? Prior to the divestiture, the Senate had already passed legislation incorporating a ban on AT&T's participation in electronic publishing. *Computer Inquiry II* had established strict structural separation between a carrier's basic and enhanced services operations. Finally, prior to divestiture, while still an integrated company, AT&T's videotex venture, its viewtron system, failed miserably. Thus, for reasons relating to both policy and the marketplace, it is not clear we would have witnessed any golden age of information services if only the MFJ had not restricted BOC participation.

Moreover, even with relief from the FCC's structural separation requirements granted in the FCC's ill-fated *Computer III* decision, as well as with Judge Greene's relaxation of the MFJ requirements regarding information storage, processing and protocol conversion, it is not certain that the BOCs would find the right technical and marketing strategy to make a success of the information services business.[29]

With respect to the manufacturing restrictions imposed by the MFJ, there has probably been a modest technological effect. The BOCs are in a position, as users of telecommunications technology, to recognize potential for new hardware and software to meet customer needs. However, to the extent that this recognition requires elaboration through applied research and development, the BOCs are not in a good position to appropriate all of the benefits of that research and development, except through arms-length royalty arrangements with manufacturers. Not all know-how is easily protectable and transferrable in this manner. While the existence of Bellcore provides a partial means of reducing the cost to any one firm of generically relevant research, it still does not allow the RBOCs to readily appropriate benefits that may be derived outside the local exchange industry. At the same time, the restrictions on manufacturing have had a substantial positive influence on standardization. Without proprietary interest in any particular technology, the RBOCs, through their agent, Bellcore, have been the most fervent proponents in the U.S. telecommunications industry of compatibility standards.

If we examine the rate and direction of technological change since divestiture, we can draw several interesting conclusions. First, changes in industry structure change the incentives for developing specific technologies. Second, competition spurs investment, which in turn, through learning curve effects, spurs the improvement of technology. The improvements in fiber optics are a good example. Third, where decisions on technology choice are in the hands of a single firm, investment (and hence technological change) can proceed rapidly. We have seen this with the diversity of software-based services introduced by the interexchange carriers or CPE vendors individually. However, where progress requires coordinated decisionmaking by multiple firms, as with ISDN, then increasing the number of players is likely to slow decisionmaking and hence technology deployment.

Bruce C. N. Greenwald

There are many things to commend in Marvin Sirbu's analysis. In setting the question as one of assessing the difference between a world with and without divestiture, he has pointed the inquiry in a valuable direction. He has made a valuable distinction by separating the technology question into one of technology development, where divestiture has had little or no detectable impact, and technology deployment, where the effects of divestiture are more readily discernable. He makes an important point, routinely ignored by pure technologists, that changes in industry structure, like divestiture, do affect the incentives for developing specific technologies.

However, Sirbu's specific conclusions seem to be considerably more problematical. Sirbu analyzes the effect of divestiture on nine basic technology areas: digital switching, Centrex systems, fiber optics, Intelligent Network architectures, ISDN, private network technologies, CPE, cellular, and CATV. In each of these areas, he seems to overestimate significantly the impact of divestiture on technology, even in cases such as CPE development, where he recognizes the effect of divestiture has been marginal.

In digital switch technology, Sirbu claims divestiture has had several important impacts. The equal access requirements of the consent decree have accelerated electromechanical switch replacement, speeding the diffusion of digital switch technology. Increased post-divestiture competition among switch manufacturers has reduced switch costs leading to more rapid deployment. Greater diversity among the RBOCs in terms of switch requirements (than in the old AT&T) has encouraged diversity in digital switch development. In none of these areas is the factual support for Sirbu's case strong.

While it is true that digital switch penetration among the RBOCs rose from a negligible level in 1983 to roughly 30 percent in 1988, the rate of installation of digital switches among the independent telcos during this period had been equally or considerably more rapid.[30] Also, although switch costs have declined by a factor of roughly three since divestiture, the prices of comparable pieces of computer equipment (e.g., one Mip machines) declined by fourfold or more.[31] Finally, whatever the diversity of demand by the RBOCs, the two major switch suppliers offer comparable general lines of switches whose broad outlines (and modular natures) were determined well in advance of divestiture. Moreover, the actual technology embodied in the current generation of digital switches was, as Sirbu concedes, developed well before and independently of divestiture. Thus, it is not at all certain that divestiture has had any significant impact on digital switch technology.

The one particular area in which Sirbu identifies a substantial impact on switch technology is in the development of Centrex software. In this case, the devotion of substantial effort by switch manufacturers is undeniable. However, it is not clear how far these development expenditures have affected the switch technology actually in use. Centrex, which according to Sirbu served approximately 30 percent of business lines in 1984, has continued to decline in market share, significant development expenditures notwithstanding. Centrex now routinely accounts for 3 percent or less of RBOC revenues. The fundamental economic advantages of CPE appear to have overwhelmed divestiture-induced investments in new Centrex technology.[32] Again, therefore, the impact of divestiture on technology, even in this area of particular interest, has been marginal at best.

In fiber optics, Sirbu notes that competition among MCI, US Sprint, and AT&T has lead to greatly increased fiber installation and a consequent reduction in fiber-optic costs as the industry moves down its learning curve. However, it is not clear whether fiber installation is due largely to competition engendered by divestiture. For many years, beginning before divestiture, local exchange carriers were using fiber optic cable as the medium of choice for interoffice trunks and feeder cable, even in areas where competition was not a serious consideration. But the extra fiber demand occasioned by the creation of competitive networks may have had only a minor impact on fiber optic systems cost. The United States market for fiber is embedded in both a global market for fiber, and a broader market for optical-electronic devices (the major current costs of fiber consist of system and termination electronics). The addition of long-distance fiber miles by MCI and US Sprint represents only a relatively marginal contribution to this worldwide and industry-wide enterprise. Except in the specific area of long-distance fiber systems, the effects noted by Sirbu are likely to be small. In terms of changing telecommunications technology, it is the economics of fiber loops to the home, not these long-distance loops that are critical.

The impact of divestiture on implementation of ISDN is, as Sirbu himself concludes, ambiguous. The RBOCs' demand for digital Centrex has, he reasons, fueled the demand for ISDN (although it may have distorted the direction of ISDN development). On the other hand, the difficulty of obtaining agreement on ISDN standards may have delayed ISDN introductions. Neither factor appears to be critical to ISDN implementation. The chief physical (and cost) components of ISDN are digital switches, already discussed above, and end-office SS7 capability. The RBOCs are now beginning to install SS7 for reasons unaffected by divestiture—chiefly the demand for enhanced calling services by households and internal telco management capabilities. The other principal component of ISDN, terminal electronics and switch interfaces, can be installed on a demand basis. Thus, the impacts of divestiture on ISDN development have not only been offsetting, but may have been marginal at most.[33]

In the area of Intelligent Network architecture, Sirbu maintains divestiture (and, in particular, the separation of switch manufacture from the local exchange carriers) has accelerated Intelligent Network development. However, he concedes that the basic concepts involved significantly predate divestiture, that currently available realizations (e.g., 800 Service) were available before divestiture, and that the architectures involved largely mirror parallel architectures in the broader area of data processing. The acceleration claimed by Sirbu must, therefore, relate to the development and deployment of more advanced forms of intelligence. Since no such developments or deployments have yet taken place, this must be almost entirely a matter of conjecture.

Moreover, it is not clear the kind of intelligence that Sirbu envisions will ever be a significant part of the basic central telephone network. In data processing, the dominant technological trend has been toward decentralization. The use of centralized facilities has greatly diminished with the development of personal computers and specialized devices (such as file-services, printers, etc.) designed to work with networks of such personal computers. Service bureaus that merely rent basic data processing capabilities of various sorts are rapidly disappearing. The reasons for this trend appear to apply equally to highly developed telecommunications network intelligence. CPE-based systems have the special advantage of being able to restrict both the user options and the kinds and generations of equipment they will accommodate. Consequently, the systems are inexpensive to develop and easy to adapt to new technology, compared to a public network which must, by its very nature, accommodate many kinds of users and many generations and types of equipment. Consider, for example, the difficulty of adapting the current telephone infrastructure of electromechanical, analog electronic and digital switches to provide ubiquitous ISDN. Those, like Sirbu, who doubt the power of this CPE advantage need only look to the expensive failure of NET 1000, AT&T's attempt to provide network-based data processing capabilities.

Sirbu's contention that divestiture has encouraged private network development rests on the claims that the continued mispricing of long-distance services post-divestiture has encouraged private networks, and that the confusion in the public network associated with divestiture may have driven customers to develop their own private networks. The first of these points actually seems to suggest that divestiture may have inhibited, if only slightly, private network development and deployment. But the overpricing of long-distance services was more severe pre-divestiture than post-divestiture, and thus divestiture should have reduced the incentives for private bypass facilities. The second claim applies only to the two years following divestiture. As the Huber Report noted, the trend toward private networks on the part of large users is a long-standing trend that continues to accelerate, despite improvements in post-divestiture telephone company service levels and the pricing of long-distance access. It is not certain, therefore, that divestiture has had any impact in this area.

Finally, in the area of CATV technology, cellular, and CPE, even Sirbu regards the impact of divestiture as minimal. In cellular, Sirbu refers only to the research efforts of some of the RBOCs (e.g., NYNEX) which are only a tiny fraction of the total global cellular industry research effort. In CPE, Sirbu notes that most of the important regulatory and industry structure changes predate divestiture. And in CATV, Sirbu properly points to the fact nothing has been done by the telephone companies either before or since divestiture, and any claims for the impact of divestiture rest on conjectured future developments. Again, therefore, the likely impact of divestiture in these technologies is negligible to nonexistent.

That basic theme appears to apply across the full range of technologies. Because telecommunications technology is developed in a global context as an intrinsic part of a broad electronics and computer industry, the effects on technology of events in the domestic United States telecommunications industry are greatly attenuated. At the same time, conditions peculiar to telecommunications (e.g., the substitution of CPE for network capabilities) have further limited the technology impact of divestiture. Thus, although in general Sirbu makes a good point when he notes the impact of industry structure on technological developments, it is not a point which applies with great force to divestiture.

Dale N. Hatfield

Prior to reading Marvin Sirbu's discussion, I prepared a very rough outline of my own relating to the changes in telecommunications technology that may have been influenced by divestiture. While Sirbu has done a much more comprehensive and thorough job of analyzing post-divestiture changes in technology, I found my own outline was basically a subset of the ideas he discusses. Indeed, I found myself in basic agreement with most of what he has written.

Before I review those areas of agreement and add some comments of my own, I should state that I am in total accord with his comments regarding the importance of other policy decisions, such as the FCC's *Computer Inquiry III* attempt. Because of the intense publicity given to divestiture and its direct impact on customers (for example, the need to select a long-distance carrier), there has been a tendency to overemphasize its role. For instance, people often credit divestiture with producing the intensely competitive market in CPE. But as Marvin Sirbu correctly points out, it was a series of FCC proceedings (beginning with the *Carterfone* decision in 1968) that led to a competitive market in CPE prior to divestiture. Thus, I think it important to avoid the tendency to place too much blame on—or give too much credit to— divestiture when it comes to analyzing post-divestiture technological development.

My original outline listed three major areas of technology change where divestiture seemed to have played an especially important, identifiable role. The three major areas were: the resurrection of Centrex and associated services; the evolution toward an Intelligent Network in the local exchange area; and the changes in the local exchange and interexchange networks directly or indirectly attributable to the equal access provisions of the MFJ.

The first area, the resurrection of Centrex, may not be the most important technological impact of divestiture, but it certainly appears to be one of the most direct and visible. As Sirbu and others in this volume have indicated, Centrex was a dying service offering prior to divestiture. It provided little more functionality than ordinary POTS and it was not being upgraded or improved—it literally appeared to be dying from neglect. Indeed, prior to divestiture, AT&T had been employing—or was allegedly employing—its so-called "migration strategy." AT&T was widely perceived to be using its market power to force customers away from Centrex and older PBXs toward more modern PBX products.

Observers at the time ascribed various motives for the migration strategy. They speculated that it was an attempt by AT&T to shift customers from month-to-month tariffed service offerings to less competitively vulnerable, and potentially more lucrative unregulated long-term equipment contracts. They speculated it was an attempt to protect—almost preemptively—an existing customer base before interconnect competition got too strong.

However, one does not have to ascribe particular motive for the strategy. Centrex service was dying, if for no other reasons than it was not keeping up with the features and functions that were and are available on modern stored program control (SPC) or "computer-like" PBXs located on the customer's premises. AT&T controlled this situation because it was essentially the only supplier of network equipment such as CO switches to the undivested BOCs. As part of AT&T and dependent upon Western Electric for their CO switches, the BOCs had little choice in the matter. The BOC control over the local loop also gave AT&T some influence over the situation. The relative attractiveness of Centrex services versus PBX services obviously depends upon the relative costs of Centrex lines versus PBX CO trunks.

Centrex was so widely perceived to be a declining service offering that I do not personally recall any analysis of it in the divestiture discussions to which I was privy. To the best of my recollection, it was not mentioned in the original divestiture agreement between AT&T and the DOJ. The situation quickly changed with divestiture, however, and the BOCs were able (1) to pressure their equipment vendors sufficiently to obtain more competitive features and functionality, and (2) to gain support from their regulators to offer rate stabilization and other plans making Centrex competitive with CPE. In going through my files to prepare these comments, I stumbled across an article published shortly after divestiture entitled "Centrex Rises from the Ashes," as indeed it did. It was quickly touted as the "flagship offering" of the divested BOCs and it was—and still is—strategically important to the companies. As Sirbu notes, the providers of the first point of switching to the customer—whether the interconnect vendor is a PBX on the customer's premises, the local telephone company at the CO, or the IXC at a toll office—has important marketplace advantages.

I believe the customer has generally benefited from the additional choice provided by resurrected and vastly improved Centrex offerings. The BOCs have repositioned Centrex somewhat to service smaller customers, and equipment vendors have responded to provide station and associated equipment specially designed to work with Centrex offerings. Moreover, the BOCs' initial ISDN offerings are being provided to large customers on a Centrex-like basis, so there is strong evidence that Centrex will remain an important and evolving service of the BOCs.

Since BOC-provided Centrex offerings do compete directly with PBXs offered by interconnect companies, and because the BOCs still have strong control of the local access lines required by both, there remains an incentive for the BOCs to discriminate or cross-subsidize in favor of Centrex offerings. As long as this is the case, effective regulatory oversight will be required to assure that the BOCs do not artificially manipulate customer choices between network and customer premises-provided services.

The second area of technological development which seems to have been impacted rather significantly by divestiture is the evolution of the local exchange network toward an Intelligent Network. The Intelligent Network concept essentially creates a new interface in the local exchange which would allow the BOCs—and perhaps even end users—to utilize a common set of basic call processing instructions or "primitives" in developing new software-based services. Speaking more broadly, the concept allows functionality to be distributed flexibly at a variety of processing/database nodes, both on and off the network.

As Sirbu points out, part of the incentive for the development of the Intelligent Network concept was for the BOCs to reduce their dependence upon network equipment vendors for the development of new and improved services. A local exchange network without Intelligent Network capabilities puts the BOCs at a competitive disadvantage compared to PBX manufacturers and interexchange carriers, especially when dealing with large customers. Hence, I agree with Sirbu's assertion that the BOCs were more or less forced to pursue the Intelligent Network concept. The additional interface within the local exchange network should lead to a more competitive network equipment market and more choices for the end user. Without divestiture, one would wonder whether AT&T would have voluntarily opened another interface to the network, facilitating competition with its own applications software development.

The Intelligent Network notion is important not only because of the competition and increased customer choices it may produce, but also because it was influential in the development of the ONA/CEI concept. In *Computer Inquiry III*, the FCC tried to relieve the BOCs of the separate subsidiary requirement for the offering of enhanced services. It wished to replace the structural separation requirements with certain nonstructural safeguards, the cornerstone of which were the ONA/CEI requirements with unbundling of their BOC networks to give enhanced service providers access to basic elements on an equal, nondiscriminatory basis. Giving the non-BOC-affiliated enhanced-service operator access to the software interface described above would both diminish the extent of the BOCs' monopoly power from control of local loops, and encourage a broader range of vendors to develop enhanced services.

Given the importance of the Intelligent Network concept to ONA, I was somewhat dismayed by Bruce Greenwald's comments that difficult implementation problems may render the concept wishful thinking. The lack of this additional network interface reduces the potential effectiveness of the ONA/CEI concept and, therefore, increases the chances of anticompetitive conduct in BOC provision of enhanced services on an unseparated basis.

The third major area of technological development directly affected by divestiture stems from the equal access provisions of the MFJ. Directly identifiable are changes in hardware, software, and network architecture necessary to create equal access. These include such things as the changes necessary to allow the subscriber to resubscribe to any competitive carrier, and then to override the resubscription and select another carrier on a call-by-call basis. They also include changes to the switching hierarchy permitting more efficient access for smaller carriers (e.g., through the addition of access tandems).

The indirect impacts of these directly identifiable changes are, as Sirbu notes, numerous and significant. They facilitated much faster growth in interLATA competition, which in turn led to much faster conversion of the long-haul network to all-digital transmission and to the rapid deployment of fiber optic facilities. This led to the faster development of at least three major long-haul networks in addition to AT&T—MCI, US Sprint, and the independent fiber carriers. This development of alternative long-distance networks no doubt played a significant role in AT&T's recent multi-billion dollar writeoffs of existing, yet dated facilities. The rapid deployment of alternative, high-capacity fiber optic facilities, with their perceived higher quality transmission characteristics, has also played an important role in driving satellite systems out of the high density, point-to-point voice network business.

Once again, I think the general public has been well-served by this accelerated pace of technological change. One of the major concerns with divestiture was the possible negative impact on national defense caused by fragmentation of the network. But, because of the careful way the interfaces between the BOC local exchange networks and the long-haul networks have been developed, the concerns about network fragmentation have been offset in part, if not totally, by the advantages of physical diversity. There have been negative consequences such as the need to develop much more sophisticated network management tools to work in a multivendor environment. Also, as I recall, the pre-divestiture AT&T was working on passing CCS information across the local exchange/long-haul boundary. With divestiture, AT&T was to retreat to an older, less sophisticated form of per-trunk signaling in order to offer equal access on a uniform basis. In short, the overall impact of divestiture on the long-haul portion of the business has been positive, but not universally so.

The equal access provisions of the MFJ also became part of the model for ONA/CEI adopted by the FCC in *Computer III*. If the BOCs could successfully be required to offer nondiscriminatory access to the local network for all long-distance carriers, it would appear they also could be required to provide nondiscriminatory access to enhanced service providers. As mentioned above, the FCC previously adopted such a requirement as a condition for the removal of the separate subsidiary requirement.

There are differences in the two situations, however. The BOCs are prohibited from entering the long-haul (interLATA) market by the MFJ line-of-business restrictions, and thus have little or no incentive to discriminate among the different long-distance carriers. On the other hand, they have been allowed to engage in certain enhanced services such as the provision of voice messaging services or electronic mail. In these areas, the incentives for the BOCs to discriminate in favor of their own enhanced service offerings are still present. Despite the presence of these incentives, the FCC has heavily relied upon ONA/CEI to protect against discrimination when the BOCs offer such enhanced services within the same (i.e., nonseparated) company. This suggests the need for effective efforts to police the boundary between basic and enhanced services to ensure that discrimination does not occur. This need is irrespective of the perceived success of the equal access provisions of the MFJ.

In summary, it is far too early to reach any final conclusions, though I believe divestiture has had a generally positive effect on technological change and generally has benefitted consumers. There is no evidence that pre-divestiture claims of disastrous consequences will ever become a reality. Indeed, some of the tools and approaches adopted in conjunction with the MFJ (e.g., the equal access requirements) can serve as useful models in other situations.

A. Daniel Kelley

Technological change was one of the most difficult issues facing the government as it weighed possible remedies in *U.S. v. AT&T.* The pre-divestiture Bell System raised the specter of a collapse in R&D funding, with a consequent plunge in the rate of technological change, as an antitrust defense.[34] The other side of the argument, however, is that a vertically integrated monopoly can retard innovation by competitive businesses and entrepreneurs.[35] If consumers must endure both the exercise of monopoly power and the loss of innovation, they are two-time losers.

Marvin Sirbu's wide-ranging review of post-divestiture technology issues provides a measure of comfort to those who advocated divestiture. The central teaching of Sirbu's analysis is that most trends in place prior to divestiture have continued. If anything, according to

Sirbu, the pace of technological change has increased in many areas as long-distance competitors have taken advantage of the opportunities created by divestiture to invest in new technology.

The introduction of new technology into the BOC's networks, or the introduction of old technology at lower prices, is another of the substantial and immediate benefits of divestiture mentioned by Sirbu. The migration of procurement away from Western Electric after divestiture was significant and sudden; by March of 1986, for example, AT&T's share of Pacific Telephone's procurement fell to less than 50 percent, from a pre-divestiture level of 90 percent.[36]

It appears that technological progress in these areas has not suffered as a result of divestiture. Indeed, as far as the diffusion of technological change is concerned, society is clearly better off. As Sirbu notes, the question of whether divestiture has had an impact on earlier steps in the process of technological change—invention and innovation—is more difficult to evaluate. However, judging by the levels of the available objective indicators, the future looks promising. As Charles Brown notes elsewhere in this volume, total R&D in the firms that comprised the pre-divestiture Bell System has increased substantially.[37] Moreover, the incentive for independent manufacturers to invest resources in invention and innovation has increased as the enormous Bell market has opened up and as AT&T's long-distance competitors have made substantial investments.[38] AT&T's R&D may now emphasize applications to a greater degree than in the past, and pure research into areas far afield from telecommunications may not receive the attention it once did at Bell Labs. However, a system of monopoly control over an industry, rationalized by the supply of a public good—pure scientific research—and funded by telephone customers' dollars, never fit comfortably with this country's capitalist philosophy. This kind of research is better funded through the National Science Foundation.

Often forgotten in debates over the effects of the divestiture is the fact that the 1956 consent decree effectively prohibited AT&T from unleashing the resources of Bell Labs on unregulated markets. A robust, highly successful computer industry developed in an environment free from the telephone company's monopoly interference. With emerging competition in long-distance, divestiture made it possible to eliminate the line-of-business restrictions on AT&T. At the same time, monopoly local exchange customers were protected from funding cross-subsidies by maintaining the 1956 decree's line-of-business restrictions on the divested BOCs, who lacked expertise in R&D and manufacturing anyway.[39]

Several of the individual examples of post-divestiture technological change cited by Sirbu deserve brief comment. Events in the Centrex market illustrate that the theory of the antitrust case and its actual implementation did not coincide perfectly. Boundaries between competitive and monopoly services are often difficult to draw. This is particularly true when there is rapid technological change. At divestiture, the boundary problems were, for the most part, resolved satisfactorily. Under the theory of the case, AT&T was to receive the competitive, or potentially competitive, Bell System lines of business. However, Centrex competes directly with customer premises switches. This is true even though the functional capacity for Centrex is located in the monopoly local switch. The BOCs were given Centrex at divestiture, despite its competitive nature, because of the technical difficulty inherent in giving it to AT&T.

As Sirbu notes, prior to divestiture, AT&T had decided to migrate customers from Centrex to PBXs. After *Computer II*, just prior to divestiture, the BOCs understandably began to market Centrex aggressively and were able to induce AT&T and other vendors to provide the upgrades to Centrex necessary to compete with PBXs. Sirbu concludes that "we have seen a wide range of feature enhancements to Centrex which ... can be directly traced to the new incentives created by divestiture."[40] Left unanswered is whether this is a good thing.

AT&T could have chosen to respond to evolving PBX competition prior to divestiture by upgrading Centrex. It did not do this, even though doing so would have allowed it more easily to cross-subsidize the Centrex service because of the high degree of common costs in local switches. This strongly suggests that Centrex is simply the wrong technological choice, but the BOCs are promoting it for their own strategic purposes. While this does not mean divestiture was a mistake, it does show it was not perfect.

Sirbu blames divestiture for a two-year delay in the implementation of ISDN standards because AT&T lost some control over the standard-setting process. The ISDN standard issue was controversial even before divestiture, and there is no guarantee that an integrated AT&T could have pushed one standard through the standard-setting bodies. This is particularly true given the interplay between domestic and international ISDN standards.[41] Moreover, many of the ISDN standards issues are related to CPE. As Sirbu indicates, the Bell System equipment monopoly was under attack prior to divestiture. This was both because of the successful FCC network interconnection standards and because the Bell System analog technology did not meet with consumer favor.

The standards issue is a serious one. There is no question monopolies have an easier time imposing standards than multiple firms have in agreeing to them. This may simply be one cost of receiving the benefits that multiple choices provide. It may also be an area in which more government involvement will be required in the future.[42]

Sirbu looks skeptically on BOC participation in the information services markets, correctly pointing out that "for reasons of both policy and the marketplace, it is not clear we would have witnessed any golden age of information services if only the MFJ had not restricted BOC participation" and that "it is not yet clear that the BOCs will find the right technical and marketing strategy to make a success of the information services business." This is a refreshing rebuttal of the BOC conventional wisdom.

Indeed, Sirbu could have gone even further to point out that the French videotex system, which he notes is used by the BOCs as an example for the U.S. to emulate, actually provides strong evidence that U.S. technology has not suffered as a result of the divestiture. Growth in usage of the French Teletel system for services other than directory information is primarily in the business market.[43] U.S. businesses already have widespread access to a wide variety of information services through PCs found in virtually any office.[44] Most non-directory services used by residential customers in France are for "chat lines" and basic sports, health, and travel information which are provided in this country at much less cost through universally available audiotext services or 800 Services. As for directory assistance, the operator-provided service in France is notoriously poor, Minitel customers are not issued the White Pages, and Minitel directory assistance is free.[45]

Sirbu finds good news and bad news in the manufacturing ban. The good news is that "without proprietary interests in any particular technology, the RBOCs, through their agent, Bellcore, have been the most fervent proponents in the U.S. telecommunications industry of compatibility standards." Loss of compatibility was a major concern at the time of divestiture. The post-divestiture experience shows that this concern has been addressed adequately. Although interexchange carriers and the BOCs have numerous disagreements over public policy issues, engineering-level working relationships are quite good.

The bad news, Sirbu believes, is that the decree's manufacturing ban impedes the flow of information between the BOCs and their equipment suppliers and prevents the local exchange carriers from appropriating the full benefits of R&D activity. However, there are arguments on the other side. Regulators can induce the BOCs to spend R&D dollars on applied telecommunications research simply by allowing the BOCs to recover the costs from their monopoly customers. This is a luxury most firms in the economy do not enjoy. Financial integration by the BOCs into manufacturing would allow information to flow only at the expense of creating the same incentives for self-dealing and discrimination that existed prior to divestiture. The costs of this must be weighed against any speculative gains from direct BOC involvement in manufacturing. Moreover, the costs are speculative. Vertical integration is not the only mode of organization in telecommunications. MCI, for example, owns no interest in any manufacturer. Yet, as Sirbu points out elsewhere in his discussion, MCI has access to state-of-the-art switching and transmission technology.

The technological benefit/cost ratio from divestiture seems quite high. Diffusion of technology increased dramatically. The evolving post-divestiture market structure seems conducive to additional gains in invention and innovation. No change of the magnitude of divestiture will be perfect, but the single largest bit of industrial policy attempted in this country to date appears to have worked.

ENDNOTES

1. Amendment of Section 64.702 of the Commission's Rules and Regulations (Third Computer Inquiry), Report and Order, 104 FCC 2d 958 (1986). *Vacated and remanded California v. FCC* No. 87-230 (9th Cir.) June 6, 1990.

2. *United States v. Western Electric Co.*, American Telephone & Telegraph Co., 552 F. Supp 131 (D.D.C. 1982).

3. Final Decision, Amendment of Section 64.702 of the Commission's Rules and Regulations *(Computer Inquiry II)*, 77 FCC 2d 384 (1980), on recon., 84 FCC 2d 50 (1980), 88 FCC 2d 512 (1981), aff'd sub nom. Computer and Communications Industry Association v. FCC, 693 F. 2d 512 (1982), cert. denied, 461 U.S. 938 (1983).

4. Use of the Carterfone Device in Message Toll Telephone Service, 13 FCC 2d 420 (1968).

5. Proposals for New or Revised Classes of Interstate and Foreign MTS and WATS, 56 FCC 2d 593 (1975), 57 FCC 2d 716 (1976).

6. North American Telecommunications Association, "1983 Telecommunications Equipment Industry Statistical Review," Tech. report, North American Telecommunications Association, 1984.

7. Eric Nelson, "PBX and Key Systems: The State of the Marketplace," *Telecommunications* (June 1989), 23:6.

8. Inan Czatdana, "Carriers Plan $24 Billion Outlay in 1986," *Telephony*, January 13, 1986, pp. 32 ff.

9. William H. Davidson, "A Comparative Assessment of National Public Telecommunications," NTIA Submission, April 9, 1990, p. 8.

10. Abudi Zein, "Switched in Time?" *Data Communications*, October 1, 1987, pp. 68 ff.

11. For example, see Peter Huber, *The Geodesic Network* (Washington, D.C.: 69O, 1987).

12. G. Pinkham, "An Intelligent Move," *Telephony*, May 15, 1989, pp. 40ff.

13. Some observers have pointed to the explosion in PCs in the corporate world and the relative decline of the mainframe and draw an analogy to suggest that putting intelligence in the network is a mistake. A more nuanced reading of the record reveals that more and more PCs are being hooked into networks, with specialized shared machines, such as file servers, print servers, database servers, and communications servers, providing support to applications through standardization protocols. Similarly, the communications network must move towards a model in which central office switches act as servers for carrier, enhanced services provider, and end-user application.

14. I. Dorros, "Evolving Capabilities of the Public Switched Telecommunications Network," in J. Schement et al., eds., *Telecommunications Policy Handbook* (New York: Praeger, 1982).

15. As of June 1987, nearly 20 percent of BOCs' subscriber lines terminated on electromechanical switches.

16. Larry Lannon and Inan Czatdana, "Spending Falls Gently in 1988," *Telephony*, January 18, 1988, pp. 36 ff.

17. John Foley, "Supernode to CO's Rescue," *Communications Week*, April 25, 1988, pp. 25ff.

18. See, for example, the debate over the introduction of 800 number call processing by the BOCs and its impact on call processing times. Kathleen Killette, "Carrier Flap Persists Over Proposed 800 System," *Communications Week*, April 18, 1988, pp. 37 ff.

19. Mark Rockwell, "Intelligent-Net Basics to Come Next Year," *Communications Week*, March 27, 1989, pp. 2 ff.

20. Michael Warr, "Bellcore Slows Program for Network Evolution," *Telephony*, May 15, 1989, p. 12.

21. Paulina Borsook, " 'U' Marks the Critical Spot for USer Interfaces to ISDN," *Data Communications* (October 1987), 16(11):70.

22. NTIA, NTIA Trade Report, Assessing the Effects of Changing AT&T Antitrust Consent Decree, Washington, D.C., 1987, Special Publication 87-19.

23. "Pacific Telesis to Get Option for Sake in Group W. Cable Arm," Dow-Jones Newswire, April 21, 8:09 A.M., 1989.

24. Federal Communications Division, Common Carrier Bureau, Industry Analysis Division, "AT&T Share of Interstate Switched Market," June 15, 1989.

25. Equal access was available on only 3.8 percent of all BOC lines on December 31, 1984. By the end of 1986 this had jumped to 74.4 percent and by the end of 1989 reached 94.9 percent. *FCC Statistics of Common Carriers,* 1988/1990 edition, p. 308.

26. M. Kerner, H. L. Lemberg, and D. M. Simmons, "An Analysis of Alternative Architecture for the Interoffice Network," JEEE JSAC, vol. SAC-4, no. 9, December 1986, pp. 1404–13.

27. Based on calculations by D. Reed and M. Sirbu.

28. M. Sirbu, D. Reed, and F. Ferrantz, "An Engineering and Policy Analysis of Fiber Introduction into the Residential Subscriber Loop," *Journal of Lightwave Technology* (November 1989).

29. While other BOCs have begun videotex trials, in October 1989, Pacific Telesis announced it had abandoned plans to test a videotex gateway service because market research turned up insufficient numbers of potential information providers.

30. The reason for this is that the independents had not installed an interim generation of electronic analog switches (e.g. the IAESS) like the RBOCs. Replacement of electromechanical by digital switches is justifiable almost entirely in terms of the superior economics of digital switches: hence the more rapid rate of digital switch installation by independents.

31. Also prices in international markets for switches equipment, which tend to be dominated by non-U.S. or Canadian competitors, have experienced price reductions comparable to those in the United States.

32. The basic advantage of CPE lies in the ability of purchasers to restrict user options. Technology in the public network must inevitably accommodate a very wide range of manufacturers and generations of equipment. The cost of doing so, which rises exponentially with the number of alternatives accommodated, accounts for the poor performance of network based solutions compared to CPE.

33. Internationally, rapid ubiquitous ISDN deployment (as in Japan) appears to depend much more on government subsidy and commitment than industry structure.

34. See, e.g., Defendant's Pretrial Brief, *U.S. v. AT&T*, Civil Action no. 74-1698, December 10, 1980, pp. 199–210.

35. See, e.g., Plaintiff's First Statement of Contentions and Proof, *U.S. v. AT&T*, Civil Action no. 74-1698, November 1, 1978, at pp. 258-514 for a discussion of the Justice Department's equipment foreclosure case.

36. Statement of Gary McBee, Pacific Telesis, to the House Subcommittee on Telecommunications, Consumer Protection and Finance, March 13, 1986, p. ii. Also see, 'Digital Switch Business Sees More Competition," *The Wall Street Journal*, January 23, 1986, p. 6.

37. Also see letter from Gerald M. Lowrie, Senior Vice President of AT&T, to Alfred C. Sikes, Assistant Secretary of Commerce for Communications and Information, Re: Docket No. 81267-8267, March 10, 1989.

38. MCI's investment in its network rose dramatically in the first full year after divestiture was announced, and continued to rise for several years thereafter. See MCI Annual Reports.

39. AT&T's difficulties in penetrating the computer market to date, even with its R&D and manufacturing expertise, may say something about the benefits of unleashing the BOCs to participate in manufacturing.

40. The fact that the BOCs were able to induce their suppliers, primarily among them AT&T, to upgrade Centrex shows that they have substantial ability to control the evolution of technology in their networks, the manufacturing ban not withstanding.

41. See Federal Communications Commission, First Report In the Matter of Integrated Services Digital Networks, April 12, 1984.

42. Jean Tirole notes that "the adoption of AM stereo radio broadcasting in the U.S. seems to have been hampered by the lack of standards and the concommitant hesitancy of stations and listeners to sink money into technological losers." *The Theory of Industrial Organization* (Cambridge, Mass.: MIT Press, 1988), p. 405. This is a case where the FCC explicitly decided not to set a standard.

43. "Minitel Loses Fad Image, Moves Towards Money," *MIS Week*, September 5, 1988.

44. NTIA Information Services Report, U.S. Department of Commerce, Reg. 4 No. 88-235, August 1988.

45. Justine DeLacy, "The Sexy Computer," *The Atlantic Monthly*, July 1987.

4
ECONOMIC ISSUES

9

Telephone Penetration

■

LEWIS J. PERL

AND WILLIAM E. TAYLOR

■

BRIDGER M. MITCHELL

ALEXANDER BELINFANTE

GENE KIMMELMAN

AND MARK N. COOPER

Lewis J. Perl and William E. Taylor

Like the comet Kahoutek and Sherlock Holmes' dog that did not bark, the most notable effect of divestiture on universal telephone service is what did *not* happen. Despite dire predictions of massive reductions in subscribership, the single largest restructuring of the U.S. telecommunications industry occurred without a visible effect on the percentage of households subscribing to telephone service or having access to a telephone. Since divestiture was accompanied by significant changes in rate structure which shifted costs from usage to access, the fact that subscribership remained largely unchanged over the period is something of a paradox.

Almost all observers of the data agree that penetration, even (especially) among disadvantaged demographic subgroups, has continued to rise since divestiture. On the other hand, some disagreement concerning the effect of divestiture (and associated rate changes) on penetration arises from three observations: the level of penetration may be too low for some demographic subgroups and the rate of growth of overall penetration may have slowed since divestiture; the implementation of federal SLCs may have reduced the level of penetration below what it otherwise might have been; and the aggregate nature of census statistics may not reveal geographic or demographic pockets in which penetration rates might be deteriorating.

We will explore three areas of inquiry: what do the current population survey (CPS) statistics and other aggregate statistics collected in the FCC "Monitoring Reports"[1] actually show about the level and change in penetration since divestiture; what changes in the environment over the post-divestiture period explain these changes in demand, and what would be the level of penetration today if divestiture (and related rate changes) had not occurred; and to what extent are analyses based on aggregate statistics—such as those produced by the Census Bureau or the series of FCC "Monitoring Reports"—inadequate to monitor the state of universal service.

Despite significant increases in residential access charges, telephone penetration—as measured by the CPS—has actually risen since divestiture. In March 1984, 91.8 percent of all U.S. households had telephone service; by March 1987, penetration had risen to 92.5 percent, and by March 1990 to 93.3 percent.[2] This change represents nearly a 10 percent drop in the number of U.S. households *without* phones, and thus it reflects a significant improvement in overall telephone availability. This outcome is quite surprising because, at divestiture, widespread increases in monthly residential access charges, due to local rate increases as well as the federal subscriber line charge, were expected by some analysts to threaten universal service.[3]

If the 6.7 percent of households without telephone service in March 1990 were average households—so that the incidence of nonsubscription were distributed uniformly among all economic and demographic groups—there would be little need to worry about universal service. However, the low level of aggregate nonsubscription hides nonsubscription rates significantly above 10 percent for identifiable subgroups of the population, and much of the concern about post-divestiture subscription rates focuses on these subgroups.

In March 1987, who did not subscribe to telephone service? As shown in figure 9.1, nonsubscribing households are more likely to be rural, black, low-income, and comprised of a single male than subscrib-

FIGURE 9.1

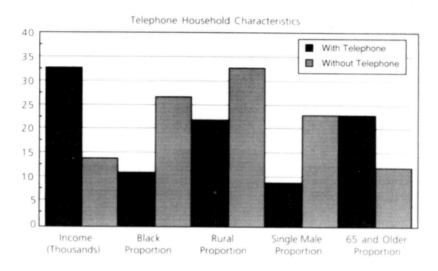

ing households. Nonsubscription rates fall sharply with income (from about 24 percent below $5,000 to above 98 percent above $30,000) and with age (from about 20 percent for household heads between 16 and 24 years of age to about 95 percent for households older than 55) as shown in figures 9.2 and 9.3. To place these levels in context, note that

FIGURE 9.2

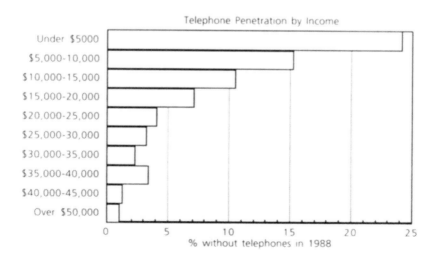

FIGURE 9.3

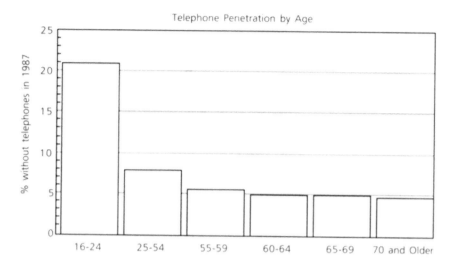

telephone nonsubscription as measured by the decennial census has ranged from 25.2 percent in 1960 to 12.8 percent in 1970 to 7.1 percent in 1980, so that the nonsubscription rate for the poorest segment of the population in 1988 was about the same as the average nonsubscription in 1960.

In the three years immediately following divestiture, not only did penetration increase on average, but, perhaps surprisingly, penetration increased most among demographic groups having the lowest initial penetration. This is illustrated in figure 9.4. While penetration increased by about 0.7 percentage points on average, it increased by over 2.1 percentage points for blacks and 3.4 percentage points for families of Hispanic origin. The increase for employed household heads was about 0.3 percentage points, compared with a 2.1 percentage point increase for unemployed household heads. An equally striking result emerges when we examine changes in penetration by income level. For those with incomes under $10,000, the increase in penetration between 1984 and 1987 was about 0.8 percentage points. For those with incomes between $10,000 and $25,000, the increase was approximately 0.2 percentage points, and for those with incomes over $25,000, there was virtually no change in penetration. Since penetration has increased most where penetration rates were lowest at the outset, this pattern mitigates distributional concerns about universal service.

Even though penetration continued to rise over the post-divestiture

FIGURE 9.4

Change in Penetration by Demographic Characteristic 1984-87

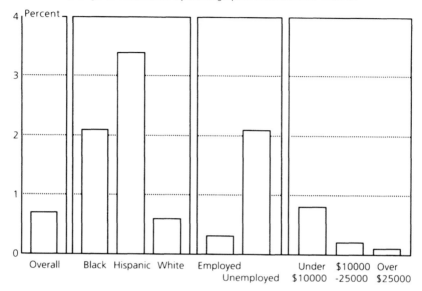

period, there may be some concern that it is rising at a diminishing rate; indeed there is some evidence that penetration actually fell between 1980 and 1983, as measured by the decennial census and the CPS respectively. Of course, since penetration is bounded by 1.0, it cannot continue to increase at a constant rate. For this reason, it is more appropriate to examine the rate of decline of nonsubscription, as opposed to the rate of increase of penetration. By this measure, there has been a small secular decline in the rate of progress towards universal service, although, as table 9.1 indicates, the decline began well before divestiture. Note that this comparison ignores differences in sampling methodologies across the decennial censuses, but does not require that the census methods be comparable to those of the CPS.

Notwithstanding a reduction in the rate of decrease of non-subscription, the pattern of change in penetration levels between 1984 and 1987 was not what was expected to occur following divestiture. At that time, two independent effects of separating the ownership of the local and long-distance networks were thought to have serious consequences for universal services. First, the requirement that the local and long-distance networks interact at arm's length through access tariffs meant

TABLE 9.1
Annual Rate of Growth
of Nonsubscription

Period	Growth
1960–1970	−6.6%
1970–1980	−5.7%
11/83–7/88	−5.0%

that the traditional support for local rates from toll rates would become difficult to sustain.[4] As a result, the FCC felt compelled to reduce the amount of interstate costs of the local network recovered from usage-based charges, and increase the amount of those costs recovered in monthly charges from subscribers. These residential subscriber line charges were implemented on June 1, 1985 at $1.00 per month, were increased to $2.00 per month one year later, and rose to $2.60 on July 1, 1987. During a period in which flat-rate local service prices averaged about $13 per month, the SLCs represented a significant increase in the price of residential access.

Second, the financial prospects for the LECs were thought to be questionable, and a number of state rate cases had been delayed due to divestiture. As a result, intrastate rates were increased by roughly $4 billion in 1984, resulting in an unusually high increase in local service rates. The combined effect of these factors is shown in figure 9.5, in which it is apparent that the real increase in local rates began before divestiture. Indeed, the real annual rate of growth of local rates between 1980 and 1984 exceeded the rate of growth between 1984 and 1987, as measured by the CPI. It is thus difficult to attribute local rate increases between 1984 and 1987 entirely to divestiture per se, and it is probably accurate to say that local rates increased much less than was forecast at the time.

In summary, the effect of divestiture and its concomitant rebalancing of local and long-distance rates on the level of penetration is nearly unobservable. Since local rates rose dramatically since 1980, this observation comes as something of a surprise to an economist, and one must look elsewhere to find other changes in the environment which offset the effects of local rate increases during this period.

There are several likely reasons for the relative stability of the penetration rate since divestiture. *First*, the increase in basic service charges has probably been less than anticipated. It was commonly thought that

FIGURE 9.5

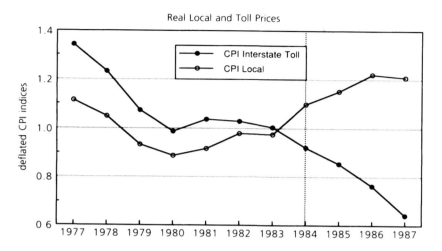

Real Local and Toll Prices

rate restructuring following divestiture would raise basic service charges by 50 to 100 percent. But, because it proved impolitic to shift all non-traffic-sensitive costs into basic service charges, actual increases to date have been under 30 percent. *Second,* the decreases in penetration that might otherwise have been caused by rising basic service charges have been offset by changes in income and other demographic characteristics. Increases in income and the age of household heads have generally led to increases in telephone penetration. *Third,* exogenous increases in demand for telephone service may have served to offset price trends. For example, from 1970 to 1980 changes in taste increased demand by roughly four percentage points. Continuation of these trends would cause a significant increase in demand in the 1980s, thereby further offsetting effects of rate increases. *Fourth,* long-distance rates fell significantly, and since access and usage are complementary goods, demand for access increased. *Finally,* changes in the structure of telephone prices may have mitigated the effects of price increases. In particular, there has been a significant increase in the availability of local measured service. Since this reduces the minimum price at which access is available, this change tends to offset the effect of any general increases in the price level. There also has been some increase in the availability of lifeline service, which has reduced the cost of telephone service for the low-income households most likely to be adversely affected by any rate increases.

To examine these influences quantitatively, we have made use of NERA's (National Economic Research Associates) 1983 access demand model[5] which relates the demand for telephone service to price, income, and demographic characteristics. This model has been used here to predict changes in penetration which might be expected to occur from 1984 to 1987 as a result of changes in price, income and demographic characteristics, and changes in taste for phone service. By comparing predicted with actual changes in penetration over this period, we can see how well the model accounts for the changes which actually occurred. If the model predicts actual changes accurately, we can determine the change in penetration which would have occurred under various assumptions about the rate of growth of basic service charges.[6]

The application of the model to explain the change in penetration over the post-divestiture period is summarized in table 9.2. For each of the key factors influencing penetration, this table describes its percentage increase or decrease from 1984 to 1987 and the effect of this change on the penetration rate. The model suggests that, taken in isolation, the increase in telephone prices occurring over this period was associated with about a 0.8 percentage point *decrease* in the fraction of

TABLE 9.2
Change in Penetration from 1984 to 1987

	Change in Characteristic	Change in Penetration	Cumulative Penetration
Actual Penetration in 1984			91.80%
(1) Prices			
Measured rate price	16.6%		
Flat-rate price	16.6%		
Installation charge	1.8%	−0.80%	90.99%
(2) Income	10.1%	0.85%	91.84%
(3) Demographics			
Age	0.2%	+0.03%	
Proportion black	2.8%	−0.01%	
Number of persons	−1.1%	+0.01%	
Income/Age	0.2%	−0.20%	
Total		−0.16%	91.68%
(4) Historical trend	—	0.95%	92.63%
(5) Measured-rate availability	12.2%	0.02%	92.65%
(6) Total predicted	—	0.85%	92.65%
Actual Penetration in 1987	—	0.70%	92.50%

households with phones. On the other hand, the 10 percent real increase in income from 1984 to 1987 would have been expected to increase penetration by about 0.85 percentage points, more than offsetting the price effect. In addition, other demographic changes, principally the aging of household heads offset by the interaction of age and income, causes penetration to fall about 0.16 percentage points.[7] Finally, the continuation of the 1970 to 1980 trend in telephone demand would account for a 0.95 percentage point rise in penetration from 1984 to 1987. In combination, these factors would predict about a 0.8 percentage point rise in penetration compared with the 0.7 percentage point rise which actually occurred. The consistency between this prediction and the actual change occurring gives us some confidence in this model of telephone demand.[8]

While we have not tried to quantify their effects, other factors could account for any remaining difference between actual and predicted changes. *First,* there was some increase in the availability of lifeline rates over this period, and this may have offset the effect of rising charges for low-income consumers. *Second,* there may have been some narrowing of income distribution from 1984 to 1987. This often occurs during upswings in economic activity. If income were rising somewhat faster for low than for high-income groups, income effects would be somewhat larger than that described above. *Finally,* there was a significant decline in toll rates over the period and since access and toll usage are complementary services, this rate reduction would mitigate some of the effects of the increase in local rates.

Although they were more than offset by other forces, these data suggest that price changes did cause some decrease in penetration. Thus, had prices not risen, 1987 penetration would have been 93.3 instead of 92.5 percent. How should this be viewed? Some clearly feel that any decrease in penetration or potential penetration is to be deplored. Others (ourselves included), would argue that since the price changes did not decrease penetration, but merely slowed its growth, they are of less concern. Thus, despite the price increases, the 1987 share of households with phones is higher than in 1984 and about even with the level observed in the 1980 census. In fact, since the census and CPS surveys are somewhat different, when adjusted for differences in the sampling approach, penetration in 1987 may in fact be higher than in 1980. Moreover, this slowdown in the growth in penetration must be viewed in context. It occurred because rates became more closely aligned with cost, and this has resulted in substantial increases in the overall value of phone service. As we have argued elsewhere,[9] the price changes occurring from 1984 to 1987 have increased the value of phone service to the *average* consumer by nearly $4.68 per month, and any losses in penetration must be balanced against these gains.

The link between divestiture per se and penetration rates is federal subscriber line charges. From a residential consumer's perspective, these charges had the same effect as an increase in local rates, and the implicit increase was quite significant. From divestiture to April 1987, these charges rose $2.00 (not counting intrastate SLCs enacted by some state commissions) which represents roughly a 17 percent increase in the flat-rate price and a 28 percent increase in the measured-rate price. Thus, one clear measure of the effect of divestiture on universal service is the effect on penetration of SLCs, holding all other variables at their observed levels.

This calculation is presented in line (1) of table 9.3. When the $2.08 federal and state SLCs are removed from the estimated 1987 rates, predicted penetration in 1987 rises by 0.76 percentage points. In March 1987, there were approximately 90.2 million households in the United States, so that a penetration increase of 0.76 percentage points would represent approximately 686,000 additional households having access to telephone service. Whether this number is large or small depends on the perspective of the reader.

Moreover, this estimate undoubtedly overstates the adverse effect of the implementation of SLCs on the penetration rate. While SLCs increased access rates between 1984 and 1987, they also resulted in declines in interstate toll rates, which would be expected to increase the demand for access. While the existing access demand model does not relate toll prices to access demand directly, it can be used to estimate this effect.[10] Doing this suggests that about 25 percent of the effect of increased subscriber line charges is offset by the corresponding fall in toll prices. Thus the net effect of subscriber line charges was to reduce penetration by roughly 0.6 percentage points.

Instead of confining the effect of divestiture on penetration to the impact of subscriber line charges, suppose we ask what penetration would have been in March 1987 if local rates had continued to grow at their pre-divestiture rate. From 1977 to 1984, the BLS CPI-Local index fell by about 12 percent in constant dollars—an annual rate of roughly 2.5 percent. Had local rates fallen in real terms at this rate between 1984 and 1987, penetration would have been approximately 1.37 percentage points higher than under observed rate increases, as shown on line (2) of table 9.3. On the other hand, if local rates had grown at the same real rate of growth as the BLS CPI-Local index grew between 1980 and 1984,[11] penetration would have been approximately 0.22 percentage points lower than under observed rate increases. As a middle ground,

TABLE 9.3
The Effect of Residential Rate Changes on Penetration, 1984–1987

	Change in Prices	*Change in Penetration*	*1987 Predicted Penetration*
Actual Price Changes: 1984–1987		−0.80%	92.65%
Measured-rate price	16.6%		
Flat-rate price	16.6%		
Installation charge	1.8%		
(1) Eliminate state and federal subscriber line charges		−0.04%	93.41%
Measured-rate price	−5.5%		
Flat-rate price	3.2%		
Installation charge	1.8%		
Difference		0.76%	
(2) Assume access rates grow at 1977–1983 growth rate		0.57%	94.02%
All access rates	−6.68%		
Difference		1.37%	
(3) Assume access rates grow at 1980–1984 growth rate		−1.60%	91.85%
All access rates	17.2%		
Difference		−0.80%	
(4) Assume access rates remain constant in real terms		0.01%	93.46%
All access rates	0.0%		
Difference		0.81%	

if local rates had remained constant in real terms over the period, penetration would have been roughly 0.83 percentage points higher than predicted under observed rate increases.[12] Without offsets, the 44 percent increase in price from 1980 to 1987 would have reduced penetration from 93 to about 90 percent. This potential decline, however, was essentially offset by a continuation in the historic trends in demand for phone service, and to a lesser extent by increases in the age of the population and increased availability of measured service.

Thus far, we have described the effect of divestiture on universal service exclusively in terms of penetration: how penetration changed in the post-divestiture period in the aggregate and among demographic groups of concern, and what underlying factors produced that change. In this section, we assume the relevant goal of public policy is universal service, and question our implicit reliance on the CPS penetration rates and on penetration rates in general in light of that goal. Two issues must be clearly distinguished. First, do the CPS reports provide a sufficient measure of penetration to guide regulatory policy? Second, is the penetration rate—even if available in a timely manner for all demographic or geographic groups of interest—sufficient information to gauge the state of universal service?

The telephone penetration questions asked by the CPS every four months were instituted at the request of the FCC to monitor the effects of its decisions on subscribership. The monitoring program began as Phase IV of the access charge docket (CC Docket 78-72) in response to concerns raised by the states. The decisions in question were initially SLCs, but since the implementation of the SLCs coincided with a reform in jurisdictional separations (which increased, on average, the intrastate share of loop costs), the Commission's charge was to monitor the effects of all its actions on universal service. For this broad requirement, a compilation of national survey data at four-month intervals seemed appropriate.

However, the effects of post-divestiture FCC decisions did not fall equally on all demographic or geographic groups. In separations policy, the transition of the subscriber plant factor[13] to a uniform 25 percent raised intrastate revenue requirements in some states and lowered them in others. Effects in some states for some local exchange companies were enormous, while on average, the intrastate assigned portion of NTS costs increased only about two percent. Subscriber line charges were assessed as a fixed dollar amount per line (at different rates for residential and multiline business subscribers) which represented a larger percentage increase for customers subscribing to lower-priced services: customers in small exchanges, rural customers, and measured-rate subscribers.

With these policy changes, one might expect small changes in national average penetration to mask unacceptably large changes among customers of particular LECs in particular states. And for this purpose, the CPS sample is inadequate. At a state level, the sample is too small to identify penetration changes with sufficient precision, and no information whatever is provided by telephone exchange or by serving LEC. More precisely, the sampling error in the national estimates is about 0.5 percentage points (at a 95 percent confidence level), while state-level sampling errors range from 2 to 6 percentage points, varying inversely with the square root of the sample size. The inability to detect penetration changes of this order of magnitude is a significant limitation on the usefulness of the CPS data for its intended purpose.

Penetration changes among particular demographic groups are observable at the national level, but with much less accuracy at the state level. An attractive benefit from additional sampling among demographic groups would be to enable analysts to gauge the effectiveness of federal and state programs focused on those groups: e.g., Lifeline and Link-Up America subsidies for low-income households. There is considerable variation in the implementation of these plans across the states, and if the results could be monitored with accuracy, improvements in assistance plans could probably be devised.

Measurement of penetration is difficult because the calculation requires knowledge of quantities which are not normally measured by the telephone companies. The numerator of the penetration estimate is total subscribership, not number of access lines. The denominator is number of households, which is difficult to monitor reliably between the decennial censuses.[14] Monitoring changes in the numerator (or changes in connection and disconnection rates) is relatively easy to do, but the vast majority of connects and disconnects are associated with moves or household formation, and thus do not reflect changes in penetration. Identifying and tracking involuntary disconnections is a more fruitful approach, but reports from the disconnect monitoring plan suggest involuntary disconnections are more related to general financial or personal distress than to the level of monthly access charges.

In sum, current monitoring of penetration rates is probably adequate to track national effects of state and federal policy changes, but probably inadequate to detect the type of universal service problem—if any —that might be caused by access charges or separations policy changes. Other, cheaper, monitoring measures are suggestive at best. The most straightforward solution—expanding the CPS sample—is prohibitively expensive. Fortunately, decisions concerning local rates are largely in the hands of state commissions, where benefits from subsidizing customers of particular telephone companies or particular demographic groups or geographic regions can be weighed against their costs.

Penetration technically measures the proportion of households which subscribe or have access to telephone service. However, the object of universal service must be the capacity to reach individuals, not households. In this view, additional lines beyond the first increase universal service, in that the probability of completing a call to a particular individual is increased. Lines to second homes, public telephones, and mobile telephones contribute towards universal service to individuals in the same sense. All of these methods of accessing the network are ignored by a penetration standard of universal service.

Penetration also measures the fraction of households which actually choose to subscribe to telephone service, as opposed to the fraction for which service is available at a reasonable and affordable price. One of the largest demographic groups with low penetration is households headed by young, single males. Similarly, elderly households exhibit high levels of penetration across all income classes. Taste for telephone service, not service quality or affordability, appears to be an important determinant of demand, acting differently among different demographic groups. A better measure of universal service would differentiate between availability and actual subscription.

Finally, the use of penetration rates for households to monitor universal service ignores entirely a large segment of the telecommunications market. One of the most significant developments in the national network since divestiture is that a majority of its capacity is no longer owned or controlled by traditional common carriers. Private networks —real or virtual, facilities-based or resold—have proliferated, and an increasingly important role of the public switched network is to provide universal service—connectivity—to these customers. The arguments which justify traditional universal service as an appropriate public policy goal apply with equal force to the interconnection of networks. Measuring the penetration rates of households does not monitor this increasingly important dimension of universal service.

Bridger M. Mitchell

Why didn't the dog bark? Perl and Taylor address three questions about the availability of residential telephone service since divestiture: What has happened? What if? What should be?

Determining what has happened to telephone penetration is an exercise in accounting. The authors provide useful statistics computed from recent CPSs. In the aftermath of divestiture, two "what if" questions remain—first, what would penetration be today in the absence of divestiture? And, second, what would it have been had the initially predicted increase in local rates actually occurred? Economic analysis is required to answer these questions, and my comments will focus on that aspect of Perl and Taylor's discussion. The normative aspects of universal service—what should be—are in the category of social and political choice. They are addressed by some of the other discussants.

Household telephone penetration did not decline following divestiture—the dog did not bark—despite widely voiced prediction to the contrary. Perl and Taylor establish that penetration has, in fact, increased in the post-divestiture years.

They then examine the counterfactual scenario of no divestiture, by predicting penetration for local telephone prices that exclude the federal subscriber line charge ($2 in 1987). After accounting for lower toll prices, the authors estimate the net effect of the price change alone was to reduce penetration by about 0.6 percentage points. This effect was, however, more than offset by higher incomes, favorable demographic shifts, and most importantly, an increased taste for a telephone.

A second, and equally interesting, "what if" question concerns the quantitative predictions of the effects of divestiture made at the time that AT&T was broken up. Many public commentators and telecommunications analysts predicted the dog would at least bark, if not howl —that penetration would decline to a considerable degree.

Why were these predictions wrong? These alternative hypotheses could be tested: local telephone rates did not increase to the extent assumed by the analysts; the effect of increasing real income was not considered, or was mismeasured; specific policies have offset higher local rates—introduction of measured service and lifeline rates; or the forecasting models were fundamentally incorrect. Using their model, Perl and Taylor provide some information bearing on these hypotheses.

Divestiture affects penetration through telephone prices—higher local flat rates, reduced toll rates, possibly greater prevalence of measured-service rates, more widely available lifeline rates, and possibly higher connection rates. Divestiture does not affect trends in income, changes in demographic factors, and changes in tastes, the net effect of which has been to increase penetration since 1984. Thus, the task for economic analysis is to model and estimate the marginal effect of prices on telephone penetration, given the changes in penetration that would have occurred due to other factors.

Perl and Taylor rely on the model developed earlier by Perl (1983)[15] using revised estimates in Perl (1984).[16] It postulates a demand function for access to the network, and estimates the factors from 1980 census and telephone operating company data. The estimated model's predictions are then checked against actual penetration rates in 1984 and 1987.

In the Perl model, an individual household's demand for access is a logistic function of prices, income, demographic characteristics, and fraction of measured service subscribers. In addition, changes in unmeasured factors, collectively labelled "tastes," cause demand for access to shift over time.

As shown in figure 9.6, demand for access—the probability of a given household subscribing to telephone service, or the percentage of similar households who subscribe—is a decreasing function of the

FIGURE 9.6

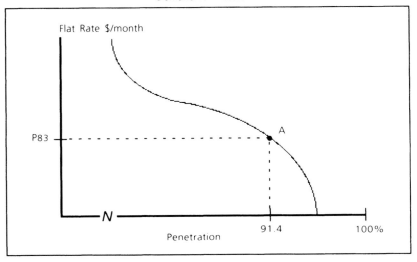

Demand for Access

monthly flat rate. In 1984, at the average flat rate, approximately 91.8 percent of U.S. households subscribed. At lower prices, penetration would increase, but even if the price were zero, penetration would fall short of 100 percent.

By 1987, the effect of higher real incomes, an older population, other demographic changes, and an increased taste for telephone service had shifted the demand curve to the right (figure 9.7). Perl's model estimates that these exogenous changes would have increased penetration to about 93.7 percent, had the flat rate remained unchanged in real terms (point B). But the increase in the local rate moved penetration up to the demand curve (point C) and reduced it to just 92.5 percent.

Perl and Taylor's tabulation of penetration by different demographic groups reveals that, since divestiture, the net effect of all factors combined has increased actual penetration. The increase has been greatest for low-income, nonwhite, and unemployed households (figure 9.4, p. 361)—generally, the groups with the lowest overall penetration. Since the local telephone rates paid by these groups rose during this period, it is non-price factors that have had the predominant effect on penetration. In terms of figure 9.7, the data suggest that access demand curves have shifted outward more rapidly for the lowest-penetration groups.

FIGURE 9.7

Demand for Access Over Time

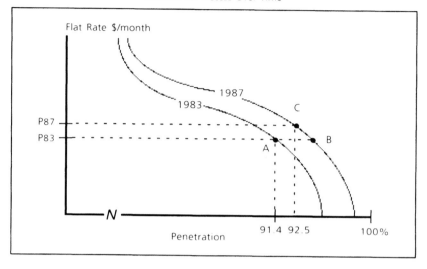

The extent to which a change in local rates affects penetration also appears to vary by income and by demographic group. For example, figure 9.8 shows the access demand curves for households with a head aged 18–24 and those with a head aged 65–69. In 1984, at the then-prevailing flat rates, only 78 percent of the younger households had a telephone, compared with some 96 percent of those age 65–69. The Perl model predicts, at a zero price, penetration would increase to 92.6 percent for those 18–24 and to 99.7 percent for those 65–69. This larger percentage increase in the predicted penetration for the younger group appears to be similar to the nonprice effect just discussed—a greater increase in penetration observed in the low-penetration groups in the 1984–1987 data. In fact, it is a consequence of the logistic functional form of the demand curve. Both age groups—and indeed all households —are assumed to have the same underlying coefficient of price-responsiveness.

In this model, when two groups of households pay the same prices, the group that has the lower penetration rate in 1984 will also have the lower rate in 1987. Furthermore, the model implies that service will always be less "universal" among younger households, even if local telephone service were free. To put it differently, in this model the effect of a lower (or higher) telephone price depends only on the group's

FIGURE 9.8

Demand for Access by Different Ages

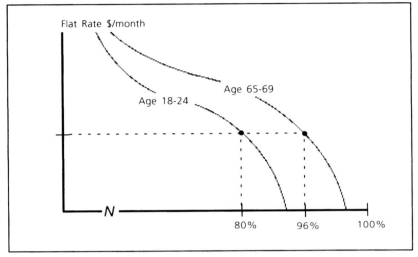

initial fraction of telephone service, not on its income or demographic characteristics.

Figure 9.9 illustrates how this assumption limits the analysis of penetration under alternative pricing scenarios. The dashed segment of the demand curve is not possible in the model—even if local rates were subsidized for young households, their telephone access would not increase to the level that would exist for older households. In similar fashion, initial differences in penetration that exist between different racial and gender groups will persist even if rates are reduced to zero. Of course, it may be the case that some groups would consistently have lower penetration if telephones were free. In the current model, however, this result is an assumption, not an empirical finding.

To the counterfactual question—to what extent would penetration in different groups have been reduced by the sharply higher rates expected at the time of divestiture?—the model has a uniform answer. Changes in predicted penetration depend only on initial penetration in each group, and one common coefficient of price responsiveness.

Because local exchange companies do not systematically collect statistics on nonsubscribers, empirical estimation of an access demand equation requires merging population survey data (census or CPS) with telephone company data on rates and number of subscribers by rate

FIGURE 9.9

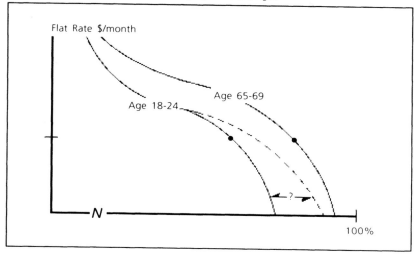

Price Sensitivity by Different Ages

plan. The access demand variable must therefore be binary-valued, and represents the sum of demand for flat-rate and demand for measured-rate service.

The availability of both flat-rate and measured-rate service in a single locality complicates the estimation of demand for access. Perl's 1983 demand model incorporates the effects of measured rates indirectly, by including, in addition to the flat-rate price, the prices of measured service. Unfortunately, this specification is not consistent with an economic model of consumers' choices of class of service, and leaves the reliability of the estimated price elasticities in some doubt.

The model could usefully be elaborated to represent the choice of class of service explicitly. In this framework, Perl and Taylor could then derive demand for access in a given market as the sum of demand for flat rate plus the demand for measured rate.[17] Telephone company data on the number of flat and measured subscribers for the same geographic areas offer the opportunity to estimate such demand functions, conditional on subscribing to some class of service. These additional data promise to improve estimates of the access demand equation, and to test its predictive accuracy.

In Perl and Taylor's analysis, the most important quantitative factor affecting penetration is one that is, in fact, not measured in the model

—an increasing "taste" for telephone service. This taste shift is estimated by the increase in actual penetration from 1970 to 1980 (measured by the decennial census) that is not predicted by the econometric model. This unmeasured effect no doubt captures many characteristics of telephone service that have made a telephone increasingly desirable —improved quality, a larger network of subscribers, and lower prices of toll service. In the current model it amounts to more than 60 percent of the total increase in penetration.

Interstate toll rates, which were declining rapidly in the pre-divestiture period, must have accounted for an important part of this unmodeled effect. And divestiture caused toll rates to fall even more rapidly (figure 9.5, p. 363). Although an unknown fraction of the residual taste effect is indeed a price effect, Perl and Taylor are unable to capture it directly in their model. However, they make a side calculation (based on the consumer surplus derived from toll calls) that suggests about one-fourth of the marginal reduction in penetration due to subscriber line charges is offset by lower toll rates. This important, but indirect, evidence may suggest that lower toll prices have contributed more to keeping penetration high than was expected when divestiture occurred.

Using data from the CPS, Perl and Taylor establish the dog did not bark—household telephone penetration has risen following divestiture. But the intriguing question remains: why did it not bark? Perl and Taylor provide one part of the answer: local rates did not rise to the expected levels. And other factors—principally, higher incomes and a trend in telephone penetration—more than offset the higher prices that did occur.

Given the exogenous forces working to increase penetration whether or not divestiture occurred, would larger access rate increases have had only minor effects on penetration anyway? Were those who proclaimed the end of universal service only crying wolf? Or was it the political constraint on higher subscriber access charges that prevented a decline in penetration among the groups with fewest telephones?

An economic analysis of the counterfactual scenarios requires a well-specified model of demand for access. The underlying model by Perl and Taylor represents an important beginning. It can be developed further to allow price response to vary by demographic group, capture choices between flat-rate and measured-rate service, and perhaps include toll calling as well. With such extensions it may be possible to answer a key "what-if" question: would full-scale local rate restructuring have jeopardized universal service?

Alexander Belinfante

I cannot argue with the general discussion of recent trends in telephone penetration by Perl and Taylor. Indeed, much of it is derived from information that I have been responsible for releasing[18] and from analysis I have conducted.[19] However, I think their analysis is incomplete, because it does not incorporate information that has recently become available. As a result, I disagree with their conclusion that penetration would have been higher if SLCs had not been introduced. In fact, I believe the restructuring of rates resulting from the access charge program has stimulated telephone penetration.

When residential SLCs were first introduced, there were many predictions that the increase in the fixed cost of subscribing to telephone service would cause many households to lose telephone service. This has clearly not happened. One question is whether this is purely because we have experienced an expanding economy. A more fundamental question is whether the FCC's access charge program has been beneficial or harmful in promoting universal service.

I think everyone agrees the increases in telephone penetration are at least partly the result of the growth in real household income in the past few years. The impression left by the use of the Perl model, however, is that penetration would have grown faster in the absence of the access charge program. I disagree with this impression.

I believe the access charge program has stimulated telephone penetration in three ways: the Lifeline and Link-Up America parts of the program have helped low-income households obtain and maintain telephone service; the restructuring of rates that resulted from the program have benefited the class of households most vulnerable to disconnection—namely, low-income high-volume users; and the efficiency gains from the program have helped stimulate the economy. I will not dwell on the third of these here, but simply note that there is at least one study which links at least a small portion of the growth in the economy to the SLC.[20]

Prior to conducting my own analysis, I tended to agree with the widely held view that subscriber line charges would be detrimental to telephone penetration. This view is bolstered by the Perl estimate of a drop in penetration of 0.76 percent due to SLCs. Estimates such as this were instrumental in causing the establishment of the Lifeline and Link-Up America programs as part of the access charge program, in causing the Joint Board and the FCC cautiously to say that the SLC would preserve (rather than promote) universal service, and in causing the Joint Board and the FCC to establish a monitoring program to assure that universal service would be preserved. My own analysis, however, indicates the increases in telephone penetration are more than can be explained by income increases alone.

The first piece of evidence that caused me to reconsider the impact of SLCs was an econometric study I conducted using cross-section and time-series data from the March CPS of 1984 through 1987.[21] Included in this model were various demographic and economic variables, including household income, the price of local service, the price of installation, the SLC, and an indicator of the availability of a lifeline program.[22] The household income and price of local service variables had signs and magnitudes that were in line with my expectations. The Lifeline and SLC variables, however, failed to meet my expectations. I had expected the SLC to have a negative coefficient, as is normally the case for a price variable. Instead, it had a significant positive coefficient. I concluded the coefficient must reflect something other than the direct effect of SLCs, and that a likely candidate was the effect of the accompanying reduction in toll rates. (My model did not include a toll rate variable.)

I attributed my failure to find a positive coefficient for my Lifeline variable to the newness of the Lifeline program, and the failure of my variable to distinguish between programs for which income is the only eligibility criterion, and programs which additionally have non-income eligibility requirements, such as being elderly or disabled. The programs that have such additional requirements generally have few households that qualify for Lifeline assistance, and thus do not effectively promote universal service. In spite of my failure thus far to find an econometrically estimated effect, however, I still believe the Lifeline and Link-Up America programs have helped stimulate penetration, judging from the number of households that have taken advantage of these programs.

The second piece of evidence causing me to reconsider the impact of SLCs was the set of disconnect studies submitted by the RHCs and GTE in the monitoring docket during 1988. Among the findings of these studies were: virtually no households disconnected due to the SLC increase, indicating a price elasticity for access of close to zero; most of the households disconnected for economic reasons were involuntarily disconnected due to nonpayment of their bills; and most involuntarily disconnected households were heavy users of telephone service, including toll service. These findings led me to conclude there are far more households without phone service because of their inability to pay for toll charges, than because of their inability to pay for SLCs. This conclusion was reinforced by the observation that involuntary disconnects declined after toll rates were reduced.

The third piece of evidence causing me to reconsider the impact of SLCs was the analysis of changes in penetration for income groups reported in the December 1988 "Monitoring Report." This analysis indicated that the only income groups having significant changes in telephone penetration in the last few years have been low-income groups, which have experienced significant increases in penetration. This led me to conclude that recent penetration increases cannot be just the result of increases in income, because the effect of such income increases would be to cause more households to move into higher income categories (which have higher penetration levels), rather than to increase the penetration rate within any one income category. The relationship between penetration and income has thus shifted, particularly in the low end of the income scale. This indicates that the Perl model overstates the magnitude of the income effect on penetration, since it does not reflect this shift.

The final piece of evidence causing me to reconsider the impact of SLCs was a study conducted by Southwestern Bell submitted in the monitoring docket. [23] This study analyzed the bills of a sample of about 500,000 of Southwestern Bell's customers, and compared them with the bills of another sample of 500,000 Southwestern Bell customers living in low-income areas. Among the conclusions of this study were: the reductions in toll rates since the introduction of SLCs have more than offset the amount of those charges for the average customer in both samples, resulting in a lower total bill; the reduction of toll rates has greatly stimulated toll usage since divestiture, the growth rate of toll usage has been about twice as great for low-income subscribers as for subscribers in general, resulting in toll usage patterns that are now nearly equal for both groups; and the SLC constitutes a small percentage of the average subscriber's total bill (including subscribers in low-income areas). This study provides evidence the reductions in toll rates have provided significant benefit to low-income households in two ways—first, by making toll calls more affordable, and removing them from the class of luxury goods and services, and, second, by reducing the total bill of average and above average users of interstate toll service. The study also shows the number of low-income high-volume users is greater than previously believed.

All of this evidence combined leads me to conclude that the restructuring of rates resulting from the access charge program has stimulated telephone penetration. While the direct effect of the SLC may have lowered penetration slightly, this effect may have been offset by the Lifeline and Link-Up America programs. On the other hand, the accompanying reduction in toll rates has undoubtedly resulted in fewer low-income heavy users of toll service being subject to disconnection because of their inability to pay their total bill.[24] Since the Perl model does not include any variable for toll rates, it largely overlooks this beneficial impact on penetration.[25]

Finally, some comments on the discussion of proposed changes in the definition of universal service. The increasing number of vacation homes and introduction of multiple telephone lines into residences forced a change in the way telephone penetration is measured. This introduction forced the abandonment of measuring penetration as the number of residential lines divided by the number of households. While multiple lines improved telephone availability, they did not increase universal service as traditionally defined. Similarly, pay phones, phones in cars, airplanes, and trains, and paging devices have increased telephone availability.

A new measure of availability, such as the percentage of time an average person can be reached by telephone, might be useful, but will probably be difficult to measure. Furthermore, it is not clear universal availability is desirable, as evidenced by the high percentage of households with unlisted numbers, and the annoyance of being called at inconvenient times, or by parties with which one does not wish to communicate. Until telephone penetration (as currently measured) for low-income households approaches the level currently enjoyed by high-income households, it will remain useful to continue to measure penetration as it is currently done.

Gene Kimmelman and Mark N. Cooper

Discussions about decreased penetration since divestiture have always involved small numbers and these discussions have never been earth-shattering. It is not death and destruction in terms of public policy, but it is a very important public policy issue and, therefore, I think the small numbers matter.

One thing everyone has mistaken about the dog that did not bark is that we, the Consumer Federation of America, *were* the dog, and we barked—and policymakers listened to some extent. Furthermore, 600,000 households within six blocks of the White House without access to the telephone network should constitute at least a small bark. And in fact, the dog was threatening to bite off our leg. At that time, the proposed SLC (previously called the access charge) was the six dollars at the state level plus another six or seven dollars at the federal level for every residential telephone subscriber. That was a policy matter the dog barked at.

Affordability of telephone service is indeed an important issue. Another reason why the dog did not bark so loudly was that requests for local rate increases were only partially granted, the SLC was decreased, and Lifeline was implemented—all measures which contributed to basic service affordability for low-income subscribers. Lifeline, however, was not a result solely of divestiture. It was implemented because many of us fought for it. Nor was divestiture the reason why many telephone companies were willing to go along with it. As Alex Belinfante points out, the FCC viewed Lifeline as an essential element of its SLC plan.

In this normative context of universal service, the elements of concern have been quite simple. We should be concerned about drop-off, about *who* drops off the network, and about failure to expand the network in a manner consistent with the historic rate of expansion. Most importantly, we should worry about the financial burden we have placed on people for whom the telephone is a necessity item—those with what some would call inelastic demand for telephone service. Is it fair to put that burden on people of low and fixed income, who may have to give up other important resources to pay for the telephone? We believe this financial burden should be minimized. These are all the consumer goals pertaining to universal service, and these goals need to be recognized because universal service is more than penetration rates.

The consumer advocate's approach to the issue of universal service lies between the two extremes presented by William Baxter and Charles Brown. On the one hand, Baxter seemed unconcerned with price increases so long as prices were based on costs; on the other hand, Brown seemed to propose that the objective affordable residential service was feasible in the monopoly environment, but now AT&T was obliged to compete. Since we believe the Consumer Federation of America's stance is often not understood completely, we will state it clearly: we espouse a kind of incrementalism, allowing competition and allowing a restructuring of the industry; with some skepticism, but not total antagonism. But we also advocate the use of regulation to protect the concept of universal service. We believe that many of the "inefficiencies" of regulation are vastly outweighed by the benefits these "inefficiencies" bring us, such as pricing policies that promote affordable universal basic phone service. That is the approach we have taken through the divestiture era, and plan to continue to take. It involves a very simple formula with the maximum contribution possible to the rate base from all interconnecting services, to keep local rates low, given what the market will bear. This is something economists hate to hear, but it is the kind of pricing approach we believe promotes both universal service and fair competitive rules.

But the most important question at this point is, do the data in figure 9.10 indicate that telephone penetration is at saturation? Have we done as much as we can? I do not think anyone has ever advocated that everyone in society should have a telephone. We have stated that everyone who wants a telephone, but who cannot afford one, should be subsidized. That was the issue in the lifeline debate, and that is the direct issue related to the comparison of the penetration data. I believe lifeline is often dismissed by those who claim, "it is done, don't worry about it." But I do not think the issue is resolved yet. As Belinfante points out quite clearly, our data show that less than half the states actually have a lifeline program. More have signed on for Link-Up, but less than half the low-income people in this country qualify for lifeline programs. And many of the programs are woefully mistargeted. They certainly should not be targeted to include people who do not need the service, while ignoring some who clearly are underrepresented on the network. However, as suggested by the following, this is the case in a number of states.

For example, Hawaii only offers discount rates to individuals who fit the following criteria: they are at least sixty years old or are handicapped, and have income below $10,000.[26] Of the states that have a lifeline program, almost half include restrictions similar to Hawaii's, which make a large segment of the low-income community ineligible for discounted service.[27] In addition, most states with broader lifeline programs exclude low-income individuals who do not go through the often complex, stigmatizing process of applying for welfare benefits. As a result of the FCC's and states' failure to mandate the availability of discounted local service for individuals below the poverty line, more than 50 percent of low-income Americans are not offered affordable local phone service today. The goal of universal service is being thwarted by these inadequate federal and state Lifeline efforts.

What about the data presented in the Perl and Taylor discussion, and the conclusions we can draw from it? First, measuring the effects of divestiture is not a straightforward exercise. Most will agree that other factors were sources of change, and divestiture did not change many things. Moreover, to the extent that the effects of divestiture are measurable, they still are not of primary concern to policymakers. It is those other factors, such as pricing policy, that matter. A basic problem with the data presented in Perl and Taylor is that 1960 was not a "benchmark." As we enter the 1990s, to say that things were pretty good in 1960 is not relevant in a policy context (see figure 9.11 and the recent trend in local prices).

Another problem with the timeframe of the data lies in the calculation of relative rates of progress toward universal service. Taylor and Perl compared 1960 to 1970, 1970 to 1980, then 1984 to 1988. But 1980 to 1983 are missing; this was a period of recession, and the end of 1983 was the bottom of the cycle. As a result, the data compare the bottom of a recession to the top of the highest, most rapid growth in a business cycle the U.S. has seen since the Second World War. Drawing conclusion from such a comparison is analogous to analyzing the effects of the air traffic controllers strike after airline deregulation. We will never be able to properly specify the effects of these two massive events, which occurred at the same time.

Accordingly, we do not know if we can draw meaningful conclusions without filling the gap. Perhaps when we look at the 1990 census and compare it to 1980, we will be able to fill that gap. It is our impression that some very important events happened during the first three years of the 1980 decade. Historically, eras of dramatic income growth have also witnessed a real decline in local rates and fairly large increases in penetration rates. We believe that during the recession of the 1980s and the real rate increases the Perl and Taylor data show, there probably was some dropoff. However, we do not have any measurements, since CPS data do not exist for that period. Neither do we know whether there was a resurgence in penetration during (1) the recent period of real income growth or (2) the real local rate increases and the beginnings of Lifeline service in some areas. The 1980s look like a rather stagnant period. We would have to go back and look carefully at the 1960s to 1970s to 1980s comparison (given that 1980–1983 data are missing) to see if the overall conclusion is correct.

But when we examine this data, we should attempt to determine how to include Lifeline programs in our modeling, in order to give them credit if it is due. On another note, second homes that qualify for Lifeline service are not the policy issues, but that is normative, and that we cannot resolve.

We need to examine the way prices are modeled. Perl's model used the Bureau of Labor Statistics' (BLS) numbers to escalate rate increases. But the BLS escalator includes Lifeline, installation prices, changes in touch-tone, and more. BLS takes a sample of bills; it is not monthly access prices, and therefore the data are escalated at an average rate

FIGURE 9.10

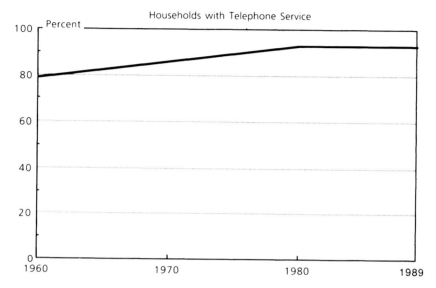

Source: Bureau of Census, *Housing Characteristics*, various issues.

that probably does not reflect actual monthly access prices. And we question whether installation charges were included separately, but obviously there is a massive federal program to offset them.

Another set of concerns has to do with toll rates. I have never seen the price elasticity of demand for access for toll rates specified. It could be treated as an income effect, but the result would be too small. Belinfante almost got it right. The answer is that by lowering toll rates, you increase the value of the phone, and therefore there is a price elasticity with respect to access. This is a legitimate issue.

Although we disagree with some details of the Perl and Taylor analysis, and concur with some of the methodological questions raised by others in this chapter, our greatest concern is in the focus of the introduction and how Perl and Taylor address concerns of universal service. We believe penetration rates could be much better. How much? We are not sure. But start with cleaning up the Lifeline programs, expanding them, and establishing them in states that do not have them.

Our interest focuses on data collection, and in getting all the data analyses debated on paper. We need to look toward the future, and we need to think about the 1990 census and whether it can in some way help us in analyzing that 1980-to-1983 data gap. I think today's public

FIGURE 9.11

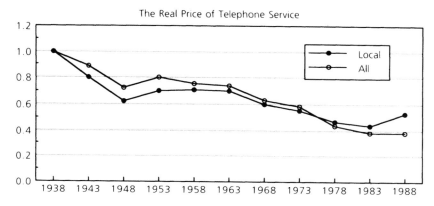

The Real Price of Telephone Service

Source: Bureau of Labor Statistics, *Consumer Price Index.*

policy debate illustrates the need to look toward information services and how that issue relates to universal service. We need greater information about low-income households, because they are obviously where the greatest affordability problem lies. We need to look toward affordability questions as we develop information services, to make sure that, this time, as we proceed into the 1990s, we actually have benchmarks (i.e. some data). We need to have an empirical basis to do an analysis of what universal service is ten years after divestiture and beyond.

ENDNOTES

1. As outlined in the quarterly "Monitoring Reports," filed in CC Docket No. 87–339. These reports typically present the basic post-divestiture data on penetration levels, lifeline assistance plans, eligibility for the high cost fund, network usage, local and long-distance rates and revenues, bypass, and the financial performance of the National Exchange Carrier Association mandatory and voluntary pools.

2. March over March penetration rates are used to eliminate seasonal effects, and March was chosen because the March reports contain more demographic information.

3. Whether or not penetration has increased since the 1980 decennial census is still an open question. National average penetration in the 1980 census was 93.4 percent while the November 1983 CPS estimate was two percentage points lower. Some analysts ascribe the drop in measured penetration to differences in sampling methodology between the census and the CPS, while others attribute the drop to federal policies. For our present purposes, it is enough to note that

the drop, if real, occurred before divestiture and cannot be associated with rate changes implemented as part of divestiture. In the next section, we show that our econometric model would have forecast a penetration drop of roughly the magnitude observed, due primarily to large increases in real telephone prices and a fall in real income over the 1980–1984 period.

4. In an integrated network, a customer would have to bypass the entire switched network in order to avoid the local support embedded in long-distance rates. When the support for the local network became a part of carrier access charges, a customer only had to bypass the local network to avoid paying local support.

5. Lewis J. Perl, "Residential Demand for Telephone Service, 1983," National Economic Research Associates Memorandum, December 1983; revised May 1984 to correct installation charge data.

6. The 1983 access demand model was developed by examining the demand for telephone service in a large sample of individual households. Data from the 1/1000 sample of the 1980 census indicated whether or not each of 80,428 households subscribed to telephone service, described the demographic characteristics of the household in detail, and assigned the household to one of 1,154 geographic areas. NERA then obtained exchange-specific rate data from the (then) BOCs for the 71,979 households assigned to Bell territory. From this large cross-section of households in 1980, a logit equation was estimated, relating the probability of a household subscribing to telephone service to the prices it faced and to its socioeconomic characteristics.

The coefficients of the demand equation are summarized in William E. Taylor and Lewis J. Perl, "Telephone Penetration and Universal Service in the 1980s," Center for Telecommunications and Information Studies, Columbia University Graduate School of Business, Working Paper, 1989. These coefficients measure the change in the natural log of the odds of a household subscribing to telephone service associated with a one-unit change in the variable in question. Price and income elasticities from this model depend upon the penetration level at which they are measured; for 1984 or 1987, the flat-rate price elasticitites are roughly -0.05 and the income elasticity is about $+0.190$.

7. Note that the race effect does not dominate despite the fact that there was a comparatively large proportionate change in percentage nonwhite, and that race has a high coefficient in the model. Average number of persons per household is 2.68 in the sample, while percentage nonwhite is roughly 10 percent. The race elasticity is thus about -0.005 ($= -0.52 * 0.11 * (1-0.918)$) while the "persons" elasticity is roughly -0.01 ($= -0.05 * 2.68 * (1-0.918)$).

8. The three factors which are important in determining the change in penetration between 1984 and 1987 are prices, income, and an exogenous trend in the taste for telephone service. The measurement of both price changes and the trend in tastes is explained in William E. Taylor and Lewis J. Perl, "Telephone Penetration and Universal Service in the 1980s."

9. Lewis J. Perl, "Welfare Consequences of Competition in Telecommunications;" presented at the International Telecommunications Society 7th bi-annual conference Cambridge; Mass., July 1988; table 7, p. 20.

10. Recall that the demand for access to the telephone network is determined by the consumer surplus associated with using the network at prevailing usage rates. In this view, a $1 change in consumer surplus has the same effect on a consumer's likelihood of subscription regardless of its source. If this is the case, the effect of a change in toll prices can be estimated by first calculating its effect on consumer surplus for a representative sample of consumers. Then, using the coefficient relating access prices to penetration, we can assess the effect of these changes in consumer surplus on access demand.

11. Between 1980 and 1984, the BLS CPI-Local index grew 24 percent in real terms or about 5.7 percent per year.

12. While the principal focus of this analysis is on changes in penetration since divestiture, it is also of some interest to examine changes from 1980 to 1984. Prices also rose during this period (about 24 percent above inflation) and published data appear to suggest that penetration fell. Penetration in 1984, as estimated in the current population survey, was 91.8 percent. By comparison, 1980 penetration, as reported in the decennial census, was 93 percent. Did the rise in prices from 1980 to 1984 *cause* the apparent decline over this period? If it did, why didn't income and taste changes also offset decreases during this period?

To resolve this question, we have sought to determine whether the apparent change in penetration from 1980 to 1984 can be explained by reference to changes in price, demographic characteristics, and a continuation of historic taste changes. The change predicted by the model matches the actual change very closely.

This result has several implications. First, the ability of the model to account for both the 1980–1984 and the 1984–1987 change increases our confidence in its predictive power. Second, since the model predicts the apparent 1980–1984 change, perhaps previous concerns that the CPS and census estimates are not comparable have been misplaced. Finally, if the model is valid, it enables us to assess the effect of price on penetration over the entire period 1980–1987. The net effect of these forces was to leave penetration essentially unchanged (it was about 0.5 percentage points less in 1987 than in 1980.)

13. The subscriber plan factor (SPF), calculated separately for each local exchange carrier in each state, is used to divide loop costs between the state and interstate jurisdictions. In the previous decade, the factor was based on a multiple of the proportion of interstate usage, and it grew rapidly with the increase in interstate usage. SPF was frozen at its 1983 level by a Federal-State Joint Board decision and transitioned to a uniform 25 percent (the gross allocator) over an eight-year period. Frozen SPF averaged about 27 percent nationally, but the average conceals about a 60 percentage point range across the states.

14. Consulting services which provide local area population estimates between census years frequently use telephone access line growth to interpolate between census estimates or to distribute more reliable aggregate population changes across geographic areas.

15. Lewis J. Perl, "Residential Demand for Telephone Service, 1983," National Economic Research Associates Memorandum, December 1983.

16. Lewis J. Perl, "Revisions to NERA's Residential Demand for Telephone Service, 1983," National Economic Research Associates Memorandum, April 24, 1984.

17. This approach is used, for example, in a simulation model of class of service choice and penetration in Park and Mitchell (1989).

18. Industry Analysis Division, Common Carrier Bureau, Federal Communications Commission, "Telephone Subscribership in the U.S.," released three times per year, in January, May, and September. Tables 2 to 6 in this report are prepared by the Current Population Survey, Bureau of the Census, U.S. Department of Commerce, under contract from the FCC, and the remaining tables are based on data provided by the Current Population Survey.

19. Staff of the Federal-State Joint Board in CC Docket No. 80-286, "Monitoring Report," and CC Docket No. 87-339, December 1988, Sec. 1, "Subscribership and Penetration Levels."

20. Wharton Econometric Forecasting Associates, "Pricing Telecommunications Service: The Impact on the U.S. Economy of Subscriber Line Charges," 1986.

21. Alexander Belinfante, "The Analysis of Telephone Penetration: An Update," *Review of Business*, (Spring 1989), 10(4):9–14, 32.

22. Link-Up America was not adopted until April 1987 and thus was not available during the period for which I had data.

23. Alexander C. Larson, Thomas J. Makarewicz, and Calvin S. Monson, "The Impact of Subscriber Line Charges on Residential Customer Bills," Southwestern Bell Telephone Company, January 17, 1989. Submitted as part of Reply Comments in the Matter of Establishment of a Program to Monitor the Impact of Joint Board Decisions, CC Docket No. 87-339.

24. In addition, the reduction of toll rates has increased the value of phone service for all users.

25. Since the Perl model is estimated from cross-sectional data alone, it is difficult to include toll rates directly in the model, because the variation in toll rates occurs mostly over time. Perl and Taylor do attempt to estimate the effect of toll rate changes indirectly through the impact on consumer surplus. However, this estimate is based on untested assumptions, and its magnitude is therefore questionable.

26. "Monitary Report," CC Docket No. 87-339, July 1989. Prepared by the staff of the Federal-State Joint Board in CC Docket No. 80-286.

27. Id. However important exceptions are New York and California.

10

Labor, Employment, and Wages

■

WALLACE HENDRICKS
AND SUSAN C. SASSALOS

Wallace Hendricks and Susan C. Sassalos

Beginning in 1978 with the deregulation of the airline industry and continuing through the divestiture and partial deregulation of telecommunications, the federal government has attempted to improve economic performance in several key industries by changing the regulatory environment. These changes, of course, could not be accomplished without significant repercussion in the labor market. Indeed, some commentators might suggest that the *major* impacts of trucking and airline deregulation were felt by organized labor rather than by the stockholders of firms in those industries.

While deregulation and divestiture go hand-in-hand in the restructuring of telecommunications, we would like to separate them in discussing their labor market impacts. The primary reason for this artificial separation is that while the deregulation of telecommunications can be compared to deregulation in trucking and airlines which occurred a few years before, the divestiture is somewhat unique in our recent experience, and therefore requires its own analysis.

Telecommunications is highly unionized and the typical contract in the industry runs for three years. The last contract signed prior to the divestiture was negotiated in 1983. Thus, as of this date, we have had only two new contract negotiations in the post-divestiture era. Obviously, generalization is difficult based on these two negotiations. Therefore we will take the approach of comparing the early experience in telecommunications with the experience in trucking and airlines, and try to predict whether or not we are likely to see a comparable result in telecommunications.

The significant declines in prices brought on by deregulation of trucking and airlines led to substantial increases in employment in both industries. In trucking, essentially all this new employment occurred in the nonunion sector. The Teamsters lost massive numbers of members as a direct result of deregulation. This brought up an interesting issue. Workers in the trucking industry were to be partially protected against job loss due to deregulation under terms of the 1980 Motor Carrier Act. If some workers lost their jobs, yet employment in the industry was increasing, should those job losses be attributed to deregulation? The government took a negative position and the workers were largely uncompensated for their losses. The most comprehensive study of the impact of deregulation on wages in trucking, published by Nancy Rose,[1] finds a similar result. Union wages were reduced by approximately 14 percent, while nonunion wages were largely unaffected by deregulation.

A slightly different result occurred in airlines. First, the advent of the "hub and spoke" system after deregulation has led to increases in concentration in many markets, rather than the decreases which were predicted. Second, many airlines were able to offset higher wages with large increases in productivity brought on by major concessions from their unions. For example, productivity increased only 0.5 percent per year during the ten-year period preceding deregulation, and increased by over 3.5 percent in the ten-year period after deregulation. As a result, neither the huge membership losses nor the declines in wages which characterize the trucking experience are found in airlines. There have been job losses and wage cuts. However, they do not dominate the overall statistics. A recent study by David Card found that between 1978 and 1986 average wages in airlines fell slightly or matched the general level of wage increases in the economy as a whole.[2] The range of wages between low and high-wage firms is much larger than in the preregulation period because firms have followed different strategies to remain competitive. Major labor-management problems have occurred in those firms (e.g., Continental Airlines and Eastern) which saw deregulation as an opportunity to improve their competitive position by cutting wages.

Like the Teamsters Union, unions in the airline industry have attempted to cushion the blow of deregulation for some of their members by having the government invoke some of the labor-protective provisions called for under the Airline Deregulation Act of 1978. Again, this effort has largely been unsuccessful.

Should deregulation in telecommunications be expected to yield results similar to airlines or trucking or neither? To evaluate this question we need to investigate how regulation influences bargaining.

Regulatory policy can theoretically influence bargaining in two general areas. First, regulation can limit the number of competitors in the product market by granting monopolies. Unions can therefore grow with existing firms and need not organize new entities. To the extent that regulation causes less competition in both the product and the labor market, union power may be higher than it otherwise would be. We label this the "structure" effect of regulation. Second, regulation may have lessened the incentive of firms to contain labor costs since these costs could be passed along to customers in the form of higher rates. If regulated firms have few incentives to operate efficiently in every market they serve, there may be a tendency to focus on the "bottom line," as opposed to specific lines of business. For example, telephone maintenance could be priced far below cost and the revenue to cover the loss could be obtained from over pricing long-distance service. Without a connection between prices and costs, there might be little incentive to operate the maintenance division efficiently. We label this the "pricing" effect of regulation. The combination of the structure and pricing effects could lead to substantially higher rates in regulated industries. Therefore, deregulation might be expected to reduce wages and employment.

Wage data suggest that the telecommunications unions had done quite well for their members prior to the divestiture. For example, the average hourly wage in the telephone industry at the end of 1982 was $11.20, as compared to $8.69 in manufacturing. This differential had existed for some time, but had actually increased during the latter 1970s (in June 1976, the figures were $6.21 and $5.15, a 21 percent differential, as opposed to the 28 percent differential in 1982). For example, average hourly earnings increased 133.5 percent between 1974 and 1983, as compared to only 106.5 percent in the automobile industry.[3]

These wage data offer a prima facie case for a regulatory impact on union power, but high wages could exist for any number of reasons. Closer study is necessary to isolate those causes. The only major study of this question for the telephone industry focused on wages at New York Telephone in 1976. The author, Ronald G. Ehrenberg, concluded, "As of the end of 1976, NYT's employees' earnings, on the average, were 15 to 20 percent above the level I had defined to be just and reasonable."[4] In this case, he defined "just and reasonable" as the wage paid employees with equal skills in the New York labor market. It should be noted that the average of the wages paid to all comparable workers in New York is considerably below the average of wages paid to comparable workers at the large, unionized firms in New York.

Ehrenberg's results, although only for a single company, probably can be generalized to most companies in the industry, since the Bell System companies bargained on a nationwide basis at the time. They suggest that union power was high, but they do not provide an easy answer to the issue of the impact of regulation on union power. N.Y. Telephone might have been a large, unionized company even in the absence of regulation. A 15 to 20 percent wage differential over the average wage in the labor market would therefore not be unexpected.

Deregulation poses two problems for telecommunications unions. First, they cannot simply organize workers by growing with existing firms. New competition requires them to attempt to organize the new firms. This is not an easy task since many of the new competitors are either foreign-based or historically nonunion (e.g., IBM). Second, unions must organize new divisions of existing firms. Although the divestiture was originally designed to separate competitive from monopoly segments in the industry, all of the RBOCs now have regulated and unregulated subsidiaries.

There is little evidence to date that would suggest that deregulation itself will likely lead to significant competition in wage rates. The most immediate threat is in the manufacturing of telecommunications equipment, with fewer possibilities of nonunion entry into long-distance service and local service markets. AT&T remains the dominant long-distance carrier. Significant competition could be added if the RBOCs are allowed to compete in the long-distance market. However, they are all large, unionized firms. It seems unlikely that a significant nonunion presence is likely to occur in the industry in the near future. Thus, the impact of deregulation on union power will probably be significantly less than in trucking or even airlines.

The fact that deregulation by itself is not likely to lead to short-run changes in the bargaining power of telecommunications unions suggests that any decrease in this power might be better attributed to the divestiture which also occurred at the same time. To investigate this possibility, we will first review the evidence on changes in wages and employment in telecommunications since divestiture. We will then review the specific impacts of divestiture on union-management relationships.

Throughout the 1980s, the telecommunications industry has experienced considerable changes in both the kind of employees it requires and the amount of labor it demands. These changes have been precipitated by both deregulation and changes in technology. Although the effect of technology on employment is not our focus in this chapter, it is still important for two reasons. First, by altering the structure of employment, technology affects the bargaining strength of the parties. Second, firms make choices where to invest and apply new technologies, and deregulation will affect these choices.

Employment trends in telecommunications, manufacturing and trucking between 1979 and 1988 are summarized in figure 10.1. We have separated telephone equipment employment from employment in the service sector. The figure makes it clear that employment has been declining in the industry throughout the 1980s. Thus, the entire decline cannot be blamed on divestiture or deregulation. However, there is a substantial difference in the rate of decline between the equipment and service sectors. Employment declined by 3.6 percent per year in the

FIGURE 10.1

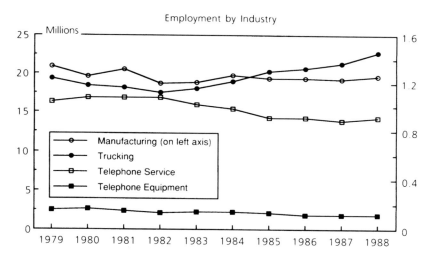

Source: U.S. Bureau of Labor Statistics.

equipment sector (5.2 percent for production employees), compared to 1.7 percent per year in the service sector (1.8 percent for production employees). The dramatic declines in manufacturing are probably attributable to the increased competition brought on by earlier deregulation in that sector and trade barriers which allow foreign competition in the United States but which restrict American companies from competing abroad.

Import penetration increased from 2 percent of the telecommunications market in 1982 to 14 percent in 1984, and the Communications Workers of America (CWA) estimated that this increase caused the loss of as many as 120,000 jobs.[5] While employment has also declined overall in the service sector, this decline follows a trend which is probably better explained by changes in technology. These results are in direct contrast to the perception that deregulation of telephone equipment was a "clear-cut public policy victory for competition," while the benefit of deregulation of long-distance service to consumers is "murky."[6] Workers in the industry probably have been hurt the most by the policy change which has benefited the consumers the most.

During the 1980s, demand for nonmanagement employees in telecommunications has been sizably affected by the application of new technology. Technological advances have contributed to substantial increases in labor productivity. As James Peoples found, this has contributed to the above-average wages of telecommunications workers (see below), but the trade-off of using technological advancements to obtain high wages has been job displacement.[7]

A study of the Canadian telecommunications industry shows that technological change had the most severe impact on the employment of telecommunication operators and clerical workers.[8] Similar evidence of decline in these occupations can be found in the United States. A BLS wage survey of the communications industry revealed that the number of telecommunications operators declined from 213,614 to 128,218 during the 1970s.[9]

Since divestiture, the employment of operators, craftsmen, and linemen has fallen, while the employment of salespeople, professionals, and R&D professionals has increased. The number of line installers increased after divestiture then stabilized. The employment of operators is still falling, from about 25 percent to only 10 percent of the work force.

Lynch and Osterman investigate the impact of technical innovation upon employment structures within one BOC from 1980 to 1985, specifically the introduction of electric system switching (ESS) and multiple loop testing (MLT), and the subsequent effects on the occupational employment distribution.[10] While the employment of workers in general corporate services, business, residence and directory services, and network installation and maintenance increased, the number of workers in operator services and network distribution and plant operations declined. Lynch and Osterman calculate that every 10 percent increase in operators' productivity results in a 4 percent decrease in employment. They also found that occupations which are heavily unionized are more likely to adjust to falling demand through exits from the firm than through internal transfers. Union workers are more likely to quit or be laid off than their nonunion counterparts (as is true in the United States in general), while the latter are more likely to take early retirement. The result is a reduction in the fraction of the firm's labor force which is unionized.

Employment figures for most of the large telecommunications companies are presented in table 10.1 for the period 1983 to 1988. The decline in total employment has not been universal. For example, Ameritech and Bell Atlantic were able to maintain their employment at approximately the same level as occurred at divestiture. On the other hand, AT&T employment declined by 4.3 percent per year during this period, reflecting large declines in manufacturing. Unions at AT&T were unsuccessful in their attempt to obtain employment security provisions in their 1989 negotiations. Among the BOCs, Pacific Telesis

TABLE 10.1

Total Employment in Selected Telecommunication Companies,
1983–1988

	1983	1984	1985	1986	1987	1988
AT&T	372,716	365,514	337,844	316,968	307,724	308,173
Ameritech	78,009	77,514	76,640	77,538	78,510	79,336
Bell Atlantic	22,145	21,493	20,271	21,381	21,742	21,142
BellSouth	91,758	89,022	80,323	77,571	74,900	75,023
NYNEX	116,839	94,662	89,354	90,196	95,313	97,400
Pac Telesis	97,812	75,733	69,461	70,746	67,777	66,125
SWestern Bell	77,135	68,133	65,836	61,793	59,642	57,975
US West [a]	89,503	70,765	70,202	69,375	68,523	69,765
GTE	109,300	105,700	103,000	102,500	101,300	98,600
Contel	16,284	15,691	15,101	14,851	14,021	14,968

Source: Direct correspondence with companies.

[a] Company annual reports.

TABLE 10.2
Ratio of Management to Nonmanagement Employees

	Mgmt	Non-Mgmt	Ratio	Mgmt	Non-Mgmt	Ratio
AT&T	111,432	261,284	42.7%	126,669	181,504	69.8%
Ameritech	23,102	54,907	42.1%	25,606	53,730	47.7%
Bell Atlantic	6,871	15,274	45.0%	5,915	15,227	38.9%
BellSouth	25,308	66,450	38.1%	19,041	55,982	34.0%
NYNEX	32,052	84,787	37.8%	16,861	59,893	28.2%
Pac Telesis	25,338	72,474	35.0%	18,766	47,359	39.6%
SWestern Bell	19,723	51,412	38.4%	16,963	41,012	41.4%
US West	—	—	—	—	—	—

Source: Direct correspondence with companies.

suffered the largest decline, primarily as a result of the transfer of 20,000 operators back to AT&T immediately following divestiture. Unions at Pacific Telesis were able to obtain employment security provisions in their 1986 negotiations, but employment in the regulated portion of the company has continued to decline since that time. In 1983, 67 percent of Pacific Telesis employees were unionized; in 1988 the figure had declined to 61.5 percent. Table 10.3 illustrates the growth of the nonregulated sector of the industry since divestiture.

While Ameritech has been able to maintain approximately the same size labor force, the mixture of this force between typically union and nonunion positions has changed significantly. In 1988 over 11,000 of the 79,000 workers were in nonregulated subsidiaries and the percentage of nonmanagement employees had declined from 70 percent in 1983 to 68 percent in 1988. Table 10.2 shows the ratio of management to nonmanagement employees for some of the other operating companies. Like Ameritech, AT&T has also increased the proportion of typically nonunion positions. The company suggests that this is the result of diversifying into new markets, such as computers and the international market, and their subsequent need for new professionals with expertise in these areas.

In May 1990 the CWA represented about 18,000 operators at AT&T. The union estimates that, if 1950s technology were still in place, there would be three million jobs for operators today! The current number of jobs for operators will be sizably reduced, perhaps even halved in the next few years because of operator system position switching (OSPS)

TABLE 10.3
Employment in Nonregulated Subsidiaries

	1984	1985	1986	1987	1988
BellSouth	6,666	12,064	16,906	18,252	19,285
NYNEX	5,658	6,163	14,196	16,424	20,646
Pac Telesis	860	1,665	3,749	3,619	3,147

Source: Direct correspondence with companies

which is expected to quadruple the productivity of operators. Also, over 15,000 top craft workers represented by the CWA have been cut due to the reorganization of the company at AT&T Information Systems, and the position of cable splicer has been completely eliminated.

Both the reduction in the unionized work force and the application of automation have already had an impact on the union's bargaining power. Striking telephone workers once had the ability to shut down the nation's entire phone system. During the 1986 and 1989 strikes, however, supervisors at AT&T and the BOCs were able to fill in for striking operators with very little interruption in service. As a result, the unions had to find innovative methods such as the "invisible picket line" to try to exert economic pressure on management.

If regulation has produced high wages in telecommunications by

FIGURE 10.2

Source: U.S. Bureau of Labor Statistics.

eliminating firms' incentives to contain costs, then deregulation ought to result in a relative wage decline. This has not, in fact, occurred in telecommunications. Average hourly earnings have grown at approximately the same rate as in manufacturing, perhaps even higher.

Average hourly earnings of telephone communication and equipment workers are compared to averages in other industries in figure 10.2 and table 10.4. The average increase in hourly earnings for both telephone communications and telephone equipment workers in the pre-divestiture period (1978–1983) was 8.7 percent, while the average increase in hourly earnings for all manufacturing workers during this same period was 7.8 percent. In the post-divestiture period (1984–1988), telephone communications workers averaged a 3.3 percent increase per year, telephone equipment workers 2.5 percent, and all manufacturing workers 2.8 percent. Thus, there was a slight closing of the wage gap between telephone equipment and other industries, but no such closing in telephone communications.

These wage trends are also reflected in the provisions of the collective bargaining agreements. The 1977 contract provided a total general wage increase of 13.79 percent plus cost of living (COLA) over three years. The 1980 contract had an even larger increase of 14.65 percent plus COLA. But general wage gains in the 1983 contract were smaller than they had been in previous years. The contract provided a total wage increase of 8.5 percent plus the same COLA formula included in the 1980 agreement. As Peoples points out, it is difficult to determine whether this moderation was the result of uncertainty over the market conditions that would accompany the impending divestiture, or if it was in reaction to the economic recession of the period.[11]

After divestiture, the CWA and the International Brotherhood of Electrical Workers (IBEW) negotiated average general wage increases of 8 percent at AT&T, but lost the use of the COLA provision. This resulted in a significant decrease in union wage growth, since the COLA typically paid 65 percent of the increase in inflation above some minimum amount.

Generally, the 1986 wage rate increases for the Regional Operating Companies were no better than those at AT&T. They ranged from a low of 3.5 percent at Mountain and Northwestern Bell, to a high of 8.5 percent at Wisconsin Bell. However, the inclusion of lump-sum and profit-sharing as well as COLA provisions provided employees of all of the BOCs except Mountain Bell with a total wage package which was superior to AT&T's. Cappelli and Perry, however, note that these types of wage gains do not add to the basic rate, and therefore make the contract cheap in the next round of negotiations.

TABLE 10.4
Average Hourly Earnings in Selected Industries

	1977	1978	1979	1980	1981	1982	1983	1984	1985	1986	1987	1988
Manufacturing	5.63	6.17	6.69	7.27	7.98	8.50	8.84	9.17	9.52	9.73	9.91	10.17
Electric equipment	5.34	5.83	6.31	6.96	7.65	8.17	8.67	8.99	9.47	9.67	9.90	10.13
Telephone & telegraph equipment	6.25	6.73	7.51	8.24	9.14	9.86	10.27	10.69	10.82	10.93	11.17	11.62
Transport. & public utilities	6.94	7.55	8.18	8.89	9.72	10.31	10.81	11.15	11.38	11.63	12.01	12.32
Telephone communication	6.94	7.50	8.07	8.72	9.80	10.66	11.45	12.00	12.47	12.83	13.21	13.46
Switchboard operators	5.89	6.26	6.67	7.15	7.99	9.04	9.93	—	—	—	—	
Line construction employees	8.24	9.13	9.77	10.64	11.38	12.35	13.15	—	—	—	—	
Electric services	7.12	7.70	8.33	9.12	10.04	10.89	11.57	12.28	12.94	13.46	13.86	14.32
Gas production & distribution	6.64	7.10	7.65	8.27	9.16	9.81	10.43	11.14	11.76	12.53	13.00	13.32
Combination utility services	7.79	8.46	9.06	9.64	11.08	12.29	13.35	14.19	14.93	15.58	16.16	16.88

Source: U.S. Department of Labor, Bureau of Labor Statistics. *Employment and Earnings*, table C-2, "Average hours and earnings on private nonagricultural payrolls by detailed industry," March 1978–1989, p. 82.

In the 1989 negotiations with AT&T, the parties settled on an increase of 4 percent in services, and an increase of 3.5 percent with an 8 percent bonus in telecommunications equipment manufacturing, plus profit-sharing in both. Since the all-industries median first-year increase in the first twenty-four weeks of 1989 was 3.5 percent (4 percent with the expected value of bonus payments),[12] the telephone unions at AT&T continued to negotiate packages similar to those found in manufacturing. Wage settlements at the RBOCs have been similar. Of the settlements in 1989 the highest occurred at US West (5 percent including a $600 bonus in the first year, followed by 2.5 percent and 2.25 percent in the remaining two years, plus possible incentive pay in the second and third years) and Southwestern Bell (5.25 percent in the first year, which includes a $1,000 lump sum bonus, followed by 2.25 percent each year for the remaining two years, plus a COLA in the last two years), and the lowest at Bell Atlantic (3 percent-2.25-percent-2.25 percent plus COLA)[13] and BellSouth (4 percent-1 percent-1 percent plus COLA)[14] and NYNEX (3 percent-1.5 percent-1.5 percent plus COLA).[15]

Early post-divestiture results suggest that wages in telecommunications have not declined relative to wages in comparable industries. Peoples[16] investigated the effect of regulation on wage levels by examining pay differentials between workers within and outside the telecommunications industry both before and after divestiture. He found that the gap between union and nonunion wages in telecommunications was quite small prior to divestiture and has actually increased since that time. Since the Bell System is extensively unionized, and new entrants into the competitive post-divestiture long-distance sector are almost entirely nonunion, these results suggest that workers employed in the regulated sector continue to benefit from restricted competition—at least in the form of higher wages.

This conclusion is further supported by an examination of the 1986 labor contracts, since organized employees at all of the BOCs except Mountain Bell received greater total wage gains than their counterparts at AT&T. Although wage growth in the nonunion sector of the telecommunications industry was decelerating, Peoples found that the growth rate still exceeded the wage gains in other industries.

Several explanations may account for the lack of any substantial decline in relative wages after deregulation. First, workers may not have earned rents under regulation. In this case, deregulation will not affect wages. Second, there may not have been any substantial shift in market power among the firms in the industry. In the following chapter of this volume, Crandall will attribute the absence of relative wage decline to the fact that much of the industry continues to be tightly regulated. The unregulated sector employs such a small fraction of the labor force in telecommunications that its impact on the average industry wage is minimal. In that case, future changes in this fraction might still undermine union ability to maintain the wage gap with other industries. Although Crandall acknowledges that the slight decrease in the relative wage of the telephone equipment industry may be the result of competitive forces, the rise of import pressures prior to the fall of the dollar may have also contributed to its decline. Finally, the stability of the telephone wage premium might indicate that the impact of deregulation has been entirely offset by significant improvements in productivity—a result that has seemed to occur in airlines.

From an industrial relations perspective, the divestiture is much more interesting than the deregulation which occurred in telecommunications because it created a natural experiment in which the parties had to reestablish bargaining structures and negotiate rules to govern the movement of workers to the newly established companies. Because the parties had been anticipating the divestiture for years, they were able to begin planning for the transfer of employees long before the reorganization actually occurred. In the 1980 contract the CWA and AT&T negotiated a Memorandum of Agreement (MOA) which guarantees employees continued employment and salary level for five years, moving and travel expenses, continued pension and insurance coverage, and a seven-year preferential right of rehire if they were laid off.[17] The MOA was amended in 1982 and 1983 in what is known as the New Entities Agreements. These guarantee continued application of the bargaining contract and continued recognition of the CWA as the bargaining representative of the transferred employees.

The CWA was also actively pursuing employee protection in the judicial arena. They argued that any changes in the pension plans ought to be determined through collective bargaining. After AT&T submitted its plan for reorganization, the CWA formally objected to it on the grounds that the one-year limit on pension portability was too restrictive. They also contended that breaking up the Bell System pension plan into eight separate plans would open up the possibility that benefits among the operating companies would no longer remain equal.[18] The final Court ruling rejected all of these objections.

Consequently, the CWA turned to the legislative arena to obtain protection for transferred employees. They were successful in obtaining a provision in the Deficit Reduction Act of 1984 which extended the period of pension portability past 1984 for workers earning less than $50,000, and extended the recognition of service credit indefinitely.[19]

Employment security continues to be an important issue with the unions due to the significant reductions in the organized work force from technological change, and the continuing threat that work may be shifted to nonunionized subsidiaries or overseas. In several of the negotiations between the CWA and the RBOCs during 1986, job security was of central importance. Workers at Pacific Telesis received a no-layoff guarantee in exchange for management having more flexibility in work assignments. Employment security was later extended to management and holding company employees and continued in the 1989 agreement. BellSouth agreed to fund a $7.8 million a year career continuation program. At NYNEX, displaced workers won the right to bid on vacancies in nonbargaining unit operations, including NYNEX subsidiaries. Management cannot lay off workers who are eligible for these jobs and willing to take them. Moderate employment security provisions were obtained at US West. As Perry and Cappelli note, job security provisions were conspicuously absent at Bell Atlantic, despite expectations of significant workforce reductions.[20]

In the 1986 negotiations with AT&T, the company agreed to contribute $21 million to an employee retraining program. Although there is a "reassignment pay protection plan" which allows employees to work for three years at their past pay, most of the jobs being eliminated are in top craft occupations, while those opening up are in clerical and administrative positions. Since most of the top craft workers are mature workers, many have opted for early retirement under the supplemental income protection plan.

The CWA continues to lobby for wage and job protection legislation. They have voiced opposition to any lifting of antitrust restraints imposed on the BOCs. The union is also lobbying Congress to require manufacturing of telecommunication equipment domestically.

The divestiture and the subsequent expansion of the RBOCs and AT&T into unregulated markets precipitated two major issues between management and the unions. First, the parties had to decide on the appropriate bargaining structure. Second, the companies had to form a policy toward the possible unionization of their new subsidiaries. Prior to 1984, bargaining in the Bell System was characterized by a high degree of centralization. The CWA had attempted to gain national bargaining for many years before it was actually codified with the 1974 agreement. This centralization was probably a direct outgrowth of restrictions on entry into the industry, which were a result of regulation. But divestiture changed the bargaining arrangements considerably. The 1983 agreement (in which the CWA and IBEW bargained at the same table for wages at AT&T and all the BOCs) was the last agreement signed on a national basis.

The CWA preferred centralized negotiations. Prior to the 1986 bargaining round, it attempted to centralize negotiations at AT&T and to form a single multi-employer unit with the RBOCs. It was successful at AT&T, although the IBEW and CWA bargained in separate negotiations, but there was no possibility of getting the RBOCs to negotiate together. Failing this, the union attempted to obtain regional level negotiations at each RBOC. This was achieved at all companies except US West and Ameritech.

Ameritech was able to settle with the IBEW prior to its settlement with the CWA in the 1986 negotiations. As a result, Ameritech was able to exert considerable pressure on the CWA to sign under similar terms. Both Ameritech and US West also achieved contracts which were not unfavorable to management with the Mountain Bell contract, widely regarded as the worst overall settlement for the union. Thus, decentralization of negotiations seemed to favor management.

In the 1989 negotiations, the CWA again pushed to centralize negotiations at US West, Ameritech and AT&T. Unlike the 1986 negotiations, the CWA and IBEW bargained together ("coordinated bargaining") at AT&T. However, AT&T was able to negotiate different patterns for service (largely organized by the CWA) and manufacturing (largely organized by the IBEW) to reflect differences in cash revenues and cash flows of these businesses.[21] The CWA was successful in combining three separate contracts with the individual BOCs at US West into a single contract. However, CWA was unsuccessful at Ameritech. Ameritech was again able to negotiate an early settlement with the IBEW at Illinois Bell, Ameritech Services and Indiana Bell. The subsequent strikes of CWA employees at the five Ameritech operating companies probably reflected, in part, management's desire to maintain separate negotiations, and the union's desire to centralize these negotiations.

These confrontations on bargaining structure are only one symptom of the overall environment in negotiations between the newly formed companies and their unions. One interesting line of inquiry is whether or not this environment carries over to the companies' position on unionization of its new subsidiaries. In their 1988 paper, Perry and Cappelli investigate this question. They examine each company's policy towards the union in the negotiations for the company's regulated businesses, and compare this with company policy regarding union representation in the new nonregulated subsidiaries. It is often the case there are considerable differences in the company's relationship with

TABLE 10.5
Characterization of Union–Management Relations, 1986

Cooperative	Co-Existence	Contentious
Pacific Telesis	Ameritech	Bell Atlantic
BellSouth	US West	NYNEX
AT&T	Southwestern Bell	

Source: Perry and Cappelli, 1988.

the union at the bargaining table, and its tolerance of union organizing activities in the new subsidiaries.

Perry and Cappelli characterize the current bargaining relationships between each of the telephone companies and the unions as either cooperative, coexisting, or contentious. A summary of their findings is provided in table 10.5.

Both Pacific Telesis and BellSouth have relationships with the union that are labeled cooperative, despite previous years of antipathy. In the 1986 negotiations with Pacific Telesis, the union agreed to remove contractual restrictions of transfers in exchange for a no-layoff guarantee. This alleviated some of the tension between the parties which had arisen during the company's efforts at labor force reductions. Still, Pacific Telesis was the target of a short strike in the 1989 negotiations. In the 1986 negotiations with BellSouth, the company agreed to regional bargaining in return for the union's sanction of contract flexibility with regard to differences across labor and product markets. The 1989 agreement was settled without a strike.

Ameritech, US West and Southwestern Bell have a relationship labeled as "coexistence" by Perry and Cappelli. Relations are generally good. In the 1986 negotiations, however, the strategy of Ameritech and US West was to settle first with the IBEW instead of allowing the two unions to bargain jointly. This alienated the CWA. Since Ameritech followed the same strategy in the 1989 negotiations, their position of "coexistence" might be tenuous. Perry and Cappelli suggest that because Southwestern Bell includes many states with right-to-work laws, the union is weakened, and this creates a tension in the relationship between the two parties.

Both NYNEX and Bell Atlantic have a contentious relationship with their unions. According to Perry and Cappelli, in the case of Bell Atlantic, the source of militancy is management. While the company has been willing to negotiate wage changes at the regional level, many of the problems have concerned work rules and grievances procedures which are negotiated at the individual companies. These local issues have caused significant difficulties in arriving at settlements. In the case of NYNEX, the unions have been historically militant. Perry and Cappelli indicate that this is a product of both the local labor-market conditions and a rivalry in this area between the CWA and the IBEW. While the two unions attempted to coordinate bargaining at the same table in the 1989 negotiations, NYNEX refused. Both NYNEX and Bell Atlantic faced strikes in their 1989 negotiations. The strike at NYNEX was particularly bitter and lasted over 100 days. Financial analysts told the *New York Times* that NYNEX was forced to take a tough stance "because much of its operations lie in dense urban areas, making its operating costs higher than those of the other companies."[22] More likely, the dense urban area makes future competition for local service a greater possibility in New York than in some other regions. High wages would put NYNEX at a competitive disadvantage in dealing with new competitors.

The unregulated sector of the telecommunications industry is largely unorganized. The union's attempts at organizing subsidiaries that have arisen in the nonregulated sector have met with a variety of reactions from the telephone companies which range from hospitable (AT&T, BellSouth) to neutral (Ameritech, NYNEX) to hostile (Bell Atlantic, Pacific Telesis, Southwestern Bell, and US West).

Both AT&T and BellSouth have been hospitable to union organizing of their subsidiaries. The New Entities Agreement between the CWA and AT&T ensures continued representation rights in any unit to emerge from existing functions or reallocation of existing employees.[23] Problems may arise in the future, however, if unorganized companies are acquired, or if competition in the industry intensifies and AT&T's rivals remain unorganized. BellSouth has been diversifying into the equipment market, and has agreed to union representation in its new subsidiaries.

Neither Ameritech nor NYNEX has opposed union organizing efforts. This is probably because employment at Ameritech's subsidiaries is only a fraction of its total work force, and NYNEX has not diversified much beyond its core industry. Bell Atlantic, Pacific Telesis, and Southwestern Bell have ambitiously launched into the unregulated market. Each company has also vigorously opposed union organizing attempts at any new subsidiaries.

Thus as Perry and Cappelli point out, the likelihood that a company will resist unionization of their unregulated subsidiaries appears to be correlated with how extensively they intend to diversify into the competitive sector. It is less likely to be linked with the company's relationship with the union in its regulated business. The future environment of union-management negotiations in the industry may therefore depend on regulatory decisions which open up new unregulated markets for the BOCs. The companies can be expected to become more militant in negotiations in an attempt to compete in labor costs with competitors who are likely to be nonunion.

As in airlines and trucking, deregulation in telecommunications brings on mixed blessings for labor. On the one hand, lifting the hand of regulation from some markets will allow firms to compete more rigorously, decrease prices and increase output. As a result, expansion of employment will occur as the firms move into these new areas. Ameritech, for example, has been able to expand employment, even though technological change has reduced the need for workers in the regulated sector. On the other hand, competition in these new areas is likely to be more severe than in the past. Some firms will take this as a sign to increase their competitiveness by reducing their labor costs. This means either a nonunion or a hostile union atmosphere. In trucking, deregulation caused virtually all markets to become highly competitive. With very little room for significant increases in productivity, this change naturally led to reduced wages and lower employment for union drivers who did not accept significant reductions in their relative wages. In airlines, significant productivity increases and continued market power (in part brought on by the new "hub and spoke" technology) cushioned the deregulation impact for some workers (although not all). It seems that telecommunications is likely to follow the airlines' example over the next few years, since many companies have regulated markets in which they experience relatively little competition, as well as newer, deregulated markets in which the competition is fierce. If experience in airlines is a good indication, a variety of approaches will ultimately be taken: some firms will follow the Frank Lorenzo lead while others will not. Some firms will be able to remain competitive even while paying relatively high union wages, because they are relatively insulated from low-wage competition or because they are leaders in technological development or in improvements in productivity.

ENDNOTES

1. Nancy Rose, "Labor Rent Sharing and Regulation: Evidence from the Trucking Industry," *Journal of Political Economy* (December 1987), 95:1146–78.

2. David Card, "Deregulation and Labor Earnings in the Airline Industry,"

Princeton University Industrial Relations Section Working Paper #247, January 1989.

3. Peter Cappelli and Charles R. Perry, "Bargaining in Telecommunications After Divestiture," Wharton School Working Paper Series #628, December 1986.

4. Ronald G. Ehrenberg, *The Regulatory Process and Labor Earnings* (New York: Academic Press, 1979), p. 40.

5. Wallace Hendricks, "Telecommunications" in D. Lipsky and C. Donn, eds., *Collective Bargaining in American Industry* (Lexington, Mass.: Lexington Books, 1987), p. 130.

6. Jerrold Oppenheim, "The Quest for Alternatives to Regulation: Are the Benefits of Competition in Public Utility Markets Worth Their Price." Presented before a Symposium of the Public Service Commission of the District of Columbia, "Regulatory Issues Posed by a Competition and Technological Change in State Telephone Markets," October 6, 1988, pp. 4, 8.

7. James Peoples, "The Impact of Regulatory Change on Wage Levels in Telecommunications," Working Paper Rutgers University, Department of Economics, 1987.

8. Michael Denny and Melvyn Fuss, "The Effect of Factor Prices and Technological Change on the Occupational Demand for Labor: Evidence from Canadian Telecommunications," *Journal of Human Resources* (Spring 1983), 18(2):161–76.

9. James Peoples, "The Impact of Regulatory Change on Wage Levels in Telecommunications," Working Paper Rutgers University, Department of Economics, 1987, p. 14.

10. L. Lynch and P. Osterman, "Technological Innovation and Employment in Telecommunications," *Industrial Relations* (Spring 1989), 28(2):188–205.

11. James Peoples, "Wage Outcomes Following the Divestiture of AT&T," Xerox, Rutgers University, May 24, 1989.

12. BNA (Bureau of National Affairs), Daily Labor Report #116, June 19, 1989, p. B-1.

13. BNA, Daily Labor Report #156, August 5, 1989, p. A-9.

14. BNA, Daily Labor Report #151, August 8, 1989, p. A-11.

15. Frank J. Prial, "NYNEX Reaches Tentative Pact with 60,000 Striking Workers," *New York Times*, November 14, 1989, pp. B1-2.

16. See note 9.

17. BNA, Daily Labor Report #19, January 28, 1982, p. C-1.

18. BNA, Daily Labor Report #31, February 16, 1983, p. A-6.

19. See note 5.

20. Charles R. Perry and Peter Cappelli, "Labor Relations in Telecommunications," University of Pennsylvania Discussion Paper #37, July 1988.

21. Janet Guyon and Albert R. Karr, "AT&T, Two Unions Reach Three-Year Pact with Only Modest Wage-Benefit Gains," *Wall Street Journal*, May 30, 1989, p. A17.

22. Supra at note 15, p. B2.

23. See note 20.

11

Efficiency and Productivity

■

ROBERT W. CRANDALL

■

M. ISHAQ NADIRI
GERALD W. BROCK
GERALD R. FAULHABER

Robert W. Crandall

When the consent decree was announced in 1982, many Americans were shocked and disbelieving. Could the U.S. government possibly think that "breaking up the most efficient telephone company in the world" would contribute to economic welfare? Service quality would undoubtedly suffer as standardization was sacrificed to the cruel forces of competition. Costs would surely rise and rates would soon follow. The crown jewel of the U.S. research establishment, Bell Labs, would doubtlessly lose its ability to pursue crucially important basic research.

The divestiture was just one of a succession of events that followed the FCC's early attempts to introduce competition into a regulated industry.[1] Some economists argued that competition was impossible in telephony.[2] Others argued that AT&T may have had an unsustainable natural monopoly.[3] Still others thought that even if AT&T were a natural monopoly, it sacrificed the critical but stagnant portions of this monopoly in a cynical attempt to rid itself of the strictures of a previous decree.[4]

It may be too early to determine if separating AT&T from its local operating companies contributed on balance to economic welfare, but it is not too early to look for some of the manifestations most feared by the decree's critics. I shall examine the rate of growth of telephone rates, employment, output, and productivity in the industry to see if the industry has begun to perform as the critics feared it might. Because other chapters in this volume discuss the implications of the MFJ on the efficiency of relative telephone rates and service quality, I do not address the rebalancing of rates and the quality of service since 1984. Nor do I attempt to analyze the effects of the MFJ on research and development, other than through its indirect effect on productivity.

If telephony is a natural monopoly, it is presumably so because of the economies of scale or scope in the delivery of various services. Substantial scale economies are thought to exist in long-distance transmission, but not in the provision of access service.[5] In the latter market, there may be economies of density, but not of scale. A single metropolitan area will have many exchanges and several switching centers. Thus, it may be true that a single exchange is more efficient than competing exchanges in a given small area, but it is far from clear that efficiency requires that the owners of adjacent exchanges be part of the same enterprise.

The issues in the 1974 AT&T antitrust suit (and its predecessors) involved the use of vertical integration, either to avoid the strictures of rate regulation, or to monopolize what would otherwise be competitive markets. As a result, in the decree settling the case, the "bottleneck" monopolies—the Bell local exchange companies—were divorced from the other functions of AT&T—namely, long-distance services, manufacturing, and enhanced "information" services. It is this vertical fragmentation that is ostensibly the source of the critics' wrath, not the sacrifice of scale economies.

At first blush, it seems unlikely that vertical fragmentation of the U.S. telephone network has been the source of *static* efficiency losses. Surely, the divested BOCs can arrange to buy from AT&T or from other suppliers the equipment that they once transferred internally. In fact, it is likely that the vertical fragmentation has led to more efficient procurement decisions. Moreover, there is no a priori reason to believe that AT&T's long-distance operations are now unable to interconnect with the BOCs as efficiently as they did when they were part of the same company. In short, it would be surprising if the U.S. sacrificed static efficiencies because it failed to keep a vertically integrated telephone sector.

The more likely argument against the vertical divestiture derives from the process of innovation. A vertically integrated AT&T could develop new equipment for delivering services through its combined long-distance and local-exchange operations. The divested BOCs, prohibited from engaging in manufacturing, are hostages to equipment suppliers and to those funding research and development, who have no stake in the delivery of local access/exchange services and could not easily obtain one. The crucial links between R&D, manufacturing, and information/communications services must have been the major reason why AT&T chose to accept a consent decree of the form of the MFJ. Otherwise, it might have chosen to offer to jettison Bell Laboratories and Western Electric to settle the antitrust suit.

On the other hand, divestiture freed the BOCs from Western Electric and forced the latter to compete with domestic foreign sellers of telephone equipment. Presumably, this competition would place downward pressure on equipment prices and perhaps even induce a more rapid adoption of new technologies.

If local access/exchange service were competitive (or contestable), the alleged evils of vertical integration would be mitigated, and we might return to a world of vertically integrated telecommunications firms, all competing with one another. This presupposes that in a competitive world there would be no need for regulation, and that the traditional capital equipment supplier/regulated firm integration would not be the source of the "evasion of the regulatory constraint" argument. We are not yet in this world, apparently, and as a result are faced with the prospects of continued vertical fragmentation of the telephone industry.

A common criticism of the MFJ is that it raised local telephone rates and, as a result, the average price of telephone service. A review of the data, however, suggests that the reversal in real telephone rates occurred at least for three years before divestiture. In 1981–1982, as inflation began to subside, telephone companies began to seek rate increases to make up for the rate compression that had occurred in the inflationary 1970s. Many of these increases were granted (table 11.1).

Real local access/exchange rates rose substantially even before the FCC began to reprice telephone service through its interstate access rate policy that substituted monthly SLCs for interexchange carrier access fees. Real interstate and even intrastate toll rates have fallen dramatically during the 1980s, in part because of the repricing of access

TABLE 11.1
The Trend in Real Consumer Price Indexes for Telephone Service,
1964–1988
(1977 = 100)

	All Telephone Service	Local Service	Interstate Toll	Intrastate Toll
1964	152.2	NA	NA	NA
1965	147.4	NA	NA	NA
1966	140.4	NA	NA	NA
1967	138.2	NA	NA	NA
1968	132.2	NA	NA	NA
1969	127.5	NA	NA	NA
1970	121.8	NA	NA	NA
1971	122.5	NA	NA	NA
1972	125.2	NA	NA	NA
1973	121.0	NA	NA	NA
1974	113.6	NA	NA	NA
1975	107.4	NA	NA	NA
1976	105.2	NA	NA	NA
1977	100.0	100.0	100.0	100.0
1978	93.9	94.0	92.1	93.1
1979	84.2	84.0	82.2	84.5
1980	76.0	77.4	73.4	73.4
1981	75.0	78.2	72.1	68.5
1982	77.8	82.1	74.8	69.0
1983	80.3	86.1	74.0	71.5
1984	83.4	94.2	69.4	72.3
1985	83.7	98.1	64.2	70.5
1986	86.1	106.0	58.6	69.1
1987	82.6	107.4	48.1	65.4
1988	79.0	104.6	44.4	60.9
Average Percentage Change:				
1977–83	−3.7	−2.5	−5.0	−5.6
1983–88	−0.3	+3.9	−10.2	−3.2

Source: Bureau of Labor Statistics.
Note: All indexes are CPI indexes deflated by CPI-U.

charges. The overall result, however, has been a rise in the weighted average of telephone rates contained in the consumer price index (CPI), an increase that has probably been exaggerated somewhat by the historical weights applied to the various services.[6]

It is interesting that the CPI for telephone service rose more rapidly in 1981–1983 than in the first few years after divestiture. More importantly, the rise in real rates has now stopped. It is likely that real consumer telephone rates will now resume the 1960s and 1970s rate of decline, and perhaps fall even more rapidly as new technology proliferates in the telephone network.

Telephone rates do not provide dispositive evidence on the effects of the MFJ on productive efficiency. Virtually all telephone service is still regulated. Regulators could have been allowing rates to rise in the face of declining costs in the early 1980s. Indeed, the market-book ratios for all major telephone company stocks rose substantially in the 1980s as inflation and regulatory pressures abated (table 11.2).

I have not attempted to estimate statistical cost functions for telephone companies as a means of inferring the effects of the MFJ on carrier efficiency. Rather, I look at input prices and productivity to gain some insight into cost behavior in the industry since divestiture.

An important element in both the 1949 and 1974 AT&T antitrust suits was the theory that the vertical integration of Western Electric and AT&T had led to excessive capital equipment costs. Freeing the BOCs from the necessity of purchasing Western Electric equipment should have eliminated a large part of this alleged problem.

We know that AT&T, since 1983, has lost a sizable share of the BOC market to competitors,[7] but this loss may be due to a number of factors, not just lower prices or better technology. The increase in competition in central office and transmission equipment markets should have placed downward pressure on equipment prices, and stimulated more rapid technological change in equipment. AT&T had lagged badly in developing a time-division, stored program-control digital switch for local exchange operations. It has now fought back successfully with its #5ESS switch. It has also made up some lost ground in the PBX market.

Given the lead time required to develop major new telecommunications technologies, it is undoubtedly too early to tell whether the vertical fragmentation of the telephone network has proved beneficial. However, the early results appear favorable. Fiber optics is developing very rapidly. Terminal equipment prices are falling rather dramatically.[8] And real digital switch prices are falling at about twice their rate of decline in the years before divestiture.[9]

Surprisingly, relative wage rates have not fallen in the telephone service industry. In trucking and airlines, there is substantial evidence that deregulation has reduced the rents earned by labor.[10] Unfortunately, the telephone industry has not been deregulated. Local telephone service remains rather tightly regulated in most states, and most

TABLE 11.2
Market-Book Ratios for Telephone Company Equities, 1964–1988

	AT&T	GTE	Rochester Telephone	United Telephone	Continental Telephone
1964	1.92	2.95	2.26	3.26	2.82
1965	1.63	3.34	2.33	3.45	3.52
1966	1.43	2.90	2.07	3.16	3.71
1967	1.25	2.54	1,84	3.26	3.47
1968	1.28	2.33	2.06	3.32	3.05
1969	1.14	1.77	1.56	2.15	1.98
1970	1.10	1.80	1.91	1.73	2.30
1971	0.98	1.72	1.87	1.70	2.04
1972	1.12	1.55	2.16	1.83	2.24
1973	1.02	1.23	1.33	1.29	1.45
1974	0.87	0.82	0.74	1.04	0.89
1975	0.94	1.17	0.80	1.12	1.01
1976	1.15	1.36	0.99	1.48	1.39
1977	1.01	1.22	1.00	1.36	1.14
1978	1.00	1.04	1.02	1.26	1.06
1979	0.82	0.99	0.98	1.26	1.12
1980	0.73	0.95	1.00	1.06	1.09
1981	0.87	1.08	1.28	1.19	1.12
1982	0.86	1.33	1.17	1.13	1.10
1983	0.88	1.30	1.25	1.09	1.28
1984	1.13[a]	1.12	1.28	1.17	1.27
1985	1.41[a]	1.43	1.43	1.40	1.34
1986	1.73[a]	1.68	1.60	1.52	1.48
1987	1.52[a]	1.48	1.48	1.62	1.58
1988	1.56[a]	1.79	1.76	2.57	2.03

Source: Company reports; Standard & Poor's.
[a] AT&T and Divested Regional Holding (Operating) Companies.

industry employment is to be found in the local operating companies. AT&T's long-distance service remains regulated. Only the new OCCs (other common carriers) are essentially unregulated, but they employ no more than 3 percent of the industry's labor force. Thus, perhaps it is not surprising that the telephone industry's wage costs have not fallen relative to other industries. (table 11.3).

In the telephone *equipment* industry, wages have fallen slightly relative to all manufacturing. The increase in competition facilitated

TABLE 11.3

Average Hourly Earnings for Production or Nonsupervisory Workers, 1972–1988

($/hour)

	Total Private (nonfarm)	Telephone Communications Services	Telephone and Telegraph Equipment
1972	3.70	4.10	4.18
1973	3.94	4.45	4.45
1974	4.24	4.90	4.73
1975	4.53	5.61	5.23
1976	4.86	6.33	5.70
1977	5.25	6.89	6.28
1978	5.69	7.50	6.73
1979	6.16	8.07	7.50
1980	6.66	8.72	8.24
1981	7.25	9.80	9.15
1982	7.68	10.66	9.86
1983	8.02	11.45	10.27
1984	8.32	12.00	10.69
1985	8.57	12.45	10.82
1986	8.76	12.85	10.94
1987	8.98	13.21	11.17
1988	9.29	13.46	11.62
	Annual Percentage Change		
1972–81	7.5	9.7	8.7
1981–88	3.5	4.5	3.4

Source: Bureau of Labor Statistics, *Employment and Earnings.*

by the MFJ is undoubtedly partly responsible, but the sharp rise in import pressures in 1983–1986 prior to the fall of the dollar must have added to this downward pressure on equipment manufacturing wages (table 11.3).

Perhaps the most surprising effect of the MFJ has been upon telephone industry employment. After rising more or less steadily through 1981, telephone industry employment began to fall dramatically in 1982. Between 1981 and 1986, the industry reduced its workforce by more than 18 percent (table 11.4). Labor productivity has continued to

TABLE 11.4
Employment and Labor Productivity for Telephone
Communications, 1975–1988

	Total Employment[a] (000s)	Production Workers[a] (000s)	Output per Employee Hour[b] (1977 = 100)
1975	966.6	739.8	85.9
1976	953.2	727.8	93.3
1977	957.3	722.4	100.0
1978	994.8	738.8	105.8
1979	1048.2	772.1	110.8
1980	1072.2	779.3	118.1
1981	1077.3	783.6	124.4
1982	1071.8	787.1	129.1
1983	956.0	701.0	145.1
1984	953.6	712.5	143.0
1985	920.9	687.3	149.9
1986	881.4	655.6	158.9
1987	893.7	661.8	166.1
1988	908.3	666.6	NA

[a] Bureau of Labor Statistics, *Employment and Earnings.*
[b] Bureau of Labor Statistics, *Productivity Measurers for Selected Industries,* SIC4811.

grow at about 5 percent since 1984—a rate equal to the average for the industry in the 1960s and 1970s.

It was widely believed that liberalized entry and divestiture would sharply increase the riskiness of holding telephone company equities, thereby raising the cost of capital to the industry. In fact, the riskiness of AT&T's equities as measured by p, in the capital-asset pricing model, has stabilized at a level approximately equal to its 1960–1980 average of 0.64. Using monthly data for the 1984–1987 period to estimate the capital asset pricing model, I find the estimate of p is 0.66 for AT&T and between 0.50 and 0.66 for the BOCs.

This rather cursory review suggests that the price of capital equipment may have fallen due to divestiture, but wage rates and the cost of capital have been little affected. The relative use of labor, however, has fallen substantially, suggesting substantial improvements in efficiency.

A better measure of industry efficiency or the rate of technical change in the industry is the rate of growth of total factor productivity (TFP). I have attempted to calculate TFP growth for the entire telephone (and telegraph) industry over the period 1961–1988, and to look for any sharp breaks that might have been caused by the competitive changes in the 1970s or the MFJ in the 1980s.

To estimate TFP, I have constructed consistent series of industry output, value added, labor input, material input, and capital stock for all common carrier, local exchange, long-distance, and telegraph carriers for whom data are available from 1960 through 1988. The output measure is constructed by deflating industry revenues from various services—local, interexchange, etc.—by the appropriate Producer Price Indexes. To obtain a measure of industry value-added, the output series was multiplied by the share of industry costs[11] estimated to be accounted for by capital and labor.[12]

Total labor input is calculated by multiplying BLS measure of average weekly hours by industry-reported employment data adjusted for labor quality per Christensen.[13] Capital services are assumed to be proportional to the level of the capital stock. The capital stock measure is equal to 74 percent of the gross capital stock, plus 25 percent of the net capital stock calculated from industry investment data by the perpetual inventory method.[14]

Material input is total (noncapital) purchases by telephone companies deflated by the GNP implicit price deflator. There was a slowdown in capital formation in 1981–1988 and a sharp decline in labor input since the announcement of divestiture.

The standard Tornquist measure of TFP is calculated by using income-share weights from the FCC's *Statistics of Communications Common Carriers* and USTA *Telephone Statistics.* The resulting three-factor (labor, capital, and materials) and two-factor (labor and capital) TFP growth estimates are shown in table 11.5.

Estimated total factor productivity grows substantially more rapidly in the 1971–1983 period than in 1961–1970, the period of no competition in interexchange services. Estimated TFP growth declines in 1984–1985, a decline that may be a reflection of measurement problems. The divestiture changed the structure of the BOCs and AT&T so radically that it is impossible to know if data reported to the FCC in 1984 are comparable with 1983 and earlier years.[15]

After 1985, total factor productivity resumed its growth at a rate in excess of 4 percent. Thus, TFP now appears to be growing even more rapidly than before divestiture. More importantly, TFP appears to rise with increases in competition over the 1970–1987 period. Given the slowdown in industry growth in the 1980s, the continued acceleration in TFP is all the more remarkable if there are increasing returns to

TABLE 11.5
Estimate of Total Factor Productivity Growth for the U.S.
Telecommunications Sector, 1961–1987
(average annual growth rate, %)

Period	Output	Value-Added	Total Factor Productivity 3-factor	2-factor
1961–70	8.2	8.0	2.8	2.7
1971–83	7.2	8.2	3.9	4.1
1984–87	5.1	3.6	3.2	3.2

scale in certain segments of the industry. It is important, however, to stress that all of these conclusions on productivity growth must be tempered by the realization that the data on which they are based are imperfect at best.[16]

Despite the rather smooth short-term transition of the industry to its new vertically fragmented state, and the desirable changes in relative prices that have been triggered by the FCC, there are a number of nagging problems to be resolved.

First, rates remain regulated at the state and federal levels, generally based upon some rate-of-return concept. Attempts to replace federal rate-of-return regulation with a less distorting form of regulation have been stalled by the Congress. In 1989, the FCC managed to introduce a limited form of price cap regulation for AT&T, a considerable accomplishment in light of the political opposition to price caps.

The prospects for full deregulation of interexchange services are obviously very poor at this time. The continued regulation of AT&T while new entrants are free to set rates without government involvement creates the obvious political pressures to protect nascent carriers by keeping AT&T rates artificially high.[17] Equally important are the political forces on state regulators who generally use intrastate toll rates and business access rates to subsidize residential access service. These distortions create obvious incentives to avoid the use of the public switched network.

In addition, there is no blueprint for releasing the divested BOCs from the line-of-business restrictions of the decree. Judge Greene appears reluctant to allow major departures from these restrictions as long as the BOCs have a "bottleneck" on local access. But state regulators are not likely to be hospitable to breaking this bottleneck, as long as they are intent on using cross-subsidies to satisfy political claimants.

At the first Triennial Review, the BOCs and the DOJ made very little headway in persuading Judge Greene to liberalize the restrictions on the BOCs. The "bypass" threat was simply not demonstrated in the documents filed before the court.[18] More recently, the BOCs and GTE filed reports before the FCC that show that about 5 percent of total minutes of use are now being syphoned off by facilities bypass.[19] If this share grows appreciably, it may suggest to the court that rate distortions are creating major incentives for users to avoid the use of regulated circuits wherever possible.

Perhaps the most disturbing evidence that regulation and the line-of-business restraints are creating incentives for unregulated private telecommunications networks is the sharp decline in the growth of output on the public network in the 1980s (see table 11.5). There is no deceleration in the apparent demand for telecommunications, as evidenced by the continuing growth in equipment sales, but the public network is growing much more slowly than in the 1970s. Capital stock growth for the public network since divestiture has been less than half of its pre-divestiture levels. If this shift from public to private networks is driven by distorted rate signals provided by regulatory authorities, the efficiency of telecommunications delivery will obviously be affected.

Finally, it is important to keep in mind that any temporal analysis of efficiency in telecommunications service delivery involves comparing today's performance under regulation with yesterday's performance under regulation. No one is able to compare current performance with that produced by a market unfettered by the deadening influence of rate-of-return regulation.

It would be presumptuous to suggest I have demonstrated the MFJ has had no unfavorable static efficiency effects on the domestic telecommunications sector. But even if I had, this conclusion would undoubtedly be of little long-term relevance. Telecommunications is an industry buffeted by rapid technical change. The real question for policymakers is whether a regulated vertically fragmented industry is more likely to encourage technical progress than a regulated vertically integrated industry, a deregulated vertically fragmented industry, or a deregulated vertically integrated industry. The post-divestiture experience is not likely to give us enough evidence to draw meaningful conclusions on this issue. My analysis simply argues divestiture has not created static efficiency losses in the delivery of telecommunications services.

M. Ishaq Nadiri

Robert Crandall has addressed a significant public policy issue—i.e., the effect of the Bell System divestiture in promoting the efficiency of the telecommunications services in the United States. This is an important but difficult question to answer: first, it involves comparing the performance of an industry structure that no longer exists with that of the new one that has replaced it; and second, the timespan for the new industry structure is not sufficiently long to provide firm conclusions. Nonetheless, Crandall provides an interesting and valuable set of results.

Crandall looks at a number of performance indices in the telecommunication industry and reaches the tentative judgment that there have been efficiency gains in provision of telecommunication services as a result of the divestiture. This judgment is based on four facts: the telephone rates, especially inter- and intrastate toll rates, have declined substantially in the post-divestiture period; the input prices, especially in price of capital, have fallen (though this is not true for wage rates); the level of employment, especially in the AT&T and BOC family of firms, has declined substantially; and both labor productivity and total factor productivity, as measures of efficiency, have improved substantially in the post-divestiture period.

His results also point to a disturbing phenomenon—a substantial decline in the rate of capital formation after the divestiture. The rate of investment declined from 5.5 percent in the 1971–1983 period to 2.6 percent in 1985–1987. Crandall correctly draws our attention to another problem: the incomplete deregulation of AT&T and the imposition of several restrictions on the activities of BOCs may have created an incentive to bypass the public telecommunication system.

I find most of Crandall's arguments very interesting and relevant; however, I shall raise a number of questions and issues. First, the dramatic decline in employment which Crandall reports requires further analysis; it would be important to identify the reasons for this decline. What role may have been played by changes in relative prices, demand changes, and technological change to generate such a decline in employment? Were there other causes? Similarly, to what should be attributed the decline in investment in the post-divestiture period? Could it be due to better utilization of existing capital stock, or some other factor?

The productivity indices reported by Crandall are somewhat fragile. If one includes the negative 1984 figures for both labor and productivity and total factor productivity, the magnitudes of these two indices change substantially. Also, there are years in the pre-divestiture period in which total factor productivity was as high as those reported for the post-divestiture period. If the high growth rate of total factor productivity in 1985–1987 is to be attributed to efficiencies due to divestiture, what would be the causes of the even higher rates of productivity growth observed for 1978 and 1979? A much more direct relationship between divestiture and productivity growth needs to be established before the inference of increased efficiency is totally acceptable.

Crandall's productivity calculation rests on the assumption of constant return technology. There are a number of studies which suggest the presence of fairly large economies of scale in this industry, at least for the pre-divestiture period. It would be important to determine how the contribution of scale of operation has affected the degree of efficiency in the industry. Similarly, we might want to know the degree to which economies of scope have changed between the two periods to which economies affect the indices of efficiency reported by Crandall. Further, there is the problem of resources used up in order to change from the pre-divestiture industry to the new post-divestiture structure. These adjustment costs could be substantial and could materially affect the magnitudes of the labor, investment, and total factor productivity.

Crandall does not specifically address the effect of divestiture on the R&D activities in the telecommunication industry. I believe the effect of divestiture on R&D investment in the telephone industry will be the most telling influence on the industry's future growth, efficiency, and structure. What has happened to the size and mix of R&D investment due to the divestiture, and how in turn these developments have affected the cost structure of the telephone industry, have a great deal to tell us about the industry's future, and in particular, its long-term efficiency.

Most of the issues I raise cannot be analyzed with the methodology adopted by Crandall. An analysis based on formal modeling of the cost structure of the industry would be required to identify the specific contributions of input prices, demand, scale, adjustment costs, degree of economies of scope, technological change in pre- and post-divestiture periods.

What Crandall has contributed is a look at first order consequences of divestiture. He has highlighted some important events of the post-divestiture period, such as low rate of capital formation, dramatic decline in employment and potential bypass of the public telecommunication system due to regulatory effects. His work will stimulate further discussion of the important issues he has raised.

Gerald W. Brock

Due to the efforts the FCC is currently making to institute a price cap form of regulation, productivity is taking a primary role in public policy debate. In the process, we are adding considerably to the education stock of our country with regard to technical economic issues. For example, the Commission is now sending information to Congress on the differences between two-factor and three-factor productivity.

Price caps are a relatively simple scheme, at least in theory. In practice it becomes complex, as does the calculation of productivity itself. Rather than looking at the observed or predicted one-year cost of telephone companies, we look at the expected productivity based primarily upon past productivity and then use that as an adjustment to expected prices in the future. Price caps focus great attention on the expected productivity, because one percentage point difference in the productivity can mean a swing over the next four years of something between three and four billion dollars between consumers and stockholders. Consequently, there is a great deal of effort and many lawyers engaged in attempting to prove that productivity is one number versus another.

For that reason, I am particularly happy to see this new study by Robert Crandall. I do have some concerns, however. First, it is not perfectly clear exactly how output was measured. Obviously the output measure is critical. Crandall indicates he took a combination of revenues and deflated them by the appropriate producer price indexes. The normal pattern is either to use a specific price index related directly to those services, and therefore construct a revenue index of the services, or to build up an index of physical output. Each of two very well-known studies covering some of the same period, one by Christensen which was presented in the divestiture case and one by Bell Labs, used one of those two methods—Christensen, a physical output; and Bell Labs, an index. For both of those, I have compared the rate of growth of output numbers with those of Crandall's. In general, they both suggest lower growth in output numbers than does Crandall. It would be of some interest to know how the various output measures affect Crandall's results.

Second, although I ought to be proud that Crandall has used the FCC's *Statistics of Communications Common Carriers,* I know what goes into those statistics, and that makes me a little nervous. In particular, I wonder whether Crandall picked up all of the nondominant interexchange carrier output. The FCC does not require full reports from nondominant carriers. Crandall may have obtained revenue figures from other sources, but it would be of interest to know how well he is tracking the effectively deregulated parts of the industry. Anyone who looks at our FCC numbers has to be very careful, and must recognize that the universe measured by our statistics is gradually shrinking as the effectively deregulated sector grows.

As an aside, I should also put out a general caution concerning the many hazards in working with telephone statistics. In the Commission's Common Carrier Bureau, we are making an effort to clarify the statistics. The FCC's Industry Analysis Division has been asked to develop a meaningful statistical series, but it will not be an easy task. There are very well-known problems when you are looking at long-term comparisons of long-distance versus local rates, because the separation ratios have changed. In the post-divestiture period, we have deregulated some companies and have made very large changes in the structure of prices. These changes have increased the difficulty of interpreting statistical series. Statistical interpretation is further complicated by the fact that on January 1, 1988, we adopted a new accounting system and also made a number of major changes in the separations rules, changes in the accounting treatment of pension expenses, and changes in the costs the companies are required to capitalize.

All of these changes create difficulties in attempts to develop a time-series statistical analysis. The FCC hopes to be able to provide better statistics for research. But my caution and my plea to anyone seriously trying to use these statistics is to seek assistance from our people in the Industry Analysis Division to ensure an accurate understanding of what the numbers represent, and what kinds of adjustments are made to them.

The Common Carrier Bureau has done a number of studies of productivity because of the current interest in a price cap approach. Because there are problems in constructing physical output measures for total factor productivity, we have also measured the dual of total factor productivity. In a regulated industry in which prices are limited to cost, the price index itself is a measure of productivity. The price index measures changes in the cost function, which is a dual of the production function, and therefore the price index measures changes in total factor productivity. Over the last fifty years the telephone CPI has declined about two percent per year relative to the overall CPI. That is one measure of the net total factor productivity. By net productivity, I mean the productivity in this industry above the average productivity in the economy that would be embedded in the price index. Consistent with results that Crandall, Christensen, and others have obtained, the FCC's Common Carrier Bureau has observed a slight rising trend in net productivity. Instead of the 2-percent fifty-year average, the average productivity improvement over the last ten years has been about 2.6 percent.

We have also attempted to develop productivity measures from the price indexes for the post-divestiture period on a disaggregate basis, looking separately at AT&T and the interstate portion of the local exchange carriers. For AT&T we have been able to develop a measure of productivity improvement with some confidence and have determined AT&T's net productivity gain to be 2.4 percent per year. With regard to the local exchange carriers, there are so many adjustments to be made, we still lack complete confidence in any of the numbers we have seen or have produced. We are still working to refine those measurements.

To summarize, productivity analysis is taking on increasing importance, not only as an academic pursuit or as a tool for evaluating broad public policies, but also in setting specific regulated prices. We at the FCC are continuing to attempt to refine the productivity numbers in the telephone industry. I greatly welcome the Crandall study, but I have some concerns about certain of its technical components.

Gerald R. Faulhaber

Robert Crandall has done his usual excellent job of tackling a tough issue. However, I think he would agree that his effort is merely a start, and much still needs to be done in studying efficiency and productivity in telecommunications.

Before making some general comments about divestiture and efficiency, I should point out an omission in Crandall's discussion. His table 11.5 unfortunately reveals only sketchily how output and capital stock are calculated. The standard measurement trick in the service sector (where we cannot count physical output because we do not know what it is) is to deflate revenues by a price deflator. But there is general agreement that telecommunications prices track quantities badly: most local calls are priced at zero, toll call prices most likely carry a subsidy burden, etc. Clearly, as real output proportions change, as is likely with the changing pattern of prices since divestiture, this approach to output estimation is poor at best.

Crandall and others in this volume have appropriately emphasized that, although the actual divestiture occurred at a particular point in time, the event which we normally subsume under the rubric of divestiture really goes back almost a decade, to the procompetitive policies of the FCC in the mid to late 1970s. The divestiture is simply the most public symbol of a very long process of introducing new players into the telecommunications game in the name of competition. When viewed in this light, we should expand our view of what constitutes "divestiture" to include, for example, the FCC CPE registration decision.

If I am allowed the license to include registration within the penumbra of divestiture, I would suggest that there were five major efficiency-affecting changes that occurred in association with this more broadly defined divestiture.

The *least* politically affected efficiency change was the very substantial market entry and product proliferation that occurred subsequent to the FCC registration decision. This change affected both the *price* at which CPE could be purchased, but even more importantly, the *set of products* consumers could purchase. The market changed from a rental market of plain vanilla (but absolutely bullet proof) telephone sets, to a highly diverse high-volume consumer electronic market. My unsupported view is that the efficiency gains from this change were very large.

The *most* affected efficiency change was the tremendous outpouring of state regulatory generosity to the BOCs just before and after the divestiture, when they feared that "their" BOCs were about to go "belly up." Difficult though it is to imagine today, there was great public sympathy for the BOCs just after the announcement of the MFJ in early 1982. Many state regulators feared the telephone behemoths under their care would be in dire financial straits. Local rates increased significantly over this two-year period. Since the service in question, access, is highly inelastic, the efficiency losses were small, but the transfers were rather great.

Similarly, the FCC made sure that AT&T's long-distance rates fully reflected every reduction the Commission engineered in carrier access charges. As a result, the period since divestiture has been marked by aggressively declining long-distance rates, just as all we economists predicted. But my guess is that the cause of that decline was due more to FCC pressure than to the competitive pressure of William McGowan and his colleagues.

On the supply side, the big post-divestiture news (but no big surprise) was that all parts of the old Bell System were overstaffed. The BOCs' as well as AT&T's blood flowed thick and fast. Crandall documents a reduction of 18 percent in the work force; I estimate it was closer to 35 percent. There are two views of this reduction: it was a human tragedy, and it was a substantial efficiency gain. I think both views are accurate.

Finally, two changes occurred on the supply side of long-distance. First, AT&T decided it had facilities sufficient to last for a very long time if only they were used more efficiently than in the past. So its construction program slowed substantially. The second change was the nationwide fiber optic binge by both MCI and US Sprint (as shown in data presented by Bolter and McConnaughey in this volume), which has resulted in more transmission capacity nationally than we are likely to need for many years. I am not sure where these two effects show up in Crandall's numbers; I suspect he is picking up AT&T-BOC only in his figures concerning capital stock. If so, I view the slowdown of capital stock growth as a very healthy signal of increasingly efficient use of capital. On the other hand, the excess capacity that now exists in long-distance transmission facilities has also been a spur to competition in a long-distance market that many of us thought would not be competitive until after 1990.

Both my comments and those of Crandall are focused on the efficiency area that economists can say something about, i.e. price and cost reductions. However, we are less able to measure what may be the far more important area of *product* innovation, such as has occurred in the CPE market. But, as Bruce Greenwald notes earlier in this volume, we have yet to see that type of flowering in the telecommunications market since the divestiture. In spite of the ritual invocation of ISDN, the "engineers' fantasy" of a brave new telecommunications world has not occurred.

Furthermore, I have the uneasy feeling we are looking into the wrong place for product innovation. Telecommunications is a "techie" business, and at the mention of innovation we all think of Bell Laboratories, because we think of innovation as *things*, as *hardware*. Let me suggest a change of thinking about what innovation can mean: shortly after Bell Labs was giving us Picturephone, one anonymous AT&T employee thought up a new service with the awkward name of "IN-WATS", now known as "800 Service." This service innovation has created an entire mail-order industry, changed the face of retail trade, and enabled firms to reach their customers in new ways undreamed of before. In my view, the telephone company added more value to the U.S. economy with the "simple" innovation of 800 Service than all the Bell Labs' hardware of the 1970s. Perhaps it is the marketeers and not the "men in the white coats" who will be the principal source of innovation in the coming decades.

ENDNOTES

1. For a discussion of these events, see Gerald W. Brock, *The Telecommunications Industry: Dynamics of Market Structure* (Cambridge, Mass.: Harvard University Press, 1981). Gerald R. Faulhaber, *Telecommunications in Turmoil: Technology and Public Policy* (Cambridge, Mass.: Ballinger, 1987). *Telecommunications in Transition: The Status of Competition in the Telecommunications Industry*, Report of the Majority Staff of the Subcommittee on Telecommunications, Consumer Protection, and Finance of the Committee on Energy and Commerce, U.S. House of Representatives, November 3, 1981.

2. Almarin Phillips, "The Impossibility of Competition in Telecommunications: Public Policy Gone Awry," in Michael A. Crew, ed., *Regulatory Reform and Public Utilities* (Lexington, Mass.: Lexington Books, 1982).

3. See Faulhaber, *Telecommunications in Turmoil*; and William J. Baumol et al., *Contestable Markets and the Theory of Industry Structure* (New York: Harcourt Brace Jovanovich, 1982).

4. Paul W. MacAvoy and Kenneth Robinson, "Winning by Losing: The AT&T Settlement and Its Impact on Telecommunications," *Yale Journal on Regulation* (1983), vol. 1.

5. For a review of the empirical evidence on this issue, see Leonard Waverman, "U.S. Interexchange Competition," in Robert W. Crandall and Kenneth S. Flamm, eds., *Changing the Rules: Technical Change, International Competition, and Regulation in the Telecommunications Industry* (Washington, D.C.: Brookings Institution, 1989).

6. The relative importance of interstate long-distance service has been increasing while local service has been declining in relative importance.

7. See Robert W. Crandall, "The Role of Local Exchange Carriers," in Crandall and Flamm, eds., *Changing the Rules*.

8. Recent data show that PBX and key telephone prices have been declining at a real rate of 7 to 8 percent per year—substantially more rapidly than in the five years prior to divestiture.

9. Bellcore and New York Telephone data on switch costs per line, 1972–1988.

10. For example, see Nancy L. Rose, "Labor Rent-Sharing and Regulation: Evidence from the Trucking Industry," *Journal of Political Economy* (1987).

11. These data are drawn from the FCC's *Statistics of Communications Common Carriers* and USTA's *Telephone Statistics*. Capital income is equal to net income before taxes, fixed charges, and depreciation and amortization. Labor costs are total compensation, including pensions.

12. The value added measure is theoretically inferior to a gross output measure if materials are not weakly separable from capital and labor in the production function. See Ference Kiss, "Productivity Gains in Bell Canada," in L. Courville et al., eds., *Economic Analysis of Telecommunications* (Amsterdam: North Holland Press, 1983), p. 97.

13. The labor hours are adjusted for quality differences, as reported by Christensen et al. through 1979, but since 1979 the BLS data show little change in

employment shares by the categories used in Christensen's analysis. Therefore, the mix of employees is assumed constant for 1979–1988.

14. This is the measure of capital suggested by Edward Denison in *Accounting for Slower Economic Growth, The United States in the 1970s* (Washington, D.C.: Brookings Institution, 1979), pp. 50–52. Alternative approaches are shown in the Appendix to his chapter. In 1984, consumer premises equipment was detariffed for BOCs. This resulted in a decline in the capital stock in service in the telecommunications sector and required a reduction of $6.9 billion from the net capital stock and $14.5 billion from the gross capital stock in 1984.

15. An adjustment was made to smooth the abrupt decline in capital's share in the *SOCCC* data that was apparently caused by the $5.5 billion writeoff taken by AT&T at the end of 1983.

16. It is reassuring, however, that the average TFP growth for 1961–1980 reported in table 11.5 is 3.4 percent. This compares with an average of 3.44 percent reported by Kiss for Bell Canada and 3.3 obtained by Christensen et al. for AT&T in 1961–1979.

17. John Haring and Kathy Levitz, "What Makes The Dominant Firm Dominant?" Federal Communications Commission, Office of Plans and Policy, OPP Working Paper #25, April 1989.

18. See U.S. Department of Justice, *The Geodesic Network: 1987 Report on Competition in the Telephone Industry* (The Huber Report), ch. 3.

19. Filed in CC Docket 87-339, 1988.

12

Issues of International Trade

■

KENNETH G. ROBINSON, JR.
·
ELI M. NOAM
ROBERT T. BLAU
MICHAEL D. BAUDHUIN
TIMOTHY J. BRENNAN

Kenneth G. Robinson, Jr.

Too often within government in the past, telecommunications has tended to be dealt with as just another international trade commodity, similar to hides, tobacco, or citrus. The most oblique reference to telecommunications trade deficits—and the possibility of special government actions or initiatives—has thus not infrequently provoked grand bureaucratic, rhetorical battles regarding the well-known hazards of dreaded "industrial policy." The notion that the United States itself does not practice such policy in some sectors has about as much validity as the view that our major trading partners have not really targeted this field for special attention. There are, however, at least three reasons why those international communications trade effects matter, or should matter, from an overall public policy standpoint.

First, whatever might be the optimal criterion by which to assess the success or failure of the Bell System breakup, international trade and competitiveness were advanced by both the breakup's proponents and defenders as an appropriate point of assessment. AT&T suggested, for example, that with the change it would "be well positioned to compete in the growing global market for communications and information services."[1] Reagan administration spokesmen also suggested that the settlement would free AT&T to compete. At the time the initial consent decree proposal was being reviewed by Judge Greene, the United States had a significant international communications trade surplus of about $275 million. No one seriously believed that surplus was threatened; most assumed, if anything, that our refurbished flagship company would prove so much more formidable that our trade surplus would inexorably grow.

Second, as the telecommunications trade provisions of the 1988 Omnibus Trade Act (among other enactments) demonstrate, communications trade is in fact an increasingly significant item on the U.S. domestic political agenda. For years, as one U.S. core industry after another has been severely affected by imports—steel, textiles, footwear, automobiles, etc.—the government responded chiefly by stressing the putative virtues of "high-tech" alternatives. Concentrating on "upstream," technology-intensive enterprises was supposed to take up the slack. But then, U.S. high technology seemed to decline as well. Between 1980 and 1986, for example, the United States reportedly went from a $26.7 billion trade surplus in high-technology markets to a $2.6 billion deficit. We developed a $4+ billion a year computer trade deficit with Japan. As one critic wryly commented, we learned "we can't all become astronauts," and politicians began to question the future strength of American technology. That anxiety was leavened with good ol' nationalistic xenophobia, as foreign-based companies began converting their trade surpluses into U.S. domestic corporate holdings. The international trade effects of the reorganization of the Bell System, in short, rose and are still fairly high on the list of political priorities.

Third, communications trade matters. Communications and associated information industry enterprises constitute some 6 percent of the U.S. gross national product and are gaining GNP share by about one-half of one percent annually—one of the relatively few sectors to be rising (figure 12.1). Business is reportedly allocating more than 30 percent of total annual investment in equipment to communications and information-processing products. Telecommunications traditionally has been a major source of profits and good jobs with a future. It is an area where our technology remains competitive internationally. And yet,

FIGURE 12.1

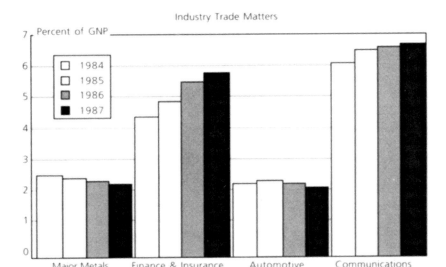

Source: U.S. Department of Commerce.

the United States will face some fairly serious problems in the relatively near-term future if it continues to lose in this key infrastructure sector of the economy at the current rate. More is at stake than the health of one industry. Other key industries are becoming increasingly dependent on the communications infrastructure to compete in the global marketplace. U.S. businesses, for example, have invested highly in computer equipment over the last ten to fifteen years, yet few have seen appreciable productivity benefits (figure 12.2). This problem is particularly acute in the service sector where 76 percent of the U.S. work force is employed. Linking individual computers together via high-speed data communications networks is increasingly recognized as a promising way to unleash more of this technology's productivity potential. It is unlikely to happen on a large scale, however, if the public communications infrastructure does not keep pace with ongoing advancements in computer technology.

If the present trends are not altered rather quickly—

By 1992, our overall trade deficit in the relatively narrow category of telephone and telegraph equipment should be about $4.9 billion, compared with $2.6 billion in 1988.

FIGURE 12.2

Computer Spending and Productivity

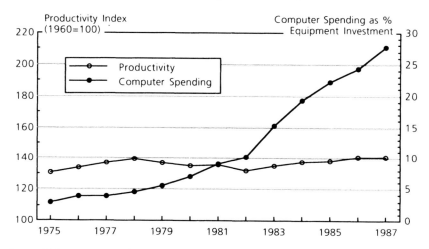

Source: U.S. Department of Commerce, Bureau of Economic Analysis, American Productivity Center.

In the broader category of "electronics-based products," our 1992 trade deficit should amount to about $18 billion—about the same as the current U.S.-Japan trade deficit in passenger cars.

The Bell companies (which represent some three-quarters of our telephone business by 1992) should be spending about 58 percent of their annual procurement budgets with foreign-based companies.

AT&T, our putative national communications leader, by 1992 should have slipped to fourth or possibly fifth among the world-class telecommunications manufacturers (behind Alcatel, Siemens, Northern Telecom, and probably Ericsson), while reducing its workforce by at least 50,000 more U.S. jobs.

In simplistic terms, the current trade statistics for the telecommunications and information sector suggest that the United States is currently moving toward becoming a technological colony, principally of Japan, but also possibly of Europe. The 1982 surplus in telephone and telegraph equipment of $275 million deteriorated to a $2.6 billion deficit in 1988—about a $3.0 billion turnaround. Our $4.7 billion surplus

FIGURE 12.3

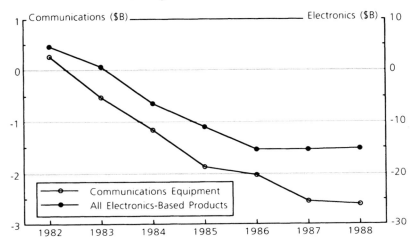

U.S. High-Tech Trade Deficits

Source: U.S. Department of Commerce.

in electronics-based products in 1982 fell precipitously to a more than
$15 billion deficit (figure 12.3). Along the way, according to AFL-CIO
estimates, the United States electronics manufacturing sector also saw
a shrinkage of 300,000 jobs.

Some of the problem no doubt stems from the kind of domestic
telecommunications industry we had on the eve of the Bell breakup.
The U.S. telecommunications goods and services sector was heavily
regulated and tightly monopolized until early in the 1980s, and did not
emphasize commercial agility or customer responsiveness. For most of
its corporate existence, AT&T had focused on meeting relatively easily
predicted, standard, basic communications requirements. Corporate
management assumed demand for conventional voice telephone service was and would remain the chief marketplace priority. It assumed
voice traffic would continue indefinitely to expand yearly by the square
of annual population growth, and built and installed plant accordingly.

AT&T concentrated on producing durable—but costly—lower technology products which were then marketed chiefly to a captive domestic market, its owned and operated telephone companies. Management
also focused on ensuring neither demand for equipment nor services
outstripped AT&T's ability to manage and supply it, which helped
minimize the likelihood of competitive entry. The prevailing regula-

tory regime, which keyed allowable telephone service profits to the magnitude of the firm's investment, induced the production of costly products which, while perhaps attractive enough for domestic purposes, were not always well-suited to appeal to the world market. It was not until the late 1970s, for example, that AT&T began producing small, relatively lower cost digital electronic switches in appreciable volumes. The firm was then obliged to play catch-up with Northern Telecom, the world's largest producer of such state-of-the-art products.

Although AT&T maintained a world-renowned research arm, Bell Labs, and pioneered many of the fundamental developments in telecommunications, its actual commercial deployment of new technology domestically was largely dictated by regulatorily established, overlong depreciation schedules. Well into the 1970s, a large portion of Western Electric's telephone switch output, for example, consisted of analog machines not technologically much more sophisticated than those produced in the 1940s and 1950s. As one critic at the time put it, "It was as if Ford Motor Company in the 1970s decided to limit its output to some 1947 Fords, plus a smattering of Model As and Ts."

Because it enjoyed a tractable captive market which could be served without incurring significant sales development or forecasting expenses, AT&T until 1978 also concentrated almost exclusively on the United States. Its only significant international equipment operations focused on selling reconditioned products in a limited number of Latin American countries. Unlike most of its Japan and Europe-based competition, it did not seek to hone its competitive skills through striving for success in world markets, as the prevailing environment did not require such action.

International politics (and its consequences) were also a factor. The fixed exchange rates that prevailed until 1971 had the effect of overvaluing the American dollar. Those countries which today account for much of our trading deficit balked at subsidizing American consumers and, in any event, faced substantial domestic demand as the communications infrastructures of Japan and West Germany were rebuilt. Technical standards were also a problem. AT&T established what was known as the North American Standard for most telephone switching and other gear, while the balance of the world generally applied standards developed by the International Telecommunication Union's CCITT. The result was Balkanization of much of the equipment market for many years.

The initial competitive difficulties which the principal U.S.-based communications equipment producers experienced in the 1970s, when the Federal Communication Commission (FCC) sanctioned competition in customer premises terminal equipment, were compounded by new regulatory impositions. AT&T was directed meticulously to segregate its service and equipment sales operations, and was placed under extensive technical and commercial plan disclosure requirements (which some Congressional critics contended benefited chiefly Japan-based competitors). AT&T was later to document regulatory requirements which cost the firm over $1 billion yearly. AT&T also continued to be subject to pervasive regulatory restrictions on its prices and profits, while most of its domestic and foreign-based competitors were not. The requirement that it obtain prior regulatory approval of new service offerings, by filing extensive market forecasts and business plans, afforded competitors both competitively valuable information and a means of imposing delays.

Just as foreign-based competition in U.S. equipment markets was intensifying, the Justice Department in 1974 filed an antitrust suit aimed at dismantling the Bell System. The filing of an antitrust suit against AT&T both preoccupied its management and dampened its penchant for hard-market competition just at the time that changes in customer demand, domestic regulatory reforms, and other factors were radically altering U.S. communications markets. AT&T also discontinued its sale of communications equipment to most of the independent, non-Bell companies, to avoid increasing its market share (and thus creating a window of opportunity for foreign-based firms).

While the U.S. government was moving to dismantle its communications flagship company, foreign administrations, most notably parts of the Japanese government, were targeting the United States market for special attention. Having orchestrated Japan's automotive industry successes, the Ministry of International Trade and Industry chose semiconductors and telecommunications as the country's next major industrial policy endeavors. A 1970 Finance Ministry white paper had discussed the desirability of focusing on these fields. Following the twin shocks of the Arab oil embargo and the Carter administration's soybean embargo, which heightened Japan's sense of dependency and vulnerability, Japanese industry was strongly encouraged to emphasize "knowledge-intensive" fields.

As Japan-based industry, with government help and encouragement, was entering communications and computers on a major scale, U.S. regulators, largely oblivious to those overseas developments, were creating new U.S. market opportunities for foreign-based firms. Prior to 1977 when the final implementing regulations were adopted by the FCC, Bell and GTE telephone companies represented almost all of the demand for telephone handsets in the United States. That demand was satisfied almost exclusively by AT&T's Western Electric and GTE's Automatic Electric subsidiaries, which manufactured equipment domestically. Customers were forbidden by regulation from using so-called "foreign attachments."

When the FCC ruled that customers had a right to employ telephone equipment of their own choosing, whether supplied by the local phone company or other firms, that lock on demand was opened. Independent U.S. equipment vendors and Japan-based suppliers formed a "marriage of convenience." That marriage, plus the difficulties which AT&T and GTE encountered trying to compete, started a surge of telecommunications equipment imports. In 1976, moreover, the FCC directed AT&T to alter its procurement practices to permit greater access to the Bell System market on the part of nonaffiliated firms. One result was the certification of Bell Canada's Northern Telecom subsidiary as an accredited supplier, an action which helps explain the large U.S. market share the firm enjoys today. As the Commerce Department noted in 1981 studies regarding the AT&T litigation, foreign equipment sales nearly quintupled to about $1.3 billion in a matter of about four years.

Divestiture was ordered with relatively little regard to the prevailing international economic environment. It was begun precisely as the value of the U.S. dollar commenced rising sharply against other major currencies. And it occurred at the same time that special federal tax incentives to invest in technology products, such as business telephone systems, were put into place. Moreover, the significant government and consumer deficit spending that started in earnest following the 1982 tax cuts, boosted the rate of economic growth for the United States, making the U.S. market even more attractive to foreign-based suppliers.

Between 1980 and 1985, the U.S. dollar rose some 75 percent in value relative to other world currencies, making imported telecommunications products especially attractive to U.S. purchasers. Accelerated depreciation and tax credits drove business demand. Between 1982 and 1985, for example, total annual U.S. telephone equipment consumption increased to $18.1 billion from $13.2 billion, or more than 11 percent compounded annually (figure 12.4). As AT&T was preoccupied with court-ordered reorganization during that time period, much of that surge in demand was satisfied by Japan-based firms.

The U.S. government and consumer deficit spending had the effect of boosting U.S. growth rates higher relative to those in Canada and Europe. Canadian and European administrations, confronting high unemployment rates and slow growth, responded to domestic labor union and other pressures and maintained (or, in some cases, raised) barriers

FIGURE 12.4

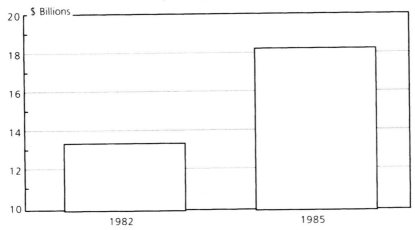

U.S. Telephone Equipment Consumption

Source: U.S. Department of Commerce.

to electronics-based imports. In developing countries, a world debt crisis dampened demand for communications products; and, in newly industrializing countries such as Brazil, Taiwan, and South Korea, import barriers in aid of indigenous communications producers were imposed.

U.S. export sales were depressed by currency misalignments plus cutbacks in Export-Import Bank subsidies. World economic conditions deflected Japanese and East Asian efforts from Canada, Europe, and the Third World and redirected them heavily toward the U.S. market. The result was to focus nearly the full force of Japan's targeting efforts on a domestic U.S. civilian market which was growing rapidly and which our indigenous producers were not serving fully.

Certain features of the 1982 AT&T consent decree had additional negative effects. The procurement requirements of the individual Bell companies—equivalent to more than 80 percent of the U.S. market for network telecommunications products—were not only opened to non-AT&T suppliers. The Bell companies were also explicitly required by the consent decree not to discriminate in AT&T's favor, and took that admonition as a requirement that they actively solicit alternative suppliers. At the same time, however, the decree placed AT&T in actual and potential competition with its main customers.

Telecommunications service and equipment expenditures are inter-

changeable in many instances. That is, the more spent on equipment—
to secure a very sophisticated PBX system, for example—the fewer
lines probably will be needed, and vice versa. Business customers also
have the option, in most cases, of purchasing their own PBX or similar
apparatus, or buying Centrex services from the local telephone company. As the largest PBX vendor, AT&T was thus competing with local
Bell companies' Centrex operations.

The consent decree was modified by Judge Greene to allow Bell
companies to market equipment. In all instances the BOCs bought
equipment from firms other than AT&T for retailing by their equipment subsidiaries. The Bell companies in short order thus became
major U.S. distributors of foreign-made communications equipment.
At the same time, they sought what were denominated "neutral suppliers" for much of their network equipment needs. In that respect,
AT&T's policy of resisting virtually any modification in the terms and
conditions of the consent decree contributed to a climate of ill-feelings
and commercial suspicions between AT&T and the Bell companies.
The predictable result was a sharp decline in the percentage of their
total procurement dollars which the Bell companies channeled to AT&T.

AT&T already confronted strong U.S. market competition from
Northern Telecom, Inc., majority-owned by Bell Canada. Northern's
Canadian base was protected not only by regulatory restrictions on
Canadian telephone customers' choice, but a 17 percent tariff on imports (vs. about a 7 percent U.S. tariff). AT&T now faced additional,
well-financed competition in the United States by several of the premier telecommunications equipment makers in the world.

The rapid expansion of parts of the U.S. domestic communications
market and declines in some other foreign markets (most notably Latin
America) resulted in U.S. entry on the part of three world-class network
communications equipment manufacturers (West Germany's Siemens
AG, Sweden's L. M. Ericsson Group, and France's Alcatel-Thomson),
and, to a lesser extent, two Japan-based multinationals, Nippon Electric
Co. (NEC) and Fujitsu. Each enjoyed a substantial home market, typically a protected market, yet perceived a need to expand sales volume
beyond what that home market could support. Initially, each company
employed "forward pricing" to some extent to build U.S. sales.

The defense buildup of the period also coincided with a tightening
of export controls. In 1981, for example, Apple Computers was embar-
goed, as was the export of digital switching gear. Fiber optics, opto-
electronics, and communications satellites became exceedingly difficult to export. The predictable result was to limit the ability of U.S.
firms to compete in the high end of communications, computers, and

electronics-based products overseas. Japan-based firms (and non-COCOM (Coordinating Committee on Export Controls) members firms, such as L. M. Ericsson of Sweden) were thus able to address third-country demand without U.S. competition.

Almost precisely as the United States was restructuring the Bell System and thus, in many regards, blunting the potential competitiveness of our leading firm, foreign administrations were making fundamental network equipment procurement decisions. Both West Germany and the United Kingdom in the mid-1980s determined to rebuild much of their backbone communications system, replacing outmoded analog, electromechanical switching apparatus with state-of-the-art digital electronic gear. It is by no means certain U.S.-based suppliers could have secured an appreciable part of these major, long-term requirements contracts. But even had those markets been fully open to U.S. competitors, we were not in a position to capitalize significantly on those opportunities.

During the Reagan years, the number of corporate takeovers also increased well beyond previous levels. In part, some contended, this was due to antitrust permissiveness, and in part, others maintained, because corporate assets were undervalued (and firms thus found it less costly and risky to buy rather than competitively capture market share). Two major U.S. electronics and telecommunications companies for a time were takeover candidates, GTE Corporation and RCA. GTE maintained its independence, but evidently in the process incurred such high costs that it was obliged to divest its extensive foreign manufacturing operations (which were bought by Siemens) as well as most of its domestic operations (which were bought by Fujitsu). RCA ultimately was acquired by General Electric, which apparently financed the acquisition, in part, by selling RCA's consumer electronics and equipment service operations. The former operations were bought by the French government majority-owned Thomson organization.

The Bell System breakup was, in some senses, the greatest unilateral removal of a nontariff trade barrier in international trade history. That action, however, was only one of several factors contributing to the U.S. telecommunications trade deficit. It made things worse, particularly as it both opened U.S. markets *and* eliminated a source of leverage that might have been used to open others that, in 1982–1984, remained essentially closed. But it would probably be a mistake to attribute to that action all of the difficulties the United States subsequently experienced in this increasingly important sector of the economy.

Communications, information, and electronics-based products are at the core of what AT&T has estimated to be a $1 trillion worldwide "information economy" by 1990. These markets are among the world's fastest growing. It is important that U.S. industry continue as a leading player. Maintaining control of "upstream," knowledge-intensive stages of production is key. Product conceptualization, design, and introduction typically count as among the highest value-added stages, while "bending the metal" or simple assembly of components counts for less. Important to delivering quality products which will sell in increasingly competitive world markets, however, is at least the ability to accomplish all stages of production.

Expanding U.S. communications, information, and electronics-based exports and reestablishing our preeminence in these high-technology sectors will require concerted efforts on the part of both the government and the American business community. While some free-market purists will criticize any government initiative, the fact is that without a coherent "offensive strategy," the United States risks further losses.

The following are measures which should be taken:

(1) *Reduce Government "Competition" with Marketplace Alternatives.* Certain large parts of the prevailing communications regulatory regime constitute the functional equivalent of an attractive nuisance in terms of impeding market competition. Through complaints and petitions to state and federal regulators, for example, economically, telephone companies typically are able to hobble any competitors which might impinge on their putatively exclusive local telephone service franchises. Conversely, cable television companies (which are essentially freed from any price controls) are able through the regulatory process to keep telephone companies from competing in their "turf." A result, as one local official phrased it, is that the public too gets neither the ostensible benefits of regulation nor the genuine benefits of actual and potential competition.

Judicial regulation of large parts of the U.S. communications business is also a problem. So long as Japan-based equipment vendors and AT&T are able through the courts to frustrate virtually any participation in the manufacturing field by the Bell companies, half of the financial and human resources that the United States has in the telephone business will stay under wraps. Foreign-based firms will have a relatively free hand to continue acquiring small, entrepreneurial American firms, probably at an accelerating rate. Once their already substantial beachhead in U.S. equipment markets is secure and consolidated, our recapturing lost ground will become even more difficult. And AT&T will tend to rely more on energizing the government to safeguard its profits, and less on improving its overall competitiveness.

(2) *Remove or Ameliorate Self-imposed Constraints.* The AT&T

antitrust consent decree prohibits the seven Bell companies (which control nearly 80 percent of the U.S. telephone's net current assets) from engaging in manufacturing in the United States for the U.S. market—they may manufacture abroad, but only for foreign consumption —or providing new, computer-related information services. An effect of the prohibition on manufacturing has been to shield both U.S. and foreign-based companies from additional competition. Another effect has been to facilitate the acquisition of U.S. firms by foreign-based companies; U.S. antitrust considerations would tend to restrict the acquisitions our few major companies such as AT&T could make domestically. If other U.S.-based companies which are likely acquirers are artificially excluded from the marketplace for corporate control, the practical effect is to assist foreign firms seeking to expand their U.S. presence.

Restricting the sophistication of the services which can be offered by the Bell companies on the public telephone network also has adverse trade effects. Many new services can be provided using either telephone company switching apparatus or CPE. Voice storage and retrieval, for example, can be offered using the capabilities of today's sophisticated digital switches or with answering machines. While U.S.-based companies such as AT&T are seeing their share of the U.S. equipment decline, those firms still have a dominant share of the network switch market. In contrast, foreign-based companies are strong in customer-premises products. Indeed, virtually none of the many answering machines sold in the United States last year was made in this country. Yet by driving the "intelligence" from the public-switched network, the information services limitations placed on the Bell companies by the AT&T consent decree effectively channel U.S. customer demand for new offerings to foreign-based producers. Similarly, by impeding the fullest possible use of telephone network resources, future investment in that system as well as the cost of using it—costs which will ripple throughout the economy—are artificially hiked.

Overall competitiveness in this field, however, is not likely to be accomplished—and, in any event, will not be achieved soon—so long as many of the major firms in this line of commerce remain subject to artificial government controls, controls which tend to benefit foreign-based firms. Success in the near term here, as in other key sectors, is dependent upon maximum possible mobilization of U.S. financial and human resources. Transitional safeguards and procedures may be needed. Unless the full resources potentially available to the country in the communications field are actually available for deployment, however, success will almost certainly prove illusive.

Telecommunications trade did not become a significant executive branch concern until 1985, by which time our $275 million surplus in 1982 had become a $1.8 billion deficit. By 1985, our deficit in the general category of electronics-based products (telecommunications, computers, most office equipment, etc.) had grown to $10.9 billion, compared with a $4.7 billion surplus in 1982. In 1985, the U.S. deficit in automobiles was about $24 billion. That deficit took more than a decade to build to then-current levels. In electronics-based products, however, a deficit almost half as large materialized in only about three years (figure 12.5).

With enactment of the 1988 Omnibus Trade Act, the Reagan administration dropped previous strong opposition to so-called "sectoral reciprocity," and the bill, as passed and signed into law, singles telecommunications out as a special area of particular U.S. trade policy emphasis. Even with the passage of this important law, however, and the 1987–1988 devaluation of the dollar, our telecommunications trade deficit continued in 1988 to grow at about the same seven percent compounded annual rate.

For 1989, the official deficit figure decreased to $1.9 billion from $2.6 billion for 1988. However, at least half of this reduction was due merely to significant changes in the method used to compute the

FIGURE 12.5

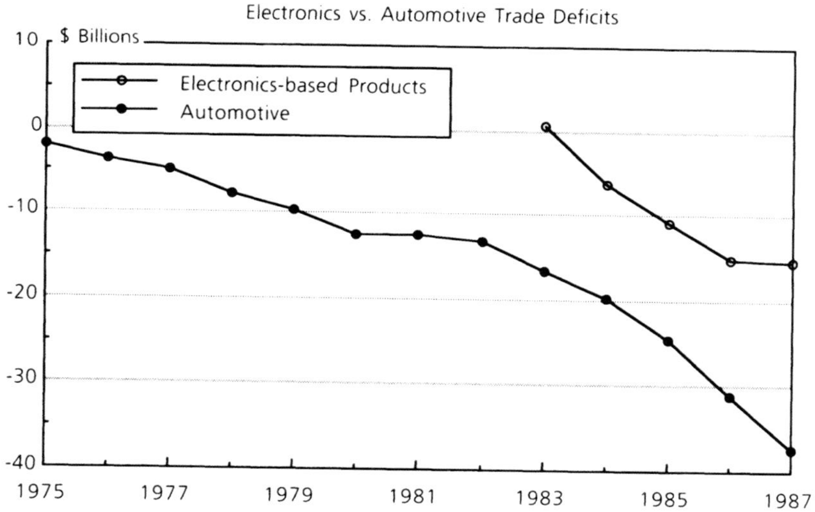

Source: U.S. Department of Commerce.

telecommunications trade balance, including reclassifying satellite technology as telecommunications equipment. Moreover, the relatively low U.S. dollar exchange rate that prevailed throughout much of 1989 also played a role in the marginal decrease in the deficit figure. It should also be noted that to the extent there was a genuine improvement in the trade picture during 1989, much of the credit must go to foreign-owned companies such as Northern Telecom and Siemens, which were largely responsible for a small U.S. trade surplus in the "high end" of telephone equipment, through exports of network switching technology made in this country.

U.S. procompetitive policies have gained some acceptance abroad over the past four years. The British government privatized British Telecom, beginning in 1981; the firm, which is the 17th largest publicly traded company in the world, is now 51 percent privately owned, and additional shares may be sold by the government in the future. Japan also passed communications liberalization legislation, and began the privatization of Nippon Telegraph & Telephone (currently the world's largest company in terms of stock market valuation), which is now about 30 percent completed. In West Germany, less ambitious deregulatory and restructuring legislation passed in July 1989, although all parts of the Deutsche Bundespost, Europe's largest single enterprise, will remain government-owned.

These trends in some regards place the United States in a dilemma. Unless foreign communications, information, and related markets are "deregulated," the export opportunities available to U.S.-based companies will remain relatively sparse. At the same time, by moving their telecommunications enterprises ostensibly beyond direct government control, the ability of the U.S. government to accomplish additional market openings through direct government-to-government talks will diminish. The potential utility of changing multilateral trade agreements to encompass communications goods and services more effectively will also decline.

What steps need to be taken? In the short run, it is important for the United States to amplify the signals already sent to our trading partners indicating that telecommunications is a sector which we value highly. Second, it is at least as important for the senior political leadership of the country to impress upon U.S. firms the importance accorded to aggressive pursuit of overseas export markets. Third, bilateral talks and discussions with foreign communications administrations should be continued and, where feasible, telecommunications trade issues should be handled by communications experts apart from overall trade discussions generally.

If the United States were to become completely dependent on foreign-based sources for telecommunications products, the result would be catastrophic. Telecommunications and related computer systems are increasingly pivotal production factors in more and more businesses. They are also, of course, critical to our national defense. Telecommunications trade concerns, in short, have an added dimension which goes beyond mere national commercial interests. The hazards with relegating those concerns to conventional trade discussions and negotiations is that they will be inadvertently subordinated or ignored, with serious long-term consequences.

Similarly, and because of the added dimension to telecommunications, rote application of familiar "freedom of investment" rules may implicate significant long-term risks. The United States, for example, is today the only country in the world which permits completely foreign-owned firms to provide regular long-distance telephone service. Others may permit U.S. firms to hold minority interests, or to provide specialized services over indigenous carriers' facilities. But the United States has foreign-ownership limitations only when radio frequency licenses are required—and today's fiber optics communications networks do not require them. Siemens, Britain's Cable & Wireless PLC, and British Telecom consequently operate long-distance telecommunications companies in the United States while, in West Germany, voice communications is now and will continue to be a state monopoly and, in Britain, only two British companies have been licensed to provide service.

In 1989, the FCC determined that foreign ownership restrictions on ownership of radio licenses do not apply when the services involved are not generally offered to the public. Under the FCC's ruling, Canadian, French, or indeed, Soviet-owned satellite communications systems could provide service within the United States, providing that it were a "private" service, without impinging on U.S. law. (Such service might implicate certain international communications treaties, although, in general, those treaties do not apply to services offered wholly within national boundaries.)

At present, the United States has no systematic reporting requirements which would permit an accurate tally of the number of foreign-based companies currently providing communications services within the country. Most of the services involved have been "deregulated" by the FCC, and regular reports are thus not required. Yet when the FCC proposed in 1987 and again in 1988 to impose modest reporting requirements on foreign-based communications companies, that initiative was strongly opposed by U.S. trade and international investment agencies, as well as the Department of State.

So long as telecommunications is treated as just another trade commodity, like meat, shingles, or citrus, the probabilities are that U.S. telecommunications interests will not be accorded priority commensurate with this sector's commercial and geopolitical strategic importance.

While ill-timed or inadequate government measures have contributed to the difficulties the United States currently confronts in communications, information, and electronics, part of the blame must also be shared by the American business community.

In general, it is easier to sell at home, and to export only what others abroad do not make (or to export products which can be produced for far less, or are benefited by government subsidies). In the United States, decades of great commercial success undermine our corporate character. A business culture evolved that taught home market dependence, while mitigating against cooperative ventures. What is needed is further action aimed at stressing the key importance to the U.S. business community of quality manufacturing for global markets.

Fifteen years ago, a nation's annual steel production, its miles of railways, housing stock, or its electricity generation were the prevailing measures of development and competitiveness. Today, it is the incidence of computers, the miles of fiber optics, and the level of research and development spending that typically are the benchmarks of national competitiveness and success.

The American communications, information, and electronics industries, as well as related fields, are today the focus of deliberate (often governmentally orchestrated) foreign programs that explicitly aim at attaining commercial as well as technological hegemony. From a fundamental policy standpoint, the United States has the option of seeking to blunt the effectiveness of those programs by fostering more open and competitive markets globally, or undertaking countervailing steps. At issue, too, is whether we are prepared to blame all our problems on foreign practices or, rather, look toward making necessary domestic reforms.

If experience is any guide, things may have to deteriorate further before there is substantial change on the domestic front. Attitudes toward proposals to alter consent decree restrictions have hardened on the part of AT&T. Proposed changes in traditional economic regulation at the federal level have encountered stern opposition; one result has been to water down proposals to the point where implementing them will make considerably less procompetitiveness difference. There is also little of a crisis atmosphere, and little strong, sustained public interest in these topics—both of which mitigate against Congress taking the initiative in the near term. The probabilities, unfortunately, are that the United States will likely continue to muddle along in this sector, as telecommunications trade deficits mount.

Eli M. Noam

The trade issue has become arguably the primary problem of the post-divestiture environment. The numbers say it loud and clear: the trade balance in terminal equipment moved from a $275 million surplus in 1982 to a $2.6 billion deficit in 1988, and things may get worse. Kenneth Robinson warns us that this deficit could grow, according to some estimates, to $4.9 billion by 1992, when the Bell companies could possibly buy an incredible 58 percent of their procurement from foreign-based companies. AT&T would cut 50,000 American jobs. One can add other horror statistics: registration of new equipment (so-called Part 68 filings) show that in 1988 only 43 percent of registrations were by American companies—many of which may well be foreign-owned subsidiaries—while 48 percent were by Asian firms. Europeans, interestingly enough, had only five percent of registrations (figures 12.6 and 12.7).

The twin reasons for the deficit are usually seen as the closed mar-

FIGURE 12.6

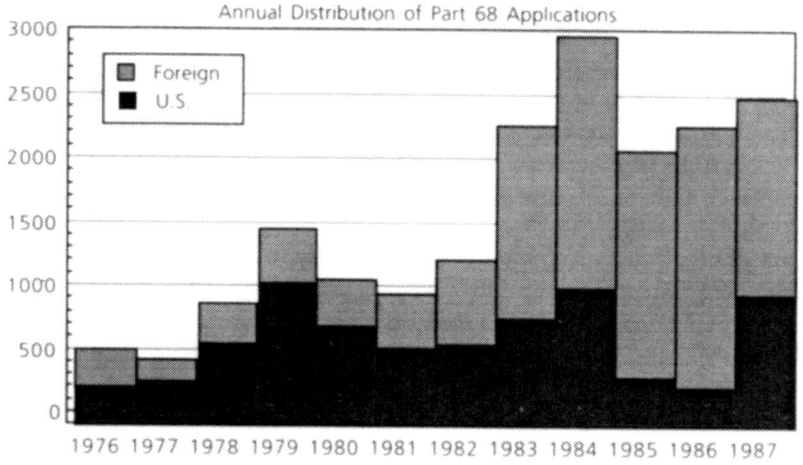

Annual Distribution of Part 68 Applications

:Source: W. Von Alven, FCC, Washington, D.C. 1988.

FIGURE 12.7

1987 Part 68 Registrations

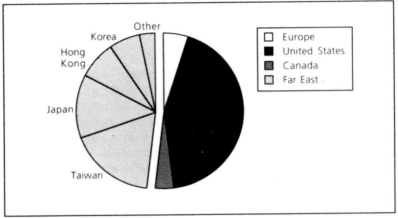

Source: W. Von Alven, FCC, Washington, D.C. 1988.

kets abroad and the open ones at home—open due to the divestiture. Both these reasons are partly correct; at the same time, things are often more complicated than they seem at first, and one needs some dispassion before blaming divestiture for our trade balance problems.

It is first necessary to understand the forces that are changing the international equipment market. Many people assign the prime role to changing technology, but one must recognize that networks in industrialized countries have reached a certain maturity, which in turn leads to a change in development strategy. The key variable is the saturation of basic service. The achievement of universal service is a very recent phenomenon; in Germany, for example, overall telephone penetration in 1960 was only 12 percent of households. A minuscule 6 percent of households headed by blue- and white-collar employees had a telephone. But in 1980, overall telephone density was up to 75 percent. In France, overall penetration in 1967 was an anemic 6 percent, and it is over 80 percent today. For the national telecommunications equipment industries, the achievement of universal service creates a serious challenge. The industry must reorient itself enormously, because its activity level would otherwise fall dramatically. Figures 12.8 and 12.9 illustrate the great drop in equipment investment in Germany.

Thus, having been successful in spreading telephony, the supplying

FIGURE 12.8

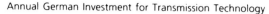

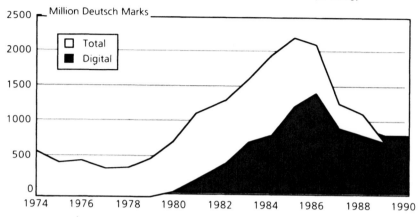

Source: Helmut Schön, "Das ISDN im Investitions, Industrie Und Fernmeldepolitischen Kontext," in W. Kaiser, ed., *Integrierte Telekommunikation, Münchner Kreis,* no. 11.

FIGURE 12.9

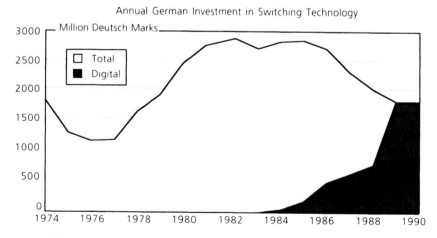

Source: Helmut Schön, "Das ISDN im Investitions, Industrie Und Fernmeldepolitischen Kontext," in W. Kaiser, ed., *Integrierte Telekommunikation, Münchner Kreis,* no. 11.

TABLE 12.1
Telephone Carriers' Share of Total Formation in Telephone and
Telegraph, 1970–1986
($B)

	Common Carrier Capital Expenditures[a]	Total Investment in Telephone and Telegraph[b]	Ratio
1970	9,275	8,835	1.05
1975	12,833	12,683	1.01
1980	23,620	26,081	1.09
1986	25,890	38,930	0.67

[a] Calculations of Robert Crandall, Brookings Institution.

[b] U.S. Department of Commerce data for equipment and structures in telephone and telegraph.

industry of several industrialized countries became a victim of its own success in saturating the basic market. Domestically, it had no place to go but down in terms of basic equipment. This left several complementary options: *Strategy 1: Upgrade* This means a supply push into videotex, ISDN, IBN, and cable television as ways to provide the industry with procurement orders. This partly explains national initiatives in that direction, and the emphasis on setting standards. *Strategy 2: Export* Increased international activities can substitute for the shrinking basic domestic market. However, most interesting markets in industrial and industrializing countries are protected by their own governments. Therefore, everyone either concentrates on those markets that are more open, most particularly the United States, or engages in bilateralism and reciprocity. Part of the U.S. problem is that it unilaterally relaxed structural protections without extracting a reciprocal lowering of barriers. *Strategy 3: Retarget* Perhaps most importantly for the long term, manufacturers should target large private *users* as a market for equipment. Whereas in 1975 virtually all of capital equipment in telecommunications in the U.S. was invested by the carriers, in 1986 it was only two-thirds (table 12.1). About $13 billion were invested by noncarriers, mostly large users.

The implication is that the equipment industry, in the past a protector of the old order, is increasingly part of the process of creating alternatives to the traditional carriers. With this supply push, the peripheral equipment market is expanding into what used to be the realm of the traditional core network. This is partly a secular trend, based on the demand pull of what may be called a pluralism in the network, as users and user groups increasingly set up specialized networks and higher-level enhanced services.

In other words, it is not just the changed market structure in the United States that leads to the changed trade situation. It is also the domestic market conditions of telecommunications manufacturing in other countries that has changed.

The manifestations exist on multiple levels: the *first* wave of imports into the United States was in terminal equipment. Here, it was not the divestiture that made CPE interconnection legal, possible, and convenient, but rather the *Carterfone* decision more than ten years earlier. Once one permits CPE interconnection, equipment can originate from Taiwan as well as from San Jose, and it would be surprising if the general strength of Asian producers in consumer electronics would not show itself in CPE, too. A country that can build cheap tape recorders can also build cheap answering machines. Of course, one could structure a set of restrictive type-approval rules on the books in order to protect the domestic manufacturers. But the European experience shows that what God wants interconnected, government cannot keep apart.

In Switzerland, for example, the PTT in 1984 set standards for cordless phones. The fifty-five pages of specifications required a virtual Rolls Royce among such equipment, including forty duplex channels and automatic scanning. The rules were supposed to protect the users from unauthorized usage, but, as it happens, only one company (a Swiss one) could meet the standards quickly. This was not surprising since the company had played a major role in writing the rules. That manufacturer's price to the PTT was about $600, and rental price to users came to over $180 per year. At the same time one could *buy* a simpler but perfectly adequate cordless phone in the United States for under $75. As one may expect, Swiss consumers started buying cheaper unlicensed equipment, willingly supplied by numerous "for export only" outlets. Pressured by industry, PTT, and unions, the Swiss Parliament passed a law, described as a liberalization. It prohibits the sale and purchase of unauthorized equipment, while making it easier to search private residences to stamp out the threat.

The implications are that for CPE, with or without the divestiture, and with or without attachment and type-approval rules, a flood of Asian imports would have entered, just as it did for VCRs, compact disc players, and television sets.

When it comes to *network* equipment, the divestiture has made a greater difference. The RHCs can now buy equipment competitively,

TABLE 12.2
Cost of Digital Central Office Switch
($M)

	1983	1984	1985[a]	1986[a]	1987[a]	1988[a]
10,000 Line Switch	2.73	2.53	2.29	2.08	1.91	1.73
20,000 Line Switch	4.60	4.16	3.80	3.36	3.08	2.88

Note: Switch costs exclude installation.
[a] Estimated by New York Telephone.

and are not tied anymore to Ma Bell's apron strings. As a result, AT&T's market share for network equipment has dropped considerably. Before we pronounce this a disaster, we should examine the price trend (table 12.2). The costs per line of a digital central office for NYNEX have come down from $230 in 1983 to an estimated $125 in 1990.

A third problem area in trade is emerging in *services*. Foreign resellers, VANs, and cellular carriers now operate in the United States; they could evolve into local and long-distance service providers. This is fine, up to a point, but provided there is reciprocity.

The trade issue had not been thought through sufficiently when the divestiture was conceived by the policymakers. But others were not much smarter, either. France's premier newspaper, *Le Monde,* once ran a series of noted articles on the divestiture, which emphasized this was part and parcel of a large American export offensive. How wrong they were. But the policies such views brought, which can be called political telematique, still haunts transatlantic telecommunications trade.[2] Both GTE and ITT, the main American participants overseas, were squeezed out of Europe, with hardly a whimper or offer of help from the U.S. government. ITT used to dominate the French market, but after several rounds of politics, plus its own internal problems, it had no place to go but sell out to the French CGE. AT&T tried to get an allocation of 16 percent of the French market by offering major concessions, but the German firm Siemens would have none of it.

And this is part of the problem. The Europeans are now preoccupied with unifying their Common Market. To reduce national compartmentalization they lower barriers and make concessions to each other, and partly at the expense of outsiders. It is difficult enough for an American firm to get a major telecommunications procurement order in Europe. But for Japanese or Koreans, the odds become even smaller. These are highly political markets dominated by governments, and to view them with somewhat rosy glasses would be to distort reality.

On the plus side, imports make the cost of telephone service cheaper in the United States. And as a state regulator, that of course pleases me. But if I stop defining my job as merely keeping residential rates low, and view the "public interest" more broadly, I, too, must be concerned with the trade problem, and do my share to address it. Also, the nationally compartmentalized markets abroad impose a direct cost on American telephone users. They cannot benefit from economies of scale if AT&T cannot sell in France, or if Ericsson cannot sell in Japan. In other words, equipment sold in America would be cheaper if other countries, too, would open their markets to international competition. And this would translate itself to lower phone rates. So there is a direct link even to the traditional concerns of state regulators.

Trade politics, however vocal, will only open the door. One still needs superior products. Ultimately, the trade balance is determined by the competitiveness of the industry. If we had better and cheaper facsimile machines than the Japanese, we would buy them here and sell them there. This does not excuse other countries, but neither does it let domestic producers off the hook.

For the future, the most worrisome area is that of technology development. And while the private sector is working hard in that regard, telecommunications with its network characteristics frequently leads to chicken-and-egg situations. This has led the New York Public Service Commission to act as a catalyst for the industry's ISDN interconnecting trials. The various federal agencies involved in telecommunications must be forward-looking in technology questions. The FCC has started to do so, and I hope it can formulate a coherent long-range vision on how telecommunications policy should assist the evolution of advanced networks. For example, it could consider developing a blueprint for interface points and interconnection standards that would permit compatibility by hardware and software suppliers.[3] NTIA has issued calls for action. Robinson lists several initiatives upon which the federal level should embark. Standards and procurement policies should be priorities. When I served on the advisory board of the FTS-2000 federal phone system, a $25 billion procurement giant, it was astonishing to learn that of all the many criteria for evaluating the bids, the factor of how the governmental network would advance civilian technology and applications, was largely missing. It is unlikely the Japanese would proceed in that fashion.

In the past, state regulators tended to be preoccupied with the domestic conflicts and turf fights with the FCC, and not focused on the interrelations with the rest of the world. Yet in a few years, the difficulties of maintaining a national policy, let alone a state policy, in an electronically interdependent world will become increasingly apparent. In the past, perhaps the United States could afford the luxury of tying itself into regulatory knots and spending ten years on developing policies governing cellular radio and AM stereo. But the times are changing, and regulators must, too. The trade balance figures are only a symptom of the more general problem of economic performance, innovation, and international interdependence. The time for localism is running out, and regulators on all levels of government must think in global terms.

Robert T. Blau

No one seriously believes that AT&T's divestiture is solely responsible for the erosion of U.S. competitiveness in global telecommunications equipment markets. But many industry observers and participants do believe that the MFJ has made a bad trade situation worse, unnecessarily. There are three principal reasons.

First, by breaking up the former Bell System in the manner it did, the government unilaterally opened the U.S. telecommunications equipment market to foreign competitors without even trying to extract reciprocity from Japan and other major industrial trading partners. Second, the MFJ restrictions have encouraged the RHCs to buy from foreign firms in order to reduce their dependence on equipment produced by AT&T, the sole U.S. manufacturer of central office switches and other major types of local telephone network technology. The RHCs have taken this step out of concern that AT&T can use its control over the introduction of new network technology to create a competitive edge in local service markets where the two compete. Third, and perhaps most important, by denying the RHCs the right to manufacture equipment or provide information services, the MFJ has eliminated virtually all incentives for seven of the nations' largest telecommunications companies (with combined revenues of $75 billion in 1988) to invest in the development of new technology that the U.S. clearly needs to compete in world markets.

In response, apologists for the AT&T consent decree assert that America's trade problems are not confined to telecommunications markets, and have far more to do with U.S. fiscal and monetary policy than with the MFJ. AT&T's Michael Baudhuin will later argue that replacing the MFJ restrictions with alternative regulatory safeguards would only encourage the RHCs to joint venture with foreign manufacturers, thereby foreclosing a large portion of the U.S. network equipment market to AT&T and other domestic firms. Should this occur, Baudhuin claims, the ensuing loss of U.S. sales to foreign rivals would add to the trade deficit, force a reduction in AT&T's own commitments to R&D, and further weaken its ability to compete in a critically important market for the nation's long-term economic welfare.

It is interesting AT&T apparently feels no shame in using the specter of joint ventures with foreign competitors as its primary rationale for keeping the manufacturing restraint on the RHCs intact. During the period since divestiture was announced, AT&T itself has shut down seven major manufacturing plants in the U.S., and cut back production capacity in sixteen others, while opening four wholly-owned offshore manufacturing facilities and entering into joint production ventures with no fewer than ten of its major foreign competitors. These initiatives have resulted in the combined loss of as many as 70,000 high-quality manufacturing jobs in this country,[4] but added little, if anything, to AT&T's share, domestic or foreign, of telecommunications equipment markets.

Other defenders of the status quo, including William Baxter in chapter 1, argue that trade considerations should have little or no bearing on the administration of the MFJ. According to this school of thought, if Asian or European manufacturers can make and sell telephone handsets and other types of "low end" telecommunications equipment in this country at a lesser cost than AT&T and other domestic producers, then federal policymakers should accept that fact and do nothing to discourage imports. If U.S. telecom manufacturers are protected, the argument goes, they will simply tie up capital and human resources that could be put to more productive use elsewhere in the economy. American consumers will end up paying more than they need to for telephone equipment and services.

Whom is one to believe? If the weight of empirical evidence and common sense have any bearing on the debate, Kenneth Robinson's views should prevail hands down. Those who might question Robinson's veracity would do well to consider just how badly U.S. trade in telecommunications has faltered since the announcement of AT&T's divestiture in January 1982, and what will need to change if the U.S. telecommunications industry is to avoid digging itself into a deeper competitive hole during the early 1990s.

The numbers clearly show that the MFJ has seriously aggravated

FIGURE 12.10

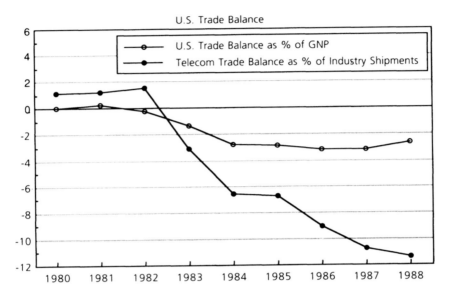

U.S. Trade Balance

Source: U.S. Department of Commerce.

U.S. trade problems in telecommunications. Since early 1982, when responsibility for procurement decisions within the former Bell System effectively moved from AT&T's corporate staff to the local BOCs, U.S. trade in telecommunications has deteriorated at a rate *almost four times faster* than the decline in the nation's overall trade balance (figure 12.10). Worse yet, between 1985 and 1987, the nation's telecommunications trade deficit more than doubled, falling from $1.2 to $2.5 billion, despite a 40 percent decline in the value of the U.S. dollar—a decline that should have boosted AT&T's competitive standing by making its products less expensive abroad while raising the cost of foreign imports in the United States.

Contrary to what AT&T and William Baxter would have us believe, trends in telecommunications trade also imply the recent erosion of U.S. competitiveness is not confined to "low end" consumer products, where the United States is thought to be at a major disadvantage by virtue of higher labor costs. If the problem were that simple, then sharply lower U.S. exchange rates should have produced at least some improvement in the trade balance. That U.S. trade deficits have continued to mount in the face of a much weaker dollar simply suggests that

FIGURE 12.11

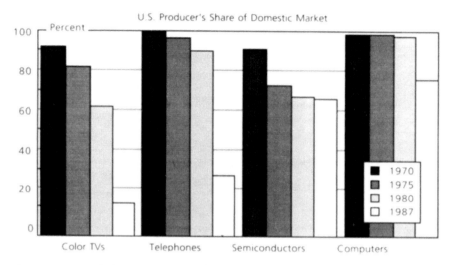

Source: *Business Week*, U.S. Department of Commerce.

FIGURE 12.12

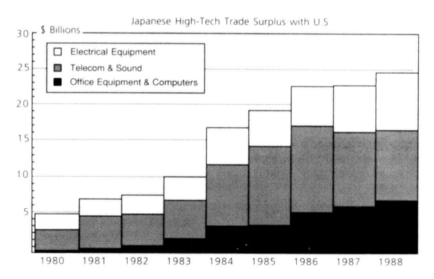

Source: U.S. Department of Commerce.

FIGURE 12.13

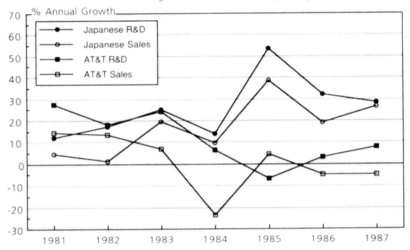

Source: COMPUSTAT and Company Annual Reports.

forces other than cost—forces such as more rapid innovation of new technology made possible by higher levels of R&D spending and more efficient production processes—are instrumental in determining who wins and who loses in the global telecommunications marketplace.

There is also no question AT&T's loss of domestic market share since divestiture has enabled foreign manufacturers to sharply increase R&D spending which, in time, will make their products and services even more competitive both here and abroad. Figure 12.12 highlights recent growth in Japan's "high-tech" trade surplus with the U.S. which, between 1982 and 1987, rose from $7 billion to nearly $23 billion. Figure 12.13 depicts corresponding growth in combined sales and R&D spending for Japan's six leading manufacturers of telecommunications equipment, computers, and electronics—NEC, Matsushita, Toshiba, Pioneer, Sony, and Hitachi—and compares those growth rates with AT&T's.

During this period, the Japanese boosted R&D spending at a compounded average annual rate of 30 percent, thanks largely to a 22 percent average increase in sales. By contrast, AT&T's outlays on R&D rose at an average annual rate of only 6 percent, constrained no doubt by a 5 percent average annual decline in total operating revenues, and an even larger percentage drop in annual equipment sales.[5]

TABLE 12.3
R&D Spending By U.S. Information Industries

Industry	R&D as % 1988 Sales	R&D % Change from 1987	1988 R&D $ per Employee
Bell cos. (+Bellcore)	1.3	8	1,721
Telecom equipment	5.7	6	6,281
Computers	8.2	16	10,680
Systems design	9.2	35	11,719
Computer peripherals	5.6	14	7,352
Software services	13.3	33	18,429
Semiconductors	8.9	15	7.461
Electronics	4.8	19	4,618
All Industry	3.4	11	5,042

Source: *Business Week.*

At the same time, the MFJ has all but eliminated incentives for the RHCs to spend competitively on R&D. The MFJ's manufacturing and information services restraints have made it virtually impossible for the local Bell companies to recover capital that they might otherwise commit to the development of new telecommunications technology. Consequently, the RHCs devoted only 1.3 percent of their sales to R&D in 1988, which is less than 40 percent of the U.S. industrial average (3.4 percent of sales) and only about one sixth of what other high-tech industry groups routinely commit to R&D (table 12.3).

In short, the MFJ in general and the line-of-business restrictions in particular, have aggravated the nation's mounting trade deficit in telecommunications equipment. Adding insult to injury, the erosion of AT&T's equipment sales since divestiture has helped the Japanese and other foreign manufacturers finance a massive build up in R&D spending that will make it all the more difficult for U.S. producers to regain lost ground in the "low end" of the equipment market, or to stay competitive in "higher," more knowledge-intensive segments of the business. So difficult in fact that in Fall 1989, AT&T's Chairman and CEO Robert Allen announced that the company may stop producing those products that do not contribute significantly to its growth in earnings. According to Allen:

> You have to look at the maturity of some of our traditional [equipment] markets. One has to conclude if we're going to realize growth and also be responsive to our customer needs, we'll have to move up

the value chain over time and be participating in faster growth areas. . . . It is clear that there is declining value added in traditional or basic manufacturing in this country, and that's true for us. There is more [value] added at the component level and more added at the software and services area.[6]

Making matters even worse, there are reasons to believe the MFJ is compromising U.S. efforts to reduce the trade deficit in telecommunications through bilateral negotiations with Japan. Post-divestiture relationships between telecommunications trade and R&D spending have created incentives for the Japanese government to prolong trade talks with the U.S. before any meaningful concessions are forthcoming. Japan can reasonably anticipate its recent buildup of R&D spending will soon give rise to new telecommunications technology which outperforms anything that Japanese users might acquire from AT&T or other American suppliers (assuming U.S. products were fairly priced and readily available). Once that technology "gap" is opened, trade negotiations will then progress, but only to the extent that government-sanctioned trade barriers are no longer needed to strengthen or preserve Japan's ability to compete worldwide.[7]

Figure 12.12 suggests that a basic shift in technological leadership from AT&T to its principal foreign rivals may already be underway. Historically, many Japanese manufacturers have avoided sizable outlays on basic research by acquiring rights to state-of-the-art technology developed in the U.S. and focusing their resources on commercializing that technology. While this process continues today, the Japanese are relying less on innovations born in the U.S., presumably because their own research capabilities are beginning to surpass what industrial laboratories in this country can now provide. It is only natural that Japan's R&D outlays have increased sharply, because they are now paying for the full cost of developing state-of-the-art technology that they used to get from Bell Labs and other U.S. sources at bargain basement prices.

Figures 12.11 and 12.12 (p. 455) illustrate one other disturbing feature about the MFJ that merits mention in this context. Because Japan's six leading manufacturers of telecommunications equipment also produce computers, electronics, and other high-tech products, they are free to share R&D resources and to transfer proprietary technology among many different lines of business (e.g., next generation computers, expert software systems, high-definition television, etc.) as market conditions warrant. This means Japanese manufacturers are positioned to derive significantly higher returns on their investment in R&D than their American counterparts. Japan's highly integrated industrial structure also implies that the adverse effects which the MFJ has had on R&D

spending and U.S. competitiveness extend well beyond telecommunications equipment markets per se.

What then might telecommunications policymakers do to improve the nation's trade prospects? In addition to several constructive suggestions outlined in the conclusion of Robinson's paper, it is obviously important that federal and state officials heed Eli Noam's advice and think through the likely effects of their actions on U.S. competitiveness, *before* they act. Had this been done in the course of finalizing terms of the consent decree, or later during the first Triennial Review, responsibility for administering the MFJ restrictions would not have remained with the Court. Instead, the FCC would have been given the authority to condition RHC entry into nonregulated markets on compliance with procompetitive federal and state regulatory safeguards. Properly administered safeguards, after all, would satisfy the public's interest in full and fair competition, without completely undermining the U.S. telecommunications industry's ability to compete globally.

Baudhuin's claims notwithstanding, MFJ relief would not prompt the RHCs to enter into joint ventures with foreign manufacturers, much as AT&T has done. On the contrary, if allowed to manufacture, some RHCs might well be interested in participating with AT&T in the development and production of central office switches or other types of local network technology. The RHCs would benefit from such arrangements because they would then be in a position to ensure that new local network technology, including central office software operating systems that are used to create new service offerings, is designed and introduced in full accord with their own competitive interests, not just AT&T's. Similarly, AT&T could benefit by collaborating with the RHCs because the local companies could help underwrite escalating R&D costs which AT&T will otherwise have to bear alone, or share with foreign joint venture partners. And the U.S. would benefit because American companies would retain control over new technologies that AT&T and the RHCs should be able to bring to the market. In addition, much-needed improvements in its relations with the RHCs should add to AT&T's share of the domestic equipment market, thereby reducing trade imbalances the Japanese and other foreign manufacturers are currently using to finance rapid growth in their R&D capabilities— growth that, if left unchecked or unchallenged, will surely result in the demise of AT&T's reputation as the world's foremost innovator of state-of-the-art telecommunications technology.

Timothy Brennan later correctly observes that the U.S. "will not have the best policy with regard to the MFJ . . . if the debate is shouldered with unrealistic expectations of and demands for 'proof,' and denigration of what [economic] theory can tell us." He is not correct, however, in suggesting that policymakers will somehow need the benefit of more involved theoretical arguments or additional econometric evidence before they can make an informed judgment concerning the merits of MFJ relief. Common sense will suffice.

Common sense and the continuing erosion of U.S. trade and technological leadership in the global telecommunications market tell us that while relaxing the MFJ restrictions will not, in and of itself, revitalize U.S. competitiveness, it will help at a time when help is sorely needed. If this is to occur, however, jurisdiction over the MFJ will have to be shifted from the court to the federal and state regulatory commissions. As long as the court continues to administer the AT&T consent decree, it will do so on the basis of facts and conclusions that emerged from the government's case against the former Bell System fifteen years ago. While this approach to policymaking may have merit from a purely judicial perspective, it ignores the fact the telecommunications industry has changed, and must continue to change, in response to circumstances that have little or nothing to do with "evidence" presented in the course of AT&T's antitrust trial. Since then, both technological advances and the emergence of a global economy have completely altered the nature and significance of the telecommunications marketplace. If the U.S. expects to compete, domestic communications policy will have to change its orientation from one that is excessively preoccupied with the "ghost" of a company that no longer exists, to one that will promote, rather than handicap, U.S. economic interests.

Michael D. Baudhuin

It has become fashionable in some circles to place the AT&T antitrust decree at the center of the current debate on telecommunications trade policy. Robert Blau claims that if only the decree were changed to permit the divested Bell companies to manufacture equipment, they could help reverse the trade deficit. I reach the opposite conclusion: the Bell companies would not help the trade balance if they manufactured; instead, they would make it worse. What is more, the industry's ability to conduct research and development, which the consent decree has uniquely fostered, would diminish.

The trade problem is not unique to telecommunications equipment. The total merchandise trade deficit for 1989 reached $109 billion, only 2 percent of which was attributable to telecommunications equipment

TABLE 12.4
U.S. Telecommunications Equipment Trade
($ million)

	Trade Balance	Year-to-Year Change
1981	+817	
		−542
1982	+275	
		−793
1983	−518	
		−633
1984	−1,151	
		−715
1985	−1,866	
		−164
1986	−2,030	
		−520
1987	−2,550	
		− 58
1988	−2,608	
		+623
1989	−1,935[a]	

Source: Office of Telecommunications, International Trade Administration, U.S. Commerce Department.

[a] 1989 figure would have been approximately −2,300 had accounting methods used in previous years not been revised.

trade. The factors contributing to this economy-wide problem are as diverse as the affected industries themselves. Some of the factors cut across the industries as a whole; others relate to the individual sectors.

In the telecommunications sector, some critics have held divestiture responsible for the telecommunications trade deficit, because it opened the American market for network products to foreign suppliers. The telecommunications trade figures do not support this theory. They clearly show that the trade problem not only predated the 1984 divestiture by two years, but that the largest year-to-year increase in the trade imbalance occurred in 1983, before divestiture (see table 12.4).

The disaggregated trade statistics also show network equipment is not causing a trade problem. The problem lies, as the North American Telecommunications Association has reported, in imports of "lower end" consumer products, which account for the bulk of all telecommunications imports.[8] In 1989, for example, the U.S. imported $978 million in facsimile machines, mostly from Japan.[9] This represented 14 percent of all telecommunications imports for 1989, 51 percent of the year's deficit, and a 95 percent increase over 1987 imports. 1989 imports of residential telephones reached $1.37 billion.[10] Cordless phone imports[11] alone have grown by 246 percent since 1985 and now comprise 43 percent of total phone imports. Answering machines from South Korea and cellular phones from Japan also swell the deficit.

Switching equipment imports, by contrast, were not only a small percentage (6.3 percent) of total 1989 telecommunications imports, but exports exceeded imports. (Exports totaled $826 million;[12] imports were $438 million.[13]) Notwithstanding the efforts of foreign firms such as NEC, Ericsson, and Siemens to establish themselves in the U.S. market, American firms plus Northern Telecom-U.S. accounted for 91 percent of 1987 U.S. sales of switching, transmission, and media equipment.[14]

It is therefore specious to blame the consent decree for U.S. trade problems. The decree did open the market for network equipment, but it did not have a negative impact on trade. Responsibility for the trade deficit lies in part in other government actions taken years before divestiture was conceived, which opened the door to a flood of foreign consumer products.

In Congressional testimony in 1976, Glenn Watts, then President of CWA, made a chilling prediction: opening the U.S. market for telephone equipment would mean the end of U.S. manufacturing capabilities for residential telephones (September 30, 1976, testimony under CCRA legislation before the Commerce Subcommittee on the Interstate and Foreign Commerce Committee). Notwithstanding, in the 1970s the FCC initiated a proceeding to end the near-monopoly of the old Bell System in supplying telephone equipment to consumers. At the end of the decade, the FCC set in place a registration program by which anyone can make and sell equipment to be attached to the AT&T public network. This was all the opening that the Far East, with its cheap labor supply, needed. Now, a decade later, the CWA's prediction has all but come to pass. Even AT&T has been forced, by extremely low margins, to move several hundred residential telephone-set manufacturing jobs offshore (leaving 90,000 other manufacturing and support jobs in the United States), or exit the residential market.

Having thus introduced competition, the FCC then adopted rules that had the effect of handicapping AT&T's ability to compete with the Far East manufacturers. In 1980, the Commission required AT&T to establish a rigid, structural separation between its regulated common carrier business and its recently-detariffed consumer products business. AT&T asked the FCC to lift those *Computer II* rules after divestiture of its monopoly exchanges, which had been the justification for the rules in the first place. However, the FCC did not grant AT&T's petition for another one-and-a-half years. In the meantime, the mandated duplication of resources cost AT&T $1 billion each year.

Unrelated, but equally relevant to the trade issue, was the government's fiscal and monetary policy, which allowed the dollar to remain expensive in international currency markets. This had the effects of making imports cheap relative to U.S. products, and exports costly. As a result of this and other government policies, the nation's exports, across the economy, were not competitive in world markets. The telecommunications equipment surplus, which policymakers had taken for granted, quickly disappeared in an avalanche of facsimiles, telephones, and other consumer products from the Orient.

Over the past several years, AT&T and other U.S. manufacturers have refocused their resources to enable them to produce the best products, incorporating the latest technologies, at the lowest cost. To compete in the global market, they have pared costs, streamlined operations, improved inventory and manufacturing controls, applied new technologies, and tightened the links between research facilities and manufacturing operations.

Signs of a more coherent telecommunications trade policy are now emerging in the government as well. A few years ago, the Treasury orchestrated the dollar's fall in relation to other currencies, making all U.S. exports more attractive to overseas buyers and making imports either more expensive or less profitable than before. The telecommunications provisions of the 1988 Trade Bill sent a strong signal overseas that Congress will not tolerate the continued protectionist policies of U.S. trading partners. The U.S. Trade Representative has now targeted the European Economic Community and South Korea for possible sanctions under the bill if they persist in closed markets. Other actions include the U.S.-Canada Free Trade Agreement, which eliminated the Canadian tariff on switching equipment, effective January 1, 1989. On the office products front, the International Trade Commission has accepted AT&T's complaint against several Far Eastern companies for dumping their key systems on the U.S. market.

It is not yet clear whether these measures will cause the demise of the trade barriers that have proved so intractable in the past. The barriers take many forms, from standards-setting practices to the cultural biases that the Recruit scandal in Japan have exposed to the world. Perhaps most pernicious is the captive-supplier relationship between a nation's monopoly carrier and its switch manufacturer. The U.S.-Canada Free Trade Agreement has removed the tariff on switching equipment, but it will have no effect on Bell Canada's practice of turning to other suppliers only if Northern Telecom is not interested. An example of the extraordinary advantages a captive market provides a firm such as Siemens is illustrated by the fact that the Bundespost pays it about $700 for each telephone line installed, while U.S. telephone companies pay around $100.[15]

This close relationship between manufacturer and monopoly carrier is what some seek to recreate for the Bell companies. It was an informal trade barrier in the old Bell System, and it would be once again. The terrible irony is that this time, America's main entry in the global sweepstakes, AT&T, would not be permitted to compete in its hometown based on the merits of its products.

The decree may be the only thing that prevents the closed market of the past from reemerging. If the manufacturing injunction were eliminated, the consequences are predictable: the Bell companies probably would not manufacture consumer products at all, and have said as much in Congressional testimony. They would manufacture network equipment, and particularly central office switches, by joint venturing with foreign partners, and they would buy exclusively from those partnerships. This means that the surplus in switching equipment would become a serious and entrenched deficit, and domestic R&D would fall. These conclusions are explained below.

The Bell companies would not help the trade problem because they have little incentive to manufacture consumer products in the U.S., if at all. The market is dominated by imports from Asia, where labor is relatively cheap. Low margins have forced American companies, including AT&T and some of the Bell companies, to obtain consumer products sold under their name from the Far East, and that would not change if the decree were altered. In the office products market, all seven Bell companies are reportedly losing money.[16] AT&T has seen its business so unfairly squeezed in this market by Asian firms that it has had to resort to the anti-dumping laws for relief.

The more serious threat to the U.S. trade position is in the central office equipment market. The Commerce and Justice Departments, and the RBOCs themselves, recognize that the Bell companies would not start a switching business from scratch; the costs are too high. Instead, they would form joint ventures with established foreign manufacturers,[17] from whom they would thereafter purchase equipment exclusively. Who are the candidates—the national switch manufacturers of Germany, Japan, France, Sweden, Canada, and Britain, many of whom are working to lift the decree's manufacturing injunction. This would have the effect of foreclosing AT&T, America's only central office switch manufacturer, and only full-line telecommunications equipment manufacturer, from making sales to the Bell companies, who represent 80 percent of the market.

The problem is not solved by the U.S.-based manufacturing facilities of Siemens, Nippon Electric, or other foreign firms. The profits of these operations are repatriated to Germany, Japan, and other foreign countries. More seriously still, the R&D and the good high-tech jobs would be in Germany and Japan. America's role, and American jobs, would then be principally confined to metal-bending.

The central office switch industry is contracting, even as the worldwide market is growing. The enormous research and development costs required to develop new products have caused mergers all over the world and more are expected. ITT has disappeared into Alcatel; Siemens has acquired the international operations of GTE; GEC and Plessey have together become GPT; AT&T has joint-ventured with GTE in the U.S. to upgrade GTE's switch with AT&T technology. Therefore, even if the Bell companies were to attempt to start their own switching business, they would not likely survive in a climate that cannot even support those already there.

Unheeded now, even within the NTIA, is the Commerce Department's warning these joint ventures "could pose the threat of destroying this country's indigenous central office equipment manufacturing capacity."[18] Yet this is precisely what is at risk. AT&T has no protected market; support for its worldwide efforts must come from success in the competitive U.S. market. If it must cede that market to the Bell companies' affiliated suppliers, AT&T and its research and development capabilities would vanish as an American presence in the global telecommunications equipment market.

Research and development in telecommunications has been a bright spot in the otherwise alarming decrease in research investment across the economy. Between 1982 and 1987, telecommunications research and development expenditures almost doubled for the industry, and more than doubled for the companies that comprised the old Bell System. AT&T Bell Laboratories' budget has increased by 35 percent over pre-divestiture levels—from $2 billion in 1983 to $2.7 billion in 1989 —at the same time that AT&T's revenues have shrunk by 50 percent. This surge in research, so essential to the country, would be blunted if the Bell company markets were to close.

In summary, the foreign trade consequences of changing the manufacturing injunction would be devastating. It would (1) foreclose American markets to American firms, (2) deny American firms the revenue needed to sustain the research and development needed to sell equipment to Asian, European, Middle Eastern, and other foreign markets, and (3) give foreign firms captive markets and guaranteed sales in this country. The consequences would be especially severe because Japanese and European manufacturers have, to date, successfully excluded AT&T and other American firms from Japan, Germany, France, and other European markets. Removal of the injunction would have the extraordinary consequence that foreign firms would, through alliances with the Bell companies, exclude American firms from the American market as well.

The AT&T antitrust decree ensures that U.S. manufacturers can compete on an equal footing with each other and with foreign companies in supplying equipment to the monopoly Bell companies. This openness is what trade policy seeks in overseas markets, and it must be the policy in the U.S. as well, or the telecommunications trade picture will dim.

For the United States to continue to reverse its $109 billion trade deficit will require cooperation between business and government in a host of areas that cut across all economic sectors. Business's focus must be on producing for world markets the best products and services at the lowest prices, and on becoming smarter at marketing those products abroad. The government should continue to pressure foreign countries to open their markets to U.S. products, but policies that focus on trade alone are not enough. Fiscal and monetary policies affect the availability of capital, and whether American products are priced out of foreign markets. The failings of the American education system must be redressed by government, with the help of parents and business. Labor policies that are expensive can also affect the competitiveness of U.S. industry. These and other areas should be the focus of business and government's collective effort to ready America for global competition.

Timothy J. Brennan

In the context of telecommunications trade, how do we know whether the MFJ restrictions are good policy? As economic policy, the MFJ debate pertaining to trade, innovation, or other policies fundamentally hinges on two issues:[19] (1) the extent to which diversification by regulated local telephone monopolies would lead to discrimination and cross-subsidization, resulting in higher prices to consumers and exclusion of more efficient firms from information services, interexchange markets, and equipment manufacturing; (2) the extent of economies of scope between local exchange service and these other businesses that could produce more efficient production and lower prices, and might outweigh any predicted harm from discrimination and cross-subsidization. Presumably, such consequential policies would not be undertaken without knowing their benefits, but they may be but an "enormous gamble," as Peter Temin has said[20] and as William Baxter observes in chapter 1. The question I want to address is not whether the MFJ restrictions are a good idea but whether, in the trade context, these questions are addressed, if not settled, on the basis of economic theory or empirical evidence?

The MFJ debate regarding trade takes on extra complications. Along with comparing the benefits of preventing abuse of the local exchange monopoly with the costs of sacrificed economies of scope, the policymaker must decide the extent of trade-related market failures or noneconomic factors that might change this cost-benefit test.[21] In addition, trade considerations can erroneously imply that the debate is turning on measurement rather than conjecture. Data that speak to the magnitude of the trade "problem" may not speak to the merit of rescinding or retaining the MFJ. If the MFJ impedes productivity and serves no purpose, it should be rescinded regardless of the sign or size of the telecommunications trade deficit. The crux of the trade and telecommunications debate is whether the MFJ should be retained even if it promotes an efficient, but import-supplied, telecommunications industry.

As both Kenneth Robinson and William Baxter observe, trade considerations figured but little in the initial divestiture decision. Robinson suggests that telecommunications trade was not running a substantial deficit at the time, and thus was not on the political agenda. Baxter's observations are more characteristically economic. Trade was not a consideration because, except as a threat to get other countries to open markets, there is no justification for policies solely to minimize imports. He says, "It certainly would not have influenced me in the negative to know I was going to increase international trade by taking the divestiture step." More bluntly, if Japan can sell CPE or central office equipment at lower cost than U.S. firms, the U.S. economy is better off buying their equipment rather than manufacturing its own. This conclusion holds, as Baxter points out, even if foreign countries maintain barriers restricting U.S. exports.

The contributors to this chapter offer three major arguments on why these trade figures matter for post-divestiture policy. (1) BellSouth's

Robert Blau indicates that trade deficit signals a decline in the productivity of the U.S. telecommunications industry relative to foreign producers. He views rescinding the MFJ as a major instrument for reversing that relative decline. (2) Eli Noam and Robinson argue that the trade deficit results in part by the unilateral opening of U.S. markets to foreign equipment, brought about by the FCC's registration program and the elimination of the "Buy Western" policy imposed on the local operating companies by AT&T prior to the divestiture. (3) Robinson also points out that the size of the telecommunication industry and its high-technology prominence make it politically important. Many jobs, profits, and political reputations are at stake.

Robinson and Noam cite data on the growth of the U.S. trade deficit in telecommunications since the divestiture. However, MFJ evaluation requires an assessment of what these trade figures mean, whether they reflect well or ill upon the U.S. economy, and how they should be weighed against the efficiency considerations underlying the divestiture. Michael Baudhuin claims that the trade data should not carry much political or economic weight. He finds that the deficit is largely in "lower end" CPE, a sector neither technologically significant nor one in which integrated BOCs would likely participate as domestic original equipment manufacturers. In his view, lifting the MFJ would result in the BOCs joining with foreign producers in production ventures and then foreclosing other firms, including AT&T, from their markets, thus exacerbating the trade deficit.

To make the trade data meaningful, the next step in the analysis should be verification of trade-related market failures that should affect MFJ policy. On this, the authors are generally silent, taking for granted that large deficits merit concern. The discussion is neither theoretical nor empirical; it seems to reflect political or business concerns rather than any clear conception of or fact about the public interest.[22] The absence of a general picture makes it difficult to take seriously the nearly explicit suggestion that AT&T's pre-divestiture procurement policy, discrimination, and cross-subsidization were good because they kept down imports.

The crucial argument is whether the MFJ keeps the U.S. telecommunications industry from being as efficient as it should be. Blau speaks of limited productivity and a decline in R&D spending, technological leadership, and competitiveness. Robinson fears that the U.S. will become a "technological colony" of the Japanese. Both suggest that the MFJ will contribute to these undesirable consequences, for reasons already familiar—that there are either economies of scope that make the BOCs especially efficient in the equipment markets subject to import competition, or that BOC entry would improve the performance of firms with few competitors. The former argument would seem to apply more to the highly competitive CPE markets; the latter may apply to the more concentrated central office equipment business.

Resolution of this controversy could turn on empirical comparisons of the likely harms of the divestiture, the magnitude of economies of scope, and the benefits of competitive entry, or it could turn on theoretical argument, spiced with anecdote or the odd piece of supporting data. The statements and responses of Brown, Baxter, McGowan, and Judge Greene together suggest in chapter 1 that the policy arguments initially surrounding the divestiture combined a general theory of inefficient behavior by diversified regulated firms with, from a variety of perspectives, particular experiences associated with the unique history of AT&T.[23] The trade presentations here suggest that the trade aspect of the divestiture debate remains theoretical and anecdotal.[24] No commentator offers empirical evidence for or against the propositions that the BOCs produce more efficiently than other suppliers, domestic or foreign, or would act anticompetitively against them. The data supplied may or may not speak to a significant trade deficit, but they do not tell us whether lifting the MFJ would either reduce the deficit or—not necessarily the same thing—improve the performance of the U.S. telecommunications industry.[25] The debate here remains primarily theoretical, complicated by the introduction of trade considerations for which there are data but no analytical framework in which they have any ready meaning.

Interest in the development of the telecommunications industry since the 1984 divestiture by AT&T of its local telephone companies is not motivated only by the academic curiosity of the industrial historian. The normative question of whether the divestiture was sound legal and economic policy remains important. It could be thought of as a subject for sophistry, for regardless of one's opinion of Humpty Dumpty, there is no way to put the egg back together. However, courts, regulators, legislators, and industry participants address this issue daily when assessing the restrictions in the MFJ[26] that keep the BOCs from entering other telecommunications markets and replicating the structural conditions that drew regulators and antitrust litigators to hamstring and then disassemble AT&T.

Despite the understandable desire to ground telecommunications policy in empirical findings, it remains a largely theoretical enterprise. Data are often nonexistent or of limited relevance, especially when major policies are at stake. We do not have the luxury of a U.S. or world economy identical in every way to our own but for the divestiture and

MFJ against which we could compare our experience. Whatever the data, MFJ proponents can claim that the data would be worse but for the MFJ, while its opponents can claim the opposite; both are protected from empirical refutation. The counterfactual nature of the debate inherently implies that it will take place on theoretical grounds.[27]

The statements included here regarding the decision to divest and the subsequent policy debates regarding trade support this conclusion.[28] We need to tolerate, if regrettably, the absence of strong empirical evidence to resolve policy disputes, even those as consequential as the MFJ restrictions. Other ways of informing judgment, including simulations and anecdotes as well as theoretical argument, need to be recognized. More econometric evidence would be helpful, but there is little reason to think it will be forthcoming, if those with such strong financial, legal, and political interests in telecommunications policy have not yet put forth such evidence.

A corollary is that policy debate needs to be conducted without false hopes regarding the availability of empirical evidence and the relative speciousness of "mere theory." Otherwise, policy debate can be biased and hampered if one side can successfully place the burden of empirical proof on the other side. If this burden is insurmountable, the burdened side may lose even if it has the better theoretical and anecdotal case, and its opponent too lacks empirical support. Moreover, since incentives, benefits, and costs are ultimately in the subjective eye of the consumer, worker, and investor who perceive them, economic policy evaluation is unavoidably theoretical. We surely would not, and will not, have the best policy with regard to the MFJ, price cap regulation, ONA, or competitive policy, if the debate is shouldered with unrealistic expectations of and demands for "proof" and denigration of what theory can tell us.

ENDNOTES

1. AT&T 1982 Annual Report, p. 18.
2. Eli Noam, *Telecommunications in Europe*, forthcoming.
3. Eli Noam, "Beyond ONA: Designing a Modular Network as a Strategy for National Competitiveness," Center for Telecommunications and Information Studies, Columbia University Graduate School of Business, Working Paper, 1989.
4. See Bell Atlantic Corp., "Response to NTIA Request For Comments Concerning The Effects of The MFJ Restrictions On Bell Company Research, Development and Manufacturing," January 31, 1989, pp. 19–21; and Communications Workers of America, "Information Industry Report," October 19, 1988.

5. See AT&T Annual Reports for the years 1984 through 1988.

6. See "Less Manufacturing for AT&T: Allen's Vision For The '90s," *Communications Week*, October 2, 1989, pp. 1, 61. For a contrasting point of view on the competitive merits of manufacturing see "A Japanese View: Why America Has Fallen Behind," *Fortune*, September 25, 1989, p. 52.

7. See Laura D'Andrea Tyson and John Zysman, "Developmental Strategy and Production Innovation In Japan," in Chalmers Johnson, Laura Tyson, and John Zysman, eds., *Politics and Productivity, How Japan's Developmental Strategy Works* (Cambridge, Mass.: Ballinger, 1989), pp. 59–130.

8. *Wall Street Journal*, January 24, 1989, p. 7.

9. HTSUS Code 851782.00.40.

10. HTSUS Codes 851710.00.20, .40, .50, .70; 851790.30.00 and 852520.50.00.

11. TSUSA Code 685.25.00 and HTSUS Code 852520.50.00.

12. HTSUS Codes 851730.10.40, .10.80, .50.00 and 851790.20.00.

13. HTSUS Codes 851730.15.00, .20.00, .25.00, .30.00, .50.00 and 851790.05.00, .10.00, .15.00, .60.00.

14. Northern Business Information Reports, Transmission Equipment Market and Central Office Equipment Market, 1988 Editions.

15. *The Economist*, December 17, 1988, p. 70.

16. *Communications Daily*, February 17, 1989.

17. NTIA 1987 Trade Report, February 4, 1987, p. 92.

18. Id., p. vi.

19. For extended discussions of the theoretical justifications for the divestiture and the line-of-business restrictions, see Brennan, "Why Regulated Firms Should be Kept Out of Unregulated Markets: Understanding the Divestiture in *U.S. v. AT&T*," *Antitrust Bulletin* (1987) 32:741–93; "Divestiture Policy Considerations in an Information Services World," *Telecommunications Policy* (1989) 13:243–54. An especially relevant precursor to this analysis is Baxter, "How Government Cases Get Selected—Comments from Academia," *Antitrust Law Journal* (Spring 1977), 46:586–91.

20. Peter Temin, with Louis Galambos, *The Fall of the Bell System* (New York: Cambridge University Press, 1987), p. 365.

21. Examples of such market failures and noneconomic considerations are the misgivings voiced by Jerrold Oppenheim and Commissioner Sharon Nelson concerning threats to privacy and First Amendment freedoms posed by monopoly telecommunications technologies in an unregulated environment.

22. Baudhuin also notes that telecommunications constituted only 2 percent of the U.S. 1988 trade deficit, and suggests that any endemic problems caused or created by this deficit spread far beyond the telecommunications industry.

23. Not all of these parties to the creation of the MFJ world may agree with this conclusion. William Baxter admits (in chapter 1) that the MFJ "implicitly made a wager" that the losses predicted by this theory outweighed the gains from any economies of scope excluded by divestiture, and that "[i]t would be absurd to pretend that [the MFJ] was made on the basis of detailed econometric data." Judge Greene, however, is "convinced" of the divestiture's benefits and

strongly rejects Prof. Baxter's characterization of the divestiture as a "gamble."

24. The same conclusion could be reached regarding the debate over the MFJ's effects on telecommunications innovation.

25. For example, one wonders how those concerned with trade would regard lifting the MFJ, if doing so would speed the development of new information services that rely on imported CPE.

26. *U.S. v. American Telephone and Telegraph*, 552 F. Supp. 131, 226 (1982).

27. An extensive discussion of the methodological problems associated with empirical and industrial policymaking is in Brennan, "Economic Theory in Industrial Policy: Lessons from *U.S. v. AT&T*," Graduate Institute for Policy Education and Research Working Paper 1989-1, George Washington University, 1989.

28. Ironically, they provide empirical support for the proposition that telecommunications is not empirically driven.

INDEX

Access charges, 377
  bypass, 109
  residential service, 107-8, 358
Access services market, 136-38, 163
Ake, John R., 268-69, 270
Alcatel-Thomson, France, 437
Allen, Robert, x, 457
Alternative operator services (AOS), 311
  market, 147-48
Ameritech, 395-96, 403, 404
  and Intelligent Network model, 333
AOS, *see* Alternative operator services (AOS)
AT&T, 210-11, 268, 346, 417
  antitrust suit, 409
  antitrust suit against (1949), 2-3,45
  antitrust suit against (1974), 3-7
  Bell Telephone Laboratories, 38-39
  communications union, 401-5
  consent decree (1956), xi-xii, 2-3, 36, 55, 101, 348
  consumer affairs, 225-26
  cost allocation issues, 214-15
  electronic publishing, 17n53, 23, 46
  information economy, 438-39
  innovation, 285, 289, 291, 319-20, 432-33
  interconnection equipment, 22-23
  inward WATS, 35
  Kingsbury Commitment, 55
  long-distance services, 177

Modified Final Judgment, 410
  post-divestiture: collective bargaining, 403-6; performance, 33-34, 131-32; potential revenue, 10; regulation, 230-31n5, 461
  price cap regulation, 111n15, 154
  private antitrust cases, 58-59
  quality of service, 252-53, 265-67
  reorganization plan, 9-10, 23, 97-98, 106-8

Baldridge, Malcolm, 6
Basic service elements (BSEs), 85, 291
Baudhuin, Michael D., 453, 459, 460-66, 468
Baxter, William F., 5-17, 21-39, 92, 186, 307, 381, 453-54, 468
Belinfante, Alexander, 377-80, 381-82, 384, 473
Bell Atlantic, 404-5
"Bell bill," 3-4
Bell Canada, 65
Bellcore, 39, 333, 338
Bell Laboratories, 2-3, 38-39, 425, 433
  innovation, 286
Bell Operating Companies (BOCs) (*see also* Regional Holding Companies [RHCs or RBOCs]), 9-16
  competition, 31, 56, 112n21
  consent decree (1982), 27
  digital capacity, 291-94, 329-30
  gateway services, 11, 53, 64

Lightning Source UK Ltd.
Milton Keynes UK
173341UK00001B/1/P